# Computer Law
## Fifth Edition

# Computer Law

## Fifth Edition

EDITED BY

Chris Reed and John Angel

OXFORD
UNIVERSITY PRESS

# OXFORD
## UNIVERSITY PRESS

Great Clarendon Street, Oxford OX2 6DP

Oxford University Press is a department of the University of Oxford.
It furthers the University's objective of excellence in research, scholarship,
and education by publishing worldwide in

Oxford New York

Auckland Bangkok Buenos Aires Cape Town Chennai
Dar es Salaam Delhi Hong Kong Istanbul Karachi Kolkata
Kuala Lumpur Madrid Melbourne Mexico City Mumbai Nairobi
São Paulo Shanghai Singapore Taipei Tokyo Toronto

with an associated company in Berlin

Oxford is a registered trade mark of Oxford University Press
in the UK and in certain other countries

Published in the United States
by Oxford University Press Inc., New York

British Library Cataloguing in Publication Data

Data available

Library of Congress Cataloging in Publication Data

Data available

ISBN 0-19-926350-7

1 3 5 7 9 10 8 6 4 2

Typeset in Times
by Cambrian Typesetters, Frimley, Surrey
Printed in Great Britain
on acid-free paper by
Antony Rowe Limited, Chippenham, Wiltshire

# Contents Summary

# Contents

# Preface to the Fifth Edition

The first edition of *Computer Law* was published in 1990. The area of law covered by the book has developed considerably over the last thirteen years but there is a sense now that computer law has become an established area of law with a more stable content. This is reflected by the fact that, while the book as a whole has been thoroughly revised, updated and extended, there are no real additional chapters to the book in contrast with previous editions. In fact we have dropped a separate chapter on semiconductor chip protection because of the lack of developments in the area. The two Internet-related chapters have been combined into one under the title of 'E-Commerce' (Chapter 9). The chapter on European computer law has been replaced by relevant updates to all the other chapters together with the addition of 'EC Competition Law and the New Economy of Information Technology' (Chapter 12) which, as its title indicates, concentrates on the increasingly new and difficult competition aspects of the subject matter of the book.

The original concept of this book came from Chris Reed's desire to provide a textbook for students on the University of London's LL M course which could also combine as a useful book for practitioners. The fact that the course is taught by academics and practitioners, and that they are the authors of the book, makes *Computer Law* a unique contribution to the field which is clearly recognized as such as it now goes into its fifth edition. Chris Reed continues to make an enormous contribution to the book but I have tried to take more of the burden from him in my co-editorial role, for example, by writing this preface.

My thanks go to all the authors, who because they are very successful academics and practitioners in their own right have little time available in their busy schedules, but have still produced excellent contributions, largely on time! Lorraine Mulpeter, our Institute's administrator, deserves particular thanks for co-ordinating all the authors and ensuring that the electronic manuscript was received by the publisher on time. Also many thanks go to OUP for continuing to support the book since their acquisition of Blackstone Press, the previous publishers. Lastly I would like to thank my co-editor Chris Reed for his inspiration which continues to make this book a success.

John Angel
March 2003

# Contributors

## THE EDITORS

**Chris Reed** is Professor of Electronic Commerce Law and Director of the Centre for Commercial Law Studies, Queen Mary, University of London. Chris is also Of counsel to the City of London law firm Tite & Lewis, in association with Ernst & Young.

He joined the Centre in 1987 and is responsible for the University of London LL M courses in Information Technology Law, Internet Law, Electronic Banking Law and Telecommunications Law. Chris has published widely on many aspects of computer law. As well as co-editing and contributing to *Computer Law*, he is the author of *Electronic Finance Law* (Woodhead Faulkner, 1991), *Digital Information Law: Electronic Documents and Requirements of Form* (Centre for Commercial Law Studies, 1996) and *Internet Law: Text and Materials* (Butterworths, 2000), and the co-editor of *Cross-Border Electronic Banking*, 2nd edn (Lloyd's of London Press, 2000). Research with which he was involved led to the EU Directives on electronic signatures and on e-commerce.

From 1997 to 2000 Chris was Joint Chairman of the Society for Computers and Law, and from 1997 to 1998 he acted as Specialist Adviser to the House of Lords Select Committee on Science and Technology. Chris participated as an Expert at the European Commission/Danish Government Copenhagen Hearing on Digital Signatures, represented the UK Government at the Hague Conference on Private International Law and has been an invited speaker at OECD and G8 international conferences.

**John Angel** is a solicitor who specialized in employment law and was a part-time Employment Tribunal chairman before leaving private practice for a period of twelve years in the IT industry. He has worked with City law firms in recent years and was formerly Head of Online Legal Services at Clifford Chance. He is a Visiting Professorial Fellow at the Institute of Computer & Communications Law which is part of the Centre for Commercial Studies, Queen Mary, University of London. John is consultant editor to *Electronic Business Law* (Butterworths Tolley), general editor of *Technology Outsourcing* (Law Society Publishing); as well as co-editing and contributing to *Computer Law*, he is joint editor of *Telecommunications Law*, also published by Oxford University Press.

## THE CONTRIBUTING AUTHORS

**Steve Anderman** is Professor of Law at the University of Essex. He has been an Expert on Competition Policy to the Economic and Social Committee of the European Union since 1984. He has worked on the Merger Control Regulation, the Technology Transfer Block Exemption Regulation and the Vertical Horizontal and Modernisation Regulations. He gave evidence to the US Department of Justice/ Federal Trade Commission hearings on the Antitrust Intellectual Property Interface 2002. Recent publications include *EC Competition Law and Intellectual Property Rights: The Regulation of Innovation* (Clarendon Press, 2000); *The Law of Unfair Dismissal*, 3rd edn (Butterworths, 2002); 'EC Competition Law and Intellectual Property Rights in the New Economy', [2002] Antitrust Bulletin; and 'Microsoft in Europe' in *International Intellectual Property Law and Policy* (Juris Publications, 2002).

**Simon Chalton** is a solicitor and a consultant to Bird & Bird, an international law firm with special interests in computer law. His experience with computers and the law relating to information technology goes back to the late 1960s. He has contributed to the specification and design of computer applications programs and their implementation, and he has served as a non-executive director and chairman of a software house. His experience has included advising on computer and software contracts, software licensing and software protection, computer-related disputes and data protection.

He has held office as Chairman of the Intellectual Property Committee of the British Computer Society, as Chairman of the National Computing Centre's Legal Group and as Chairman of the International Bar Association's Computer and Database Committee. He has also served as a member of the US Society for Information Management's Procurement Working Group and as a Vice-Chair within the Computer Division of the Economics of Law Practice Section of the American Bar Association. He is a Fellow of the American Bar Foundation and a Fellow of the College of Law Practice Management. A World Intellectual Property Organization-listed mediator, he is a Fellow of the Chartered Institute of Arbitrators, and a Fellow of the Society for Advanced Legal Studies.

The senior founding editor of Sweet and Maxwell's *Encyclopedia of Data Protection*, a co-editor of *Database Law* (Jordan Publishing, 1998), Chalton is also the author of *The Legal Protection of Databases* (Hawksmere, 2001) and a contributor to other publications and professional journals relating to computer law. He is an experienced practitioner and speaker at an international level, and writes extensively on the legal aspects of computing.

**Allison Coleman** is Director of Culturenet Cymru Ltd, a company, funded by the Welsh Assembly Government, to promote the culture and heritage of Wales on the web. Allison is a former Senior Lecturer in Law at the University of Wales, Aberystwyth where she specialized in Intellectual Property and International Copyright Law. She is the author of many books and articles, including *The Legal Protection of Trade Secrets* (Sweet and Maxwell, 1992) and is a co-author of a forthcoming book on Copyright Exceptions in the Digital Age, to be published by Cambridge University Press.

**Christopher Millard** is a partner in the London office of Linklaters where he leads the firm's global IT & Communications Group. He has 20 years experience in the technology and communications law fields and has led many multi-jurisdictional e-commerce and data protection compliance projects. As a Visiting Professorial Fellow of Queen Mary, University of London, he teaches on courses in IT Law, Internet Law and Telecommunications Law. He is the author of *Legal Protection of Computer Programs and Data* (Carswell/Sweet & Maxwell, 1985) and has subsequently published many articles and book chapters on data protection, IT and communications law. He is a General Editor of the *International Journal of Law and Information Technology* (Oxford University Press) and is a founding editor of *Data Protection Laws of the World* (Sweet & Maxwell). He is Co-Chair of the Technology and Ecommerce Law Committee of the International Bar Association (2003–5), is a past Chair of the Society for Computers and Law and a past President of the International Federation of Computer Law Associations. He has an LLB from the University of Sheffield and an MA and an LLM from the University of Toronto. Prior to joining Linklaters in June 2002, Christopher was with Clifford Chance for 18 years. He can be contacted at: christopher.millard@linklaters.com

**Jeremy Newton** is a partner in the Technology Media and Telecommunications Group at Nabarro Nathanson, which he joined in September 2001 after a period as Assistant General Counsel with Sun Microsystems. He has specialized in IT and e-commerce law for over 10 years, and is noted as a leader in the field in Chambers Guide to the Legal Profession and the Euromoney Guide to the World's Leading IT Advisers. Jeremy is on the editorial advisory board of Electronic Business Law magazine, and he writes and lectures extensively on IT law and contracts.

**Tim Press** BA (Chem) Oxon, solicitor, joined the legal profession after leaving University in 1980 and qualified as a solicitor in 1984. He practised in London with Woodham Smith and Taylor Joynson Garrett, as a partner from 1988, specialising mainly in contentious and non-contentious intellectual property work and general commercial litigation. He left practice in 1992, moved to Cardiff University and embarked upon a new career as an academic. He teaches litigation and advocacy and commercial litigation on the Legal Practice Course.

**Gavin Stutter** is a Research Fellow at the Institute of Computer & Communications Law, Centre for Commercial Law Studies (Queen Mary, University of London). He manages the ICCL's LLM IT Law course, teaches content regulation issues on the Internet law course, and is responsible for the Internet Content Regulation module on the Institutes's Internet-based LLM distance learning programme. In addition to his teaching duties, Gavin has also played an active role in ICCL research projects, including the ECLIP (Electronic Commerce Legasl Issues Platform). He has published various papers in several academic volumes and journals, and is pleased to note that his professional views on Internet pornography and sexual harassment in the workplace have been quoted in *Shine*, a glossy magazine marketed at women in their late twenties. Gavin also sits on the executive committee of BILETA (British and Irish Law, Education & Technology Association). In his spare time, he is undertaking PhD research.

**Ian Walden** is Head of the Institute of Computer and Communications Law in the Centre for Commercial Law Studies, Queen Mary, University of London, and Director of Queen Mary's Computer-Related Crime Research Centre. He is editor of *EDI and the Law* (Blackwell Publishers, 1989) and joint editor of *Information Technology and the Law* (Palgrave Macmillan, 1990), *EDI Audit and Control* (Blackwell Publishers, 1993), *Cross-border Electronic Banking* (Informa Business Publishing, 1995, 2000), *Telecommunications Law Handbook* (Blackstone Press, 1997), *E-Commerce Law and Practice in Europe* (Woodhead Publishing, 2001) and *Telecommunications Law* (Blackstone Press, 2001). Ian is joint editor of Sweet & Maxwell's *Encyclopedia of Data Protection* and is a member of the Legal Advisory Board to the Information Society Directorate-General of the European Commission and a consultant to the global law firm, Baker & McKenzie.

**Alison Welterveden** is a partner in the Technology & Outsourcing Group at Tite & Lewis, the associated law firm of Ernst & Young in the UK. Alison has published a number of articles on various aspects of information technology and e-commerce law. She is also co-author of the chapter on 'IS Outsourcing' in the *Outsourcing Practice Manual* (Sweet & Maxwell, 1998) and the chapter on 'IT Outsourcing' in *Technology Outsourcing* (Law Society Publications, 2003). Alison specializes in technology, outsourcing (both IT and business-process outsourcing) and digital security law.

# Table of Cases

# Tables of Legislation

# International Legislation

**Table of Statutory Instruments and European Secondary Legislation**

# Abbreviations

| | |
|---|---|
| ASP | application service provision |
| BBS | Bulletin Board Service |
| BPO | business process outsourcing |
| CDPA 1988 | Copyright, Design and Patents Act 1988 |
| CL&P | Computer Law and Practice |
| CLSR | Computer Law and Security Reports |
| DG Comp | Directorate General Competition of the European Commission |
| DMCA 1998 | Digital Millennium Copyright Act 1998 |
| EDI | Electronic Data Interchange |
| EPC | European Patent Convention |
| EPO | European Patent Office |
| IP | intellectual property |
| IPRs | intellectual property rights |
| IS | information systems |
| ISP | Internet Service Provider |
| IT | information technology |
| ITT | invitation to tender |
| PFI | private finance initiative |
| PIDA 1998 | Public Interest Disclosure Act 1998 |
| PPP | public–private partnership |
| RFP | request for proposal |
| RIPA 2000 | Regulation of Investigatory Powers Act 2000 |
| SGA 1979 | Sale of Goods Act 1979 |
| SGSA 1982 | Supply of Goods and Services Act 1982 |
| SME | small and medium-sized enterprises |
| TRIPs | Trade Related Aspects of Intellectual Property Rights |
| TUPE 1981 | Transfer of Undertakings (Protection of Employment) Regulations 1981 |
| UCTA 1977 | Unfair Contract Terms Act 1977 |
| USPTO | United States Patent and Trademark Office |
| VAN | Value Added Network Service |
| VPN | virtual private network |
| WIPO | World Intellectual Property Organization |

# INTRODUCTION

*Chris Reed*

In about 1950 the then chairman of IBM was rumoured to have predicted that the world market for computers at the end of the century might approach one hundred machines. The degree to which his prediction fell short is a measure of how far computing technology has pervaded our lives. The result of this dramatic increase in the use of and reliance upon computing technology is that new and qualitatively different legal problems have arisen. These problems are the focus of this book.

The Introduction to earlier editions of this work discussed the argument that there is no need to treat computer law as a separate topic because it is no more than the application of existing principles to novel sets of facts. Today there can be no disagreement that computing technology does indeed give rise to novel legal problems which are not resolvable by applying existing legal principles. This is particularly apparent where transactions are carried out through the exchange of digital information rather than by human interaction. The developing law which seeks to resolve those problems is the heart of computer law.

## 0.1 DEFINING COMPUTER LAW

Computer law is that branch of the law which regulates the *technological* aspects of information,[1] ie, it is the law which governs information *processing*. Information

---

[1] Thus, eg, the law of defamation is not specifically part of computer law, but those aspects of defamation which arise uniquely from information-processing activities will fall to be treated under this heading, particularly if the legal principles involved are common to those applied to similar problems which would traditionally be examined under different legal headings. A particularly good example of such an issue is the question of when an Internet Service Provider ('ISP') is liable for the information which passes across its servers, even though it is not the author and did not originate the transmission of that information. This issue is discussed in detail in Chapter 9.

processing is the automated transformation or transmission of digital information, and the subject area extends to the information-processing aspects of the technology used. At present this primarily, though not exclusively, means computers and other information-processing devices.[2]

The transformation in society which has been brought about by information technology ('IT') has given rise to qualitatively different types of legal issue. Traditionally, the law divided the subject matter of commerce into goods and services and dealt with information either as an aspect of human behaviour (for example, negligent advice) or through intellectual property rights ('IPRs'). Manufacturing industry processed physical entities into other physical entities, which were distributed under a well-defined legal framework. Services, such as advice or labour, were essentially ephemeral matters which had no permanent existence and could thus be regulated mainly as a question of whether the provider of the service did so with proper care and in the proper manner. Intellectual property ('IP') was generated through human effort and ingenuity, and produced delimited and static results (such as a book or an invention) which could be exploited in a limited number of ways.

All these things still happen, of course, but IT has enabled information, formerly an ephemeral phenomenon, to be turned into something that has a quasi-physical existence and which can be traded as if it were a physical commodity. Thus, database services sell pure information whilst software houses sell applied information in the form of computer software, and much of this information is generated not by human effort but as the result of computer-controlled processes. Fixed physical documents turn into dynamic digital data, and are 'signed' in non-physical ways. Music recordings lose their physical support and, when associated with rights-management technology, become in many ways closer to programs than data.

Some chapters of this book record the ways in which traditional divisions of the law are adapting themselves to these new phenomena, while others examine entirely new fields of law which are in the process of development. Because of the constant change in the law, some of the suggestions made in the following chapters must necessarily be speculative. Nonetheless, those working with IT or advising others on the legal aspects of its use require guidance, and the authors have used their experience in their own particular specialisms to provide the best predictions that can be made at the moment. In an increasing number of areas there is now technology-specific legislation, though its precise application often has yet to be decided by the courts. Even where new legislation is unlikely to be forthcoming, new problems still arise and will therefore have to be dealt with by judicial adaptation of existing principles. This book attempts to identify those problems and suggest the solutions likely to be adopted by the courts.

---

[2] These include obvious devices such as mobile telephones but also encompass far more obscure machines, like electronic toasters, which contain specially designed semiconductor chips, or washing machines which are connected to the Internet.

## 0.2 COMMON THEMES

Throughout the law relating to computers run a number of common themes, which the reader should bear in mind.

### 0.2.1 Information or knowledge as a species of property

IP law already recognizes that certain types of knowledge should be treated to some extent as if it were private property and thus capable of 'ownership', for reasons such as the invention shown by its devisor, the creative effort put into its compilation or because it has been kept confidential. Other types of knowledge are incapable of ownership because of their nature as fundamental concepts or because they are mere ideas, and these are instead free to be used by all mankind. Thus the equation $e=mc^2$ cannot be the subject of a patent or of the law of copyright, nor can the basic concept of the internal combustion engine (though of course a specific implementation of that concept can be). Because IT concerns itself with applied information, however, it is difficult to classify it into either of these categories. Such information is normally very valuable, and in general most things which have a market value are dealt with by the law as a species of property. IP law has developed techniques to decide which IT products are to be treated as belonging only to one particular individual, and which are incapable of ownership and thus available to all.

### 0.2.2 The distribution of resources and effort

The newest challenge to IPRs comes from the rise of global information networks, of which the Internet is the prime example. Copyright law, in particular, is based on the assumption that a protectable intellectual asset exists in fixed form, and thus only protects it against copying. Networks make it possible for an information resource, such as a program or a digital image, to be used without copying it to a different computer, or to be incorporated in an activity in such a way that the person controlling the incorporation does not undertake any copying (for example, linking to a resource on another's website). In other words, there are new ways of using another's IP, and the question whether those uses infringe the owner's rights is still in the process of being answered.

Distribution of resources and effort is even challenging specific computer laws, such as those on data protection. Personal data is now gathered from multiple activities and sources, held in different places (which may change regularly in both location and content) and used by searching across holdings of data controlled by different persons. Data-protection laws are based on the concept of a single database controlled by a single entity, and are struggling to adapt.

### 0.2.3 Controlling the use of information

The capacity which computing technology provides allows the aggregation of scattered information, and can make it available worldwide. Data which might formerly have had to be kept in a number of small collections for access to be feasible (such as an individual doctor's patient records) can now be brought together and made globally searchable (for example, the medical records for the whole of the UK). Moreover, data can be collated across multiple data sources to produce new information about individuals and corporations. For example, it would technically be feasible to produce a detailed financial profile of any individual from his tax, investment and spending information, if coordinated access to the databases held by the tax authorities, credit-card companies, pension funds and supermarkets were permitted.

These technical possibilities have the potential to conflict with the fundamental human right of privacy. They also question the nature of privacy itself—is it merely the right not to disclose personal information, in which case once disclosure has taken place there is no further privacy interest in that information, or does it extend to controlling the use which others make of that information? A consensus seems to have been achieved that it is the latter, but there is still no international agreement on what the use restrictions should be and how they should be monitored and enforced. The absence of international agreement here raises special legal difficulties in an era in which the Internet has made all data equally accessible, regardless of the geographical location of its storage device.

New control issues also arise in respect of IPRs. The move from dealings in physical copies of works to digital information products has weakened the control which rightsowners and publishers can exert over further uses of these works. This is most clearly exemplified in the extensive litigation over online distribution of unauthorized copies of music recordings. However, the digital nature of these new products also gives new control opportunities, both through technology which monitors and controls further uses of digital products, and through online contracts direct between rightsowner and customer which can be used to impose restrictions on use. Recent copyright legislation accepts and legitimizes the first method of control, subject to some limitations, and even grants the rightsowner a new right not to have this technology disabled. Control through contracts is more controversial, however, and the courts have yet to decide how far a rightsowner can use contract to extend the scope of the monopolies granted by statute.

Finally, the psychological characteristics of data stored and processed by computer creates legal problems, as humans still have an unjustified belief in the infallibility of computers whilst failing to recognize that the information comes, directly or indirectly (as software-processing results) from fallible humans. The effects this belief has on human behaviour in response to a computer's output will be of particular relevance to the law of negligence.

### 0.2.4 IT as a substitute for human endeavour

In many fields of human activity IT is used to substitute for some or all of the functions previously undertaken by humans, or to perform functions that could not previously be performed at all. This has of course happened before in the history of technology, for example, the motor car has in part been substituted for walking, but in each previous case the mechanism has remained largely under the control of its human user. The whole point of using IT, however, is that the machine should control itself. This raises a number of problems that the law must eventually resolve:

(a) Where does responsibility lie when someone who, in the absence of his using a computer to perform some task would be personally responsible for loss caused to another, relies on the computer's proper operation, rather than his own expertise, to avoid causing such injury?

(b) How are the courts to cope when the only evidence of a fact lies solely within the 'knowledge' of a machine, particularly where the machine also has the ability to alter that information? The basic evidential difficulties seem largely to have been solved, but where complex electronic transactions are carried out through largely automated processes, which often cross jurisdictional borders, new legal issues of identity and attribution arise. Legislation is rapidly being introduced to address some of these, and the EU Directives on electronic signatures and electronic commerce introduce some important new principles of law.

(c) The enhanced abilities of machines inevitably lead to increased expectations, and standards of performance that were acceptable before the introduction of computer technology may well now fall short of what ought to be achieved. Older readers may remember the public outcry after the Great Storm of 1987 when many people complained that the UK Meteorological Office had failed to predict the violence and extent of the storm in spite of substantial investment in IT. It has still to be decided how far the law's allocation of responsibility (mainly in tort and contract) should reflect these increased expectations.

### 0.2.5 The move from products to information services

The first generation of computing technology concentrated on the electronic hardware used to process information; the second on the software which controlled that processing. Today, it is possible to identify a clear shift from these discrete products to pure trade in information services. From a user's perspective this makes a great deal of sense—what is required is the final output of the information-processing process, such as a document or a set of accounts, and the precise equipment and software used to produce that output are merely means to an end.

This shift generates a further fundamental challenge to the law. Services were previously the result of human effort or skill, and the quality of service to be provided could be judged against the standards expected from other humans. Now, most information-based services are provided by computing technology, and the human input is increasingly remote from the point of service delivery. It is clearly inappropriate to judge an automated bank teller or an online share dealing service by the standards to be expected of a human, for example, and the law is still in the process of determining the new quality and liability tests which should apply to services provided in this way.

### 0.2.6 Trading in information products

Closely linked to the question of information as property is the legal classification of trade in information products. This is particularly relevant to the supply of computer software, information services and entertainment products and services. Initially, when the only computers were mainframe systems and software was only available from the manufacturer, it was generally accepted that the relationship between software producer and user could be classified solely as a licence of IPRs and thus as a supply of services for liability purposes. Information was marketed in two forms: products, which were static (such as books), and bespoke information (such as legal advice) which was not reusable. Entertainment either came in static form (for example, an audio tape), or was supplied in real time in a reasonably fixed form (for example, theatre performances or television broadcasts).

Today, we have entered into an age of mass customization. Most software products are multifunctional, and capable of further extension and customization by downloading additional elements. Online delivery of information and entertainment allows the 'product' to be modified to the recipient's exact requirements. However, the nature of the software market has changed radically. The relationship between the producer of these information products and the ultimate consumer is often remote, with new types of intermediary springing up to make information products and services available on the market. It is now far harder to say exactly what is being traded—goods? services?—or something entirely new which does not fit into any existing classification?

### 0.2.7 Paperless and people-less trading

In the business-to-business (or 'B2B') arena, computers have for some years been selling and buying on behalf of their owners without any human intervention or decision making. The stock-control systems of supermarkets discover, through links to the tills, that a product line is running low and immediately generate an online order to the supplier's computer, which accepts it and puts in train the process of production and delivery. Many other industries and commercial sectors undertake automated trading. More recently, this phenomenon has begun to extend to the business-to-consumer (or 'B2C') market. Human consumers now buy from software-controlled traders, leading to interesting discussions when the software erroneously discounts prices by 90 per cent or more. In the longer term it is predicted that a consumer's automated software agent will scour the Internet for bargains, negotiate an agreement within the parameters set by its human principal and arrange for payment in electronic form.

These activities do not always accord with the existing legal and regulatory framework. The law of contract has traditionally assumed the meeting of human minds, and requirements to undertake business transactions via written and signed documents are found in every country's laws. Major legislative reform is under way to assimilate these new, online transactions within an extended legal structure, and the most relevant laws and proposals are examined in the applicable chapters.

### 0.2.8  Globalization

Until quite recently the users of IT acted locally, even if the IT industry was global. This meant that national laws still had the ability to provide meaningful solutions to most legal problems. Now, both commercial and private users act globally as well. Commercial websites are visible in almost all parts of the world, often doing business online with customers in unknown countries, and private websites disclose personal information, abuse individuals and companies and make music downloads available, all across national boundaries.

This globalization of computer technology use has highlighted the different ways in which national laws approach particular issues. An activity which is known to be lawful in the user's own country is suddenly exposed to legal challenge when it goes online and has effects abroad. The EU's resolution of this problem, through the Electronic Commerce Directive and its country-of-origin regulation provisions, is radical but effective. However, that approach cannot easily be translated to the rest of the world, which is only just beginning to react to the challenges posed to both business and non-commercial online activities.

### 0.2.9  Convergence of national laws

The IT industry, and the dissemination and consumption of information products and services, transcends national boundaries. Differences in national treatment of these phenomena can result in major distortions of the market; for example, the current tax treatment of electronic commerce (which is beyond the scope of this work) often discriminates in favour of exporters of information products and against the domestic supplier.

In the long term it is possible to detect a natural trend towards convergence[3] of national laws. Indeed, countries whose laws take a different direction to the trend

---

[3] 'Convergence' is used here, rather than 'harmonization' or 'approximation', because it is a value-free term which carries no connotations of a supranational legislator. Additionally, it recognizes that legislators do not always set out consciously to match their laws with those of another state. In some instances (the law concerning digital signatures being, perhaps, the prime example) convergence may simply happen, driven by the needs of the market rather than any legislative planning.

may be forced by the requirements of the global market to enact amending legislation. One of the earliest examples was the Australian amendment to its copyright
laws following the High Court's decision that no copyright subsisted in object code,[4]
and more recently the US spent several years in negotiation with the European
Commission over the transborder effect of data-protection laws.[5]

A particularly strong force towards convergence is the Internet and the commercial and non-commercial activities it allows. These impose substantial pressure on
national legislators to eradicate the differences between their own laws and those of
other states. Convergence also reduces the severe difficulties of enforcing laws and
regulations against an online actor, as compliance with the laws of the actor's home
state is likely to mean that it is also compliant abroad. The trend is towards recognition of a basic principle that information-processing activities should primarily be
regulated in their home countries,[6] which in its turn requires that laws converge.

Convergence can happen in one of three ways:

- Through the mechanism of international conventions—normally too slow a
  process for computer-law issues.

- Through harmonization or approximation of national laws, as the result of a
  conscious decision of national governments to remove the differences between
  them. The European Union provides the classic case study for harmonization, and
  where powers to enforce the adoption of new laws are lacking, approximation of
  national laws through bilateral or multilateral agreement is a possible alternative
  route.

- Through what might be described as accidental or fortuitous convergence, driven
  by pressure from IT enterprises and influential policy organizations.

The last of these is by far the most common, and means that many of the principles
of English law described in this book are likely to be replicated, now or in the future,
in the laws of other countries. As a corollary, when English law changes it will often
be possible to identify the inspiration for the change in another country's laws.
Globalization is a phenomenon which is not limited to trading activities—it also
drives legal innovation, and computer law is more strongly affected than most areas
of law.

---

[4] *Apple Computer Inc v Computer Edge Pty Ltd* [1986] FSR 537.
[5] For the outcome, see www.export.gov/safeharbor/sh_overview.html.
[6] See, eg, Directive 95/46/EC on the protection of individuals with regard to the processing of
personal data and on the free movement of such data ('the Data Protection Directive'), art 4; Directive
2000/31/EC on certain legal aspects of information society services, in particular electronic commerce, in
the Internal Market ('the E-Commerce Directive'), art 3(2).

# 1

# SYSTEM SUPPLY CONTRACTS

*Jeremy Newton*
*Partner, Nabarro Nathanson*

## 1.1 INTRODUCTION

### 1.1.1 System supply contracts

1.1.1.1 *What is a 'system supply contract'?*

Expressions like 'system supply contracts' and 'computer contracts' cover a multitude of commercial transactions, ranging from the purchase of a single CD-ROM from a high-street retailer through to multimillion pound systems or communications outsourcing projects. The traditional approach to examining such contracts drew a distinction between hardware and software agreements, but this distinction is becoming increasingly irrelevant. For the purposes of this chapter, then, a system supply contract is one under which the customer is to receive one or more of the following:

(a) hardware;
(b) software;
(c) other equipment (such as cabling or power supply); and
(d) services (such as consultancy, installation, support and maintenance).

### 1.1.1.2 *Contract structures*

System supply contracts can be structured in numerous ways. One common structure is known as the 'turnkey' arrangement, whereby the supplier undertakes to supply all the elements of the system under one contract, or as prime contractor at the top of a chain of connected subcontracts. More complex structures are also possible, whereby the supplier acts effectively as a broker between the customer and third-party suppliers.

## 1.1.2 The contract process

### 1.1.2.1 *Function of a written contract*

In most commercial transactions, the terms of contracts will be recorded in writing, and understanding the reasons for having a written contract can help the parties to negotiate it effectively. The function of a written contract is to record the terms governing the supply of goods and services. In the absence of a clear, express understanding between the parties, the law implies certain terms into the contract (discussed in more detail in section 1.2.1 below) which may run counter to the actual intentions of the parties, so a written agreement gives certainty to the terms of the transaction.

### 1.1.2.2 *Significance of the negotiation process*

There is also an important function to the negotiation process that leads up to signature of a written agreement. This process should help to ensure that the parties understand each other's expectations about the deal in question, and to draw out differences in those expectations that can then be resolved before they lead to problems. Many information technology ('IT') projects fail precisely because the parties do not exercise sufficient care to ensure that the supplier's and the customer's expectations match. Ensuring that these do match is, in the opinion of this author, the key role of the legal adviser in the contract process.

### 1.1.2.3 *Use of standard terms*

It is a feature of doing business in the IT sector that most suppliers will attempt to deal on their own set of standard terms. However, these are always negotiable to some degree. How far the supplier is willing to deviate from his standard terms depends mainly on the customer's bargaining power. Probably the only negotiable term in a contract for a single PC is the price, whereas a buyer who is paying several million pounds per annum as part of a major outsourcing deal will be able to negotiate most of the terms. The danger of uncritically accepting the standard terms of even the most respectable supplier can be illustrated by *Mackenzie Patten v British Olivetti*.[1] In that case, a law firm bought an Olivetti computer system to run its

---

[1] (1984) 1 CL&P 92, 95.

accounts. They discussed their needs with the salesperson, and signed up on Olivetti's standard terms. These dealt only with the system's technical performance, but did not address certain other important issues. The system proved unsuitable for the firm's purposes; it was slow, difficult to use, and could not expand to cope with new business. None of these matters was dealt with in the contract. In the event, the court found that Olivetti was bound by the salesperson's claims that the system would be suitable for the law firm's needs, but by that stage the firm had expended time and money in the litigation, and then of course had to find a replacement system.

Put another way, 'standard' forms are only suitable for 'standard' transactions. No matter how comprehensive the standard contract, it will usually fail to cover some essential point envisaged by the particular parties to any particular deal.

### 1.1.2.4 *Negotiating for the long term*
There is a further reason for negotiating a detailed contract for any significant deal: unlike many sale of goods contracts, the delivery of a computer system (or the commencement of service provision) is only the beginning of the relationship, not its culmination. Further work will be necessary to install the system and get it working properly, to obtain upgrades, and to monitor service levels. So although the aim of the negotiator is to get the best possible deal for the client, this should not mean gaining at the expense of the other side. The aim is to produce a mutually satisfactory contract which will provide a comprehensive basis for the continuing relationship between them.

### 1.1.2.5 *Types of contractual provision*
Any well-drawn contract will have provisions relating to three broad categories of expectation:

(a) Contract mechanics: for example, who delivers what, and when?

(b) Commercial highlights: for example, what is the price, who owns any resulting intellectual property rights ('IPRs'), what warranties are given in respect of the system?

(c) Problem management: what happens if the project goes wrong, and what remedies are available?

The objective is to ensure that no essential terms are missing from the contract. Some of these are discussed in section 1.2 below, and others relevant to the particular circumstances should come out of the negotiations themselves. However, before looking at specific contractual provisions, this chapter will discuss some of the principal legal aspects of system supply agreements.

### 1.1.3 Terminology

As a general point on terminology, there are a number of expressions that may correctly be used to denote the different parties to any system supply contract. In the context of the software-licensing elements, it is common to refer to 'licensor' and 'licensee'. Hardware sale agreements usually refer to 'buyers' and 'sellers'. Consultancy or software-development contracts will tend to refer to 'consultant' and 'client'. However, as a system supply contract may comprise any combination of these various elements, the author refers generally in this chapter to 'supplier' and 'customer' unless there is a sound reason for using the narrower expressions (such as in the discussion of Sale of Goods legislation which specifically refers to buyers and sellers).

## 1.2  PRINCIPAL LEGAL ISSUES APPLICABLE TO SYSTEM SUPPLY CONTRACTS

### 1.2.1  Implied terms

#### 1.2.1.1  *Background to the statutory implied terms*

Certain terms may be implied into contracts (both consumer and business contracts) as a matter of statute law or common law. The main statutory implied terms arise under the Sale of Goods Act 1979 ('SGA 1979') and under the Supply of Goods and Services Act 1982 ('SGSA 1982'). These terms are generally characterized as either conditions or warranties, the distinction being that breach of a condition entitles the innocent party to terminate the contract outright, whereas breach of a warranty entitles him to sue for damages only (but he remains committed to perform his side of the deal).

#### 1.2.1.2  *Section 12(1) of the SGA 1979: the right to sell*

Section 12(1) of the SGA 1979 implies a term[2] into all contracts of sale that the seller has the right to sell the goods. If the seller fails to transfer ownership, then he will be in breach of this term, and the buyer can reject the goods and recover the price, plus damages if they can be proved.[3]

#### 1.2.1.3  *Implications of section 12(1) of the SGA 1979 for hardware sales*

In order to satisfy section 12(1), the buyer must receive full and unfettered rights of ownership (unless the contrary has been agreed under section 12(3)). This means that the seller will be in breach of the condition if the goods are subject to rights belonging to a third party. The most obvious rights which exist independent of ownership are IPRs, so hardware producers risk running into difficulty if the product

---

[2] In England, Wales and Northern Ireland, this term is a condition by virtue of section 12(5A), added by the Sale and Supply of Goods Act 1994.

[3] This is not affected by any use of the goods by the buyer. The essence of a sale of goods contract is the transfer of ownership from seller to buyer, and a failure to effect this means that there is a total failure of consideration (*Rowland v Divall* [1923] 2 KB 500).

infringes someone else's IPR. In that eventuality, a patentee or copyright owner might prevent the buyer using any infringing equipment (or software loaded on legitimate equipment), so an innocent buyer could be prevented from using the hardware he has purchased. This is a clear breach of section 12(1) on the seller's part, even if the IPR owner chooses not to exercise his rights.

### 1.2.1.4 *Section 12(2) of the SGA 1979: quiet possession*

The seller will be in breach of section 12(1) if the third party's rights existed at the time of sale. However, some IPRs (for example, patents and trade marks) only come into existence on registration, so it is possible that such rights might only arise *after* the sale was made. In that case, the seller is not in breach of section 12(1), but is in breach of the term[4] in section 12(2)(b) that the buyer will have quiet possession of the goods.[5] This is in effect a promise by the seller that no person will in the future acquire rights over the goods and enforce them against the buyer. The warranty is broken only when the third party enforces his rights, at which point the buyer becomes entitled to claim damages from the seller (but not to reject the goods). However, if the third party prevents the buyer from using the goods, the buyer's damages will be assessed as the cost of buying a replacement, in effect returning the price.

### 1.2.1.5 *Section 13 of the SGA 1979: correspondence with description*

Section 13 of the SGA 1979 provides for an implied condition that goods will correspond with their description. In general, the description of hardware will be contained in a 'user requirements specification' attached to the contract. However, the question arises whether any claims made by salespeople or contained in the manufacturer's publicity material amount also to a description for these purposes. The traditional test is to ask whether the words used are a term of the contract or a mere representation. This is answered by examining whether the seller intended to promise, as part of the contract, that the words were true. In practice, however, it is impossible to ascertain the seller's real intention (indeed, the seller may have had none) and what the courts appear to be asking themselves is whether the buyer got that which he was led to believe he was buying. The test would thus be whether a reasonable person in the buyer's position would have been led to believe that the seller was promising a true description of the goods. As a general rule, only if the buyer examines the goods thoroughly before he buys will the court decide that descriptive words which had no influence on his decision to buy are not part of the description of the goods for the purposes of section 13.

---

[4] In England, Wales and Northern Ireland a warranty by virtue of section 12(5A), added by the Sale and Supply of Goods Act 1994.
[5] For a clear illustration of the distinction, see *Microbeads AG v Vinhurst Road Markings Ltd* [1975] 1 WLR 218.

### 1.2.1.6  *Section 14 of the SGA 1979: quality and fitness for purpose*
Section 14 of the SGA 1979 provides for an implied condition that goods will be of satisfactory quality (s 14(2)) and reasonably fit for their purpose (s 14(3)). However, obligations of quality raise particular problems in relation to IT systems as it is often difficult to define a system's purposes with sufficient precision, let alone decide if it is reasonably fit. In this respect, the description[6] of the goods can be very impor- tant—in some cases, it is almost the sole determinant of the quality the buyer is enti- tled to expect.

### 1.2.1.7  *Section 14 of the SGA 1979: satisfactory quality*
'Satisfactory quality' is defined in section 14(2A) and (2B) of the SGA 1979 Act (inserted by the Sale and Supply of Goods Act 1994) which state:

(2A)  For the purposes of this Act, goods are of satisfactory quality if they meet the standard that a reasonable person would regard as satisfactory, taking account of any description of the goods, the price (if relevant) and all the other relevant circumstances.

(2B)  For the purposes of this Act, the quality of goods includes their state and condition and the following (among others) are in appropriate cases aspects of the quality of goods—

   (a)  fitness for all the purposes for which goods of the kind in question are commonly supplied;
   (b)  appearance and finish;
   (c)  freedom from minor defects;
   (d)  safety; and
   (e)  durability.

It will be clear from the above definition that no hard and fast rule can ever be drawn as to whether goods fulfil the obligation of satisfactory quality. Instead, the courts will examine the circumstances of the contract in an attempt to decide whether a reasonable buyer would have been satisfied with the quality of the goods.

### 1.2.1.8  *Exceptions to section 14(2) of the SGA 1979*
The obligation set out in section 14(2) does not extend to defects that the seller specifically reveals, nor to those defects that should have been discovered by the inspection (if any) that was *actually made* by the buyer.[7] It should also be noted that it is not only the goods sold that must be satisfactory—any goods *supplied* under the contract (for example, manuals or magnetic media) must also be of satisfactory qual- ity, even if they remain the seller's property and are to be returned to him.

### 1.2.1.9  *Implications of section 14(2) of the SGA 1979 for system supply agreements*
The problem of ascertaining whether a system fulfils section 14(2) is likely to turn almost exclusively on the question of whether the system is fit for all its common

---

[6] ie, the user requirements specification, assuming one has been negotiated.
[7] SGA 1979, s 14(2C), as amended by the Sale and Supply of Goods Act 1994.

purposes. In this context, freedom from minor defects is probably an aspect of that fitness, unless the defects are merely cosmetic (perhaps, for example, a small dent in a computer case). The court's task is to determine what purposes systems *of the kind in question* are commonly supplied for. This is a very difficult matter, particularly in relation to hardware, the functioning of which is determined by the software which runs upon it. Similarly, in relation to software, programs invariably contain programming errors or 'bugs', and it is likely that a court will take note of this in determining whether a program is of satisfactory quality. Indeed, in *Saphena Computing Ltd v Allied Collection Agencies Ltd* the recorder acknowledged precisely this when he observed that 'even programs that are reasonably fit for their purpose may contain bugs'.[8] So the real question to be determined is what functions the seller might reasonably foresee the buyer as requiring. Predictably, no clear answers can be given, and for this reason it is common in substantial computer contracts to agree a detailed specification, listing the functions to be performed and objective criteria for testing that performance, and then to exclude the terms implied by section 14(2) and (3). (Note that different considerations apply to the purchase of commodity items such as PCs and peripherals as individual transactions, where the contract value is likely to be too low to permit the negotiation of detailed specifications. In many such cases, it may become necessary to rely on section 14(2).)

### 1.2.1.10 *Fitness for the buyer's particular purpose*

If the seller sells in the course of a business and the buyer expressly or impliedly makes known a particular purpose or purposes for which he intends to use the hardware, section 14(3) implies a term[9] that it will be reasonably fit for those purposes. This condition is imposed because the buyer relies on the seller to use his expertise to select goods suitable for the buyer's needs. If the buyer produces the user requirements specification himself, this would normally suggest that he is not relying on the seller's skill and judgment to select appropriate equipment, and that section 14(3) accordingly has no relevance. However, the seller will still be liable under that subsection in respect of matters not covered by the specification, as illustrated by *Cammell Laird & Co Ltd v Manganese Bronze & Brass Co Ltd.*[10] In that case, the buyer entered into a contract for the supply of a ship's propeller, to be manufactured to the buyer's specification and used on a named ship. The propeller proved unsuitable for the ship because its pitch was incorrect, a matter not provided for in the specification. The court held that as this had been left to the seller's discretion it clearly showed reliance on the buyer's part. The court also made it clear that if the defect had been in the buyer's specification the seller would not have been in breach of the condition.

In the context of IT systems, standard hardware and software are not of course

---

[8] [1995] FSR 616, 637, per Recorder Havery QC.
[9] In England, Wales and Northern Ireland, this term is a condition by virtue of section 14(6), substituted by the Sale and Supply of Goods Act 1994.
[10] [1934] AC 402 (followed in *Ashington Piggeries v Christopher Hill Ltd* [1972] AC 441).

designed for any particular user, and will be unlikely to meet all the requirements of any user. However, where customized hardware or bespoke software is supplied, the user may more reasonably expect to receive a warranty that it will comply with his requirements: indeed, it is far from unusual for the buyer to expect the seller to check his specification, particularly where the specification has been arrived at in consultation between them. In such cases, the buyer will claim to have relied on the seller's skill and judgment.

### 1.2.1.11 *Exceptions to section 14(3) of the SGA 1979*
The condition is not implied where it is unreasonable for the buyer to rely on the seller's expertise. This might be the case where the seller makes it clear that he cannot say whether the hardware will be suitable (for example, where it is purchased for research purposes) or where the buyer fails to give him the information he needs to exercise his judgment properly.[11]

### 1.2.1.12 *Section 13 of the SGSA 1982: reasonable care and skill*
The implied terms discussed above all apply to contracts for goods. Section 13 of the SGSA 1982 implies a different term into contracts for services, to the effect that the services will be provided with 'reasonable care and skill'.

### 1.2.1.13 *Implications of section 13 of the SGSA 1982 for system supply contracts*
Although section 13 of the SGSA 1982 may have little significance for contracts for hardware alone, the implied term is of course important to the supply of related services, for example, hardware maintenance, software development and support, consultancy and training. There is also a possibility that the supply of software *per se* may be viewed by the courts as a supply of services, for the reasons set out below.

### 1.2.1.14 *Classification of software as goods or services*
Until the late 1990s there did not appear to have been any reported cases in which the statutory implied terms had been held to apply to software, but four cases illustrate the development of judicial thinking on this point:

(a) In *Eurodynamics Systems plc v General Automation Ltd*[12] Steyn J refused to decide whether software was goods, or whether the terms implied by the SGA 1979 applied to the software licence in question, as he was able to decide the case without reaching a view on these issues.

(b) By contrast, in *Saphena Computing Ltd v Allied Collection Agencies Ltd* the recorder decided that 'it was an implied term of each contract for the supply of software that the software would be reasonably fit for any purpose which had been communicated to the plaintiff [claimant]'.[13] This decision is unsatisfactory,

---

[11] See *Griffiths v Peter Conway Ltd* [1939] 1 All ER 685.
[12] 6 September 1988 (unreported).     [13] [1995] FSR 616, 644.

however, since the recorder did not explain the basis on which he found that the term was implied. He did find, however, that the software had been supplied on terms that the software might not be lent, sold or hired to any third party without the licensor's consent, which might suggest a hiring rather than a sale, though this is by no means conclusive. On appeal Staughton LJ stated:

... it was, we are told, common ground that the law governing these contracts was precisely the same whether they were contracts for the sale of goods or the supply of services. It is therefore unnecessary to consider into which category they might come.

On the face of it that is an extraordinary statement since the law relating to goods as against services is quite different: the only term implied into a contract for services is that reasonable skill and care will be used, not that the result will be fit for any particular purpose or meet any standard of quality.[14]

(c)  A clearer statement that the SGA 1979 applies to the supply of software appears in the *obiter dictum* of Scott Baker J in *St Albans City and District Council v International Computers Ltd*.[15] The judge concluded that although the disks or tapes on which a program is recorded certainly are goods, the program of itself is not.

(d)  In the most recent reported decision on the point, *Horace Holman Group Ltd v Sherwood International Group Ltd*,[16] the court found that the computer program that a supplier had contracted to provide did not constitute 'goods' for the purposes of section 6 of the Unfair Contract Terms Act 1977 ('UCTA 1977') (discussed below at section 1.2.2.6).

Against this line of cases, the Scottish decision of *Beta Computers (Europe) Ltd v Adobe Systems (Europe) Ltd*,[17] holding that a supply of 'shrink-wrapped' software was not a sale of goods, should also be noted, although the decision is only of persuasive authority in England.

To what extent are these decisions helpful in determining whether the supply of software amounts to the provision of 'goods' or of 'services'? The view of this author is that a more subtle distinction is required, and that the classification (and hence the legal rules that apply to the supply) should really depend on the circumstances in which the software is procured. The purchase of, say, a standard computer game should be regarded as a sale of goods irrespective of the medium by which the software is delivered, whereas a bespoke system written specially by the supplier for a particular customer necessarily entails the supply of services. (Whether the terms implied by section 13 of the SGSA 1982 provide adequate protection for the customer in this latter case is an argument beyond the scope of this chapter.)

### 1.2.1.15  *Common-law implied terms*
It should be remembered that apart from terms implied by statute, terms may also be

---

[14]  Ibid, 652.     [15]  [1996] 4 All ER 481, CA.
[16]  (2002) 146 SJLB 35.     [17]  [1996] FSR 367.

implied from the facts and circumstances of the particular contract. Here the courts use the 'officious bystander' and 'business efficacy' tests to determine whether the implication of a term is proper, as illustrated by *Greaves & Co (Contractors) Ltd v Baynham Meikle & Partners*.[18] In a contract for the provision of engineering consultancy services there was an implied term that the design which was the subject of the contract should be fit for certain specific purposes. Similarly, in a software contract that is a mere contract for services (for example, programming), it may be possible to imply a term that the software supplied should comply with particular criteria, over and above the statutory term that the work be carried out with reasonable skill and care.

### 1.2.2 Limitations and exclusions of liability

#### 1.2.2.1 *Introduction*
It is common for system supply contracts to contain provisions excluding or limiting the supplier's liability. The most common exclusions or limitations refer to a breach of description or quality, and in particular it is common to exclude all liability for loss consequential on a breakdown or malfunction of the equipment. Such provisions need to be carefully drafted if they are to be effective, and some exclusions are not permitted by law. There are two levels of legal control over exclusion clauses: the common law, and statutory control under UCTA 1977 and the EC Directive on unfair terms in consumer contracts 1993.[19]

#### 1.2.2.2 *Common-law rules: incorporation of terms*[20]
In order for an exclusion clause to protect the supplier, it must be contractually binding on the customer. This is most easily effected if it is contained in a written contract signed by the buyer. Many contracts for goods of low value, however, are made by exchange of letters, each referring to the other's standard terms, and it may be a difficult matter to decide whether the clause in question is part of the contract.[21]

#### 1.2.2.3 *Common-law rules: construction and the* 'contra proferentem' *rule*
Even if it is duly incorporated, an exclusion clause will only protect the seller if, as a matter of construction, it covers the breach that has occurred. The rules of construction are complicated but in general the more serious the breach of contract, the more clearly worded the clause must be if it is to exclude liability for that breach: it is interpreted against the party seeking to rely on it (the *contra proferentem* rule). A good illustration of this principle at work can be found in *Salvage Association v CAP*

---

[18] [1975] 1 WLR 1095.

[19] Council Directive 93/13/EEC of 5 April 1993 on unfair terms in consumer contracts, OJ L95, 21 April 1993.

[20] See, generally, P S Atiyah, *The Sale of Goods*, 9th edn (Pitman, 1995), ch 13.

[21] This point is beyond the scope of the present work, but the rules for construing such an agreement can be found in any standard work on the law of contract.

*Financial Services Ltd.*[22] There, a contract to supply bespoke software contained a warranty (clause 11.1) which provided that the limitation (clause 12) applied 'if CAP fails to perform its obligations under this condition [11.1]'. The wording of clause 11.1 was sufficiently ambiguous that the official referee could construe it as meaning that the warranty did not come into effect until after acceptance by the claimant, and as the claimant's claim arose from breaches occurring prior to acceptance (which in fact never occurred because the dispute began before the contract's acceptance procedures were reached), the warranty in clause 11.1 never came into effect, and thus the exclusion in clause 12 also never came into effect. The result was that the defendant's liability for breach of contract was completely unlimited.

Similarly, in *Pegler v Wang*,[23] the clause in question purported to exclude liability for 'consequential loss in connection with or arising out of the supply, functioning or use of the system'. The court interpreted this language as not excluding liability for consequential loss arising from the *failure* to supply or the *delay* in supplying the system.

### 1.2.2.4 *Unfair Contract Terms Directive: background*
The newest statutory control on exclusion clauses is the EC Directive on Unfair Terms in Consumer Contracts,[24] implemented in the UK by the Unfair Terms in Consumer Contracts Regulations 1994.[25] The Directive provides that in a contract between a seller or supplier and a consumer unfair terms shall not be enforceable against the consumer, although the remainder of the contract remains in force so far as that is feasible.

### 1.2.2.5 *Unfair Contract Terms Directive: terms which may be regarded as 'unfair'*
A term is unfair for the purposes of the Directive if: (i) it has not been individually negotiated; and (ii) 'contrary to the requirement of good faith, it causes a significant imbalance in the parties' rights and obligations arising under the contract, to the detriment of the consumer' (art 3(1)). The annex to the Directive contains a list of terms which 'may be regarded as unfair' (art 3(3)).[26] Examples from that list which are particularly relevant to computer contracts include terms:

(b) Inappropriately excluding or limiting the legal rights of the consumer . . . in the event of total or partial non-performance . . .

(f) Authorising the seller or supplier to dissolve the contract on a discretionary basis where the same facility is not granted to the consumer . . .

---

[22] [1995] FSR 654.  [23] [2002] BLR 218.
[24] Directive 93/13/EEC, OJ L95, 21 April 1993.  [25] SI 1994/3159.
[26] In a consultative document, *Implementation of the EC Directive on Unfair Terms in Consumer Contracts* (DTI, 1993), the DTI took this wording to mean that the terms in the list may be, but are not necessarily, unfair. Other Member States may take a stronger position on this point, and in any event sellers should realize that including any of the terms in the annex is likely to give rise to a presumption of unfairness.

(h) Automatically extending a contract of fixed duration where the consumer does not indicate otherwise, when the deadline fixed for the consumer to express this desire not to extend the contract is unreasonably early.[27]

(i) Irrevocably binding the consumer to terms with which he had no real opportunity of becoming acquainted before the conclusion of the contract.[28]

(k) Enabling the seller or supplier to alter unilaterally without a valid reason any characteristics of the product or service to be provided.

(p) Giving the seller or supplier the possibility of transferring his rights and obligations under the contract, where this may serve to reduce the guarantees for the consumer, without the latter's agreement.[29]

(q) Excluding or hindering the consumer's right to take legal action or exercise any other legal remedy, particularly by . . . unduly restricting the evidence available to him or imposing on him a burden of proof which, according to the applicable law, should lie with another party to the contract.

These examples are not exhaustive—others from the annex may be applicable to particular computer contracts, and in any case the annex is purely indicative, so that terms having a similar effect are likely also to be construed as unfair.

### 1.2.2.6 *UCTA 1977: background*
UCTA 1977 is of more general application than the Directive, as it applies to contracts between businesses as well as to those between businesses and consumers. Suppliers of IT systems to consumers will need to consider both forms of control, whereas suppliers only to businesses can ignore the Directive.

### 1.2.2.7 *Section 6 of UCTA 1977: exclusions of liability under the SGA 1979*
Section 6 of UCTA 1977 deals with attempts to exclude liability under the SGA 1979. In particular:

(a) Section 6(1) provides that it is not possible to exclude the condition that the seller has the right to sell the goods (see sections 1.2.1.2–1.2.1.4 above).

(b) Section 6(2) provides that where the buyer deals as a consumer, it is not possible to exclude the seller's liability for correspondence to description, quality and fitness for purposes (see sections 1.2.1.5–1.2.1.13 above). A buyer 'deals as a consumer' if: (i) he does not buy in the course of a business; (ii) the seller sells in the course of a business; and (iii) the goods are of a type normally supplied for private use or consumption (see UCTA 1977, s 12).

(c) Section 6(3) provides that, where the buyer does *not* deal as a consumer, the seller's liability for correspondence to description, quality and fitness *may* be excluded, provided the exclusion clause satisfies the test of reasonableness.

---

[27] Examples (f) and (h) are particularly likely to arise in maintenance contracts.
[28] This is a particular problem in mail-order sales, especially where the order is placed by telephone.
[29] This too is a term which may be found in a maintenance contract.

### 1.2.2.8  Section 3 of UCTA 1977: exclusions of liability for breaches other than of the SGA 1979 implied terms

UCTA 1977 also affects clauses that attempt to exclude liability for breaches of terms other than those imposed by the SGA 1979. The most relevant provision is section 3, which provides that where the buyer deals as a consumer, or where he deals on the seller's written standard terms, the clause must satisfy the test of reasonableness to be effective. In most IT contracts, section 3 will apply as well as section 6, in which case the section that provides the best protection for the buyer will be applied.

### 1.2.2.9  When does UCTA 1977 not apply?

The only obvious case in which UCTA 1977 will be irrelevant is where the parties depart substantially from the seller's standard terms, and the breach is not of one of the implied terms. The theory is perhaps that if the parties are of such equal bargaining power that they can negotiate a non-standard contract, any exclusion clause is seen by both sides as fair. The question remains whether the entire contract needs to be in standard form, or whether it is sufficient to bring the case within section 3 if the exclusion clause alone is the seller's standard term. These issues have been examined in some depth in a line of recent cases:

(a)  In *Salvage Association v CAP Financial Services Ltd*,[30] which related to the supply of bespoke software, CAP had put forward its standard contract and had negotiated certain changes to it. In deciding whether section 3 of UCTA 1977 applied to those attempted exclusions, the official referee set out a list of factors which would be relevant:

(i)   the degree to which the standard terms are considered by the other party;

(ii)  the degree to which the terms are imposed on the other party;

(iii) the respective bargaining power of the parties;

(iv)  the willingness of the party putting forward the terms to negotiate them;

(v)   how far any alterations to the terms were agreed; and

(vi)  the extent and duration of the negotiations.

On the facts of the case, because the Salvage Association had considered various drafts and taken legal advice on them and persuaded CAP to agree to changes (though not, it is implicit, in the relevant exclusion terms), this was enough to show that the contract was not made on CAP's written standard terms. The exclusion and limitation clause therefore only fell under section 2(2), because it limited liability for breach of the express and implied terms that reasonable care and skill would be exercised by CAP.

---

[30] [1995] FSR 654.

(b) In *St Albans City and District Council v International Computers Ltd*[31] ICL had developed a complex package ('COMCIS') to calculate and administer the community-charge or poll-tax system of local taxation. St Albans used COMCIS to calculate the number of community-charge payers in its area, and used that figure to set its community-charge rate. The COMCIS software contained an error, so that although the St Albans database contained all the necessary details, the population figure reported was too high and, as a result, St Albans suffered a financial loss.

The contract contained a clause purporting to limit ICL's liability to the price or charge payable for the item of equipment, program or service in respect of which the liability arose or £100,000 (whichever was the lesser); and purporting to completely exclude liability for, *inter alia*, any indirect or consequential loss or loss of business or profits sustained by the customer. Liability turned on whether this clause was reasonable under section 11 of UCTA 1977.

ICL contested that UCTA 1977 applied at all, arguing that the contract had not been on standard terms. However, the judge held that UCTA 1977 did apply: in other words, that St Albans had contracted on ICL's written standard terms. Even though many elements of the contract were negotiated at length (for example, delivery dates, specification), ICL's General Conditions (which contained the limitation and exclusion clauses) 'remained effectively untouched in the negotiations',[32] and indeed were referred to by ICL staff as ICL's Standard Terms and Conditions in witness statements and letters.[33]

(c) In *South West Water Services Ltd v International Computers Ltd*[34] SWW and ICL had entered into two contracts—a turnkey agreement and a project-management agreement—under which ICL was to deliver a customer-service system to SWW. After ICL accepted that it would be unable to deliver the system to specification and in accordance with a planned timetable, SWW sued for breach of contract, claiming that ICL had failed to deliver the system as agreed, or at all, and also for misrepresentation.

Both agreements had contained a clause based on a standard ICL contract which purported to limit ICL's liability for any claim for loss or damage. The evidence was that, during the negotiations, SWW had originally submitted its own standard procurement conditions to ICL, and that ICL had rejected these. The question then arose whether, in these circumstances, the ICL limitations could be regarded as ICL's 'standard terms'.

Toulmin J followed the *St Albans* decision in finding that, even though SWW originally offered its own terms in negotiations, in the event ICL had dealt on ICL's

---

[31] [1996] 4 All ER 481, CA.                    [32] [1996] 4 All ER 481, per Nourse LJ.

[33] In the earlier case of *Flamar Interocean Ltd v Denmac Ltd* [1990] 1 Lloyd's Rep 434, the judge suggested (though did not specifically decide) that the fact that many parts of the defendant's standard terms, other than the exclusion clause, were modified in negotiations meant that section 3 did not apply. One clear difference between that case and *St Albans v ICL* is that in *St Albans* there was a clear distinction between the particular terms, which were negotiated, and the General Conditions, which were not. This is consistent with the decision in *Salvage Association v CAP*, though it is still not clear how much negotiation will take standard terms outside the provisions of section 3.

[34] Technology and Construction Court, 29 June 1999 (unreported).

own standard terms which had been only slightly adapted. The fact that one fairly predictable eventuality—failure to progress the project to a point where there was a system in place for SWW and capable of being tested—had not been addressed in the documentation also tended to suggest that the contract should be regarded as 'standard terms'.

(d) In *Pegler v Wang*,[35] the contract in question consisted of a set of standard terms with an attached schedule of variations and additional terms. One of these additional terms was a provision entitling the customer, Pegler, to recover any financial loss in the event that it terminated the contract for material breach. This conflicted with an exclusion clause in the main contract which set out a broadly worded exclusion of liability.

Purely on the question of whether the contract was on 'standard terms', the court found—perhaps somewhat counter-intuitively—that the contract was on standard terms notwithstanding the schedule of variations, as the standard exclusion clause itself had been included without any material variation to its wording.

(e) A similar approach was adopted by the court in *Horace Holman Group Ltd v Sherwood International Group Ltd*.[36] In this case, as in *Pegler*, the contract had taken the form of a set of the supplier's standard terms together with an attached annex of amendments, additions and deletions. The court took the view that the fact that some degree of negotiation had taken place was not relevant to the question of whether any particular term had ceased to be 'standard'. In fact, as the changes to the supplier's standard limitation clauses were only minor in this instance, these terms in particular were to be treated as 'standard terms', so UCTA 1977 did apply.

### 1.2.2.10 *The UCTA 1977 reasonableness test*

The test of reasonableness is set out in section 11 of, and Schedule 2 to, UCTA 1977. Section 11(1) provides that it must have been fair and reasonable to include the clause at the time the contract was made. The court will take account of the matters mentioned in Schedule 2, including:

(a) The strength of the bargaining position of the parties.

(b) Whether the buyer received some benefit (for example, a lower price) for agreeing to the clause.

(c) How far the buyer knew or ought to have known of the existence and extent of the clause.

(d) If the exclusion is contingent on compliance with some condition (for example, regular maintenance) whether it was reasonable to expect the condition to be complied with.

(e) Whether the goods were specially made or adapted to the customer's order.

---

[35] [2000] BLR 218.    [36] (2002) 146 SJLB 35.

The courts have also held that the question as to which of the parties can most readily insure against the loss is a relevant consideration, and that a limitation of liability is more likely to be reasonable than a complete exclusion.[37]

### 1.2.2.11 *The reasonableness test in practice (1): towards the high watermark*
The earlier cases in the line of decisions mentioned in section 1.2.2.9 above illustrate how the reasonableness test has historically been applied in practice:

(a) In *Salvage Association v CAP Financial Services Ltd*[38] the official referee found the following factors tended to support the supplier's contention that the exclusion was reasonable: first, the parties were of equal bargaining power and, secondly, the Salvage Association had taken legal advice and advice from its insurers and auditors. Against those factors, however, were the following:

(i)   UCTA 1977 puts the burden of proof of reasonableness on CAP;
(ii)  CAP had insurance up to £5,000,000, and could thus stand a greater liability, whilst the Salvage Association could not easily obtain insurance against CAP's failure;
(iii) the risk of CAP's failure should have been low;
(iv)  CAP assured the Salvage Association that it would succeed in constructing the software as required under the contract, and the Salvage Association had no reason to doubt this;
(v)   CAP had already decided to increase the maximum limit of its liability from £25,000 to £1,000,000, but failed to do so in this contract for unexplained reasons; and
(vi)  CAP called no evidence to justify the £25,000 limit in relation to CAP's turnover or insurance, or the contract value, or the financial risk the Salvage Association was running.

The official referee found that the factors in favour of the clause being unreasonable far outweighed those in favour of its reasonableness, and held the clause to be invalid so that CAP's liability for the breaches of contract was unlimited.

(b) Similarly, the judge in *St Albans City and District Council v International Computers Ltd*[39] held that the term was not fair and reasonable, and was thus ineffective to exclude or limit ICL's liability. Although St Albans knew of the limitation and had attempted to negotiate it, the following factors operated to render the clause unreasonable:

(i)   ICL had substantially more resources than St Albans;

---

[37] *George Mitchell (Chesterhall) Ltd v Finney Lock Seeds Ltd* [1983] 2 AC 803. This was a case decided under the slightly different provisions of the Supply of Goods (Implied Terms) Act 1973 as its facts occurred before the 1977 Act came into force, but it was nonetheless clearly decided with at least one eye on that Act.
[38] [1995] FSR 654.
[39] [1996] 4 All ER 481, CA.

(ii)    ICL held product liability insurance in an aggregate sum of £50 million worldwide;[40]

(iii)   ICL called no evidence to show that the limitation to £100,000 was reasonable, either in relation to the potential risk or the actual loss;

(iv)    as in *Salvage Association v CAP Financial Services Ltd*, the contract had mistakenly been made on an outmoded version of the General Conditions. In the current version the limitation was £125,000;

(v)     local authorities are not in the same position as private-sector businesses; their operations are constrained by statute and financial restraints and they cannot necessarily be expected to insure against commercial risks;[41]

(vi)    St Albans received no inducement to agree to the limitation, and there was evidence that all ICL's competitors imposed similar limitations of liability; and

(vii)   when St Albans tried to negotiate the limitation, albeit at the last moment, ICL in effect said that this was not possible because it would delay the provision of the software to St Albans beyond the date for implementation of the community charge.

The judge accordingly found that ICL had not discharged its burden of proving that the term was fair and reasonable, and also that financially ICL was best placed to bear a risk of this kind through insurance and thus spread it across its customer base.

(c)  The judge in *South West Water Services Ltd v International Computers Ltd*[42] noted further that the extent to which a party has had discussions and has freely entered into a contract on the other party's standard terms may be relevant as an important circumstance in considering whether those terms are reasonable. ICL argued that its standard limitation clause should be treated as reasonable in this case because its terms had been subject to arm's-length discussion and negotiation, but this was found not to be the case on the evidence.

### 1.2.2.12  The reasonableness test in practice (2): the high watermark

*Horace Holman Group Ltd v Sherwood International Group Ltd*[43] probably represents the high watermark of the courts' stringent application of the *contra proferentem* rule and the reasonableness test in favour of the customer. The contract had provided that the supplier, Sherwood, would have no liability for 'indirect, special,

---

[40]  It is not clear how this figure was discovered by St Albans. In *Flamar Interocean Ltd v Denmac Ltd* [1990] 1 Lloyd's Rep 434 the judge specifically held that details of the defendant's insurance cover did not have to be disclosed on discovery, as the relevant question under UCTA 1977 was not the specific cover that the defendant held but the availability of insurance cover in similar situations.

[41]  The case has received substantial criticism on this ground, which appears to reflect a somewhat idealized view of the relationship between local authorities and their suppliers. It seems unlikely to survive serious argument before another court.

[42]  Technology and Construction Court, 29 June 1999 (unreported).

[43]  LTL 27 July 2002.

consequential or economic loss or loss of contracts, goodwill, revenue, profits, anticipated savings or other benefits . . . or for any loss [arising from third-party claims]',
and that certain other losses were subject to a 'price paid' cap.

On the specific issue of reasonableness, the court made several observations
which seem a little counter-intuitive. For example:

(a) the court said that whilst both parties were large and capable of negotiating
on their own behalf, this was not a major consideration to the determination of the
reasonableness of the limitation;

(b) the court observed that as Sherwood's system was the best on the market at
that time, and the equivalent could not have been got elsewhere without a lot of extra
work, this also tended to undermine the reasonableness of the limitation—though it
is unclear to this author why a supplier's standard limitation clause should be treated
particularly unfavourably just because the supplier happens to have the best product
on the market;

(c) there was evidence from both parties that all the terms were commonplace in
the software industry, and the court held that Holman could not have obtained a
contract from a different supplier without substantially similar clauses—though
again, it is not clear why this should tend to undermine the reasonableness of a
clause;

(d) with regard to the price-paid cap, the court observed that the potential for loss
was significantly greater than the financial limits in question—but this is precisely the
reason for seeking to put a financial cap on the supplier's liability in the first place;

(e) with regard to the exclusion of liability for loss of savings, the court said in a
memorable phrase, 'people buy software to make savings because . . . if it works
properly, one computer loaded with the right software can replace a dozen Bob
Cratchits sitting at their stools with pens'.[44] On that basis, the court emphasized
again that a good reason was required to justify the exclusion and none was found, so
the exclusion of lost savings failed as well.

### 1.2.2.13  *The reasonableness test in practice (3): the tide turns*

As a result of that line of cases leading up to *Holman v Sherwood*, the question
started to arise whether the English courts 'have it in' for the IT industry.[45]
However, the tide now seems to have turned back in favour of the supplier, following the Court of Appeal's decision in *Watford Electronics v Sanderson*.[46]

---

[44] Ibid, 21–2.

[45] 'Do the Courts Have It In for the IT Industry?' was the title of a discussion at the Computing
Services and Software Association at the end of 2001, where the panellists included the chairman of ICL
and the judge in *Watford v Sanderson*. One of the themes at that session was that the IT industry does not
help itself with poorly drafted specifications and contracting processes, and with multiple personalities
within different parts of the supplier, eg, different individuals dealing with software, hardware and
support sales, etc.

[46] [2001] All ER 290.

In this matter, Watford had purchased an integrated sales accounts and warehouse package for use in its mail-order business. Total software and hardware costs and licence fees were in the region of £100,000, with damages claimed in excess of £5 million.

The contract was on standard terms, and also contained an exclusion of consequential loss and a price-paid limitation clause. At first instance, the judge found that these limitations taken together were unreasonable, and the supplier Sanderson appealed on this point to the Court of Appeal.

The Court of Appeal overruled the 'broad brush' approach taken by the lower court in treating the consequential loss and the price-paid limitation clauses as interconnected terms. This represents good news for suppliers, as these clauses will henceforth be construed separately so that if one is found to be unenforceable, there is at least a chance of succeeding under the other.

With regard to the exclusion of consequential loss specifically, the Court of Appeal went back to some first principles, and the logical argument was expressed as follows:

(a) there is a significant risk that a customized software product may not perform to a customer's satisfaction;

(b) if that happens, the customer will not make the savings it had expected to make, and this risk is (or at least ought to be) in the contemplation of the parties at the outset of the contract;

(c) in this particular case, the supplier was better able to appreciate the risk of *whether* the product might fail; but the customer was in a better position to *quantify* that risk;

(d) the risk of loss can generally be covered by insurance, although this may be available only at a cost which will in turn be reflected in the contract price.

Given all that background, when parties of equal bargaining power negotiate a price under an agreement which provides for the risk to fall on one particular party, the Court of Appeal said that the judiciary should be 'cautious' about saying that the term is not reasonable. The parties should be taken to be the best judges of the commercial fairness of the agreement, with a court not intervening unless one party has in effect taken unfair advantage of the other. In the circumstances of *Watford v Sanderson* itself, the exclusion of consequential loss was upheld.

The most important conclusion which can be drawn from all these cases is that a clause which is devised in standard form and then used in every transaction, without considering whether it is appropriate to that transaction and modifying it as necessary, is likely to be held unreasonable by the courts. Suppliers will therefore need to examine this issue in every case, except perhaps if a category of transactions can be identified where it is appropriate for the same clause to be used each time. Suppliers point out, quite reasonably, that it is commercially impossible for them to do this, as both the time required for individual negotiation and the costs of doing so are prohibitive. The only response must be that the benefits of contracting using standard contracts carry with them the cost that, from time to time, the standard exclusions will be held unreasonable.

### 1.2.3 Remedies

#### 1.2.3.1 *Conditions and warranties*
Some of the terms of the contract of sale are defined by the SGA 1979 or by case law as *conditions*,[47] terms whose breach is considered so serious that the buyer has the right to bring the contract to an end by rejecting the goods. The buyer is not, however, required to reject: he may elect to continue with the contract and claim damages for the breach. Other terms are defined in the Act as *warranties*. Although the Act provides that breach of such terms gives rise to a claim for damages only, the position adopted by the courts is rather different. If one of these terms is broken, the buyer will still have the right to reject if the breach 'goes to the root of the contract'—that is, if it is so serious that further performance is rendered pointless.[48] If the breach is not sufficiently serious to permit rejection, the buyer's only claim is for damages. This type of obligation is often known as an *innominate term*.

#### 1.2.3.2 *Rejection of goods*
Where the supplier is in breach of a condition of the contract, or where the breach is of an innominate term and sufficiently serious to go to the root of the contract, the customer will be entitled to reject the goods and recover the purchase price in full. It is not necessary for the customer physically to return the goods to the seller—all he is required to do by section 36 of the SGA 1979 is to inform the seller that he is rejecting and to make the goods available for collection. Rejection is a powerful remedy where the price has not yet been paid, as it forces the seller to initiate proceedings if he disputes that he is in breach. However, there are a number of reasons why the customer will find this remedy less useful than at first sight it might appear:

(a) Rejection may be undesirable because the process of specifying the system and negotiating terms has taken so long that finding an alternative supplier would result in too great a delay in the installation of replacement equipment. In such a case the buyer's only real option is to negotiate with the seller for the faults to be rectified and to claim damages. Indeed, the buyer may be 'locked in' to one particular supplier because the new system needs to be compatible with existing infrastructure.

(b) The right to reject can be lost, for one of three reasons: acceptance, election or waiver. These are discussed below.

---

[47] Under the law of England, Wales and Northern Ireland. Scots law uses different terminology, though the effect is similar.

[48] *Hong Kong Fir Shipping Co Ltd v Kawasaki Kisen Kaisha Ltd* [1962] QB 26.

### 1.2.3.3 *Acts constituting 'acceptance'*

In its legal sense, 'acceptance' means that the customer has performed some act which indicates that he intends to keep the goods. The relevant provision is section 35 of the SGA 1979, as amended by the Sale and Supply of Goods Act 1994, which essentially sets out three ways in which goods may be 'accepted':

(a) The buyer intimates to the seller that he accepts them, for example, by telling the seller that he is satisfied with them (s 35(1)(a)).

(b) The buyer, having received the goods, does some act 'inconsistent with the seller's continued ownership', for example, active use of the goods that goes beyond what is required merely for testing and evaluation, or physical modification of the goods such as to show that the buyer is treating them as his own (s 35(1)(b)).

(c) The buyer retains the goods beyond a reasonable time without rejecting—a question of fact in each case, though express contractual time limits for rejection are generally accepted by the courts as the parties' view of the time that would be reasonable for the buyer to retain the goods (s 35(4)).

### 1.2.3.4 *Acceptance of goods comprising a 'commercial unit'*

One further provision to note in relation to system contracts—which will often involve delivery of numerous goods such as CPUs, monitors, printers, cabling and software media (whether all at once or over a period of time)—appears in section 35(7) of the SGA 1979. This provides that where the contract is for the sale of goods making a commercial unit (that is, a unit division of which would materially impair the value of the goods or the character of the overall unit), then a buyer accepting *any* goods in a unit is thereby deemed to have accepted *all* the goods in the unit.

### 1.2.3.5 *Acts not amounting to acceptance*

Section 35 of the SGA 1979 goes on to specify certain acts that do *not* amount to acceptance. These are having the goods repaired under an arrangement with the seller (such as a guarantee) (s 35(6)(a)), and delivering the goods to a third party under a subsale or other disposition (s 35(6)(b)). Neither of these acts *in themselves* constitutes acceptance.

### 1.2.3.6 *Election*

Election involves the buyer making a choice between two remedies. Under section 11(2) of the SGA 1979, the buyer has the right to decide not to reject the goods but to claim damages instead. If he leads the seller to believe that this is what he is doing, he has made an election and accordingly loses his right to reject. This typically occurs in the case of late delivery, where the buyer accepts delivery but reserves his right to damages. By doing so in the knowledge that the delivery is defective (ie, late) he loses his right to reject and is relegated to a claim in damages.

### 1.2.3.7 *Waiver*

Waiver is similar to election, in that it involves the buyer leading the seller to believe that he will not enforce the right to reject the goods. However, waiver entails a more complete renunciation of rights, and requires a representation that the buyer will not enforce a particular contractual right at all. The most common examples of waiver occur where the goods are not delivered on time and the buyer, instead of immediately rejecting, presses the seller to make delivery as soon as possible. This amounts to a representation by the buyer that he is not insisting on the original date, and not only does he lose his right to reject for that breach but also any claim to damages. This is not necessarily as final as it might seem, for if the seller has still to perform his obligation the buyer can reimpose the condition by giving reasonable notice.[49]

### 1.2.3.8 *Damages payable to a buyer of goods*

The buyer's claim for damages will fall into one of two categories, depending on the nature of the breach of contract:

(a) Damages for failure to deliver goods (either on time or at all)—these damages are governed by section 51 of the SGA 1979, which provides that the normal measure of damages is 'the estimated loss directly and naturally resulting, in the ordinary course of events, from the seller's breach of contract' (s 51(2)).

(b) Damages for breach of warranty—these damages generally are governed by section 53(2) of the SGA 1979, which is in substantially the same terms as section 51(2). However, if the breach is of a 'warranty of quality', the statutory measure of damages will be '*prima facie* the difference between the value of the goods at the time of delivery to the buyer and the value they would have had if they had fulfilled the warranty' (s 53(3)).

### 1.2.3.9 *Damages payable to a seller of goods*

The preferred remedy of any seller will be the price of the goods, as this is what he contracted for. The basic assumption of the SGA 1979 is that he is not obliged to deliver the goods to the buyer until he has been paid, and so he has a right of lien (ie, a right to retain possession) if payment is not forthcoming. However, if the buyer wrongfully fails or refuses to accept delivery, the seller will have a claim for damages against him. Damages are assessed under section 50, which is in almost identical terms to section 51, and the majority of what has already been said about that section will apply here.

### 1.2.3.10 *Specific performance*

Under section 52 of the SGA 1979, the court has a discretion to award specific performance where the contract relates to specific or ascertained goods. If the subject matter of the contract is generic—in other words, it merely refers to a partic-

---

[49] *Charles Rickards Ltd v Oppenhaim* [1950] 1 KB 616.

ular description of goods—it is generally assumed that the buyer will be able to obtain replacement goods elsewhere.[50]

## 1.3 COMMERCIAL AND DRAFTING ASPECTS

### 1.3.1 Introduction

#### 1.3.1.1 *The need for express contract terms*
It will be clear from the above discussion that there is no shortage of contractual terms that can be implied by law into contracts for the provision of computer systems. These implied terms will not always reflect the commercial intentions of the parties, and to that extent it is preferable for the parties to set out in express terms the position they are trying to achieve. However, the contract is more than just a 'legal' document. Its function should be to record all the terms governing the supply of the system—in terms of what is being delivered, how it is paid for, what happens if the goods or services supplied are unsatisfactory, and so on. The function of the negotiation process that leads to a written contract is to ensure that the parties understand each other's expectations (and their own) about the deal in question, and to draw out differences in understanding that can then be addressed before they lead to problems. Many projects go wrong precisely because, for whatever reason—time pressure, pushy salesmen, deliberate misrepresentation—the parties do not exercise sufficient care to ensure that the supplier's and the customer's expectations match.

#### 1.3.1.2 *The role of the legal adviser*
As noted at section 1.1.2 above, a well-drawn system supply contract will have certain features that require the parties to consider their expectations and record them. Ensuring that these expectations do match, and are properly recorded in the contract document, is the key role of the legal adviser in the contract process.

There is a common misconception in the IT industry that contract documentation is purely a matter for lawyers, and is somehow separate from the commercial realities of a transaction. As a result, the legal adviser is often left out of the early stages of negotiation, and frequently has to raise key issues such as limitations of liability at a very late stage in the process. Putting together the right team for the procurement or sale should mean involving the legal team at the outset, and using their expertise to help draft and structure the documentation generally.

---

[50] An exception to this general rule is where a dealer has a long-term contract with a manufacturer for regular deliveries of hardware, and there is no alternative source of supply; see *Worldwide Dryers Ltd v Warner Howard Ltd, The Times*, 9 December 1982.

### 1.3.2 Specification

#### 1.3.2.1 *Need for a written specification*
A clear specification is the foundation stone of a successful system supply contract. It defines what the supplier will provide, sets out the quality standards to be achieved, and forces both sides to think seriously about what is really wanted, and what is achievable. In every case, the specification should address:

(a)  Functionality (ie, what the system is to do).
(b)  Performance (ie, how well it is supposed to do it).
(c)  Compatibility (ie, any software and hardware with which the system is likely to be used).

The importance of including a suitably detailed specification can be illustrated by two cases. In *Micron Computer Systems Ltd v Wang (UK) Ltd*[51] one of Micron's complaints was that a system bought from Wang did not provide 'transaction logging'. The judge observed that 'the acknowledged absence of a transaction logging facility is not in reality a fault in the system which was sold. Micron can only complain about its absence if Micron can establish a contractual term, express or implied, or an actionable representation, to the effect that the system included such a facility. In order to make good its case on transaction logging, Micron must therefore establish that they made known to Wang that they required such a facility'.[52] In the event, the judge found on the evidence that Micron had not made its requirement for transaction logging clear to Wang, and accordingly that part of Micron's case failed.

By contrast, in *St Albans City and District Council v International Computers Ltd*[53] the local authority had made its requirements clear in its invitation to tender which had itself been expressly incorporated into the contract. When the system supplied failed to meet those requirements, the authority claimed successfully against the supplier on the basis of breach of an express term.

### 1.3.3 Delivery and acceptance arrangements

#### 1.3.3.1 *Delivery*
The arrangements for delivery should always be dealt with by express provisions in the supply contract. The contract should set out the date (or dates) on which delivery is to be made, whether all the elements of the system are to be delivered at one time or whether it is to arrive in instalments, and who has responsibility for installation and testing. From the point of view of contractual certainty, the ideal situation is for the contract to set out specific delivery dates. This may not be possible if, say, there is a lengthy development project prior to delivery, but even in that eventuality the

---

[51] 9 May 1990, QBD (unreported).       [52] Ibid.
[53] [1996] 4 All ER 481, CA.

contract should set out a timetable or project plan showing roughly how long each phase is likely to take. If no clear date is identified or identifiable, then as a matter of law the system will have to be delivered within 'a reasonable time': a position of contractual uncertainty that is unlikely to provide significant advantage to either party in the event of a dispute.

*Consequences of late delivery and non-delivery.* What commonly happens if delivery is late is that the buyer waives the seller's obligation to achieve that date, and so loses the right to reject: for example, by continuing to request delivery after the contractual date has passed. This means that there is now *no* contractual date for delivery, and at best the seller is obliged to deliver within a reasonable time. In order to regain the right to reject, the buyer must reimpose a date by giving the seller reasonable notice that the buyer will refuse to accept that part of the system after a particular date.[54] Such notice is normally express, but it may be given impliedly (for example, by service of a writ[55]). As an additional protection for the buyer, the contract should ideally contain an express provision permitting cancellation of the contract, with or without compensation to the buyer, if the goods are not delivered by some cut-off date. Alternatively, if the supplier does not agree to a clear target date for delivery, the contract may provide for a notice period after which the buyer can withdraw, with an appeal against the notice to a third party.[56]

### 1.3.3.2   *Acceptance arrangements*

Formal acceptance procedures are a crucial aspect of any successful system procurement. Systems are acquired in order to perform a specified set of functions, within particular performance requirements. Until the system has been tested, the buyer will not be able to assess whether what has been delivered accords with the contract.

*Defining acceptance criteria.* The nature of acceptance tests varies widely between projects. Where a major piece of development work is involved, the parties may negotiate and document detailed testing arrangements as part of the contract document. At the other extreme, the acceptance procedure may simply be that if the buyer uses the system 'live' for, say, thirty days without rejecting it, then it is deemed to have been accepted. The vital features of any acceptance procedure, however, are:

(a) That it provides for an objective and measurable 'yardstick' as to the standards of performance and functionality to be demonstrated.

(b) From the buyer's point of view, that this yardstick will demonstrate to its full satisfaction that the system meets its requirements.

---

[54]   *Charles Rickards Ltd v Oppenhaim* [1950] 1 KB 616.
[55]   *Tool Metal Manufacturing Co Ltd v Tungsten Electric Co Ltd* [1955] 1 WLR 761.
[56]   eg, an arbitrator, the engineer in construction contracts, etc.

(c) That the procedure is clear as to the consequences of both the passing and failing of the acceptance test.

*Consequences of acceptance.* On successful completion of the testing, the system will be deemed to have been accepted. Acceptance will generally trigger payment of the whole or the final instalment of any lump-sum charges, or the commencement of periodic charges, and following acceptance the buyer's remedies will be limited to a claim under the warranty provision. The contract should also provide expressly for the consequences of failure to achieve acceptance. Typically, there will be a period during which the supplier may rectify problems and then retest; but further failure will signal the premature end of the contract, with the buyer able to return the hardware and software in exchange for a refund of any moneys paid.

### 1.3.4  Timetable

#### 1.3.4.1  *Need for the timetable*
The preparation of the specification should enable the parties to assess the likely timescale for the project and so to prepare a project plan setting out key deliverables (or 'milestones') and their expected dates. In almost all implementations of major systems staged payments will be triggered by the achievement of individual milestones. It is accordingly essential that these are identified with as much precision as possible, and reflect the terminology of the contract generally. The buyer will generally have in mind a timescale within which it wants the system provided, although the sophistication of the timetable will vary according to:

(a) The complexity of the project in question—a major development contract may include target dates for numerous stages, each of which may be divided up into smaller phases such as functional specification, systems specification, program specification, development, program testing, systems testing, debugging, retesting and acceptance.

(b) Payment arrangements—in particular, whether the price and payment arrangements are tied in to specified 'milestones', and the implications for both parties of any failure to meet target deadlines.

### 1.3.5  Pricing and payment

#### 1.3.5.1  *Pricing and payment structures generally*
From the supplier's point of view, the heart of the contract is ensuring that he gets paid for the goods or services he provides. There are as many pricing and payment structures as there are types of IT deal. For example:

(a) a single charge for the entire development and implementation project; and/or

(b) periodic charges for ongoing maintenance and support; and/or

(c) separate purchase and licence fees in respect of the hardware and software elements of the system (for which licence fees may themselves be periodic or a single lump sum).

As a result, there is little to be gained from making generalizations about pricing and payment terms. The one point worth making is that, where payments are tied into specific targets (such as system acceptance), the terminology and structure of the payment schedule should accurately reflect that of the timetable.

### 1.3.5.2 *Timing of payments*

The time of payment will generally not be of the essence unless it is expressed as such. However, for the sake of contractual certainty, it is of course desirable to specify precisely when sums become due. This links in with delivery dates. A common practice in systems contracts is to pay by instalments as the various parts of the system are delivered, retaining a proportion of the price until the complete system has been tested. This arrangement will incentivize the supplier to perform these obligations in accordance with the contractual timetable, while the retention of a significant proportion of the fee until acceptance will give the buyer some security for performance. Suppliers will also often seek an express right to payment of interest on overdue amounts.

In respect of periodic fees specifically, the buyer will be concerned about the supplier's rights to increase the fee, and may seek to circumscribe these in some way. For example, he may seek to incorporate a term so that only one increase a year may be permitted or so that rises are limited by reference to an appropriate index. The buyer may also seek to delay the first payment until after the system has been accepted.

### 1.3.5.3 *Retention of title*

Where the seller gives credit to the buyer, there is always some doubt whether the seller will be paid. If the buyer is a well-established organization this doubt is extremely small, but newer or smaller organizations may present a greater risk. For this reason, it is common for hardware suppliers to retain title in the goods they supply as security for payment. A retention-of-title clause is a provision in the contract that although the buyer is to be given possession of the goods, ownership is to remain with the seller until certain conditions (normally payment in full) are complied with. If the buyer fails to comply with the conditions, the seller is entitled to repossess the goods, and can then sell them to recoup his losses.

Retention-of-title clauses are permitted under section 19 of the SGA 1979. It is important that the seller retains title, property or legal ownership (all these terms are equivalent).[57] As risk normally passes with property, a retention-of-title clause will also provide that the goods are at the buyer's risk from the moment of delivery. It should contain a clear statement of when the seller is entitled to repossess the goods,

---

[57] Note that any drafting which amounts to a retention of equitable ownership will result in the creation of a charge which must be registered under the Companies Act 1985 or the Bills of Sale Act 1878.

normally if payment is not made within the credit period, or if the buyer commits an act of insolvency or a receiver is appointed. It is also common to include a provision that the seller has the right to enter the buyer's premises to repossess the goods.

### 1.3.6 Intellectual property rights

#### 1.3.6.1 *The need for express treatment of IPR issues*
System supply contracts generally entail the transfer of information, in some form, from one party to another, for example, program specifications (in a consultancy agreement), software (in a software licence), data for processing (in a bureau services agreement) or confidential business information (in a development agreement). The lawful use of such information is dependent on compliance with the laws relating to copyright, confidentiality, database rights and other forms of intellectual property ('IP'). In addition, the use of certain computer equipment may constitute an infringement of patent or similar rights if it is undertaken without the consent of the rights owner. As a result, it is essential that any system supply contract deals comprehensively with IPR issues, and in particular addresses:

(a) ownership; and
(b) IPR warranties and indemnities.

#### 1.3.6.2 *Ownership*
The contract should specify what IPRs are to be created or used, and precisely who owns them. This is particularly important in contracts for software development or consultancy work because of section 11 of the Copyright, Designs and Patents Act 1988 ('CDPA 1988') which contains a common trap for the unwary: work done under a consultancy contract will normally vest in the supplier, not the customer, so a formal written assignment of copyright is needed if the aim is for the customer to own the work product outright.

#### 1.3.6.3 *Treatment of third-party software*
For similar reasons, where the system incorporates any third-party software, the prudent customer will want an express assurance that the supplier has authority to grant the licence or sub-licence in respect of those third-party rights. As a practical matter, it is essential to ensure that there is no 'hiatus' between the scope of the third-party licence and the uses envisaged in respect of all other aspects of the system.

#### 1.3.6.4 *IPR warranties and indemnities*
Although section 12 of the SGA 1979 provides a remedy for the customer if the seller should turn out not to have the right to sell the products in question,[58] in practical terms, the parties are unlikely to be happy to rely on this general law position:

---

[58] See section 1.2.1.2 above.

(a) The customer will often impose a formal obligation to take curative action to deal with any allegations of third-party IPR infringement. This is particularly so if the system is a critical part of the customer's business and merely rejecting it and claiming back the purchase price would leave the customer in a difficult position.

(b) Equally, the supplier may wish to reserve the right to dispute the existence or extent of the third party's claims, in order to preserve its reputation and position in the market.

As a result, most system supply contracts will contain a warranty in favour of the customer that use of the system will not infringe third-party rights, and an indemnity in respect of any claims that may arise. (Similar provisions are commonplace in distribution and agency contracts, to protect the distributor/agent and its end-user customers against IPR claims brought in respect of products supplied by the principal.) The contract should set out any express warranties as to the supplier's ownership or entitlement in respect of the IPRs comprised in the system, together with a process for addressing any breach of those warranties. A clause which incorporates the following points should assist in removing some of the potential complications:

(a) A right on the supplier's part to take over and litigate (in the customer's name) any such action by a third party, and to settle the action.

(b) A right for the supplier to modify the system so that it does not infringe the alleged right, provided that it still conforms with the specification.[59]

(c) An indemnity given by the supplier against the customer's losses in the event of a successful third-party claim.

### 1.3.6.5 *Confidentiality*
A further feature of the transfer of information between suppliers and customers is that provision needs to be made to ensure that the information is treated in confidence. In the context of a consultancy agreement or a bureau services contract, for example, the consultant may have access to all kinds of commercially sensitive information about the customer's business and systems. The customer will want to ensure that this information is only used for the express, permitted purposes. Similarly, where a software house is licensing programs for use by its customer, the supplier will want to ensure that its proprietary software is not disclosed to third parties.

### 1.3.6.6 *Access to source code*
Software elements of the system will usually be delivered to the customer in object code form, with the source code being retained by the supplier. The practical

---

[59] It must be noted that a seller cannot exclude or restrict the condition in the SGA 1979, s 12(1); see sections 1.2.1.2–1.2.1.3 above. However, until the third party has established that the right has in fact been infringed, the seller is arguably not in breach of that condition. In any event, most buyers should be satisfied with effective cure.

consequence of this will be that, whilst the buyer is able to use the software, he will not be able to modify or maintain it. He is dependent on the supplier for software maintenance, although he may be able to protect himself against the more dire consequences of such dependence by reason of the error-correction rights conferred in section 50C of the CDPA 1988. Again, however, the prudent customer would be unwise to rely on this general law provision, for which reason the contract should expressly provide for either:

(a) An express right to call for and to use the source code for development or maintenance purposes (a requirement which will often be vigorously resisted by suppliers), perhaps subject to confidentiality conditions, in order to protect the supplier's legitimate interests in the secrecy of this material.

(b) An escrow arrangement, whereby the supplier agrees to deposit a copy of the source code with an independent third party (the escrow agent) and then the supplier, customer and escrow agent enter into a tripartite agreement to govern its release. The escrow agreement will provide for the initial deposit of the source code, and for its updating with error corrections and new releases. On the happening of certain specified events (for example, such as the supplier going into liquidation, or failing to provide maintenance services as contracted for), the escrow agent will release the source code to the customer for the purposes of maintaining the software. At least two bodies provide an escrow service along these lines, namely the National Computing Centre and the Computing Services and Software Association, and so far it would seem that the arrangements work successfully.

### 1.3.7  Other express warranties

#### 1.3.7.1  *The need for express warranties*
The existence or otherwise of implied terms in system supply contracts is, as we have seen, a matter of some uncertainty. In reality, such terms are unlikely to be of much assistance to the customer as they will be pitched in general terms, and the limited usefulness of these provisions can be illustrated by reference to two decisions:

(a) In *Saphena Computing Ltd v Allied Collection Agencies Ltd*[60] the court found that there was an implied term that software should be fit for all purposes communicated to the supplier before the contract was made, and any further purpose subsequently communicated, provided that in the latter case the supplier accepted the customer's instructions to make the relevant modification.

(b) *Micron Computer Systems Ltd v Wang (UK) Ltd*[61] illustrates the consequences of failing to make a requirement known. In that case, Micron failed on the evidence to show that it had made its requirement for 'transaction logging' known to

---

[60] [1995] FSR 616.        [61] 9 May 1990, QBD (unreported).

Wang, and its claim that the system supplied by Wang was defective accordingly failed in that respect.

A further problem in the real world is that software licences are nearly always written, and nearly always exclude or limit the operation of all implied conditions and warranties. The efficacy of such exclusions and limitations is examined at section 1.2.2 above.

### 1.3.7.2 *Forms of warranty*

Express warranties given by suppliers are accordingly of considerable importance. Such express warranties normally take one of two forms:

(a) The warranty may state that the system will comply with its functional specification or user manual, or meet certain specified performance criteria, or the like. Such a warranty has the advantage that compliance or breach can be objectively measured, and is usually the best form of express warranty that a licensee can obtain.

(b) The warranty may provide that defects will be corrected by the supplier or licensor, though the disadvantage here is that it begs the question of what constitutes a defect. For example, in the event of failure to perform a particular function, there may be a dispute about whether the lack of the particular function in fact amounts to a defect (which was precisely the issue in *Micron*).

### 1.3.7.3 *Restrictions on warranties*

Whatever the form of warranty, it is likely to be subject to a number of restrictions:

(a) It will generally be limited to a fairly short period of time, probably between three and twelve months. After this time the system may be covered by the maintenance and support arrangements: in other words, ongoing maintenance after expiry of the warranty period has a separate price attached to it.

(b) Some warranty clauses also state that the supplier's only liability is to correct the non-compliance or the defect. The purpose would seem to be to exclude any liability for damages. To the extent that the supplier complies with the warranty this would seem to be effective, but if he fails to remedy the non-compliance or defect, an action for damages would lie for that failure.

(c) Warranties often state that they cease to apply if the customer makes any additions or modifications to the system. Customers would be well advised to limit the qualification to errors or defects in the system that are actually caused by the addition or modification.

## 1.3.8 Limitations and exclusions of liability

### 1.3.8.1 *Drafting effective exclusion clauses*

IT suppliers generally seek to restrict their potential exposure to users resulting from breach of contract or defects in the system. This is treated by some as purely a 'legal' issue, but in fact it is a major practical question of commercial risk assessment and allocation. This type of provision is commonplace in system supply contracts, particularly where the contract is based on the supplier's standard terms, which typically contain a limitation clause along the following lines:

(a) The supplier does not exclude liability for death or personal injury caused by negligence (which cannot by law be excluded).

(b) The supplier seeks to exclude liability altogether for 'special', 'indirect' or 'consequential' losses.

(c) The supplier accepts a limited degree of liability for certain other classes of 'direct' loss.

The general legal issues as to the enforceability of limitation and exclusion clauses are discussed at section 1.2.2 above. The first point in (a) above requires little further discussion: liability for death or personal injury caused by negligence *cannot* be limited, as a matter of law.[62] The second and third points in (b) and (c) are discussed below.

### 1.3.8.2 *Consequential loss: general principles*
The parties need to consider what kinds of loss might result from a system failure, and who takes the risk. The basis of the supplier's argument to exclude liability for consequential loss or loss of profits is essentially that the nature of IT products means that their uses (and thus the potential consequential losses) are not easily foreseeable at the time the contract is made, and that the potential exposure is in any case disproportionate to the contract value. Whether this is an acceptable commercial stance depends on the nature of the system and the extent of the customer's dependence on it.

### 1.3.8.3 *Consequential loss: drafting issues*
However, turning that commercial position into effective (and commercially acceptable) drafting can be more problematic. There is no consensus as to the meaning of the expressions 'special', 'indirect' and 'consequential' in the context of contractual claims, and there is often a resulting lack of certainty as to the precise effect of the intended exclusion. It is not the purpose of this chapter to try to offer a definitive interpretation of these terms, but it may be helpful to summarize the semantic and philosophical problems encountered by judges and academics in trying to pin down their meanings.

### 1.3.8.4 *Consequential loss:* Hadley v Baxendale
The starting point for any discussion of consequential damages is *Hadley v Baxendale*[63] which distinguished two classes of loss recoverable for breach of contract. These are:

---

[62] UCTA 1977, s 2(1).        [63] (1854) 9 Exch 341.

(a) 'such [damages] as may fairly and reasonably be considered either as arising naturally, that is, according to the usual course of things . . . or such as may reasonably be supposed to have been in the contemplation of both parties at the time they made the contract as the probable result of the breach of it';[64] and

(b) if the parties were aware of 'special circumstances' at the time the contract was made, the damages 'which they would reasonably contemplate would be the amount of injury which would ordinarily flow from a breach under these special circumstances'.[65]

That basic distinction has been recast on a number of occasions over the last 140 years. However, the difficulty for the draftsman is that the terminology in common usage—'indirect' or 'consequential' loss, or 'special' damages—does not fit neatly into the *Hadley v Baxendale* rules, nor is it used in a consistent fashion. For example, the expression 'consequential loss' is taken by some to mean pecuniary loss consequent on physical damage. However, when used in an exclusion clause, 'consequential' means losses arising under the second rule in *Hadley v Baxendale*, and so does *not* preclude recovery of pecuniary losses under the first rule.[66]

### 1.3.8.5 *Consequential loss:* British Sugar plc v NEI Power Projects Ltd

The most recent authoritative discussion of the meaning of 'consequential loss' is *British Sugar plc v NEI Power Projects Ltd.*[67] It is also a good example of the confusion that can be caused by trying to use *Hadley v Baxendale* terminology to define concepts like 'direct', 'indirect' or 'consequential' loss. In the *British Sugar* case NEI supplied some defective power equipment to British Sugar, with a headline value of about £100,000. The sale contract expressly limited the seller's liability for 'consequential loss'. As a result of breakdowns, increased production costs and resulting loss of profits, British Sugar put in a claim of over £5 million. British Sugar argued for the narrowest construction of the term 'consequential loss', interpreting it to mean 'loss not resulting directly and naturally from breach of contract'; whereas NEI argued that the term meant 'all loss other than the normal loss which might be suffered as a result of the breach of contract, negligence or other breach of duty'. The courts found for the claimant, and approved earlier authorities that 'consequential damages' means the damages recoverable under the second limb of *Hadley v Baxendale*. By this analysis, where loss of profits or loss of business (commonly regarded as typical examples of 'consequential loss') arise naturally from the breach of contract, they should be recoverable by the user: a result that may surprise many IT suppliers.

### 1.3.8.6 *Consequential loss: defining 'indirect loss' and 'special damages'*

Similar confusion applies in relation to the effect of other commonly used terms:

---

[64] Ibid, 354.                              [65] Ibid.
[66] See *Saint Line Ltd v Richardsons, Westgarth & Co* [1940] 2 KB 99.
[67] [1998] ITCLR 118.

(a) In relation to 'indirect loss', it used to be the case that the courts would hold a defendant liable (particularly in negligence) for all 'direct consequences' whether foreseeable or not, but they have long since ceased to try to define issues of remoteness and quantum in terms of 'direct', 'natural' or 'ordinary'. Instead, following the *Wagon Mound*[68] cases in the 1960s, the test of liability (in tort at least) is analysed simply in terms of foreseeability.

(b) To complicate matters further, the term 'consequential' has at one point been defined simply to mean 'not direct'[69] but there is also an argument, following certain observations of Lord Diplock in *P & M Kaye v Hosier*[70] that the expression 'direct' could include 'consequential' losses provided these were not too remote.

(c) The term 'special damages' has at least four possible meanings, including: (i) past (pecuniary) loss calculable as at the trial date, as opposed to all other items of unliquidated 'general damages'; and (ii) losses falling under the second rule in *Hadley v Baxendale*, as opposed to 'general damages' being losses recoverable under the first rule.

### 1.3.8.7  *Consequential loss: towards a risk-allocation analysis*

In summary, the meanings of the terms 'indirect', 'consequential' and 'special' are at best unclear in the context of IT contracts, and it is surprising that they should continue routinely to be used. The inclusion of such imprecise terminology inevitably delays the contract process, creates uncertainty for users and suppliers alike, and reflects badly on the IT industry and its legal advisers. Instead, both suppliers and customers should focus on the specific risks associated with the particular system. The customer will generally accept that the supplier has a legitimate concern about exposure to unspecified types of liability: but the kinds of loss that will flow from a breach of an IT supply contract *can* be classified, at least in general terms.

In this respect, the hearing on assessment of damages in *Holman v Sherwood* provides some helpful headings for consideration. Once the limitation clauses had been overturned, the parties went back to court to determine the heads of damage for which Sherwood would be liable. Holman had claimed under six heads of damage:

(a) third-party costs (including disaster recovery, maintenance, contractors' fees and the costs of upgrading its PCs to cope with the replacement system);

(b) other costs savings (which included savings which Holman had expected to make by bringing the preparation of its insurance policy work in-house, but which it was unable to achieve until three years after the original target date);

(c) audit savings, which it was unable to achieve for the same reason;

---

[68] *Overseas Tankship (UK) v Morts Dock and Engineering Co ('The Wagon Mound')* [1961] AC 388 and *Overseas Tankship (UK) v Miller Steamship Co Pty ('The Wagon Mound' (No 2))* [1967] 1 AC 617.
[69] See *Millar's Machinery v David Way* (1935) 40 Com Cas 204.
[70] [1972] 1 All ER 121.

(d) the costs of employing staff who *would* have been made redundant if the system had gone live when promised;

(e) time wasted by directors and staff in attempting to implement the Sherwood system; and

(f) lost revenue opportunities—the work which the company might have won had it been administratively geared up to have handled the extra volume that the system was supposed to be able to manage—together with interest that might have been earned on those revenue opportunities.

### 1.3.8.8 *Consequential loss: negotiating issues*

These categories of loss are not intended to be definitive: there is no 'definitive list' as such, and each customer and supplier will have its own specific concerns. However, the starting point for constructing an effective provision must be to identify what categories of loss are foreseeable and how the parties intend to allocate these risks between themselves. The aim is to avoid the (ultimately futile) job of trying to *define* 'direct' or 'consequential' loss, and instead—having regard to all the commercial circumstances of the particular transaction—to try to allocate responsibility for those *specific* types of loss that the parties might have in mind: upfront, and without resorting to semantic contortions. Any unspecified types of loss will then fall to be determined by the court according to normal foreseeability principles. In any case, whether the exclusions are fully negotiated or whether they are unilaterally imposed (in the supplier's standard terms, for example), records of the negotiations in respect of exclusion clauses will clearly be of great utility in the event of a dispute, and should therefore be preserved.

### 1.3.8.9 *Financial caps on liability*

The recovery of other classes of potential loss is often limited to an agreed financial cap. It is common to place a financial cap on the supplier's liability, both for any one breach and also as a global limit (for example, £100,000 for any breach, £500,000 in total). It is likely that any figures of this nature will be subject to negotiation, and it is clear from the limited case law under UCTA 1977 that where the parties have genuinely negotiated a limitation the court will be likely to find that limitation to be reasonable.[71] Some sellers limit liability to the contract price, though this seems to set the limits rather too low.

---

[71] *Phillips Products Ltd v Hyland* [1987] 1 WLR 659. See also the discussions of *Salvage Association v CAP Financial Services Ltd* [1995] FSR 645, *St Albans City and District Council v International Computers Ltd* [1996] 4 All ER 481, CA, and *South West Water Services Ltd v International Computers Ltd*, Technology and Construction Court, 29 June 1999 (unreported) at section 1.2.2 above as illustrations of the consequences of the failure properly to negotiate such limits.

### 1.3.9 Contractual remedies

#### 1.3.9.1 *Introduction*
Consideration needs to be given to the question of what happens if a contract does not go according to plan—for example, if the supplier fails to deliver a working system within the contracted timeframes. The general law principles as to the remedies available for breaches of contract are set out in section 1.2.3 above. However, for the reasons discussed in that section, it is often desirable for the contract documentation to provide for specific remedies in particular situations.

#### 1.3.9.2 *Customer remedies: liquidated damages*
One typical solution to that particular problem is to provide for payment of liquidated damages to the customer for each day or week the system is overdue. This will involve an attempt in good faith to estimate the cost to the customer of such delay; and if the delay persists for a specified length of time, the customer may also want a right to terminate. The liquidated damages clause sets in advance the precise sum to be paid as compensation for certain breaches (for example, late delivery at £x per day). Provided that sum is a *genuine pre-estimate* of the likely losses, and not a *penalty* to force the supplier to perform, the clause will be enforceable. This is so even if the customer's loss is in fact less than the agreed sum.

#### 1.3.9.3 *Supplier remedies: interest on late payment*
Similarly, on the supplier's side, the supplier may want an express right to withhold its services or to charge interest in the event of late payment, and in the last resort to terminate the contract altogether.

### 1.3.10 Change control

#### 1.3.10.1 *The need for change control provisions*
The successful implementation of a complex IT system imposes responsibilities not just on the supplier, but also on the customer. Unlike the supply of a simple package, a bespoke contract is more of a joint effort and, whilst the primary obligation will be on the supplier to write any software and to deliver the system, the supplier will depend on the customer providing information about his business, testing the software, providing employees to be trained and so on. Crucially, since the customer's requirements may change as the project progresses, the contract should provide a procedure for specifying and agreeing changes to the scope of work. These will involve adjustments to the functional specification, the price and probably also the timing of the project.

#### 1.3.10.2 *Documenting change procedures*
The proper documentation of these changes will avoid disputes later about what the supplier's obligations actually were. The contract should accordingly include a

formal 'change control' clause, setting out a mechanism whereby the customer can request (and the supplier can recommend) changes to the specification, the project plan, or any other aspect of the deal. Any such change would need to be considered from the point of view of technical feasibility and its impact on timing and pricing generally, and no change should take effect unless it has been formally agreed by both parties and documented in the manner envisaged by the change control clause.

### 1.3.11 Termination

Provision has to be made for termination of the contract, setting out the circumstances in which the contract may be brought to an end and the consequences of that action. These provisions will vary according to the nature of the contract and the deliverables. Apart from a general right to terminate the contract in the event of material breach or the insolvency of the other party, the following points should be considered:

(a) Hardware procurement—the customer may wish to cancel/terminate the contract before the delivery date, and in that event the contract should set out the compensation payable to the supplier.

(b) Software development—contracts for development services are typically terminable by the customer if specific time-critical milestones are significantly overdue. Provision should be made for treatment of the developed software on termination, including delivery up of all copies (and source code) and certification that no copies have been retained.

(c) Contracts for continuing services—consultancy, support and maintenance services, and bureau services should in any event be terminable on notice. The length of the notice, and the earliest dates on which it may be effective, are matters of negotiation in each case.

## 1.4  ADDITIONAL CONSIDERATIONS FOR SPECIFIC CONTRACTS

### 1.4.1 Introduction

The general legal and drafting issues discussed in sections 1.1 to 1.3 of this chapter will apply to the full range of system supply contracts. However, there are additional specific considerations that may apply to particular agreements, and these are discussed in this section.

### 1.4.2 Software licences

1.4.2.1 *Why is software different?*
Software comprises the instructions which cause hardware to work in a particular

way, for example, to process a company's payroll. Looked at in this way, software is intangible, and difficult to classify in legal terms. Some of the relevant case law, as to whether the supply of software comprises 'goods' or 'services', is discussed at section 1.2.1 above. Equally important from the contractual point of view is the fact that software is primarily protected by the law of copyright, as a consequence of which the use of software generally requires a licence from the rightsowner.

### 1.4.2.2 *Types of software*

There are various distinctions that need to be kept in mind when discussing software contracts:

(a) *Standard, bespoke and customized software*: 'Standard' or (package) software, such as commonly used business applications like Microsoft Word or Excel, is marketed as an off-the-shelf product to meet the requirements of a large number of users. By contrast, 'bespoke' software is specially written to meet the requirements of the particular customer. 'Customized' software falls somewhere in between, involving the supplier altering his standard package so that it fits the customer's needs more closely. Predictably, standard software will tend to be cheaper than bespoke, but may not reflect the way the customer's business operates, while bespoke will be more expensive but should be exactly tailored to the customer's requirements.

(b) *System software and application software*: System software organizes the way in which the hardware operates, whereas application software performs the functions actually required by the user (word processing, accounts or whatever). System software is generally supplied by the manufacturer of the hardware, as a standard package, while application software might be standard, bespoke or customized.

(c) *Source code and object code*: A final distinction to be aware of is that between source code and object code. This distinction is discussed at greater length in Chapter 6 but for the purposes of this chapter 'source code' may be defined as a version of a program, using alphanumeric symbols, which cannot be processed directly by a computer without first being 'translated' (or 'compiled') into a machine-readable form. 'Object code' is the machine-readable form of that program, which essentially comprises long series of ones and zeroes, corresponding to the complex 'on-off' instructions used to process data. (The significance of the distinction in the context of this chapter is that it is difficult for a person to read object code, and hence access to source code is needed in order to enable a person to support or modify a computer program.)

### 1.4.2.3 *Types of software contract*

Standard software is often supplied by retailers or distributors, without the customer entering into any direct contract with the software owner. The technique of 'shrink-wrap' licensing (discussed in section 1.4.2.6 below) is commonly used to try to establish this kind of direct contractual relationship. Contracts for bespoke software tend to be entered into on a more formal basis, because of the need to agree a specification and to address other issues arising out of the development process.

### 1.4.2.4 *Why is software licensed?*
Copyright subsists in computer software, so the use of software requires the grant of a licence. Apart from legitimizing the customer's use, however, the licence also enables the software owner to impose restrictions on the use of the software. For this reason, even where a copy of the software is sold without a direct agreement between the software owner and the customer, software owners still seek to impose shrink-wrap licence terms. The efficacy of such licences is discussed at section 1.4.2.6 below. (A further discussion of the requirement for a licence, and the extent of implied rights in relation to acts such as decompilation and error correction, appears in Chapter 6 (section 6.5).)

### 1.4.2.5 *The main licence clause*
There is a broad range of possible licensing structures for computer software. These include, by way of illustration:

(a) the right to use the software on a single computer (sometimes identified by reference to a specific CPU number) at a single location;

(b) the right to use the software on any number of networked or clustered computers at different sites; or any combination of numbers and sites.

*Limitations on use.* The use permitted is often restricted to the 'internal purposes' of the customer. This restriction is justified by the supplier on the basis that using the software for other purposes, particularly by using it to provide a bureau service for third parties, might adversely affect the supplier's ability to charge licence fees that it might otherwise receive from those third parties. The licence terms may also restrict the customer from transferring the software to any third party, again on the basis that the supplier has a right to know precisely who is using its software. Although these concerns appear reasonable, customers should be aware that these provisions have a number of serious implications:

(a) Companies which are members of a corporate group may find that such wording restricts their ability to process data for their associated companies.

(b) The restriction on assignment may be invoked by the supplier as an opportunity to charge increased fees in the event that the system has to be transferred, whether between companies in the same group (as part of a group restructuring, say) or to a third party (perhaps in the context of a business sale).

(c) Such restrictions are also sometimes invoked by the supplier as a means to prevent the customer engaging a third party to manage the system, or as a bar to outsourcing the system to third parties. (Outsourcing is discussed in more detail in Chapter 2.)

It is accordingly vital that the customer considers the business effect of licence restrictions at the very outset of its relationship with the supplier (and does so in the context of its long-term plans for its IT function and the business as a whole), and where necessary negotiates appropriate changes to the contract documentation. Failure to do so may leave the customer exposed to a claim for copyright infringement if it exceeds the scope of the permitted use, or to being charged additional licence fees for the right to do so.

*Licence duration.*   The licence will often be expressed as perpetual, or for a long fixed term (say ninety-nine years). In the absence of any express contractual provision, the normal rule is that an IP licence is determinable by 'reasonable notice'. However, in determining what is reasonable (and indeed whether the licence should in fact be treated as unlimited as to duration), the court might have regard to the consequences of termination for the licensee: these consequences might be severe in the context of business-critical systems or software.

### 1.4.2.6 *Shrink-wrap licensing*

*Background.*   Software is often mass-marketed through a distribution chain (or by mail order), in a similar manner to records or CDs, with the result that there is no opportunity for the customer to enter into a formal licence agreement with the software owner. Many software owners have accordingly adopted the technique of the 'shrink-wrap licence': a licence agreement the terms of which are set out on the outside of the packaging, visible through clear plastic film, and the terms of which are deemed to be accepted if the packaging is opened. The shrink-wrap licence purports to be a direct contract between the software owner and the customer (quite separate from the contract of sale by which the customer acquired the software) which takes effect when the customer breaks the shrink-wrap seal in order to remove the disk.

*Enforceability.*   Although the 'headline' terms of shrink-wrap licences are broadly the same as can be found in other forms of software licence (scope of use, duration, restrictions and so on), there is a question as to whether shrink-wrap licences are actually enforceable as a matter of law, for two reasons:

(a) *Can a shrink-wrap licence embody all the elements of a contract?* Any valid contract requires three basic elements—offer, acceptance and consideration—but the shrink-wrap structure does not 'map' cleanly onto these formal legal requirements. The visible display of the licence terms clearly constitutes an offer, and consideration is given by the licensee by virtue of the promises set out in the licence. However, it is unclear whether the licensee validly accepts the offer by breaking the seal, as the usual rule is that acceptance of an offer must be communicated to the offeror.

It is of course open to the offeror to waive that requirement for communication, and a court anxious to enforce the licence against the licensor may well find that the wording on the licence constitutes such a waiver. However, when considering enforcement against the licensee, the same considerations do not apply: an offeror cannot unilaterally declare that silence will constitute consent, nor can a party impose a contract by ultimatum. In the absence of clear acceptance by words (such as by signing a user registration card) or conduct (such as returning a defective disk for replacement), the enforceability of the licence by the licensor is uncertain.

(b) *Does the doctrine of privity of contract operate to prevent enforcement of the shrink-wrap licence?* The doctrine of privity provides that a person cannot take the benefit of a contract unless he is also a party to it. This principle has historically posed problems for suppliers of shrink-wrap software in England and Wales, as it has been open to question whether they are legally entitled to enforce such licence terms in the absence of a direct contract with the customer.

This situation has now been clarified by the Contracts (Rights of Third Parties) Act 1999, which applies to all contracts entered into after 10 May 2000. A non-party to a contract will henceforth be entitled to enforce a term in it where:

(a)  the contract expressly provides that he may (s 1(1)(a)); or
(b)  the term purports to confer a benefit on him (and it does not appear from the contract that the parties did *not* intend it to be enforceable by him) (s 1(1)(b)).

*Beta v Adobe.*  As a result of the Contracts (Rights of Third Parties) Act 1999, many of the English law concerns as to the enforceability of shrink-wrap licences have evaporated. However, as noted above, the new Act only applies to contracts entered into after 10 May 2000, so there remain many contracts in respect of which the supplier will not have the benefit of the new legislation. The Scottish case of *Beta Computers (Europe) Ltd v Adobe Systems (Europe) Ltd*[72] illustrates the difficulties that these legal issues can cause in practice. The customer (Adobe) had placed a telephone order with its supplier (Beta) to provide a standard package owned by a third-party software house (Informix). Beta delivered a copy of the program to Adobe, which came in shrink-wrap packaging which included the statement 'Opening the Informix software package indicates your acceptance of these conditions'. Adobe did not use the software, and sought to return the package (unopened) to Beta. Beta refused to accept it back, and sued for the price. In its defence, Adobe argued that its transaction with Beta was conditional on Adobe seeing and approving the licence terms: in other words, that there was no effective contract until Adobe had accepted the terms of the shrink-wrap licence by breaking the seal. Lord Penrose found:

(a)  That a contract for the supply of a standard package made over the telephone was not completed until the customer had seen and accepted the shrink-wrap licence

[72] [1996] FSR 367.

terms—and since Adobe had not in fact accepted the terms and had rejected the software, there was accordingly no contract.

(b) That if the customer *had* accepted the licence terms by opening the package, then the licensor would have been able to enforce those terms under the Scottish doctrine of *ius quaesitum tertio* (ie, as a third-party beneficiary).

(c) That the licence terms were not in themselves capable of constituting a contract between Informix and Adobe that was discrete from the main transaction between Adobe and Beta.

However, as already noted in section 1.2.1.14 above, this decision is heavily dependent upon a doctrine of Scottish law for which there is no English equivalent, and so is of dubious value as an authority in England.

### 1.4.2.7 *Specific issues applicable to bespoke software*

Contracts for bespoke software development work have many similarities to licences of standard software, but there are also important differences that arise from the fact that the bespoke software does not exist at the time the contract is made. The main differences are summarized below.

*Unique specification.*  The essence of a bespoke software contract is that the software is written, or a package is to be tailored, to the requirements of the user. This means that the functional specification is of critical importance, just as in other system supply contracts (see sections 1.2.1 and 1.3.2 above). In the context of software development, the functional specification is best prepared by the user alone (possibly with the help of outside independent consultants) or by a combination of the user and the software house, with the user maintaining ultimate control of its contents. Indeed, where a large and complex system is proposed there may be a contract with the software house or a consultant for the production of the specification, quite separate from the contract for the writing of the software.

*Acceptance testing.*  Acceptance testing will also occupy a more important role in relation to bespoke software than it does in relation to a standard package.[73] If package software has been seen working at other users' sites or has been used on a trial basis by the user, the requirement for a formal acceptance test of the package may not be so important. However, in the case of completely new software, acceptance testing is clearly crucial to determine whether or not the software house has delivered software conforming with the contract and to determine whether or not it is entitled to be paid.

*IPR ownership.*  By contrast with contracts for the supply of standard packages, the IPRs in which necessarily remain with the software supplier, a bespoke contract may

---

[73] See S Charlton, 'Product Testing: Liability, Acceptance, Contract Terms' (1989) 4(5) CLSR 23.

vest the IPRs to the software in the user. The property rights that are relevant are primarily copyright and (to a lesser extent) confidential information, although patent rights cannot be totally ignored. The general rule of English copyright law is that where a person commissions another to produce a copyright work, the copyright in that work vests in the author, and not in the commissioning party. If there is no express provision as to ownership it would be open to the court to imply that notwithstanding the general rule, in equity the copyright belongs to the user, but to reach such a conclusion there would have to be some evidence that this was the intention of the parties.

All these matters should be explicitly addressed in any bespoke software contract.

### 1.4.3 Maintenance and support contracts

#### 1.4.3.1 *Introduction*
Almost all new systems are supplied with a warranty as to functionality and performance, though this warranty will generally be of limited duration. It is quite common for the supplier, in addition to this warranty, to offer a maintenance contract which covers part or all of the expected lifetime of the system, subject to payment of additional periodic charges.

#### 1.4.3.2 *General maintenance obligations*
The extent of the maintenance offered will vary according to the particular contract. It may be:

(a) Regular preventative maintenance.

(b) Repair on a time-plus-parts cost basis.

(c) Remote diagnostics with on-site attendance where required (primarily in respect of hardware).

(d) Full maintenance service with every fault attended to within a certain number of hours of its reporting, in accordance with a set Service Level Agreement ('SLA').

The precise service will depend on the customer's requirements, the supplier's ability to provide maintenance, and the charges agreed between the parties. Some important points that should be covered by any maintenance agreement are:

(a) *Response time*: The supplier should guarantee that problems will be attended to within a specified time, with 'target' times for activities such as responding to initial calls, provision of telephone assistance, attendance on site, and time actually to fix the problem. The shorter the response time required, the more expensive the contract. Whilst it is not possible to guarantee in advance how long any actual repair will take, the contract should be clear as to the consequences of failing to meet these target times, which may include liquidated damages in the event of late response or delayed repair.

A related point on time limits is that contractual response times to calls for assistance are often less stringent in software maintenance contracts than in hardware maintenance contracts. This is curious, since the consequences of faulty software are at least as serious as those of faulty hardware, if not more so.

(b) *Fault classification*: Faults vary in importance, depending upon the extent to which the functionality and performance of the system is affected, and the supplier may agree to respond more quickly to more important faults. For example, a 'level 1' fault might be one that effectively stops the customer doing business and to which an urgent fix is required; whereas a 'level 3' fault may be some defect in the system that is trivial or annoying, but not directly harmful. There are no universally recognized classifications of fault severity, and the classifications are a frequent sticking point in contract negotiations. However, it is essential that there is a clear and effective mechanism for classifying faults quickly: leaving classification 'to be agreed at the time' is just as risky as providing that either party has the unilateral right to classify faults in its sole discretion.

(c) *Replacement*: The contract should make it clear what is to happen if a part of the system (particularly any hardware element) needs to be removed for repair or replacement, and in particular whether the supplier will provide temporary replacement equipment and within what period of time.

(d) *Duration, increase of charges and renewal*: As the system ages, maintenance charges will necessarily increase. The contract should set out a minimum period of time for which the supplier will provide maintenance, and some way of assessing the charges that will be made in future years, for example, by reference to indexation. Phrases like 'the supplier's current charges as amended from time to time' should not be acceptable, as there is no ceiling on what he might decide to charge. The agreement should also, from the customer's point of view at least, contain a right of renewal.

(e) *Transferability*: If the customer wishes to resell the system at some later date, or to transfer it intra-group, he will also need to transfer the benefit of the maintenance agreement. The contract should therefore contain a provision to this effect. The supplier might also wish to transfer the burden of the contract to another organization, but a provision permitting this should be resisted by the customer: there is no guarantee that the new supplier will have sufficient expertise or experience of the system in question.

1.4.3.3 *Specific issues relating to software maintenance: source code*
Software maintenance usually comprises two elements:

(a)  the correction of software errors (or 'bugs'); and
(b)  the provision of enhancements and updates to the software.

Software maintenance—sometimes also called 'support'—has to date typically been provided by the supplier of the software because of the need to have access to the program source code. However, as noted in Chapter 6 (section 6.5.1), the customer has a limited right to decompile the object code to produce source code for the purpose of error correction (though not for any other form of maintenance such as the development of enhancements or updates).[74] The source code may in any case be made available to the customer, either because it is the policy of the supplier to do so,[75] or because the IPRs vest in the customer (under a bespoke contract, for example), or because the customer has obtained access to the source code pursuant to an escrow agreement. In such cases the customer should be able to maintain the software on its own account (or appoint a third party to do so).

### 1.4.3.4 *Specific issues relating to software maintenance: upgrades*

Apart from error correction, the supplier will usually agree to supply a copy of all enhancements and updates developed by him during the term of the maintenance agreement. These fall into a number of categories:

(a) Corrections of previously reported errors.
(b) Updates necessitated by changes in the law.
(c) Variations necessitated by changes in the system software that runs on the hardware in question.
(d) Improvements or new functions.

The customer will often be obliged to accept and install the enhancements and updates, so that the whole of the maintenance company's customer base is using the same version of the software. For this reason, it will often be a requirement of the software licence that the licensee enters into a software maintenance agreement in the first place.

### 1.4.3.5 *Warranties and liability*

Maintenance agreements are contracts for the provision of services and accordingly, by virtue of section 13 of the SGSA 1982, there will be an implied term that the maintenance company will use reasonable skill and care in carrying out the service. It is fairly unusual to find express warranties as to the *quality* of the maintenance services, although ideally the supplier should agree to maintain the system's functionality and performance to the standards set out in the original system supply agreement. Suppliers will often seek to impose limitations to their liability similar to those in other system supply contracts, and the observations already made in that regard apply equally in this context.

---

[74] However, the right can be excluded by contract, at least as implemented in the UK; see the new section 50C of the CDPA 1988.

[75] In *Andersen Consulting v CHP Consulting Ltd*, 26 July 1991, Ch D (unreported) the judge described the standard licence agreement of the claimants relating to the program in question, under which the program source code was supplied to licensees for a fee of £125,000. The judge noted that 'the result is that the plain intent of the contract was that the licensee should have the ability, the material and the right to alter and amend the programme [*sic*] by persons other than those who had written it'.

### 1.4.4 Hardware and software leases

#### 1.4.4.1 *Introduction*

It is not unusual for the customer in a systems procurement to finance the transaction by entering into some form of leasing arrangement. This involves the supplier selling the system (in other words, the hardware elements and the right to use the software elements) to a third-party finance company (termed the 'lessor'), which in turn leases it on to the customer to use. However, as leasing comprises a discrete (and substantial) body of law in its own right, it is not proposed to address it in this chapter, other than to make some general observations about two important contractual implications of the leasing structure. These are:

(a) The ability of the customer to enforce performance and other warranties in respect of the system.

(b) The licensing structures required in respect of software elements of the system.

#### 1.4.4.2 *Enforcement of warranties by customer*

The SGSA 1982 (or the Supply of Goods (Implied Terms) Act 1973 if it is a hire-purchase contract[76]) imply terms into the contract which are broadly the same as those implied by the SGA 1979 into a sale contract. However, as the customer's only contractual relationship (at least under a finance lease as opposed to an operating lease) is with the lessor, the question arises as to how the customer can enforce rights against the original supplier. There are three broad ways of achieving this:

(a) *Assignment by the lessor*: the lessor agrees to assign to the customer its rights under its own contract with the supplier (or occasionally to enforce them for the customer's benefit). The problem with such a solution is that the customer's claim is limited to the damages the lessor could have recovered, which in many cases will be nothing.[77]

(b) *Novation*: the deal is structured initially as a direct sale between the supplier and the customer, with the 'day-to-day' obligations—such as delivery, acceptance arrangements, and payments—being subsequently novated in favour of the lessor. The intention is to leave the supplier liable to the customer in respect of matters such as warranties, although there seems to be no clear legal authority that such a partial novation is possible.

(c) *Direct collateral contract*: the deal is structured as three separate contracts, namely (i) a sale agreement between supplier and lessor, (ii) a lease agreement between lessor and customer, and (iii) a collateral contract containing the various warranties given by the supplier to the customer (the consideration for which is the

---

[76] ie, if it contains an option to purchase.
[77] eg, if the lease excludes liability for defects and rental is payable irrespective of such defects.

customer's entering into the lease). This is thought to be the most effective of all three methods of conferring the benefit of supplier warranties on the ultimate customer, provided the supplier's warranties and the customer's remedies are drafted in the light of the terms of the lease agreement.

### 1.4.4.3 *Software licensing structures*

The need to ensure that software is properly licensed gives rise to particular concerns in the context of a leasing arrangement. First, the lessor will need to ensure that the licence permits it to do any of the acts it might be required to do in connection with the financing arrangements, including (for example) assigning or sublicensing its rights to third parties in case the customer should default on its payment obligations. Secondly, the customer will want to ensure that its own licence (from the lessor) covers the full range of its intended activities in relation to the system in the same way as if it were taking a direct licence from the supplier.

## 1.5 CONCLUSION

The delivery of a working system which meets the customer's needs is a difficult enough task, but it is even more difficult to achieve in a contractual vacuum. In summary, there are three main advantages to a properly negotiated and well-drawn contract:

(a) Identification of the issues.
(b) Clarity as to the obligations of each party.
(c) Agreement in advance on how disagreements are to be resolved.

The overall aim is a good working relationship, leading to successful performance of the contract and the installation of an effective system. Whilst it is tempting to produce standard form contracts, particularly given the cost of negotiating individual agreements, this factor is far outweighed by the expense of resolving disputes and complications when contingencies not explicity covered by the terms of the contract occur.

# 2

# INFORMATION SYSTEMS OUTSOURCING

*Alison Welterveden*

## 2.1 INTRODUCTION

### 2.1.1 What is an IS outsourcing contract?

An information systems ('IS') outsourcing contract involves the transfer of all or a substantial part of the IS functions of a customer's business to a third-party service provider. Typically, an IS outsourcing arrangement will therefore involve the transfer of assets and, frequently, staff that were previously used to support the activity or operation, to the supplier. Those assets are then used to provide a service back to the customer, to an agreed level of service. These contracts are frequently referred to as IS outsourcing contracts or information technology ('IT') outsourcing contracts.

IS outsourcing has been utilized for many years now, although IS outsourcing in its modern format has developed from the introduction of the early time-sharing, facilities management and service bureau arrangements from the 1960s and 1970s. The nature of these facilities management and service bureau arrangements are described below.[1] Although facilities management and service bureau contracts are different in nature to a pure IS outsourcing, they heavily influenced its development.

---

[1] See section 2.1.2.

It is generally agreed that the first landmark IS outsourcing contract that was signed was the contract entered into in 1989 between Eastman Kodak and an IBM subsidiary, Integrated Systems Solutions Corporation. Under the terms of that agreement Integrated Systems Solutions Corporation built and operated a computer centre for Kodak taking on some 300 Kodak staff in the process.[2] Since this date the IS outsourcing market has expanded rapidly as a growing number of corporate and government entities alike have rushed to jump on the outsourcing bandwagon and take advantage of the perceived benefits that an outsourced function could bring.[3]

IS functions which are now outsourced typically include one or more of the following:

(a) data centres;
(b) voice and data networks;
(c) telecommunications;
(d) applications development;
(e) applications support and maintenance;
(f) desktop;
(g) project management;
(h) contract and vendor management;
(i) helpdesk and call centre;
(j) IS training; and
(k) disaster recovery.

IS outsourcing contracts will frequently include a bundle of functions which are transferred to the supplier, especially given the natural dependencies that exist between many different IS functions.

Although most IS functions are capable of being outsourced, the crucial decision for any business will be which elements of their IS function should be outsourced in practice. Generally, where an IS function is critical to the business (such as where a particular system enables the business to distinguish itself from its competitors) a degree of caution should be exercised before the running of that function is entrusted to a third party.

### 2.1.2 IS outsourcing contracts distinguished from service bureau and facilities management contracts

The early time-sharing and bureaux-based contracts from which the modern IS

---

[2] See Thomas R. Mylott, *Computer Outsourcing: Managing the Transfer of Information Systems* (Prentice Hall, 1995), p 15 and Robert Klepper and Wendell O. Jones, *Outsourcing Information Technology Systems and Services* (Prentice Hall, 1998), p xxii.

[3] Mary Lacity and Leslie Wilcocks have estimated that the global IT outsourcing market will be worth $150 billion by 2004. Similarly, the Sourcing Interests Group Report currently estimates the outsourcing market to be worth $72 billion and projects it to grow to over $100 billion by 2005. The future for IS outsourcing currently looks very rosy indeed.

outsourcing contract has evolved were more limited in scope and did not involve the transfer of assets to the supplier. Instead, under time-sharing arrangements the customer would be given a connection to enable it to access the supplier's systems at the supplier's site. The customer remained responsible for the use to which he put those systems. Similarly with service bureau arrangements, the supplier would process an application, such as payroll, using its mainframes to provide similar processes for a number of customers.

Under facilities management contracts, it is generally the customer's IS systems (whether they are owned by the customer or licensed to it from third parties) that are used by the supplier to deliver the services to the customer. Again, there is no change of ownership in the assets which traditionally remain under the ownership of the customer or are licensed to it and which remain located at the customer's premises. The supplier is merely granted access to use those IS systems which are needed to provide the managed service.

It should, however, be borne in mind that the question of whether a particular arrangement is an IS outsourcing contract is really a question of degree. For example, most private finance initiative ('PFI') and public–private partnerships ('PPP') transactions are outsourcing contracts in all but name. Although it may not be Government policy to refer to these deals as outsourcing they typically involve a supplier building or supplying, owning and operating IS and then providing a service to the government entity concerned using those systems. One of the principal conditions of PFI/PPP treatment is that the supplier owns the IT asset so that it remains on the supplier's balance sheet and thereby avoids the Government taking the capital asset into its own books. So, as with IS outsourcing, assets which are owned by the supplier are used by the supplier to deliver a service back to the Government customer. The structure of such a PFI/PPP contract looks very similar to that of the typical IS outsourcing contract.

Even where the transaction is not a pure IS outsourcing involving the transfer of assets and the related activity, and instead falls under the guise of, for example, a facilities management contract, many of the issues referred to in this chapter will still be relevant.

### 2.1.3 Recent trends

It is clear that the IS outsourcing market is not a static one and over the past decade a number of new variants on the traditional structure have surfaced. The increasingly global nature of business is driving a shift towards more complex outsourcing contracts. Organizations are frequently looking to outsource their IT operations not on a country-by-country basis, but under a global deal to a single provider. These global transactions raise important structural and legal issues. The contract itself can be structured in a number of ways. Frequently, a relationship agreement is adopted at the highest level, which prescribes a framework under which local agreements can be entered into by local subsidiaries. Standard templates for local agreements are often then provided in order to reduce the scope for negotiation at a local level and to ensure that services are provided on as uniform a basis as possible. Nevertheless, some amendment of those local agreements may be necessary, for example, to reflect local law requirements in relation to employee, data protection or competition issues.

In addition to the move towards global contracts, flexibility is seen as an increasingly important goal to ensure that the contract can develop to mirror changes to the business. This means, in practice, setting up a contract which takes into account the need for technical changes (such as the introduction of new technology or the refreshment of existing systems) together with business change (such as the need to absorb a newly acquired subsidiary into a business structure or, conversely, to allow for partial termination of a contract where a particular service is no longer required). Change mechanisms are discussed in greater detail in section 2.2.2.7 below.

Other forms of outsourcing, in particular business process outsourcing ('BPO') continues to grow.[4] BPO, as its name suggests, involves the outsourcing of business processes (such as finance and accounting or payroll processes). It often comes hand in hand with the outsourcing of the applications that support the business processes, which would be the subject of a typical IS outsourcing contract.

The future of the application service provision outsourcing ('ASP') market is more difficult to predict. In ASP deals the power of the Internet is utilized to enable the supplier to provide the customer with access to services (such as hardware platforms, applications, systems management and support) using a standard web browser. ASP contracts ironically see a return to the days of time-sharing where the customer uses a connection to access systems owned by a third party. The current focus of such ASP contracts is very much on enterprise resource-planning programs and is proving popular with the smaller- to medium-sized corporate entity which can utilize the ASP concept to gain access to more sophisticated technology than it would otherwise be able to and without the need to develop in-house resources to support it. Growth forecasts for ASP in the late 1990s when the concept really took off were, like most forecasts for anything to do with the dotcom economy at that time, stratospheric. Take up of ASP services has, however, been slower than expected—partly due to the current economic climate but perhaps also due to the limited interest in the market in ASP outside of the small- and medium-sized enterprise ('SME') sector. Ultimately, if ASP develops into the management not just of applications but of the entire business process supported by those applications, then the ASP concept will merge into BPO.

---

[4] Ovum Holway has predicted that the UK BPO market will be worth more than £10 billion. It is particularly noteworthy how quickly this market is growing compared to IS outsourcing. For example, the BPO market in the UK was said to be worth £3.5 billion in 2001, compared with £6.9 billion for IT outsourcing. When looking at the predicted growth figures for the years ahead, the IT outsourcing in the market in the UK is likely to be worth £11.9 billion, according to Ovum Holway, compared to a figure of £10.3 billion for BPO.

The outsourcing of shared service centres is also often an attractive business proposition. Shared service centres typically arise from the rationalization of a corporate entity's IS functions or on the introduction of new enterprise-wide applications that are then provided to the business. External service providers may be called in to run a shared service centre which is used by one particular corporate group, or a shared service centre which is used to provide services to a number of external customers to achieve economies of scale.

### 2.1.4 The partnership myth

One of the common myths in outsourcing is that the relationship between the customer and supplier can be likened to a partnership. Whilst commendable on a commercial level, the legal reality is somewhat different. A true partnership involves the equal sharing of risk and reward. Suppliers may be keen to reap the benefits of the outsourcing relationship but there is no making of a 'common profit' from the outsourcing relationship, a concept at the heart of the legal definition of a partnership. Indeed, the converse is true. The supplier provides services to the customer at a carefully calculated charge to make a profit from the customer. It is also virtually unheard of for the risks to be divided equally. This is evidenced most clearly in the detailed clauses purporting to limit their liability that suppliers will seek to impose to control their risk exposure.

References to the relationship being a true partnership should therefore be avoided by the supplier and treated with a healthy dose of cynicism from the customer.[5]

The term 'partnership' is also sometimes used in a slightly different context to refer to the creation of an ongoing relationship where it is envisaged that a number of contracts will be awarded over time to the supplier. In these circumstances, the supplier is effectively a preferred supplier for any future outsourcing. For example, a framework agreement may be entered into governing the overall business relationship and acknowledging the intention that the supplier is a preferred supplier provided certain key terms (such as pricing for any outsourced service) are met. The terms of any such framework agreement should be negotiated carefully. The customer should not be influenced by the anticipated costs savings achievable from appointing an entity as its preferred supplier to the detriment of a well thought out contract. Any key terms specified in a framework agreement should be subject to the same, if not greater, scrutiny as a one-off outsourcing contract. Again, the relationship could not be classified as a partnership in the legal sense and any references to it being one should be avoided.

---

[5] This is not intended to belittle the outsourcing relationship. A high degree of trust and a solid working relationship will be vital to maximize the benefits that can be achieved by both parties.

### 2.1.5 Reasons for outsourcing

The reasons for outsourcing are varied. The most frequently quoted incentives in the private sector are the added value that third-party expertise and experience can bring, and the costs benefits.[6] The added value is evidenced through the enhanced levels of service that a supplier will usually offer which, because of the experience and economies of scale available to the supplier, are often provided at a cheaper cost than that achievable in-house. Whether the first wave of outsourcing contracts entered into in the early 1990s brought the anticipated costs savings and improved service is unclear. It is apparent that at least in some cases that this was not the result.[7]

In the public sector the motivators for outsourcing are somewhat different. The nature of government bodies means that there is no need to reduce costs to increase profitability. Instead, the focus is very much on 'value for money'. This means that public-sector organizations will typically want to increase the quality of service for the charges paid and thereby make better use of taxpayers' money.

The technology industry is highly competitive and grows at a rapid rate as the modern economy becomes increasingly reliant on IT. Consequently, over recent years staff costs in this sector have spiralled upwards. Outsourcing obviates the need to recruit and, crucially, to retain IT staff and enables the business to focus on its core competencies. Provided a good contract manager is appointed by the customer to oversee the operation of the contract, management will generally need to spend considerably less time in overseeing the IS function. The role required will be that of strategic input and direction, rather than managing day-to-day operational issues.

The outsourcing of an IS function or functions necessitates the transfer of the assets used to support and run that function to the supplier. Accordingly, responsibility for maintaining and updating those systems will also pass. The financial burden for the customer is translated from that of the costs of resources to provide an in-house service and the fluctuating costs of improving the existing, and acquiring any new, technology to a more stable regular service charge. Not only do the costs of

---

[6] A survey carried out by the Outsourcing Institute on current and potential outsourcing end-users cited costs reduction as the primary reason and access to world-class capabilities as third (see www.outsourcing.com/howandwhy/research/surveyresults.htm). It seems that companies are, however, moving away from costs reduction as a primary reason for outsourcing and are looking at other factors (see Formation Consulting's November 1999 report at www.formation-consulting.co.uk/survey_questions.html and the study conducted by Lacity and Willcocks reported at www.outsourcing-academics.com/html/acad2.html).

[7] Rudy Hirschheim, who with Mary Lacity researched IS outsourcing over a nine-year period, has commented that 'many companies that have gone through large-scale outsourcing exercises are finding that their flexibility is not as enhanced as they thought it would be with outsourcing, and that service levels they thought would improve have actually dropped . . . They're beginning to find that outsourcing is not the panacea they hoped for when they initially outsourced' (*Backsourcing: An Emerging Trend?* at www/outsourcing-academics.com/html/acad1.html). Accordingly, some companies are beginning to take back in-house functions that they had previously outsourced as a result of this dissatisfaction. This chapter will show that a well-drafted contract can ensure that many of the customer's expectations as to the level of service and costs are realized.

receiving the service become more certain but the use of a third-party supplier should improve access to new technology. Suppliers can acquire such technology more quickly, being able to spread the cost over a number of customers. In addition, the supplier will have the resources and skill available to evaluate and implement that new technology more rapidly than the typical corporate or government entity. The larger-scale supplier will also often be able to negotiate substantial discounts from the price of any new software or hardware. This rapid access to, and potentially lower cost of, new technology can make IS outsourcing a very attractive proposition.

These are some of the more common reasons for outsourcing. With any corporate or government customer, the business case will differ and a careful evaluation of the pros and cons of outsourcing any IS function should always be undertaken.

### 2.1.6 Disadvantages of outsourcing

One of the distinctions between the typical IS outsourcing contract and other computer contracts (such as software and hardware procurement or maintenance contracts) is the ongoing cooperation which will be required from the parties over the life of the contract. Without a close working relationship and an understanding of the parties' respective obligations and responsibilities (in both the strict contractual sense and more generally) the IS outsourcing relationship may be doomed to failure.

As with any business proposition, there are potential downsides to be considered. As noted above, although costs reduction is often cited as a primary motivator, the much sought after savings do not always happen in practice. Indeed, with some contracts the cost to the customer has increased as a result of the contract. This is particularly the case where the service requirements are ill-defined in the initial contract, enabling the supplier to demand additional charges through any contract-change mechanism as the scope of the contract is formally increased to cover service requirements of the customer (which, although always intended by the customer to form part of the outsourced function, fall outside the strict wording of the service schedule).[8]

The transfer of staff to the supplier as part of the outsourcing process[9] results in the loss of specialist skill and expertise within the business. This can be a particular problem if the business is left without any person with the technical skills required to oversee the running of the contract. Obviously, the more of the IS functions of any business which are outsourced the more likely this will be an issue. This problem can also effectively lock a customer into a relationship with a supplier. If the business lacks the technical skills required to bring the service back in-house, it may be easier to leave the service provision with an under-performing supplier rather than to expend the necessary time and management resource to locate an alternative vendor.

---

[8] The importance of the service description cannot be overstated. See section 2.2.2 (in particular section 2.2.2.1) below.

[9] The Transfer of Undertakings (Protection of Employment) Regulations 1981, SI 1981/1794 ('TUPE 1981'), will usually apply to transfer staff associated with the function that is outsourced to the supplier. See section 2.4 below.

A decision to outsource should be treated with some sensitivity within an organization, particularly as regards the dissemination of information to employees. Staff are not always receptive to the prospect of outsourcing and to the transfer of their employment to a third-party IS supplier, although the manner in which the proposal to outsource is communicated to employees can reduce some of this negativity. An effective communications process will therefore be required to avoid negative publicity, or even the risk of strikes or other industrial action by disgruntled employees.[10].

Outsourcing invariably involves the transfer of a number of assets to the supplier. This may result in a lack of control over the nature of the IT infrastructure used to deliver the services—which may be a particular problem when the infrastructure is returned to the customer on the expiry or termination of the contract and the customer is left with an outdated system and with little or no knowledge as to its detailed operation. Although the essence of the IS outsourcing contract is the delivery of services to a specified level it is nevertheless advisable to include provisions requiring technology refreshment on a regular basis to ensure an acceptable standard of infrastructure is maintained. An adequate flow of information throughout the duration of the contract regarding the composition of the technology architecture used by the supplier will also be essential.

Another consequence of having part of a business function run by a third party is the potentially increased security risk. In particular, there is an increased risk that others may access, and misuse, information which is confidential to the business and that the staff of the supplier may unintentionally or otherwise misuse the customer's intellectual property. Detailed provisions regarding the use of, and access to, confidential information and intellectual property are the norm in IS outsourcing contracts. Suppliers should also be compelled to comply with the customer's security policies and procedures.

Rigid contracts may also prevent future expansion and growth of the customer's business. One of the inevitable consequences of the outsourcing relationship will be that the supplier's consent must be obtained before any changes can be made to the scope of the service. Contract-change provisions will therefore play an important role in any contract.[11]

The constant expansion of the IS outsourcing market is testament to its popularity. The disadvantages and risks of IS outsourcing seem rarely, in practice, to outweigh the perceived benefits. For those contemplating an outsourcing contract, it will therefore be comforting to know that many of the risks outlined above can be controlled or minimized through appropriate contractual provisions.

---

[10] In addition to the commercial necessity of such an effective communications process, where TUPE 1981 apply, there are legal stipulations about the consultation process which must take place. See section 2.4.4 below.

[11] See section 2.2.2 below.

### 2.1.7 The outsourcing contract

The essence of an IS outsourcing contract is a commitment by the supplier to deliver services to predefined service levels. The contract will then go on to define what happens in the event that these service levels are not met. A failure to meet a particular service level will often result in the payment of service credits, a specified sum of money which becomes payable automatically in the event of a breach. Without service credits being stipulated, the customer would need to prove on each occasion that any failure to meet the service levels is a breach of contract and that they are entitled to damages from the supplier accordingly. To specify the service credits that will become payable in this way therefore gives certainty to both parties and helps to avoid protracted disputes as to whether any breach of contract has occurred and, if so, whether it has caused any loss and damage to the customer which should be recoverable from the supplier. These service-credit regimes differentiate the IS outsourcing contract from other IT contracts, such as system supply contracts, where such schemes are found more rarely.

The contract will contain other provisions which are key to the effective management of the ongoing relationship between the parties. IS outsourcing contracts are usually long in nature, with contracts for seven- to ten-year periods being relatively standard industry market practice. Flexibility will therefore be crucial, in terms of adapting the contract to reflect the customer's changing business requirements and to introduce new forms of technology and other service improvements.

This chapter will examine some of the key features of the IS outsourcing contract in turn.

### 2.1.8 The outsourcing process

#### 2.1.8.1 *Board/business decision*

The process will begin with an evaluation by the customer of the business case for outsourcing. The evaluation process will review both the benefits and any disadvantages of outsourcing the particular IS function in question.[12]

The evaluation team should ideally be comprised of those who will be involved in the entire outsourcing process to ensure continuity in approach and full accountability for the outsourcing decision. The team should include those with appropriate IS technical skills and suitable management or board representation. Finance and human resources managers may also need to play an important role, depending on the size and scope of the outsourcing in question.

#### 2.1.8.2 *Specifying requirements/service levels*

Assuming a decision to outsource is made, the customer will initially need to put

---

[12] See section 2.1.5 above for a description of some of the popular reasons to outsource and section 2.1.6 above for some of the disadvantages of outsourcing.

together a statement of its requirements for the outsourced function. The importance of this exercise cannot be underestimated. A detailed requirements specification which clearly specifies the business need will help to attract the correct suppliers competent to provide the relevant services and avoid (or, at least, minimize) later disagreements about the scope (and consequent cost) of the service that suppliers are tendering for. Cost will be an important factor for any customer and the evaluation process should undertake a thorough review of the cost that is currently incurred in providing the service in-house and an assessment of the likely costs savings that can be achieved through outsourcing.

As well as identifying the particular function that is to be outsourced, due consideration must be given to associated issues. For example, which of the assets that are currently used by the customer to deliver the service in-house are to be transferred to the supplier? Who owns those assets and where are they located? Are there staff who are to transfer? What dependencies are there between the function to be outsourced and other functions that are to be retained in-house by the customer? Should assets used to provide the service be returned to the customer at the termination or expiry of the outsourcing arrangement? Once these, and other, questions have been considered, the customer will be in a position to go out to the marketplace and tender for a supplier.

Putting together the tender documentation is a skilled and time-consuming process and one in relation to which external consultants are often employed. Such consultants help draft the tender documentation, evaluate the responses, sit on the negotiation team and generally steer the client through the outsourcing process. External specialist IS outsourcing lawyers are also usually engaged from the early stages. They will define the contract requirements to be included in the tender, together with advising on associated legal issues (such as confidentiality agreements). Lawyers will also play a key role in the negotiation process, reducing the client's requirements to contractual form.

### 2.1.8.3 *Going out to tender*

The tender documentation needs to include a detailed description of the services required and the service levels to which they should be delivered. This information is contained in either an invitation to tender ('ITT') or request for proposal ('RFP'). The ITT or RFP will need to be sufficiently detailed to enable the supplier to provide a detailed costing. This means information regarding assets and staff to transfer, contract duration, reporting requirements and any business processes the supplier must adhere to should be included.

Whether or not the contract should be attached to the ITT is often a subject of debate. This can take the form of either the entire contract or an outline of key terms only. It enables the customer to specify the terms on which they wish to do business and compels the supplier to indicate at an early stage which of those terms are acceptable (or otherwise) to it. The supplier will therefore be reviewing and commenting on those contractual terms when their negotiating power is at their weakest and the desire to win an attractive contract may force them into making more concessions than they would otherwise do so.

In some circumstances, time constraints may mean that it is simply not feasible to include contract terms at the ITT stage, especially where the customer is new to outsourcing and has no standard contract terms in place. In any event it must also be accepted that a certain amount of negotiation will be inevitable, even where the contract was included as part of the ITT and a supplier has indicated their acceptance of its terms in their tender response.

### 2.1.8.4 *Choosing a preferred supplier*

Essentially, there are two methods that can be adopted in selecting a supplier. The first is to produce a shortlist with a number of preferred suppliers and to run negotiations in tandem with each of them. The disadvantage of such an approach is that it is very costly in terms of the management time required to participate in several negotiations at once and the associated expense of external advisers evaluating and negotiating a number of draft contracts. This acts as a considerable deterrent in smaller-value contracts. The advantages can be considerable though. Suppliers who know that they are in competition with others will adopt a far more flexible approach in negotiations than they would if they were the sole preferred supplier. Suppliers will inevitably end up in a 'contract race' with the first to agree acceptable terms and price winning the contract. This can assist to speed up the contract negotiation process (although this must be balanced against the management resource required to undertake negotiations with several suppliers).

An objective set of assessment criteria should be adopted against which any potential supplier is assessed, with a review of all aspects of the tender response. In addition to the obvious considerations, such as capability to provide the service and price, other factors may be relevant. The relationship between the parties will usually be a long one and it is important to ensure that there is a 'cultural fit' between the two entities. Without this, the parties may simply be unable to work together effectively.

Visits to other customer sites may also be beneficial to assess the supplier's performance in practice compared to any assurances given as part of their tender response. It also enables the customer to gain a valuable insight into the day-to-day working methods of the supplier.

### 2.1.8.5 *Due diligence*

Due diligence plays an important role, enabling the supplier to verify that information provided regarding the assets and employees is correct, to ascertain the condition of any assets which are to be transferred and to consider whether the supplier believes the desired service levels can be achieved using them. Due diligence is also used to investigate any other matters which may impact on the supplier's costs model. This process helps to flush out any potential issues and, more importantly, ensures that they are resolved prior to contract signature. Due diligence also helps to foster an early working relationship between the parties.

One of the key aspects to be investigated will be software and databases licensed to the customer where the supplier needs to use those tools to continue providing the service. Many licences are drafted so as to prevent access to, or use of, software or databases by anyone other than the customer. To allow access and use by the IS outsourcing provider without obtaining the third-party supplier's consent would therefore place the customer in breach of its licence terms, with the risk of that licence being terminated and a damages claim made against it.[13] In addition, the supplier may itself be making copies of such software or databases in the course of the service provision and thereby infringing the intellectual property rights ('IPRs') of the third-party owner. Some third-party suppliers are renowned for the considerable fees they seek to impose for allowing access and/or use by a service provider and the allocation of these costs between the parties will often be a hotly contended issue.[14]

Due diligence is usually carried out prior to contract signature following selection of the preferred supplier. This is most desirable for both parties enabling certainty to be achieved before the contractual relationship begins. This is particularly the case where software is licensed to the customer and third-party consent must be obtained to allow the service provider to gain access to that software or for a new licence to be granted direct to the service provider. Identifying licences where consents must be obtained, and the procedure to obtain this consent, can take many months.

The alternative is for due diligence to take place in a period after the contract is entered into with an adjustment to the contract charges to take into account any inaccuracies in the information provided to the supplier which impact on the cost of providing the services. This approach can lead to disputes as to whether correct information was or was not provided initially which can sour relations between the parties at a very early stage in the relationship. For this reason, it is best avoided.

### 2.1.8.6 *Negotiating the contract*
There will usually be much debate about the detailed terms of an IS outsourcing contract. These contracts are complex in nature providing a well-defined service requirement whilst allowing for future change and flexibility in terms of the customer's changing business requirements and the rapid developments in the technology market.

Even where the draft contract forms part of the tender documentation, it is common to find considerable negotiation over its terms, especially where the

---

[13] eg, in October 1990 the UK press reported that Computer Associates ('CA') had started legal proceedings against Hosykns, claiming alleged copyright infringement of 39 of CA's programs. This related to the use by Hoskyns of CA software that CA licensees had transferred to Hoskyns under facilities management contracts. This dispute was settled out of court.

[14] Competition remedies may be available when the owner is demanding royalties, although this is at best an open question. The argument is that such a demand may be an abuse of a dominant position contrary to article 82 of the EU Treaty. Also, it could be argued that the restriction on licensing can be regarded as anticompetitive contrary to article 81(1). This would only be the case if the restriction is appreciable, which is unlikely in most outsourcing contracts.

supplier's tender indicates that the terms are acceptable in principle but subject to detailed negotiation (a commonplace, and understandable, response). This sort of response allows a 'get out' enabling the supplier to defer lengthy negotiation until after its selection as the preferred supplier.

In consequence, it can take some months to finalize the detailed contract terms and a suitable amount of time should be scheduled accordingly for this process to take place.

### 2.1.8.7 *Public-sector outsourcing*

The public sector has embraced IS outsourcing with as much zeal as the private sector. The focus of such an outsourcing is different—concepts such as profitability and shareholder value which drive the private sector are irrelevant. Instead, the public sector looks for value for money in allocating outsourcing contracts.

An entity within the public sector will approach the outsourcing process in a very different manner. There are a number of laws and regulations which will impact on the procurement process, including the manner in which a tender is carried out, the negotiation process and contract award.

Various EU Directives on public procurement have been adopted which relate to procedures for the award of service contracts, supply contracts and work contracts in the public sector. Of particular importance to the outsourcing sector is the EU Services Directive[15] which was implemented into English law in 1994 by the Public Services Contract Regulations 1993[16] ('the 1993 Regulations'). In very simple terms these Regulations state that if a 'contracting authority' wants to award a contract for public services which exceeds specified financial thresholds then it must follow certain rules. The term 'contracting authority' encompasses central, regional and local government as well as bodies that are controlled by the state (like NHS Trusts) or state-funded (like universities). The 1993 Regulations ensure that contracts are openly advertised and that the evaluation of bidders is carried out on a fair and open basis. There must be no unfair discrimination in the selection of suppliers and national buy campaigns (for example, 'Buy British') are outlawed. The rules apply to all such public-services contracts, other than those below a minimum estimated contract value or which fall into certain very narrow exceptions.

There are a number of requirements in the 1993 Regulations about notices which contracting authorities must publish regarding contracts to be entered into and their final award. These notices are published in the *Official Journal* of the European Union.

The 1993 Regulations provide fairly detailed procedures for awarding contracts. The process must be open to all applicants by way of an open procedure (a one-step bidding process without negotiation), a restricted procedure (a two-stage registration

---

[15] Directive 92/50/EC, as amended by Directive 97/52/EC.

[16] SI 1993/3228, as amended by the Public Supply Contracts Regulations 1995, SI 1995/201, the Utilities Contracts Regulations 1996, SI 1996/2911, and the Public Contracts (Works, Services and Supply) (Amendment) Regulations 2000, SI 2000/2009.

and shortlist bidding process but without negotiation) or a negotiated procedure (where the contracting authority negotiates with several suppliers, entering into a contract with one of them). The last type of procedure, the negotiated procedure, is particularly favoured in outsourcing projects, although the contracting authority must be able to justify its use of the negotiated procedure in accordance with the requirements of the 1993 Regulations.

In shortlisting bidders contracting authorities can only evaluate them on the basis of certain selection criteria (such as their economic and financial standing and their technical ability). Similarly, contracting authorities are also required to base their decision to award the contract to a particular bidder on the grounds of lowest price or, more flexibly, the most economically advantageous tender.

Action can be taken by third parties where the correct procurement procedure has not been followed which, where successful before the contract is awarded, may lead to the suspension of the procurement process pending a decision being made by the courts. Otherwise, damages may be awarded.

## 2.2 THE IS OUTSOURCING CONTRACT

### 2.2.1 The services agreement and related documents

The central document in any outsourcing relationship will be the services agreement. This documents the services to be provided by the supplier and the levels to which those services must be provided. It also includes other provisions relating to the ongoing management of the outsourcing relationship. There are, however, other contractual documents which may be entered into leading up to, and in the course of, the outsourcing contract.

Heads of agreement (also known as memorandums of understanding) are sometimes used to reflect the early commercial agreement reached between the parties prior to entering into the detailed outsourcing contract. For the most part, these heads of agreement simply reflect the commercial intent of the parties and are little more than an agreement to agree future detailed contract terms. As agreements to agree, they are unenforceable under English law. The exceptions to this are terms such as confidentiality and exclusivity undertakings (ie, that during a fixed time period negotiations will not be conducted with any other third parties) which will be legally binding. Their value is therefore for the most part in the commercial comfort that they give to each party that there is a mutual understanding that an outsourcing relationship will be embarked on and, very broadly, what the scope of any contract will be.

Frequently, suppliers may be asked to commence work, or may themselves suggest that certain activities should be performed, before the services agreement itself is signed. This is a reflection of the time that is usually required in order to complete the process of due diligence and contract negotiations. Once a supplier has been selected as the preferred supplier it may make business sense for certain investments to be made prior to contract signature in order to minimize any period of delay once the contract is up and running. This sort of investment may include acquiring new technology or employees in order to provide the services. Suppliers will seek to cover their risk exposure during this period leading up to contract signature by obtaining from the customer its written consent to specified activities being carried out by the supplier on behalf of the customer (for example, the acquisition of a specific piece of hardware or software) and an indemnity in favour of the supplier in respect of the costs relating to those activities (such as the price of that piece of hardware or software). Relatively informal letter agreements are frequently used to record the parties' understanding in relation to any such arrangements. The letter agreement can also formally acknowledge the customer's intention to enter into a contract with the supplier, on the assumption that suitable contract terms can be agreed.

Suppliers may seek to expand the scope of these undertakings by the customer to cover other activities and costs prior to contract signature. It should be accepted that a certain amount of time and resource should be invested by any supplier in order to achieve a successful contract. However, where there are activities which should genuinely be rewarded on a time and materials basis, the supplier should not be left out of pocket if the contract negotiations later fail. Any recovery under these sorts of arrangements should be on the basis of specified fee rates. In order to avoid rapidly escalating costs of which the customer is unaware, the supplier should be required to obtain the prior consent of the customer before incurring the costs. It will be in neither party's best interests for these sorts of informal arrangements to continue on an indefinite basis and it is therefore common to find time limits imposed on the expiry of which the letter agreement terminates if no outsourcing contract has been entered into by the specified date.

A consequence of the detailed process of discussion and disclosure which takes place prior to contract signature is that the supplier inevitably has access to a large amount of the customer's confidential information. It will therefore be important to ensure that the supplier is required to enter into a confidentiality (or non-disclosure) agreement. This will govern the use that can be made of the confidential information (essentially, to evaluate whether a contract should be entered into) and will prevent the disclosure of that information to third parties. The supplier should also be restricted in the internal disclosures it can make of the confidential information within its own organization—disclosure should be limited to those who are part of the bid team. This agreement should be put in place before any information or documentation, which is confidential in nature, is disclosed to the supplier. Where a letter (or other agreement) is used to cover any pre-contract investments or activities (as referred to above) these obligations can be incorporated into that letter agreement. Otherwise, a separate confidentiality agreement can be used.

As part of the outsourcing arrangement there will be a transfer of assets from the customer to the supplier. This will include third-party computer programs, hardware, related contracts (such as hardware and support arrangements), software which has been developed and is owned by the customer, buildings and land and other assets, items, contracts and arrangements. The transfer of these assets can take place either within the principal services agreement or alternatively as a separate contract. In any event, the terms regarding the asset transfer will be the same.[17]

In some of the more sophisticated outsourcing arrangements, two established entities may join together in order to provide a combined service to a particular customer. This can be done by establishing a joint-venture vehicle into which each of the two entities contributes staff and assets. In such circumstances, a joint-venture agreement will therefore be required to record the establishment and operation of the joint-venture vehicle. The customer will need to be satisfied that the joint-venture company is not merely a shell company but is a substantive entity backed up by sufficient value and assets.[18] In any event, it may be appropriate to seek a finance-and-performance guarantee by the original two parent entities in the event of any failure to perform by the joint-venture company. A joint venture created in this way may, in addition, require merger clearance from the relevant European or national competition authorities, as the compulsory merger-control regimes mostly have triggers based on group turnover size.[19] A merger authorization is particularly likely to be required if the joint venture is expected to be able to operate independently and to be able to sell similar outsourced services to other customers in its own right within a fairly short time.

### 2.2.2 The services agreement

As noted above, the services agreement is the principal contract between the parties governing the delivery of the services to the customer. Contracts are usually long in length reflecting the complex nature of the relationship and the need for the service provider to have a relatively long period in order to achieve the promised costs savings. Contracts for seven- to ten-year periods are still relatively common in the industry, although there is now a movement to shorter, typically five-year, contracts. The negotiation of the contract terms will often take many months and in light of the very commercial nature of their subject context, they will usually be highly tailored to meet any particular customer's requirements.

This section outlines some of the key provisions that will appear in any IS outsourcing contract. There will, of course, be many other terms regarding the ongoing service provision and outsourcing relationship.

#### 2.2.2.1 *Definition of the services*
The description of the services (and the service levels that must be attained) lies at

---

[17] See section 2.3 below for a discussion of the main elements of an asset-transfer agreement.

[18] Not least so that the customer can effectively pursue that company for damages claims or for service credits in the event of any failure to provide the services.

[19] See section 2.2.2.16 below.

the very heart of the outsourcing contract. It is essential to ensure that the service description captures all of the IS services to be provided by the supplier under the outsourcing arrangements. For example, where data-centre operations are to be outsourced to a supplier it will not be sufficient simply to give a description of the data-centre operations themselves. Other questions which should be considered by the customer will include:

(a) What other ancillary services are to be provided by the supplier?

(b) Who will be providing the disaster-recovery service?

(c) Who is providing the service that links the data centre to desktop and other IS environments?

(d) How is the supplier to interact with the customer's in-house IS function and other third-party service providers?

(e) What additional services or duties should the main outsourcing supplier have, recognizing the need that it should work effectively with the customer's in-house and external IS suppliers?

(f) Are there any other services that the customer is likely to need in the future that should be covered within the scope of the services agreement?

Similar sorts of issues will be relevant to any other type of IS function to be outsourced.

The answers to these and other questions should result in the outsourcing contract listing, in addition to the core IS services to be outsourced, a number of related and ancillary services and obligations.

The value of a well-defined service description cannot be underestimated. It will avoid, or at least minimize, subsequent disputes as to what is in included within the scope of the contract. Hastily drawn up service schedules frequently lead to a large number of contract-change requests being entered into after the contract has been commenced to incorporate elements which have been simply overlooked during the negotiation phase, with the attendant cost increases for the customer. All too often, it is inadequately drafted service schedules which provoke disputes that can fundamentally damage the outsourcing relationship. The service schedule should include as much detail as possible regarding the exact scope of any activity to be performed by the supplier and should be intelligible to someone who was not involved in its negotiation. Although it may be tempting to reduce the schedule to a fairly high-level set of obligations it should always be borne in mind that at a later date a court, or some other third-party expert or mediator, may be called on to interpret the terms of that schedule.

A distinction is sometimes drawn between services provided during an initial transitional period and those fully developed services to be provided afterwards. This reflects the fact that services provided during the initial transitional phase might be very different—in scope, duration, level of service and possibly even in the charges—from the services to be provided after that phase. Where an exception is to be made in respect of transitional services, the contract should specify very clearly to which of the contract provisions they are subject.

In some circumstances, it is not always possible for the customer to list in detail at the outset of any contract all of the services it would like to see provided in the future. It may be appropriate to include a section of additional services which the customer is entitled to require the supplier to provide at a later date on the terms of the services agreement. One advantage of such an approach will be to set out a clear fees structure which will apply to these additional services.

The services agreement will obviously need to identify the entities who are to benefit from the services provided. In a simple outsourcing arrangement one corporate entity will constitute the customer. In more complex arrangements, there may be an entire customer group which is to benefit and the contract therefore needs to be very clear about how the customer group is comprised. Where there are group companies involved, it may be the case that not all of the corporate entities are to receive the services from the commencement date. There is an increasing trend instead for companies to put in place framework contracts with outsourcing vendors under which the centralized outsourced service is provided to the holding company or principal operating vehicle, with provision to roll out the outsourced services to other group companies as and when they decide to take those services.

Clauses which restrict the customer's ability to purchase services from other third parties or which restrict the supplier's ability to deliver services of a similar nature to other customers may infringe national or EU competition regulation.[20]

### 2.2.2.2 *Service levels*

Service levels are at the core of any IS outsourcing contract, as they define the quality of the service to be provided by the supplier. Specifically, the customer will want to be assured:

(a) That the services will be available when the customer needs them (ie, with limited 'down time' or 'outage').

(b) That the services will be responsive and speedy.

(c) That they will be effective in supporting the customer's business operations.

(d) Above all, that they will deliver the cost savings and other benefits promised by the supplier, as reflected in the services agreement.

Service levels therefore play a very important role. However, producing a defined set of service levels to be attached to the contract can often be a difficult and time-consuming process. For many customers, there will simply be no documented records as to the level of service which has been provided in-house prior to the outsourcing contract being entered into. It may be tempting to adopt the commonly

---

[20] See section 2.2.2.16 below for a more detailed discussion of the competition issues. And see, further, Chapter 12.

used process of entering into a contract without any service levels attached, merely incorporating a contractual provision that the service levels will be reviewed and agreed during an initial stated time period. To follow this approach simply defers discussion regarding the required service levels to a stage when the customer is in a very unfavourable negotiating position, which, from the customer's perspective, is a recipe for disaster.

If this approach is adopted then the contract must also deal with the issue of what should happen if the parties still can not agree service levels even after the contract has been signed and the initial review period during which agreement was to be reached has passed. In these circumstances, it would be sensible to allow the customer to terminate the agreement in respect of those services for which no service levels have been agreed with the resulting changes to be made to other provisions of the agreement through the contract-change mechanism, such as a reduction in charges.

Service levels may not be attached to every type of service to be provided by the supplier as part of the services agreement. For example, there may be certain categories of service which are not seen as being a crucial part of the agreement or activities to which no objectively measurable service level can be set.

Importantly, the service level schedule needs to set out not only the service level to be attained but also how that service level will be measured (in terms of both method and frequency). In the event of any failure to achieve the service levels, service credits will usually be payable to the customer by the supplier.[21]

### 2.2.2.3 *Customer obligations*

Performance by the supplier of its obligations will, by varying degrees, depend on the customer meeting its own obligations. As a result, many contracts specify certain obligations which the customer must perform in order for the supplier to provide the services or other service dependencies. For example, any failure to transfer assets which it has been agreed by the parties should be transferred or any defects discovered in those assets which were not disclosed previously will obviously have an impact on the services that can be provided. Any obligations which are imposed on the customer should be specified clearly within the contract to avoid any later disputes.

Where the supplier will need access to the customer's premises to provide the services, standard provisions should be incorporated regarding the access to and use of those premises and other facilities.

### 2.2.2.4 *Performance improvement*

Although a customer may be prepared to accept that the duration of the contract should span typically five to ten years to allow the supplier to achieve the promised

---

[21] See section 2.2.2.10 below for a description of how service-credit regimes operate. Service credits are a valuable remedy and the 'teeth' by which the agreement is enforced.

costs savings, in return the customer will want to ensure that they continue to receive a cost-effective and high-quality service for the duration of that contract. This is one of the primary reasons for the inclusion of such provisions in a typical contract.

Under performance-improvement mechanisms, reviews of the service provision will be carried out by either the supplier themselves or by external third-party consultants. For example, suppliers are often required to carry out annual reviews of the services to identify areas for development or improvement and to identify ways in which the services can exploit falling technology costs within the marketplace. Any changes which the parties agree should be made are then implemented through the contract change-control mechanism.

In order to bring a degree of independence to the contractual arrangements, third-party review procedures can be incorporated. Under such procedures external third-party consultants conduct an assessment of the services to see if services of an equivalent nature can be obtained more cheaply or at increased service levels from elsewhere. These procedures are known as benchmarking procedures. Again, these benchmarking reviews usually take place on a yearly basis. In order for these reviews to take place the supplier will need to agree to allow the third-party consultant access to its data, software, hardware and networks which are used in providing the services. Such third parties will, as a matter of course, be required to sign up to stringent confidentiality undertakings regarding the information and assets they have access to.

These performance mechanisms with their yearly reviews form a useful function in ensuring that the services are continually assessed and improved. However, they should not replace regular detailed reporting and meeting requirements which provide for the day-to-day review and discussion of the supplier's performance under the contract.

### 2.2.2.5 *Relationship management*
Any IS outsourcing relationship necessitates a cooperative working relationship between the parties and an open exchange of information. The contract should formalize the discussion and reporting process without creating an unnecessary administrative burden for the supplier. With a trend towards more complex, high-value and global transactions, the importance of relationship management increases.

Typically, contracts will stipulate regular meetings at two levels. First, regular (perhaps monthly) meetings between the respective project managers of the parties to discuss day-to-day operational issues, resolve any disagreements and generally oversee the running of the contract. Secondly, meetings of representatives at a more senior level (such as Chief Information Officer or Finance Director). These need to occur less frequently (for example, on a quarterly basis) and their purpose should be to review the overall strategic direction of the contract and the outsourcing relationship, to build the relationship at an executive level, to resolve any disputes or issues submitted to them and to review any annual benchmarking survey results.

Meetings should be supplemented by a detailed reporting process. Regular reports should be submitted by the supplier regarding the performance of the services, any failures to achieve the service levels (and why this occurred) and any service credits that are paid. Reports should also be tailored to meet the specific requirements of a particular customer, for example, detailing any security breaches that have occurred or on specific aspects of the services provided. These reports will provide an invaluable tool to track performance, display any trends in over- or under-performance and generally to monitor the performance of the contract.

### 2.2.2.6 *Acceptance testing*
In some circumstances, the supplier is required to build and supply or integrate new systems before starting to provide the outsourced services. Where the supplier is to own such a system then traditional acceptance testing is likely to be inappropriate. This is because of the nature of an IS outsourcing contract, ie, an obligation on the supplier to deliver services to an agreed service level. How these service levels are achieved (ie, whether or not the system conforms to any particular detailed design build and specification) is irrelevant. In this scenario, any evaluation testing is only likely to be appropriate where it enables the customer to check that the system is capable of delivering the output required to support the outsourced services.

In the event that the customer is to own the system from which the outsourced services are to be provided then it will be more appropriate to impose traditional acceptance testing. Contractual procedures will need to specify the method by which such acceptance testing is to be carried out, provide detailed obligations on the supplier to remedy or fix any defects that are located during the testing period, specify details of the tests that are to take place and provide the consequences of a failure to pass the acceptance-testing procedure.

In addition, if further deliverables are to be provided by the supplier during the course of the outsourcing contract, such as new items of software or hardware, it may be appropriate to include a general acceptance-testing provision governing the procedure to apply and which is to be used on the delivery of any such items.

### 2.2.2.7 *Contract-change mechanisms*
Contract-change provisions will have a particular role to play in an IS outsourcing contract. The purpose of these provisions is to allow the contract to evolve over its life as the scope of existing services is changed, as new services are introduced and as new forms of technology are utilized.

Contracts need to incorporate a formal process by which any changes to the contract's scope will be discussed and implemented. Any changes to the scope of the contract or the services to be provided, however small, should be subjected to this procedure to enable a proper evaluation to take place. It is important to ensure that a detailed assessment is carried out by the supplier to review the impact of the change on the terms of the contract and the provision of the existing services. This then enables the customer to make an informed decision as to whether, and the basis on which, to proceed with any change. Any consequent amendments to the charges will be agreed through this procedure.

Mutual agreement is always at the core of any change-control procedure, although in some contracts where the negotiating power of the customer is particularly strong, the ultimate decision as to whether or not to accept or reject the proposal for the change may lie with the customer.

### 2.2.2.8 *The charges*

As in any contract, the charging structure which is to be adopted will very much be a matter of negotiation for the parties. The charges can either be fixed or variable or a combination of the two. One of the prime concerns of a customer will be how to predict and control those costs over the life of the contract, in particular to ensure that the opportunity for the supplier to introduce any increases to the charges is limited. The contract should therefore state those circumstances in which the charges may be changed.

Suppliers will naturally seek to ensure that the charges are linked to indexation with changes being made on an annual basis to reflect any change in an appropriate inflationary index. A matter which is frequently debated is the appropriate index to apply in these circumstances. The retail prices index as published by the Office for National Statistics is used in many contracts, both within the IT industry and otherwise, to govern future price increases. However, this index reflects the general rate of inflation in the economy and is based on the price of goods. It therefore fails to take into account the rather special circumstances of the technology industry and the spiralling labour costs within that market. Suppliers may therefore look to other indices specific to the IT industry as the basis on which charges should be increased. Any other changes to the charges should only be made if agreed through the contract change-control mechanism.

As with any contract, provisions regarding the mechanism for payment will need to be included. Issues such as the timing of payments (for example, whether charges are paid in arrears or in advance) and the frequency of payments must be stipulated, together with the mechanism by which any penalties under the contract, such as service credits, are to be paid. Service credits can be paid direct to the customer from the supplier or they may be deducted from invoices for the charges. Suppliers invariably favour the latter approach, not least because of the reluctance to incur costs as opposed to a loss of revenue.

As noted above, contracts will often be put in place with a certain degree of flexibility, enabling the customer to require the supplier to provide certain additional services as and when required. Ideally, the costs for any additional services which can be predicted as being a likely future requirement should be agreed at the outset and specified in the services agreement. This will not always be possible. For services that cannot be foreseen at the outset it may nevertheless be possible to specify a price formula within the contract by which the charges for any additional service will be calculated. This may be a cost-plus basis with the supplier being able to recover the cost of the new element of the services, together with an additional fixed profit element.

### 2.2.2.9 *Contract duration*

At first sight, this may appear to be a straightforward issue. In reality, the position will be more complex. The length of the contract term will be determined by a number of factors, most of which are strategic in nature. The key factor is whether the customer and supplier will realize their respective financial returns and other benefits from the IS outsourcing over the proposed term.

A view widely held by both customers and supplier is that, because IS outsourcing contracts are difficult to enter into and exit costs need to be amortized, such contracts must necessarily be long term. So for this reason there are still many IS outsourcing contracts which are entered into for a ten-year period. However, there are a number of other factors which should also be borne in mind which favour a shorter contract period. These include the fact that the customer's business changes over time and long-term contracts may often be inflexible and, also, that it may not always be in its best interests to enter into outsourcing contracts that will run beyond the life expectancy of the customer's technology. For these and other reasons many advisers now tend to recommend shorter contract durations, such as a three- to five-year term.

Contract renewal can be another contentious issue. Many customers will seek the right to extend the basic contract term for a certain time period without having to renegotiate the contract. This will be particularly important if the contract is for a shorter duration, such as a three-year period. In practice, suppliers will often be happy to extend the contract term provided that an acceptable charging basis for that extension period can be agreed. The exercise of an option to extend the contract term may also be used by the supplier to renegotiate other terms which it sees as being less than favourable, such as service levels or exit arrangements. Attempts to renegotiate any terms other than those which are directly impacted by the contract extension should be firmly resisted.

### 2.2.2.10 *Service credits and debits*

If the essence of the services agreement is a commitment by the supplier to deliver services to a stated level of service then the contract must define any consequences of a failure to achieve those service levels. Traditionally, service-credit regimes have been adopted. Service credits are a stated monetary amount which becomes payable by the supplier to the customer on a failure to achieve a service level to which those service credits apply. They are often expressed as being a certain percentage of the monthly charges.

The advantage of such a service-credit regime is that it provides the customer with an automatic financial remedy in the event of a service failure, thereby avoiding the customer being required to pursue formal legal claims for damages against the supplier. It also removes the potential for disputes between the parties as to the amount of loss and damage which has occurred in practice as a result of any failure to reach a specified service level and whether that loss and damage is of a type which should be recoverable from the supplier.

The imposition of service credits therefore incentivizes the supplier to ensure the service levels are achieved and, in the event that they are not, provides an effective form of financial recourse to the customer.

It usually takes some time to calculate and negotiate the monetary amount which should constitute a service credit. Contracts will typically set service credits either at a relatively nominal level or at a much higher level which aims to provide true compensation for the breach of the particular service level that has occurred.

Under English law, an amount stated in a contract which operates as a penalty is not enforceable. Accordingly, service credits which are set at too high a level run the risk of being struck out. It will therefore be important to ensure that any service credits reflect a genuine pre-estimate of the likely loss and damage that will be suffered in the event of a service failure. Those involved in calculating service credits should retain records from the time of contract negotiations in the event of any later disputes as to the validity of the amounts specified.

The imposition of service credits will usually provoke a response from a supplier that the converse should also apply, ie, that in the event that the service levels are exceeded the supplier should receive some form of compensation. For many, the idea that a supplier should be compensated for performing in excess of a level required and whilst the customer is still paying for that service is counter-intuitive. If it is accepted that some form of service debit should be payable then the most frequent way of incorporating them into the contractual framework is to set up a service-credit/debit bank. This requires an account, either real or notional, to be established. Service credits are then paid into the account as they are triggered. The supplier is then given the opportunity to reduce the amounts of credits payable by performing in excess of the service levels. On any over-performance, service debits will be paid into the account having the effect of reducing the balance of credits in that account. The account should then be settled on a regular basis with an appropriate payment to the customer, either directly or by a reduction against the charges which are invoiced for. Where such mechanisms are used, it is usual to ensure that service debts can only reduce the amount of credits that are payable to a zero amount and that service debits never become an amount which the customer is actually liable to pay direct to the supplier.

Service-credit regimes are, of course, only one method of compensating for failures to reach the specified levels of service. Other remedies include termination rights and damages claims.[22] On a more practical note, suppliers are also usually contractually required to provide such additional resources as may be necessary to remedy the service-level failure with, occasionally, the right for the customer to call on a third party to provide that failing service where the supplier has failed to remedy the situation within a specified time period.

---

[22] See section 2.2.2.11 below regarding the relationship between service credits and damages claims.

## 2.2.2.11 *Liability*

Suppliers will inevitably seek to limit their risk exposure under any IS outsourcing contract through the imposition of detailed limitation-of-liability clauses. Such clauses will usually impose a limit on the amount of any loss or damage, whether arising from a breach of contract, tort or otherwise, to a stated amount. Customers should also limit their own liability to the customer in the same way.

Under English law, liability for certain types of loss and damage cannot be excluded. These include, most notably, exclusions or limitations for death or personal injury caused by a party's negligence,[23] and, where the IS outsourcing contract involves the sale of goods (such as the sale of hardware from the customer to the supplier as part of the initial asset transfer), the term that the seller has the right to sell those goods.[24]

English law also provides that certain exclusions and limitations of liability must be subject to the test of reasonableness. For example, where the parties contract on the basis of one party's standard terms of business, the exclusions and limitations of liability for loss and damage in respect of any contract breach must be reasonable.[25] Although it is likely that many IS outsourcing contracts will be the subject of extensive and detailed negotiations so that the negotiated 'deal' can no longer be said to be on one party's standard terms of business, those negotiating and drafting contracts should be aware of this principle.[26]

Suppliers generally seek to exclude their liability for indirect or consequential loss and damage. This type of loss includes loss beyond the damage to the value of the property itself, such as loss of profits and loss of revenue. Suppliers who do wish to exclude their liability for consequential loss will need to draft appropriate provisions with care. Recent case law has thrown doubts over the effectiveness of the, until now, standard formulations of exclusions for 'indirect and consequential damage'.[27] (See also Chapter 3 for a detailed discussion of liability generally and the effectiveness of exclusion clauses.)

---

[23] Unfair Contract Terms Act 1977 ('UCTA 1977'), s 2.

[24] Sale of Goods Act 1979 ('SGA 1979'), s 12; Supply of Goods and Services Act 1982 ('SGSA 1982'), s 7.

[25] UCTA 1977, s 3. Whether or not the exclusion/limitation is 'reasonable' will be assessed in light of a number of factors specified in Schedule 2 to that Act.

[26] Especially given the willingness of courts recently to strike out liability clauses which were in breach of UCTA 1977, s 3. See, in particular, *St Albans City and District Council v International Computers Ltd* [1995] FSR 686 and *South West Water Services Ltd v International Computers Ltd*, 29 June 1999, Technology and Construction Court (unreported), although both of these cases involved rather specific facts which may well enable courts later to distinguish from them in future judgments.

[27] The Court of Appeal in *British Sugar v NEI Power Projects Ltd* (1998) 87 BLR 42 suggested that the meaning of the word 'consequential' was loss which flows from special circumstances and therefore within the second limb of the *Hadley v Baxendale* (1854) 9 Exch 341 damages test. This reasoning contradicts the widespread opinion that certain types of consequential loss can constitute direct loss within the first limb of *Hadley v Baxendale*. However, until further guidance is received from the courts those drafting contracts must navigate the rather confusing judgment in *British Sugar* as best they can.

The services agreement will include a number of provisions regarding the supplier's liability in specific circumstances. Common examples include liability in the event of an infringement of a third party's IPRs, specific indemnities (for example, regarding employee transfers and the application of TUPE 1981) and in the event of a failure to achieve service levels. The services agreement must bring together all of these forms of the supplier's liability under the contract and detail how these specific liabilities are linked to the general caps on the supplier's liability for contract breaches, if at all.

The relationship between the liability provisions and the supplier's liability to pay service credits in the event of a failure to achieve a service level to which service credits relate will merit special consideration. The liability for such service credits can fall within the general cap, be subject to a separate cap or be unlimited. The services agreement will need to find a balance between ensuring that the customer can recover appropriately in the event of a service failure (bearing in mind that including service credits within a general liability cap of, say, the total contract price, may not provide adequate compensation to the customer or incentive to the supplier to avoid breaches) against the supplier's understandable desire to limit its total liability exposure.

The services agreement will typically include some specific remedies which are available to the customer in the event of a contract breach. A good example comes from provisions stipulating what will happen in the event that any of the customer's data is lost or corrupted. This loss of data is a consequential loss and one for which typically (as noted above) the supplier will seek to exclude its liability. However, to leave a customer with no remedy in these circumstances where the potential for damage to the customer's business as a result of that loss is so great, would be unacceptable. Services agreements therefore often require the supplier to restore or procure the restoration of any data that has been lost or corrupted to the last transaction processed. This data recovery is carried out at the supplier's cost.

In any event due consideration should be given not only to what liability provisions can be negotiated but also as to the likely ability of the supplier to pay out under any claims. This is particularly important where the supplier is either one of the smaller, newer, entrants to the market or where services are provided through a particular subsidiary (with limited assets) of a more well-known market player. In these circumstances, obtaining contractual assurances as to insurance cover or seeking parent-company guarantees is advisable.

### 2.2.2.12 *Warranties*

The services agreement will need to incorporate a number of warranties to deal both with the status and performance of the supplier generally and then to cover a number of specific issues arising in relation to IS outsourcing contracts.

English law will imply certain terms into any contract. In relation to a contract for the provision of services, as an IS outsourcing contract will be characterized, the supplier will be required to use reasonable care in the provision of the services.[28] In practice, this implied warranty will usually be replaced by detailed contractual assurances regarding the nature of the services to be provided. Accordingly, the application of implied terms is often expressly excluded.[29]

Assuming that the contract will therefore replace warranties implied by law with express warranties, general warranties to be included regarding service performance will include those regarding the performance by the supplier of its obligations in accordance with all applicable laws, the use of skilled and experienced personnel and performance of obligations in accordance with good industry practice. Warranties are also included regarding the general standing of the supplier at the time the contract is entered into, such as warranties that the supplier has full capacity and all necessary consents and licences to enter into the contract, that it is not subject to insolvency (or similar) proceedings and that there is no material litigation pending to which the supplier is a party. Equivalent warranties may also be sought regarding the general standing of the customer at the time the contract is entered into.

Specific issues to be covered include euro-compliance and the absence of any viruses in systems provided or used. Assurances should be obtained regarding euro-compliance where any IT system provided or used by the supplier needs to recognize and deal in euros. Legal requirements relating to the euro are currently contained within two Council Regulations[30] and the definition of euro-compliance is traditionally based on the system in question performing in accordance with them.

As noted above, the position regarding viruses should also be considered. Where software is provided by a supplier, contractual assurances may be obtained acknowledging that the software does not contain any virus or lock or any other device which enables the supplier to prevent its continued operation, such as a facility to disable software if a customer fails to make payment. Such locks and time bombs will be illegal under the terms of the Computer Misuse Act 1990 unless the supplier has notified the customer in advance of its intention to use such devices in the software and their effect.

### 2.2.2.13 *Data and data protection*

Most IS outsourcing contracts will involve the supplier handling a considerable volume of the customer's data, either where the supplier generates data using systems which are utilized by the supplier as part of the services or data which the supplier itself directly generates in the course of performing the services.

---

[28] SGSA 1982, s 13. Where goods are supplied, the SGA 1979 requires them to be of satisfactory quality (s 14) and fit for their purpose (s 15).

[29] As with any exclusion or limitation of liability, caution must be exercised to ensure that UCTA 1977 (in particular, sections 2(2) and 3) is adhered to.

[30] Council Regulation (EC) No 1103/97 dated 17 June 1997 and Council Regulation (EC) No 974/98 dated 3 May 1998. These Regulations cover conversion (from ecu and national currencies to the euro) and rounding requirements, together with a number of other legal issues.

Customers should therefore ensure that they own all of the rights in their data and that appropriate assignments are obtained from the supplier of the IPRs in the data.

Data-protection law will also have a considerable impact on outsourcing activities. Data-protection law has recently undergone some important changes with the introduction in the UK of the Data Protection Act 1998 which came into force on 1 March 2000. It has been implemented as a result of the Data Protection Directive[31] and applies to any data relating to a living individual and from which the individual can be identified.

The Act replaces the earlier provisions relating to computer service bureaux which were contained in the predecessor to the 1998 Act, the Data Protection Act 1984, with the concept of the data processor.

A data processor is someone who carries out the processing of personal data on behalf of a data controller. The data controller is an entity which (either alone or jointly or in common with other persons) determines the purposes for which, and the manner in which, any personal data are processed. In a standard outsourcing contract the customer will usually take the role of the data controller and the supplier the role of a data processor.

The Act requires that a data controller should impose certain obligations on any data processor that it appoints. Data processors must be appointed under a written contract and must carry out any processing activities only on the instructions of the data controller. Importantly, the data controller must choose a data processor with sufficient guarantees in respect of the security measures it takes to protect the data processed against unlawful or accidental loss or destruction.

One of the further changes arising from the new data-protection legislation is the introduction of the much-publicized eighth principle under Schedule 1 to the Act. Schedule 1 lists a number of principles with which a data controller must comply. This eighth principle states that personal data cannot be transferred to a country outside the European Economic Area unless that third country offers an adequate level of protection for the data concerned. With the increasingly global nature of business, today's modern IT systems will invariably involve the transfer of personal data between a number of countries. In addition, with the current trend towards utilizing outsourcing suppliers based overseas, often in countries such as India, South Africa or Malaysia, the data-protection considerations become even more key. Businesses therefore need to be aware of the eighth principle and that further steps may need to be taken to ensure compliance with it.

### 2.2.2.14 *Termination*
As with any IT contract, a number of standard termination rights should be incorporated. These should include rights of termination in the event that the other party to the contract breaches one of its terms or becomes insolvent.

---

[31] Directive 95/46/EC on the protection of individuals with regard to the processing of personal data and on the free movement of such data, OJ 1995 L281.

More specific termination rights should then be catered for. These will often include defining a minimum service level and providing that if the service drops below this minimum level then the customer has a right of immediate termination. Defining a minimum service level in this way effectively defines what the parties consider amounts to a material breach and avoids protracted disputes about whether any particular service level failure is of sufficient impact otherwise to entitle the customer to terminate under standard provisions regarding material breach.

It is not only one-off breaches of the service levels that should be considered for specific treatment within the termination provisions but also persistent, albeit more minor, breaches of service levels. It may be unacceptable for the parties to be locked into a contract indefinitely where there are repeated more minor breaches (even where this triggers service credits) and it may therefore be useful to define further termination rights as existing after there have been a specified number of these more minor breaches within any fixed time period.

Under many IS outsourcing contracts there is a mix of a different number of services which are provided by the suppliers. For this reason, rights to partial termination may be appropriate, and highly desirable, enabling the customer to retain a high degree of flexibility as to how its business develops in the future. In each circumstance, those drafting a contract will need to consider the extent to which the services are bundled together and whether they can be easily separated. If it is possible to separate the services, or part of a service, partial termination rights may be appropriate. In practice, any partial termination rights are likely to be resisted heavily by the supplier. Where the services are partially terminated there will inevitably be an impact on the remaining provisions of the contract (such as the other services being provided, the service levels and the charges). Accordingly, any necessary changes to the remaining contract terms should be made through the contract-change provisions.

Break options are also a popular remedy, entitling the customer to terminate a contract at will after a number of years. The customer therefore does not need to prove any breach by the supplier or any other cause entitling them to terminate. Many suppliers will calculate their cost models on the basis of recovery of various investment costs over a relatively long period and to allow termination in this way would potentially leave a supplier seriously out of pocket. For this reason, break options are usually accompanied by large financial penalties under which the supplier seeks to recoup this type of investment cost.

As has been seen, IS outsourcing contracts require a close working relationship to be established between the parties and a number of the customer's assets will have transferred to the supplier at the beginning of that relationship. The exercise of termination rights can therefore pose difficult issues for the customer. It is not a relationship from which the customer is likely to be able to extricate itself in a number of weeks. Assets will need to be transferred back to the customer or to a replacement service provider to enable the customer to maintain continuity in the provision of service. There will need to be a flow of information and assistance between the parties. Consequently, exit provisions dealing with the handover of assets and information and ensuring ongoing service provision whilst the customer or its replacement service provider take over the service provision will be vital to ensure a seamless transition of the services. The importance and nature of exit provisions are discussed in more detail in section 2.5 below.

### 2.2.2.15 *Dispute resolution*

It is being increasingly common to formalize escalation procedures within a contract providing for stated levels within each entity to which any dispute will be escalated (within fixed timescales) before the matter can be referred to the courts. For example, project managers may initially be required to resolve any dispute and, on their failing to do so within a specified time, the issue may be referred to the finance director of each organization. The purpose of these provisions is to encourage settlement of any dispute at an early stage.

There are a number of matters which should be excluded from the scope of these escalation procedures as there are some circumstances in which it will not be appropriate to follow this type of process before being free to pursue legal action. For example, where one party has committed a material breach of the contract the other party will want the immediate right to terminate and to pursue any other legal remedies (such as a damages claim) without being required first to discuss the dispute with the other party. Also, if one party suspects that its IPRs have been, or are about to be, infringed or if it thinks that its confidential information has been, or is about to be, disclosed then immediate action will be required (for example, through seeking an injunction) to protect the rights of that party.

Contracts may also provide for other forms of dispute resolution in the event that the internal escalation process does not resolve the matter. This is particularly the case given an increasing reluctance to refer matters to the court due to the fact that the costs of court action can be extremely high and the length of time that court proceedings can take. In addition, disputes arising out of IS outsourcing contracts can often be of a highly technical nature and it may be more appropriate to refer the issue to an expert with suitable knowledge and understanding rather than to the courts.

Third-party experts may therefore be used to resolve disputes of a technical nature. The contract will need to specify the processes the expert will adhere to and how that expert is appointed. The decisions of such expert adjudicators are usually expressed as being binding. Mediation is often used to resolve other disputes (ie, those of a non-technical nature) and the contract will need to specify a body which, in the event of a failure by the parties to agree on the identity of a mediator, will be required to appoint one. The Centre for Dispute Resolution is often used in this context. Again, the contract will need to specify the process which will be adopted where mediation is used.

The use of such dispute-resolution mechanisms in any contract also reflects the increasing trend to consider appropriate forms of alternative dispute resolution as a result of the Woolf reforms to the UK litigation process. Litigants are now asked whether they considered or participated in other dispute-resolution mechanisms before resorting to the courts. For those who have not, there are significant costs implications.

### 2.2.2.16 *Competition issues*

The typical outsourcing contract rarely raises many competition issues. Where they do arise, they are likely to take one of three forms: exclusivity (for example, preventing the customer purchasing further services from anyone other than the supplier); limits on pricing policies; or merger control where the outsourcing is to be achieved through a joint venture.

Competition rules are now effectively applicable worldwide. They are also not limited to the governing law of the contract. It is therefore possible for more than one competition regime to apply at a time where, as can be the case, the parties operate in several jurisdictions. Clauses that infringe competition rules will be void under the rules of the UK, EU and most other countries. Government authorities also have wide rights to investigate companies for infringements and then to impose fines. Such investigations are inevitably time consuming. Finally, others who have suffered loss and damage as a result of the competition infringement can sue to recover this.

Exclusivity can apply to either the customer or the supplier. A supplier may wish to tie in a customer so that it cannot buy related services from one of the supplier's competitors. A customer may feel that the outsourcing gives them a competitive advantage and wish to prevent their core competitors from outsourcing with the same supplier. Not all limits are objectionable. Competition law instead looks to the effect of the restrictions considering the market strength of the parties, whether everyone else in the market will have the same limitations and the exact scope of the provision. The stronger the market position of either party, the longer the duration and the more aggressive the restriction, the higher the competition risk. Each contract needs to be assessed on its own merits and it is difficult to draw general conclusions. However, restrictions for market shares of less than 15 per cent are unlikely to be problematic. Restrictions for market shares in excess of 40 per cent are unlikely to be possible with restrictions for market shares between 15 to 40 per cent and the accompanying risk requiring careful analysis.

If the supplier is very strong in its market then an additional range of obligations will apply. The dominant supplier must treat all its equivalent customers on a similar basis. This means, for example, that the price or core terms that a customer is given must match those for an equivalent deal. It is of considerable value to the customer to identify whether this is the case.

Finally, where a new entity is created to operate the outsourcing, particularly if that entity will also take the outsourced services to the market more generally, merger control may apply.

## 2.3 SALE AGREEMENTS

### 2.3.1 Purpose of sale agreements

One of the features of an IS outsourcing contract is the transfer of assets from the customer to the supplier. A formal document of transfer will be required to identify those assets which are to be transferred, the mechanism by which they are to be transferred and the price which the supplier is to pay for them.

Provisions can be incorporated into the principal services agreement dealing with the assets transfer. It may, however, be easier to use a separate sale agreement to document the provisions regarding the one-off transfer of assets. This is particularly likely to be the case where there are a considerable number of assets to be transferred.

### 2.3.2 Identification of assets

Early in the outsourcing process the customer should identify the assets which are currently used by it to deliver the service in-house. This should include a listing of the assets themselves and any related contracts. Ultimately, this information will need to be attached as a schedule to the sale agreement. It is important not to underestimate the length of time that will be required to compile this listing. Unfortunately, it is often found to be the case that customers have poorly documented the systems that are used in providing services in-house, especially regarding pieces of software which are developed on a fairly *ad hoc* basis for use by the company. It can therefore be a difficult and time-consuming task to piece together the relevant information.

The types of assets which are likely to have been used by the customer and which the supplier may require will include software and hardware and their related support arrangements, together with other items such as premises, equipment and contracts. In respect of items of software, hardware or other equipment which are owned by the customer the position will be relatively straightforward. A decision will need to be taken whether these assets are to be transferred to the supplier for an appropriate payment or whether a lease or licence of them will be provided and, if so, the terms of that lease or licence.

Items of software or hardware that are owned by third parties and leased or licensed to the business may cause more difficulties. Often the terms of those contracts will prevent the use of that item by a third party, even where the third party is acting on behalf of the customer, let alone an outright transfer of it to the supplier. Any use by a supplier of those items will therefore be in breach of the contract provisions exposing the customer to a claim for damages and to termination of the contract for material breach of its terms. In addition, such unauthorized use will infringe the IPRs (usually copyright) of the third party and the supplier may therefore be liable accordingly.

The third parties who provide those items of software, hardware or other equip-ment will therefore need to be approached to give their consent to the transfer of the relevant item by the third-party supplier. If this consent cannot be obtained then the primary alternative will be to seek a licence in favour of the supplier from the third-party owner of the item involved. Obviously, the consequences of either of these two methods is the sum of money which the third party imposes on the supplier to provide its consent or provide the licence. Traditionally, the customer is forced to bear the costs associated with obtaining any necessary consents from third parties. This will, however, very much depend on the negotiating power of the parties. Also, it should be noted that the process for approaching those third parties and obtaining consents from them can be a lengthy one and it should therefore be started well in advance of the anticipated contract commencement date.

The contract should also specify the consequences if relevant third-party consents cannot be procured. It may be that an alternative item can be found or that the customer continues to operate the item of software or hardware that cannot be trans-ferred. This is discussed in more detail in section 2.3.3 below.

### 2.3.3  The sale agreement

The sale agreement will thus identify all of the assets which are to be transferred to the supplier and will specify the date on which this is to take effect. As the supplier will usually take over the obligations and liabilities in relation to third-party items after the transfer date, the customer will usually warrant that it has fulfilled all of those obligations and liabilities up to that date.

The supplier will be in control of those third-party items after the transfer date, so the customer will want to have assurance that, if there are any problems that arise after that date, the supplier will be legally responsible for them. It is therefore usual for the customer to seek an indemnity from the supplier in respect of any claims and expenses arising after the transfer date. Often, the supplier then seeks a counter-indemnity from the customer in respect of the fulfilment of the customer's obliga-tions in relation to the third-party items prior to the transfer date.

The supplier may seek warranties from the customer regarding the performance and quality of assets which are to be transferred to it. Whether these warranties are ultimately incorporated into the sale agreement will be a question of the respective bargaining power of the parties. Where, as is usually the case, the supplier under-takes a detailed process of due diligence prior to entering into the contract,[32] then one of the primary purposes of this exercise will have been for the supplier to ascer-tain the quality and condition of the assets and for this to be reflected in the purchase price accordingly. On this basis, warranties should be resisted. Where no, or little, due diligence has taken place prior to entering into the contract it may be necessary to incorporate some limited warranties for the benefit of the supplier.

---

[32] See section 2.1.8.5 above.

A great deal of cooperation will be required between the customer and the supplier to ensure the smooth transition of the assets to the supplier. As mentioned above, it should be accepted that there may be some items where consent simply cannot be obtained from the relevant third party prior to the commencement of the services agreement. In this circumstance, it will be necessary to consider other options in order to ensure that the services can nevertheless still be provided by the supplier. Contracts may therefore need to build in a mechanism to deal with this scenario, including, for example, removing those third-party items from the scope of the outsourcing or for the third-party vendor simply to manage those contracts on behalf of the customer until such time as the third party consents to the transfer.[33]

In relation to any particular IS function that is being outsourced, there may well be assets which although related to the function are not to be transferred and will be retained by the customer. For the sake of clarity, contracts may also need to identify the assets and contracts which are to be retained by the customer in this way and which are therefore outside the scope of the sale agreement.

As far as the transfer of third-party contracts is concerned, the most effective form of legal transfer will be novation. The legal effect of novating a contract is to terminate the existing legal arrangement between the customer and third party and to create a new legal arrangement (on the same terms as the previous contract) between the supplier and the third party. The other method of transfer which may be referred to is an assignment. However, generally, an assignment can only transfer benefits and not burdens.[34]

Where property is involved, the supplier may need to be sold or leased premises, or a sublease may need to be granted. Where the customer is granting a sublease of property, it will need to get the owner's consent. As with other third-party assets that are transferred, there are likely to be costs implications in obtaining these consents and other conditions may be imposed. The sale or leasing of property will also raise issues of property law (which are beyond the scope of this book) and specialist advice should be obtained in this regard.

Staff may also transfer to the supplier, together with the valuable body of knowledge that each staff member will have built up regarding the IS systems and generally in relation to the business operations of the customer.

---

[33] Note that these arrangements too can be problematic as many third-party contracts will contain standard provisions preventing or restricting the customer's ability to assign, transfer or otherwise dispose of its rights under that contract. Also, there are often confidentiality obligations imposed on the parties to such contracts which will effectively prevent the access to, and use of, that item by a third party. The management option may therefore not always be a viable option.

[34] So, where the customer has obligations to perform, as in a standard software licence, novation is the more effective and complete way of transferring that licence.

## 2.4 STAFF

### 2.4.1 TUPE 1981 and the Acquired Rights Directive

The impact on the customer's staff will need to be considered carefully in any potential IS outsourcing. The law gives considerable rights to employees to ensure that they are fully protected where they undergo a change of employer which results from a transfer of the undertaking that they work for.

TUPE 1981 (discussed in relation to liability under the service agreement at section 2.2.2.11 above) give effect to the earlier European Acquired Rights Directive[35] in the UK. The 1981 Regulations will apply on any relevant transfer of an undertaking. An undertaking is defined in TUPE 1981 as including any 'trade or business' and will include a self-contained, separate or separable part of the business capable of operating as a going concern.

For the purposes of TUPE 1981, a transfer can be exercised by a sale of that undertaking (or part of it) or, of perhaps more importance in the outsourcing scenario, on an alternative form of disposition.

The application of TUPE 1981 encompasses the scenario of an outsourcing of an undertaking's business and a change in the contractors carrying out the business of an undertaking. It does not matter that the legal ownership of the undertaking is consistent pre- and post-transfer. The key question is whether there is an undertaking which retains its pre-transfer identity at the post-transfer stage.[36]

Importantly, later cases have emphasized the need for there to be an accompanying transfer of assets and that the transfer of an activity alone would not be sufficient to trigger the application of the legislation. To date, these cases have been confined to the re-tendering of contracts on their expiry or termination. They are discussed in detail at section 2.4.3 below. There is no reason why some of their logic should not be applied to the initial grant of a contract, although further clarification from the courts is awaited on this issue.[37]

In relation to IS outsourcing, one of the difficult issues will be to determine which employees 'belong' to the undertaking (or part of it) that is being transferred. Where only part of the IS function is being outsourced and where employees previously carried out duties both in relation to the functions being outsourced and those being retained, it is not always apparent whether or not they will transfer. There are no clear rules on this and ultimately it is a question of fact to be determined by looking

---

[35] Directive 77/187/EC.

[36] See *Spijkers v Gebroeders Benedik Abattoir* (Case 24/85) [1996] ECR 119. In determining the issue the Court of Justice laid down a helpful set of factors to be taken into account when determining whether the undertaking remains the same, although subsequent case law has established that these factors cannot be considered in isolation and the overriding criteria will be whether or not there is an economic entity which retains its identity.

[37] In *Suzen*, referred to in section 2.4.3 below, there was some suggestion that the case was clarifying some of the earlier case law and from this it may therefore be possible to predict that the courts will take a similar approach when looking at the initial grant of the contract as they will on its subsequent re-tender.

at all the relevant circumstances, such as the proportion of time allocated to the undertaking that is being transferred by each employee and the description of their duties contained in their employment contract.

The application of TUPE 1981 has caused some uncertainty in the UK. For example, it was unclear for many years whether the 1981 Regulations would always apply to an outsourcing in the public sector and it was not until 1993 that this issue was finally resolved.[38] Fortunately, case law (on a European and national basis) has assisted to clarify a number of issues, although there are still areas where the potential effect of the legislation is not yet fully understood.

A further Directive[39] amending the Acquired Rights Directive was adopted in 2001 but awaits implementation in the UK. The Government is currently undertaking a review of TUPE 1981 in this regard. A consultation paper was issued in September 2001[40] and the consultation period under that paper closed three months later in December 2001. Unfortunately, the results of that consultation paper are still awaited and it is therefore likely to be some time yet before we see any legislative overhaul to the UK regime. The Government is considering a number of key areas, some of which are particularly relevant in the outsourcing context.

The Government is, in particular, seeking views as to whether there should be a presumption that TUPE 1981 applies in an outsourcing transaction. It is proposed that if there is a service-provision change (and a service-provision change would encompass the initial outsourcing of a service and where an outsourced service is either brought back in-house or transferred to a new contractor) and prior to the change, there are employees assigned to an organized grouping which performs activities on behalf of the company concerned, then TUPE 1981 would apply to transfer those employees. Such an approach would at least provide some certainty to all concerned in the outsourcing transaction although inevitably there is still likely to be room for argument in each case as to whether such an organized grouping exists.

Also under consideration is the treatment of occupational pension rights. Currently, there is no automatic transfer of such rights under TUPE 1981 as rights and liabilities in respect of continuing membership of occupational pension schemes were excluded from the scope of the original Acquired Rights Directive. The consultation paper seeks views on whether some protection should be provided for rights under occupational pensions on transfer, with a range of options under consideration dependent on the nature of the transferor's and the transferee's pension schemes in existence at the time of the transfer.

---

[38] Through a combination of the Trade Union Reform and Employment Rights Act 1993 (which removed the previous exclusion from TUPE 1981 of undertakings that were 'not in the nature of a commercial venture') and *Wren v Eastbourne Borough Council* [1993] IRCL 425 it became apparent that TUPE 1981 would apply to public-sector outsourcings.

[39] Directive 98/50/EC.

[40] *Transfer of Undertakings (Protection of Employment) Regulations 1981: Government Proposals for Reform* (DTI, September 2001) (URN 0111158).

Finally, there are proposals for the introduction of a statutory requirement for information to be provided in writing to the transferee about the rights and obligations in relation to employees that will be transferred. It is also suggested that in the event that those rights or obligations change between the time of the original notification and completion of the transfer, then the transferee must again be notified in writing. This would help considerably in ensuring an adequate flow of information to the transferee to enable a better evaluation of the impact of any proposed outsourcing arrangement.

Changes of this nature would clearly have a significant impact on the ability of the parties to determine with some degree of certainty whether TUPE 1981 can be said to apply to any contemplated outsourcing and the rights and liabilities that will pass to the transferee. It is difficult to predict, however, at present the detailed shape of any likely changes to the existing Regulations.

### 2.4.2 Effects of TUPE 1981

In circumstances where TUPE 1981 applies, there will be a transfer of the existing employment contracts of employees connected to the undertaking on the transfer of that undertaking. This means that the supplier will become responsible for those employees and any associated liabilities arising from their employment from the date of the transfer. Consequently, the customer will relinquish all liability (except in relation to any occupational pension scheme, as discussed in section 2.4.1 above).

TUPE 1981 also operates to protect employees from being dismissed merely as a result of the transfer of the relevant undertaking. In relation to employees that are dismissed prior to the transfer of the undertaking for reasons unconnected to the transfer then those employees will remain the responsibility of the transferor. TUPE 1981 will, however, apply to employees who are dismissed prior to the transfer for a reason connected to the transfer.[41]

Employees who lose their jobs as a result of the transfer will automatically be considered to be unfairly dismissed[42] unless there are economic, technical or organizational reasons justifying the job loss. Even where there are apparently justifiable reasons for that job loss an employee of the transferred undertaking can make a claim for constructive dismissal.

In practice, the services agreement will normally incorporate the allocation of liability between the customer and the supplier relating to the potential liabilities attached to the customer's staff who will transfer. For example, the customer may be required to indemnify the supplier in relation to any such liabilities which have arisen due to acts of the customer prior to the contract commencement date with a reciprocal indemnity from the supplier in favour of the customer for the period thereafter.

---

[41] *Lister v Forth Dry Dock & Engineering Co* [1989] IRLR 161.
[42] Provided they have had two years' continuous employment before the effective date of termination.

As a result of the transfer, the employee will be shown to have a continuous record of employment and his time spent with the undertaking pre- and post-transfer will therefore be treated as a continuous period of employment.

Agreements reached between the transferor (ie, the customer on the grant of the outsourcing contract) and a trade union representing the transferor's employees will also transfer to the transferee.

### 2.4.3 Effect of TUPE 1981 on expiry or termination of the services agreement

There has previously been some debate as to the extent to which TUPE 1981 would apply on the expiry or termination of an outsourcing contract automatically to transfer employees engaged in the service provision either back in-house to the customer or to a third-party replacement service provider. Recent case law has shed some light upon this issue.

In *Suzen v Zehnacker Gebaudereinigung GmbH Krankenhausservice*[43] it was found that the Acquired Rights Directive did not apply to a situation in which a person who had entrusted the cleaning of premises to a first undertaking terminated their contract with that undertaking and, for the performance of similar work, entered into a new contract with a second undertaking if there was no accompanying transfer from the first undertaking to the second of a significant amount of tangible or intangible assets, or by taking over a major part of the workforce, in terms of their number and skill, assigned by the previous undertaking to the performance of the contract.

The *Suzen* case therefore establishes that whether or not TUPE 1981 will apply on the termination or expiry of an outsourcing contract will depend on the extent to which there is a transfer of associated assets.

The findings of the *Suzen* case have subsequently been applied by the Court of Appeal in *Betts v Brintel Helicopters*.[44] Again, in the *Betts* case it was held that there was no relevant transfer for the purposes of the Directive and TUPE 1981 where a replacement contractor did not take on any of the initial contractor's employees or assets. This has subsequently led to some concern that replacement contractors may try to avoid the effect of TUPE 1981 by not employing any of the employees following the transfer. The courts have gone some way to rectify this and in the case of *ECM (Vehicle Delivery Services) Ltd v Cox*[45] the courts stressed the importance of looking at why employees were not taken on by a new contractor so as to prevent transferors being able to circumvent the application of TUPE 1981.[46]

---

[43] Case 13/95; [1997] ECR 1259.

[44] [1997] IRLR 361. And in a stream of further cases, including *Allen* [2000] IRLR 119 and *Oy Liikene AB* [2001] IRLR 17.

[45] [1998] IRLR 416.

[46] This approach was also adopted in *ADI (UK) Ltd v Willer* [2001] IRLR 542 where it was noted that if an incoming contractor declines to take on the workforce, due regard should be given as to whether this was done to avoid the application of TUPE 1981.

### 2.4.4  Consultation

As good commercial practice, many employers will wish to embark on a full consultation process with their employees well in advance of any IS outsourcing. For many
employees, the prospect of transferring their employment to a specialist IT firm will
be viewed as an exciting one with the new career-development opportunities it may
bring. The way in which the possibility, or decision, to outsource is notified to
employees will be very influential in determining whether it is seen in a positive
light or not.

Aside from such practical considerations, TUPE 1981 imposes legal obligations
on employers to notify and consult with employees. The notification and consultation process should relate to the transfer and also as to any redundancies. Employees
must be informed about the transfer, its implications for them and any measures that
the employer anticipates he will take in relation to affected employees. Where there
are proposed redundancies, the notification obligations will vary according to the
number of employees who will be affected. Those who fail to comply with the
consultation obligations risk seeing their deals delayed or prevented.[47]

## 2.5  EXIT ISSUES

### 2.5.1  Importance of service continuity

Many customers find it difficult to tackle the issue of exit provisions with the
supplier during negotiation for the services agreement. To contemplate the end of
the relationship before it has begun can seem at best like being overly detailed and,
at worst, may be perceived as damaging to the future partnership between customer
and supplier. However, detailed provisions which specify the rights and obligations
of the parties on any termination or expiry of the contract will be important to ensure
that the customer is able to exit the relationship without undue disruption to its business and to ensure a seamless transition of the services either back in-house or to a
replacement third-party service provider.

Just as the services agreement (or, in some cases, the sales agreement) incorporates detailed provisions regarding the transfer of assets from the customer to the
supplier on the commencement of the contract, the contractual documentation
should also specify how relevant assets will be transferred to the customer or the
replacement service provider on the termination or expiry of the relationship.
Obviously, the customer will be in a far better position to negotiate favourable exit
provisions prior to entering into the original outsourcing contract when the
supplier is anxious to win the business rather than at the time of termination when

---

[47] Recently, Prudential was threatened by legal action from trade-union officials after the insurance
company announced plans to outsource its call-centre function to India. It was claimed that a proper
consultation exercise had not been followed.

the relationship has broken down and any goodwill between the parties may be limited or non-existent.

Typically, these provisions will be incorporated into a separate schedule of the services agreement specifying the consequences of any termination or expiry.

## 2.5.2 Exit provisions

The contract will need to deal with a number of issues relating to the transfer of information and assets from the supplier to the customer. Some of the principal provisions are outlined below in this section. There will, of course, be other ancillary obligations which any contract will need to deal with.

### 2.5.2.1 *Assets register*

In order for the customer to continue itself to provide the service or to engage a third party to do so on its behalf, it will need to have knowledge of the assets used by the supplier during the term of the services agreement. Many customers seek the option to choose the particular assets they wish to have transferred from the supplier rather than being under any general obligation to take over all the relevant assets used.

The supplier should therefore be required to maintain on a regular basis an inventory record which lists all of the assets used by the supplier to provide the services, such as any software, hardware, data, documentation, manuals and details of licences, leases, or other arrangements relating to the services provided. A customer should have access to or receive copies of this inventory on a regular basis and should be provided with a copy of it on any expiry or termination. The customer will then be able to select which items it wishes to acquire from the supplier on the expiry or termination of the contract. The issues regarding the transfer of such assets are discussed in more detail below.

### 2.5.2.2 *Ongoing service provision*

The typical IS outsourcing contract will take a number of months from selection of a preferred supplier to the 'go live' date from which services are provided. This should serve as an indication of the complexity of exiting from an existing outsourcing relationship. For the services to be discontinued immediately by the supplier on the service of a notice of termination will be unacceptable to the customer as it will find itself without crucial services for a potentially significant time period until it is able to identify a replacement service provider and enter into a suitable contract with it for the new service provision. It is therefore typical to include provisions which require the supplier to continue providing the services, at the customer's option, for specified blocks of time. For example, it may be that a customer has a right to buy chunks of service from the supplier for three-month periods up to a total period of one year.

During the period for which such run-off services are provided, services should be delivered in accordance with all the existing terms of the contractual arrangements, including the terms relating to charges and to service levels. The supplier may wish to carve out certain provisions which are not to apply, such as those relating to performance improvement.

### 2.5.2.3 *Assets transfer*
Provisions should be incorporated regarding the transfer of assets from the supplier back to the customer.

The supplier should return copies of any of the customer's proprietary software, including copies of any modifications that are to be made to that software.

In relation to third-party items, such as software, hardware and related support arrangements, the supplier should novate such licences and other agreements to the customer.

It is also quite likely that the supplier may have used some of its own proprietary software for the purpose of providing the services. Customers may therefore also seek a licence to use this proprietary software as a minimum during the exit period for which any ongoing services are provided and, quite possibly, beyond the expiry of that time. Licence fees will obviously need to be negotiated for any ongoing licences which are granted.

Where the supplier has used its own premises to provide the services which the customer requires further access to on termination, it may be possible to obtain a lease to use part (or all) of those premises from the supplier. Where the premises are leased to the supplier from a third party, this will usually be done by granting a sublease to the customer for the appropriate areas of the premises. The terms of the sublease will generally need to mirror those of the head lease. Consents may well be required from the original head lessor to any sublease and, in addition, the head lease may stipulate terms which must be incorporated into a sublease.

In addition to the tangible and intangible assets that may be required by the customer, there will also be a considerable amount of knowledge obtained by the supplier's personnel regarding the operation and use of any IS systems and other procedures involved. Exit provisions should therefore also provide for a transfer of knowledge from the technical staff of the supplier to the customer through the provision of general information and assistance, as required by the customer. Access should also be given to the supplier's premises and equipment used to provide the services and to staff deployed in the provision of the services.

TUPE 1981 might apply at the expiry of the IS outsourcing contract to transfer the staff of the supplier who have been substantially employed in providing the services to the customer (or the replacement contractor), although whether TUPE 1981 does apply is likely to depend on the extent of any related asset transfer.[48]

### 2.5.2.4 *Exit plans*
Although the contractual provisions should specify as much detail as possible

---

[48] See section 2.4.3 above.

regarding the respective rights and obligations of the parties, it will be impossible to stipulate every act that should take place on termination at the time that the services agreement is entered into. It is therefore common to include general provisions requiring the supplier to draw up an exit plan on any exit or termination. The exit plan will then specify in detail how all of the exit obligations are to be carried out.

The overall purpose of the exit plan is to ensure the smooth transition of services from the supplier either back in-house to the customer or to its replacement third-party service provider. Contractual assurances should be obtained so that the exit plan will achieve this if it is followed by both parties.

### 2.5.2.5  *Costs issues*

There will always be a considerable amount of negotiation over the extent to which the supplier is permitted to charge in respect of performing its obligations under the exit provisions. As part of the exit provisions, and as noted above, the customer should have the right to buy further periods of service provision up to a maximum specified time period. Obviously, the charging provisions will continue to apply and the supplier will therefore be paid in respect of the base service provision. There are, however, likely to be a number of additional costs arising as a result of the exit provisions, including the costs of obtaining any necessary third-party consents and the additional resource costs of drawing up and implementing the exit plan. Suppliers are therefore likely to seek payment on a time-and-materials basis for any assistance provided under the exit provisions. Ultimately, the contract should specify which types of obligations the supplier is entitled to recover additional amounts for and those which the supplier is expected to bear as part of its internal costs.

## 2.6  CONCLUSION

The outsourcing concept has evolved from a relatively simple service relationship in the days of the early time-sharing and bureau agreements into a complex arrangement between supplier and customer that is often compared to a partnership. The future for outsourcing looks very bright indeed, with significant growth predicted over the next few years.

The importance of getting the contract right cannot be overstated. With contracts typically for a long duration and for high values, those responsible for drafting the contract need to be aware that the contract will often raise issues not seen in the typical contract for the provision of IT or related services. It is the service description and the service levels that are at the heart of the contract. Adequate time must be spent on these areas so that both parties are confident that there is a clear understanding as to what is to be delivered. They also have a complex interaction with other contract provisions, including those relating to liability, loss of data and service credits.

It is not the contract alone that requires detailed consideration. The outsourcing relationship also raises a number of regulatory issues. One of the most complex areas will relate to the transfer of staff to the supplier and the application of TUPE 1981, with contractual terms governing the allocation of liability between the customer and supplier for potential liabilities attaching to transferring employees and terms relating to the impact of TUPE 1981 on termination or expiry of the contract hotly debated. Competition law may also need to be taken into account, depending on the nature of the contract and market position of the contracting parties. The processing of data by the supplier on behalf of the customer will also (as a result of the Data Protection Act 1998) require certain contractual provisions to be incorporated to take account of the data processor relationship and where data is to be transferred outside of the European Economic Area as part of the outsourcing contract, additional complexities arise.

The time invested in the contract and related issues upfront will reap rewards, providing a clear definition of the services to be provided and the performance levels expected, facilitating the relationship between the parties with clear information flows and reporting obligations and with adequate exit provisions striking a sufficient balance between the competing interests of supplier and customer on any termination or expiry of the contract. And although the contract alone cannot guarantee the ultimate success of the outsourcing relationship, it can certainly help.

# 3

# LIABILITY

*Chris Reed and Alison Welterveden*

It is probably impossible to live a day in the developed world without at some point becoming involved with a computer-controlled process, although it may not be obvious that this is happening. Everyday objects such as washing machines and toasters are now microprocessor-controlled, the telephone system is fully computerized, and a high proportion of employees now use computers as part of their normal work activities. If a computer-controlled process does not function properly, loss may occur and thus potential liability may arise.

Losses can be caused by three basic types of malfunction:

(a) Hardware malfunctions, for example, a computer catches fire.

(b) Software produces incorrect information which feeds directly into a physical process, for example, in a car's anti-lock braking system, or a bank ATM dispensing currency notes.

(c) Software produces incorrect information which is relied on by a human mind, for example, computer-controlled traffic signals, and reliance on spreadsheet calculations to build a bridge or calculate tax liability.

This apparently simple classification is complicated by the fact that hardware and software interact. Deciding whether a malfunction is caused by hardware or software defects, or by a combination of both, often requires expert evaluation. This interaction also means that defectiveness may be a relative, rather than an absolute, concept as the software in question might run perfectly on a different hardware platform, and the hardware platform operate correctly if different software is running.

Liability claims may be based on a number of different causes of action:

(a)  Breach of contract, which can be subdivided into:
     (i)    contracts of sale or supply;
     (ii)   contracts to provide services; and
     (iii)  licence contracts.

(b)  Product liability, for physical injury or property damage caused by a defective product.

(c)  Negligence claims for physical injury or property damage.

(d)  Negligence claims for financial loss, divided into:
     (i)    consequential losses because the software is unusable; and
     (ii)   losses caused by reliance on information, produced by the software and addressed to the human mind.

Additionally, a claim in negligence or contract may be made on the basis that the defendant has *acted* negligently, either in the way the software was used or by failing to use appropriate software.

This chapter will concentrate on liability in respect of defective software. Software is important because its whole purpose is to produce results—instructions for process control, financial or other information, and even advice—which will be acted upon. These results will almost always be uncheckable (in practice if not in theory) or there would be little point in employing a computer to produce them. Reliance on those results where the results, or the action taken upon them, are in some way defective gives rise to questions of liability. How far is the producer or user of computer software to be held responsible for losses caused by his production or use?

Once it is accepted that liability for losses caused by software requires particular investigation, it should also be clear that the most relevant areas of the law will be contract and negligence. However, European legislation has imposed strict liability on the producers of products, and it is necessary also to examine that area of liability. It is also important to remember that where there is contractual liability for defective software, the position will be very similar to that in negligence except where this liability arises from the express terms of the contract or the terms implied into contracts for the supply of goods.

## 3.1 CONTRACTUAL LIABILITY

In liability terms it is important to distinguish between the two different elements of software supply: the licence of intellectual property ('IP') and the development and/or supply of a copy of the software. So far as licensing is concerned, the only real *contractual* risk is that a third party may possess intellectual property rights ('IPRs') which are superior to those of the licensee. The nature and extent of this risk is quite clear, and the drafting of suitable provisions to control it is a comparatively simple matter. By contrast, the development of software under a contract with the user, or the supply of a copy of a package, gives rise to potential contractual liability which is less certain in scope. Liability will arise either from the express terms of the contract or from those implied by law, and the terms in development contracts will be quite different from those in supply contracts.

Liability under more complex service-based contracts will primarily arise in relation to the quality of the service delivered. Although implied terms have a role to play, it will become apparent that express contractual terms will be at the heart of any such contract.

### 3.1.1 Software-development contracts

If a client commissions a software house to write an application, this will certainly create a contract between them. In almost every case the terms of this contract will be in writing, and will normally contain clauses purporting to exclude the software house's liability; but what is this potential liability?

The answer is that the software house has contracted to provide a service, the production of software to the client's specific requirements. Subject to any express contractual provisions setting out the software house's obligations more fully, its liability to the client is governed by section 13 of the Supply of Goods and Services Act 1982 ('SGSA 1982'). This section implies into the contract a term that the provider of the service will take reasonable care in its provision.[1] In the context of software-production contracts, the obligation is to take reasonable care to ensure that the software performs the functions specified by the client, together with any other functions which a reasonable software producer would realize to be necessary if the software is to work effectively. For software supplied prior to 1 January 2000 this might have obliged the software house to use all reasonable skill and care to ensure that the software was Year 2000 compliant, although this would very much have depended on the time at which the software was developed and the anticipated lifespan of the product at the time of development. This duty should be distinguished from the stricter liability placed on the supplier of goods by sections 13 and 14 of the

---

[1] *Salvage Association v CAP Financial Services Ltd* [1995] FSR 654. The review of the evidence in the transcript of this case, which unfortunately is omitted from the published report, is a splendid case study of the ways in which a software-development contract can go wrong.

Sale of Goods Act 1979 ('SGA 1979'). Although that obligation is not absolute, in the sense that goods need only be *reasonably* fit for their common or specified purposes, the supplier is not excused by reason of the fact that he took all reasonable precautions to ensure that the goods were reasonably fit. However, if in our example the software house wrote an application that totally failed to perform, it would not be liable unless it could be proved that the cause of that failure was a lack of care on the part of the software house. The fact of making a contract establishes the duty to take reasonable care. The defendant will be in breach if he has failed to take as much care in producing his software as a reasonable man in the same position, professing the same expertise, would have done. An attempt to prove that the defendant did not take sufficient care may run into a number of difficulties.

First, the fault may not be self-contained, but due to interaction with the hardware. If the fault is caused by a feature of the hardware which a reasonable software producer would not have expected, then he will not be in breach of his duty. For example, many of the programs written to run on the PC family of computers use functions provided by the machine's BIOS chip, but some BIOSs do not implement all functions in a standard manner. In some cases the result is that the software fails to recognize the machine, often part-way through the execution of the program, and the results can be unpredictable. If the producer should have recognized and dealt with the incompatibility he will be in breach, but in many cases this will be hard to demonstrate, particularly if the hardware in question was not commercially available when the software was designed. The burden of proving breach is on the claimant and clearly in some cases it will be difficult to discharge this burden. Of course, the problem will sometimes be entirely due to malfunction of the hardware, but it may be impossible to decide whether this is the case if the fault is one-off or intermittent.

Second, much software is, or could be claimed to be, of an experimental nature. Software released as version X.0 is generally updated within a few months as faults are discovered and corrected, and new versions appear on a regular basis. As the duty is to take such care as other reasonable producers would take, it is arguable that, in the current state of the art, the production of software which works perfectly is impracticable. It may not be careless to release slightly defective software. Again, it will be for the claimant to show that the defects are such that a reasonable producer would not have released that version.

Third, the output of the system is in most cases produced by the interaction of the software with data or instructions provided by the user. Before it can be shown that the software is defective, its workings must be disentangled from the data—this will not normally be easy. The problem may arise from a particular combination of circumstances with which the software could not cope—again, should a reasonable producer have foreseen this possibility? It is also conceivable that the use to which the software has been put is not a use that the producer had expected. Should he then be liable? Again, it depends on the foresight of a reasonable producer.

Given these uncertainties, it is essential to establish clearly in the contract the quality standards to be attained, rather than relying on the term implied by the SGSA

1982. This can only be done through a combination of careful specification and clear provisions for acceptance testing against that specification. A properly drafted software development contract would contain an express warranty of quality linked to a detailed specification of what is to be achieved, along the same lines as a system supply contract (see, further, Chapter 1 (sections 1.3.2 and 1.3.7)). Where the developer has produced similar software in the past, he may give an absolute warranty that the system will perform as specified. In other instances, though, the parties may recognize that achieving all the functions in the specification is not feasible, or not feasible at an acceptable price. In that case the warranty is likely to be that the developer will use reasonable care and skill to achieve the initial specification, together with a procedure for modifying the specification and price as the development proceeds. This will be coupled with a further warranty that the software will comply with the final agreed specification.

Although express warranties of quality are clearly desirable and will be found in most bespoke software contracts, the term implied by section 13 of the 1982 Act will still be important. Any term which reduces the rights the customer would have had under that Act is an exclusion clause,[2] and thus subject to the test of reasonableness by virtue of sections 2(2) or 3 of the Unfair Contract Terms Act 1977 ('UCTA 1977').[3] The foregoing only applies, however, to those software development contracts which can be classified as contracts for the provision of services. In most cases bespoke or custom software contracts will normally fall into this category as any physical component, such as the manuals or even the media on which the software is supplied, is clearly subsidiary to the main purpose of the contract, which is the design and writing of a unique software package. Problems with the classification of bespoke software will arise, however, where what is contracted for is not a completely new package but one which has already been created and which is modified to meet the customer's requirements. If the modifications are not substantial the main purpose of the contract is the provision of the basic package, and if this is supplied on physical media the contract might well be construed as one for the sale of goods.[4] This point will be increasingly relevant as modular software engineering methods become more common. If all that the software house is doing is combining standard program modules from its library, it will be difficult to discern the same 'service' element as in a complete rewrite.[5] As Hilbery J said, referring to the manufacture of a fur coat:

---

[2] *Smith v Eric Bush* [1990] 1 AC 831.

[3] See Chapter 1 (section 1.2.2) and section 3.2 below.

[4] By analogy with the 'work and materials' cases such as *Robinson v Graves* [1935] 1 KB 579 and *Marcel (Furriers) Ltd v Tapper* [1953] 1 WLR 49. See, further, Chapter 1 (section 1.2.1) and section 3.1.2 below.

[5] To take an example from a different part of the IT industry, the DEC VAX computer used to be individually configured to the customer's requirements from standard DEC components. There were many thousands of possible configurations, so many that DEC used an expert system, XCON, to design each VAX. Nonetheless, it would be a brave lawyer who was prepared to argue that the supply of a VAX was a contract for services rather than a sale of goods.

I cannot uncover anything to distinguish this from the case of any article which it is part of someone's business to supply and which he makes up to special measurements for the customer. It requires skill, labour and materials to make it but the purpose of the transaction is the supply of the complete article and the receipt of the price.[6]

### 3.1.2 The supply of software packages

The legal classification of software is likely to bear little relation to commercial classifications. English law essentially divides the subject matter of commerce into real property, choses in action, goods and services. Only the last two categories are potentially appropriate for software. The legal regime governing the contract to supply software is thus dependent on which of these categories best fits the software in question. The establishment of the appropriate legal regime is important as it defines the default set of obligations which are modified by the express contract. We have already seen that bespoke or custom software will usually be classified as services. Package software will normally be goods, as it is supplied on physical media in multiple copies. However, software downloaded from websites or similar sources will probably be treated as services, or perhaps it is *sui generis* because it has no tangible component.

This classification of software into goods and services is completely illogical, if the normal rules for classifying the products of commerce are followed. These rules are based not on the software's purpose or its format, but on how it is supplied. Goods are defined in section 61 of the SGA 1979 as personal chattels, which requires them to possess some tangible or corporeal element, so it is clear that pure information cannot be goods.[7] Nonetheless, a supplier of standard, packaged software will normally be selling goods. The supply of software is, in part at least, a sale of goods if the main purpose of the transaction is that the purchaser will become the owner of some tangible property containing the software, that is, the medium on which it is supplied, usually a CD-ROM or a series of floppy disks. Software which is installed by copying it onto the purchaser's system from a medium that remains the property of the supplier will lack the necessary tangibility.

Software producers might attempt to argue that, even though some tangible medium is supplied, it is only that medium that is goods, so that the software recorded on it is merely information and thus not covered by the SGA 1979. The argument is that, because the value of packaged software subsists mainly in the IP element which is licensed rather than 'sold' to the user, what is supplied is a service and thus subject only to standards of reasonable care. This argument fails to distinguish between the contract *supplying* the package, which is between the dealer and the user and could well be a sale, and the licence of IPRs granted by the *software house* which is clearly not a sale.[8] It is analogous to the seller of a pre-recorded

---

[6] *Marcel (Furriers) Ltd v Tapper* [1953] 1 WLR 49, 51.

[7] *Oxford v Moss* (1978) 68 Cr App Rep 183.

[8] This argument has been accepted in Sir Ian Glidewell's judgment in *St Albans City and District Council v International Computers Ltd* [1995] FSR 686.

cassette tape arguing that the tape is not defective because the only fault is that the music is distorted whilst the tape itself is perfect. The reason that the purchaser pays more for a pre-recorded than a blank tape is precisely because it has information (music) on it. This point appears to have been recognized in *Cox v Riley*[9] where the defendant was charged with criminal damage. He had erased the programs from a magnetic card that controlled a programmable saw, rendering the card almost value-less. In spite of his argument that he had not damaged the card itself he was convicted, on the ground that he had damaged the 'card as programmed', which was property for the purposes of the Criminal Damage Act 1971.

This rather technical approach may turn out to be unnecessary, as in *St Albans City and District Council v International Computers Ltd*[10] the judge at first instance was firmly of the view that software is goods, although a final determination on that point was not necessary for the decision in the case. The software in question was a substantial package, for which the council was to pay £1.3 million over five years, and it is unlikely that it was supplied on a tangible medium ownership of which was to pass to the council. A strongly influential factor in forming the judge's opinion was his finding that, if software were not goods, it would fall entirely outside any regime of statutorily implied terms. However, in the Court of Appeal Sir Ian Glidewell held that the contract was not a sale of goods, because property in the tangible medium of a disk had not been transferred, but that nevertheless:

In the absence of any express term to the contrary, such a contract is subject to an implied term that the program will be reasonably fit for (ie, reasonably capable of achieving) the intended purpose.[11]

Although the difference between the first-instance and Court of Appeal judgments is of theoretical importance, in practical terms the result is identical. If package soft-ware *is* goods, the seller is obliged under section 14 of the SGA 1979 to supply soft-ware that is of satisfactory quality and reasonably fit for the purposes the buyer has made known to him. This is assessed in relation either to the common purposes for which software of that type is purchased or by reference to the purpose that the buyer has made known. Software, however, does not have the same degree of homogeneity within its various categories as, say, motor cars. Different word-processing or data-base systems may go about the task in entirely different ways, and prove more or less suitable for entirely different tasks. It is likely that the only clear guidance available to the court will be the claims the producer has made in his advertising and promo-tional material. This may amount to a description of the goods, or may be some other relevant factor the courts may take into account in deciding if the software is of adequate quality. Depending on the time of supply of the software package and the nature of the software, Year 2000 compliance might have been a typical requirement

---

[9] (1986) 83 Cr App R 54. See also *R v Whiteley* (1991) 93 Cr App R 25. This issue is discussed in greater depth in Chapter 8 (section 8.4.4).
[10] [1995] FSR 686, 698–9, [1996] 4 All ER 481, CA.
[11] [1996] 4 All ER 481, 494.

which the courts could consider to determine whether a software package was of satisfactory quality. Suppliers often incorporated express provisions into their contracts regarding Year 2000 compliance (and, in particular, their liability for non-compliance and any steps they would take to remedy a failure to comply) rather than risk more general implied terms being applied.

It is obviously possible to overcome some of these classification problems by including express provisions as to quality, etc in the contract and providing that these are in substitution for all other rights. However, it must be remembered that if these provisions impose lower obligations on the seller than would be the case under, for example, the SGA 1979, the term will amount to an exclusion clause and be potentially subject to attack under UCTA 1977.[12]

### 3.1.3 Service contracts

Service-based contracts are frequently used in the IT industry, whether they relate to the development of a bespoke software package or the provision of consultancy services to more complex projects, such as outsourcing or facilities-management arrangements. (The position in relation to software-development contracts has already been dealt with at section 3.1.1 above.)

As noted above, section 13 of the SGSA 1982 will apply to imply into service contracts a term that the service provider will take reasonable skill and care in the service provision. However, customers (and service providers) under service-based contracts will rarely want to rely on this general term and instead will want to agree more detailed provisions regarding the scope of the obligation. In such contracts it is the quality of the supplier's personnel which will be key. A relatively simple contract for consultancy services will therefore typically include warranties by the consultancy firm regarding the use of appropriately experienced personnel and the use of good industry practice (or similar standards).

Customers under more complex outsourcing and facilities-management contracts are likely to seek detailed warranties specifying (in addition to those regarding experienced personnel and the use of good industry practice) that services will be provided in accordance with applicable laws and with any relevant policies and procedures. The services will usually also be provided to stated service levels. Failure to achieve those service levels will usually expose the supplier to contractually pre-determined financial penalties, such as service credits or liquidated damages. Reliance on the basic provisions under the SGSA 1982 alone is of little use in these more complex, high-value transactions. Indeed, its application is frequently expressly excluded in the business-to-business context although care must be taken in doing so to avoid breaching the provisions of UCTA 1977, in particular sections 2(2) and 3.

---

[12] Although Schedule 2 to UCTA 1977 excludes from the operation of the Act contracts creating or transferring IPRs, the consensus interpretation is that the Act still applies to other parts of the contract, eg, obligations of quality, delivery dates, etc.

## 3.2  EXCLUSION CLAUSES

It is by no means uncommon to find a clause in contracts of US origin that provides: (a) that the software house warrants only that the media on which the software is supplied are free from defects in normal use; (b) that this warranty is in lieu of all other liabilities, express or implied, whether by statute or otherwise; (c) that liability for breach is limited to rectification of defects in or replacement of the media; and (d) that no liability is accepted for consequential loss.

In the light of UCTA 1977 such a clause is almost worse than useless. If the software is goods, the terms that the seller or supplier has the right to sell[13] or supply[14] cannot be excluded at all, and the implied terms as to description and quality cannot be excluded at all if it is a consumer sale or supply, and only subject to the test of reasonableness if not.[15] In the case of bespoke software, the term as to reasonable care under section 13 of the SGSA 1982 can only be excluded subject to the test of reasonableness,[16] and exclusion of liability for breach of other terms in the software house's standard form contract are subjected to the same test by section 3 of UCTA 1977.

The test of reasonableness is set out in section 11 of UCTA 1977, which provides that it must have been fair and reasonable to include the clause at the time the contract was made. Schedule 2 of the 1977 Act[17] sets out a number of factors for the court to take into account—the strength of bargaining position of the parties; whether the party bound by the clause received some benefit (for example, a lower price) for agreeing to it; how far he knew or ought to have known of the existence and extent of the clause; if the exclusion is contingent on compliance with some condition (for example, informing the software house of defects in the software within twenty-eight days of the end of acceptance testing) whether it was reasonable to expect the condition to be complied with; and, in a sale of goods contract, whether the goods were specially made or adapted to the customer's order. The courts have also held that the question as to which of the parties can most readily insure against the loss is a relevant consideration.[18]

The principles which will be applied by the courts in determining whether an exclusion clause satisfies the test of reasonableness have already been examined in Chapter 1 (see, in particular, section 1.2.2). The cases make it clear that to pass the test there should have been a proper assessment of the potential consequences of

---

[13] SGA 1979, s 12.    [14] SGSA 1982, s 7.
[15] UCTA 1977, ss 6, 7.    [16] Ibid, s 2.

[17] In theory, Schedule 2 applies only to contracts where the possession of goods is transferred; in practice, however, the courts are likely to take its provisions into account when deciding on the reasonableness of other exclusion clauses.

[18] At present the insurance market has limited experience of the software industry, and insurance may be difficult to obtain on reasonable terms. This fact may make limitations of liability more likely to satisfy the section 11 test. However, as the claims record of the industry becomes clearer, this position is likely to change.

breach, and the clause should allocate these risks in accordance with the financial strengths of the parties and their respective abilities to insure.

In the UK, the Court of Appeal judgment in *St Albans City and District Council v International Computers Ltd*[19] has caused some concern and, consequently, it may indicate the beginning of a stricter approach to exclusion and limitation clauses by the English courts. In that case the court considered that a clause limiting liability to the price payable for the item of equipment, program or service in respect of which the liability arose or £100,000 (whichever was the lesser) was found not to be reasonable within the terms of UCTA 1977 and was struck out. However the very specific facts of *St Albans*, most notably the existence of a relatively unsophisticated local authority as a contracting party, the low value of the liability cap (£100,000) compared to the overall contract value (£1,300,000) and the availability of resources and insurance cover to meet the claim, means that it is perhaps unlikely to be applied widely.[20]

Similar points apply to the earlier case of *Salvage Association v Cap Financial Services Ltd*.[21] *Obiter* comments were made by Judge Thayne Forbes regarding the reasonableness of a limitation clause to £25,000. The availability of insurance cover for Cap's financial exposure and the fact that Cap's standard contract was being revised to increase (significantly) the amount for which Cap would be liable were strong factors in the judge's reasoning that the limitation of liability was not reasonable. Again, the specific facts mean the case can be distinguished.

This tendency of the courts to intervene in contracts and strike out liability provisions has been balanced by the more recent decision of *Watford Electronics Ltd v Sanderson CFC Ltd*.[22] Sanderson sought to rely on an exclusion clause in its standard terms of business that purported to exclude liability for indirect and consequential loss and a limitation provision that attempted to limit its liability to the price paid by Watford under the contract. The system delivered had failed to perform and Watford was seeking damages of £5.5 million. The total price paid was £104,596. The Court of Appeal held that it was clear that the contract had been negotiated between experienced businessmen of equal bargaining power and skills and that

---

[19] [1995] FSR 686.

[20] See also the rather specific facts of *South West Water Services Ltd v International Computers Ltd* (2002) 146 SJLB 35 where it was held that South West Water Services Ltd had entered into contracts made on ICL's standard terms of business and that, under UCTA 1977, ss 3 and 11(1), the exclusion clauses were manifestly unreasonable and so unenforceable. The case concerned a system which, following a series of project delays, failed even to reach acceptance testing, and the effect of the exclusion clauses would have meant that South West Water Services Ltd would have been in a far worse position than if the system failed after acceptance testing. Also, in *Horace Holman Group Ltd v Sherwood International Group Ltd*, 12 April 2000, Technology and Construction Court (unreported) liability clauses which purported to exclude liability for consequential loss and impose a limit on other liability equal to the value of the licence fee were found unreasonable for a number of reasons (including the lack of insurance cover, the lack of better terms from alternative suppliers and the absence of any negotiation on the liability provisions).

[21] [1995] FSR 654.

[22] [2001] 1 All ER (Comm) 696.

unless the court was satisfied that one party had effectively taken unfair advantage of the other or that a term was so unreasonable as plainly not to have been understood or considered, the court should not interfere. On this basis the exclusion and limitation clauses were found to be reasonable.

In the UK, a common approach in IT contracts is the purported limitation of a supplier's liability in direct damages to the overall value of the contract or the price paid over a twelve-month period prior to the breach. It is difficult to assess whether such limitations would always be held to be reasonable, given the approach of the English courts to date. In any event, suppliers should be careful to record and keep written calculations of how liability limits have been arrived at, rather than relying on arbitrary figures. Suppliers should also reconsider the standard approach when contracting under larger contracts, such as outsourcing arrangements. Arguably, in such contracts the fees paid by the customer may be less relevant to the question of reasonableness than the importance and value to the customer of the contract and IT systems being outsourced, and liability limits may need to be reconsidered accordingly.

It has been common practice for suppliers in the UK to draft exclusion clauses to attempt to exclude their liability for indirect or consequential loss. The phrase is generally used to encompass loss beyond the damage to the value of the property itself, such as loss of profits and loss of revenue. The Court of Appeal decision in *British Sugar v NEI Power Projects Ltd and Another*[23] suggested that such clauses may no longer be sufficient to exclude the supplier's liability as desired. In this case the defendant was relying on a clause which purported to limit liability for consequential loss to a maximum of the value of the contract in question. Lord Justice Waller approved Parker J's earlier judgment that the word 'consequential' does not 'cover any loss which directly and naturally results in the ordinary course of events'[24] and went on to state that such consequential loss therefore equated to loss which is not direct, such as damage flowing from special circumstances within the second limb of *Hadley v Baxendale*.[25] This contradicted the long-standing view of many commentators[26] that direct loss (ie, that under the first limb of *Hadley v Baxendale*) can include some types of financial (consequential) loss and introduces a confusing link between the definition of consequential loss and the rules for remoteness of damage. For example, in circumstances where a supplier has been made aware of further contracts the customer intends to enter into and the customer's reliance on the supplier for that purpose, it was generally thought that the loss of profits on those further contracts would be capable of being recovered under the first limb of *Hadley v Baxendale*. Following the approach of *British Sugar*, this would no longer be the case.

---

[23]  (1998) 87 BLR 42.
[24]  Ibid, 50.
[25]  (1854) 9 Exch 341.
[26]  See, eg, *McGregor on Damages*, 16th edn (Sweet & Maxwell, 1997), p 25.

Further decisions have provided some clarification. In *Hilton International Hotels (UK) Ltd v Hotel Services Ltd*[27] Hotel Services rented minibars to Hilton International Hotels. The minibars developed problems with their refrigeration devices. Hotel Services sought to rely on an exemption clause which purported to exclude liability for indirect and consequential loss to escape liability for loss of profits. The Court of Appeal held that Hotel Services had represented the minibars as an opportunity for Hilton to sell drink at a profit and therefore lost profits were a direct and natural consequence of the faulty minibars.[28]

The effect of these cases is to render unclear the meaning of the phrase 'consequential loss' and when such loss is recoverable. Those drafting exclusion clauses would therefore be prudent to define exactly what is meant by the phrase and to state precisely what a supplier is liable for and what types of liability are excluded. This needs to be done in the context of the restrictions and test of reasonableness imposed by UCTA 1977 with an appropriate allocation of risk accordingly.

Whilst it may be tempting to attempt to exclude as much liability as possible, the danger of such an approach is that the software house supplier will be left completely unprotected against claims if a court finds the clause unreasonable. It should also be apparent that there is no point in merely copying a clause used by one's competitors, particularly if (as is often the case) it was drafted with US law in mind. Conversely, when contracting with a US or other foreign client it is essential to take advice on the effect of any standard exclusions under the client's domestic law. Although a clause providing that the contract is to be governed by English law and adjudicated in England may be effective, it may not be so where the contract is to be performed primarily abroad. Again, advice should be taken on the specific circumstances.

## 3.3  THIRD-PARTY RIGHTS

The Contracts (Rights of Third Parties) Act 1999 introduced an important change to the long-standing rule of privity of contract (ie, that only the parties to a contract can sue in relation to its terms). The Act came into force on 11 November 1999, but applies only to contracts entered into following the expiry of six months after that date.

The Act gives third parties rights in two circumstances, set out in section 1(1). A contract can provide expressly for a benefit to be conferred upon a third party. Alternatively, a contract can expressly provide that a third party is entitled to enforce its provisions. In either circumstance the third party is entitled to enforce that contract against the other parties to it. Given the frequent use of multi-party relation-

---

[27]  (2000) BLR 235.
[28]  In *Pegler Limited v Wang* [2002] BLR 218 the court also interpreted an exclusion clause narrowly, finding that an exclusion of indirect and consequential loss applied only to loss of profits arising under the second limb of *Hadley v Baxendale* but not to lost profits arising under the first limb.

ships in the IT industry (for example, customer–licensor–reseller relationships and licensor–licensee licences for the benefit of a number of licensee-group companies) liability provisions and contractual provisions will need to be reassessed to ensure that liability to third parties is provided for and excluded, where appropriate.

Contracts will, under the 1999 Act, only be able to provide for a benefit to a third party. They cannot impose a burden. Any exclusions or limitations of liability contained in the contract will also be effective as against the third party seeking to enforce its rights. Generally, the third party is afforded the remedies the contracting party would have had. It should be noted though that section 2(2) of UCTA 1977 does not apply regarding negligence consisting of the breach of an obligation arising from a term of the contract and where it is the third party seeking to enforce that contract term.

## 3.4 STRICT LIABILITY: THE CONSUMER PROTECTION ACT 1987

Following the EC Directive on Product Liability,[29] the Consumer Protection Act 1987 came into force on 1 March 1988. The essence of the Act is that producers or suppliers of products in the course of a business[30] should be liable to anyone who suffers personal injury or property damage caused by a defect in that product, irrespective of any fault on the producer's part. As we shall see, however, the effect of the 'state of the art' defence (included largely at the request of the pharmaceutical industry) is to retain the requirement of fault though placing the burden of disproof on the producer.

The main requirements for liability are set out in section 2(1) of the 1987 Act, which provides that subject to the remaining provisions of the Act:

where any damage is caused wholly or partly by a defect in a product, every person to whom subsection (2) below applies shall be liable for the damage.

The obvious question raised by this subsection is whether computer software is a 'product', for if it is not the Act is irrelevant to our discussion. 'Product' is defined in section 1(2) as 'any goods or electricity' including components. 'Goods' are defined in section 45 as including (amongst other things such as crops and aircraft which clearly do not cover software) 'substances', and the same section defines 'substance' as 'any natural or artificial substance . . .'. In spite of the circularity of this definition, it is clear that computer software will only qualify as a product if it is a 'substance', which suggests that it must have the tangible quality normally associated with goods. This is supported by the text of the Directive which defines 'product' as any moveable. It seems likely, therefore, that the Act applies only to software which is marketed on some form of tangible medium (for example, a tape or disk) ownership of which is transferred to the purchaser. Software which is installed by

---

[29] 85/374.     [30] Consumer Protection Act 1987, s 4(1)(c).

copying it onto the purchaser's system from a medium that remains the property of the supplier will lack the necessary tangibility to fall within the definition. The Act is to be interpreted in accordance with EU law and the Directive, and it has been held that television programmes, which similarly consist of information transmitted as electric signals, are not goods but services.[31]

The Act also limits liability to death or personal injury[32] or damage to property (including land) which is ordinarily intended for private use or consumption and was so intended to be used by the claimant.[33] It does not cover damage to the product itself or to any product containing the defective product[34] and the damage must exceed £275.[35] Thus where software is purchased by a business and used solely within the business, claims can only be expected from outsiders who are injured by the business's activities where the cause was a defect in the software. The most obvious case where the Act might otherwise apply, air-traffic control, will not be covered as the software in question is unlikely to be a product. Even so there are a number of situations which will at present fall within the Act—computer-controlled lifts, microchips in washing machines, etc—and with the growth in the number of computers in the home, the Act will become increasingly important.

Section 2(1) of the 1987 Act requires that the damage be caused by a 'defect' in the product, and this is defined in section 3. A product is defective if it does not provide the level of safety (in respect of property as well as the person) that persons generally are entitled to expect. This raises no problems so far as manufacturing defects are concerned, but if the defect is in the design of the product it is suggested that this test is little more than the existing test for negligence. The courts are required to consider such matters as the manner of marketing, instructions and warnings, what the producer might reasonably expect to be done with the product, and the time at which it was supplied. This is the kind of risk/utility balancing that is used to decide liability in negligence, and it may well be the case that a manufacturer who would not be liable in negligence will escape liability under the Act as well.[36]

Once the claimant has established that he has suffered damage through a defective product, he has a choice of defendants. The obvious person against whom to claim is the producer (defined in section 1(2)), but he may also claim against any person who holds himself out as the producer or against the importer of the product into the EU if it is produced outside.[37] In some cases, however, it may not be

---

[31] *Italy v Saachi* [1974] ECR 409. Note though that this finding was in the context of the Treaty of Rome provisions on the free movement of goods. Whether the same is true in the context of the Product Liability Directive is a matter of some doubt. It has been argued that some non-UK jurisdictions may take a purposive approach to the definition of 'product', and decide the issue on whether the item in question is effectively mass-marketed or produced only on a one-off basis; see J Herschbaeck, 'Is Software a Product?' (1989) 5 CL&P 154. See also *St Albans City and District Council v International Computers Ltd* [1995] FSR 686, discussed at section 3.1.2 above, which suggests that the English courts might adopt a similar approach.

[32] Consumer Protection Act 1987, s 5(1).                        [33] Ibid, 5(1) and (3).

[34] Ibid, 5(2).                                                  [35] Ibid, 5(4).

[36] See, eg, *Evans v Triplex Safety Glass Co Ltd* [1936] 1 All ER 283.

[37] Consumer Protection Act 1987, s 2(2).

obvious who the producer is, and so the claimant is given a right of action against the supplier under section 2(3). The supplier is only liable, however, if the claimant requests from him the name of the producer or importer and the supplier fails to give that name within a reasonable time.

Finally, mention should be made of the 'state of the art' defence. Whilst section 4 contains a number of defences, some of which might be useful to a software producer, the most relevant by far is that contained in section 4(1)(e). This provides that the producer can escape liability if he can show that the defect is such that a reasonable producer would not, in the current state of the art in that industry, have discovered the defect. The practice in the software industry is to release software that is not entirely 'bug-free', on the not unreasonable ground that the use made of the software is not totally predictable and thus exhaustive testing is, commercially at least, impracticable. It has even been suggested that it is impossible to produce bug-free software, though this proposition appears to depend on the logical proof that it is impossible to write a program that can be guaranteed to debug another program. Given this practice, it is arguable that a software producer who failed to discover even a quite serious defect in his software would nevertheless be able to take advantage of the defence, so long as the defect is not in an area of the program that would be tested as a matter of course by others in the industry. If this is so, the effect of the defence is merely to permit the producer to *disprove* negligence, a very different matter from the strict liability that the Act apparently introduces.

As the application of the Consumer Protection Act 1987 is so limited in scope and the majority of claims in respect of software will be for financial loss, it seems likely that the Act will have a comparatively small impact on the liability of software producers. Nonetheless, where the claim is for physical injury or property damage the evidential burdens placed on the claimant are much lighter than in negligence, and the Act would be the obvious first line of attack. For most claims, however, the common-law of negligence will remain the most fruitful hope of recovery.

## 3.5 NEGLIGENCE

Although the general heading 'tort' covers a wide range of legal wrongs, it becomes clear on closer examination that the only real tortious problems posed by information technology arise in the field of negligence. It is quite possible to imagine situations where a computer might play a part in the commission of another tort, but almost certainly some question of negligence would be involved. Thus in the American case of *Scott v District of Columbia*[38] where the claimant alleged false arrest and wrongful imprisonment against the police, who had relied on a warrant erroneously issued by a computer system, her suit failed because the officers who arrested her had not been negligent in relying on the computer. In other false arrest

---

[38] (1985) 493 A 2d 319.

cases, if there were no question of carelessness in the use of the computer, it would be legally irrelevant that a computer was somehow involved. This is true for other torts, for example, where the noise from a computer printer constituted a nuisance or an information-retrieval system contained defamatory material. These cases would normally raise the same legal problems as noise from a typewriter or defamation in a book, except for the special case of intermediary liability (see Chapter 9).

Before going any further, it is necessary to recognize that the question of liability may be affected by the type of damage suffered by the claimant. If this is physical injury or damage to property few problems will arise; the test for the existence of a duty of care will be that in *Donoghue v Stevenson*,[39] and breach and causation will be dealt with as in any other negligence action. The real problems arise when the claimant's losses, as is likely to be the case almost every time in relation to software cases, are purely economic. If this is so, the question of whether the defendant owes him a duty of care will depend to a large degree on the type of damage that was sustained.

### 3.5.1  Loss of use of the software

Any producer of software will, to some degree, be aware of the potential that his product has for causing loss to someone who makes use of it. If he fails to take sufficient care when designing the product, and so causes loss to users, his commercial interests will suffer. This does not necessarily mean that he is under a legal duty to take such care. The general principle laid down in *Donoghue v Stevenson* that one person owes a duty of care to another if he ought reasonably to have foreseen that his actions or inaction will cause harm to that other, expresses the duty very widely. It might therefore be thought that the producer of software is in the same position as, say, the producer of electric toasters, who clearly owes a duty of care to any person who uses the toaster. In such a case the duty is to design the toaster so as to avoid injuring the user or damaging the user's property. In the case of a software designer the position is rather different. It is unlikely that defective software will cause any loss that is not purely financial,[40] and the attitude of the law towards financial losses is less favourable than towards physical or property damage.

For many years the position appeared to be settled that a claimant could only recover for economic loss if it was consequent on physical injury or damage to property[41] or caused by reliance on a negligent misstatement. However, in *Junior Books Ltd v Veitchi Co Ltd*[42] the possibility of a more relaxed attitude to pure economic loss was recognized. In that case the defendants were building subcontractors who

---

[39] [1932] AC 562.

[40] Though we should note that common physical processes are increasingly becoming computerized, eg, Honda has produced a four-wheel steering system which replaces the physical link between the steering wheel and the road wheels with a computerized link, and 'fly-by-wire' airliners are now commonplace. These types of applications, which include anti-lock braking systems and such mundane things as washing machines, are generally implemented by turning the software into an application-specific integrated circuit, ie, a physical microchip, which is clearly both goods and a product.

[41] *Spartan Steel and Alloys Ltd v Martin* [1973] QB 27.          [42] [1983] 1 AC 520.

laid a floor at the claimant's premises. The floor quickly proved defective and unsuitable for use. The claimants successfully recovered the cost of replacing the floor and lost profits while this was done, in spite of the defendant's argument that these losses were purely financial and thus not recoverable. The House of Lords held that a duty to take care to avoid financial losses could be owed if there was sufficient proximity between claimant and defendant, and that in this case, the defendants having been nominated as subcontractor by the claimants, a sufficiently close relationship did exist.

However, *Junior Books* has proved a source of worry to the courts, for the fear of opening the floodgates is ever-present. In *Muirhead v Industrial Tank Specialties Ltd*[43] the Court of Appeal distinguished it, holding that in *Muirhead* the claimant and defendant (the supplier of a defective pump to the builder of a tank for the claimant's lobsters) were not in a sufficiently proximate relationship for the defendant to owe the claimant a duty to take care to avoid causing financial loss. Robert Goff LJ explained *Junior Books* as deciding that such a relationship would only arise if the claimant relied on the defendant to avoid such losses, and if the defendant could be seen as undertaking responsibility to do so. Similarly in *Simaan General Contracting Co v Pilkington Glass Ltd*[44] the Court of Appeal held that the defendants, who supplied glass to a subcontractor of the claimants, owed no duty to the claimants to supply glass that was of a consistent colour. There was no reliance on the defendant's expertise and no discussion with them as to the nature of the glass to be supplied. Any remedy that the claimants might have would be in contract against the subcontractor. Finally in *D & F Estates v Church Commissioners*,[45] a case almost identical to *Junior Books* except for the fact that the subcontractor was not nominated by the claimant, the House of Lords refused to follow that case and held that *Junior Books* was a case which turned on its own special facts, although the following year the House of Lords refused to disapprove or overrule it, recognizing that in a few special cases there would be sufficient proximity to give rise to a duty of care in respect of pure economic loss.[46]

More recently, a series of House of Lords cases has re-examined the circumstances in which a duty to avoid causing economic loss will arise, whilst carefully avoiding a re-examination of *Junior Books*. The basic principle adopted is that laid down in *Caparo Industries plc v Dickman*,[47] a negligent misstatement case, that liability is based on the defendant's undertaking of responsibility for achieving a particular result where economic loss is a foreseeable result of failure to meet that responsibility.[48] This is perhaps most clearly explained in *Marc Rich & Co AG v*

---

[43] [1986] QB 507.                                          [44] [1988] QB 758.
[45] [1989] AC 177.
[46] *Murphy v Brentwood District Council* [1990] 2 All ER 908.        [47] [1990] 2 AC 605.
[48] In negligent misstatement cases an additional requirement, that of reliance on the statement, is also imposed, but *White v Jones* [1995] 2 AC 207, a case in which a solicitor failed to draft a will in time to ensure that the claimant-beneficiary received a legacy, shows that the requirement of reliance is not essential in non-misstatement cases, as its purpose is to show a causal link between the negligent misstatement and the loss.

*Bishops Rock Marine Co Ltd.*[49] A bulk carrier vessel developed faults and the surveyor acting for the ship's classification society recommended that it could proceed to its next scheduled port for repairs. The following day, the ship sank with a total loss of cargo. The cargo owners claimed in negligence against the classification society. The House of Lords held that the same test should apply to physical and financial losses. The question of whether there was sufficient proximity between claimant and defendant, which in physical damage cases is normally determined almost exclusively by foreseeability of the likelihood of harm, is decided in economic loss cases by seeking the relevant undertaking of responsibility.[50]

However, even on the assumption that there was sufficient proximity between the cargo owners and the surveyor, the court also held that on the facts it was not fair, just and reasonable to impose a duty of care because of the agreed contractual structure adopted in the shipping industry which allocates losses of this type between shipowners and cargo owners. This recognition that the imposition of a duty of care can upset carefully crafted contractual arrangements is also found in Lord Nolan's judgment in *White v Jones* in which he said:

I would for my part leave open the question whether . . . the defendant who engages in the relevant activity pursuant to a contract can exclude or limit his liability to third parties by some provision in the contract. I would prefer to say that the existence and terms of the contract may be relevant in determining what the law of tort may reasonably require of the defendant in all the circumstances.[51]

It appears from these cases that the kind of circumstances in which a duty of care to avoid economic losses will arise would be where one software producer is employed to devise software specifically for the user, and subcontracts some or all of the work to another software house. In such a case, provided there is evidence that it is the subcontractor rather than the main contractor who is undertaking responsibility for that part of the work, which is likely to require there to have been sufficient discussion between user and subcontractor to show that the user is relying on the subcontractor's expertise, the user will have an arguable case in tort for the cost of replacement or repair. However, the role of contracts in determining whether it is just and reasonable to impose a duty of care will need to be examined. If, as is quite likely, the subcontractor has effectively[52] limited his liability to the main contractor, the fact that imposing direct tortious liability would evade that limit might be sufficient to persuade a court that it would not be fair, just and reasonable to impose a duty.

---

[49] [1996] AC 211.

[50] See also *Henderson v Merrett Syndicates Ltd* [1995] 2 AC 145; *White v Jones* [1995] 2 AC 207; and *Spring v Guardian Assurance plc* [1995] 2 AC 296, all of which stress assumption of responsibility as the test for proximity.

[51] [1995] 2 AC 207, 294.

[52] If the subcontractor's limitation of liability were ineffective, it would clearly not for that reason be unfair, unjust or unreasonable to impose a duty of care on him. This raises the interesting spectacle of a court being required to give judgment on the effectiveness of a contract term which is not actually in dispute.

### 3.5.2  Consequential losses caused by reliance on the output of the software

In a standard negligence action, the question whether economic loss can be recovered at all is dealt with as a matter of the scope of the defendant's duty, as explained above. It is arguable, however, that if the loss is consequential on reliance on the output of the software a less stringent test should be imposed, a test similar to that used in the cases on negligent misstatements. The results produced by the software are similar to (and in many cases treated by the user as) statements of fact. If reliance on those statements is foreseeable it would seem reasonable to assume that the considerations influencing the courts in negligent misstatement cases will also be relevant in deciding the extent of the duty owed by a software producer.

In 1998 a similar argument was applied by the courts in deciding whether a software package which assisted users to decide which stocks and shares to buy constituted the giving of investment advice under the Financial Services Act 1976.[53] In *Re Market Wizard Systems (UK) Ltd*[54] the Secretary of State petitioned for the compulsory winding up of the company on the ground that it was engaged in an unlawful activity, the carrying on of an investment business without authorization contrary to section 3 of the 1976 Act. The company's business consisted of supplying computer software to end-users. The software required users to enter share prices and other information about a selected set of securities on a daily basis, and then calculated the financial futures positions which the user should hold in respect of those stocks. The software was advertised on the basis that users could expect to make substantial profits if they followed its recommendations. The user manual described the Market Wizard program as a 'computerised trading tool' which 'generates detailed trading advice for a specific range of exchange traded securities'.

Carnwath J, holding that the company should be wound up, made two findings which are relevant here:

(a)  That the output of the Market Wizard program constituted advice:

I have no doubt that the signals generated by the use of the system constitute the kind of advice with which para. 15 [of the Financial Services Act 1976] is concerned. The signals provide guidance as to the course of action which the user should take in relation to the buying or selling of the investments. Such guidance, in the ordinary use of English, is 'advice on the merits' of purchasing those investments. It matters not that the user is free to follow or disregard the advice; nor that he may receive further advice from his broker before making a final decision.

---

[53] Activities which require authorization under section 3 of the Act (now replaced by the Financial Services and Markets Act 2000) include giving, or offering or agreeing to give, to persons in their capacity as investors or potential investors advice on the merits of their purchasing, selling, subscribing for or underwriting an investment, or exercising any right conferred by an investment to acquire, dispose of, underwrite or convert an investment (Financial Services Act 1976, Sch 1, Pt II, para 15).

[54] *The Times*, 31 July 1998.

(b) That the company was responsible for that output, and was therefore giving investment advice to users through the medium of the program's output:

> The question is whether the company is carrying on the business of giving advice. It is not necessary to identify a particular point in time at which the advice is given. It is enough, in my view, that it is providing the customer with a medium by which its purported expertise in the analysis of historical trading patterns is communicated in the form of advice related to a particular investment. If the programme were being operated by the company itself to produce the signals, in response to specific requests from customers, there would be no doubt that it was the company which was providing the advice. The fact that it is the customer who is operating the programme does not change the nature of the advice or its source.[55]

This judgment is the first acceptance by the English courts that the output of software might constitute advice, although it must be recognized that there were a number of special factors in this case which led to that finding, in particular the way in which the company advertised the software. Nonetheless, the decision in *Re Market Wizard* is strongly supportive of the argument that non-contractual liability for defects in the output of a program should be dealt with on the basis that they are, or are closely analogous to, negligent misstatements.

Software may cause reliance-losses in a number of different ways, and the potential causes of action may be classified as follows:

(a) Negligence in designing the system.
(b) Negligence in operating the system.
(c) Negligence in relying on the output of the system.
(d) Failure to use a computer system.

### 3.5.2.1 *Negligent design*

The greatest difficulty that a defendant will have in suing a software producer for losses caused by a negligently designed piece of software is establishing that the producer owed him a duty of care.[56] If, as the decision in *Re Market Wizard Systems (UK) Ltd* suggests, the relevant test[57] will be based on the same principles as are used in establishing liability for negligent misstatements, those principles need to be examined here. In *Hedley Byrne & Co Ltd v Heller & Partners*[58] the claimant suffered loss when he gave credit to a firm called Easipower in reliance on a reference given by the defendant bank. The court held that because the claimant and the defendant were in such a close relationship, the defendant owed a duty to take care in giving the reference. This case established the possibility of claiming for negligent

---

[55] The link between the company and the advice was, in the judge's opinion, reinforced by a requirement to update the software on a daily basis via the Internet from the company's website.

[56] The House of Lords in *IBA v EMI and BICC* (1980) 14 Build LR 1 has recognized that the designer (in this case of a building) can owe a duty to take reasonable care in making the design.

[57] For an alternative approach based on the liability of professionals for careless advice, which nonetheless also examines the misstatement cases, see D Rowland, 'Negligence, Professional Competence and Computer Systems' (1999) 2 The Journal of Information, Law and Technology.

[58] [1964] AC 465.

misstatements. The problem that troubled the court most was the danger of 'opening the floodgates' to litigation. The difficulty with careless words as opposed to careless actions is that the range of those affected is potentially very large indeed. The example given by Denning LJ in *Candler v Crane Christmas & Co*[59] of the marine hydrographer is instructive: we are asked to envisage that the hydrographer, in drawing up a chart of a particular part of the oceans, negligently fails to mark in a reef that is a danger to shipping. The chart is published, and is used by the masters of ships sailing in those waters. One or more ships run on the reef, entirely due to the fact that it is not marked on the chart. Should the hydrographer be liable to compensate the master of the ship, the shipowners, and any passengers or cargo owners, all of whom will suffer loss because of his carelessness? Clearly the hydrographer satisfies the test of foreseeability laid down in *Donoghue v Stevenson*.[60] Clearly, also, his liability is potentially so wide, and extends so far in time (the charts might well be used for many years) that it seems wrong to say that he ought to be held liable.

The solution adopted in *Hedley Byrne & Co Ltd v Heller & Partners* was to limit the duty of care to those who were in a 'special relationship' with the maker of the statement. This special relationship was variously defined as being 'equivalent to contract' (per Lord Devlin), a voluntary undertaking given to the claimant to undertake skill and care (per Lords Morris and Hodson), or knowledge by the defendant that the claimant would rely on the statement (per Lord Reid). In any event, it was clear that the mere fact that it was foreseeable that some person in the defendant's position *might* rely on the statement would not be enough to establish a duty of care.

The position has been somewhat clarified in *JEB Fasteners v Marks, Bloom & Co*[61] where the defendant accountants negligently overvalued a company's assets in a report prepared for the company. As the defendants knew, the report was intended to be shown to prospective investors in the company. The claimants, who were the eventual purchasers, brought an action against the defendants based on the negligent misstatement in the report. The court held that although the defendants did not specifically know that the report was to be shown to the claimants, they did know that the report would be shown to, and relied on by, the class of intending purchasers, a class of which the claimants were a member. There was, therefore, sufficient proximity for the defendants to owe the claimants a duty of care, though in the event their action failed as they had not relied on that statement in deciding to purchase the company.[62] An important element in deciding the proximity question appears to be the purpose for which the advice was produced. In *Caparo Industries plc v Dickman*[63] the House of Lords held that a company's auditors owed no duty of care to the shareholders in respect of the accounts because the accounts were not produced for the purpose of being relied on when making investments (even though it was *foreseeable* that they would be relied on[64]). This question is likely to be

[59] [1951] 2 KB 164.      [60] [1932] AC 562.      [61] [1983] 1 All ER 583.
[62] See also *Haig v Bamford* (1977) 72 DLR (3d) 68 (Canada).      [63] [1990] 2 AC 605.
[64] See the judgment of the Court of Appeal.

answered in the affirmative in the case of most software producers—if the output of the software is not intended to be relied on, it is difficult to see why the user bought it.

Applying these principles to the question of whether a software producer owes a duty of care to the ultimate user, the following position seems a likely one:

(a) If the software was commissioned by, or modified for, the user, the producer will owe him a duty of care. This appears to follow from *Hedley Byrne* and is supported by *Junior Books Ltd v Veitchi Co Ltd.*[65]

(b) If the software was produced for use by a limited class of users, for example, for a trade organization which would market the software to its members, then a duty of care would seem to exist following *JEB Fasteners v Marks, Bloom & Co*, provided it was intended to be used and relied on by that group.

(c) If the software was produced for release to the general public, then it appears unlikely that the producer owes a duty of care to the user, as the class of users is too indeterminate to satisfy the tests laid down in *Hedley Byrne* and *JEB Fasteners*. It is still the case, however, that the user might have a contractual claim against his supplier.

It should also be recognized that even if the designer of the system does not owe a duty of care in the design itself, if defects become apparent he, or the manufacturer or distributor, may well then owe a duty to users to warn them of the defect. This is well-illustrated by the case of *Walton v British Leyland.*[66] Here the claimants were injured when a wheel came off their Austin Allegro car. The defendants had known of this danger for some time, but instead of recalling the model and publicizing the danger, they simply instructed their dealers to deal with the problem as the cars came into the dealers' garages. The claimant's car had been purchased from, and was serviced by, a non-Leyland dealer, so it was never modified. The court held that the defendants were liable in negligence, on the ground that once the danger became apparent they were under a duty to warn users, and they had failed to carry out this duty.

Even if a duty of care can be established, it is still necessary for the claimant to prove that the defendant was in breach of that duty, and that there is a sufficient causal connection between the breach and the loss that the claimant has suffered. The defendant will be in breach if he has failed to take as much care in producing his software as a reasonable man in the same position, professing the same expertise, would have done. The questions which arise here are the same as when a breach of a contractual duty of care is alleged, and have already been examined in section 3.1 above.

The requirement that there be a sufficient causal link between breach and loss may also raise problems. The test for sufficiency is a simple one: is the loss a fore-

---

[65] [1983] 1 AC 520.    [66] (1980) Product Liability International 156.

seeable result of the breach? This test was laid down in *Overseas Tankship (UK) v Morts Dock and Engineering Co ('The Wagon Mound')*[67] where oil that had carelessly been discharged from the defendant's ship was ignited by sparks from the claimant's welding operations and burnt down the claimant's wharf. On the evidence before it, the court held that fire damage was not a foreseeable consequence of the discharge, and thus the claimant's case failed.

More recent cases such as *Anns v Merton London Borough Council*[68] and *Junior Books Ltd v Veitchi Co Ltd*[69] have emphasized the close connection between duty and causation. The test for a duty of care is, in part at least, whether the defendant ought to have foreseen that damage of that type might occur. Nevertheless, it is possible to envisage situations where a duty of care is owed but the loss is an unforeseeable consequence of the breach of duty. Let us imagine that, owing to a defect in its design, an accounting program destroys all its data, and that for some reason the user has failed to make back-up copies of the data. Assuming the designer of the program owes the user a duty of care (for example, the program was specially modified for the user) then it is clear that some loss of data is foreseeable. Nevertheless, it is not foreseeable that all data would be lost, as it is standard practice to make regular back-ups. It follows that further consequential losses, perhaps loss of business, penalties imposed by the Inland Revenue, etc, will also be unforeseeable consequences of the breach.

One final point that should be considered here is that many users of software, in addition to their contract with the supplier, are bound by a licensing agreement entered into between the producer and themselves. This licence operates as a collateral contract,[70] and in many cases will contain clauses purporting to exclude the producer's liability for negligent design. It is quite likely that such a clause, insofar as it amounts to a promise by the user not to sue in negligence, will be caught by section 2(2) or section 3 of UCTA 1977 and thus fail to protect the producer unless it satisfies the test of reasonableness. The question of whether a clause does satisfy this test can, of course, only be decided by reference to the particular facts of the case, though relevant factors are likely to be the price of the software, how clearly its limitations are spelt out in the documentation, and whether the function performed is innovative or commonplace.[71] Even if the clause fails the test, it may still have a residual importance as a warning to the user of the reliance he may safely put on the results of the software. In *Hedley Byrne & Co Ltd v Heller & Partners*[72] the bank was in the end held not liable in negligence to the claimant because it had issued its reference 'without responsibility', thus making it clear to the claimant that reliance could not be placed upon it.

---

[67] [1961] AC 388.  [68] [1978] AC 728.  [69] [1983] 1 AC 520.

[70] If it operates at all when the software is mass-marketed (see Chapter 1 (section 1.4.2.2)); see also G Smith, ' "Tear-open Licences": Are they Enforceable in England?' (1986) 2 CL&P 128 and C Millard, 'Shrink-wrap Licensing' (1987) 4 CLSR 8.

[71] See section 3.2 above.  [72] [1964] AC 465.

### 3.5.2.2 *Negligent operation*

The allegation that the claimant's loss was caused by the defendant's negligent operation of his computer system will generally give rise to few special legal problems. In most, if not all cases, the defendant will be performing some function affecting the claimant, and the computer will merely be the means by which he performs the function, for example, an air-traffic controller. The question, 'did he take sufficient care in operating the computer?' is really part of the larger question, 'did he take sufficient care in performing that function?'.

The problem of duty of care was considered in the American case of *Independent School District No 454, Fairmont, Minnesota v Statistical Tabulating Corporation*.[73] In that case, a firm of surveyors had been employed by the claimant school to value its buildings for insurance purposes. The surveyors employed the defendants to carry out the computational work on their measurements. Unfortunately this work was performed carelessly, with the result that the school was under-insured and suffered losses when buildings caught fire. There was no point in bringing an action against the surveyors as they had performed their work with care and skill, so the school brought an action against the defendants. The court held that the defendants did owe a duty of care to the claimants, as they knew that the school would rely on their work in insuring the buildings, and the class of potential claimants was small (in this case, one member). It can be seen that the approach here is similar to that adopted in *Junior Books Ltd v Veitchi Co Ltd*,[74] probably because in both cases the losses caused by the negligence were purely financial.

However, it seems fair to say that the courts will be less reluctant to find a duty to take care in operating a computer system than in designing one precisely because the class of claimants will, in the end, be small. The analogy may be drawn with road works; although the number of people at risk is potentially very large, in the end only one or two are likely to fall into the hole. Similarly, a negligently *operated* computerized accounting system is likely to cause loss to a few clients only. A negligently *designed* accounting system may cause loss to *all* those potentially at risk (its users) and for this reason a duty of care may be held not to exist.

With regard to the question whether the defendant was in breach of his duty of care, that is whether he took sufficient care in performing that function, it should be recognized that the introduction of new technology will have an effect on the required standard of performance. The fact that a computer has been used may lead those who are affected by the defendant's performance of his function to expect a higher standard of performance than they would be entitled to expect if a computer had not been used. A failure to perform at this standard may well be evidence of negligence, precisely because proper operation of the computer would produce a higher standard. Thus in the American case of *Southwestern Bell*

---

[73] (1973) 359 F Supp 1095.      [74] [1983] 1 AC 520.

*Telephone Co v Ray P Reeves*[75] in which the telephone company failed for a year to re-route the claimant lawyer's telephone calls to his new number, the jury inferred negligence on the telephone company's part from the fact that the only reasonable explanation was some malfunctioning of the computer or other equipment involved, all of which were under the company's control. The First Court of Civil Appeals, Houston, refused to hold that there was insufficient evidence on which to base this inference.[76]

Nevertheless, it is reasonable to expect 'teething problems' in the introduction of any new technology, and the fact that these problems are foreseeable does not mean that it will be negligent to introduce the new system. The question is whether the new system will, in the end, produce an improvement, and of course whether sufficient care was taken in its introduction and operation, and in curing the initial difficulties. It was for this reason that in the American case of *Gosney v State of California*[77] the court refused to grant an injunction to force the state to operate its new computerized system of social security payments properly and to introduce new checks and 'fail-safe' procedures. Overall the new system reduced the number of errors; the question of negligence in respect of individual cases could be left to the trial of those actions.

### 3.5.2.3 *Negligence in relying on the system's output*

We have already seen that a person who relies on the output of a negligently designed or operated computer system may have a claim against the designer or operator. Is it possible, though, that the very act of relying on the system might be negligent?

Clearly the answer to this question must be 'yes' if the defendant who relied on the system knew, or ought to have known, that the system was defective in design or operation. Generally, however, the defendant's reliance will not be negligent if he had no reason to suppose that the output was defective and had acted reasonably in choosing to rely on it. Thus in the *Independent School District No 454* case (discussed in section 3.5.2.2 above) it is clear that the surveyors were not negligent as they had no reason to suspect that the data had been carelessly processed, and had chosen an apparently competent firm to undertake the work. Similarly in *Scott v District of Columbia* (see section 3.5 above) the police officer who arrested the claimant on the erroneous warrant had not been negligent because '[the claimant's] protests gave [the officer] no factual basis for questioning the accuracy of a computer system regularly relied on by officers throughout the metropolitan area'.[78] Once there is evidence, however, that the system has produced an incorrect output, reliance on that output will be a breach of duty. This is similar to

---

[75] (1979) 578 SW 2d 795.
[76] See also *County Trust Co v Pascack Valley Bank* 225 A 2d 605 (1966).
[77] (1970) 89 Cal Rptr 390.      [78] (1985) 493 A 2d 319, 322.

*Prendergast v Sam & Dee Ltd*[79] where a pharmacist misread a doctor's writing on a prescription form and as a result supplied drugs to the claimant which caused him to suffer brain damage. The court held that, even on the misreading made by the pharmacist, the prescription was clearly defective (the drug he thought had been prescribed was not made in the strength stipulated on the prescription) and thus the pharmacist was under a duty to check the prescription with the doctor before he dispensed it. His failure to do so was therefore negligent.

It should also be recognized that where a computer system is under the defendant's control the fact that it produced incorrect results may suggest so strongly that the work was undertaken negligently that the doctrine of *res ipsa loquitur* comes into operation. It will then be for the defendant to show that the system of work was sufficiently well-planned and designed that it was reasonable for him to rely on the results. The position is similar to that in *Henderson v Henry E Jenkins & Sons*[80] where a lorry's brakes failed when a brake pipe fractured, injuring the claimant. The defendants showed that they operated a safe system of inspection, and argued that this demonstrated that they had taken sufficient care. However, they failed to show that they had no knowledge of special facts that might render their system inadequate (for example, that the brake pipe had been exposed to corrosive agents such as salt water) and as a result were held liable.[81]

It is quite possible to imagine situations where it might be insufficiently careful to rely on the output of the system even though there is no particular reason to suspect that the system has worked incorrectly, because the general possibility of its inaccuracy ought to be in the defendant's mind. One example was suggested in 'Computer Horizons' in *The Times* of 1 October 1987, where it was pointed out that auditors of a company's accounts may well be negligent in declaring the accounts to be a 'true and fair' picture of the financial position of the company precisely *because* the accounting system runs on a computer. The dynamic nature of a 'real-time' system, where the information is constantly changing, and the fact that data can simply and untraceably be altered, means that the auditor cannot be certain that the information on which he bases his audit is accurate.

In America, this point has been considered in *Chernick v Fasig-Tipton Kentucky Inc.*[82] In that case, the defendants were intermediaries in the sale of racehorses. They sold a horse belonging to the claimants to Cloverfield Farm Inc, who intervened in the action. The horse was described in the sale catalogue as 'barren and free from infection', which suggested that the horse would be suitable for breeding purposes. In fact the horse, a mare, had twice spontaneously aborted foals, a fact which substantially affected the horse's value. When Cloverfield discovered this, they complained to the defendants, and eventually a case came to trial in which the claimant sellers sued the defendants for the purchase money

---

[79] *The Times*, 24 March 1988.
[80] [1970] AC 282.
[81] See also *CK Security Systems Inc v Hartford Accident and Indemnity* (1976) *Co* 137 Ga App 159.
[82] 1986 (unreported).

(which the defendants had refused to hand over) and Cloverfield sued both the claimants and the defendants. It is the action by Cloverfield against the defendants that concerns us here. The defendants had prepared their sale catalogue from information supplied by the claimants, and from information on the Jockey Club computer. It was well known that the information on the computer was likely to be inaccurate. Nevertheless, the defendants relied on this information to check the claimant's assertions. Not surprisingly, the court at first instance held that the defendants had been negligent, and the Court of Appeals of Kentucky agreed. Unfortunately for Cloverfield, in spite of this negligence their action against the defendants failed on a technicality.

A similar point was made in *Brown v United States*[83] where two fishing boats had been lost at sea due to an inaccurate weather forecast. The National Oceanographic and Atmospheric Administration, which produced the forecast, knew that the relevant weather buoy was out of action but nevertheless issued the forecast without adding a warning that it was potentially inaccurate. It was held that this amounted to negligence, and thus the claimant's case succeeded.

Another reason why relying on the output of the system might be negligent is that, although the output is accurate, it is not sufficient on its own to justify the reliance that was placed on it. In *The Lady Gwendolen*[84] a ship was fitted with the new technology of radar to assist the master in avoiding collisions at sea. In fact, the radar induced the master of the ship to travel at high speeds, even in fog. At the time he collided with another ship, in dense fog and in the restricted channel of the Mersey, he was not only travelling at top speed, but was operating the radar incorrectly. The court was clear that even if the master had operated the radar properly, he would still have been negligent because the radar did not give sufficient warning of other shipping to allow him to proceed at such a speed. Similarly in *Central Maine Power Co v Foster Wheeler Corporation*[85] a power company brought an action in negligence against the designer of a condenser which leaked and damaged other parts of the plant. It was held that the power company was contributorily negligent as its employees had relied solely on the computer system to bring any alarms to their notice, though at the time it was not programmed to do so, and thus failed to prevent the damage.

Problems in this area will often arise when professionals give advice which is based on the output of a computer program. For example, if a solicitor were to undertake a LEXIS search in an attempt to discover the answer to his client's problem, and, having discovered an apparently relevant case, based his advice entirely on the results of the search, he would undoubtedly be liable in negligence if it transpired that the case had been overruled or superseded by statute.

---

[83] (1984) 599 F Supp 877.     [84] [1965] P 294.     [85] 1988 (unreported).

### 3.5.3  Failure to use a computer system

The question of when a failure to use a computer system might amount to a failure to be sufficiently careful, and thus a breach of duty, will always depend on the particular circumstances of the case. The mere fact that the use of a computer would have prevented harm to the claimant is not, in itself, proof of negligence, though it must be proved in order to establish the necessary element of causation. If non-use did cause the claimant's loss the question whether a reasonable man in the defendant's position would have used the computer so as to avoid the loss will then arise. This will be decided by reference, amongst other things, to the 'state of the art' in that particular field.

If the possibility of harm through non-use of the computer is not known at the time of the loss, then it can not be negligent to fail to use one. For example, it is obvious that a solicitor who advises his client wrongly may cause the client loss. At the time of writing, however, expert systems that might prevent this happening have not been developed to the stage of commercial availability, with the result that it cannot be negligent not to use them. If such systems are developed and prove successful, it will, at some time in the future, be negligent not to use them, provided that they are sufficiently cheap and easy to use that a reasonable solicitor would provide himself with them. Once the 'state of the art' both recognizes the problem and produces usable solutions, it will be negligent not to adopt those solutions even if the custom in that area is not to use them. In the American case of *The TJ Hooper*[86] the claimant's barges were lost in a storm at sea whilst being towed by the defendant's tugs. If the tugs had been fitted with radios, they could have received warning of the storm and taken shelter, thus avoiding the loss of the barges. In spite of the fact that it was not common practice to fit radios to tugs, the court held that the defendant was negligent—the technology was easily available, comparatively cheap, and its utility was clear. More recently in *United States Fire Insurance Co v United States*[87] it was held that the action of the coastguard in calculating the site of a navigation beacon by manual rather than computerized means, when the computer system was both available and known to be many times more accurate, was potentially negligent and thus an issue to be decided by the jury at the trial. Similarly, in *Chandler v United States*[88] the claimant was awarded $1,000 for negligent disclosure of tax-return information. The disclosure took place when the IRS instructed Ms Chandler's employers to deduct arrears of tax from her salary, although a computer search (which was not made) would have revealed that the arrears had already been paid. This was held to be negligent.

The position is much the same in English law. In *General Cleaning Contractors v Christmas*[89] the claimant was a window cleaner who was injured when the lower sash of a window suddenly fell. He claimed that his employers had been negligent

---

[86]  (1932) 60 F 2d 737.          [87]  (1986) 806 F 2d 1529.
[88]  (1988) 687 F Supp 1515.          [89]  [1953] AC 180.

in not instituting a system of precautions to prevent this from happening. The defence put forward by the employers was that the trade took no such precautions. Lord Reid said: 'even if it were proved that it is the general practice to neglect this danger, I would hold that it ought not to be neglected and that precautions should be taken'[90] because the danger was so obvious, and because although it was not clear exactly what precautions could be taken, it was apparent that the problem could very easily be solved, for example, by wedging the window.

It follows from *General Cleaning Contractors v Christmas* that there is scope for a court to decide that failure to invent or modify a computer system to prevent harm might amount to negligence if the invention or modification would be simple to effect. In order to decide whether a reasonable man would make such an invention or modification, it is necessary to balance the seriousness of the potential loss, the likelihood of its occurrence, and the expense of invention or modification. It should, however, be noted that in the cases that establish this principle[91] there was in each case a precaution that could have been taken that would *certainly* have prevented the claimant's loss. Whether the courts would be prepared to hold that a failure to innovate a system which *might* prevent loss (for example, an expert system) amounts to negligence remains a matter for speculation.[92]

In areas where new technology has already provided some new service, the question of whether a failure to use it amounts to negligence is greatly exercising the minds of practitioners. For example, is it negligent for a solicitor not to use a legal database when advising a client? The answer to this question is probably 'no', if the matter is a straightforward one. If the matter is complex, or is in an area where the law is constantly being modified, then it would seem likely that a solicitor would be negligent if he did not either use a database or take counsel's opinion. This again must remain a matter for speculation until the courts have pronounced on it. It is, however, known that many firms of solicitors are insisting that work is checked in this way before it goes out to clients.

## 3.6 CONCLUSION

As yet the English courts have not been called upon to decide the negligence issues raised in this chapter. The problems, however, lie not so much in the technology as in the application of existing principles to facts that are entirely novel and which have few conceptual similarities with the kind of facts the judiciary is accustomed to encounter. This need not be an insoluble problem; its solution requires the education of the legal profession not merely in how to use the new technology but also in how it works. A lawyer who is entirely ignorant of the

---

[90] Ibid.

[91] eg, *Paris v Stepney Borough Council* [1951] AC 367; *Bolton v Stone* [1951] AC 850.

[92] See, further, *Midgen v Chase Manhattan Bank* (1981) 32 UCC Rep 937.

processes involved in the creation and running of software can hardly be expected to understand how the principles of negligence, or indeed any other rules of law, should be applied to it. In *Ministry of Housing v Sharp* Salmon LJ referring to a proposal to computerize the Land Registry, said, 'Computers might produce an inaccurate certificate without negligence on the part of anyone'.[93] As we have seen, this proposition is unlikely to be true, and the number of judges who would support it is significantly smaller than in 1970.

[93] [1970] 2 QB 223, 276.

# 4

# PATENT PROTECTION FOR
# COMPUTER-RELATED INVENTIONS

## *Tim Press*

## 4.1 AN OVERVIEW OF THE PATENT SYSTEM

### 4.1.1 The UK and European legal framework

Patent protection in the UK is governed by the Patents Act 1977 and rules made under it relating to the procedure for obtaining patents.

The Patents Act 1977 was passed in order to implement the European Patent Convention ('the EPC'), to which the UK and most of the other major European countries, including all the then members of the EEC, were signatories.[1] The Convention provides for harmonization of all major aspects of domestic patent law of the signatory states and also provides for the setting up of the European Patent Office ('the EPO') to grant European patents. The national systems of granting patents via national patent offices remained in force, although patents granted at the national level were subject to the newly harmonized patent laws.

The EPO is concerned solely with the granting of patents. An applicant makes an application to the EPO indicating which convention states protection is desired in

---

[1] The current EPC states are the EU states plus Cyprus, Liechtenstein, Monaco, Switzerland and Turkey plus (since July 2002) Bulgaria, the Czech Republic, Estonia and Slovakia.

(the fees are lower if fewer states are designated). The application is examined within the EPO, and EPO examiners decide whether a patent should issue. But any patent that is eventually granted takes effect as if it were a bundle of national patents granted by the domestic patent offices of each of the designated states. So proceedings to restrain acts of infringement would be commenced before the German courts if the acts were committed in Bonn and the English courts if the acts were committed in Liverpool. Any remedy would only cover the territory of that court, so the English injunction would only operate within the UK and any enquiry as to damages ordered by the UK court would only cover acts of infringement carried out within the UK.[2]

The UK part of a patent granted by the EPO and designating the UK is referred to as a European patent (UK). After grant, subject to a nine-month opposition period, all influence of the EPO over a patent ceases and this applies to challenges to the validity of or applications to amend patents after grant, which are decided by national courts or patent offices just as they would be for domestically granted patents, as well as to issues of infringement. It is possible for the UK part of a European patent to be revoked whilst the Swedish or Spanish parts remain in force and perfectly enforceable in those jurisdictions. Of course, the basis for granting and revoking the domestic patents will be the same as that applied by the EPO because the provisions of the Treaty provide for harmonization of the key principles.

Thus in theory, when matters relating to the validity or infringement of the German part of a European patent are considered by the German courts, the same considerations will be applied as when the same matters are considered in relation to the UK part of the same European patent by the English (or Northern Irish or Scottish) courts or the UK Patent Office. In practice there is not as much consistency as might be desired. Not only are the procedures whereby validity and infringement are considered (for example, rules relating to evidence and disclosure of documents) very different in the different states, but the respective histories of national patent law against which the Treaty-inspired current domestic legal provisions are construed are quite different.

In the case of issues of validity, there is a source of moderation between the EPC states in the decisions arising from the appeals procedure of the EPO. The Patents Act 1977 expressly allows reference to be made to the EPC in matters of interpretation and the courts have shown themselves quite willing to pay careful heed to decisions of the Technical Boards of Appeal of the EPO when the validity of UK patents

[2] Pursuant to the European Convention on Judgments and Jurisdiction, there are limited circumstances where issues of infringement of a national patent forming part of a European patent granted in one country can be litigated in another. Specifically, these are, first, where a summary remedy can be granted and, secondly, where the dispute between the parties concerns more than one of the national patents granted pursuant to a European patent and the infringing articles are the same. Issues of validity must always be litigated in the national courts of the country for the relevant part of the European patent. This has led to great difficulty; see *Expandable Grafts Partnership and Others v Boston Scientific BV and Others* [1999] FSR 352 (CA, The Hague) and *Coin Controls Ltd v Suzo International (UK) Ltd and Others* [1997] FSR 660.

or European patents (UK) is in issue. However, in the case of issues of infringement, although the EPC lays down a general definition there is no supranational body with jurisdiction to decide issues of infringement or review domestic decisions. There has indeed been considerable debate concerning whether the provisions of the Patents Act 1977 relating to infringement as interpreted by the UK courts comply with the EPC. Decisions from other states (notably Germany) have been considered by the UK courts in relation to this issue, but German decisions are no more authoritative than French or Swedish ones in this regard, so there is no authority to say which EPC state has 'got it right'.

It must be stressed that the EPO is not a creature of the European Union and decisions of its tribunals do not have the same force as decisions of the European Court of Justice. Nevertheless decisions from the EPO will be referred to in this chapter and are of great weight in practice. The legislative outline is in place (in the EPC and the Act) to enable the creation of genuine European patents covering the whole of the EC ('Community Patents') but the scheme has not been implemented.[3]

### 4.1.2 International considerations

Beyond the European system noted above, there is a system of international conventions in the field of patents covering essentially all the industrialized countries of the world:

(a) The Paris Convention[4] allows for the nationals of one Convention country to be granted patent protection in any other. Most importantly, it provides for an application filed in one state to give priority to subsequent applications, based on that first filing, made in any Convention country provided the subsequent applications are made within one year from the first.

(b) The Patent Co-operation Treaty allows for an 'international application' to be made at a 'receiving office' which will generally be the applicant's national patent office. An applicant can ask for an 'international search' to be carried out in respect of an application, the results of which will be used in subsequent prosecution proceedings in the various jurisdictions.

These provisions are of course of immense importance in enabling effective worldwide protection to be obtained without excessive costs having to be incurred at an early stage when an invention's true value may not be apparent. Patent applications will still ultimately have to be prosecuted in all states (or supranational granting bodies such as the EPO) where protection is required, but the inventor has a year to decide whether the invention is of value and where protection should be sought, and search fees may be reduced.

---

[3] This lack of a genuinely unified European patent system is generally regarded as unsatisfactory and change may be on the horizon; see, further, section 4.5 below.

[4] The International Convention for the Protection of Industrial Property.

This chapter will also consider aspects of the law relating specifically to computer-related inventions from the United States. The US and European practices represent two different approaches, and other patent laws often tend to follow one or other model. It should further be noted that, whilst differences within the problem areas (and computer-related inventions are a problem area) between patent laws are interesting, patent law is an area where there is considerable congruence at the level of general principles between the laws of the countries of the world.

### 4.1.3 The nature of patentable inventions

Patents granted by most countries or bodies now follow a similar form. First, they set out information about the inventor, the owner and the history of applications and dates leading up to the grant of the patent. There will then be a descriptive part forming the bulk of the patent in which the invention is explained. Lastly, there will be the numbered claims where the inventor sets out precisely what the monopoly covers. In deciding whether a patent is infringed, one looks at the claims and asks the question, 'does what is complained of fall within the scope of what is described in the claims?'. The description can be used to provide definition to or resolve ambiguities in the claims. The precise latitude allowed in interpreting the scope of the claims varies from jurisdiction to jurisdiction.

The claims and their precise wording are thus central to the patent system. In many cases where an inventor disagrees with the decision of a patent office, the disagreement is not about whether a patent should be granted but about the precise scope of the claims that should be allowed. Patent examiners are naturally concerned that the monopoly granted should not be wider than the law permits, whereas from the inventor's point of view, the broader the claims the better.

Claims may describe machines, articles, materials or processes for doing or making things. The claims to patents are arranged in series (normally only one or two of them), each headed by an 'independent claim'. All non-independent claims in a series incorporate by reference the description of a product, process or whatever from an earlier claim in the series and add further elements which serve to narrow down the scope of the claim. Thus, for example, claim 2 of a (hypothetical) patent might be worded thus: 'A cigarette rolling machine according to claim 1 in which the main shaft rotates at above 2,000 rpm'.

The purpose of the explanatory part of a patent is to enable the invention (as claimed in the claims) to be carried out by any person reasonably skilled in the area of technology in question—to teach how to do it. This teaching is considered part of the *quid pro quo* for the granting of the patent monopoly: an inventor can either try to keep his technology secret or apply for a patent, but if the latter course is adopted the invention must be explained. The explanation is assumed to be of benefit to society by advancing the general corpus of knowledge available to other researchers who may use it to make further advances. It appears beyond doubt that the pace of technological development is hastened in some instances by the publication of matter in patent specifications. Whether the public benefit in each case justifies the monopoly granted is of course another matter.

The need for teaching in a patent is enforced by virtue of a rule in most jurisdictions (including Europe and the United States) that any claim in a patent that is not sufficiently well taught is invalid. Lack of adequate teaching is a not uncommon ground for objection to a patent. Apart from this issue of 'internal validity', for a patent to be granted the invention claimed in the claims has to be:

(a) an invention that is capable of industrial application and not excluded from patentability;

(b) new; and

(c) not obvious, that is containing an inventive step.

These concepts will be discussed below, particularly the concept of patentable inventions, in which area the status of computer-related inventions has been a cause of much debate.

## 4.2 PATENTS FOR COMPUTER-RELATED INVENTIONS IN DETAIL

### 4.2.1 An overview of the problem

The precise scope of what is a patentable invention is an important issue because, traditionally, patents have been granted for industrially useful things such as new machines, chemical compounds and materials and processes for making such things or otherwise achieving a useful result. A computer program of itself is not, to many minds, such a thing. We tend to use the term 'computer program' to describe a sequence of instructions to a computer in the abstract sense, much as we talk of a novel or play as an abstract entity which is separate from the book (disk) it is recorded on or any particular performance (reading, running) of it. The example below illustrates a computer-related invention, and the distinction between that and a computer program.

In 1970 Albert and John Carter invented the 'nudge' feature on fruit machines.[5] Claim 1 of their patent read:

A coin-operated . . . gaming machine . . . wherein at least one drum . . . displays at least two symbols and this or each such drum has associated therewith . . . an adjustment button or mechanism the operation of which after the machine has been played, causes the respective drum . . . to be indexed to display on the combination line another symbol which was previously visible to the player but not on the combination line and which thereby completes or contributes to a winning combination.

Note that this claim specifies a machine with reference to what it does rather than how it does it. The body of the patent sets out a method of achieving this using

---

[5] UK patent 1,292,712.

electromechanical means (switches, relays and so on). By the time the patent expired, fruit machines operated under microprocessor control. In such machines the nudge was achieved by the nudge button sending a message to the microprocessor which arranged for signals to be sent to the stepping electric motor for the relevant reel which turned so as to rotate the reel by exactly one position. Such computerized machines still infringed the patent and their manufacturers paid royalties under it.

The nudge feature is an example of an invention that can be achieved by computer or mechanical means. Apart from the provision of a nudge button and suitable information on the machine, in modern machines the nudge feature is contained solely in the program that runs on the microprocessor, whereas at the time of its invention it was hard-wired by the use of conventional electromechanical components. This patent also provides a good example of the importance of careful claim drafting in ensuring that economically useful protection will last for the legal duration of the patent.

There is generally no problem with claims of the above type, that is claims to machines or processes that happen to be implemented with the aid of a suitably programmed computer. The important point to such inventions is generally not the development of the program but the realization that a better (more useful, cheaper to make, etc) machine results from making the machine behave in that particular way. All the program does is take a series of inputs (numbers), operate upon them in a certain way and produce an output (different numbers). Consider a program used to control, say, a welding arc by relating the voltage to various measured parameters of the arc. If the method of controlling the arc was new, a patent would be granted. The same program could be used to operate a food processor or toy car if the same mathematical relationship was useful in those areas, but the patent would not cover those uses nor would previous uses in food processors or toy cars invalidate the welding equipment patent.

In fact a program on its own is nothing more than a representation, in the form of instructions how to carry it out, of a mathematical formula or relationship,[6] which could be applied in any number of ways. Such descriptions of processes are also referred to as 'algorithms' and this term has formed a central feature of discussions about the patentability of computer-related inventions. Prior to the invention of computers it had always been held that scientific discoveries, laws of nature, mathematical formulae and the like were not suitable subject matter for patents—the formula or discovery had to be applied and only the particular application developed could be patented.

Broadly speaking it is still the position that mathematical formulae and so on are not patentable, but great difficulties have been experienced in applying this apparently simple concept in the field of many computer-related inventions. In the examples given above the distinction between the program/algorithm and its application is quite clear. But cases arise where the distinctions are more blurred and this is

---

[6] It must be understood that this term is used in a broad sense to cover matters of logic as well as arithmetic. Many modern programs are far too complex for a precise mathematical description of their operation to be written down, but at least in theory one does exist.

particularly so where the subject matter of the invention is not an obvious industrial process such as welding but is itself of a more abstract nature, such as methods of analysing electronic data, or an aspect of computer design, architecture or organization. The distinction between a fruit machine and the mathematical relationships underpinning its operation is clear. The distinction between a computer and the logical and mathematical rules by which it operates is altogether more tricky. What is a computer other than an assembly of things obeying logical (mathematical) relationships? Yet patents are granted for developments in computer technology.

Another area that has caused acute problems more recently is where the subject matter of the computer-related invention is a method of doing business. In such cases the problem lies in disentangling the technological (and therefore potentially patentable) aspects of the invention from those aspects which represent developments in fields such as finance, commerce and marketing which do not normally attract patent protection.

### 4.2.2 The European position

#### 4.2.2.1 *The basic provisions of the EPC and the UK Patents Act*

The fundamental provisions of the EPC are found in article 52(1), which states that 'European patents shall be granted for any inventions which are susceptible of industrial application, which are new and which involve an inventive step'. Article 57 further states that 'An invention shall be considered as susceptible of industrial application if it can be made or used in any kind of industry, including agriculture'.

Article 52(2) provides exclusions to patentability:

The following in particular shall not be regarded as inventions within the meaning of paragraph 1:

   (a)  discoveries, scientific theories and mathematical methods;
   (b)  aesthetic creations;
   (c)  schemes, rules and methods for performing mental acts, playing games or doing business, and programs for computers;
   (d)  presentations of information.

The scope of the exclusions is explained (not as helpfully as might have been hoped) by article 52(3):

The provisions of paragraph 2 shall exclude patentability of the subject-matter or activities referred to in that provision only to the extent to which a European patent application or a European patent relates to such subject-matter or activities as such.

It had been suggested that anything was capable of being an 'invention' for the purposes of article 52(1) of the EPC (although the exclusions of article 52(2) would then have to be applied). The case of *Genentech Inc's Patent*[7] stated that this was not

---

[7] [1989] RPC 147, CA.

so, it being held that the word 'invention' in the similar provisions of section 1 of the Patents Act 1977 had to be given a meaning and that some things were not 'inventions' even though they fell outside the scope of the article 52(2) exclusions.[8]

The EPC does not elucidate on what a claim for a computer program is or indeed define a 'computer program' at all. It can be seen, however, that the restriction applies only to programs, not software in the more general sense. As will be seen, the specific 'computer program as such' exclusion is by no means the only hurdle in the way of protection for computer-related inventions.

### 4.2.2.2  The basic approach of the EPO: 'technical content' needed

The discussion of patents for computer-related inventions before the EPO has largely concentrated on the concept that patentable inventions must be 'technical'. This concept is difficult to explain, but the first clear explanation of the requirement for technical content was given in *IBM/Document abstracting and retrieving*:

Whatever their differences [they being the things excluded under article 52(2) of the EPC] these exclusions have in common that they refer to activities which do not aim at any direct technical result but are rather of an abstract and intellectual character.[9]

The decision goes on to point out that the Implementing Regulations of the EPC require a claim to have 'technical features' and therefore that the EPC requires inventions to have a 'technical' character. Reference to the histories of patent law of the contracting states is made, apparently to assist in construing a technical character as being a fundamental principle underlying the concept of what is an invention and the exclusions of article 52(2).

*Vicom/Computer-related invention*[10] is the leading decision in the area of computer-related inventions. The claims concerned a general method and apparatus for processing digitized images within a computer in particular ways. The process consisted of operating on the data representing an image mathematically so as to alter the nature of the image in some way, for example, sharpening or smoothing out edges. It was accepted that the process could be carried out by suitably programming a known computer. The Examining Division rejected the claims but the Technical Board of Appeal remitted them for further consideration. It was held that:

---

[8]  The court was concerned not to allow a claim drafted so as to cover a wide field of which the innovation actually made by the inventor was only a small part. It was no doubt influenced by concern (not so prominent following *Biogen Inc v Medeva plc* [1997] RPC 1) that in the EPC and the UK Act the provisions which require claims to be 'supported by' the description cannot found applications to revoke after grant. The claim was for a known product when made by any process of genetic engineering, the inventors having been the first to find a way to make the product by a genetic-engineering process. The majority held that the applicant had not 'invented' everything within the scope of these wide claims, so they were not for 'inventions' at all. It has also been held in the EPO decision *Christian Franceries/Traffic regulation* [1988] 2 EPOR 65 that the list of what is not an invention in article 52(2) is not exhaustive.

[9]  [1990] EPOR 99.

[10]  [1987] EPOR 74.

(a) Manipulating an image was an industrial process, which could be used, for example, in the design field.

(b) Just because the claims might be drafted in terms of an algorithm, that did not make them unpatentable if the invention related to a *technical process*. The distinction was drawn between claims for 'a method for digitally filtering data' (which would be unpatentable as being merely for a mathematical method), and the invention as claimed. In the former case, no physical entity is represented by the data whereas in the latter it is (an image).

(c) Similarly, a claim to a *technical process* carried out under the control of a computer program is not a claim to a computer program *as such*.

(d) A known computer which is set up to operate a new computer program cannot be said to form part of the state of the art (ie, lack novelty).

(e) It would not be appropriate to draw a distinction between an invention when carried out in hardware and the same invention when carried out in software when the choice between the two ways of doing it would be based on technical and economic considerations unrelated to the inventive concept as such.

In *Koch and Sterzel/X-ray apparatus*[11] there was no problem in finding a link with a real-world object of a technical character, but the question arose of how any technical features should be related to the teaching of the invention. The claim was for standard X-ray apparatus which was linked to and controlled by a data-processing unit. This unit stored information about different exposure parameters and used that information to set the tube voltages so as to obtain the optimum desired exposure. Clearly an X-ray apparatus is a technical thing, but the opponents to the patent cited German authority to the effect that the main area of the teaching of the patent had to be of a technical nature (ie, not relate to unpatentable matter such as computer programs or mathematical methods). They argued that in this case no technical effect was achieved because any technical effect occurred after the operation of the program. The opponents also argued that *Vicom/Computer-related invention*[12] was wrong and effectively allowed any computer when programmed to evade the exclusion of computer programs. The Technical Board of Appeal held that:

(a) The German approach did not conform with the EPC and was fraught with the difficulty of identifying what the essential contribution to the invention's success is. If the invention defined in a claim 'uses technical means' it is not a claim to a computer program 'as such', regardless of whether it also contains non-patentable matter such as computer programs.

(b) When the technical effect occurs is irrelevant, so long as the invention does produce a technical effect.[13]

---

[11] [1988] 2 EPOR 72.  [12] [1987] EPOR 74.

[13] A very similar problem caused somewhat more difficulty in the United States; see the discussion of *Parker v Flook* (1978) 437 US 584 at section 4.2.3.2 below.

(c) A program used in a general-purpose computer is a computer program as such. But if the program controls the operation of the computer 'so as to technically alter its functioning', the unit consisting of the program and computer combined may be a patentable invention. In the present case, the technical effect was the manner of operation of the X-ray apparatus.

(d) The invention claimed was patentable whether or not the apparatus without the program formed part of the state of the art.

This case illustrates the difference between deciding whether what is new about the alleged invention is excluded (not the correct test) and looking at the invention as a whole. In a narrow sense the novelty resided in a computer program, but the 'real contribution to the art' of the invention was a way of operating an X-ray machine. In the language of the decision, the program altered the functioning of the computer technically. One can attempt to give an everyday language explanation of the 'real contribution to the art' as 'the thing people got from the invention that they didn't have before and that was ultimately useful to them', although this should not be taken as a strict statement of the law.

Two relatively recent developments have changed this basic position. *IBM's Application*[14] has meant that claims which read 'a computer program in which . . .' are now allowable. *PBS Partnership/controlling pension benefits system*[15] has held that the 'contribution approach' outlined above is wrong, and the necessary technical content must be sought when identifying the inventive step (if any) of the invention. These are discussed below.

Until the 1999 case of *IBM's Application* it was the position that claims relating to computer programs were only allowed when cast in the form of a claim to a computer or a method of doing something using a computer. It was held that claims to the program itself, or the program when recorded on a 'carrier' (ie, a disk or memory chip) were claims to computer programs 'as such' and therefore not patentable. In this decision the Technical Board found that it was not consistent with the reasoning in cases such as *Vicom* and *Koch and Sterzel* to limit claims to computer programs in this way. The Board's position on this point is set out below:

In the view of the Board, a computer program claimed by itself is not excluded from patentability if the program, when running on a computer or loaded into a computer, brings about, or is capable of bringing about, a technical effect which goes beyond the 'normal' physical interactions between the program (software) and the computer (hardware) on which it is run.

'Running on a computer' means that the system comprising the computer program plus the computer carries out a method (or process) which may be of the kind according to claim 1.[16]

---

[14] [1999] RPC 563.

[15] T-931/95.

[16] The claims related to a system for use in a windowing environment which rearranged the information on underlying windows so that it could all be seen in the part of the underlying window still visible. Claim 1 was for 'A method in a data processing system for displaying information, wherein . . .'.

'Loaded into a computer' means that the computer programmed in this way is capable of or adapted to carrying out a method which may be of the kind according to claim 1 and thus constitutes a system (or device or apparatus) which may be of the kind according to claim 5.[17]

... Furthermore, the Board is of the opinion that with regard to the exclusion under Article 52(2) and (3) of the EPC, it does not make any difference whether a computer program is claimed by itself or as a record on a carrier (following decision T 163/85 BBC/Colour television signal, as cited above).

The main claim which the Examiner had objected to read:

8. A computer program element comprising: computer program code means to make the computer execute procedure to display information within a first window in a display; and responsive to the obstruction of a portion of said first window information by a second window, to display in said first window said portion of said information that had been obscured by said second window, including moving said portion of said information that had been obscured by said second window to a location within said first window that is not obscured by said second window.

9. A computer program element as claimed in claim 8 embodied on a computer readable medium.

The other EPO cases that are referred to in this chapter should be read with *IBM's Application*[18] in mind. The patent claims involved will have been framed so as not to offend the erstwhile requirement that program-related claims be drafted as claims to computers which operate in a specific way. But the relaxing of this requirement has not changed the fact that technical content is required:

9.6 A computer program product which (implicitly) comprises all the features of a patentable method (for operating a computer, for instance) is therefore in principle considered as not being excluded from patentability under Article 52(2) and (3) of the EPC.

It is self-evident that a claim to such a computer program product must comprise all the features which assure the patentability of the method it is intended to carry out when being run on a computer. When this computer program product is loaded into a computer, the programmed computer constitutes an apparatus which in turn is able to carry out the said method.

The main effect of this decision is thus on the way in which claims to inventions can be drawn, rather than on the inventions for which protection in some form can be achieved. This is not insignificant, as it will affect the scope of activities that will infringe the patent granted. But a claim for a program which is expressed purely in terms of abstract numerical or logical inputs and outputs will still fail as having no technical character, even if a program having that effect could be incorporated into a system which did have a technical character.

It should follow from this decision that claims to data structures can similarly be made. Such claims would not have to refer to a machine or method which operates

---

[17] Claim 5 was for 'A data processing system for displaying information, wherein . . .'.
[18] [1999] RPC 563.

on the data, provided that the data structure is adapted to be useful in a technical way when operated on by a known computer. So far, claims that have been pursued before the Technical Boards have addressed machines or methods that make use of a data structure, rather than the data structure itself. The door would now appear to be open for technically useful data structures to be claimed as such in Europe. Data structures have been patented in the US.[19]

In *PBS Partnership/controlling pension benefits system*,[20] a claim to an apparatus (a programmed computer) for carrying out a non-technical activity (determining pension benefits) was held not to be excluded under article 52(2) on the grounds that the apparatus was a physical thing and thus of a technical nature. The 'contribution approach' developed in the cases noted above was held to be wrong. However, the Board went on to consider the question of obviousness/lack of inventive step. They held that the step from the prior art to the invention, if it was inventive at all, involved invention in a non-technical field of activity (calculating pension benefits). To the extent that there was a development in a technical field (computerization) it was not inventive, the task of computerizing the process used being achieved using standard methods. The Board itself threw out the claims on the ground of lack of inventive step, rather than adopting the more normal approach of sending the matter back to the examining division to consider this issue.

It has always been an aspect of European patent law that the inventive step must lie in a technical field (see section 4.3.2 below). But prior to *Pensions* it was believed that the requirement for technical subject matter was a separate (and not necessarily identical) issue relating to patentability. *Pensions* clearly represents a major shift from a doctrinal perspective; what is less clear is the effect it will have on the substantive patentability of claimed inventions: is the same question being asked but under a different heading, or has the question changed?[21] Only further developments in the case law can answer this (the existing cases on inventive step do not address typical computer-related problems because, hitherto, such problems have been dealt with in relation to patentable subject matter). However, what is clear is that the Technical Board did not intend to change the underlying concept of what things are technical in nature and what things are not.

This approach to technical content has been embodied in the draft EU Directive on the Patentability of Computer-Related Inventions (see section 4.5 below). Despite the earlier comment that UK courts attempt to track the development of EPO doctrine by the Technical Boards, it appears that *Pensions* may have stretched this flexibility to breaking point. In *Hutchins Application*,[22] the Patent Office Hearing

---

[19]  See section 4.2.3.5 below.

[20]  Case T 931/95.

[21]  For a robust criticism of the case, see Laakonen and Whaite, 'The EPO Leads the Way, But Where To?' (2001) 23(5) EIPR 244–9.

[22]  [2002] RPC 8. This case may be appealed. But it does illustrate the strains that can arise when trying to harmonize decisions between a system of looking at the law based on civil-law notions (as in the EPO) and the more precedent-led common-law system of the UK.

Officer felt constrained by earlier UK court decisions which followed the 'contribution approach' and thus unable to adopt the new doctrine.

As with *IBM*, therefore, any discussion of pre-*Pensions* cases must be prefaced with a caveat that now the argument would centre on the nature of the inventive step involved rather than the contribution to the art. But as with *IBM*, such cases are nevertheless useful in helping to develop an understanding of what is and is not regarded as technical. This is discussed, under headings related to the broad subject matter of the invention, below.

### 4.2.2.3  *The internal operation of computers*

The concept of 'technically altering the functioning' of a computer is (relatively) easy to apply where the properties claimed for the computer/program combination relate to the effect of the combination on the outside world, for example the exposure times of the X-ray tubes in *Koch and Sterzel*. But where the claimed properties of the combination are matters of the internal working of the computer, the 'technical effect' test is more difficult to apply. Which aspects of computer technology are to be considered 'technical' and which are not?

In *IBM/Data processor network*[23] the claim concerned a data-processing system comprising a number of data processors forming the nodes of a communications network. In the invention claimed the processors are so arranged that a transaction request originating at one node may be split up and part or parts of the transaction carried out at another node. The claims specified in general terms a method of carrying this out but did not give any detail of the computer programming structures used to achieve the method. The Technical Board of Appeal decided that 'the coordination and control of the internal communication between programs and data files held at different processors in a data processing system . . . is to be regarded as solving a problem which is essentially technical'.[24] Again no attempt was made in the decision to state any general rule defining what is and is not 'technical', which was treated as simply a matter of fact to be decided in each instance.

In *Bosch/Electronic computer components*[25] the claims covered a 'device for monitoring computer components' which was capable of resetting the computer's processor. The contents of the computer's volatile memories were compared with a pattern contained in non-volatile memory to establish whether, when the computer's processor had been reset, it was the result of the device or an operation of the manual reset circuit. On the basis of this decision, the reset procedure could be made significantly shorter than would otherwise be possible because it would not be necessary to reload all programs into memory. This process was held to have the necessary technical content by applying the reasoning of *Vicom*.[26]

---

[23] [1990] EPOR 91.          [24] Ibid.          [25] [1995] EPOR 587.

[26] In *Bosch* it was also held that notwithstanding the provisions of the Patent Co-Operation Treaty which relieve the requirement to search in the field of computer programs, if an office was equipped (ie, had the necessary personnel) to search or examine against computer programs then it should do so. This illustrates an acceptance that computer programs can lie at the heart of inventions that are nevertheless potentially patentable.

It is comparatively easy to understand why the Board was prepared to classify both of the above inventions as having a technical character, although difficult to define a clear dividing line between such 'hardware' inventions and programs as such which effect the operation of a computer. In *IBM/Computer-related invention*[27] the claim was for a method of displaying one of a set of predetermined messages in response to events occurring to or within the computer. The method is achieved on a known computer, and involves using tables containing words used in the messages from which each message is built up by a 'message build program'. The problem of extracting any theoretical basis from EPO decisions is illustrated by quoting from the Board's reasons: 'Generally the Board takes the view that giving visual indications automatically about conditions prevailing in an apparatus or system is basically a technical problem.' It was held that IBM's claim, in claiming one way of overcoming such a technical problem, was not to a computer program as such even though the basic idea resides in a computer program.[28]

#### 4.2.2.4 *Data processing, data structures and business methods*
As with *IBM/Computer-related invention,*[29] where data manipulation is concerned the approach has been to cast around for some real-world, non-digital analogies in looking for technical content. The vastly increased commercial use of computer networks has shifted the focus in this area to data-processing claims where the underlying process can be viewed as a business method. Claims to such inventions are as likely to give rise to objection on the 'method of doing business' ground as the 'computer program' ground.

In *Vicom/Computer-related invention*[30] the claim dealt with the manipulation of digital images. Although the Board talks of an image as a 'physical entity' and as a 'real world object', it is made clear that an image stored in any form, hard copy or electronic, will be regarded as a physical entity. The crux of the decision was the finding that images could be used in the design field, which was an industrial area. It was this point which enabled the Board to find the necessary technical content. It appears that the fact that images could be used in the *industrial* design field was important to this finding, although of course the invention would be equally applicable to images whose sole purpose was aesthetic.

In the light of subsequent cases, the 'real world' test needs elucidating. The reference to the 'real world' is in the context of distinguishing between digital data which represent numbers with no meaning (clearly not technical things) and data which represent numbers which represent something more, something outside the confines

---

[27] [1990] EPOR 107.

[28] The finding on the facts of this relatively early case can be criticized. In subsequent decisions less reliance is placed upon drawing analogies with non-computer things that have been found before to be technical. If the rules are applied to these facts, it can be seen that numerical error messages, where the operator has to look the number up in a manual to find out the error, were known. The real contribution is an automated way of performing this looking-up operation, which is a mental process, an excluded thing.

[29] [1990] EPOR 107.

[30] [1987] EPOR 74.

of the purely theoretical. It is clear that real-world content is not enough: in addition the real-world impact of the invention must have a technical (as opposed to a purely aesthetic) character.

In *Sohei/General purpose management system*[31] Claim 1 was directed to 'A computer system for plural types of independent management including at least financial and inventory management . . .'. A common 'transfer slip' is displayed on a screen from which entries can be made affecting all of the different 'types of management', a 'memory' is provided for which holds data in various 'files' and 'processing means' are provided for which operate on inputs, outputs and data. Claim 2 was directed to a 'method for operating a general-purpose computer management system' along very similar lines.

The reasoning of the Board in finding (as they did) technical content in *Sohei* is at times impenetrable. First, they did not regard the requirement for financial and inventory elements as restricting the claims to just those elements, and therefore when considering technical content considered the claims as covering different types of generalized management. This assisted them in not raising an objection on the grounds that the claims were directed to a method of doing business. The crux of this part of the decision is that if an invention can cover a number of fields, some of which are excluded and some not, it is a patentable invention. The example of management of construction work and workers is given as comparable with managing manufacturing processes (technical), whereas other kinds of management would be of a more abstract character and therefore excluded as business methods. This echoes the reasoning in *Vicom* where the fact that images could serve technical as well as non-technical purposes was significant.

The Board also had to deal with the 'computer program as such' exclusion. The basis of its decision here was that the 'transfer slip' amounted to a 'user interface' and as such was patentable as having technical content. They held that the provision of this 'interface' constituted neither only presentation of information nor only computer programs as such, because it allowed two kinds of systems to be combined by a common input device:

. . . it is noted that programming may be implied also in the subject matter as presently claimed. Mere programming as such would . . . also be excluded from patentability by virtue of the fact that it is an activity which essentially involves mental acts . . . However, the implementation . . . of the said 'interface' . . . is not merely an act of programming but rather concerns a stage of activities involving technical considerations to be carried out before programming can start.[32]

Presumably, 'before' is not to be taken literally so as to require program 'front ends' to be created before their 'back ends'. The interesting point here is that the Board held that the technical content would arise from the implementation of the user interface, in other words it was implicit in the invention, rather than being explicitly

[31] [1996] EPOR 253.    [32] Ibid.

taught in the specification. The Board held that this did not matter, the result was still a technical contribution to the art.

In *PBS Partnership/controlling pension benefits system*[33] the claim was to a method of calculating pensions benefits, rather than to a method of processing data with more general applicability that could include application to technical fields (as was the case with *Sohei*). The claim failed (albeit for lack of inventive step under the new doctrine) because there was held to be no technical character in this process.

### 4.2.2.5 *Text-processing decisions*

The former requirement for the real contribution to the art to have a technical effect was developed in a number of cases involving text manipulation. Almost by definition, text is a set of symbols (alphanumeric characters) whose combination as words is addressed to the human mind, and processed by that mind in a non-technical way. The Technical Boards have been ready to find in such cases that the real contribution to the art lies not in any technical area but in areas such as semantics which are the same thing as (or analogous to) a series of mental steps.

In *IBM/Document abstracting and retrieving*[34] the claim was for a system for automatically abstracting a document and storing the resulting abstract. The system involved comparing the words used in a document with a dictionary held on a computer, thereby noting proper names and the occurrence of other words which would be of assistance in characterizing the document, and incorporating these words in the abstract. This information was to be used to assist in identifying documents in response to enquiries. It was held that (*inter alia*):

(a) The claims were unpatentable by reason of lack of a technical character and 'more particularly as falling within the category of schemes, rules and methods for performing mental acts'.[35]

(b) The fact that technical means were used in carrying out the abstracting process did not make the process patentable, because the contribution made to the art by the invention was not technical but purely associated with the set of rules whereby the abstracting process was carried out.

(c) There were no changes to the documents themselves as 'technical entities', only changes in the electrical signals representing the information stored. By contrast, in *Vicom* there had been a change in the image.

The last point is not made with great clarity. It appears to build upon the finding that the abstracting process itself is not patentable as lacking technical content by affirming that the body of documents themselves, whilst changed as digital files by the addition of the abstracting information, are not changed in any other way and therefore not in any technical way.

An IBM application refused for essentially the same reasons was *IBM/Text clar-*

---

[33] Case T 931/95.          [34] [1990] EPOR 99. See section 4.2.2.3 above.          [35] Ibid.

*ity processing.*[36] The invention claimed was a method of identifying expressions in a text processing system which fell below a determined level of 'understandability' and replacing them with more 'understandable' expressions. It was held that evaluating understandability was a series of mental acts and that once this was given, it would have been obvious to any skilled programmer how to instruct a computer to do it, so the real contribution to the art was not in a technical field.

Similarly in *IBM/Semantically-related expressions*[37] the claim concerned a system for automatically generating a list of expressions semantically related to an input linguistic expression. It was held, as a matter of fact, that matters of semantic relationship are not technical matters. Reference to the excluded matters under article 52 of the Convention was made by pointing out that a semantic relationship can only be found by performing mental acts. Again it was stressed that these claims were refused because the contribution to the art was found not to stray beyond the matter of identifying semantically related expressions, and that an invention directed to semantic relationships might be patentable provided a contribution was made outside the range of excluded things.

The refusals of the latter two cases are perhaps not surprising. A case which causes more difficulty is *Siemens/Character form.*[38] This concerned a process for displaying on a VDU screen characters which have different forms depending on whether they are used in isolation, or at the beginning, middle or end of words, such as occur in Arabic. The process involved initially choosing the most likely form and subsequently altering the form if necessary depending on the following character. The application was initially rejected (perhaps unsurprisingly) for lack of inventive step. On appeal, the Technical Board of Appeal rejected the application on the grounds that the invention lacked technical content. *Koch and Sterzel/X-ray apparatus*[39] was distinguished on the basis that there no technical means were used but the effect was technical.

Here, the problem of identifying technical content is split into two parts: are technical means used to achieve a result, and if not, is the result to be achieved a technical one? On applying these tests it was held that the claim was directed to a non-technical procedure in that all that was achieved by the program was the retrieval of a character in one form and its replacement in another form. These two pieces of data were held to differ 'only in the information they contain, not technically'.[40] Furthermore, the purpose of the procedure (the problem to be overcome) was of a non-technical nature as it related to improving the 'mental registering of the character' by the viewer of the VDU.

In contrast to these decisions where the text-processing application was rejected, the application in *IBM/Editable document form*[41] succeeded before the Technical Board. The application claimed a method of transforming text stored in one editable

---

[36]  [1990] EPOR 607.      [37] [1989] 8 EPOR 454.       [38] [1992] EPOR 69.
[39]  [1988] 2 EPOR 72. See section 4.2.2.3 above.       [40] Ibid.
[41]  [1995] EPOR 185.

form to another (basically, translating word-processing formats). On appeal the claim was amended to restrict its scope to documents stored as digital data and was allowed. The technical features of text processing were said to include 'printer control items' and so transforming these from one system to another was a method having a technical character. The objection overcome had been that the method for transforming the documents was no more than a mental act.

This decision apparently allowed a claim for a method of conversion between word-processor file formats. But the types of text file referred to are said to contain formatting information that substantially overlaps with the printer control codes which would be used to direct a line or character type of printer. It was this close relationship with the control of a piece of everyday hardware that made the claims allowable.

An analysis of these text-processing decisions reveals that the reasons (or possible reasons) for rejection were related to the 'mental acts' exclusion. The exception is *Siemens/Character form*[42] from which it is not entirely clear whether the ground for rejection was non-technicality as a mental act or because the claim was for a computer program as such (the Technical Board described claim 1 as being for 'an idea for a program'[43]). It can be seen that the Technical Boards have developed a more sophisticated means for finding 'technical content' (or perhaps seeking out the lack of it) than that used in *Vicom/Computer-related invention*.[44] In *Vicom* the usefulness of the images in a technical area (industrial design) appeared determinative. Documents are of course useful in all technical and non-technical industries, as are images, but that has not been sufficient.

#### 4.2.2.6 *Inventions relating to programming itself*
Many decisions of the EPO have referred to the possibility that computer programs may have technical content. In all of them, it appears that the Board concerned was referring to the fact that the computer program might, when run on a computer, have a technical effect in the outside world or on the operation of the computer itself. This begs the question of whether developments in the field of computer programming itself can be patented.

In *IBM's Application*[45] the Board affirmed the unreported decision *ATT/System for generating software source code*.[46] They identified its real reasoning as being that the activity of programming a computer was essentially a 'mental act'. (They needed to overrule the decision to the extent that it relied upon the rule that computer programs, even if they had a technical character, could not be patented as such.)

The Board in *IBM* did not directly address the question of whether inventions which relate solely to the field of computer programming itself are patentable. But taking the Board's discussion of *ATT* overall, it appears that the *IBM* Board would

---

[42] [1992] EPOR 69.
[43] In the UK, Laddie J has described the distinction between the 'mental acts' and 'computer program' exclusions as a mere matter of semantics; see the discussion of the *Fujitsu* case at section 4.2.2.8 below.
[44] [1987] EPOR 74.          [45] [1999] RPC 563.          [46] Case T 204/93.

exclude inventions which did not go outside the field of computer programming as mental acts which lack any technical character. Claims to such inventions would be refused whether they were directed to computer programs or to computer devices operating under the control of such a program.

This does not mean that claims to all aspects of programming will be unpatentable. As in *Bosch/Electronic computer components*,[47] programs which enhance the operation of a computer in a technical way are patentable. Inventions which apparently concern programming may be patentable if some technical content can be found for them.

### 4.2.2.7 *Analysis of the EPO cases*

Prior to *Pensions*[48] technical content was found in the contribution to the art if:

(a) technical means are used to produce a result or solve a problem or,

(b) the invention produced a technical result and (following *Sohei*[49]) the technical means of solution or technical problem to be overcome may be implicit, in the sense that they only occur in the implementation of the invention and may not be apparent from the invention as claimed.

Since *Pensions* the technical content must be evident in the inventive step that led to it. In either case, it is clear that the search for technical subject matter is not superficial, but involves an enquiry that goes to the fundamental nature of the underlying invention, regardless of the form into which the claims have been cast.

It is difficult to derive from the cases any satisfying general test for what is and is not technical content or effect. In the case of text processing it can be tentatively proposed that ways of manipulating the bytes of a text file on a mechanical basis would be patentable by analogy with the ways of manipulating the images of *Vicom*,[50] but that ways of manipulation that are based on the meaning of the text will not if there is no invention at the byte-swapping level.[51]

This principle can be used to distinguish the finding in *Siemens/Character form*[52] from that in *Vicom*. Both these cases claimed processes for altering digital files, *inter alia*, to make them easier for humans to perceive. But no specific industrial use for the documents made up by the characters of *Siemens* was identified. Also, the *Siemens* invention was based upon rules of writing and depended on the characters forming words having meaning; it would be irrelevant to random text. By contrast the invention of *Vicom* could apply to any image, even an abstract one and was independent of the meaning of the image.[53] Presumably ways of manipulating images

---

[47] See section 4.2.2.4 above.                    [48] See section 4.2.2.2 above.
[49] See section 4.2.2.5 above.                    [50] See section 4.2.2.3 above.
[51] eg *IBM/Text clarity processing* [1990] EPOR 607. See section 4.2.2.6 above.
[52] [1992] EPOR 69. See section 4.2.2.6 above.
[53] One can also make the distinction in terms of the type of human perception required to receive the benefit of the invention. The appreciation of the lines and edges in images operated on by the *Vicom* invention is a lower-level, more fundamental human ability than the deciphering of text, which is a

that altered the meaning of what was represented, for example, by detecting grimaces and replacing them with smiles, would not be patentable as smile detection would be considered a series of mental steps based on the theories of human behaviour and perception.[54] To put it simply, making images or text meaningful to humans is not considered technical, whereas making them intelligible to printers,[55] is. Of course, both tasks can be frustratingly difficult.

In relation to the internal operations of a computer the reasoning discussed above is not helpful as there is no connection with the non-computer world. Any information will only have meaning to a computer and the invention will only be useful to a computer. The result of the invention will clearly be a computer, a technical thing. But the problem of identifying a technical change in it, or technical means in its achievement, remains peculiarly difficult. The most that can be said is that it appears that the problem addressed has to be a low-level one, close to the hardware. Thus, the method of generating messages in response to events of *IBM/Computer-related invention*[56] would be of general usefulness, yet its patentability was based on its use to monitor hardware-related events. (It has been noted that on its facts this decision might well go the other way if decided in recent times.) By contrast the method of generating a data file of abstracting information (a high-level concept clearly in the software domain) in *IBM/Document abstracting and retrieving*[57] was not technical.

It is a fact that all manners of computer operation are the result of logical relationships between things that could be defined in terms of mathematics and carried out as a series of mental processes by a human (and should perhaps thus be excluded). Of course some things are too complex or difficult for any human to model mathematically or carry out in person. In the UK, *Fujitsu*[58] has said expressly that this is an irrelevant consideration. EPO cases such as *Sohei*,[59] which involved the computerization of a task that could clearly have been carried out with pencil and paper, indicate that this is not a useful approach.

*Sohei* perhaps illustrates either a general softening of approach, or a more liberal approach in cases involving the use of computers to operate on data that relates to an activity carried on outside the computer. The lengths gone to by the Technical Board to identify technical content in that case, even looking outside the words of the patent, make a clear contrast with some of the earlier text-processing decisions. The

---

socially or culturally developed ability. One can extend an analogy to inventions affecting the internal operation of computers (mechanical minds), where it appears that low-level, basic features stand a greater chance of forming the subject of patentable inventions.

[54] Subject always to the caveat that if 'technical means' are used in the process then they may be patentable if they form part of the real contribution to the art of the invention. But general programming means do not generally form part of the real contribution to the art of a computer-related invention; see, eg, *Koch and Sterzel* discussed at section 4.2.2.3 above. And if the real contribution to the art did lie in matters of programming, the claim would fail as being for a computer program or series of mental steps.

[55] *IBM/Editable document form* [1995] EPOR 185. See section 4.2.2.6 above.

[56] [1990] EPOR 107. See section 4.2.2.4 above.          [57] [1990] EPOR 99.

[58] See section 4.2.2.9 below.          [59] See section 4.2.2.5 above.

reasoning in all cases involving the application, rather than the operation, of computers tends to focus on non-computer arguments, on the real-world uses to which the data can be put. It is thus informative to look more generally at how the EPO deals with inventions for excluded things.

To give further examples not specifically related to computers, the following have been held to represent non-technical subject matter: methods of directing the flow of traffic ('economic activity' according to the French text of the EPC);[60] methods of marking sound-recording carriers and their packaging to avoid counterfeiting (business method);[61] a marker for facilitating the reading and playing of music (teaching method which was a method for performing mental acts);[62] a coloured jacket for flexible disks which was claimed to be writeable on, easily distinguished and to resist fingerprints (aesthetic creation and a presentation of information);[63] an automatic self-service machine in which the user could use any machine-readable card he possessed once that card had been recognized by the machine (method of doing business).[64] By way of contrast, a television signal has been held to constitute technical subject matter,[65] as has a system (incidentally, computer controlled) for controlling a queue sequence for serving customers at a number of service points.[66]

### 4.2.2.8 *The UK perspective*

The terms of the EPC are directly reflected, so far as patentable inventions are concerned, in the Patents Act 1977. Section 1(2) of the 1977 Act sets out, essentially verbatim, the exclusions of article 52(2) of the EPC and the 'as such' caveat of article 52(3). The most directly relevant authorities on the interpretation of the Act are decisions from the UK courts.

There are a number of situations when UK courts are required to decide issues of the validity of patents and interpret the legislation:

(a) The validity of a patent can be put in issue in infringement proceedings.

(b) Petitions to revoke patents after grant can be made to the courts.

(c) Appeals lie to the courts from decisions of the Patent Office made during the prosecution of UK patents.

In addition to handling applications for UK patents, the Patent Office can hear applications to revoke UK patents and European patents (UK).

The UK legislative tradition in the field of patents is somewhat different from that of most other EPC countries, and in particular the concept of 'technical content' is alien to UK patent lawyers and judges. A certain difficulty in understanding and

---

[60] *Christian Franceries/Traffic regulation* [1988] 2 EPOR 65, agreed with by Aldous J in *Lux Traffic Controls Ltd v Pike Signals Ltd* [1993] RPC 107.
[61] *Stockburger/Coded distinctive mark* [1986] 5 EPOR 229.
[62] *Beattie/Marker* [1992] EPOR 221.    [63] *Fuji/Coloured disk jacket* [1990] EPOR 615.
[64] *IBM/Card reader* [1994] EPOR 89.    [65] *BBC/Colour television signal* [1990] EPOR 599.
[66] *Pettersson/Queuing system* [1996] EPOR 3 where the ground of objection considered was 'scheme, rule or method of doing business'.

applying this concept is often expressed in the judgments, although the UK courts have sought to reach decisions in conformity with those from the EPO.

In *Merrill Lynch's Application*[67] the claim was for a computerized method of setting up a trading market in securities, using a known computer which could be suitably programmed by known techniques. It was held by the Court of Appeal (in accordance with the decision in *Genentech Inc's Patent*[68]) that an invention was not excluded simply because the novelty lay in an excluded thing (namely a computer program)[69] and that the claim had to be looked at as a whole. However, because *Vicom/Computer-related invention*[70] was followed the Court of Appeal also held that the contribution to the prior art must not itself be excluded, and in this case the result of the claimed invention was a method for doing business. Fox LJ postulated that a 'technical advance on the prior art'[71] could nevertheless be excluded as a business method. This last comment must be qualified. In the terminology used by the EPO, and most recently made clear in *IBM's Application*,[72] anything within the excluded categories is deemed to be non-technical and anything of a non-technical nature is non-patentable.

In *Gale's Application*[73] Aldous J held that a computer program held on a ROM chip was patentable although the program itself did nothing more than provide the computer in which it was installed with a new method of calculating square roots. The Court of Appeal reversed this, holding that differences in the physical structures holding the program were not material and that the program did not produce a novel technical effect. The approach of *IBM/Document abstracting and retrieving* was followed and it was held that the instructions embodied in the program did not represent a technical process outside the computer or a solution to a technical problem inside the computer. It was accepted that a new method for finding square roots had been discovered.

In *Wang Laboratories Inc's Application*[74] the approach of the EPO was also approved of and followed, albeit in a characteristically English way.[75] There the claim was for an 'expert system' program, but was phrased to include programming a conventional computer with the program. It was held that the contribution made to the art was by the program and nothing more. In this case Aldous J complained that the meaning to be attributed to the word 'technical' in all the various ways it was used in the EPO decisions was unclear. In his judgment he therefore avoids reliance on this concept:

---

[67] [1989] RPC 561.　　　　　　　　　　　　[68] [1989] RPC 147, CA. See section 4.2.2.1 above.

[69] This had been the approach at first instance at [1988] RPC 1. A similarly erroneous approach was taken and overruled in the US case of *In re Abele*, discussed at section 4.2.3.3 above.

[70] [1987] EPOR 74. See section 4.2.2.3 above.　　　　　　　　　　　　　　　[71] Ibid.

[72] [1999] RPC 563.　　　　　　[73] [1991] RPC 305.　　　　　　[74] [1991] RPC 463.

[75] In many aspects of patent law, the UK courts have found that the tests they apply under the Patents Act 1977 are effectively the same as those applied by the EPO and other EPC states under equivalent provisions although the words used to define the test seem starkly at variance. See, eg, the debate over the construction of claims addressed by Aldous J in *Assidoman Multipack v The Mead Corporation* [1995] RPC 321 and in *Kastner v Rizla* [1995] RPC 585, CA.

The machine, the computer, remains the same even when programmed. The computer and the program do not combine together to produce a 'new computer'. They remain separate and amount to a collocation rather than a combination making a different whole. The contribution is, to my mind, made by the program and nothing more.[76]

This attempt to Anglicize the EPO's formula was not entirely successful, the concept of a 'new computer' being every bit as intractable as that of a 'technical alteration of behaviour'. Whenever a computer is operating a unique program it exists in a unique electrical configuration that could in theory be measured with physical apparatus. Yet the distinction cannot be between permanent and temporary changes because that would be contrary to the sensible and necessary *Gale* test. The problem is to distinguish those aspects of computer configuration (whether permanent or temporary, 'hardware' or 'software') in which developments are deemed patentable from those that are not.

The most recent UK case is *Fujitsu Ltd's Application*[77] where we see a continued divergence of interpretation between the UK courts and the Technical Boards of Appeal. The invention was for a method of generating and manipulating graphical representations of the crystal structures of known chemicals on a computer monitor to assist chemical engineers in developing new compounds with a desired functionality. The claims were refused, and this demanded comparison with *Vicom*. Whilst it is unclear what the *Vicom* Board would have made of the *Fujitsu* claim, it is arguable that the EPO would now also refuse it. The somewhat unsophisticated finding in *Vicom* that 'manipulating images is technical' is not binding as a general principle and the EPO interpretation of technical content has progressed since that case.[78]

Aldous LJ sought to explain *Vicom* by saying that the technical contribution there was the way that the image was reproduced and that the case was not authority for the proposition that anything to do with image manipulation was patentable. The requirement (then current in the EPO) for a 'technical contribution' as the defining ingredient of a patentable invention was difficult to reconcile with section 1(2)(a) and (d) of the Patents Act 1977. At first instance Laddie J had stated that whether the claims were refused as being for a 'computer program' or a 'method for performing a mental act' was a matter of mere semantics. Aldous LJ effectively approved this view by identifying the key question as 'whether the application consists of a program for a computer as such or whether it is a program for a computer with a technical contribution'[79] (implicitly, that a technical contribution will always mean patentability).

Aldous LJ also considered the 'Method for performing a mental act' exclusion,

---

[76] [1991] RPC 463.                                           [77] [1997] RPC 608.

[78] The argument would be that, assuming no technical contribution in the basic fields of crystal-structure generation and image production and manipulation, what is left is the mental process of manipulating and comparing shapes one with another, which could in theory be carried out with physical models or by manual calculation. This can be seen as a higher level of processing of information derived from images than that addressed by *Vicom*; see n 10 above.

[79] [1997] RPC 608.

and in this respect he was at one with the Technical Boards in finding that 'Methods for performing mental acts, which means methods of the type performed mentally, are unpatentable unless some concept of technical contribution is present'.[80] In the same passage Aldous LJ rejected arguments that the 'mental acts exclusion' should only apply to acts which were actually carried out by human minds: 'A claim to a method of carrying out a calculation (a method of performing a mental act) is no more patentable when claimed as being done by a computer than when done on a piece of paper.'

As can be seen, the words used by UK judges can if closely analysed lead to a conclusion that the test applied is different from that used by the EPO. Such conclusions are to be viewed with caution in view of the frequently expressed opinion that the courts are in fact applying the same doctrine. It is submitted that the courts are doing their best to achieve results in conformity with those of the EPO whilst working within a different procedural framework and legal tradition. It is not clear that there are material differences.

The position under the Patents Act 1949 had developed along different lines. Claims for computers when programmed to perform specified functions were allowed on the basis that a computer programmed to perform a task was a machine and if that machine was novel and inventive then a patent should be granted.[81] The 1949 Act contained no specific exclusions so the courts based their reasoning upon general considerations of what an invention was. In some respects it can be seen that this approach persisted in decisions under the 1977 Act.[82] In the United States the statutory framework remains more similar to the 1949 Act and, as is demonstrated below, the US Patent and Trademark Office ('the USPTO') and Federal courts have in effect continued to develop (not always in the same direction) this type of approach.

### 4.2.3 The US position

#### 4.2.3.1 *The statutory provisions*

The US Constitution grants Congress the power 'to promote the progress of . . . useful arts, by securing for limited times to . . . inventors the exclusive right to their respective . . . discoveries'. Cases have interpreted 'the useful arts' to mean 'the technological arts', but not in a limiting way. Indeed, anything useful (as opposed to only of artistic or intellectual value) is considered part of the 'technological arts'.[83] This power is currently exercised by Congress in the form of the Patent Act of 1952, Title 35 USC. The section of particular interest from the point of view of computer-related inventions is section 101 which states:

---

[80] *Fujitsu Ltd's Application* [1997] RPC 608, 621.

[81] See, eg, *IBM Corporation's Application* [1980] FSR 564.

[82] Which Act applies depends broadly upon when the patent was applied for, the provisions of the 1977 Act applying to applications made on or after 1 January 1978.

[83] In *Re Musgrave* (1970) 431 F 2d 882 where the claims essentially related to a method of analysing seismic data and were held to form part of the technological arts.

Whoever invents or discovers any new and useful process, machine, manufacture, or composition of matter, or any new and useful improvement thereof, may obtain a patent therefor, subject to the conditions and requirements of this title.

The US statutory regime contains no reference to computer programs; indeed, there is no list of excluded things comparable to that contained in article 52(2) of the EPC. The approach to computer programs taken by the USPTO and the US Federal courts has fluctuated somewhat over the years, but has generally been to exclude fewer computer-related inventions than would be excluded under the EPC. The current position in the United States is to exclude only a narrow range of claims from patentability. It is worth considering how this position was arrived at because the arguments are of general relevance and cast an interesting sidelight in the European position.

The words of section 101 are taken to limit what may be patented to:

(a)  processes;
(b)  machines;
(c)  manufactures; and
(d)  compositions of matter,

provided they are new and useful. In decided cases, judges and examiners do not always trouble to identify clearly which of the four headings an invention falls under, preferring instead to concentrate on whether the invention falls into a general category of things outside those allowed. This judge-defined excluded category includes mental acts and thus, by reason of arguments that should now be familiar, may exclude some computer-related inventions. It must be borne in mind that in the United States there are no statutory exclusions to worry about, let alone one for computer programs. This is probably the main reason why the scope of what is patentable in the United States is wider in many respects than that in Europe.

### 4.2.3.2  *Early case law: a liberal approach*
It has been held that a process is:

a mode of treatment of certain materials to produce a given result. It is an act, or a series of acts, performed upon the subject matter to be transformed and reduced to a different state or thing.[84]

These words have been explained in the light of technological developments so that the matter to be transformed may form electrical signals representing data about something.

*Gottschalk v Benson*[85] specifically identified ideas, mental steps and discoveries of physical phenomena or laws of nature as not falling within the scope of what was patentable. Thus it was held that if a patent claim wholly pre-empts a mathematical

---

[84] *Re Musgrave* (1970) 431 F 2d 882.
[85] (1972) 409 US 63.

formula used in a general-purpose digital computer, then the patent is directed to the formula and therefore does not define patentable subject matter under section 101. This decision was based upon the proposition that the formula was not patentable as a law of nature and therefore should be free for anybody to use in a computer. It was held:

> The mathematical formula involved here has no substantial practical application except in connection with a digital computer, which means that if the judgment below is affirmed, the patent would wholly pre-empt the mathematical formula and in practical effect would be a patent on the algorithm itself.[86]

*Gottschalk v Benson* used the term 'algorithm' synonymously with 'mathematical formula' and defined it as a 'procedure for solving a given type of mathematical problem'.[87] Among the concerns expressed about allowing such patents was the reported incapability of the USPTO to search the literature on programs so as to discover the prior art. This concern seems to have fallen away in later cases. The current *Guidelines for Examination*[88] in respect of computer-related inventions issued by the USPTO now envisage searching computer program material when assessing computer-related claims.

In *Parker v Flook*[89] the claim concerned a process for updating alarm limits in a chemical process involving a programmed computer.[90] However, despite stressing that the claim is to be looked at as a whole, the court decided that since the only novel thing about the invention was a formula, the claim viewed as a whole contained no patentable invention. It was held that a new use of a known mathematical formula may be patented, and the discovery of a new mathematical formula cannot support a patent unless there is some other inventive concept involved in applying it. In this case use of the formula could not be said to have been totally 'pre-empted' but the claim failed nevertheless. The court expressed concern that skilful claim drafting could allow any formula to be patented by including irrelevant 'post-solution activity' in a process claim.

---

[86] Ibid. The claims were directed to a process of mathematical or logical steps for converting numbers between two common formats for storing them in the binary forms used in computers, 'binary coded decimal' and 'pure binary'. Claim 8 commenced 'The method of converting signals from binary coded decimal form . . .' The claims would have prevented the use of the process on any digital computer whether electrical or mechanical, but not by a human using pencil and paper.

[87] Ibid. Subsequent cases have favoured more general definitions and stressed that numbers in the mathematical sense are not necessary, eg, quoting *Webster's New College Dictionary*: 'a step-by step procedure for solving a problem or accomplishing some end' (*In Re Iwahashi* (1989) 888 F 2d 1370, discussed further at section 4.2.3.3 below).

[88] Discussed further at section 4.2.3.6.

[89] (1978) 437 US 584.

[90] In the catalytic conversion of hydrocarbons, various parameters such as temperature, pressure and flow rates are monitored and if they exceed predetermined limits an alarm is triggered. It was known that to take care of transient conditions, these 'alarm limits' required constant monitoring and sometimes updating. The process of automatically monitoring the parameters and generating alarms was also known and the court assumed that the mathematical formula used was known. What appears to have been new was the use of that particular formula for the purpose of alarm-limit updating. The court was concerned that the formula contained variables yet the patent did not teach how to select any of them. An example of using a finding of non-patentable subject matter to disallow claims that appear too wide or vague?

*Diamond v Diehr*[91] followed the 'claim as a whole' approach whilst allowing the claim to proceed. The claims covered a process for curing rubber moulded products. The cure has to take place at an elevated temperature and for a time which depends on the precise temperature–time history. Known methods involved measuring the temperature and making calculations, but these were not completely accurate because temperature was not constantly monitored. In the claimed process, temperature was continually monitored and the expected cure time recalculated using a computer which automatically opened the mould at precisely the right time. It was held that the claims here were for a new method of curing moulded rubber products, which was clearly a patentable process, and not merely claims for a process of calculating a formula. *Gottschalk v Benson* and *Parker v Flook* were distinguished on the grounds that the claims were not seeking to patent or pre-empt a formula. The warning against irrelevant 'post-solution activity' was repeated.

### 4.2.3.3  *A restrictive approach to algorithms: Freeman-Walter-Abele*

After *Gottschalk v Benson*[92] the courts applied a two-part test for establishing whether process claims were 'drawn to statutory subject matter' (ie, whether they claimed patentable inventions). This was developed after *Diamond v Diehr*[93] into the '*Freeman-Walter-Abele*' test. The two parts of the test were set out in *In Re Abele* as:

1. (first part)

do the claims directly or indirectly recite an algorithm, if so

2. (second part)

2.1  is the algorithm applied in any manner to physical elements or process steps; and

2.2  is this application circumscribed by more than a field of use limitation or non-essential post-solution activity?[94]

It can be seen that claims to processes are particularly liable to objection on the 'algorithm' ground in a way that claims to physical things ('machines' or 'manufactures' in the language of section 101) are not. But many claims relating to computer-related inventions are addressed to 'machines' but delimited solely or mainly with reference to the processes carried out by the machine (for 'machine' read 'computer'). This contrasts with ways of claiming machines which describe the physical nature of the elements of the machine and their interconnections. A claim to a computer-related invention in the former form would be largely hardware- and software-independent, whereas a claim in the latter form would be limited in its scope to only certain hardware and/or software configurations. Concerns were raised at the prospect of claims to machines being drawn which did no more than implement otherwise unpatentable processes.

---

[91]  (1981) 450 US 175.          [92]  (1972) 409 US 63.
[93]  (1981) 450 US 175.          [94]  (1982) 684 F 2d 902.

Prompted by such concerns, 'means plus function'[95] (also known as 'means for') claims were included within the ambit of the test.[96] This led to many computer-related inventions being refused protection because they were considered to amount to no more than mathematical processes notwithstanding that the claims were directed generally to apparatus involving computers.

In *Abele* itself the invention involved a system of computerized tomography ('CAT scanning'). Claim 5 (which was rejected) claimed simply a method of manipulating data followed by the display of that data. Claim 6 (accepted) was in essence claim 5 when the data concerned were X-ray attenuation data. The interpretation of *Parker v Flook*[97] made by the examiner, who held that the non-algorithm part of the claim must itself be novel and unobvious, was held to be erroneous. It was held, comparing with *Diamond v Diehr*, that 'The improvement in either case resides in the application of a mathematical formula within the context of a process which encompasses significantly more than the algorithm alone'.[98]

In *In Re Iwahashi*[99] Rich J sought to overturn the rule that 'means for' claims should be interpreted widely for the purposes of examination.[100] The result was that a claim addressed to an 'autocorrelation unit' for use in pattern recognition (for example, speech recognition) was allowable, despite the fact that the invention could have been achieved purely by programming a general-purpose computer. However the claims, whilst containing a large number of 'means for' elements, also contained reference to specific hardware elements, namely ROM and RAM, in which the program was stored.

*Iwahashi* was viewed as allowing great freedom in patenting computer-based processes and machines for carrying them out, but there was still the question of the extent to which it was necessary to specify physical hardware elements as part of the

---

[95] *In Re Walter* (1980) 618 F 2d 758. Section 112 of the US Patent Act deals expressly with such claims. For the purpose of infringement, such claims only cover the actual means taught in the body of the patent and its 'reasonable equivalents', not any means that achieve the desired function, even though the wording of the claim contains no such limitation. *In Re Walter* held that this claim-interpretation rule did not apply when considering claims for validity, thus widening the scope of claims and rendering them more likely to a section 101 objection. Such claims are frequently used when claiming computer-related inventions. The EPC contains no such interpretative provision, and 'means for' claims will be interpreted as including any means suitable for the specified function. Widely drawn claims may be held not to be 'supported by' the specification under EPC, art 84; see, eg, *General Electric/Disclosure of computer-related apparatus* [1992] EPOR 446.

[96] The USPTO and courts have had more problems with basing their rules on matters of claim form rather than substance than the EPO has. In Europe the 'real contribution to the art' concept allows examiners to look at the process underlying a claim to an article or apparatus if that is the important development. The case of *In Re Alappat* (discussed at section 4.2.3.4 below) has simplified the nature of the enquiry by effectively banning these processes of looking behind the literal wording of the claims.

[97] (1978) 437 US 584.

[98] Ibid.

[99] (1989) 888 F 2d 1370.

[100] The claim was for a new method of calculating autocorrelation coefficients used in pattern recognition that involved calculations that were simpler to implement on a computer. A ROM was specified to store squares of numbers that would be used in calculations. It should be noted that the claims apply to apparatus for comparing stored signal samples generally and are not limited to voice recognition.

claims, which had been done in that case. The *Freeman-Walter-Abele* test was still criticized for deviating from the simple 'claim as a whole' test of *Diamond v Diehr* and losing sight of section 101.

### 4.2.3.4 In Re Alappat: *Judge Rich removes the restrictions*

*In Re Alappat*[101] can be viewed in part as a return to the *Diamond v Diehr*[102] test. The claim involved a scheme for displaying a smooth waveform on a digital oscilloscope.[103] In a digital oscilloscope, the input signal is sampled and digitized. The numerical values are then portrayed by illuminating the pixels at the appropriate position on the screen in accordance with the value of the signal and its position in the waveform. A problem was experienced with this type of machine in the form of momentary aberrant signal values which made rapidly rising or falling sections of the waveform appear discontinuous. The invention used an anti-aliasing system to illuminate each pixel along the waveform differently so as to give the appearance of smoothness.

The majority opinion of Rich J in *Alappat* amounted to a direct attack on the *Freeman-Walter-Abele* test as applied by the USPTO and a complete re-evaluation of section 101, *Gottschalk v Benson*,[104] *Parker v Flook*[105] and *Diamond v Diehr*. Among his conclusions were:

(a) When considering a 'means plus function' claim for patentability, the same rule of interpretation should be used as when considering 'means plus function' claims for infringement, that is, the claim should be taken to be limited to the actual 'means' taught in the patent and its 'reasonable equivalents'[106] (relying on an earlier opinion delivered by Rich J in *In Re Donaldson*[107]). Construing the claim in issue in this way, the claim was held to cover patentable material, that is, a 'machine'. The USPTO in this case had ignored Judge Rich's comments to this effect in *In Re Iwahashi*[108] as being *obiter dicta*. Rich J approved the findings in *Abele* and other cases but sought to distinguish them by pointing out that in those cases there had been no specific teaching of how to achieve the means in the specification.

(b) A machine must perform a function that the laws were designed to protect (for example, transforming or reducing an article to a different state or thing). But in the instant case the invention claimed calculations to transform digitized waveforms into anti-aliased pixel illumination data and that was sufficient.[109]

---

[101] (1994) 33 F 3d 1526.    [102] (1981) 450 US 175.
[103] An oscilloscope displays a signal representing something that fluctuates regularly with time, such as the sound pressure in the vicinity of a musical instrument or the electrical signal given off by a human heart, as a static waveform on a television screen.
[104] (1972) 409 US 63.    [105] (1978) 437 US 584.
[106] US Patent Act, s 106.    [107] (1994) 16 F 3d 1189.
[108] (1989) 888 F 2d 137.
[109] The comparison between this case and the European case *Vicom/Computer-related invention* [1987] EPOR 74 (discussed at section 4.2.2.3 above) is instructive. In *Alappat* the waveform display was held to be a thing forming suitable subject matter for an invention in a very similar fashion to the way images were held to be 'real world objects' in *Vicom*. *Alappat* talked in more down-to-earth terms of electrical

(c) It was accepted that the 'mathematical algorithm' exception could apply to genuine machine claims, but section 101 should be given its widest interpretation. Thus if a machine produced a 'useful, concrete and tangible result' it was patentable and to be contrasted with a disembodied mathematical concept.

(d) A general-purpose computer when programmed in a particular way amounted to a 'machine' which would be patentable if the other requirements for patentability were met.[110]

Apart from reversing the claim interpretation rule of *Freeman-Walter-Abele* and effectively confining the application of the rule to genuine process claims, the important contribution of this decision is in the approach adopted in analysing a claim. The accent has shifted back to looking at the claim as a whole to see whether it is for a patentable thing (machine, manufacture, process, etc) rather than on searching out algorithms in the claim and then seeing if the claim goes beyond that (the *Freeman-Walter-Abele* approach).

### 4.2.3.5 *Post-*Alappat*: programmed computers are 'machines' and data structures in a memory are 'manufactures'*

Whilst many computer-related inventions are apt to be claimed as processes or the means for carrying them out, things such as computer memories or disks can also form the basis of claims. In *In Re Lowry*[111] the claim was for a computer memory organized in accordance with the 'attributive data model'. This comprised a way of organizing data into primitive data objects which were arranged in a hierarchy whilst also providing links between objects separate from the hierarchy. Improved data access when such structures were used in combination with programs running on the computer was claimed. The USPTO Appeals Board had allowed the claims under section 101, holding that a computer memory was an 'article of manufacture' (and this was confirmed by the Federal Circuit). However, the Appeals Board had held the claims not novel, relying on a line of cases relating to printed matter and holding that the only novelty rested in the information content and so did not count.

The Federal Circuit cautioned against overzealous use of the printed matter exception and held that the proper test was simply, 'is the article [ie, the computer memory] useful [in the technological sense identified above]'. On this basis the

---

signals, no doubt influenced by the need to read the facts on to the well-established definition of a 'process' (see section 4.2.3.2 above), but the basic reasoning is similar. The important difference between the two cases is that in *Alappat* the transformation had merely to be found 'useful' to found patentability. In *Vicom* it was necessary to find 'technical content'. It seems likely that a suitable claim to the invention of *Alappat* would issue in the EPO without problems over the patentable nature of the invention because of the clear technical nature of the subject matter, an illustration that whilst the European approach may be overall more restrictive, the 'real contribution to the art' concept can operate in favour of inventors as well as against them.

[110] It can be seen that this position is now the same as that which the UK courts were working towards under the Patents Act 1949; see the discussion at section 4.2.2.8 below.

[111] (1994) 32 F 3d 1579.

claim defined a functional thing with new attributes. These were not simply the data itself, but the organization of those data. The fact that the claims specified no particular physical organization for the data structure, only a set of logical relationships, was not material; the data structure was represented by physical (electrical or magnetic) structures. The Federal Circuit were careful to point out that the attributive data model was not being patented in the abstract.

*In Re Warmerdam*[112] concerned an improved method for navigating robotic machines which avoided collisions by using 'bubbles', imaginary spherical objects encompassing real objects to be avoided. The basic bubble idea was known, but the invention added a layer of sophistication by using a 'bubble hierarchy' whereby once a bubble was violated it was replaced with a set of smaller bubbles and so on. A technique of collision avoidance known as 'bubble bursting' is provided. Claims 1–4 were for 'A method for generating a data structure which represents the shape of physical object [*sic*] . . .' Claim 5 was for a machine but did not use any 'means for' language. In fact the function of the machine was not referred to in any way and the only features claimed for the machine were the presence and contents of memory. It read: 'A machine having a memory which contains data representing a bubble hierarchy generated by . . . the method of claims 1–4'. Claim 6 was for a data structure generated by the method of claims 1 to 4. The Board of Appeals rejected claims 1 to 4 and 6 under section 101 and claim 5 for indefiniteness under section 112.

In *Warmerdam* the USPTO had applied *Freeman-Walter-Abele* to claims 1–4. When the case came before the court *In Re Alappat*[113] had recently been decided and the court did not feel constrained to follow the two-part test precisely. It held that in this case the crucial question in relation to section 101 was whether the claim went beyond simply manipulating 'abstract ideas' or 'natural phenomena'. The court affirmed the rejection of these claims and rejected the applicant's arguments that one first had to measure real objects to apply the process because the claims themselves did not require this, nor would such a limitation be implied into them. The court also upheld the rejection of claim 6. This was on the basis that the structure as described 'is nothing more than another way of describing the manipulation of ideas contained in claims 1–4'[114] and so had to stand or fall with them.

However, claim 5 was allowed by the court as sufficiently claiming a 'machine'. It was held that a person skilled in the art would have no problems identifying whether a machine fell within the claims because 'the ideas expressed in claims 1–4 are well-known mathematical constructs'. It should be pointed out as a note of caution that the question of the utility of the invention of claim 5 was not in issue in the appeal. The USPTO had not applied *Freeman-Walter-Abele* to claim 5 (it had not rejected under section 101) and the court did not apply it either. Although considering the claim under section 101 and acknowledging that it contained process

---

[112] (1994) 33 F 3d 1361.
[113] (1994) 33 F 3d 1526.
[114] Ibid.

elements, the court did not look at the claim from the point of view of the underlying process to be carried out by the machine.

Subsequent cases[115] reaching the Court of Appeals for the Federal Circuit have confirmed that *Alappat* should be regarded as the leading authority in relation to application of the 'mathematical method' exclusion. In *State Street v Signature* the court re-examined the 'mathematical algorithm' exclusion and explained the effect of its earlier decisions in cases such as *Alappat* and *In Re Iwahashi*.[116] Rich J again delivered the judgment, and some of his comments are worthy of note:

... the mere fact that a claimed invention involves inputting numbers, calculating numbers, outputting numbers, and storing numbers, in and of itself, would not render it nonstatutory subject matter unless, of course, its operation does not produce a useful, concrete and tangible result.

... The question of whether a claim encompasses statutory subject matter should not focus on *which* of the four categories of subject matter a claim is directed to—process, machine, manufacture, or composition of matter—but rather on the essential characteristics of the subject matter, in particular, its practical utility.[117]

Rich J also pointed out that every step-by-step process involves an algorithm in the broad sense of the term, and discouraged any use of *Freeman-Walter-Abele*.[118] In *State Street* the claim was essentially for a general-purpose programmable computer programmed with so-called 'hub and spoke' software for use in assisting the management of State Street's business of an administrator and accounting agent for mutual funds. Such claims were allowed, and in allowing them Rich J buried the 'Business Method Exception' so far as the United States was concerned: 'Whether the claims are directed to subject matter within section 101 should not turn on whether the claimed subject matter does "business" instead of something else'.[119]

### 4.2.3.6 *Current US practice*

As a result of the developments in the case law, noted above, in which the USPTO policy had been criticized as lagging behind judicial pronouncement, the USPTO has revised its manual of patent-examining procedure. The current version (eighth edition, August 2001) now fully incorporates the reasoning of *State Street*. The policy can be summarized as follows:

(a) Examiners should look at the claim and specification as a whole to decide what the alleged invention is.

(b) The subject matter so identified must have practical utility.

---

[115] *State Street v Signature* (1998) 149 F 3d 1368 and *AT&T v Excel Communications*, case 98-1338, which followed.

[116] (1989) 888 F 2d 1370.

[117] (1998) 149 F 3d 1368.

[118] It was arguably still an optional method of analysis, and is still permitted by the revised USPTO guidelines (discussed below), which were issued after *Alappat* but before *State Street*.

[119] (1998) 149 F 3d 1368.

(c)  A computer, even a known general-purpose computer when programmed in a particular way, will be patentable if it has practical utility.

(d)  A known type of computer memory (disk, ROM, whatever) that carries information in a particular form is patentable if it has practical utility.

(e)  A claim which only covers a mathematical algorithm and cannot be construed so as to cover something of practical utility is not patentable.

The key revisions to the manual were issued after a period of consultation. Some of the proposals made during that process[120] were not adopted. These include:

(a)  Allowing claims for data structures and computer programs *per se*.

(b)  Allowing claims for 'non-functional descriptive material' embodied on computer-readable media.

(c)  Allowing claims which only infer (*sic*) that 'functional descriptive material' is embodied on a computer-readable medium.

The distinction between functional and non-functional descriptive material is interesting. To be functional, material must 'exhibit a functional inter-relationship with the way in which computing processes are performed'. It is easily seen that the memories of *In re Warmerdam*[121] and *In re Lowry*[122] would satisfy this test whereas plain text or music files would not.[123] The use of this definition neatly side-steps the somewhat arbitrary distinction between what is considered 'a program' and what is considered mere data. As a matter of strict theory, all computer-readable information consists of binary numbers which are capable of influencing the sequence of instructions performed by a computer, whether those numbers were intended as instructions to the computer's processor or not.

### 4.2.3.7  *Everything under the sun?*

It can be seen that, after a period of fluctuation, US law has now adopted a very liberal position on the patentability of computer-related and other inventions whose subject matter is essentially the manipulation of numbers: the 'algorithm' exclusion still holds, but it has shrunk to an essentially literal interpretation. Claims to any new and useful machine or article will be allowed protection regardless of any fears that an algorithm is being patented by the back door. It is instructive to consider earlier

---

[120] 'Examination Guidelines for Computer-Related Inventions' published in the 28 February 1996 Federal Register (61 Fed Reg 7478).

[121]  (1994) 33 F 3d 1361.

[122]  (1994) 32 F 3d 1579.

[123]  Assuming the invention claimed lay in the words or music content rather than the data structure in which they were recorded. The data structure could found an invention if it assisted in the playing, display or manipulation of the words or music on a computer. The requirement of 'usefulness' of *Alappat* must (and clearly would) be construed as meaning useful other than for the reason that you can sell the disk at a healthy profit margin because people will enjoy experiencing the data recorded on it. This would be consistent with the direction in *Diehr* that 'laws of nature, natural phenomena, and abstract ideas' are not patentable.

refused claims from cases such as *Gottschalk v Benson*[124] and *Parker v Flook*.[125] They would appear to stand a good chance of acceptance since *In Re Alappat*,[126] perhaps after casting into forms similar to those used in *In Re Warmerdam*[127] or *In Re Lowry*.[128]

These cases and *Alappat* also illustrate the lack of zeal on the part of US examiners and judges, when compared to their European counterparts, for digging for the essence of an invention in order to find that it addresses non-patentable matter. In *Warmerdam* the examination stopped at a relatively superficial level in finding that a machine was claimed: there was no further investigation of what that machine did. *Alappat* has also had the effect that claims for processes, machines as processes and articles of manufacture will be looked at in accordance with broadly the same overall test in mind. The claims in *Lowry* and *Warmerdam* may have been drafted to avoid 'means for' language so as to avoid the effects of *Freeman-Walter-Abele* (and were successful in this). Now the issue of the form of a claim, which was important when the *Freeman-Walter-Abele* test held sway, will no longer be of such significance.

*State Street* is a highly significant case not so much because it moved the doctrinal development forward but because it highlighted the wide scope for patenting claims to computerized business methods inherent in the earlier developments. Applications in this area have mushroomed in the US, and this gave rise to fears that patents covering essentially trivial business methods could stifle commercial activity. Partly in response to such concerns, the US Patent Act was amended by the American Inventors Protection Act of 1999. This provides a defence to infringement of a patent for a business method where the defendant reduced the claimed business method to practice at least one year prior to the effective date of filing the application and used the method in good faith.

The USPTO has also responded to these concerns by issuing special guidance to patent examiners as to how to deal with business-method applications in relation to obviousness.[129] These address the problem of the computerization, or implementation via the Internet, of a known process. They indicate through a number of worked examples that, for example, if the method of implementation is obvious, then the invention claimed will be obvious. In addition it has implemented a revised system of quality control for examination procedures and a programme of training examiners in developments in computerization and business methods.

This shift of focus towards obviousness as the key ground on which ambitiously drawn computer-related claims should be challenged mirrors the developments in Europe and calls for a brief discussion of the US approach to obviousness. The

---

[124] (1972) 409 US 63.                                   [125] (1978) 437 US 584.
[126] (1994) 33 F 3d 1526.                                [127] (1994) 33 F 3d 1361.
[128] (1994) 32 F 3d 1579.
[129] 'Formulating And Communicating Rejections Under 35 U.S.C. 103 For Applications Directed To Computer-Implemented Business Method Inventions', part of the *Training and Implementation Guide* issued pursuant to the American Inventors Protection Act. Given the decision in *State Street*, lack of patentable subject matter will not form a ground of objection to such claims.

current USPTO *Manual of Patent Examining Procedure*, which reflects case law interpreting 35 USC 103, summarizes the main test as follows:

To establish a prima facie case of obviousness, three basic criteria must be met. First, there must be some suggestion or motivation, either in the [prior art] references themselves or in the knowledge generally available to one of ordinary skill in the art, to modify the reference or to combine reference teachings. Second, there must be a reasonable expectation of success. Finally, the prior art reference (or references when combined) must teach or suggest all the claim limitations. The teaching or suggestion to make the claimed combination and the reasonable expectation of success must both be found in the prior art, and not based on applicant's disclosure.[130]

If the examiner finds a *prima facie* case of obviousness, the applicant can respond with evidence supporting inventive step. Unlike in Europe, there is no stress on the area of invention being technical (to put it another way, that the reason why the skilled man would not have got to the invention were not technical ones). To give a striking example, in the utility patent case of *In Re Dembiczak*[131] the patent was for orange-coloured plastic trash bags with markings which expanded when the bag was filled to show a pumpkin-lantern style of face. The prior art included similar but undecorated gusseted bags, the inventor's own prior design patent for bags with similar designs and references to the design in children's craft books. The Board of Patent Appeals and Interferences rejected the application for obviousness, but this was reversed by the Court of Appeals for the Federal Circuit. In their reasoning the Court stressed the need to guard against hindsight in combining prior art references, and held it was not obvious to combine the children's art references with known trash bags. There was no 'suggestion, teaching or motivation' in the prior art to combine the references in that way.[132] The technical (or non-technical) nature of the inventive step played no part in the decision.

A number of business-method patents of breadth and simplicity have been issued and there has been some litigation, with mixed results. No decisions have yet been reported which directly address the issue of the inventive step in a business-method application since *State Street*. (In *State Street* itself, there was no obviousness objection raised by the defendants, who ran the non-patentable subject matter argument on an application for summary judgment.) But in *Amazon.com Inc v Barnesandnoble.com Inc*[133] Amazon were (on appeal) refused interim injunctive relief on a claim for 'one-click' Internet shopping, on the basis that the defendants had mounted a substantial challenge to validity on the basis of obviousness.

Nevertheless it remains the case that a claim to a computer program (dare we say 'as such') will be refused in the United States on the grounds that it is not a manufacture, machine or process. A mathematical process will not be patentable, but should

---

[130] Section 2142.
[131] (1999) 175 F 3d 994.
[132] If the distinction over the prior art had been purely decorative, that would not have been patentable.
[133] (1999) 239 F 3d 1343

there be any practical application of it, claims to computers or memories to carry out the process or embody it will be held patentable and proceed to examination on the grounds of novelty and non-obviousness. Whether the USPTO's revised and strengthened procedures for assessing obviousness prevent the patenting of trite computerized business methods (and whether its approach will be supported by the courts) remains to be seen.

### 4.2.4  A comparison and discussion of the two approaches

The European approach to patentability of computer-related inventions is based around the requirement for technical content. This has resulted in a wide interpretation of the exclusions from patentability set out in article 52(2) of the EPC. It appears that claims draftspersons have become adept at framing claims that address machinery or processes for achieving specified ends in technical fields rather than computer programs, so few claims are refused on the 'computer program' ground. The move away from the 'contribution approach' resulting from *Pensions* has meant that very few computer-related inventions will fail because of the exclusions in article 52(2). But the development of the concept of technical content as embracing all non-excluded areas (and of the theory that the non-patentability of non-technical subject matter lies at the heart of the EPC) has ensured that some inventions will remain unpatentable because of what they cover. The difference is that, since *Pensions*, the reason for refusal of such applications will be that the inventive step does not lie in a technical field of activity.

Either pre- or post-*Pensions*, the key feature of the European approach is the way that non-patentable subject matter is sought out in claims. Whether looking for the contribution to the art or the inventive step, the enquiry demands looking behind the form of the claims to the inventive concept underlying the invention. It is in this deeper view of what the invention is that technical content must be found. On taking this deeper view, most computer-related and business-method applications will fail, if at all, on the ground of mental acts or mathematical formulae (as has proved to be the case in the decisions of the Technical Boards of Appeal). It is thus not the 'computer program' exclusion that results in applications being refused but a similar objection to that which remains in the United States, that a patent should not be granted for an algorithm.

So why is the position in Europe commonly viewed as being more restrictive? First, there is the gap between perception and reality—the existence of a specific exclusion in the EPC leads to considerable misconception as to the true position. But there is also a real difference between Europe and the US, certainly in relation to the recent explosion of activity in the field of patents for computerized business methods. As we have seen, in the US (as now in Europe), such claims will be most unlikely to be refused because the subject matter is non-patentable or excluded. In both jurisdictions also, the claim will have to proceed to examination for novelty and non-obviousness/inventive step. But in the US, in contrast to Europe, there is no specific requirement that the inventive step be of a technical nature. This difference in approach will result in a wider scope of matter being held unpatentable in Europe than is the case in the US.

The difference between the two jurisdictions is particularly marked in the case of business-method patents where *State Street* killed off the US equivalent of a 'business method' exclusion. By contrast in Europe, the development of business methods would, without more, be regarded as a non-technical field of activity and thus inventiveness restricted to such areas not rewarded with the grant of a patent. The difference is also clear if one considers the facts of the US case of *In Re Dembiczak*.[134] The approach to this case in Europe would simply be that any inventiveness did not lie in the field of the technical arts and therefore the patent was invalid. In cases where the objection in Europe would be a mathematical method, the difference will be likely to be less marked, but here too the focus on the nature of the inventive step will make the European position more restrictive. This can be seen by considering the US case of *Warmerdam*.

In *In Re Warmerdam*[135] claims were allowed in the United States essentially for a computer programmed to carry out a mathematical method and a memory carrying data in a particular structure. The claims were not limited to any particular use for such a computer or memory. It seems unlikely that any such general claims would succeed in the EPO. The inventive step would be a matter of mathematics only. Once this is proposed, the programming and hardware means for putting it into effect as a computer or memory (which might well have a 'technical' character) will be obvious. To comply with the requirement for technical content, any claims to the *Warmerdam* invention would have to be directed to a machine with an identifiable real-world use, such as a robot. Furthermore, the idea of using that mathematical method to navigate a robot (as opposed to the task of coming up with the mathematical idea) would have to be inventive (a question of fact). After *IBM's Application*[136] such claims could be addressed to a computer program or perhaps even a data structure without the need for a reference to a carrier. But they would only cover such a program or data structure to the extent that it was adapted to operate in a computer so as to achieve a technical effect. Whilst it might be thought that such matters of claim drafting are mere technicalities, this is not so. Claims in the form upheld in the US will afford significantly greater protection to the patentee, which might well be of economic value.

A superficial reading of *IBM's Application* might suggest that the European position is now more liberal than that in the US since programs can be claimed without reference to any medium for carrying them. But the Technical Board's reason for not making a distinction between the program and the medium on which it is stored was that there is no point in making such a distinction. Current scientific theory holds that information is incapable of existing other than as a result of a particular physical

---

[134] See p 165 above.        [135] (1994) 33 F 3d 1361. See section 4.2.3.5 above.
[136] [1999] RPC 563.

state of matter. So it is impossible to infringe a claim to a computer program without having it stored on a data-storage medium, because the program will not exist otherwise. Thus claims for 'computer programs . . .' are not practically any more useful than US-style claims to the storage medium as a 'useful manufacture'. *IBM's Application* made no changes to the requirement for technical content, which remains the main difference between the two systems.


## 4.3 OTHER ASPECTS OF PATENT LAW

This section contains an outline of the UK interpretation of the position under the EPC (in the form of the Patents Act 1977 as interpreted by the courts). A detailed treatment of these matters, which are largely independent of the nature of the subject matter of the invention, is beyond the scope of this chapter and readers should consult relevant works on patent law.[137] The position in other EPC jurisdictions is likely to be broadly similar as to the general principles concerned, although different in matters of detail.


### 4.3.1 Novelty

Article 54 of the EPC (Patents Act 1977, s 1(1)) states that an invention is novel if it 'does not form part of the state of the art'. The state of the art is defined in article 54(2) (s 1(2)) as 'comprising everything made available to the public by means of a written or oral description, by use, or in any other way'. The date on which the state of the art is considered is the priority date of the claim in question, which will be the date of the application for the patent or a date within one year prior to that on which another document was filed from which priority is claimed. US readers should note this (the 'first to file' system) most particularly. The US system of 'first to invent' means that a disclosure by the inventor of their invention cannot invalidate any patent that is subsequently duly applied for within a year of the date the invention was made. In Europe and many other jurisdictions it can, and frequently does (and US inventors are often the culprits).

It is established law that the phrase 'made available to the public' means that any disclosure will only contribute to the art that which it 'enables'. In respect of any particular invention, an enabling disclosure is one which would enable the skilled man, using only his general knowledge in his field and not having to exercise any inventive capacity, to achieve the invention, that is make the product or carry out the process claimed. There are several important points that follow from this:

(a) The skilled man is a hypothetical person who was skilled in the relevant areas of technology as at the priority date. The relevant areas are those which are relevant

---

[137] See, eg, Thorley et al, *Terrell on the Law of Patents*, 15th edn (Sweet & Maxwell, 2000).

to a particular claim of a patent whose novelty might be under consideration. It is thus not strictly relevant to consider a disclosure in a vacuum—there has to be an invention in mind to focus attention on a particular recipient of the information and what that recipient is enabled to do.

(b) 'Mosaicing' is not allowed. That is, different disclosures cannot be combined to add up to an enabling disclosure, each disclosure must be looked at separately.[138] A combination of disclosures might render the patent obvious, but that is a separate ground of invalidity.

(c) Disclosures made under conditions whereby all recipients of information were under duties of confidence make nothing available to the public and are disregarded. In English legal terms, the recipient has to be 'free in law and equity' to do what they will with whatever is gleaned from the disclosure. There are savings for information published in breach of duties of confidence.

(d) The fact that nothing actually was disclosed to anybody is irrelevant, what matters is availability. If nobody ever read an article in a journal that was published, the matter would still be available to the public. (And since this is a work on computer law, it should be pointed out that publication by placing information on a computer to which there is unrestricted dial-up or Internet access makes matter available to the public.)

(e) In the case of public demonstrations, the use of machines in public places and the distribution to the public of objects or substances, the scope of disclosure is determined by considering what the skilled man could have gleaned by inspecting the material had he got his hands on it (again it is irrelevant that no recipient of the object actually had the relevant skill).

(f) There are complex rules governing the situations that arise when a patent application anticipating a later application is not actually published (made available to the public) before the priority date of the later application.

Thus where the use on a public road of traffic-control apparatus would have revealed the claimed manner of operation to a passing skilled man had he simply observed the operation of the system, the claim was held to lack novelty.[139] In the case of computer-related inventions it will normally be the case that public distribution of computers or disks containing all the relevant software will make available all relevant matter to the skilled man (a complete decompilation and understanding of the code may not be necessary to understand the alleged invention sufficiently to reproduce it). If development products are to be distributed, this must either be done after any patent filing or conditions of confidence must be imposed on all recipients.

Generally novelty can reside in a new thing or a new process, which can include a

---

[138] There are exceptions where, eg, two documents cross-refer.
[139] *Lux Traffic Controls Ltd v Pike Signals Ltd* [1993] RPC 107.

new use for an old thing. The case of *Mobil Oil/Friction reducing additive*[140] represents a high point in this area. Mobil found that a certain chemical additive to engine oil reduced friction in the engine. The identical compound had been known and used as a wear-reducing agent in engine oil but it had not been realized that it reduced friction. The enlarged Technical Board of Appeals held that a claim to use of the additive 'as a friction-reducing additive' was novel. This has been criticized as effectively allowing claims to old uses of old products for new purposes, although the Board held that the use was new.[141] Subsequent patentees do not appear to have sought claims in precisely these circumstances and generally it will be possible to find some physical distinction in the product or the use over the prior art.

### 4.3.2 Obviousness

The requirement for an inventive step is set out in article 52(1) of the EPC (Patents Act 1977, s 1(1)). Article 56 (s 3) defines an invention as having an 'inventive step' if the invention would not have been obvious to a person skilled in the art having regard to the state of the art. Whilst the basic idea of obviousness is clear and similar across the jurisdictions, as a practical matter it is the most difficult fact to address in any judicial process and a number of principles and approaches have emerged from courts and patent offices around the world. It is generally thought that the UK courts are more ready to find a patent obvious than the EPO or some European courts. This may be related to the different procedures, particularly the reliance on live expert evidence in the UK compared with a more paper-based approach elsewhere. It should also be pointed out that it is difficult for patent offices to deal with the issue of obviousness at the examination stage in the same way as a civil court would do on hearing an opposition to the patent. Many successful post-grant oppositions are based on obviousness.

The basic principles applied in Europe are that the skilled man is assumed to possess common general knowledge and is also assumed to know of each piece of prior art (but no subsequent disclosure). He is therefore a highly theoretical construction. Commonly, expert testimony is led on this issue and the expert is asked to put herself in the position of the hypothetical skilled man. An example of an obvious invention is the English 'sausage machine case'.[142] It was held that there was no

---

[140] [1990] EPOR 514.

[141] The Board held that since the friction-reducing properties were not known to the public the invention was not made available. But the friction-reducing properties were available in the practical sense in every motor car using the prior additive. In the English courts at least, the claim appears unenforceable because the only difference between the prior use of the additive (which, it is axiomatic, the public can carry out as well after the patent as before) and the claim is effectively the purpose for which the additive is used, a wholly mental distinction. To find infringement one would have to postulate a mental element to the tort of patent infringement. The 'Gillette defence' which may be paraphrased as 'I am only doing what is disclosed in the prior art so either the claim doesn't cover what I am doing or it is not novel (and I don't care which)' would appear to be applicable in all cases unless a mental element is postulated.

[142] *Williams v Nye* (1890) 7 RPC 62.

inventiveness in combining a known machine for making sausage filling with a known machine for filling sausages since there was no difficulty in making the connection and it was obvious that the elements could be combined to produce an all-in-one machine if such was desired.

The approaches of the UK courts and the EPO to this issue have differed. The UK approach is summarized in the test postulated in the *Windsurfing*[143] case:

(a) First the court identifies the inventive concept in the claim in suit.

 (b) Next the court will assume the mantle of the normally skilled but unimaginative addressee in the art at the relevant date and will impute to him what was, at that date, common general knowledge.

(c) The court should then identify what, if any, differences exist between the matters cited as being known or used and the alleged invention.

(d) Finally the court has to decide whether, viewed without any knowledge of the alleged invention, those differences constitute steps which would have been obvious to the skilled man or whether they required any degree of invention.

The approach of the EPO has been to identify the technical problem to be overcome and consider the possibility of moving to a solution from the 'closest' piece of prior art. However, the Technical Board of Appeal has recognized that this approach is not appropriate in all cases, especially where there is no obvious closest piece of prior art, and that the EPC does not specify any method of finding obviousness (which is ultimately a question of fact). In *Alcan/Aluminium alloys*[144] it was pointed out that the problem-and-solution approach led to a step-by-step analysis that was based on hindsight and unreliable, although most EPO cases still use it. Cases on obviousness are strewn with admonitions about the care that must be taken to avoid hindsight and rejections of step-by-step arguments whereby each step on the road to the invention is painted as obvious whilst losing sight of the overall inventive contribution. Obviousness is and will remain a difficult question of fact to decide whatever theoretical frameworks it is placed into.

In *Bosch/Electronic computer components*[145] the audacious claim was made by an applicant that since prior documents cited against the application were written partly in program code and not 'ordinary language', the code listings therein should be ignored when considering obviousness. Thankfully for the sanity of commentators, this claim was rejected on the basis that the skilled man in that case would have been or have had access to a sufficiently skilled programmer to understand the prior citations. It was also held that the skilled man could in fact comprise a team of mixed skills.

The test is objective, and is sometimes stated as looking at what *could* the skilled man have done rather than *would* he have decided to do.[146] The inventiveness must

[143] *Windsurfing International v Tabur Marine (Great Britain) Ltd*[1985] RPC 59, 73–4.
[144] [1995] EPOR 501.            [145] [1995] EPOR 587.
[146] In *Perkins/Piston* [1996] EPOR 449 'would' is preferred over 'could', but on the basis that the skilled man is already assumed to be looking to improve the technology.

also be of a technical nature. Where the inventor spotted a previously unfulfilled market need for an improved corkscrew but, given the task of developing such a product, it would have been obvious how to achieve it from a technical point of view, the invention was obvious.[147]

It is the test of obviousness that ensures that mere clever programming will not found an invention. The skilled man is deemed to be a clever programmer, he is just not inventive—a different matter. This is why the patent claims discussed in this chapter have been addressed to principles of operation and organization of computers and data structures and have not recited detailed code. In a trivial sense many original programs are likely to be new, in that nothing identical has been written before, but few will be inventive.

In general, applications written by software houses for clients or for general sale are unlikely to involve anything patentable for reasons of obviousness. Inventive data structures or modes of operation may be involved in the programming tools used to create the products (for example, database 'engines' or image-manipulation tools) but any patents to those will belong to the owner of the tools not the writer of the end product. For most software developers therefore, limiting access to source code and enforcement of copyright are likely to be the main avenues for protection of their investment in production.

### 4.3.3 The need for disclosure

In return for the monopoly granted by the patent (see section 4.3.4), the applicant is required to disclose how the invention works. The specification must describe the invention claimed clearly and completely enough to enable the skilled man to put it into effect (article 83 of the EPC; Patents Act 1977, s 14(3)). It does not have to do more, so detailed design issues need not be addressed. One reason why the drawings to patent specifications can appear old-fashioned and unworkable is because they are there to teach principles, not to give away detailed designs.

In the case of computer-related inventions, what this means is that full code listings for programs may not need to be given. Schematics or flow diagrams may suffice to teach the principles involved. The comments made about what is assumed of the relevant skilled man in relation to obviousness apply equally here.

### 4.3.4 The rights granted by a patent

Article 64 of the EPC states that holders of European patents should have the same rights as holders of national patents. A patent grants the exclusive rights to the commercial exploitation of the invention claimed. Thus the manufacture, importa-

---

[147] *Hallen Company and Another v Brabantia (UK) Ltd, The Financial Times*, 24 October 1990, CA, approving the judgment of Aldous J at [1989] RPC 307. This approach was also taken in *Esswein/Automatic programmer* [1991] EPOR 121 where the 'invention' consisted of the appreciation that many consumers only required three programmes on their washing machines!

tion, sale or use in the course of trade of products falling within the claims of a patent may be prevented by the patent owner.[148] In the case of patents for processes, it is an infringement to use the process or to dispose of, use or import any product obtained directly by means of the process. A detailed description of the various ways of infringing a UK patent is set out in section 60 of the Patents Act 1977.

Two immediate contrasts can be drawn with the remedy for breach of copyright:

(a) Copying is irrelevant, as is knowledge of the patent (although absence of the latter can provide a seller with a defence to a claim for damages): the monopoly is in this sense absolute.

(b) Private and experimental use is permitted[149] so end-users of products who do not use them in the course of a trade (ie, consumers) cannot infringe patents—not even when purchasing the product from a retailer (who would be an infringer). But note that where there is dual purpose use, that will infringe.

It is necessary to provide a word of warning concerning use in the course of trade versus private or experimental use. It has been held[150] that experiments may have an ultimate commercial end in view and still fall within the exception, but that experiments to obtain regulatory approval or to demonstrate to a third party that a product works are not covered by the exception. It is clear from this that if a product or software forming part of an invention is investigated to find out how it works, for example, by disassembling program code, that will not infringe any patent.[151] But as steps are made towards a commercial product, infringement is likely to occur prior to launch or beta-testing.

It is also an infringement for a person to supply or offer to supply 'any of the means, relating to an essential element of the invention, for putting the invention into effect when he knows, or it is obvious to a reasonable person in the circumstances, that those means are suitable for putting, and are intended to put, the invention into effect in the United Kingdom'.[152] This is known as 'indirect infringement' and may be of considerable relevance to computer-related inventions. If a patent doesn't cover a program as such or in the form of a recorded medium such as a disk, suppliers of disks (or providers of services from which the code may be downloaded) may nevertheless be liable if the code or data on the disk forms an essential element of the invention. A possible let-out is that if the means supplied is a 'staple commercial product' then for there to be infringement the supply must be for the purpose of inducing the person supplied to do an infringing act.[153] 'Staple commercial product' is not defined but it is submitted that whereas it would include a blank disk or ROM, it would not include one on which a particular program or data had been recorded.

---

[148] Patents Act 1977, s 60(1).   [149] Ibid, s 60(5).
[150] *Monsanto Co v Stauffer Chemical Co* [1985] RPC 515.
[151] cf the position under copyright law discussed in Chapter 5.
[152] Patents Act 1977, s 60(2).   [153] Ibid, s 60(3).

This still leaves the question of how to decide when a product or process falls within the scope of a claim of a patent. This is the problem of construing the claims of a patent. Article 69 of the EPC and the Protocol thereto provide a general test to be applied, but from this apparently very different tests have grown. In the UK the approach of purposive construction originally applied under the Patents Act 1949 has been used under the 1977 Act as well, and has been held (by the UK courts) to comply with the EPC. Other EPC countries adopt what is known as the 'doctrine of equivalents'. The former is based on an analysis of what the patentee intended to claim (and not to claim) as disclosed in the whole specification, whereas in the latter test the invention is identified and its equivalents may be considered infringing even if on a strict analysis of the wording of the claims there would be no infringement. There has been much debate concerning whether the UK approach really does comply with the EPC and how different in practice the two tests are (despite coming at the problem from different angles, they do seem to converge on detailed analysis).[154] Whatever test is adopted, it does not alter the fact that careful drafting of the claim is the key to obtaining a commercially useful, easily enforceable patent.

The remedies for infringement of patent are similar to those available for other intellectual property rights ('IPRs'), that is damages (based on lost profits) or an account of profits earned by the infringer, an injunction to restrain further infringement and delivery up of infringing items. The full range of pre-emptive interlocutory remedies (early injunctions, search orders and so on) are available in patent actions in accordance with the normal principles. (A detailed consideration of these remedies is beyond the scope of this chapter.)

### 4.3.5  Duration, revocation and amendment

Under the EPC patents last for twenty years from the date of the full application, although priority can be claimed from a filing made up to a year prior to that. In the case of US patents filed prior to 8 June 1995 the term ran from the date of issue of the patent but was for seventeen years. For subsequently filed applications the position is the same as the European position. This was necessary to take account of the TRIPS agreement[155] which provides for a degree of uniformity between patent laws.

The validity of patents can generally be challenged after grant in the course of infringement proceedings or upon application by an opponent. In the UK the court hears such applications in the course of infringement proceedings, although in some jurisdictions matters of validity are considered by the Patent Office in separate proceedings. In the UK a patentee can apply to amend a patent after grant subject to certain safeguards. This is generally undertaken so as to narrow down the patent to give it a better chance of survival in the face of an opposition to validity.

---

[154] See the *Assidoman* and *Kastner* cases, n 75 above.
[155] Part of the GATT, discussed further at section 4.5 below.

### 4.3.6  Ownership, transmission and employee inventions

The EPC states that the inventor should be the first owner of any patent, but leaves rules regarding the ownership of inventions by employees to the laws of the EPC state in which the invention is made. In the UK the basic rule is that inventions made in the course of employment belong to the employer,[156] although there are provisions for compensation to be provided to employee-inventors.[157]

UK employers should note the following potential pitfalls:

(a) If an employee whose normal duties do not include programming or computer-related developments and who has not been specifically assigned a computer-related task makes a computer-related invention, the employer may not own it.

(b) Workers who are on contract (not strictly employees in the employment law sense), will own any inventions they make pursuant to a contract unless the contract specifically provides, by express or implied term, for ownership of inventions (which of course it should!).

Patents can be assigned and licensed like any other right, but assignments are only effective if in writing. The national patent offices of the EPC states have systems for the registration of transfers of ownership and generally registration is necessary for an assignment to be fully effective. After grant, a European patent is no different from a portfolio of national patents and the administrative requirements of each national system must be complied with. The separate national patents can be disposed of or licensed separately.

## 4.4  WHY EXCLUDE ANYTHING FROM PATENTABILITY?

A great deal of intellectual effort has been expended in addressing the more theoretical aspects of the issue of IP protection for computer software. Some of the main arguments that are put forward in relation to patentability are discussed below.

### 4.4.1  Which form of protection?

It has been questioned whether patent protection (as opposed to copyright protection, some other protection or no protection at all) is the right form of protection for computer programs or computer software.

It will be noted that this chapter has tended to use the rather cumbersome expression 'computer-related inventions'. The reason for this is that by their nature patents tend to protect matters of fundamental structure and functional features rather than the details of how things are written, and thus will only protect some

---

[156] Patents Act 1977, s 39.     [157] Ibid, ss 40–3.

aspects of software.[158] By contrast, copyright tends to protect the actual way a program is written and the actual data recorded in a data structure (as well as only preventing copying). This is not to say that there can be no overlap. There is no rule which says that a description of the function of a program that is sufficiently brief and general to form the substance of a patent claim would not amount to a substantial part of that program for the purposes of copyright infringement.[159] But if there is overlap it will be at the margins.

The distinction between patent and copyright protection is easily illustrated by the following example. A document setting out a novel chemical process would attract copyright protection, but that protection would protect the document against copying, not the process from being carried out. A patent for the process would prevent it from being carried out but not from being written about or broadcast. Here there is no difficulty in separating the creative literary content from the inventive technical content. In general, prior to the introduction of computers and digital methods of recording data, literary and artistic works were easily identifiable, as were technical inventions, and problems in classifying something as one or the other were rare (although they did arise).

The work of the programmer or computer technologist can fall into both the 'technical' and 'creative' camps. Whilst the chemist of the preceding paragraph clearly utilized artistic literary skill to write out the instructions and technical skill to develop the process, in programming the separation of the two is more problematical (indeed it is a similar problem to that addressed by the EPO when it looks for 'technical content'). Programming clearly involves an understanding of numbers and logic and some sympathy with the technical restraints imposed by the physical apparatus on which the program is to run, which are abilities we associate with the technologist. Yet it may also require the creation of things whose performance cannot be accurately measured and an understanding of the psychology and reactions, likes and dislikes of the user of the computer on which the program will eventually run. These are abilities we associate with people in the creative trades such as copy-writing, design and publishing.

Separating the 'technical' aspects of a piece of program code from its 'artistic' elements may not be an easy or even meaningful process. Nevertheless the patent system allows for principles to be extracted and afforded one form of protection whereas the copyright system gives protection to other aspects of the programmer's work. It is not sensible to take any area of human creative endeavour and arbitrarily say 'this should be protected by patents not copyright' or vice versa. In appropriate circumstances both a patent and copyright will protect different aspects of a computer programmer's work.

---

[158] Because, as we have seen, the detailed working out of the principles may be difficult or time-consuming, but is unlikely to be inventive.

[159] This is to apply the UK concept of copyright infringement. Perhaps the idea/expression test favoured in the US is more likely to preclude the taking of this type of feature from ever amounting to copyright infringement. See, further, Chapter 6.

### 4.4.2 Scientific consistency

Against a restrictive approach can be ranged arguments based upon considerations of the technical reality of the situation. According to these, the problem with trying to exclude programs from patentability is that a sharp dividing line is sought where none exists. Most involved in the computer industry would say they knew what was a program and what was not, but a computer program is a disembodied concept, whereas a patent claim must define the scope of an industrially useful monopoly. Knowing what a program is does not help to define the limits of patentability.

When a computer runs a program, all or parts of the program code are copied from the computer's hard disk and stored in the computer's temporary memory. As the program runs, instructions are fetched from the memory and executed by the processor, and the computer then goes on to execute further instructions. Execution of instructions may involve the creation or transposition of data in the computer's memory or the performance of input/output operations to the screen, a printer or a hard disk. All these operations occur inside the computer's integrated circuits as changes in the electrical values at various points. Data pathways are physically opened and closed and electrical circuits re-configured by the act of running the program.

Instead of being loaded into temporary memory from a disk, some programs are permanently held in ROM chips on the computer's circuit boards. They stay in place and are readable even when the computer is turned off. These programs are often low-level routines dealing with matters of the internal operation of the computer. Some program routines may be stored on the processor chip itself and built into it at the time of manufacture, so that they are embodied in the way the circuit elements of the chip are arranged and interconnected. These would deal with complex arithmetical instructions such as division and so on. The distinction between 'hardware' and 'software' is not sharp, there is a continuum. And however a program is executed, it results in a computer that is physically, electrically configured in a special way so as to operate that program.[160] So, the argument goes, there is no scientific basis for distinguishing computer-related inventions from those relating to bits of bent metal and plastic.

But it can also be argued that a solely scientifically driven view misses the point about patents. Patents are about monopolies for inventions that are useful to people. It is generally recognized that running a computer program produces a physical change in a computer. We have seen that both in the US and in Europe, questions of patentability of computer-related inventions are dealt with by applying general principles that apply

---

[160] It is interesting to note that this congruity between program and circuit is mirrored in the field of UK copyright law, where electrical circuit diagrams have been viewed as literary works (*Anacon Corporation Ltd v Environmental Research Technology Ltd* [1994] FSR 659), just as programs are. But this does not suggest that excluding 'electrical circuits' from patentability would provide an answer to the problems discussed. Indeed one can see that precisely the same problems of what amounts to an electric circuit 'as such', and whether in any event the claim really relates to a mental process will present themselves.

equally to non-computer applications. It is difficult to argue that computer-related inventions are being discriminated against in any way.

### 4.4.3 Upholding the basic principles of patent law

The 'bargain' theory of patent protection has already been mentioned. The purpose of patent protection in accordance with this theory is to grant a monopoly which will be commercially useful to the patentee whilst making available practically useful things and processes to society at large. Theories, scientific discoveries, mathematical formulae and artistic works are not useful in this practical sense although their consideration might affect our quality of life in the spiritual or intellectual sense.

The notion that the scope of patent protection granted should in some way reflect the scope of what the patent teaches people to do (referred to above) satisfies a basic consideration of fairness yet is inconsistent with allowing patent protection for mere discoveries. If a discovery or mathematical relationship were to be patentable in some way, then all industrial developments building on it (whether foreseen by the original 'inventor' or totally unexpected) would be covered by the scope of the claim. There are obvious moral and economic arguments to be mounted against the grant of excessively wide monopolies of this type. The general rule has emerged therefore that a principle or discovery must be applied to a practical purpose in some way for patent protection to be possible, and reasonable protection will be given to that particular application. Thus useful things, machines or processes designed to exploit scientific discoveries or mathematical relationships are patentable provided they satisfy the various other tests for patentability.

It is not clear that the above principle is violated by excluding or not excluding particular things since, as we have seen, any exclusionary rule will have to be applied to a patent claim and the question 'what is this claim actually for?' asked. At this stage, questions of the fundamental nature of patents come into play. It is here that differences of approach between the US and the countries that follow it and Europe become apparent. The convergence (in some respects) between the approaches adopted in the two jurisdictions over the past decade has served only to highlight the key difference: the European principle that patent protection should only cover technical advances and the absence of such a principle in the US. The issue is of a more fundamental nature than the question 'should computer programs be patentable?'.[161]

It can be pointed out that the requirements of novelty, unobviousness and sufficiency of teaching will be adequate to ensure that unwarranted and restrictive monopolies are not granted and that exclusions from patentability are not necessary. But as we have seen in Europe, since fundamental issues of what should be patented inform decisions on those topics as well as on questions of patentable subject matter

---

[161] The answer to that question, from both a US or European standpoint is 'yes, sometimes' or, perhaps, 'that's not the relevant question'.

*per se*, this approach cannot help resolve those very same fundamental issues. It is submitted that questions as to the scope of what may be patented are matters of policy and recourse to legal doctrine should not be made when answering them. Thus the US position stems from the absence of restrictive words in the relevant provisions of the US Constitution, whereas the European position derives from the identification of a requirement for technical content as an underlying principle behind the EPC. The legal doctrines have developed from those principles

### 4.4.4 Economic and social expedience

Perhaps the most sensible basis for deciding these issues is simply to ask 'what do we actually want?' There is a body of opinion that all software should be free from IP restraints (understandably, many computer users subscribe to this view). Yet the software industry is an industry like any other and if IPRs are deemed desirable to reward invention and protect creative skill and labour in other industries, why make exceptions?

Having said that, it is not clear to what extent patents are a real commercial force in the computer industry (other than in relation to definite hardware elements) in the way that they are in some other industries. The pace of technological development will clearly affect the commercial lifetime of many computer-related inventions and the time involved in obtaining a patent may make it commercially pointless to apply. It is also worth repeating that patent protection will not be relevant to most new computer programs regardless of which patent system protection is sought under.

As noted below, considerations of competitiveness between trade areas can also influence IP policy. The perception of such pressures is often that they dictate strong IPRs, although in some areas of business and industry a loose regime is more conducive to innovation and wealth creation. As with other IPRs, there has to be a balance: make the rights too strong and development is stifled; make them too weak and it will not be promoted. The fact that Congress passed the American Inventors Protection Act perhaps indicates unease at the possibly stifling effect of the current regime of patentability in the US. In addition, the tenor of the recently proposed EU draft Directive on the Patentability of Computer-Related Inventions takes a more balanced view than earlier papers where the 'strong IP: good, weak IP: bad' assumption prevailed. The policy pendulum may have reached the end of its swing.

### 4.5 THE FUTURE

The position of computer-related inventions under US law has stabilized at what might be viewed as an extreme position. The difference of approach in Europe has caused concern amongst European commentators and legislators. In 1997 the European Commission published its Green Paper on *The Community Patent and the*

*Patent System in Europe.*[162] This sought wide-ranging comment, including on how or whether to proceed with a Community Patent and on the issue of patent protection for computer-related inventions.

Following the consultation period, the Commission has issued a Communication[163] indicating its intended follow-up measures. These include:

(a) There is a real need for a Community Patent. This is to be implemented by a Regulation, not under the existing Treaty provisions, which it now appears will never be implemented.

(b) The consultation process revealed that the current position concerning legal protection for computer programs 'did not provide sufficient transparency', and that there were national differences in interpretation within the EPC area. The Commission has concluded that the difficulties in obtaining protection for some computer-related inventions in Europe when compared to the United States is damaging to European economic interests, and a more liberal regime should be put in place. It will issue a draft Directive on the patentability of computer programs (with which all EU states will have to comply) and has recognized that article 52(2)(c)[164] of the EPC will have to be 'modified' so that the EPC does not conflict with the duty of states to comply with the Directive.

(c) The Commission also concluded that the perception of Europeans is that European patent protection for computer-related inventions is less widely available than is actually the case. According to their statistics, the bulk of what they refer to as 'software patents' in Europe are held by non-Europeans.

Following up this intention, the Commission published two draft pieces of legislation relating to patents. The first, a proposed Regulation on the Community Patent, proposes that Community-wide patent protection is achieved by the EU acceding to the EPC and there being a 'symbiosis' between the two systems (EPC and Regulation). The Regulation proposes the establishment of a European Intellectual Property Court to deal with infringement disputes (other than remedies) for the purposes of ensuring harmonization. This proposal acknowledges that the existing Community Patent Convention will now never see implementation. It is not certain when (or indeed if) the proposals will reach implementation and it is understood that disagreements have arisen between Member States over languages, translations and

---

[162] COM (97) 314 Final.

[163] 'Communication from the Commission dated 5 February 1999 to the Council, the European Parliament and the Economic and Social Committee—Promoting innovation through patents—the follow-up to the Green Paper on the Community Patent and the Patent System in Europe' COM (99) 42, also published at EPO 01 4/1999 201.

[164] This is what excludes from protection 'schemes . . . and programs for computers'. In fact, article 52(2)(a), which excludes mathematical methods, could also prove a stumbling block. As we have seen, the amendments will have to make it clear that a requirement for a 'technical contribution' is not necessary if the position under the EPC is to approximate to that in the US. This will involve following 35 USC s 101 and defining what *is* patentable rather than what is not.

so on (such differences were eventually overcome in relation to the Community Trade Mark Regulation, but not quickly).

The second, a proposed Directive on the patentability of computer-related inventions, essentially follows the *Pensions*[165] approach in focusing on the nature of the inventive step in enforcing the requirement for technical content. If Member States were to adopt *Pensions* in their national laws, implementation would not appear to require any further changes.

This activity in the field of patents at EU level has been mirrored in the European Patent Organization. An amended version of the EPC has been agreed, but not ratified, by the current EPC states. This is a comprehensive updating of the text and of particular relevance to this Chapter is an amendment to article 52:

European patents shall be granted for any inventions, in all fields of technology, provided that they are new, involve an inventive step and are susceptible of industrial application.

The words 'in all fields of technology' being the substantive addition. The list of excluded things in article 52(2) remains unaltered. This wording mirrors that of the TRIPs agreement. The full name of the TRIPs agreement is the 'Agreement on Trade-Related Aspects of Intellectual Property Rights', agreed as part of the Uruguay round of the GATT ('General Agreement on Tariffs and Trade') and enforced via the World Trade Organization ('WTO'). The EC and United States, among many others, are signatories to this agreement. Under TRIPs broad harmonization of the scope of patent rights is provided for. Article 27.1 states that '. . . patents shall be available for any inventions, whether products or processes, in all fields of technology, provided that they are new, involve an inventive step and are capable of industrial application . . . patents shall be available and patent rights enjoyable without discrimination as to the field of technology'. US lawyers will point out that 'capable of industrial application' may be taken to mean the same as 'useful', whilst Europeans may point out that the reference to 'fields of technology' means that, despite the fact that TRIPs does not apparently allow for specific exclusions, the European approach of limiting the scope of the exclusions to non-technical matter means that the European approach is also compliant.

The decision in *IBM's Application*[166] recognized the possibility of conflict with the TRIPs agreement. Whilst finding that it was not possible for the EPC to be reinterpreted in the light of TRIPs, the Technical Board in that case did arrive at an interpretation of the EPC which is much more in accordance with TRIPs than the previous position. In addition, the Technical Board in that case appears to have accepted the Commission's view that the European patent system must compete on the world patent stage. The following extract from the decision indicates, perhaps, the dawn of a more flexible approach which is responsive to the rapid changes in technology:

---

[165] See section 4.2.2.3 above.     [166] [1999] RPC 563.

2.5 The appellant also referred to current practice in the U.S. and Japanese patent offices. The Board has taken due notice of these developments, but wishes to emphasise that the situation under these two legal systems (U.S., JP) differs greatly from that under the EPC in that it is only the EPC which contains an exclusion such as the one in Article 52(2) and (3).

2.6 Nevertheless these developments represent a useful indication of modem trends. In the Board's opinion they may contribute to the further highly desirable (world-wide) harmonisation of patent law.[167]

In parallel with the drive towards harmonization from the EU, the European Patent Organization has also been working on reducing the problems that arise from separate national interpretations of the Convention.[168] A working party has been set up to develop a protocol for European patent litigation and plans for a European patent judiciary.

The European Commission has published a proposal[169] for a Directive regarding Utility Models. Some EU states grant these, which are similar to patents but with sometimes less stringent novelty and obviousness criteria. In some states they apply only to three-dimensional forms. The preferred approach is a patent-like system with a similar range of excluded areas to that of the EPC, a ten-year term, a lower inventiveness threshold and with Community-wide novelty. It is therefore possible that many computer-related developments would become registrable under the rights introduced or amended pursuant to any eventual Directive.

---

[167] [1999] RPC 563.

[168] At a diplomatic level, the countries taking part in EU policy debates and those participating in the European Patent Organisation are to a considerable extent the same. Thus although the EU and EPO are separate organizations, similar policy objectives are likely to be pursued by both.

[169] 'Amended proposal for a European Parliament and Council Directive approximating the legal arrangements for the protection of inventions by utility model' COM (99) 0309 final.

# 5

# COPYRIGHT

*Christopher Millard*

## 5.1 INTRODUCTION

### 5.1.1 The nature of copyright

Notwithstanding its considerable and ever-increasing significance to business, intellectual property ('IP') continues to be one of the law's more obscure and esoteric fields. In popular parlance, confusion often reigns and talk of copyrighting an invention or patenting a trade mark is not uncommon. Such misunderstandings are, perhaps, not surprising given the highly technical nature of much of the law in this area and the scope for overlaps and conflicts between the various rights.

Nevertheless, the effective protection and exploitation of intellectual property rights ('IPRs') is crucial to the success, and in some cases the survival, of a growing number of businesses. Nowhere is this more strikingly the case than in the computer industry. For example, the right to manufacture, sell, buy or use a complex product such as a computer system comprising hardware and software may depend on licences of any or all of patents, copyrights, design rights, know-how and trade marks. Similarly, the primary assets of a software house will usually be its copyright works. The focus of this chapter will be on copyright. Other IPRs are covered elsewhere in this book.

What then is copyright? Copyright is, in essence, a right given to authors or creators of 'works', such as books, films or computer programs, to control the copying or other exploitation of such works. In marked contrast to patent rights, copyright begins automatically on the creation of a 'work' without the need for compliance with any formalities. The only prerequisites for protection, which apply to all works, are that the work must be of a type in which copyright can subsist, and that either the author is a 'qualifying person', or the work has been published or broadcast in an appropriate manner. In the case of certain types of works, including literary works such as books and computer programs, the work must also be 'original' and it must be 'recorded' in some form (for example, written down or stored in computer memory).

In addition to controlling the making of copies, the owner of copyright in a work has the exclusive right to control publication, performance, broadcasting and the making of adaptations of the work. In certain cases, the author, director or commissioner of a work may be entitled to exercise certain 'moral rights' which may include the right to be identified with a work and to object to distortion or unjustified treatment of the work.

Where any of the various exclusive rights that collectively make up copyright in a work have been exercised without permission, civil remedies may be available to the owner or author. In certain cases criminal sanctions may also be brought to bear, principally where copyright is being infringed with a view to commercial gain. Most of these concepts and terms are discussed in more detail in the rest of this chapter.

### 5.1.2 Evolution of UK copyright law

English copyright law has a history going back five centuries and has been regulated by statute for almost three.[1] The first modern copyright law, the Copyright Act 1709, was an attempt to balance the interests of authors and publishers in the case of the leading-edge technology of the day, the printing press. Technology has since moved on and so has the law. The two have not, however, always been in step. Notwithstanding regular piecemeal amendment of the law, the gap between copyright law and new media has periodically had to be closed, or at least narrowed, by means of a radical overhaul of the law. Increased sophistication in the means for commercial exploitation of the economic value of copyright has been a particularly powerful catalyst for change. Cable and satellite broadcasting of films and other works, and the distribution of computer programs and other works in digital form are examples.

A major realignment occurred with the enactment of the Copyright, Designs and Patents Act 1988 ('the CDPA 1988').[2] Its predecessor in the copyright field, the

---

[1] For an interesting historical review, see Stephen Breyer, 'The Uneasy Case for Copyright: A Study of Copyright in Books, Photocopies and Computer Programs' (1970) 84 Harv L Rev 281.

[2] Royal assent, 15 November 1988. Unless otherwise indicated, references to sections in this chapter are to those of the CDPA 1988.

Copyright Act 1956 ('the 1956 Act'), had been the subject both of detailed reform discussions[3] and temporary piecemeal amendments[4] for half of its time on the statute book. The CDPA 1988, most of the provisions of which came into force on 1 August 1989,[5] represents an attempt to start again with a clean slate. On this slate are written both a restatement of the general principles of copyright, and also various sets of rules to deal with specific types of copyright work and their commercial exploitation. Although there is considerable scope for criticizing the CDPA 1988 at a detailed level, on the whole it is a far more coherent, comprehensive and accessible statement of the law than the statutes that it replaced.

### 5.1.3 The Copyright, Designs and Patents Act 1988

The CDPA 1988, as its name suggests, does not deal solely with copyright. It established a significant new property right, known as 'design right'; the law relating to registered designs was changed; changes were made to patent and trade-mark law; and the law relating to performers' protection was reformed and restated.[6]

Although judges have provided some guidance on interpreting the CDPA 1988, there remain many areas that have not yet been considered by the courts. In the meantime, some pointers can be obtained from court decisions based on the 1956 Act (as amended), and indeed on earlier statutes, such as the Copyright Act 1911. The extent to which reliance can be placed on such old decisions is, unfortunately, not at all clear. This is because section 172 of the CDPA 1988, given the marginal note 'General provisions as to construction', provides:

(1) This Part restates and amends the law of copyright, that is, the provisions of the Copyright Act 1956, as amended.

(2) A provision of this Part which corresponds to a provision of the previous law shall not be construed as departing from the previous law merely because of a change of expression.

(3) Decisions under the previous law may be referred to for the purpose of establishing whether a provision of this Part departs from the previous law, or otherwise for establishing the true construction of this Part.

---

[3] A committee set up in 1973 under the chairmanship of Mr Justice Whitford reported in 1977 that the time had come for a general revision of the 1956 Act; see *Copyright and Designs Law: Report of the Committee to Consider the Law on Copyright and Designs* (Cmnd 6732) (HMSO, 1977). This was followed by two Green Papers which did little to advance the reform process: *Reform of the Law Relating to Copyright, Designs and Performers' Protection* (Cmnd 8302) (HMSO, 1981) and *Intellectual Property Rights and Innovation* (Cmnd 9117) (HMSO, 1983). The publication in 1986 of a White Paper, *Intellectual Property and Innovation* (Cmnd 9712) (HMSO, 1986), set the stage for a general overhaul of the law.

[4] Design Copyright Act 1968; Copyright Act 1956 (Amendment) Act 1982; Copyright (Amendment) Act 1983; Cable and Broadcasting Act 1984; Copyright (Computer Software) Amendment Act 1985.

[5] The Copyright, Designs and Patents Act 1988 (Commencement No 1) Order 1989, SI 1989/816.

[6] For a helpful introduction to the Act as a whole, which incorporates the full text of the statute, see G Dworkin and R D Taylor, *Blackstone's Guide to the Copyright, Designs and Patents Act 1988* (Blackstone Press, 1998). For a more detailed analysis, see H Laddie, P Prescott and M Vitoria, *The Modern Law of Copyright and Designs*, 3rd edn (Butterworths, 2000).

Each part of this section seems to introduce a layer of confusion. The first subsection states that the CDPA 1988 is both a restatement and an amendment of the old law. The second provides that a change in language does not necessarily indicate a change in meaning although, by implication, it may do. The third suggests that we look to court decisions based on the 1956 Act to see whether there has in fact been a change in meaning and generally to assist in understanding the new Act. Thus, even if it can be shown that a particular provision of the CDPA 1988 'corresponds' to a provision of the 1956 Act, the fact that the provision has been redrafted in different language may or may not indicate anything about its meaning. It is particularly difficult to see how cases decided under the 1956 Act could illuminate Parliament's intentions in 1988 in including, excluding or substituting specific words in the CDPA 1988. There is no reference to the status, if any, of cases decided under older statutes such as the Copyright Act 1911. Taken as a whole, section 172 gives advocates plenty of scope for argument over semantics, and leaves courts with considerable discretion as to whether to rely on or to disregard particular precedents as they seek to interpret and apply the new law.

### 5.1.4  EU Directives and their implementation in the UK

Differences in the nature and scope of the IPRs available in the fifteen EU Member States have frequently given rise to trade barriers. In seeking to limit the effects of such restrictions, the European Commission and the European Court have drawn distinctions between the existence and the exercise of IPRs. Ownership of an IPR is not inherently anticompetitive, indeed the Treaty of Rome sanctions import and export restrictions that can be justified as being 'for the protection of industrial or commercial property'.[7] However, attempts to use IPRs as a means of carving up the internal market are vulnerable to challenge under the Treaty. According to the 'exhaustion of rights' doctrine developed by the European Court, goods that have been put on the market lawfully in one of the Member States by or with the consent of the owner, must be permitted to circulate freely throughout the European Union. Of particular significance to the computer industry is the availability and scope of copyright protection for software products. In June 1988 the Commission published a Green Paper entitled *Copyright and the Challenge of Technology*.[8] In that discussion document the Commission inclined towards the view that copyright is the most appropriate form of protection for computer programs and should provide the foundation for a Directive on software protection. Comments were, however, invited on a number of issues relating to the precise nature and scope of the exclusive rights that Member States should be required to grant software owners.

Following a period of consultation that ended in December 1988, a Directive on the Legal Protection of Computer Programs ('the Software Directive') was adopted

---

[7] Treaty of Rome, art 30.      [8] COM (88) 172 final.

by the Council of Ministers on 14 May 1991.[9] Legislation to implement the Software Directive in the UK, the Copyright (Computer Programs) Regulations 1992,[10] was enacted in time for the implementation deadline of 1 January 1993. Specific aspects of the Software Directive and UK implementing legislation are discussed later in this chapter.

The EU has also adopted a Directive on the legal protection of databases.[11] The copyright provisions in the Directive only deal with the structure of databases (recital 15 and art 5) and not the contents of databases.[12] The contents of databases remain governed by national copyright laws and a novel and separate property right introduced by the Directive, the so-called '*sui generis*' or database right, which exists independently of any copyright (art 7(4)) (see, further, Chapter 7). The Directive effectively creates three tiers of protection: databases may contain contents that are copyrighted, the contents may also attract the *sui generis* protection and the database itself may also be protected. The Copyright and Rights in Databases Regulations 1997[13] implemented the Directive in the UK by amending the CDPA 1988 to include a new test of originality for copyright databases[14] and introducing the *sui generis* database right.

The 'Conditional Access' Directive,[15] which was implemented in the UK on 28 May 2000[16] by the inclusion of a new section 297A in the CDPA 1988, requires Member States to prohibit the supply of devices (including software) for circumventing technical means for limiting entry to protected, and other conditional access, services.

A Directive on the harmonization of certain aspects of copyright and related rights in the information society[17] (the 'Information Society Copyright Directive') came into force on 22 June 2001. The objectives of this Directive are to:

(a) ensure that copyright-protected works enjoy adequate protection across the Member States thereby responding to the challenges of new technology and the Information Society;

(b) facilitate cross-border trade in copyrighted goods and services relevant to the Information Society, including online and physical carriers (for example, CDs);

(c) protect technological systems for the identification and protection of works; and

(d) ratify international treaties on the protection of authors, performers and phonogram producers, agreed in December 1996 by the World Intellectual Property Organisation ('WIPO') (see section 5.1.5 below).[18]

---

[9] 91/250/EEC, OJ L122, 17 May 1991, p 42.                                    [10] SI 1992/3233.
[11] 96/9/EC, OJ L77, 27 March 1996.              [12] See the Berne Convention, art 2(5).
[13] SI 1997/3032, entry into force 1 January 1998.
[14] By reason of the selection or arrangement it must be its author's 'own intellectual creation' (reg 6, inserting s 3A(1)). See, further, section 5.2.1.3 below.
[15] 98/84/EC, adopted 20 November 1998.                                        [16] SI 2000/1175.
[17] Directive 2001/29/EC.              [18] See, further, S Saxby, 'CLSR Briefing' (1999) 15(5) CLSR 355.

The Information Society Copyright Directive was due to be implemented by Member States by 22 December 2002. At the time of writing, the UK had already missed the deadline, although draft regulations to amend the CDPA 1988 have been published for consultation.[19] It is envisaged that the amendments to the current legislation which are necessary for implementation of the Information Society Copyright Directive will relate to:

(a) the introduction of performers' exclusive rights (as opposed to remuneration rights) to control 'on demand' transmissions of recordings of their performances;[20]

(b) amendments to the acts permitted in relation to copyright works;[21]

(c) amendments to extend legal protection for technological systems which protect copyright;[22]

(d) the introduction of new provisions protecting electronic rights management information;[23] and

(e) reinforcement of certain sanctions and remedies, including the introduction of a new offence of communicating a copyright work to the public with the knowledge that by so doing copyright in the work will be infringed.[24]

### 5.1.5 International copyright conventions

International copyright conventions have had significant effects upon the development of copyright law. The Universal Copyright Convention[25] and the Berne Convention for the Protection of Literary and Artistic Works[26] oblige Member States to provide the same rights to nationals of another Member State as they provide to their own authors (the so-called 'national treatment' rule). The TRIPS Agreement[27] provides for national treatment[28] and most-favoured-nation treatment. The latter requires Member States to apply immediately and unconditionally any advantage, favour, privilege or immunity granted by a Member State to nationals of any other country.

---

[19] The Patent Office has indicated that it intended to implement the Information Society Copyright Directive by 31 March 2003 at the latest ('A Progress Report on UK Implementation of the Copyright Directive' (2001/29/EC) 19 November 2002). The target was not met.

[20] Information Society Copyright Directive, art 3(2).          [21] Ibid, art 5.

[22] Ibid, art 6.          [23] Ibid, art 7.          [24] Ibid, art 8.

[25] 6 September 1952, 6 UST 2713 (1955), TIAS No 3324, 216 UNTS 132 (effective 16 September 1955) ('Geneva Act'); revised 24 July 1971, 25 UST 1341 (1974), TIAS No 7868, 943 UNTS 178 (effective 10 July 1971) ('Paris Act'); which requires contracting states to give adequate and effective protection to the rights of authors and other copyright proprietors of literary, scientific and artistic work (art 1).

[26] 9 September 1886; Paris Act of 24 July 1971, as amended on 28 September 1979.

[27] Trade Related Aspects of Intellectual Property Rights, concluded under the Uruguay Round of the General Agreement on Tariffs and Trade, Final Act Embodying the Results of the Uruguay Round of Trade Negotiations, Marrakech, 15 April 1994.

[28] Subject to the exceptions under the Paris Convention (1967) on Industrial Property, the Berne Convention (1971), the Rome Convention (1961) on Sound Recordings, Producers and Performers and the Washington Treaty (1989) on Integrated Circuits.

The TRIPS Agreement provides that, under the Berne Convention, the object and source codes of a computer program are to be protected as literary works (TRIPS, art 10). Specific rights are provided for under TRIPS, such as the author's right to authorize and prohibit the commercial rental of a computer program, except where the computer program is not the 'essential object' of the rental (TRIPS, art 11). The TRIPS Agreement provides that, in accordance with the Washington Treaty (1989) on the protection of integrated circuits, semiconductor chips are to be protected (TRIPS, art 36). Infringement of integrated circuits, the term of copyright protection, compulsory licensing and the treatment of innocent infringers are also addressed (TRIPS, arts 37 and 38). In relation to databases, the compilation of these works is to be protected by copyright provided that it constitutes an 'intellectual creation' (TRIPS, art 10(2)).[29] This contrasts with the position in the UK up to 31 December 1997 (prior to the Copyright and Rights in Databases Regulations 1997), in that 'originality' was sufficient to establish copyright protection (see section 5.2.1.3 below).

The WIPO Copyright Treaty supplements the Berne Convention (see art 1) and applies the following 'traditional' copyright rules to the digital environment:

(a) the reproduction right (as set out in article 9 of the Berne Convention),[30] particularly in the context of the use and storage of works in digital form;

(b) the fair use principle for online communications, whereby the making of a limited number of copies of a protected work is permitted provided the 'legitimate interests' of the copyright owner are not harmed (which is generally limited to use of a non-commercial nature);[31] and

(c) the right of making available to the public, which rests with the rightholder.

The WIPO Copyright Treaty provides for protection against the circumvention of technological protection devices for controlled access to copyrighted material (art 11) and against the removal of electronic rights management information without authorization (art 12). The following provisions of the TRIPS Agreement are restated: computer programs are to be protected as literary works within the meaning of article 2 of the Berne Convention;[32] and compilations of data or other material may be protected by copyright where they are intellectual creations[33] (but the protection does not extend to the material contained in the database[34]).

The treaty on intellectual property in databases initially proposed as part of the WIPO Diplomatic Conference of 20 December 1996, which was to include the *sui generis* right for data contained in databases, was not adopted. However, article 5 of the WIPO Copyright Treaty seems to allow for the possibility of such a right in providing that:

---

[29] See, further, Louwers and Prins, *International Computer Law* (Matthew Bender, ch 8).
[30] This is by way of an 'Agreed Statement' in the Treaty.     [31] Article 10(2).
[32] The Agreed Statement to article 4 notes this restatement of the TRIPS Agreement.
[33] The Agreed Statement to article 5 notes this restatement of the TRIPS Agreement.
[34] cf the EU Database Directive, n 11 above, and Chapter 6.

Compilations of data or other material, in any form, which by reason of the selection or arrangement of their contents constitute intellectual creations, are protected as such. This protection does not extend to the data or the material itself and is without prejudice to any copyright subsisting in the data or material in the compilation.

The database right created by the EU Database Directive appears to be consistent with article 5 of the WIPO Copyright Treaty. The question of adopting a *sui generis* right, similar to that of the Database Directive, was again discussed by WIPO at a meeting on database protection between 17 and 19 September 1997, but any action at an international level seems to have been postponed indefinitely.[35]

## 5.2  IN WHAT CAN COPYRIGHT SUBSIST?

### 5.2.1  General criteria for protection

#### 5.2.1.1  *Works*
Section 1 of the CDPA 1988 provides that:

(1) Copyright is a property right which subsists in accordance with this Part in the following descriptions of work—
>  (a)  original literary, dramatic, musical or artistic works,
>  (b)  sound recordings, films, broadcasts or cable programmes, and
>  (c)  the typographical arrangement of published editions.

(2) In this Part 'copyright work' means a work of any of those descriptions in which copyright subsists.

Many products that are protected by copyright do not fit neatly into any single category from this list. On the contrary, by the time they are brought to market, most films, books, software packages, multimedia products and other composite works comprise a complex bundle of discrete copyright works. Most of the categories of work listed above are of relevance in the computer context. For example, a software product such as a word-processing package could be analysed as a collection of copyright works as follows:

(a) The program code which, when run on a computer system, provides word-processing functions would be a literary work: section 3(1) of the CDPA 1988 defines 'literary work' as including 'a computer program' (s 3(1)(b)).

(b) The preparatory design material for the computer program would itself be a literary work (s 3(1)(c)).[36]

---

[35] For further discussion of international copyright conventions, see C Rees and S Chalton, *Database Law* (Jordans, 1998).

[36] Inserted by the Copyright (Computer Programs) Regulations 1992, SI 1992/3233, reg 3, in force 1 January 1993.

(c) Any documentation or other written materials supplied with the package would be one or more conventional literary works.

(d) Any built-in dictionary, thesaurus, or help-screen files would be literary works, but would probably not be computer programs.

(e) Artwork included on packaging or in documentation would be one or more artistic works (s 4).

(f) Graphic works or photographs used to produce screen images would be artistic works (s 4(1)(a)).

(g) Copyright would subsist in the typographical arrangement of the documentation supplied with the package: section 1(1) defines 'the typographical arrangement of published editions' as a separate category of copyright work (s 1(1)(c)).

In addition to these seven categories of work, three other types of work may be embodied in an audiovisual product such as a video game:

(h) The sounds which are produced when the game is run or played might include a recording of one or more musical works: section 3(1) defines 'musical work' as 'a work consisting of music, exclusive of any words or action intended to be sung, spoken or performed with the music'.

(i) The code producing the sounds would itself be a sound recording: section 5A(1)[37] defines 'sound recording' as '(a) a recording of sounds, from which the sounds may be reproduced, or (b) a recording of the whole or any part of a literary, dramatic or musical work, from which sounds reproducing the work or part may be produced, regardless of the medium on which the recording is made or the method by which the sounds are reproduced or produced'.

(j) Any set sequence of images that is produced when the program is run would be a film: section 5B(1)[38] defines 'film' as meaning 'a recording on any medium from which a moving image may by any means be produced'.

A further four bases for protection may be relevant in relation to a database[39] or multimedia product:

(k) A database itself may attract copyright protection: section 3(1) defines 'literary work' as including a database (s 3(1)(d)).[40] A database will fall within the scope of the CDPA 1988, as amended, if it consists of a collection of independent works, data or other materials arranged in a systematic or methodical way and individually

---

[37] Substituted by the Duration of Copyright and Rights in Performances Regulations 1995, SI 1995/3297, reg 9, subject to transitional and savings provisions specified in regs 12–35.

[38] Ibid.

[39] Note that the contents of a database may also attract a *sui generis* right, which protects the investment made by database makers rather than the author's creativity in the selection or arrangement of the contents of databases, as is the case with copyright.

[40] Inserted by the Copyright and Rights in Databases Regulations 1997, SI 1997/3032, reg 5, in force 1 January 1998.

accessible by electronic or other means.[41] Databases are to be protected by copyright only so far as they are original by reason of their 'selection or arrangement' and if they constitute the 'author's own intellectual creation'.[42] Therefore, a computer-generated database would not be protected by copyright as a database.

(l)  A computer program used in the making or operation of a database would be a literary work (s 3(1)(b))[43] and may also comprise preparatory design material (s 3(1)(c)).

(m)  Some or all of the items comprised in the product may be protected separately as literary, dramatic, musical or artistic works or as sound recordings or films.

(n)  If made available to subscribers to a broadcast videotext or cable service, the product would be a broadcast or cable programme: see definitions of 'broadcast' in section 6(1) and of 'cable programme service' in section 7(1).

While it is clear that compilations attract copyright protection,[44] the fact that, for example, a software product is not a single work for copyright purposes has a number of significant consequences. First, many different authors, graphic designers, programmers, publishers, etc, may be involved in the production and marketing of the product and, as individual authors, may have separate claims to copyright in their respective contributions (see section 5.3.1 below). Secondly, copyright protection will expire at different times in respect of different component parts of the product (see section 5.3.3 below). Thirdly, the scope of copyright protection will not be the same for all of the works that make up a package. For example, unauthorized adaptation of the program code would infringe copyright, whereas there would be no copyright restriction on adaptation of the various artistic works, provided it did not amount to copying or some other restricted act (see sections 5.4.2.1 and 5.5.2 below). Fourthly, an author of the text or designer of artwork included in the documentation might be able to exercise moral rights in respect of the works he contributed, whereas a programmer would have no such rights in respect of the program code (see section 5.6 below).

### 5.2.1.2  *Recording*
There can be no copyright in a literary, dramatic or musical work 'unless and until it is recorded, in writing or otherwise'. The term of copyright starts to run from the time of such recording (CDPA 1988, s 3(2)). 'Writing' is given an expansive definition in the CDPA 1988 as including 'any form of notation or code, whether by hand

---

[41]  Section 3A(1), inserted by the Copyright and Rights in Databases Regulations 1997, SI 1997/3032. Presumably databases where the contents are automatically calculated using other data in the database, for example, would be excluded.

[42]  Section 3A(2), inserted by the Copyright and Rights in Databases Regulations 1997, SI 1997/3032.

[43]  Such programs are excluded from protection as a database (see the Directive on the Legal Protection of Databases, art 1(3)).

[44]  See, eg, *Exchange Telegraph v Gregory* [1896] 1 QB 147, concerning the unauthorized dissemination of lists of London Stock Exchange price data; and *Waterlow Directories Ltd v Reed Information Services Ltd* [1992] FSR 409, concerning a compilation of practising solicitors in the UK.

or otherwise and regardless of the method by which, or medium in or on which, it is recorded, and "written" shall be construed accordingly' (CDPA 1988, s 178). Storage in any form of machine-readable media would thus appear to qualify as 'writing'. The words 'or otherwise' would cover fixation in the form of, for example, an analogue recording of sounds or spoken words.

The CDPA 1988 does not contain a definition of 'recording' as such. It is not clear whether a degree of permanence is implied. By analogy with 'sound recording', which is defined, the essence of the concept of recording of a work is probably that there is something from which the work, or part of it, can be reproduced. Presumably, once a work has been fixed in such a form, copyright will continue to subsist in the work notwithstanding the subsequent destruction of the original recording of the work, even where no copy has ever been made in a material form. This issue might be significant if a substantial part of a program, or other work, were to be reproduced from human memory after the author had accidentally or deliberately deleted the original from the memory of the computer on which it was created.

### 5.2.1.3 *Originality*

Literary, dramatic, musical or artistic works are only protected under the CDPA 1988 if they are original (CDPA 1988, s 1(1)(a)). There is no definition or explanation of the concept of originality. However, the word 'original' was used in both the 1911 and 1956 Copyright Acts and, almost invariably, was interpreted by the courts as relating essentially to origin rather than to substantive considerations such as novelty. Thus, a work will usually be original provided merely that it originates with the author or creator and has not been copied. In many cases originality has been found to exist where the work was created either independently or by the exercise of the author's own skill, knowledge, mental labour or judgment. While one (or more) of these attributes is usually required in order to secure copyright protection, courts have tended to resist arguments that the originality requirement should be interpreted as importing connotations of aesthetic quality or innovation.[45]

The low level at which the originality threshold has tended to be fixed by the courts means that even relatively simple and utterly mundane works can be protected by copyright. This is very important in the computer context where programs and other functional works may lack aesthetic appeal and display little apparent creativity yet be of tremendous commercial value. Were a higher threshold to be set for the originality test, it is probable that much computer software and data would fall completely outside copyright.[46] The one area where, under the 1956 Copyright Act, the originality criterion was a particular cause for concern for the UK computer

---

[45] See, eg, *Victoria Park Racing & Recreation Grounds Co Ltd v Taylor* (1937) 58 CLR 479; *Football League Ltd v Littlewoods Pools Ltd* [1959] Ch 637; *Ladbroke (Football) Ltd v William Hill (Football) Ltd* [1964] 1 WLR 273, applied *John Richardson Computers Ltd v Flanders* [1993] FSR 497 (Ferris J).

[46] As was the case, eg, in West Germany prior to implementation of the Software Directive. See M Rottinger, 'The Legal Protection of Computer Programs in Germany: Renunciation of Copyrights?' (1987) 4 CL&P 34.

industry, computer-generated works, was specifically addressed in the CDPA 1988 and is discussed in section 5.2.2.2 below.

Since 1 January 1998, subject to transitional provisions, a collection within the definition of a 'database' (that is, a literary work consisting of a database) will not qualify for copyright protection unless it achieves a certain level of originality. The requisite standard is that, by reason of the selection or arrangement of the contents of the database, the database constitutes the author's own intellectual creation.[47] The standard of originality for a literary work consisting of a database remains, at this stage, untested before the English courts. It could be argued that the standard is higher than that required for other literary, dramatic, musical or artistic works, because of the inherent difficulties associated with gauging intellect and/or requisite mental effort. Note, however, that while the 'own intellectual creation' test was contained in the Software Directive,[48] the implementing legislation for that Directive did not alter the basic 'originality' test, which suggests that the new standard was not seen to be significantly different from the old. Irrespective, this will not prevent such a database from being protected by the Database Directive's *sui generis* right (the database right under the Database Regulations), provided sufficiently substantial investment in the obtaining, verification or presentation of the database's contents can be demonstrated (art 7 and reg 13(1)). The database right will be infringed by the extraction or reutilization of all or a substantial part of the contents of the database (see Chapter 6).

### 5.2.1.4 *Qualification*

Copyright will not subsist in any work unless certain 'qualification requirements' are met. The rules, which are set out in Part IX of the CDPA 1988 (ss 153–62), are complex. For most types of work, however, the general rule is that either the author must be a 'qualifying person' at the time the work is made or, alternatively, the work must be first published in the UK or some other country to which the Act extends. An author will be a qualifying person if he is a citizen of, or domiciled or resident in, the UK or some other country to which the Act extends. The qualification requirements will also be satisfied if the author is a citizen of, or domiciled or resident in, or first publication is in, a country to which the Act has been 'applied'.

By virtue of a statutory instrument that came into force along with most of the provisions of the CDPA 1988 on 1 August 1989, Part I of the Act has been applied to works of different types originating in over 100 specified countries.[49] Special rules apply to certain countries which are not members of either the Berne Copyright

---

[47] CDPA 1988, s 3A(2), inserted by the Copyright and Rights in Databases Regulations 1997, SI 1997/3032.

[48] See n 9 above.

[49] The Copyright (Application to Other Countries) Order 1989 (No 2), SI 1989/1293. This was replaced by a statutory instrument in similar terms, which came into force on 4 May 1993, the Copyright (Application to Other Countries) Order 1993, SI 1993/942, which was in turn replaced by the Copyright (Application to Other Countries) Order 1999, SI 1999/1751, which came into force on 22 July 1999.

Convention or the Universal Copyright Convention but in which the UK Government is satisfied that there exists adequate protection for copyright. An Order has also been made applying Part I of the Act to works made by officers or employees of the United Nations and certain other international organizations that would otherwise not qualify for protection.[50]

### 5.2.2 Protection of programs and computer-generated works

#### 5.2.2.1 *Computer programs*
Whereas, in its original form, the Copyright Act 1956 contained no reference whatsoever to computers or computing, in the CDPA 1988 computers make their first appearance in section 3. Further direct and indirect references are scattered throughout the Act. Section 3(1) of the CDPA 1988 defines 'literary work' as including:

(a) a table or compilation other than a database;
(b) a computer program;
(c) preparatory design material for a computer program; and
(d) a database.

This form of words has made it completely clear that programs are literary works and not merely to be protected as though they were literary works.[51]

What remains unclear is the scope of the term 'computer program', which has still not been defined. Foreign legislatures and international organizations that have defined the term have tended to characterize programs in terms of their information-processing capabilities, with specific emphasis on their ability to cause hardware to perform functions.[52] We have already seen that a software package such as a video game is in fact a complex collection of separate copyright works. Only some of the works will be computer programs. To take another example, most of the material supplied in printed or electronic form in a word-processing package will not be 'programs' in the sense of computer code that will cause a computer to process information. The printed materials will be conventional literary and other works. Moreover a great deal of the material supplied in electronic form will be digital versions of a dictionary, a thesaurus, and help-screen information, all of which, again, will be conventional literary and possibly artistic works.

The existence of special provisions in the CDPA 1988 that apply to computer

---

[50] The Copyright (International Organisations) Order 1989, SI 1989/989. In force, 1 August 1989.

[51] As was the case under the 1956 Act, as amended by the Copyright (Computer Software) Amendment Act 1985, s 1.

[52] eg, 'A "computer program" is a set of statements or instructions to be used directly or indirectly in a computer in order to bring about a certain result' (United States Copyright Act 1976, 17 USC s 101); 'A "computer program" is a set of instructions expressed in words, codes, schemes or in any other form, which is capable, when incorporated in a machine-readable medium, of causing a "computer"—an electronic or similar device having information-processing capabilities—to perform or achieve a particular task or result' (World Intellectual Property Organisation, Model Provisions on the Protection of Computer Software, 1978, restated in Memorandum on a Possible Protocol to the Berne Convention, 1991).

programs but not to literary works in general means that the two terms are certainly not coextensive. Moreover, the inclusion in the Act of many provisions that deal with the use and distribution of conventional works in electronic form makes it clear that a work is not a program just because it is stored digitally.

Neither the Software Directive nor the Copyright (Computer Programs) Regulations 1992 shed much light on the definitional issue. The preamble (recitals) to the Directive merely includes a statement that 'the function of a computer program is to communicate and work together with other components of a computer system'. Article 1(1) is a little more explicit in stating that 'for the purpose of this Directive, the term "computer programs" shall include their preparatory design material'. The Copyright (Computer Programs) Regulations 1992 contain no reference to the meaning of the term 'computer program' except to restate that 'preparatory design material for a computer program' shall be protected (see also section 3(1)(c) of the CDPA 1988).

### 5.2.2.2 *Computer-generated works*

As already noted (see section 5.2.1.4 above) for copyright to subsist in a work, certain qualification requirements must be met. In most cases, the criterion will be whether the author of a work was 'a qualifying person' at the time the work was made. With the widespread use of programming 'tools' and automated processes for collecting, processing and compiling data, it is likely that an increasing number of works, including computer programs and databases, will have no identifiable human author or authors. Prior to the CDPA 1988, there was considerable doubt as to whether such works were eligible for copyright protection.[53]

To ensure that substantial categories of works did not gradually fall out of the realm of copyright, provisions were included in the CDPA 1988 to enable copyright to subsist in a literary, dramatic, musical or artistic work 'generated by a computer in circumstances such that there is no human author of the work' (ss 9(3) and 178). The author of such a 'computer-generated' work 'shall be taken to be the person by whom the arrangements necessary for the creation of the work are undertaken' (s 9(3)). Whilst providing a welcome safety net for useful and valuable works that would otherwise fall outside copyright law, determining whether these provisions apply to a particular work will still require a careful analysis of the facts.

In particular, care should be taken to distinguish between 'computer-generated' and 'computer-assisted' (or 'computer-aided' works). The latter type of work does not receive special treatment under the CDPA 1988. The availability of copyright protection for such works was in effect recognized in a decision under the 1956 Act. In pre-trial proceedings in *Express Newspapers plc v Liverpool Daily Post & Echo plc*[54] the court ruled that grids of letters produced with the aid of a computer for use

---

[53] See C J Millard, *Legal Protection of Computer Programs and Data* (Sweet & Maxwell, 1985), pp 25–30.

[54] [1985] FSR 306.

in prize draws were authored by the programmer who wrote the relevant software. Rejecting an argument to the contrary advanced by counsel for the defendants, Whitford J stated:

I reject this submission. The computer was no more than the tool by which the varying grids of five-letter sequences were produced to the instructions, via the computer, of Mr Ertel. It is as unrealistic as it would be to suggest that, if you write your work with a pen, it is the pen which is the author of the work rather than the person who drives the pen.[55]

It was perhaps convenient for the court in the *Express Newspapers* case that the programmer was also the person who ran the program on the particular occasion in question and checked the results. The nexus between one person and the finished work was thus very close. It is not clear how the court would have resolved conflicting claims between several programmers, data providers, system operators and so on.

In cases where the association between any individual or individuals and a finished work is so remote that it can fairly be said the work has been created without a human author, there is now the possibility that it will qualify for copyright as a computer-generated work. However, it is unlikely that the CDPA 1988 provisions will be dispositive of all doubts as to the subsistence and ownership of copyright in computer output. Disputes may still arise where a number of competing individuals claim to have made the 'arrangements necessary for the creation of the work'. Would, for example, a person using a mass-marketed program generator be entitled to copyright in all such output? Would the author of the underlying software have any claim to copyright in the output? Would two or more identical works produced by different individuals using the same program generator all qualify for protection as original literary works?[56]

## 5.3 OWNERSHIP AND DURATION OF COPYRIGHT

### 5.3.1 First ownership

The first owner of copyright in a work is usually the author of the work (CDPA 1988, s 11(1)). This is the case regardless of whose ideas underlie the work and of who commissions or pays for the work. This general rule is, however, subject to several significant exceptions. Of widest importance is the special rule that, subject to contrary agreement, the first owner of copyright in a work created by an employee during the course of his or her employment is the employer, not the employee (s

---

[55] Ibid, 310. This passage echoes a statement in paragraph 514 of the Whitford Committee Report (see n 3 above) in which it was stated that a computer used in the creation of a copyright work was a 'mere tool in much the same way as a slide-rule or even, in a simple sense, a paintbrush'.

[56] For further discussion, see J A L Sterling, 'The Copyright, Designs and Patents Bill 1987' (1988) 3(5) CLSR 2.

11(2)).[57] Whilst this rule seems straightforward in principle, in practice its consequences are frequently overlooked.

The most common difficulty arises where a software house or freelance programmer is commissioned to write software under a contract *for* services (as distinct from
a contract *of* service, that is, an employment agreement). Such scenarios are often
complicated where contributions to the program development process are made by
employees of the company that has commissioned the work and possibly also by
independent consultants. The automatic operation of the rules as to first ownership
may produce results that are contrary to the reasonable commercial expectations of
one or more of the parties. For example, the commissioning party may contribute a
brilliant original concept and pay all the costs of its subsequent development and
implementation, yet end up with no legal rights of ownership in the final product.
Even if it had been understood from the start, and possibly even agreed orally, that
the commissioner would in all respects 'own' the product, this will not be sufficient
to alter the operation of the first-ownership rules. This is because, as will be
discussed below, assignments of copyright and agreements as to future ownership of
copyright will only be enforceable if they are evidenced in writing (CDPA 1988, ss
90(3) and 91(1); see section 5.3.2 below). It is possible in such a case that the
commissioner will be able to persuade a court of equity to order the developer to
execute an assignment of copyright. This might be justified on the basis that such an
assignment was an implied term of an agreement between the parties.[58] The mere
fact that the commissioner paid for the work would not normally be sufficient
grounds for inferring such a term, although such an arrangement may be evidence of
an implied licence to use the work for the purpose for which it was commissioned.[59]

Further potential for dispute arises where there is joint authorship and/or joint
ownership of copyright. In the computer industry it is common for several people,
sometimes a large number, to be involved in the initial development of a software
package. Thereafter, still more people may be involved in the preparation of revised
versions and updates. Multiple authorship and divided ownership are, however, by
no means uncommon in the copyright field. Section 10(1) of the CDPA 1988 defines
a 'work of joint authorship' as 'a work produced by the collaboration of two or more
distinct authors in which the contribution of each author is not distinct from that of
the other author or authors'. Thus, where the development of a program really is a
joint effort copyright will, subject to the rules governing employee works just
discussed, vest in the various contributors jointly. This scenario must be distinguished, however, from that in which a number of people have made separate contri-

---

[57] The other exceptions to the rule relate to Crown and Parliamentary copyright, and the copyright of
certain international organizations (CDPA 1988, s 11(3)).

[58] See, eg, *Merchant Adventurers Ltd v M Grew & Co Ltd* [1973] RPC 1. The ruling is probably
limited to the special facts of that case, however. Where ownership is disputed, courts will be unlikely to
upset the automatic operation of the statutory ownership rules.

[59] For judicial discussion on this point, see *John Richardson Computers Ltd v Flanders* [1993] FSR
497, 516 and *Ibcos Computers Ltd v Barclays Mercantile Highland Finance Ltd* [1994] FSR 275, 293.

butions to a software development project each of which can be identified as such. It may well be that in the latter case there will be a number of quite distinct copyrights in a program or package.

An example of the potential problems associated with divided ownership is where a software house or contractor writes software code for a specific customer. In such an instance, there is often a great deal of collaboration with the customer or third party with resulting issues of joint authorship or implied licence to exploit the software. The degree and kind of collaboration necessary to support a claim of joint authorship or warrant an implied licence to exploit the software was dealt with by the Chancery Division of the High Court in *Flyde Microsystems v Key Radio Systems Limited*.[60] Laddie J found that while the defendant, who cooperated in the design of software to be used in a new generation of radios to be sold by the defendant, did in fact improve the software by ironing out 'bugs' this was more akin to the skill exhibited by a proofreader not an author. As a result, it was held that the level of 'creative' skill was not sufficient to evidence copyright ownership or give rise to an implied licence to exploit the software. In *Robin Ray v Classic FM plc*[61] Lightman J found that to establish joint authorship, it was necessary to show that: (a) there was a direct responsibility for the work by providing a creative contribution that was not distinct from that of the author (CDPA 1988, ss 9 and 10); (b) there was more than a mere contribution of ideas to the author or some division of labour in the creation of the copyright work; and (c) there was no employment contract whereby copyright would be legally owned by the defendant. Further, if joint authorship did in fact exist, the consent of the other joint author to the exploitation of the work would need to be obtained (ss 16 and 173). It was also found that an implied licence to exploit copyright material would only arise where strictly necessary to make sense of the relevant commercial arrangements.[62]

Serious difficulties may arise at the exploitation stage where a software package either has a number of joint owners, or is made up of a number of programs or modules each separately owned. In either case, infringement of copyright will occur if any of the owners seeks to exploit the package as a whole without the consent of all the others. Where the various owners have quite distinct copyrights and one owner refuses to cooperate with the rest, the others may choose to rewrite the relevant part of the package and proceed to market the software without the objecting contributor being involved. This solution will not, however, be available in the case of a single work if various people are joint owners of the whole of it. Unless the rights of the uncooperative party or parties can somehow be severed, attempts to exploit the package may be thwarted permanently.

There are thus many circumstances in which there is a possibility of more than one party claiming copyright and of disagreements about how multiple owners

---

[60] [1998] FSR 449. Applied in *Pierce v Promco SA and Others* [1998] All ER (D) 780.
[61] 18 March 1998 (unreported).
[62] See, further, J Warchus, 'CSLR Briefing' (1988) 14(6) CLSR 424.

should exercise their rights. Such issues may arise where there is a misunderstanding about ownership of a work that has been commissioned; where a work has been or is likely to be computer-generated; where there are multiple authors; and where ownership is divided. In all such cases, the most satisfactory arrangement for all concerned will usually be for agreement about ownership and exploitation of any rights to be reached in advance and be evidenced in writing. Where the potential for disputes has not been successfully pre-empted, assignments or confirmatory assignments of copyright may be appropriate to resolve doubts about rights in existing works.

### 5.3.2 Assignments and licences

A copyright can be given away, be bought and sold, or be left as an inheritance under a will as personal or movable property (CDPA 1988, s 90(1)). An assignment, or other transfer, of copyright may be outright or may relate only to certain of the exclusive rights enjoyed by the owner. Thus, for example, an assignee may be given the right solely to translate a software package into a particular language. A transfer may also be limited to any part of the remaining term of the copyright (CDPA 1988, s 90(2)). In practice, limited rights, such as to convert a program for use with a particular operating system or for foreign-language users, are more often granted by way of licence than by partial assignment. Where such a licence is 'exclusive', the licensee will in effect be treated as the owner in terms of rights and remedies and the distinction between such a licence and a corresponding assignment will, for most purposes, be academic.[63] Assignments of copyright and of 'future copyright' (that is, copyright which will or may come into existence in the future, for example, in a commissioned work) will only be effective if made in writing and signed by or on behalf of the assignor (CDPA 1988, ss 90(3) and 91(1)).

Licences other than exclusive licences can be made informally without being evidenced in writing. Indeed, they may even be inferred from the circumstances of a transaction or the general or specific conduct of the parties. Licences relating to the use of software are generally recorded in a written statement of terms, though frequently there is no signed agreement or contract as such.[64] The CDPA 1988 provides, in limited circumstances, for deemed licences to use second-hand copies of programs and other works distributed in electronic form (see section 5.5.9 below).

The circumstances in which a copyright owner has the right to refuse to grant a licence were at issue in the European Court of Justice case of *Radio Telefis Eireann v Commission*.[65] The case concerned the attempted production of a weekly television guide by Magill TV Guide Ltd covering programmes broadcast by the BBC, ITV and the Irish network RTE. The networks obtained an injunction against Magill

---

[63] Section 101(1) of the CDPA 1988 provides that 'An exclusive licensee has, except against the copyright owner, the same rights and remedies in respect of matters occurring after the grant of the licence as if the licence had been an assignment'.

[64] See C J Millard, 'Shrink-wrap Licensing' (1987) 4 CLSR 8.

[65] Cases C-241 and 242/91, [1995] ECR I-743.

on the basis that they were entitled to refuse to grant licences of copyright. The case was then taken to the Commission where it was decided that each of the networks had abused a dominant position contrary to article 86 of the EC Treaty.[66] This decision was later upheld in the Court of First Instance.[67] Despite an opinion of the Advocate-General proposing that the Court of Justice set aside the judgments of the Court of First Instance, the final judgment of the Court upheld the first-instance judgment. This ruling has left considerable uncertainty amongst copyright owners as to the circumstances in which they are entitled to refuse to grant licences. Although the case only impacts upon copyright owners in a dominant position, the ability of Community authorities to invoke competition principles to curtail the rights of copyright owners may in future have significant consequences for the computer industry.

### 5.3.3 Term of protection

The term of protection afforded to various forms of copyright has been modified by the Duration of Copyright and Rights in Performances Regulations 1995[68] and the Copyright and Related Rights Regulations 1996.[69] These Regulations implemented an EU Directive on the subject, which aimed to make copyright coterminous in all Member States.[70] The CDPA 1988 originally stipulated, subject to certain exceptions, a period of fifty years from the end of the year in which the author dies for literary, dramatic, musical or artistic works (s 12(1)). This was extended for those works to a period of seventy years from the author's death by the 1995 Regulations.[71] In the case of films, the duration of copyright was extended by the 1995 Regulations from fifty years from the making or release of the film to a period of seventy years from the death of the last to die of the principal director and the author of the screenplay, dialogue or music. The 1996 Regulations[72] introduce an innovative new right, known as the 'publication right' Regulation 16 provides that a person who publishes a previously unpublished work after the expiry of copyright protection will be entitled to a period of protection for twenty-five years from the end of the year of first publication. This right is described as a property right equivalent to copyright and is intended to cover, for example, the publication of freshly discovered works of well-known authors. The CDPA 1988 provides, unamended by the 1995 Regulations and 1996 Regulations, that, in the case of computer-generated work, copyright expires after fifty years from the end of the year in which the work was made (CDPA 1988, s 12(3)). This latter rule is similar to the rules applying to

---

[66] *Magill TV Guide/ITP* OJ 1989 L 78/43 1989. Note that the relevant article of the EC Treaty is now article 82.
[67] *Radio Telefis Eireann v Commission* (case T-69/89) [1991] ECR II-485 and *Independent Television Publications Ltd v Commission* (case T-76/89) [1991] ECR II-575.
[68] SI 1995/3297, which came into force on 1 January 1996.
[69] SI 1996/2967, which came into force on 1 December 1996.
[70] Council Directive of 29 October 1993 harmonizing the term of protection of copyright and certain related rights (93/98/EEC), OJ L 290, 24 November 1993.
[71] SI 1995/3297.                                                            [72] SI 1996/2967.

sound recordings, broadcasts and cable programmes (ss 13 and 14). The typographi-cal arrangement of a published edition, which is itself a work for copyright purposes, is protected for twenty-five years from the end of the year of first publication (s 15). Thus, in the case of a product such as a software package comprising multiple works, copyright in the various component parts will run out on a number of differ-ent dates. Duration of copyright may depend, for example, on the life expectancy of various human contributors, the year in which any computer-generated works were made, and the year of first publication of the documentation.

The lengthening of the term of protection of various forms of copyright has two consequences, which further complicate matters in relation to those types of works. One is the extension of copyright in works whose protection in the UK would have expired under the provisions of the CDPA 1988 and the other is the revival of copy-right in works whose protection has expired in the UK within the last twenty years. In respect of copyright extension, regulation 21 of the 1995 Regulations provides that copyright licences which subsisted immediately before 1 January 1996 and were not to expire before the end of the copyright period as it was under the CDPA 1988 shall continue to have effect during the period of any extended copyright. In cases of copyright revival, regulation 22 provides that any waiver or assertion of moral rights, which subsisted immediately before the expiry of copyright, shall continue to have effect during the period of revived copyright. In addition, by regulation 23, no act done before 1 January 1996 shall be regarded as infringing revived copyright in a work and, by regulation 24, where revived copyright subsists, any acts restricted by copyright shall be treated as licensed by the copyright owner, subject to the payment of a reasonable royalty, to be determined, in case of dispute, by the Copyright Tribunal. By regulation 16, the revival provisions will apply to works in which copy-right has expired, but which were, on 1 July 1995, protected in another EEA state.

The provisions of the CDPA 1988 dealing with the duration of copyright (ss 12–14, which apply respectively to literary, dramatic, musical or artistic works, to sound recordings, to films and to broadcasts or cable programmes) require that, in circumstances where the country of origin or the nationality of an author is not an EEA state, the duration of copyright is that to which the work is entitled in the coun-try of origin, provided the period does not exceed that provided for under the CDPA 1988. Section 15A of the CDPA 1988[73] provides that in respect of the duration of copyright protection, the country of origin is: the country of first publication if it is a Berne Convention country (s 15A(2)); a Berne Convention country if the work is simultaneously published in a non-Berne Convention country (s 15A(3)); or an EEA state or otherwise the Berne Convention country that grants the shortest period of protection (s 15A(4)).

---

[73] Inserted by the Duration of Copyright and Rights in Performances Regulations 1995, SI 1995/3297, reg 8(1), which came into force on 1 January 1996.

## 5.4 INFRINGEMENT OF COPYRIGHT

### 5.4.1 Types of infringing act

Space does not permit a full discussion of all of the acts that can constitute infringement of the copyright in a work. Instead, the focus will be on the principal acts of so-called 'primary infringement' with reference also being made to the various acts of 'secondary infringement'. A primary infringement occurs where a person directly commits an infringing act or authorizes someone else to do so. Secondary infringers, as their name suggests, are generally one stage removed from the relevant primary infringing acts, but may be implicated by, for example, importing or distributing infringing copies without the consent of the copyright owner. A crucial distinction between primary infringers and secondary infringers is that those in the former category can be liable for infringing copyright whether or not they realize they are doing so, whereas those in the latter category are only liable if they know, or have reason to believe, that they are committing an act of secondary infringement. Three of the most relevant primary infringing acts (copying, adaptation, and issuing copies to the public) are discussed in section 5.4.2 below and the various acts of secondary infringement are outlined in section 5.4.3 below.

### 5.4.2 Primary infringement

#### 5.4.2.1 *Copying*

Whereas the 1956 Act gave the owner of copyright in a work control over the act of 'reproducing the work in any material form' (s 2(5)(a)), the CDPA 1988 contains the much simpler statement that a copyright owner has the exclusive right 'to copy the work' and to authorize anyone else to do so (s 16(1)(a) and (2)). The CDPA 1988 provides that control over copying applies in relation to the whole or any substantial part of a work, and regardless of whether copying occurs directly or indirectly (s 16(3)). As will be seen in section 5.5 below, it may be difficult to establish whether the reproduction of certain structural or other characteristics of a computer program will constitute either direct or indirect copying of a substantial part of the program.

Section 17(2) of the CDPA 1988 defines copying, in relation to a literary, dramatic, musical or artistic work, as 'reproducing the work in a material form' including 'storing the work in any medium by electronic means'. This provision is reinforced by section 17(6) which provides that 'Copying in relation to any description of work includes the making of copies which are transient or are incidental to some other use of the work'. As will be seen in section 5.5.2 below, these provisions have significant consequences when applied to computer programs and other works distributed in electronic form.

#### 5.4.2.2 *Making adaptations*

Section 21(1) of the CDPA 1988 restricts the making of an adaptation of a literary, dramatic or musical work. 'Adaptation' means, amongst other things, making a translation of a literary work, and 'in relation to a computer program a "translation" includes a version of the program in which it is converted into or out of a computer language or code or into a different computer language or code' (CDPA 1988, s 21(3) and (4), as amended by the Copyright (Computer Programs) Regulations 1992, reg 5). In relation to a computer program 'adaptation' means an arrangement or altered version of the program or a translation of it (s 21(3)(ab))[74] and in relation to a database 'adaptation' means an arrangement or altered version of the database or a translation of it (s 21(3)(ac)).[75] The possible implications of section 21 for the scope of a program copyright owner's control over simple 'use' of software are discussed in section 5.5.2 below.

### 5.4.2.3 *Issuing copies to the public*

Section 18(1) of the CDPA 1988 provides that 'the issue to the public of copies of the work is an act restricted by copyright in every description of copyright work'. The issuing of copies of a work includes the issue of the original (s 18(4)).[76] The act of issuing copies of a work to the public is defined in terms of 'putting into circulation in the EEA copies not previously put into circulation in the EEA by or with the consent of the copyright owner' (s 18(2)(a)) or 'putting into circulation outside the EEA copies not previously put into circulation in the EEA or elsewhere' (s 18(2)(b)). Broadly speaking, this gives the owner of copyright in a work control over publication of the work. Specifically excluded, however, from the ambit of section 18 are distribution, sale, hiring, loan, or importation into the UK of copies that have lawfully been issued to the public anywhere in the world (s 18(3)). Previously this exclusion was, in turn, qualified in a most significant respect with the words 'except that in relation to sound recordings, films and computer programs the restricted act of issuing copies to the public includes any rental of copies to the public'.

This restriction on the rental of copies of certain categories of works, including computer programs, was an innovative feature of the CDPA 1988. Prior to the 1988 Act no such automatic restriction existed. Copyright owners were, of course, able to restrict rental of their works by agreement and, in addition, the absence of a restriction on rental did not give a person who rented a copy any right to make a further copy. In practice, however, copies of works are often distributed in circumstances such that it is not feasible for appropriate restrictions to be imposed in that way. An obvious example is mass-market distribution of 'shrink-wrapped' software packages.[77] Moreover, a theoretical right to restrict the making of further copies from a

---

[74] Inserted by the Copyright (Computer Programs) Regulations 1992, SI 1992/3233, reg 5(2), which came into force on 1 January 1993.

[75] Inserted by the Copyright and Rights in Databases Regulations 1997, SI 1997/3032, reg 7(b), which came into force on 1 January 1998.

[76] Inserted by the Copyright and Related Rights Regulations 1996, SI 1996/2967, reg 9(3), which came into force 1 December 1996.

[77] See C J Millard, 'Shrink-wrap Licensing' (1987) 4 CLSR 8.

rented copy is of limited efficacy in the face of widespread private copying of works such as compact discs, videos and software packages. Of far greater use to copyright owners was the new right to prevent, or regulate at source, the rental of copies of such works to the public.

In response to an EU Directive on rental and lending rights adopted in 1992 ('the Rental Directive')[78] and one concerning satellite broadcasting and cable retransmission in 1993 ('the Satellite Directive'),[79] the Copyright and Related Rights Regulations 1996[80] were issued. The Regulations amend the definition of 'rental' in the CDPA 1988[81] and add a new definition of 'lending'.[82] Section 18A(2) of the CDPA 1988 defines 'rental' as 'making a copy of the work available for use, on terms that it will or may be returned, for direct or indirect commercial advantage' (s 18A(2)(a)) and 'lending' as 'making a copy of the work available for use, on terms that it will or may be returned, otherwise than for direct or indirect economic or commercial advantage' by means accessible to the public (s 18A(2)(b)). These definitions exclude any arrangement by which copies are made available for the purpose of public performance, exhibition or for on-the-spot referencing (s 18A(3)). The Regulations also provide for an extension of rental rights to all literary, musical and dramatic works and most artistic ones.[83] The rental right is the right of the owner of copyright to authorize or prohibit the rental or copies of the work, which are deemed to be restricted acts under section 18A (s 179). As a result of the changes brought about by the Regulations, performers are accorded some additional rights, including rental, lending and distribution rights and rights to income for performances in films and sound recordings. The Rental Directive provides that Member States must implement a right to authorize or prohibit the rental and lending of originals and copies of copyright works,[84] but derogations may be made in respect of the grant of exclusive lending rights provided authors, at least, are remunerated for lending. A derogation is made to cover films and sound recordings in the Regulations. In addition, certain exemptions apply to libraries and educational establishments. The Regulations also cover the requirements of the Satellite Directive and contain provisions to determine applicable law where broadcasts are made within or outside the EEA and received in more than one Member State. They also address cable retransmission, requiring the

---

[78] Directive 92/100/EEC of 19 November 1992 on rental right and lending right and certain rights related to copyright in the field of intellectual property, OJ L346, 27 November 1992.

[79] Directive 93/83/EEC of 27 September 1993 on the coordination of certain rules concerning copyright and rights related to copyright applicable to satellite broadcasting and cable retransmission, OJ L248, 6 October 1993.

[80] SI 1996/2967, entry into force 1 December 1996.

[81] Substituted by the Copyright and Related Rights Regulations 1996, SI 1996/2967, reg 10(4), in force 1 December 1996. See sections 179 and 18A(2)–(6).

[82] Inserted by the Copyright and Related Rights Regulations 1996, SI 1996/2967, reg 10(4), in force 1 December 1996. See sections 179 and 18A(2)–(6).

[83] Inserted by the Copyright and Related Rights Regulations 1996, SI 1996/2967, reg 10(4), in force 1 December 1996. See section 178.

[84] Article 1(1). By article 2(1) the right is granted, in special circumstances, to authors, performers and phonogram and film producers. See section 18A(1) and (6).

exercise of rights by persons other than broadcasting organizations to be exercised through a licensing body.

### 5.4.3 Secondary infringement

#### 5.4.3.1 *Dealing in infringing copies*

Secondary infringement occurs where, without the consent of the copyright owner, a person 'imports into the United Kingdom, otherwise than for his own private and domestic use, an article which is, and which he knows or has reason to believe is, an infringing copy of the work' (CDPA 1988, s 22). Infringement also occurs where a person, again without consent, 'possesses in the course of a business' or deals in articles which he knows or has reason to believe are infringing copies. Relevant dealings are selling, hiring, offering for sale or hire, commercial exhibition or distribution of copies of the work, and any other distribution 'otherwise than in the course of business to such an extent as to affect prejudicially the owner of the copyright' (s 23).

#### 5.4.3.2 *Providing articles for making infringing copies*

Copyright in a work is infringed where, without the consent of the copyright owner, 'an article specifically designed or adapted for making copies of that work' is manufactured, imported or commercially dealt in by a person who knows or has reason to believe that it will be used for that purpose (CDPA 1988, s 24(1)). The scope of this infringing act is not clear. It is not necessary that an article be intended specifically for use in making *infringing* copies, merely that the article is 'specifically designed or adapted' for making copies and that such copies may infringe copyright. Thus, at its broadest, the provision arguably could be construed as covering commonplace articles such as photocopiers, tape recorders, and personal computers which every importer, manufacturer, or dealer should suspect may be used to make infringing copies of works. Such a construction of the section would, however, be absurd. An extremely limited interpretation would probably be nearer the mark. The basis for a narrow construction is the reference to the making of copies of *that* work, meaning that the device in question must have been specifically designed or adapted to make copies of a particular work owned by a particular person, and not merely for making copies of works generally.

#### 5.4.3.3 *Facilitating infringement by transmission*

As where a copy of a work is rented out and copied by the renter, where a copy of a work is made available by transmission over a telecommunications system, there may in theory be a cause of action against each recipient who stores, and thus copies, the work on reception. However, the practical difficulties inherent in enforcing this right to sue each ultimate infringer render it of little practical use to copyright owners. Section 24(2) of the CDPA 1988 provides copyright owners with a basis for regulating such dissemination of a work at source, as follows:

Copyright in a work is infringed by a person who without the licence of the copyright owner transmits the work by means of a telecommunications system (otherwise than by broadcasting or inclusion in a cable programme service), knowing or having reason to believe that infringing copies of the work will be made by means of the reception of the transmission in the United Kingdom or elsewhere.

Accordingly, a supply down a telephone line of software, data, or any other work protected by copyright, may be an act of secondary infringement if done without an appropriate licence.

### 5.4.3.4 *Circumvention of copy-protection*

A further area in which the CDPA 1988 strengthened the right of owners of works distributed in electronic form relates to devices or information intended to facilitate the circumvention of copy-protection measures. The relevant provision is not grouped with the other sections that deal with secondary infringement but appears quite separately in Part VII of the Act under the heading 'Miscellaneous and general'. Section 296 provides that a copyright owner who issues a work in copy-protected electronic form has the same rights against a person who, with intent, makes available any device or means designed or adapted to circumvent the copy-protection as would be available against a copyright infringer. 'Copy protection' is defined as including 'any device or means intended to prevent or restrict copying of a work or to impair the quality of copies made' (s 296(4)).

As with the discussion of the restriction on providing articles to be used for making infringing copies (see section 5.4.3.2 above), it is not clear how broadly the circumvention of copy-protection provision will be interpreted by the courts. At its widest, section 296 could be construed as encompassing any hardware, software, or information intended to facilitate the copying of, or access to, encrypted files, or even recovery of corrupted data. Thus, suppliers of bit-copiers and utilities designed to restore garbled or incomplete data might be vulnerable to attack under the provision. Similarly, distributors of hardware devices such as 'ROM blowers', which are designed for copying data from one chip to another, might be caught. In *Sony Computer Entertainment v Owen*[85] the defendants imported a 'Messiah' chip which could be inserted into a Sony Play Station 2 in order to bypass codes embedded into CDs or DVDs which were intended to prevent copying of Sony games. Sony brought an action under section 296. The court considered the defendant's argument that the chip also had lawful uses because once the code was circumvented the machine could read material that was not protected by copyright. Jacob J concluded that the Messiah chip was specifically designed or adapted to circumvent the copy-protection code and therefore 'it does not matter that once circumvented the machine may read non-infringing material'. In the *Sony* case, the chip did not have any use other than to circumvent the protective code. The court may well have come to a

---

[85] [2002] EWHC 45.

different conclusion if the device had multiple uses, at least some of which were legitimate. It seems unlikely that section 296 would be applicable in cases where an article also has legitimate uses.

### 5.4.4 Copyright infringement via the Internet[86]

The law of copyright, as has been seen, has sometimes been hard pressed to keep pace with the legal implications of technological advances. Probably the most difficult challenge to legislators and courts to date has been regulating the use and abuse of copyright material accessed via the Internet.

Three of the most fundamental questions are these. First, who may be liable for copyright infringement? Secondly, what is the appropriate law and jurisdiction? Thirdly, what acts of infringement may have been committed under the relevant law? Possible infringers fall into three main categories: originators of material, recipients of it and network operators. Some of the ways in which they could find themselves liable under English law are as follows.

An originator who transmits infringing material via the Internet may, by the act of transmission, be infringing copyright. The originator may also infringe if he is regarded variously as performing, displaying, showing, playing or broadcasting[87] the material. This is because the act of sending a message containing infringing material in the knowledge that it will necessarily be copied along the way may constitute infringement of copyright by transmission. It may also be the case that the originator will be liable for merely making material available on his or her computer to be browsed or copied by means of an instruction by another computer to send the material to it (for example, via the World Wide Web or File Transfer Protocol). However, in the case of piracy at least, the greatest problem may not be in identifying whether or not an originator of material has infringed copyright, but in identifying who and where the originator is. Sophisticated techniques exist for ensuring the anonymity of persons making material available via the Internet.[88]

Likewise, the recipient of material may be infringing copyright if he receives material which infringed copyright at the time of sending,[89] and someone who browses material on a website, or accesses it by instructing the originator's computer

---

[86] See also Chapter 9, section 9.6 in relation to the liability of Internet Service Providers ('ISPs') for third-party activities which infringe copyright.

[87] See, eg, *Shetland Times Ltd v Dr Jonathan Wills and Another* [1998] Masons CLR 159, where, in finding that the balance of convenience fell in favour of awarding an interim injunction against the use of a website containing headlines of the pursuer, Lord Hamilton accepted the argument that there was a *prima facie* case of infringement of a cable broadcast service in that the information was conveyed to the user's site, and that constituted sending within the meaning of section 20 of the CDPA 1988.

[88] eg, 'spoofing', which involves obtaining a false Internet protocol address, or the use of anonymous remailers.

[89] This would be the case if the recipient were in possession of the infringing copies in the course of a business and had the requisite *mens rea*.

to send the material, may infringe copyright. Material may be downloaded deliberately or a copy of part or all of a file held on a remote website may be made automatically by a process known as 'caching' whereby material is copied on to a user's PC to speed up future access to a website.

On a strict application of copyright principles, network operators that carry packets of data containing infringing material, and there may be several such operators in different jurisdictions along the route of transmission, may be liable for infringement of copyright by the fact of having copied the material en route, even though copying may be automatic and though the network operator may never 'see' the material in question. The Electronic Commerce (EC Directive) Regulations 2002[90] introduced three exemptions from liability for network operators relating to mere conduit, caching, and hosting. The 'mere conduit' exemption[91] applies where a network operator is transmitting information, provided that the network operator:

(a) did not initiate the transmission;

(b) did not select the receiver of the transmission; and

(c) did not select or modify the information contained in the transmission.

If these conditions are fulfilled the network operator will not be liable for 'damages or for any other pecuniary remedy or for any criminal sanction as a result of that transmission'.

The second exemption relates to 'caching'[92] and is relevant in circumstances where a network operator is storing information solely for the purpose of making more efficient onward transmission of the information to other recipients of the transmission service. Certain conditions must be fulfilled before this exemption will apply. The network operator must:

(a) not modify the information;

(b) comply with conditions on access to the information;

(c) comply with rules regarding updating of the information; not interfere with the lawful use of technology, widely recognized and used by industry, to obtain data on the use of the information; and

(d) act expeditiously to remove or disable access to the information upon obtaining actual knowledge that the information at the initial source of the transmission has been removed from the network, or access to it has been disabled, or that a court or an administrative authority has ordered such removal or disablement. In determining whether a network operator has 'actual knowledge' for these purposes a court shall take account of all matters which appear to it to be relevant.[93]

---

[90] SI 2002/2013, implementing Directive 2000/31/EC on certain legal aspects of information society services, in particular electronic commerce, in the Internal Market.
[91] Electronic Commerce (EC Directive) Regulations 2002, SI 2002/2013, reg 17.
[92] Ibid, reg 18.
[93] Ibid, reg 22.

The third exemption relates to hosting[94] and will apply when a network operator stores information without actual knowledge of unlawful activity or where upon obtaining such knowledge, the network operator expeditiously removes or disables access to the information. The same test of actual knowledge applies as for the caching exemption.

The question is what degree of knowledge is necessary to constitute 'actual knowledge' for these purposes? Would it be sufficient for a software house to issue a letter to, say, a public network operator, stating that, in all probability, that operator's network was being used for the purpose of creating infringing copies? Would it be sufficient to produce evidence that a specific customer was using the network in this manner? Would it be sufficient that the network operator knew that the material being stored was sourced from a copy of the material on a neighbouring network, which was unlikely to have received explicit permission to copy the work? The answers to such questions are unknown at this point, but network operators would probably not be held to have the requisite knowledge unless they had received very specific and detailed information concerning the activities of a specific customer.[95]

As yet, there has been no English court decision concerning the potential liability of network operators for copyright infringement via the Internet. In the United States, however, there have been several cases already, of which we shall look briefly at two. In *Playboy Enterprises Inc v Frena*[96] it was held that there had been infringement of the claimant's right publicly to distribute and display copyrighted photographs by the defendant, on whose bulletin board the photographs had been posted by some of the defendant's subscribers without his knowledge. A different conclusion was reached in the more recent case of *Religious Technology Center v Netcom Online Communications Services*[97] which signalled a move away from the imposition of liability for direct infringement upon service providers despite strict liability under the Copyright Act 1976 (17 USC, s 501). In the *Netcom* case the District Court of the Northern District of California held that 'it does not make sense to adopt a rule that could lead to the liability of countless parties whose role in the infringement is nothing more than setting up and operating a system that is necessary for the functioning of the Internet'.[98]

The Digital Millennium Copyright Act 1998 ('DMCA 1998') came into force in the US on 28 October 1998. The DMCA 1998 codifies the result of the *Netcom* case and distinguishes between direct infringement and secondary liability of ISPs. In *ALS Scan Inc v RemarQ Communities Inc*[99] the US Court of Appeals for the Fourth Circuit held that the DMCA 1998 overrules the *Playboy* case, insofar as it suggests

---

[94]  Ibid, reg 19.

[95]  For a more detailed discussion of the position of network operators in relation to copyright infringement issues, see C Millard and R Carolina, 'Commercial Transactions on The Global Information Infrastructure: A European Perspective' (1996) 14(2) John Marshall Journal of Computer and Information Law.

[96]  (1993) 4 CCH Computer Cases 47,020.                    [97]  907 F Supp 1361 (ND Cal 1995).

[98]  Ibid.                                                  [99]  (2001) 57 USPQ 2d 1996.

that acts by ISPs could constitute direct infringement.[100] Unless ISPs have actual or constructive knowledge of infringement they will be immune from liability under the DMCA 1998.

Two further cases of interest here relate to the downloading of music from the Internet. In the US case *A&M Records Inc v Napster DC*[101] A&M Records were successful in suing Napster for contributory and vicarious copyright infringement. Napster used a central server through which users linked to files on the PCs of other users. Users' files were catalogued on the central server and users could search for specific files and then copy them. Even though Napster was not itself hosting the material that was being copied, Napster was ordered to take reasonable steps to prevent distribution of works of which it had been notified of copyright ownership. This court order effectively disabled Napster because of the huge logistical task of identifying which materials could lawfully be swapped.

The *Napster* judgment accelerated the development and deployment of systems which do not rely on a central server. KaZaA.com is one such company which distributes programs that enable file swapping over the Internet. The Dutch music licensing body Burma/Stemra brought an action against KaZaA.com for copyright infringement by users of its downloadable software. At first instance the Amsterdam District Court ordered KaZaA.com to stop offering its free software online because it encouraged copyright infringement. However, the Court of Appeals in Amsterdam overturned this judgement on the basis that KaZaA.com was not responsible for the actions of its users and because the software was also being used for non-infringement purposes.[102]

A key question is whether jurisdiction should be determined by reference to where material originated, where it went along the way or where it ended up being displayed, stored or printed out. It may, of course, be correct to say that an infringement has taken place in more than one jurisdiction and under more than one law. Possibilities for 'forum shopping' undoubtedly flow from this.

## 5.5  SCOPE OF PROTECTION FOR COMPUTER PROGRAMS AND DATA

### 5.5.1  Idea and expression, symbolism and functionality

In the UK there is no statutory rule that bars ideas from copyright protection.[103]

---

[100] The District Court of Maryland in *CoStar Group Inc v LoopNet Inc* (2001) 164 F Supp 2d 688 applied the *Remarq* case and confirmed the rejection of the *Playboy* case.
[101] No CV-99-05783MHP.                                              [102]  KG 01/2264 OdC.
[103] cf, eg, the position in the United States, where section 102(b) of Title 17 USC provides 'in no case does copyright protection ... extend to any idea, procedure, process, system, method of operation, concept, principle, or discovery, regardless of the form in which it is described, explained, illustrated, or embodied in such work'.

However, article 1(2) of the Software Directive[104] provides that 'Ideas and principles which underlie any element of a computer program, including those which underlie its interfaces, are not protected by copyright under this Directive'. The Copyright (Computer Programs) Regulations 1992 are silent on this point. However, a number of English, and other Commonwealth, precedents appear to exclude ideas *per se* from copyright protection.[105] The apparent logic behind the rule was illustrated by the Supreme Court of Canada in *Cuisenaire v South West Imports Ltd*[106] with the observation that 'were the law otherwise . . . everybody who made a rabbit pie in accordance with the recipe of Mrs Beeton's cookery book would infringe the literary copyright in that book'.[107]

The claimed distinction then is between an idea that cannot be protected by copyright, such as the procedure for making a rabbit pie, and an expression of that idea, such as a written recipe describing the process for making rabbit pie, which can be protected by copyright. In the case of a computer program, however, such a tidy analysis is not possible. Indeed, it may be that the statement that ideas can never be protected by copyright is a misleading oversimplification.[108] Take, for example, ideas such as the algorithms on which a program is based, or perhaps the methods or processes that the program implements. Because of the nature of the interaction between software and hardware, a program, unlike a page from a recipe book, can simultaneously be *symbolic* (ie, a representation of instructions to be given to the computer) and *functional* (ie, the means by which the computer is actually instructed to carry out operations). Lines of code that describe an operation or procedure can also be used to implement it. It is as though by putting the relevant pages from Mrs Beeton's cookery book into an oven one could produce a rabbit pie. This special characteristic of computer programs has a number of significant consequences in copyright law. One is that use of a program is almost impossible without copying and/or adaptation occurring (see section 5.5.2 below). Another is that there may be no way to achieve functional compatibility between two or more items of hardware or software without reproducing a substantial amount of code to effect the desired interface or communication (see section 5.5.3 below).

### 5.5.2 Infringement of program copyright by use of a program

In relation to conventional works, the 'use' of a legitimate copy of a work is not generally restricted by copyright. For example, the simple act of reading a book is not controlled by copyright. It is only on the occurrence of one of the specifically restricted acts, for example, the copying or adaptation of a substantial part of the

---

[104] Directive 91/250/EEC.
[105] eg, in *Donoghue v Allied Newspapers Ltd* [1938] Ch 106, 109 Farwell J stated unequivocally that 'there is no copyright in an idea, or in ideas'.
[106] [1969] SCR 208.
[107] Ibid, 212, citing Pape J in *Cuisenaire v Reed* [1963] VR 719.
[108] This theme is developed in more detail in section 5.5.6 below.

book, that a question of infringement can arise. However, because computer programs in machine-code form are both symbolic and functional, normal use may necessitate such copying or adaptation. Loading or running a computer program typically entails the copying of part or all of the program from a disk (or other permanent storage medium) to the computer's random access memory ('RAM') and central processing unit ('CPU'). Section 17(6) of the CDPA 1988 makes it clear that such copying of a work, even though it may be 'transient' or 'incidental to some other use of the work', is nevertheless an infringement of copyright if done without authorization. Even screen displays generated during the running of a program may constitute infringing copies of copyright material. Because the restriction on copying applies even to simple use of a program, legitimate use can normally only take place pursuant to a licence or permission of some kind. Such a licence may be express or implied. Typically, a software house will seek to attach various conditions to a licence to use. A special provision in the CDPA 1988 dealing with transfers of second-hand copies of programs is dealt with in section 5.5.9 below.

Hence, UK copyright law appears to give indirect protection to the ideas underlying a program by making the literal copying inherent in simple use of the program an infringing act. Thus, unlike the ideas and procedures described in a cookery recipe which can be used without infringing copyright in the recipe book, the ideas and procedures embodied in a computer program are regulated by copyright along with the code which implements them whenever the program is used. It is interesting to note, by way of comparison, that under United States copyright law the owner of a copy of a program does not need a licence to make or authorize the making of another copy or adaptation if doing so is 'an essential step in the utilisation of the computer program in conjunction with a machine'.[109]

A similar approach was adopted in the EU Software Directive,[110] though the deemed right to make copies or adaptations necessary for use seems to be subject to agreement to the contrary. Article 5(1) provides that 'In the absence of specific contractual provisions', copying and adaptation 'shall not require authorisation by the rightholder where they are necessary for the use of the computer program by the lawful acquirer in accordance with its intended purpose, including for error correction'. The words 'in the absence of specific contractual provisions' seem to make it clear that it remains open to a copyright owner to restrict by contract these acts of copying and adaptation necessary for use.[111] This is the interpretation adopted by the UK Government in the implementing regulations. Whether copyright can also be used to prevent non-literal copying, for example, where a person analyses or reverse

---

[109] Title 17 USC, s 117. This derogation from the copyright owner's normal rights to prevent the making of copies and adaptations does not seem to apply where title to the physical copy does not pass to the software user.

[110] Directive 91/250/EEC.

[111] Confusingly, the relevant recital is inconsistent with article 5 and provides that 'the acts of loading and running necessary for the use of a copy of a program that has been lawfully acquired, and the act of correction of its errors, may not be prohibited by contract'. Presumably, article 5 will prevail.

engineers a program and writes new but functionally equivalent code, is a rather more complex issue.

### 5.5.3 Copying, compatibility and reverse engineering

There may be a limited number of ways, in extreme cases possibly only one, of achieving a particular functional result using a specific configuration of hardware and/or software. Sometimes a single manufacturer can establish an almost universal standard or set of standards for carrying out particular operations, perhaps by being there first, by skilful marketing, by dominance in the industry, or sometimes by being truly innovative. Where, for whatever reason, a *de facto* industry standard has emerged, such as the BIOS ('basic input-output system') for IBM-compatible personal computers, the possibility of copyright being used to monopolize the specification of interfaces between hardware and hardware, hardware and software, software and software, and humans and software, has enormous policy implications. Much of the rapid growth and diversity that has characterized the computer industry in the last two decades has resulted from the widespread development of hardware and software products that are 'compatible' with those most popular in the market. Such compatible products frequently improve substantially on the products offered by the company that initiated the standard both in terms of price and performance, and often also in terms of innovation. A user who has invested in a particular 'environment' in terms of hardware, software, or training, will often wish to build on that investment without being tied into a particular supplier or suppliers for all future development purposes.

The development of compatible products can, of course, be effected in a number of ways with varying consequences in copyright terms. At one end of the spectrum, a clone may consist of or contain crude copies of key parts, or indeed the whole, of an established product. The maker of such a clone will be vulnerable to be sued for infringement of copyright and a number of other IPRs. Certainly, the literal copying of the whole or a substantial part of an existing program will almost invariably infringe copyright. At the other end of the spectrum, a developer of a compatible product may invest substantial resources in achieving functional compatibility by independent development without making a verbatim or literal copy of any part of the product that is being emulated. To ensure that it can be proved that the competing product is the result of such original labour and skill, a manufacturer may resort to a rigorous and exhaustively documented 'clean-room' procedure. Such a procedure would normally necessitate independent work being undertaken by two discrete groups of software engineers, the first analysing the product to be emulated and producing a functional specification, the second writing code to implement that specification.[112] In between these extremes of crude copying and sophisticated

---

[112] For an interesting discussion of the issues inherent in duplication of the functionality of the IBM BIOS, see G Gervaise Davis III, 'IBM PC Software and Hardware Compatibility' [1984] EIPR 273.

reverse engineering, there are various ways in which software may be developed using particular ideas or functions derived from pre-existing software products without any substantial literal copying taking place.

Various tests have been suggested for determining whether products developed using either of the latter two approaches will infringe copyright and a certain amount of judicial consideration has been given to these issues in the UK. However, most reported cases and current litigation in the area are concentrated in the United States. Much of the argument there has concerned the extent to which copyright law can provide protection against copying of either the 'structure, sequence and organization' of a program, or of its 'look and feel'. The former concerns the internal structure and workings of a program, the latter its external appearance and user interfaces. Underlying both issues is the fundamental dichotomy in United States law between ideas, which cannot be protected by copyright, and expressions of those ideas, which can. Before looking briefly at some of the American cases, one other general issue should be noted.

### 5.5.4 Difficulties of proving non-literal infringement

A further consequence of the simultaneously symbolic and functional nature of software is that the traditional tests for establishing that copying of a work has occurred may be wholly inappropriate. It is by no means always the case that functional similarity between two programs is indicative of similarity in the underlying symbolic codes. To extend the rabbit-pie analogy one final stage further, just because a rabbit pie looks, smells and tastes very similar to one made by Mrs Beeton is not in itself proof that both have been made from the same recipe. As Megarry V-C put it in *Thrustcode Ltd v WW Computing Ltd*:

... where, as here, the claim is to copyright in the program itself, the results produced by operating the program must not be confused with the program in which copyright is claimed. If I may take an absurdly simple example, 2 and 2 make 4. But so does 2 times 2, or 6 minus 2, or 2 percent of 200, or 6 squared divided by 9, or many other things. Many different processes may produce the same answer and yet remain different processes that have not been copied one from another.[113]

On the facts before it, the court was at a loss to see 'any real evidence of copying'[114] and accordingly dismissed the claimant's case. In *LB (Plastics) Ltd v Swish Products Ltd* Lord Wilberforce observed:

The protection given by the law of copyright is against copying, the basis of protection being that one man must not be permitted to appropriate the result of another's labour. That copying has taken place, is for the plaintiff [claimant] to establish and prove as a matter of fact. The beginning of the necessary proof normally lies in the establishment of similarity combined with proof of access to the plaintiff's [claimant's] productions.[115]

---

[113] [1983] FSR 502, 505.      [114] Ibid, 507.      [115] [1979] FSR 145, 149.

In *Cantor Fitzgerald International v Tradition (UK) Ltd*[116] Pumfrey J held, in finding that copyright infringement had occurred where 3,000 out of 77,000 lines of the claimant's code were copied by the defendant, that it is the function of copyright to protect the relevant skill and labour expended by the author of the work and that it follows that a copyist infringes the copyright if he appropriates a part of the work upon which a substantial part of the author's skill and labour was expended. It is not determined by whether the system would work without the copied code or the amount of use the system makes of the code.

This issue is of fundamental importance in the context of software copyright infringement. It is not enough for a claimant to allege that program code has been copied merely on the basis that a later program is similar to an earlier one in terms of its functionality or its appearance to a user. Actual copying of a substantial part is the key to copyright infringement under UK law.[117] In this case, Pumfrey J accepted that the general architecture of a computer program was capable of protection provided a substantial part of the programmer's skill and labour was used. Therefore, it was possible for specific software modules to be infringed, even though only a small proportion of the code had been copied.[118]

### 5.5.5 Infringement by non-literal copying under United States law

A full discussion of the many reported and pending American cases in the field of software copyright is well beyond the scope of this chapter. However, a brief consideration of some of the issues that have been raised in the United States may assist, sometimes by analogy, sometimes by way of contrast, in evaluating the position under UK copyright law.

In its landmark ruling in *Apple Computer Inc v Franklin Computer Corporation*[119] the United States Court of Appeals for the Third Circuit confirmed unequivocally that computer programs in both source and object code are capable of protection as 'literary works' and that such protection extends to programs in machine code embedded in integrated circuit chips. The court then considered whether program copyright extended to operating systems, and in particular whether a merger of idea and expression would prevent Apple from claiming protection for various operating programs supplied with the Apple II microcomputer. The court ruled that 'If other programs can be written or created which perform the same function as an Apple's operating system program, then that program is an expression of the idea and hence copyrightable'.[120] In response to claims by the defendants that there was only a limited number of ways of writing a compatible operating system:

---

[116] [1999] Masons CLR 157.

[117] See *Catnic Components v Hill & Smith* [1982] RPC 182, 223, followed in *Ibcos Computers Ltd v Barclays Mercantile Highland Finance Ltd* [1994] FSR 275; *Cantor Fitzgerald International v Tradition (UK) Ltd and Others* [1999] Masons CLR 157.

[118] See the comments of Colin Tapper at [1999] Masons CLR 265–6.

[119] (1983) 714 F 2d 1240.

[120] Ibid, 1253.

Franklin may wish to achieve total compatibility with independently developed application programs written for Apple II, but that is a commercial and competitive objective which does not enter into the somewhat metaphysical issue of whether particular ideas and expressions have merged.[121]

The court concluded that operating system programs are not *per se* excluded from copyright protection.

Three years later, a different panel of judges in the same Third Circuit Court of Appeals addressed in rather more detail the application to computer programs of the idea–expression dichotomy. In *Whelan Associates Inc v Jaslow Dental Laboratory Inc*[122] the claimants alleged that a program developed by the defendant in the PC language BASIC infringed their copyright in a similar program written in the mini-computer language EDL. It was accepted that no literal copying had occurred yet the Third Circuit ruled that substantial similarities between the BASIC and EDL programs in terms of their 'structure, sequence and organisation' provided sufficient grounds for a finding of infringement. As regards drawing a line between idea and expression, the court ruled that 'the line between idea and expression may be drawn by reference to the end sought to be achieved by the work in question'.[123] Where the desired purpose can be achieved in more than one way, then any particular means of achieving it will be expression, not idea. On the facts before it, the Third Circuit found that 'the idea of the Dentalab program was the efficient management of a dental laboratory . . . Because that idea could be accomplished in a number of different ways with a number of different structures, the structure of the Dentalab program is part of the program's expression, not its idea.'[124]

The Third Circuit's analysis in *Whelan Associates Inc v Jaslow Dental Laboratory Inc* has been widely criticized by academic writers.[125] A particular concern has been that the court's 'sweeping rule and broad language extend copyright protection too far' by moving towards a degree of monopoly protection previously only given to patent holders.[126] An indication of how widely the *Whelan* ruling could be applied came in *Broderbund Software Inc v Unison World Inc* where it was cited as 'stand[ing] for the proposition that copyright protection is not limited to the literal aspects of a computer program, but rather that it extends to the overall structure of a program, including its audiovisual displays'.[127] The last part of this statement is rather surprising, given that the *Whelan* case was about infringement of a copyright in program code (ie, a literary work), not infringement of copyright in screen displays (ie, audiovisual works). Moreover, in place of the structural analysis conducted by the *Whelan* court, the *Broderbund* court was more concerned with

---

[121] Ibid.        [122] [1987] FSR 1.

[123] Ibid, 19.        [124] Ibid.

[125] eg, D Nimmer, R L Bernacchi and G N Frischling, 'A Structured Approach to Analysing the Substantial Similarity of Computer Software in Copyright Infringement Cases' (1988) 20 Ariz St LJ 625.

[126] Ibid, 630. See also Robert E Ganz, '*Whelan* and "Work Made for Hire" Threaten Job Mobility' (1988) 4 Computer Law Strategist 1.

[127] (1986) 648 F Supp 1127, 1133.

whether 'the infringing work captures the "total concept and feel" of the protected work'. Noting 'the eerie resemblance between the screens of the two programs', the court found that infringement had indeed occurred.[128]

An illustration of the flexibility of the 'total concept and feel' or 'look and feel' approach can be seen in the analysis of an Ohio District Court in *Worlds of Wonder Inc v Vector Intercontinental Inc.*[129] The case concerned allegations of infringement of copyright in a talking animated toy bear known as Teddy Ruxpin. The bear was designed to be used with cassette tapes containing a soundtrack together with software to control the bear's movements. The defendants, in competition with the claimant, produced various tapes containing stories and software for Teddy Ruxpin. The court found infringement of copyright in the bear as an audiovisual work on the ground that:

the general feel and concept of Teddy Ruxpin when telling a fairy tale is the same regardless of whether a WOW or Vector tape is used; the visual effects are identical, and the voices are similar, and the difference in stories does not alter the aesthetic appeal . . . At least, the work created by the Vector tapes is a derivative work, if not an exact copy.[130]

These and other look-and-feel cases set the scene for an action brought by Lotus against alleged infringers of copyright in the look and feel of the user interfaces of its enormously successful '1-2-3' spreadsheet product.

Before identifying the principal issues at stake in the Lotus case, however, consideration should be given to a move by a District Court in California to limit the breadth of the monopoly given to software copyright owners. In *NEC Corporation v Intel Corporation*[131] the court confirmed that microcodes embodied in various Intel chips were protected by copyright as computer programs, yet ruled that the reverse engineering of those programs by NEC did not infringe the relevant copyrights.[132] The court found that 'overall, and particularly with respect to the microroutines, NEC's microcode is not substantially similar to Intel's; but some of the shorter, simpler microroutines resemble Intel's. None, however, are identical'. To resolve the issue of whether those of the shorter microroutines which were similar infringed Intel's copyrights, the court placed great emphasis on the possibility of a merger of idea and expression, not as a basis for denying copyrightability but as a justification for the production of substantially similar code:

In determining an idea's range of expression, constraints are relevant factors to consider . . . In this case, the expression of NEC's microcode was constrained by the use of the macroinstruction set and hardware of the 8086/88 . . . Accordingly, it is the conclusion of this court that the expression of the ideas underlying the shorter, simpler microroutines (including those identified earlier as substantially similar) may be protected only against virtually identical copying,

---

[128] Ibid, 1137.                                          [129] (1986) unreported.
[130] Transcript, p 9.                          [131] (1989) 1 CCH Computer Cases 46,020.
[132] In addition, the court ruled that Intel's failure to ensure that chips containing its microcode were properly marked with appropriate copyright notices had resulted in a forfeiture of its copyrights (1 CCH Computer Cases at 60,845).

and that NEC properly used the underlying ideas, without virtually identically copying their limited expression.[133]

In *Lotus Development Corporation v Paperback Software International*[134] the District Court for the District of Massachusetts was called upon to decide whether the defendant's software package 'VP-Planner' infringed the copyright in Lotus's '1-2-3' package. Both products are electronic spreadsheets intended to facilitate accounting and other processes that involve the manipulation and display of numerical data. District Judge Keeton identified three elements that appeared to him to be 'the principal factors relevant to a decision of copyrightability of a computer program such as Lotus 1-2-3'.[135] These were, first 'some conception or definition of the "idea" '—for the purpose of distinguishing between the idea and its expression'. Secondly, the court must determine 'whether an alleged expression of the idea is limited to elements essential to expression of *that* idea (or is one of only a few ways of expressing the idea) or instead includes identifiable elements of expression not essential to every expression of that idea'. Finally, 'having identified elements of expression not essential to every expression of the idea, the decision-maker must focus on whether those elements are a substantial part of the allegedly copyrightable "work".'[136]

Interestingly, the District Court judge was fairly dismissive of the 'look and feel' concept. He did not find the concept 'significantly helpful' because it was a 'conclusion' rather than a means of reaching a conclusion. Instead, in applying his three-limb test, Judge Keeton looked at the 'user interface' of the two programs. He seemed to accept as a basis for analysis the claimant's description of the user interface as including such elements 'as the menus (and their structure and organization), the long prompts, the screens on which they appear, the function key assignments [and] the macro commands language'.[137] Applying his three-stage test to these elements of the user interface, Judge Keeton found that neither the idea of developing an electronic spreadsheet nor the idea of a two-line moving cursor menu were copyrightable. Both elements thus failed to get beyond the first stage. The basic screen display of a 'rotated L' layout used in most spreadsheet packages to set out columns and rows failed to pass the second stage as 'there is a rather low limit, as a factual matter, on the number of ways of making a computer screen resemble a spreadsheet'. Similarly the use of a particular key to invoke the menu command system was found to be 'Another expressive element that merges with the idea of an electronic spreadsheet'.[138]

One element of the 1-2-3 package did, however, satisfy all three elements of the copyrightability test. The menu command system itself was capable of many types of expression and its precise 'structure, sequence and organization' was 'distinctive'. Reaching the third element of his test, Judge Keeton found it to be 'incontrovertible' that the menu command system was a substantial part of the alleged copyrighted work:

---

[133] 1 CCH Computer Cases 60,853.     [134] (1990) 2 CCH Computer Cases 46,310.
[135] Ibid, 62,264.          [136] Ibid.          [137] Ibid, 62,266.          [138] Ibid, 62,268.

The user interface of 1-2-3 is its most unique element, and is the aspect that has made 1-2-3 so popular. That defendants went to such trouble to copy that element is a testament to its substantiality. Accordingly, evaluation of the third element of the legal test weighs heavily in favour of Lotus.[139]

The court's conclusion was that it was 'indisputable that defendants have copied substantial copyrightable elements of plaintiff's [claimant's] copyrighted work . . . therefore . . . liability has been established'.[140]

However, subsequently, in *Brown Bag Software v Symantec Corp*[141] the Ninth Circuit rejected the claimant's argument that the *Lotus* approach should be applied in deciding whether the graphical user interface of the defendant's outlining program infringed the claimant's copyright. Instead, the court held that it should engage in 'analytical dissection not for the purposes of comparing similarities and identifying infringement, but for the purposes of defining the scope of plaintiff's [claimant's] copyright'.[142] Thus, the court should first determine which elements are uncopyrightable, applying the ideaexpression dichotomy and the merger doctrine to each element. Only then should it compare the protectable elements of expression to determine whether infringement may have occurred.

Many district and circuit judges have also been critical of the Third Circuit's approach in *Whelan Associates Inc v Jaslow Dental Laboratory Inc* to the separation of ideas, which may not be protected, from expressions which may be.[143] In *Plains Cotton Cooperative Association of Lubbock Texas v Goodpasture Computer Services Inc*[144] the Court of Appeals for the Fifth Circuit 'declined to embrace' *Whelan*. Subsequently the Second Circuit, in *Computer Associates v Altai*[145] has commented that the *Whelan* approach to separating idea and expression 'relies too heavily on metaphysical distinctions'. Instead, the *Altai* court suggested that District Courts would be 'well advised' to adopt a three-step procedure for determining substantial similarity of non-literal elements of computer programs. First, the court should break down the allegedly infringed program into its constituent structural parts. Secondly, the court should examine each of these parts for such things as incorporated ideas, expression that is necessarily incidental to those ideas, and elements that are taken from the public domain, thus sifting out all non-protectable material. Thirdly, 'left with a kernel, or possibly kernels, of creative expression after following this process of elimination, the court's last step would be to compare this material with the structure of an allegedly infringing program'.[146] This has become known as the 'abstraction-filtration-comparison' analysis.

---

[139] Ibid, 62,269.                                                  [140] Ibid, 62,271.
[141] (1992) 960 F 2d 1465.                                          [142] Ibid, 1475–6.
[143] See, eg, *Comprehensive Technologies Int'l v Software Artisans Inc* Civil No 90-1143-A (ED Va 2 June 1992).
[144] (1987) 807 F 2d 1256.
[145] (1992) 3 CCH Computer Cases 46,505.
[146] *Computer Associates v Altai* (22 June 1992), transcript, p 28.

The court concluded that 'we seek to ensure two things: (1) that programmers may receive appropriate copyright protection for innovative utilitarian works containing expression; and (2) that non-protectable technical expression remains in the public domain for others to use freely as building blocks in their own work'.[147] It is interesting to note that the court relied heavily on the Supreme Court's decision in *Feist Publications Inc v Rural Telephone Service Co Inc*,[148] noting that '*Feist* teaches that substantial effort alone cannot confer copyright status on an otherwise uncopyrightable work' and that 'despite the fact that significant labor and expense often goes into computer program flow-charting and debugging, that process does not always result in inherently protectable expression'.[149]

In recent cases it appears that the trend is shifting away from the 'look and feel' approach towards *Altai*'s analytical three-step test. In *Gates Rubber Co v Bando Chemical Industries Ltd*[150] the Court of Appeals for the Tenth Circuit formulated a refined version of the *Altai* test. The court suggested that before beginning the abstraction-filtration-comparison process it would normally be helpful for the court to compare the programs as a whole, as 'an initial holistic comparison may reveal a pattern of copying that is not obvious when only certain components are examined'.[151] The abstraction-filtration-comparison test itself remained comparable to the *Altai* version:

First, in order to provide a framework for analysis, we conclude that a court should dissect the program according to its varying levels of generality as provided in the abstraction test. Second, poised with this framework, the court should examine each level of abstraction in order to filter out those elements of the program that are unprotectable. Filtration should eliminate from comparison the unprotectable elements of ideas, processes, facts, public domain information, merger material, *scènes à faire* material, and other unprotectable elements suggested by the particular facts of the program under examination. Third, the court should then compare the remaining protectable elements with the allegedly infringing program to determine whether the defendants have misappropriated substantial elements of the plaintiff's [claimant's] program.[152]

Applying this test the court found that certain mathematical constants in a computer program were not protectable because they represented scientific observations of relationships that existed and were not invented or created by the claimant.

In the case of *Kepner-Tregoe v Leadership Software Inc*[153] concerning management-training software, the Court of Appeals for the Fifth Circuit held that non-literal aspects of copyrighted works may be protected. This decision was applied in *Engineering Dynamics Inc v Structural Software Inc*[154] to apply to non-literal aspects of a computer program, reversing a District Court's decision that input and output formats were uncopyrightable. The District Court, in coming to its conclusion, had thought *Lotus* was 'persuasive' but had declined to follow the decision.

---

[147] Ibid, 58.                                                                   [148] (1990) 113 L Ed 2d 358.
[149] *Computer Associates v Altai* (22 June 1992), transcript, 41.
[150] (1993) 4 CCH Computer Cases 46,971.      [151] Ibid, 65,812.              [152] Ibid, 65,806.
[153] (1994) 4 CCH Computer Cases 47,019.               [154] (1994) 4 CCH Computer Cases 47,095.

The Court of Appeals for the Fifth Circuit stated that the District Court had 'erred' and that the abstraction-filtration-comparison of *Gates Rubber* and *Altai* was appropriate on the facts albeit that:

Describing this approach as abstraction-filtration-comparison should not convey a deceptive air of certitude about the outcome of any particular computer copyright case. Protectable originality can manifest itself in many ways, so the analytic approach may need to be varied to accommodate each case's facts.[155]

Since *Engineering Dynamics, Altai's* abstraction-filtration-comparison analysis has tended to be applied more or less as a matter of course to determine the scope of copyright protection in cases involving non-literal copying.[156]

### 5.5.6 Infringement by non-literal copying under UK law

As already noted, the extent to which ideas are excluded from protection under UK copyright law has perhaps tended to be exaggerated. Some commentators have suggested that there is, on the contrary, considerable scope for protection of ideas provided merely that they have been reduced to writing or some other material form. Laddie, Prescott and Vitoria, for example, identify the 'pithy catch-phrase' that 'there is no copyright in ideas or information but only in the form in which they are expressed' and comment:

A moment's thought will reveal that the maxim is obscure, or in its broadest sense suspect. For example, in the case of a book the ideas it contains are necessarily expressed in words. Hence, if it were really true that the copyright is confined to the form of expression, one would expect to find that anyone was at liberty to borrow the contents of the book provided he took care not to employ the same or similar language. This is not so, of course. Thus, it is an infringement of the copyright to make a version of a novel in which the story or action is conveyed wholly by means of pictures; or to turn it into a play, although not a line of dialogue is similar to any sentence in the book. Again, a translation of a work into another language can be an infringement; yet, since the form of expression is necessarily different—indeed, if it is turned into a language such as Chinese the translation will consist of ideograms—the only connecting factor must be the detailed ideas and information.[157]

Laddie, Prescott and Vitoria also note that most of the cases commonly cited in support of the exclusion of ideas from protection were decided prior to the 1956 Act, many indeed prior to the 1911 Act, and would probably be decided differently

---

[155] (1994) 4 CCH Computer Cases 47,095, 66,555.

[156] See, eg, *Cognotec Services Ltd v Morgan Guarantee Trust Company of New York* 862 F Supp 45, 49–51 (SDNY 1994) 5 CCH Computer Cases 47,143; *Mitek Holdings Inc v ARCE Engineering Co Inc* 864 F Supp 1568, 1577–8 (SD Fla 1994) 5 CCH Computer Cases 47,203; *Bateman v Mnemonics Inc* 79 F 3d 1532 (11th Cir 1996) 6 CCH Computer Cases 47,356; and *Country Kids 'n Slicks Inc v Sheen* 77 F 3d 1280, 1288–9 (10th Cir 1996).

[157] H Laddie, P Prescott and M Vitoria, *The Modern Law of Copyright and Designs*, 2nd edn (Butterworths, 1998), paras 2.73 and 2.75 (footnotes omitted).

today.[158] Similar scepticism about the blanket exclusion of ideas from copyright has been expressed in judicial circles. In *LB (Plastics) Ltd v Swish Products Ltd* Lord Hailsham of St Marylebone LC observed:

... it is trite law that there is no copyright in ideas ... But, of course, as the late Professor Joad used to observe, it all depends on what you mean by 'ideas'. What the respondents in fact copied from the appellants was no mere general idea.[159]

More recently, in *Plix Products Ltd v Frank M Winstone (Merchants)*,[160] a case concerning infringement of artistic copyright, Pritchard J of the High Court of New Zealand has suggested that the so-called 'idea–expression dichotomy' can perhaps best be understood by distinguishing two different kinds, or levels, of 'ideas'. The first type of idea, 'the general idea or basic concept of the work', cannot be protected by copyright. Copyright can, however, subsist in the second type, namely 'the ideas which are applied in the exercise of giving expression to basic concepts'. As Pritchard J then observed:

The difficulty, of course, is to determine just where the general concept ends and the exercise of expressing the concept begins ... The basic idea (or concept) is not necessarily simple—it may be complex. It may be something innovative; or it may be commonplace, utilitarian or banal. The way the author treats the subject, the forms he uses to express the basic concept, may range from the crude and simplistic to the ornate, complicated—and involving the collation and application of a great number of constructive ideas. It is in this area that the author expends the skill and industry which (even though they may be slight) give the work its originality and entitle him to copyright. Anyone is free to use the basic idea—unless, of course, it is a novel invention that is protected by the grant of a patent. But no one can appropriate the forms or shapes evolved by the author in the process of giving expression to the basic idea. So he who seeks to make a product of the same description as that in which another owns copyright must tread with care.[161]

This analysis has interesting implications for the debates relating to the development of compatible software by means of reverse engineering, and the emulation of the look and feel of the user interfaces of popular software packages. The UK courts may tend, like the High Court of New Zealand, to be concerned more with whether a significant amount of an author's labour and skill has been misappropriated, than with whether what has been taken is 'merely' an idea, though there is as yet insufficient case law in the UK to be sure. To date, there have been only four reported software copyright infringement cases under the CDPA 1988 and a number of reported interlocutory (pre-trial) rulings relating to alleged infringements.[162]

---

[158] Ibid, paras 2.50–2.54.          [159] [1979] FSR 145, 160.
[160] [1986] FSR 63.          [161] Ibid, 93–4.
[162] The interlocutory judgments are *Gates v Swift* [1981] FSR 57; *Sega Enterprises Ltd v Richards* [1983] FSR 73; *Systematica Ltd v London Computer Centre Ltd* [1983] FSR 313; *Thrustcode Ltd v WW Computing Ltd* [1983] FSR 502; *MS Associates Ltd v Power* [1988] FSR 242; *Leisure Data v Bell* [1988] FSR 367; *Total Information Processing Systems Ltd v Daman Ltd* [1992] FSR 171; *Shetland Times Ltd v Jonathan Wills and Another* [1997] SLT 669; and *Microsoft Corp v Electro-Wide Ltd* [1997] FSR 580.

*John Richardson Computers Ltd v Flanders*[163] was the first full English trial for alleged infringement of software copyright. The case concerned allegations of literal and semi-literal copying of the claimant's program as evidenced at the user interface level. The defendant had worked for the claimant when the claimant was developing his program and had later developed his own. The programs were for use by pharmacists and had a number of idiosyncratic user features and routines in common. Ferris J referred to US case law and commented:

at the stage at which the substantiality of any copying falls to be assessed in an English case the question which has to be answered, in relation to the originality of the plaintiff's [claimant's] program and the separation of an idea from its expression, is essentially the same question as the United States court was addressing in *Computer Associates v Altai*. In my judgment it would be right to adopt a similar approach in England.[164]

In deciding the case he drew on the filtration and comparison parts of *Computer Associates v Altai*[165] but rejected the abstraction test as inappropriate in the circumstances. The reliance he placed on United States law, which is, after all, based on a statutory bar on the grant of copyright protection for ideas, was somewhat surprising. Such an approach might result in computer programs being treated differently from other kinds of work. This would be an undesirable outcome both in terms of the functioning of copyright law and for the computer industry in its production of multimedia products. Moreover, the *Richardson* case was evidentially somewhat unclear. Ferris J did not attempt to compare the codes of the two programs, relying entirely on visual evidence at the user interface level. Although understandable given the complexities of the case and the genuine difficulty of comparing code, this tended to obscure what the work in issue really was.

The following year in *Ibcos Computers Ltd v Barclays Mercantile Highland Finance Ltd*[166] Jacob J took a markedly different approach. He rejected the idea that United States precedents should be applied by the English courts, instead favouring a more traditional copyright analysis based on English legal principles. The facts were somewhat simpler than in *Richardson*, involving the literal or semi-literal copying of source code in an agricultural dealer system. Jacob J discussed at length not only the *Richardson* case, but also one of the interlocutory judgments, *Total Information Processing Systems Ltd v Daman Ltd*.[167] In that case Paul Baker QC, sitting as a deputy High Court judge, had not been prepared to find *prima facie* evidence of infringement notwithstanding admitted copying. He gave a preliminary ruling that there was no arguable case that the claimant had infringed copyright by copying various field and record specifications in the defendant's costing program. The defendant claimed, first, that the three-program package was a compilation, copyright in which was infringed when the claimant substituted its payroll program for the defendant's. Secondly, the defendant claimed that the copying of the specifi-

---

[163] [1993] FSR 497.                                         [164] Ibid.
[165] (1992) 3 CCH Computer Cases 46,505.        [166] [1994] FSR 275.
[167] [1992] FSR 171.

cation of the files and records from the costing program infringed copyright in that program. The judge rejected the argument that the compilation was protected, partly because:

> to accord it copyright protection would lead to great inconvenience. It would mean that the copyright owners of one of the components could not interface with another similar program to that of the other components without the licence of the compiler.[168]

Regarding the specification that had been copied, he ruled that:

> The part copied can be likened to a table of contents. It would be very unusual that that part of a book could be described as a substantial part of it. The specification in high-level language of fields and records in the data division tells one little or nothing about the costing program and so, in my judgment, cannot be regarded as a substantial part of it.[169]

Both of these conclusions are curious. Regarding the first, it has never been a criterion for copyright protection that the partial monopoly afforded by a copyright must not lead to 'great inconvenience'. In *Ibcos Computers Ltd v Barclays Mercantile Highland Finance Ltd* Jacob J commented:

> I cannot agree. Of course the owner of the copyright in an individual program could interface his program with that of another. What he could not do is to put his program into an *original* compilation of another without that other's licence. The same is true of any other copyright works, be they poems, songs or whatever.[170]

Regarding the second of Mr Baker's conclusions, it seems quite likely that a detailed table of contents for a book could constitute not only a substantial part of a work but might even be a work in its own right. Similarly, a program specification could qualify as either a substantial part of a work or as a discrete work. Jacob J commented:

> Very often the working out of a reasonably detailed arrangement of topics, sub-topics and sub-sub-topics is the key to a successful work of non-fiction. I see no reason why the taking of that could not amount to an infringement. Likewise, there may be a considerable degree of skill involved in setting up the data division of a program. In practice, this is done with the operating division in mind and its construction may well involve enough skill, labour and, I add, judgment, for it to be considered a substantial part of the program as a whole.[171]

Paul Baker QC further stated that there could be no copyright in the expression of an idea if the expression has a function and there is only one or a limited number of ways of achieving it. Jacob J took the view that, unlike United States law, English law does protect certain types of ideas. Rather:

> The true position is that where an 'idea' is sufficiently general, then even if an original work embodies it, the mere taking of that idea will not infringe. But if the 'idea' is detailed, then there may be infringement. It is a question of degree. The same applies whether the work is fictional or not, and whether visual or literary.[172]

---

[168] Ibid, 179.          [169] Ibid, 180–1.          [170] [1994] FSR 275, 290.
[171] Ibid, 303.          [172] Ibid, 291.

Paul Baker QC also suggested that copyright could not subsist in source code because the industry makes copious efforts to protect itself via confidentiality. Jacob J disagreed, saying:

> I do not understand this observation . . . Because people keep confidential material which would be of considerable use to pirates is no reason for saying that copyright does not protect it . . . I unhesitatingly say that source code can be the subject of copyright.[173]

Moving on to discuss *Richardson*, Jacob J noted that Ferris J had supported the United States approach of looking for the core of protectable expression and separating it from the unprotectable idea, leaving only 'expression' to be taken into account in determining substantiality. Jacob J found this method unhelpful. Instead, he returned to a more traditional English legal analysis, whereby ideas are not precluded from protection and the test is a question of degree, a 'good guide' being:

> the notion of overborrowing of the skill, labour and judgment which went into the copyright work. Going via the complication of the concept of a 'core of protectable expression' merely complicates the matter so far as our law is concerned. It is likely to lead to an overcitation of United States authority based on a statute different from ours.[174]

Jacob J's straightforward approach towards finding substantiality and his rejection of some of Paul Baker's views in *Total Information Processing Systems Ltd v Daman Ltd* were well received in the industry.

There are currently three trends that might result, generally, in a weakening of copyright protection for software. One trend which, if developed, would significantly weaken the scope of copyright protection for software is reliance on the principle of non-derogation from grant as a basis for permitting what would otherwise be infringing acts. The limited 'repair right' recognized by the House of Lords in *British Leyland Motor Corporation Ltd v Armstrong Patents Co Ltd*[175] has been applied by the Official Referee's Court in *Saphena Computing Ltd v Allied Collection Agencies Ltd*[176] to permit acts necessary for software maintenance which would normally infringe copyright.[177] However, Jacob J considered a similar issue in the *Ibcos* case and held that the right to repair held to exist in *British Leyland* could not be relied upon by analogy to establish a right to copy file-transfer utilities.[178]

A second basis for a weakening of the monopoly given by copyright would rest

---

[173] Ibid, 296.                                                                                  [174] Ibid, 302.
[175] [1986] AC 577.                                                                          [176] [1995] FSR 616.
[177] *British Leyland Motor Corporation Ltd v Armstrong Patents Co Ltd* concerned the protection of the designs of functional objects, spare parts for cars, through artistic copyright in the underlying design drawings. This basis of claim has been severely restricted by the CDPA 1988. On appeal in *Saphena Computing Ltd v Allied Collection Agencies Ltd* [1995] FSR 616 the Court of Appeal did not comment on the Official Referee's finding. See also *Canon Kabushiki Kaisha v Green Cartridge Company (Hong Kong) Ltd* [1997] FSR 817.
[178] See also *Mars UK Ltd v Teknowledge Ltd (No 2)*, *The Times*, 23 June 1999 where it was held that *British Leyland* had been decided under the Copyright Act 1956 and there was no longer room for such a common-law exception because there was now a complete statutory code to cover any exceptions.

on a development of competition-law principles. How would a UK court respond if asked to decide on the scope of copyright protection in circumstances where, for example, a single set of machine instructions was the only way to achieve a particular functional result, such as interfacing with a particular item of hardware or software? In such a case, it might be possible for the court to conclude that the subject matter in question is not protected by copyright due to lack of originality. However, a particular interface specification or procedure may be highly original and the result of considerable labour and skill. As has already been established, UK courts cannot invoke a 'merger doctrine' as a justification for excluding material from copyright on the ground that idea and expression have merged. In practice, however, a person who sought to use copyright as a basis for monopolizing a *de facto* industry standard might be vulnerable to challenge under UK or EU competition law (see Chapter 14).

A third, and related, consideration is the Software Directive.[179] Article 1(2) of the Software Directive requires all EU Member States to protect programs as literary works but to exclude from protection 'Ideas and principles which underlie any element of a computer program, including those which underlie its interfaces'. The Copyright (Computer Programs) Regulations 1992 contain no reference to the exclusion of ideas from copyright protection. This is presumably because the UK Government believed that ideas were already excluded from protection as a result of judicial pronouncements to that effect. However, even if English law is already consistent with article 1(2), there will remain considerable scope for dispute about what constitutes an 'idea' for the 'decompilation' right is so hedged about by restrictions as to give developers of compatible products limited comfort regarding risks that their reverse engineering activities may infringe copyright.

### 5.5.7 Decompilation of computer programs

During the Software Directive's turbulent passage through the EU legislative process, by far the most contentious issue concerned the new right to be given to users permitting them to decompile a program where necessary to achieve the interoperability of that program with another program. The complex compromise agreed by the principal protagonists, after many months of heated debate and lobbying, is now enshrined in article 6 of the Directive. The wording of the Directive is altered somewhat in the Copyright (Computer Programs) Regulations 1992 but, in effect, the provisions of article 6(1) and (2) are implemented in full. The Regulations state that it is not an infringement of copyright for a 'lawful user' of a copy of a computer program which is 'expressed in a low level language' to convert it into a higher level language, so copying it, provided two conditions are met. These are that such decompilation is necessary 'to obtain the information necessary to create an independent program which can be operated with the program decompiled or with

---

[179] Directive 91/250/EEC.

another program', which is defined as the 'permitted objective', and that 'the information so obtained is not used for any purpose other than the permitted objective'.

Exercise of the decompilation right is hedged about by four further restrictions. The Regulations state that the two conditions described above are not met if the lawful user has the information necessary to achieve the permitted objective readily available to him; does not confine decompilation to acts necessary to achieve the permitted objective; supplies information obtained by decompiling to a third party to whom it is not necessary to supply it to achieve the permitted objective; or uses the information to create a program which is substantially similar in its expression to the decompiled program or to do any act restricted by copyright.[180]

Consistent with article 9(1) of the Directive, the Regulations render void any provisions which purport to prohibit or restrict the decompilation right.

### 5.5.8 Back-up copies of computer programs

Article 5(2) of the Software Directive provides that 'The making of a back-up copy by a person having a right to use the computer program may not be prevented by contract insofar as it is necessary for that use'. The Copyright (Computer Programs) Regulations 1992 have implemented article 5(2). Section 50A of the CDPA 1988 permits the making of an additional copy of a program by a lawful user 'which it is necessary for him to have for the purposes of his lawful use'. In practice, most PC software must be loaded on to the hard disk of a PC before it can be run. The loading process often entails the 'explosion' of compressed files and the installation of the package for a particular configuration of hardware and software. The making of a back-up copy, in the sense of a verbatim copy of the original disks, may be unnecessary, as the original CD or disks will be available for back-up purposes. Thus, the back-up exemption may be of limited application.

### 5.5.9 Second-hand copies of works in electronic form

Section 56 of the CDPA 1988 contains a complex and somewhat convoluted statement of the rights to be enjoyed by a person taking a transfer from the original purchaser of a copy of a program or other work in electronic form. The provision is applicable where a copy of such a work 'has been purchased on terms which, expressly or impliedly or by virtue of any rule of law, allow the purchaser to copy the work, or to adapt it or make copies of an adaptation, in connection with his use of it'. Subject to any express terms to the contrary, where the copy is transferred to a third party, that person is entitled to do anything with the copy which the original purchaser was permitted to do. From the moment of transfer, however, any copy or adaptation retained by the original purchaser will be treated as an infringing copy.

---

[180] CDPA 1988, s 50B(3), inserted by the Copyright (Computer Programs) Regulations 1992, SI 1992/3233, reg 8.

The same rules apply to any subsequent transfers made by the new owner and that person's successors in title.

Section 56 is not a model of clarity. Taking its application to computer programs, packaged software is typically distributed with a licence 'agreement' in which the software producer purports to retain title to part or all of the product. Where title to the physical copy of the program does not pass, it will make no sense to speak of the 'purchaser' of the copy. Moreover, the scope for inferring licences in this area is quite uncertain and thus the reference to terms which the purchaser has the benefit of 'impliedly or by virtue of any rule of law' is not particularly illuminating. In practice, quite apart from the theoretical question of whether or not there is a 'purchaser', it is likely to continue to be the norm for computer programs, and many other works published in electronic form, to be distributed with an express prohibition, or at least restriction, on transfers to third parties. In all such cases, the operation of section 56 will be completely pre-empted.

## 5.6 MORAL RIGHTS

### 5.6.1 The nature of moral rights

The Berne Union, of which the UK is a member, provides for its members to give authors various 'moral rights'. Such rights are to be personal to the author or creator of a work and are to be capable of exercise independently of the economic exploitation rights in the work. For the first time in the UK, the CDPA 1988 gave the author of a work or director of a film the right, in certain circumstances, to be identified as such (s 77). Relevant circumstances include commercial publication of the work or any adaptation of it. This right is otherwise known as the right of 'paternity'. Authors and directors also have the right to object to 'derogatory treatment' of their works (s 80(1)), which right is otherwise known as the right of 'integrity'. Treatment of a work will be deemed derogatory 'if it amounts to distortion or mutilation of the work or is otherwise prejudicial to the honour or reputation of the author or director' (s 80(2)). Two other moral rights give protection against false attribution of a work,[181] and the right to privacy of certain photographs and films (s 85). With the exception of the false-attribution right, which expires twenty years after a person's death, all of the moral rights continue to subsist for as long as copyright subsists in the work in question (s 86). The rest of the discussion here will be focused on the rights of paternity and integrity as they apply to literary, dramatic, musical and artistic works.

---

[181] ie, the right not to have a work wrongly attributed to one (s 84).

## 5.6.2 Restrictions on scope

The right of paternity must be asserted in writing and will in most cases only bind third parties who have notice of it (CDPA 1988, s 78). In the case of works created in the course of employment, the right does not apply to anything done by, or with the authority of, the employer or any subsequent owner of copyright in the work (s 79(3)). The right of integrity is also severely cut back in relation to works created by employees, copyright in which originally vested in their employers (s 82(1)).[182] Neither right applies, in any event, in relation to computer programs and computer-generated works (ss 79(2) and 81(2)).

These exclusions appear, at first sight, to abrogate moral rights as they apply to works produced by the computer industry. Moral rights will, nevertheless, have significant implications for the computer and related industries and those who work in them. As already noted in this chapter, software packages, for example, are much more than computer programs for copyright purposes. While moral rights will not be available in respect of any programs and computer-generated works incorporated in a package nor any work owned automatically by an employer, moral rights will be available in respect of many other works produced on a commissioning basis. For example, a freelance technical author would be able to assert the right of paternity and object to unjust modification of published manuals or other documentation, and a freelance artist may make such claims with regard to published artwork. Moreover, moral rights will be applicable to many works that are included in databases and in that context it is difficult to see how the right of paternity could be exercised without becoming unduly cumbersome. Protection against false attribution applies to all categories of works but is less likely to cause problems in practice.

## 5.6.3 Consents and waivers

Although moral rights are 'inalienable' and thus cannot be assigned like the economic rights in a work,[183] a person entitled to moral rights can forgo the right to exercise the rights in part or completely. In general, it is not an infringement of moral rights to do anything to which the rightholder has consented. Moreover, any of the moral rights 'may be waived by instrument in writing signed by the person giving up the right'. Such waivers may relate to specific works or to works generally, may be conditional or unconditional, and may be made subject to revocation (CDPA 1988, s 87). Given the potential difficulties that were identified in section 5.6.2 above, it is probable that many organizations will include express consents or waivers of moral rights in their standard terms of business for commissioned works.

---

[182] The right will only apply if the author '(a) is identified at the time of the relevant act, or (b) has previously been identified in or on published copies of the work' (s 82(2)).

[183] Although they do form part of an author's estate on death and consequently can pass to third parties under a will or on intestacy (s 95).

### 5.6.4 Remedies

Infringements of moral rights are actionable as breaches of statutory duty owed to the person entitled to the right (CDPA 1988, s 103(1)). In relation to infringement of the right to object to derogatory treatment of a work, a court may grant an injunction requiring a disclaimer to be given, for example, on publication, dissociating the author from the treatment of the work (s 103(2)). In relation to the right of paternity, a court must, in considering what remedy should be given for an infringement, take into account any delay in asserting the right (s 78(5)). Both of these qualifications on remedies have the effect of further limiting the potential commercial leverage which moral rights may confer on an author. Where, for example, a publisher has incurred considerable expense over a period of time in preparing a work for publication, instead of stopping publication because of derogatory treatment a court may merely order that a disclaimer be printed. Likewise, the author's right of paternity may effectively be undermined as a result of any delay in asserting the right.

## 5.7 CIVIL REMEDIES, CRIMINAL SANCTIONS AND PROCEDURAL MATTERS

### 5.7.1 Civil remedies

Copyright is a property right, and where infringement has been proved, the copyright owner can, subject to certain special rules, benefit from 'all such relief . . . as is available in respect of the infringement of any other property right' (CDPA 1988, s 96). In practice, the principal remedies are injunctions to prevent further breaches of copyright, damages for breach of copyright and orders for delivery up of infringing copies. Other remedies include accounts of profits (used relatively rarely because of the difficulty of proving the precise profits made) and orders for disposal of infringing copies which have been seized or delivered up to a claimant (see generally the CDPA 1988, ss 96–106 and 113–15).

Various court orders can be obtained at the pre-trial stage, in some circumstances without the alleged infringer being given any warning or opportunity to make representations to the court. One such order that has been used with particular success against audio, video and software pirates is the 'search order'.[184] Such an order can authorize a claimant to enter a defendant's premises, without prior warning, to seize evidentiary material which might otherwise be tampered with or disappear before trial. This is obviously a powerful remedy capable of abuse in the hands of overenthusiastic claimants and the courts now supervise its use quite strictly.[185]

---

[184] Formerly called an 'Anton Piller order' after the case in which it was first obtained, *Anton Piller KG v Manufacturing Processes Ltd* [1976] Ch 55. For an example of the grant of such an order in a case of alleged software piracy, see *Gates v Swift* [1981] FSR 57.

[185] In another software copyright case, *Systematica Ltd v London Computer Centre Ltd* [1983] FSR

Whilst a final injunction may be granted at trial, it is quite common in cases of alleged software copyright infringement for an 'interim' injunction to be granted in pre-trial proceedings. An injunction may be prohibitory, for example, enjoining a defendant from copying or in any way dealing with the material that is the subject of the dispute.[186] Alternatively, or in addition, an injunction may be mandatory, for example, requiring delivery up of source code pending trial.[187]

As a general rule, damages for copyright infringement are intended to compensate a claimant for actual loss incurred as a result of the infringement. This might typically be calculated on the basis of royalties which would have been payable to the claimant had the defendant, instead of infringing copyright, obtained a licence for the acts in question. The CDPA 1988 specifies one set of circumstances in which damages must not be awarded, and one in which they may be increased beyond the compensatory level. The former arises where it is shown that the defendant did not know and had no reason to believe that copyright subsisted in the work in question at the time of infringement. In such circumstances, 'the plaintiff [claimant] is not entitled to damages against him, but without prejudice to any other remedy' (s 97(1)). In other cases, however, the court may award 'such additional damages as the justice of the case may require' in all the circumstances, with particular reference to '(a) the flagrancy of the infringement, and (b) any benefit accruing to the defendant by reason of the infringement' (s 97(2)).[188]

### 5.7.2 Criminal sanctions

The CDPA 1988 sets out a number of categories of criminal copyright infringement which, in general, are intended to penalize those who deliberately infringe copyright with a view to commercial gain. Specifically, it is an offence, if done without a licence, to manufacture for sale or hire, import into the UK other than for private and domestic use, distribute in the course of business or otherwise 'to such an extent as to affect prejudicially' the rights of the copyright owner, an article which the

---

313, 316, Whitford J observed that 'A situation is developing where I think rather too free a use is being made by plaintiffs [claimants] of the *Anton Piller* provision'. Subsequently, in *Columbia Picture Industries v Robinson* [1986] FSR 367, 439, Scott J commented 'that the practice of the court has allowed the balance to swing too far in favour of the plaintiffs [claimants] and that *Anton Piller* orders have been too readily granted and with insufficient safeguards for respondents'. The court laid down a number of procedural safeguards which should be complied with to ensure minimum protection for defendants.

[186] eg, *Raindrop Data Systems Ltd v Systematics Ltd* [1988] FSR 354; *Leisure Data v Bell* [1988] FSR 367.

[187] eg, *Redwood Music Ltd v Chappell & Co Ltd* [1982] RPC 109.

[188] In *Nottinghamshire Healthcare National Health Service Trust v News Group Newspapers Limited*, 14 March 2002 (unreported), a photograph of a patient was published by the *Sun* newspaper in breach of copyright. Under section 96 damages of £450 were awarded on the basis that this would have been the agency fee payable if the photograph had been published with consent. A further £10,000 was awarded under section 97 as additional damages. Factors taken into consideration in reaching this figure included the fact that the photograph was stolen; the conduct of the defendant (in particular destruction of evidence); and the failure to apologize to the claimant.

offender knows to be, or has reason to believe to be, an infringing copy of a work (CDPA 1988, s 107(1)(a), (b), (d)(iv) and (e)). On summary conviction the penalties for such an offence are imprisonment for up to six months and a fine not exceeding the statutory maximum, or both (s 107(4)(a)).[189] On conviction on indictment the maximum penalties are imprisonment for up to ten years or a fine.[190]

It is an offence, if done without a licence, to possess in the course of a business with a view to committing an infringing act, or in the course of business to sell or let for hire, to offer or expose for sale or hire, or exhibit in public, an article which the offender knows to be, or has reason to believe to be, an infringing copy of a work (s 107(1)(c), (d)(i), (ii) and (iii)). It is also an offence to make or possess 'an article specifically designed or adapted for making infringing copies of a particular copyright work' if the offender knows or has reason to believe that the article will be used to make infringing copies for sale or hire or use in the course of a business (s 107(2)).[191] These latter categories of offences are only triable summarily and the maximum penalties are imprisonment for up to six months or a fine not exceeding level 5 on the standard scale, or both (s 107(5)).[192]

Where a person is charged with any of the criminal offences under the CDPA 1988, the court before which proceedings are brought may order delivery up of any infringing copy or article for making infringing copies (s 108). The CDPA 1988 also provides for a magistrate, if satisfied that one of the offences which are triable either way has been or is about to be committed and that relevant evidence is in specified premises, to 'issue a warrant authorising a constable to enter and search the premises, using such reasonable force as is necessary' (s 109). Moreover, where any of the offences is committed by a company 'with the consent or connivance of a director, manager, secretary or other similar officer . . . or a person purporting to act in any such capacity' that person is also guilty of the offence, and liable to be prosecuted and punished accordingly (s 110).

Taken as a whole, these criminal offences set high stakes for commercial copyright infringement and are intended to provide an effective deterrent against commercial infringement of copyright in software and other works. Moreover, a software pirate who fraudulently uses a trade mark may be convicted of a counterfeiting offence, the maximum penalty for which is ten years' imprisonment.[193]

---

[189] At the time of writing the statutory maximum was £5,000.

[190] Section 107(4)(b). There is no statutory limit on the fine which may be imposed on conviction for one of these offences on indictment. In practice, however, the amount will be governed by the general principle that a fine should be within an offender's capacity to pay (*R v Churchill (No 2)* [1967] 1 QB 190).

[191] Interpretation of the equivalent civil infringement is discussed at section 5.4.2 above.

[192] At the time of writing, level 5 on the standard scale was £5,000.

[193] Trade Marks Act 1994, s 92(6). An offender convicted on indictment may also be liable to pay an unlimited fine. The penalty limits for summary conviction are six months' imprisonment and a fine not exceeding the statutory maximum.

### 5.7.3 Presumptions

A prerequisite to a successful action for copyright infringement, whether in civil or criminal proceedings, is proof of authorship and ownership of the relevant copyright(s). For practical and procedural reasons, proof of such facts can sometimes constitute a substantial hurdle to a claimant or prosecutor, as the case may be. The CDPA 1988 provides that various presumptions will apply in proceedings relating to various types of copyright work. These include a presumption that where a name purporting to be that of the author of a literary, dramatic, musical or artistic work appears on published copies of the work, the named person shall, until the contrary is proved, be deemed to be the author. It is, moreover, presumed that the special rules as to first ownership of works created during the course of employment, etc, were not applicable and thus that the named person was the first owner (s 104).

A special rule applies to copyright notices appearing on copies of computer programs. In litigation relating to program copyright, 'where copies of the program are issued to the public in electronic form bearing a statement—(a) that a named person was the owner of copyright in the program at the date of issue of the copies, or (b) that the program was first published in a specified country or that copies of it were first issued to the public in electronic form in a specified year, the statement shall be admissible as evidence of the facts stated and shall be presumed to be correct until the contrary is proved' (s 105(3)). This special presumption is likely, on occasions at least, to be of major assistance to claimant in civil cases and the prosecution in criminal proceedings. As a result, program copyright owners should ensure that they affix appropriate copyright notices to all copies of a program they publish and that any licensees are obliged to do likewise.

# 6

# PROPERTY IN DATABASES

*Simon Chalton*

## 6.1 THE CASE FOR LEGAL PROTECTION OF DATABASES

Databases are useful collections of materials which consequently have value independently of their several items of content. They are often creative, and are usually costly to compile, present and maintain. In the Information Society, they are of increasing economic importance.

Those who create databases, and those who invest in their development and maintenance, may reasonably expect to enjoy a return on their investments, but once a database has been made publicly available securing a financial return from it is likely to be difficult, if not impracticable, unless some form of property right is recognized in the database as such.

Traditionally, UK law has recognized copyright as protecting tables and compilations as literary works. More recently, the EU Directive on the legal protection of databases ('the Database Directive')[1] has required the Member States of the European Union, and so the countries of the European Economic Area, to harmonize this form of copyright protection. The Directive also introduced a new form of *sui generis* right (so-called, because it is a right of its own special kind) to protect databases. The new right is complementary to copyright but can exist independently of it, and is known in the UK as 'database right'. This chapter gives a high-level view of the UK law of copyright in relation to databases and other tables and compilations, of the development and provisions of the Directive and of the current UK law on the new *sui generis* database right.

## 6.2 COPYRIGHT PROTECTION OF COLLECTIONS UNDER PRE-1998 UK LAW

The Copyright, Designs and Patents Act 1988 ('CDPA 1988'), as at 31 December 1997, provided as follows:

| | |
|---|---|
| Section 1(1)(a): | Copyright is a property right which subsists in . . . original literary . . . works. |
| Section 3(1): | . . . 'literary work' means any work, other than a dramatic or musical work, which is written, spoken or sung, and accordingly includes . . . a table or compilation. |
| Section 9(1) and (3): | 'author' in relation to a work means the person who creates it. In the case of a literary . . . work which is computer-generated, the author shall be taken to be the person by whom the arrangements necessary for the creation of the work are undertaken. |
| Section 178: | 'Computer-generated', in relation to a work, means that the work is generated by computer in circumstances such that there is no human author of the work. |

Under the pre-1998 UK law, collections of materials in the form of tables or compilations were capable of protection by copyright as literary works. This principle still applies today and protects anthologies, dictionaries and other collections. These collections may be of works created by different authors, or of non-copyright materials derived from different sources. What is protected is the selection and/or arrangement of the collection. Copyright in the collection as such is distinct from copyright, if any, in the several items of content within the collection. As with all works, the collection as such must achieve the criterion of originality before it can qualify for protection by copyright. In the UK, this criterion requires that there shall have been sufficient skill, industry or experience applied in the production of the collection,

---

[1] Directive 96/9/EC of 11 March 1996, OJ L77, 27 March 1996.

which must not have been copied from another work. Mere random collections of information will not be protected nor will 'a selection or arrangement of scraps of information' not involving any real exercise of labour, judgment or skill.[2] However, a football pool betting coupon has been held to be protected,[3] as have railway timetables,[4] professional directories[5] and electrical circuit diagrams.[6]

In the United States, the Supreme Court has held that a listing of subscribers' names, addresses and telephone numbers in the white pages of a telephone directory does not contain any modicum of creativity, and so is not protected by copyright under the US Federal Copyright Act.[7] This is to be contrasted with the selection or arrangement of *Yellow Pages*-type classified directories, which have been held to be protected in the United States.[8]

The position under UK law down to 31 December 1997 may thus be broadly stated as:

(a) The selection and/or arrangement of a collection of materials may be protected by copyright as a literary work, whether or not the individual items of content in the collection are so protected.

(b) Where a collection is computer-generated, the person deemed to be the author of the collection, as a work, is the person who made the arrangements necessary for its creation.

(c) In any case, sufficient skill, industry or experience must have been applied by the author to the production of the work as a collection if the work is to qualify for copyright protection (the so-called criterion of originality).

## 6.3 DEVELOPMENT OF THE DATABASE DIRECTIVE

The European Commission's 1988 Green Paper on *Copyright and the Challenge of Technology*[9] concluded that there was a need for Europe to give copyright protection to collections or compilations as such. The Green Paper also stated that the Commission was considering whether there was an additional need to protect collections or compilations which were not capable of qualifying for copyright protection.

The central difficulty found by the Commission in formulating a Directive to harmonize the laws of the Member States on the legal protection of such collections was in reconciling the different approaches of, respectively, the copyright and

---

[2] *GA Cramp and Sons Ltd v Frank Smythson Ltd* [1944] AC 329, 340.
[3] *Ladbroke (Football) Ltd v William Hill (Football) Ltd* [1964] 1 WLR 273.
[4] *Leslie v Young and Sons* [1917] 2 KB 469.
[5] *Waterlow Directories Ltd v Reed Information Services Ltd* [1984] FSR 64.
[6] *Anacon Corporation Ltd v Environmental Research Technology Ltd* [1994] FSR 659.
[7] *Feist Publications Inc v Rural Telephone Co Inc* (1991) 111 S Ct 1282.
[8] *BellSouth Advertising & Publishing Corp v Donnelly Information Publishing Inc* (1991) 933 F 2d 952 (US Ct of Appeals 11th Circuit No 89-5131).
[9] COM (88) 172 final, 7 June 1988, para 215.

authors' right systems of law on these issues. Civil-law systems see authors' rights as recognitions of the author's creative intellectual activity: without such creativity, the application of time, trouble and expense are generally considered in civil-law countries to be insufficient to justify protection. Furthermore, the absence of a human author precludes any possibility of human creativity, and so of protection. The same strict view is not taken in common-law jurisdictions, but even in common-law countries there is a growing tendency to emphasize the requirement of skill or creativity at the expense of the requirement of labour: in *Feist Publications Inc v Rural Telephone Co Inc*[10] the US Supreme Court held that the application of 'sweat of the brow' was insufficient, in the absence of a modicum of creativity.

In May 1992 a first proposal for a Directive[11] was issued by the Commission. It included provision for a new *sui generis* form of protection for compilations, but withheld the new protection from compilations of materials which were themselves protected by copyright. The new *sui generis* right was to protect against 'unfair' extraction, a concept which was re-expressed as 'unauthorised' extraction in an amended proposal issued in October 1993.[12]

After October 1993 major changes to the form of the proposed Directive were made and a Common Position was reached in July 1995. On 11 March 1996 the Database Directive[13] was adopted substantially in the terms of the Common Position and was required to be transposed into the laws of each of the Member States by 1 January 1998.

In August 1997 the Copyright Directorate at the Patent Office published draft implementing regulations under the European Communities Act, with a consultative paper. Following this consultation an amended draft was laid before Parliament. The amended draft was adopted as the Copyright and Rights in Databases Regulations 1997[14] (the 'Database Regulations') which came into force on 1 January 1998.

The changes from the Commission's 1993 proposal, which were incorporated into the Database Directive and reflected in the Database Regulations, simplified its provisions and continued the concept of creating a new *sui generis* right, called in the Database Regulations 'database right'. This new right applies to all databases as defined by the Database Directive, including those which are accessible by other than electronic means and including databases of materials which are themselves protected by copyright. The new *sui generis* database right protects against unauthorized extraction or reutilization of the whole or a substantial part, evaluated qualitatively and/or quantitatively, of the contents of any such database.[15] In contrast with copyright in databases, the new *sui generis* database right requires substantial investment in the obtaining, verification or presentation of the contents of a protected database but does not require intellectual creativity.

---

[10]  (1991) 111 S Ct 1282.
[11]  COM (92) 24 final–SYN 383, 13 May 1992.
[12]  COM (93) 464 final–SYN 393, 4 October 1993.
[13]  Directive 96/9/EC of 11 March 1996, OJ L77, 27 March 1996.
[14]  SI 1997/3032.                  [15]  Database Directive, art 7.

The simplifications achieved by the Commission in the adopted form of the Database Directive were welcomed, though there are parts of the Directive which are so broadly stated as to be potentially uncertain in their effect.[16] Since the *sui generis* right is new, elaboration by the Member States is needed beyond the provisions of the Directive. The process of elaboration has produced results which differ from Member State to Member State, so creating inconsistencies between the new laws adopted by different Member States. Optional provisions in the Directive have also resulted in some disharmony.

## 6.4 THE SCOPE OF THE DATABASE DIRECTIVE

A major point of change from the form of the Commission's earlier proposals is extension of the Database Directive to all databases in any form, including those capable of being accessed by other than electronic means. 'Other means' includes the human eye, so extending the scope of the Database Directive to include collections of materials held, for example, in filing cabinets, provided that such collections fit within the remaining provisions of the Directive's definition of a database in article 1(2):

'Database' shall mean a collection of independent works, data or other materials arranged in a systematic or methodical way and capable of being individually accessed by electronic or other means.

The inclusion of non-electronic databases avoids the difficulties which might otherwise have arisen from conflicts between legal provisions applying only to electronically accessible databases, as being within the scope of the Database Directive, and other provisions applying to similar or identical collections of materials held in non-electronic form, which would have been outside the Directive's scope. However, conflicts may still arise between legal provisions applying only to databases as defined by the Directive and those applying to collections which do not fall within that definition.

Although the CDPA 1988 protects by copyright tables and compilations as literary works, prior to the coming into force of the Database Regulations it made no reference to databases as such. The Database Directive's definition of 'database' is both broader and in some respects narrower than the concept of a table or compilation. The Database Regulations have amended the CDPA 1988 so as to leave tables and compilations as a subclassification of literary works, and to add databases, as defined by the Database Directive, as a new and additional subclassification. This could have significant consequences. The form of protection available to a given collection may depend on the application of relatively complex classification criteria, for example, whether or not the contents of the collection are 'independent' of

---

[16] eg, the meaning of the term 'lawful user of a database'; see arts 8 and 9.

one another. The resulting classification, either as a non-database table or compilation or as a database, will affect, amongst other things, the identity of the rightholder, the term of protection, the applicable restricted acts and whether or not the collection is eligible for protection under the *sui generis* database right (see section 6.5 below).

From the standpoint of UK database rightholders, generous transitional provisions included in the Database Directive and reflected in the Database Regulations allow those databases within the Directive's definition which, at 31 December 1997, qualified for UK copyright protection and which were in existence on 27 March 1996, the date of the Directive's publication in the *Official Journal*, to continue to enjoy copyright protection under the pre-1998 UK law for the full copyright term of life of the author plus seventy years. This permitted continuing protection is notwithstanding that such databases may lack the necessary element of author's creativity required to meet the Directive's criterion for copyright protection,[17] and may be important for rightholders of computer-generated databases which lack a human creative author.

The copyright seventy-year term is to be contrasted with the *sui generis* database right's fifteen-year term. Successive *sui generis* right terms of fifteen years each, available when a database is updated so as to create a substantial change to its contents,[18] may prove capable of producing indefinitely extendable protection outlasting the seventy-year term allowed for copyright. This will be of particular value to databases such as telephone directories, statistical tables and factual compilations which may not attract copyright protection as lacking author's creativity but which need regular and costly updating. It may not help static databases, for example, those in fixed electronic form such as databases marketed on CD-ROM, which are not capable of being updated or re-presented.

## 6.5  THE MEANING OF 'DATABASE'

The term 'database' is defined in article 1(2) of the Database Directive as:

A collection of independent works, data or other materials arranged in a systematic or methodical way and capable of being individually accessed by electronic or other means.

A similar definition is contained in the Database Regulations. The significant elements in this definition are the references to 'independent works, data or other materials', to arrangement in a 'systematic or methodical' way, and to individual access 'by electronic or other means'.

'Independent works, data or other materials' is apparently intended to exclude from the definition works such as films, musical compositions and books which comprise distinct but related elements or materials (for example, frames, movements or chapters) and which, though separately accessible, are interrelated within the

---

[17] Article 14(2).    [18] Article 10(3).

collection. It may also exclude many tables or compilations already protected by copyright as literary works under UK law. 'Independent' is not defined, either in the Database Directive or in the Database Regulations. It is suggested that independence in relation to items of content in a collection should be judged from the standpoint of those items as they appear in the compiled collection: it is not sufficient for an item to be capable of being read or used by itself if reading or use of other items in the collection, or the collection as a whole, is dependent on reading or use of that item.

Arrangement in a 'systematic or methodical way' is an essential part of the definition, and may lead to difficulty. Some electronic databases are created in free form, leaving access dependent on a computer's searching capability to find relevant items. If there is no arrangement of material in a systematic or methodical way, a collection of materials may fail to qualify as a database: alternatively, it may be said that electronic arrangement of the database may be sufficient.

As mentioned in section 6.4 above, access 'by electronic or other means' includes access by the human eye. Since the scope of the Database Directive extends to databases in any form,[19] collections of individual materials arranged in a systematic or methodical way which are held in filing cabinets and capable of individual access by means of the human eye will apparently be included. By contrast, if the materials in a collection are not independent of each other or are not individually accessible that collection will apparently be excluded, though it may continue to be protected by copyright under UK law as a compilation.

The Database Directive expressly excludes from its protection computer programs used in the manufacture or operation of databases which can be accessed by electronic means.[20]

## 6.6 COPYRIGHT IN DATABASES

Article 3 of the Database Directive states that databases which, by reason of the selection or arrangement of their contents, constitute the author's own intellectual creation shall be protected as such by copyright, and that no other criteria shall be applied to determine their eligibility for that protection.[21]

The Database Directive refers to 'the expression of the database which is protectable by copyright', but does not define clearly what elements amount to protectable expression: presumably, the phrase is intended to include the expressed selection or arrangement, but not the ideas or concepts behind them.

To qualify for protection by copyright under the Directive, and to be subject to the Directive's requirement of human creativity, a collection of materials must first come within the definition of 'database' set out in article 1(2).[22] In consequence, a

---

[19] Article 1(1).                [20] Article 1(3).                [21] Article 3(1).
[22] Article 1(2) reads: 'a collection of works, data or other independent materials arranged in a systematic or methodical way and capable of being individually accessed by electronic or other means'.

collection of non-independent materials, not being a database within the meaning of the Directive, may be both outside the scope of the Directive and capable of attracting protection as a copyright compilation under the CDPA 1988, provided that the collection conforms to the criterion of originality and other requirements of UK law.

The criterion of intellectual creativity for copyright protection of a database[23] under the Database Directive reflects a similar provision in the Software Directive,[24] namely that a computer program is only to be protected by copyright if it is original in the sense that it is the author's own intellectual creation, and that no other criteria are to be applied to determine its eligibility for that protection. Both provisions are in apparent conflict with section 9(3) of the CDPA 1988 which provides that, in the case of a literary, dramatic, musical or artistic work which is computer-generated, the author shall be taken to be the person by whom the arrangements necessary for the creation of the work were undertaken. Section 178 of the CDPA 1988 defines 'computer-generated', in relation to a work, as meaning that the work is generated by computer in circumstances such that there is no human author of the work. The implication of these provisions in combination is that a computer-generated work, as so defined, can attract copyright protection in the UK for the benefit of the deemed author by whom the arrangements necessary for the creation of the work were undertaken.

An exclusive criterion of originality for copyright, that a work shall be the author's own intellectual creation, now applies to databases both under the Database Directive and under the Database Regulations. No such express provision was included in the Regulations implementing the Software Directive.[25]

Subject to generous transitional provisions in the Database Directive (see section 6.8 as to the term of protection) a computer-generated collection conforming to the Directive's definition of a database may in future not qualify for copyright protection either in the UK or in any other Member State. Such a database will then be protectable only by the new *sui generis* database right, and even that protection will be available only if the database's maker can demonstrate substantial investment in the obtaining, verification or presentation of its contents and is a national of a Member State or has habitual residence in the territory of the Community.[26]

For those databases which qualify for copyright protection under the Database Directive the copyright-restricted acts provided for by that Directive[27] are familiar and comprise, in summary:

(a) Temporary or permanent reproduction by any means and in any form, in whole or in part.

(b) Any form of distribution to the public, but subject to exhaustion of the right to

---

[23] Article 3(1).
[24] Directive 91/250/EEC on the legal protection of computer programs, OJ L122, 17 May 1991.
[25] The Copyright (Computer Programs) Regulations 1992, SI 1992/3233.
[26] Article 11.
[27] Article 5.

control resale of any copy of a database after that copy's first sale within the Community by the rightholder or with his consent.

(c)  Any communication, display or performance to the public.

(d)  Translation, adaptation, arrangement and any other alteration.

(e)  Reproduction, distribution, communication, display or performance to the public of the results of any translation, adaptation, arrangement or other alteration.

These restricted acts broadly control use of any electronic database where use necessarily requires temporary reproduction in machine memory or on screen of any part of the database. For non-electronic databases control may not be so strong, but the risks to the rightholder of economic loss may not be so great.

Moral rights are outside the scope of the Database Directive.[28] Under UK law, moral rights are capable of applying to databases as to other literary works but do not apply to computer programs or to computer-generated works.[29] The UK is to be free to continue these provisions, and other Member States are to be equally free to set their own laws for the application of moral rights to databases.

## 6.7  THE NEW *SUI GENERIS* DATABASE RIGHT

Whereas copyright protects the creativity of authors in the selection and arrangement of the contents of databases, the new *sui generis* 'database right' is designed to protect investment in databases by their makers. Recital 40 of the Database Directive states that the required investment 'may consist of the deployment of financial resources and/or the expending of time, effort and energy'. The Database Regulations define 'investment' as 'including any investment, whether of financial, human or technical resources'.[30] The investment made may be in the obtaining, verification or presentation of the contents of a database: these terms appear to be capable of including and extending beyond the selection or arrangement of database contents. The investment made must have been substantial, but substantiality may be measured either qualitatively or quantitatively, or both.[31]

The maker of a database in which there has been the necessary investment may also be an author of the same database, or may be a different natural or legal person. A database which is protected by copyright may also be protected by the new *sui generis* database right, but is not necessarily so protected if there has been no substantial investment in the obtaining, verification or presentation of the database's contents. Conversely, a database which is protected by the *sui generis* database right may also be protected by copyright, but is not necessarily so protected if the database lacks human creativity in the selection or arrangement of its contents. The *sui generis* database right cannot protect a collection which does not conform to the

---

[28]  Recital 28.          [29]  CDPA 1988, ss 79(2) and 81(2).
[30]  Regulation 12(1).     [31]  Article 7 and regulation 13(2).

Database Directive's definition of a 'database', even though that collection may be protected by copyright under national law.

Both copyright and the *sui generis* database right can thus subsist in the same database but:

(a) Each form of protection requires different criteria.
(b) Each provides different forms and terms of protection.
(c) Each may be vested in different rightholders.
(d) Each affects the use of the contents of the database, but is expressly made independent of any copyright in such contents.[32]

Presumably, if part of the contents of a database comprises a subcollection of materials which itself qualifies for the *sui generis* database right, the protection by database right of that subcollection is independent of the protection of the parent compiled collection, whether by copyright or by the *sui generis* database right.

The *sui generis* database right protects against acts of extraction and/or 're-utilisation' of the whole, or of a substantial part of, the contents of the protected database.[33] 'Substantial' in this context is to be evaluated qualitatively and/or quantitatively.[34] 'Extraction' means the permanent or temporary transfer of all, or a substantial part of, the contents of a database to another medium by any means or in any form,[35] and 're-utilisation' means 'any form of making available to the public [of] all, or a substantial part of, the contents of a database by the distribution of copies, by renting, by on-line or other forms of transmission'.[36] The definitions of 'extraction' and 're-utilisation' are exhaustive.

'Extraction' appears to include a permanent or temporary transfer of a substantial part of the contents of a database to machine memory for the purpose of processing as a necessary preliminary to searching or to screen display.[37] If these steps involve the temporary transfer of a substantial part of the database into machine memory in order to find and display a single item, control of extraction may have broadly the same effect on electronic use of a database as the copyright-restricted act of temporary or permanent reproduction in whole or in part by any means and in any form.[38] Each of these rights may prove therefore to be sufficient to prevent electronic access to, or other electronic processing of, a protected database. The *sui generis* database right is however weaker than copyright in that it restricts only extraction of substantial parts, whereas copyright is expressed to restrict any reproduction in whole or in part, thus presumably also restricting reproduction of insubstantial parts.[39]

---

[32] Article 3(2) (copyright) and article 7(4) (*sui generis* right).     [33] Article 7(1).
[34] Article 7(1).                                                        [35] Article 7(2)(a).
[36] Article 7(2)(b).                                                     [37] Recital 44.
[38] Article 5(a). For copyright, see section 6.4.2.1 above.
[39] Article 5(a). But see *Cantor Fitzgerald International v Tradition (UK) Ltd* [2000] RPC 94 as to copyright and copying of a substantial part of a protected work under UK copyright law.

Both copyright and the *sui generis* database right appear to prevent searching of an electronic database to establish that a particular item of information is not represented in it (so-called meta information). This may prove to be a valuable control.

### 6.7.1 Limitations to the *sui generis* database right

The definition of 're-utilisation' distinguishes between online databases and databases which are made available to the public by the distribution of copies, including rental.[40] Such copies may be either electronic or printed, and their distribution may be by any means and is not restricted to sale or rental. However, the first sale of a copy of a database within the Community by the rightholder or with his consent exhausts the right to control resale within the Community of that copy.[41]

Taken literally, the first-sale exhaustion provision does not appear to apply if property in a database copy is retained by the rightholder and that copy is provided on free loan to a user. Making available to the public a substantial part of the contents of a database is a restricted act only to the extent that availability is either 'by the distribution of copies, by renting, by on-line or [by] other forms of transmission'.[42] Public lending is expressly excluded from the meaning of either 'extraction' or 're-utilisation',[43] but making a copy of a database available for use for direct or indirect economic or commercial advantage, on terms that it will or may be returned, is not excluded.[44]

Once a database has been made available to the public, which availability may be by public lending, the maker of the database may not prevent a lawful user from extracting and/or reutilizing insubstantial parts of the database's contents for any purpose whatsoever.[45] This is subject to the qualification that, 'when a lawful user is authorised to extract and/or re-utilise only part of a database, this provision shall apply only to that part.'[46]

This lawful-user right is subject to further qualifications:

(a) The lawful user may not perform acts which conflict with normal exploitation of the database or unreasonably prejudice the legitimate interests of its maker.[47]

(b) The lawful user may not cause prejudice to the holder of a copyright or related right in respect of the works or services contained in the database.[48]

These qualifications are in broad terms and are not further defined or elaborated: they reflect the so-called three-step test under article 9(2) of the Berne Convention.

The concepts of a lawful acquirer of a computer program and of a person having a right to use a computer program were introduced by the Software Directive.[49] The UK's implementation of this latter Directive amended the CDPA 1988[50] to provide that a person is a lawful user of a computer program if (whether under a licence to do any

[40] Article 7(2)(b).   [41] Article 7(2)(b) and regulation 12(5).
[42] Article 7(2)(b).                                    [43] Article 7(2).
[44] Regulation 12(2).   [45] Article 8(1).
[47] Article 8(2).                        [48] Article 8(3).
[49] Software Directive, art 5.   [50] Section 50A(2).

acts restricted by copyright in the program or otherwise) he has a right to use the program. The same principle is adopted by the Database Regulations, so that a lawful user is a person having a licence or other right to extract and/or reutilize the whole or substantial parts of a database.[51] Where the database is in electronic form and a copy of it has been purchased, the provisions of the CDPA 1988 relating to transfers of copies of works in electronic form may apply,[52] but this section relates only to copyright; both the Database Directive and the Database Regulations prohibit contractual restraints on lawful-user rights.[53]

The net result of these complex provisions appears to be:

(a) *sui generis* right enables the rightholder to prevent extraction and/or reutilization of substantial parts of a database otherwise than by public lending; but

(b) once that database has been made available to the public, the combined effects of the exhaustion of rights by sale of a copy of the database and the lawful-user provisions will prevent the rightholder from using either the *sui generis* database right or a contract term to stop a subsequent lawful acquirer of a sold copy of the database from extracting or reutilizing insubstantial parts of the database for any purpose whatsoever.

This freedom for a lawful user to use insubstantial parts of such a database for any purpose whatsoever is subject to the two qualifications noted above and set out in articles 8(2) and 8(3) (conflict with normal exploitation and prejudice to rightholder).

These provisions may prejudice those who make databases available to the public by sale of distributed copies, for example, electronic copies on CD-ROM or printed copies, and may favour those who license the use of their databases through online access agreements which impose confidence and contractual terms and which limit access to parts of a database. In preparing or renewing any licence or use agreement, regard should be had to article 15 which makes null and void any contractual provision contrary to articles 6(1) and 8 (lawful-user rights). This provision is reflected in the Database Regulations and their amendments to the CDPA 1988.[54]

### 6.7.2 Exceptions to the *sui generis* database right

While much of the Database Directive is prescriptive and sets out provisions which Member States are required to adopt, certain exceptions to the *sui generis* right are permissive, and so optional.

These provisions allow Member States to create additional rights for lawful users of a database made available to the public to extract or reutilize substantial parts of the contents of the database:

---

[51] Regulation 12(1).                                    [52] CDPA 1988, s 56.
[53] Database Directive, art 15 and Database Regulations, regs 10 (copyright) and 19 (database right).
[54] Regulations 15 and 19: CDPA 1988, ss 50D and 296B.

(a) for private purposes, where the extraction is of contents of a non-electronic database;

(b) for teaching or scientific research purposes, provided the source of the extraction is indicated and the extraction is only to the extent justified by the non-commercial purpose to be attained; and/or

(c) for purposes of public security or for the proper performance of an administrative or judicial procedure.[55]

These provisions apply only to the *sui generis* right,[56] and would not appear to permit, for example, the extraction of articles from a printed journal for private purposes if the extraction involves copying, and so copyright infringement, of the article itself. The copyright provisions of the Database Directive do not affect copyright in the contents of a database. Such copying may thus be fair dealing in the contents but, if done for a commercial purpose, may not be fair dealing in the database.[57] The Database Regulations set out exceptions to database right for public administration, which include use of databases for parliamentary and judicial proceedings, Royal Commissions and statutory enquiries, material open to public inspection on an official register, material communicated to the Crown in the course of public business, public records and acts done under statutory authority.[58]

The Database Regulations also include a special provision declaring that the doing of anything in relation to a database for the purposes of research for a commercial purpose is not fair dealing with the database.[59]

## 6.8 TERMS OF PROTECTION

The term of protection by copyright of databases under the Database Directive is as for other literary works, namely the author's life plus seventy years. This is not expressly stated in the Database Directive or the Database Regulations, but is a necessary consequence of recognizing copyright for databases as literary works.

The term of protection under the *sui generis* right is fifteen years from 1 January of the year following the year in which the database was completed. If the database is made available to the public in any manner whatever during that period, the term of protection is extended so as to expire fifteen years from the 1 January following the date on which the database was first made available to the public.[60]

It follows that, if a database was completed on 2 January 1999 and is first made available to the public on 31 December 2014, the initial term of protection will not expire until 1 January 2030.

---

[55] Article 9.
[56] Broadly similar optional exceptions to the copyright-restricted acts are contained in article 6.
[57] CDPA 1988, s 29, and Database Regulations, reg 8 (amending s 29).
[58] Database Regulations, Sch 2.    [59] Ibid.
[60] Article 10(1), (2) and regulation 17(2).

If the making of a database was completed on or after 1 January 1983, and that database qualified for database right on 1 January 1998, its term of protection is fifteen years from 1 January 1998.[61]

If at any time, either during the term of protection or after its expiry, any substantial change is made to the contents of a database which would result in the changed database being considered to be a substantial new investment then that database may qualify for its own fifteen-year term of *sui generis* protection.[62]

For these purposes:

(a) 'Substantial change' is to be evaluated either qualitatively or quantitatively.

(b) 'Substantial change' includes any substantial change resulting from the accumulation of successive additions, deletions or alterations.

Databases, like telephone directories, which may lack the necessary quality of human creativity to achieve the criterion of originality for copyright protection under the Database Directive, may nevertheless achieve *sui generis* protection by virtue of substantial investment made in obtaining, verifying or presenting the contents of such databases.[63] Similar substantial investments made to update the database may qualify each updated version of the database for its own fifteen-year term.

The consequence may be that successive issues of an annually updated directory based around a common format or core of information may attract successive fifteen-year terms, to give in effect potentially perpetual *sui generis* database right protection, whether or not copyright protection is available. Such a directory could acquire a monopoly position, making it difficult commercially for a competing new directory to break into the market. This may have competition-law consequences.[64]

The Database Directive does not attempt to deal with competition issues, and does not repeat the provisions about compulsory licensing which were contained in earlier proposals in relation to the *sui generis* right. These provisions applied to databases which had been made publicly available either by a public body or by an entity enjoying a monopoly status derived from an exclusive concession granted by a public body. Instead, the Directive leaves these issues to be dealt with under Community competition law,[65] and is content to rely on the rights referred to in section 6.7 above for lawful users of databases which have been made available to the public.[66]

---

[61] Regulation 30.
[62] Article 10(3) and regulation 17(3).
[63] Recital 40 and article 7.
[64] See European Treaty, art 82 (formerly art 86) on abuse of a dominant position; *RTE & ITP v EC Commission* [1995] 4 CMLR 718 ('the *Magill* case').
[65] Recital 47.
[66] Article 8.

## 6.9  TRANSITIONAL PROVISIONS

Databases created before 1 January 1998, the date on which the Database Regulations came into force, are protected by copyright under the Database Directive and the Database Regulations if they fulfil the requirements laid down by the Database Directive and the Database Regulations for copyright protection. This does not extend to UK databases in existence at 31 December 1997 which lack any element of author's creativity in their selection or arrangement. Such databases do not fulfil the Directive's requirements for copyright protection and, but for savings in the Directive and the Regulations, would have ceased to enjoy copyright protection under the Directive on 1 January 1998. The same principle applies to pre-1998 computer-generated UK databases, which would appear to have fallen out of copyright protection on 1 January 1998 and to have been left with only the *sui generis* right.

To cushion this effect, the Database Directive provides[67] that, where a pre-1998 database had been created and was protected by a copyright system in a Member State on or before the date of publication of the Directive (27 March 1996) but that database does not fulfil the Directive's eligibility requirement for copyright protection,[68] for example, because the selection or arrangement of its contents does not constitute the author's own intellectual creation, the Directive shall not result in any curtailing in that Member State of the remaining term of protection afforded under that Member State's copyright system. This saving is reflected in the Database Regulations.[69]

This generous provision will allow UK computer-generated databases which qualified for UK copyright protection at 27 March 1996 to continue to do so for the full term of copyright remaining applicable to them. Such databases created after 27 March 1996 appear to be excluded from protection by copyright as from 1 January 1998.

For databases made after 1 January 1983 (ie, during the fifteen years prior to 1 January 1998), whether or not protected by copyright, the *sui generis* database right is to be available[70] provided that such databases meet the requirements for the *sui generis* right, namely that they show a sufficiently substantial investment in obtaining, verification or presentation of their contents. Since the *sui generis* right can apply to a database in addition to the protection of that database by copyright, UK computer-generated databases created on or after 1 January 1983 and in existence on 27 March 1996 can be protected both by copyright and by the *sui generis* right.[71] Computer-generated databases made after 27 March 1996, although apparently excluded from copyright protection as from 1 January 1998, will be capable of protection under the *sui generis* right.

---

[67] Article 14(2).           [68] As set out in article 3(1).
[69] Regulation 29.
[70] Database Directive, art 14(3) and Database Regulations, reg 30.
[71] Combined effects of article 14(1), (2) and (3).

For the *sui generis* right, the term of protection will be fifteen years from 1 January 1998.[72] Databases qualifying for *sui generis* right protection will have the possibility of creating successive new fifteen-year *sui generis* right terms by regular updating of their contents.

For databases in existence at 1 January 1998, the terms of protection provided both for copyright and for *sui generis* right are to be without prejudice to acts accomplished and rights acquired prior to 1 January 1998.[73]

## 6.10  RECIPROCITY AND THE *SUI GENERIS* RIGHT

The principle of national treatment will apply to copyright protection for databases which meet the originality and other requirements for protection by copyright under the Database Directive. This means that rightholders of copyright-protected databases, whether nationals of Member States or nationals of other states which are members of the Berne Convention, will be entitled within Europe as elsewhere to copyright protection for their databases in accordance with the law of the Berne Union State in which an alleged act of infringement occurs. The same principle will apply to databases which meet the Berne Convention's requirement of first publication in a state which is a member of Berne.

Since the *sui generis* right is a creation of the European Union, this new right is to be available, broadly, only within that Union and only to nationals of Member States of that Union. This principle is elaborated by the Database Directive into a series of complex subrules.[74]

(a) The right is to apply to databases whose makers or successors in title are nationals of a Member State who have their habitual residence in the territory of the Community.[75]

(b) The right is also to apply to companies and firms formed in accordance with the law of a Member State and having either their registered office, central administration or principal place of business within the Community. Where only the registered office of the company or firm is within the Community, the company or firm's operations must have an effective and continuing link with the economy of one of the Member States.[76]

The Commission may put a proposal to the Council for extending the *sui generis* right to third countries, and the Council may enter into negotiations with such countries providing that the term of protection so agreed does not exceed that available under article 10 of the Database Directive (broadly, fifteen years).[77]

---

[72] Article 14(5).     [73] Ibid.     [74] Article 11.
[75] Article 11(1).     [76] Ibid.     [77] Article 11(3).

## 6.11  *BRITISH HORSERACING BOARD LTD AND OTHERS v WILLIAM HILL ORGANIZATION LTD*[78]

The British Horseracing Board ('BHB'), as the governing authority for the British horseracing industry, has developed and maintains an elaborate database including details of racing fixtures, runners, owners and jockeys. Expensive to create, the database is also expensive to update and is in a constant state of change. Racegoers, bookmakers and others, including newspapers, make regular use of the database which is licensed to William Hill Organization Limited ('William Hill') for use in their licensed betting offices and telephone betting businesses.

In May 1999 William Hill established a new Internet service for horserace betting, for which they began using information derived directly or indirectly from the BHB database. Since the information was publicly available through the *Racing Post* and other newspapers, William Hill considered it to be in the public domain: on that basis they sought no licence, and paid no fee or royalty to BHB, for use of the information. BHB sued William Hill for unauthorized extraction and/or reutilization of the information on the basis that it had been derived from the BHB database in contravention, said BHB, of their *sui generis* right.

In February 2001 Laddie J gave judgment at first instance in the High Court in favour of the claimants BHB and its co-owners of the database. Interpreting and applying the Database Directive, he found that BHB and its fellow claimants, as makers of the database, had made substantial investments in obtaining, verifying and presenting its contents and were accordingly entitled to protection from unauthorized extraction and/or reutilization of any substantial part of those contents. This protection extended to important, and thus substantial, information derived and extracted from the database's contents. The claimants were also entitled to protection against repeated and systematic extraction and/or reutilization of insubstantial parts of the database's contents and information derived from them when those activities were carried out in ways which conflicted with exploitation of the database by its makers, or which unreasonably prejudiced their legitimate interests as makers of the database.

In March 2001 William Hill appealed Laddie J's judgment and on 24 May 2002 the Court of Appeal made an order requesting a preliminary ruling of the European Court of Justice on issues raised in the proceedings and relating to the Database Directive.

The Schedule to the Court of Appeal's order for reference sets out the relevant parts of the Directive, details of the parties, the facts giving rise to the dispute, details of the national proceedings before the High Court and the Court of Appeal, the issues between the parties and the questions referred by the Court of Appeal to the European Court.

---

[78]  CHANL/2001/0632/A3.

The questions referred centre round the interpretation of Chapter III of the Directive, which is headed '*Sui generis* right', and in particular article 7 and article 10. Article 7 is headed 'Object of protection' and article 10 is headed 'Term of protection'. The questions referred to the European Court go primarily to identification of the object of protection and the extent of the protection given by the Directive. Since the Directive, with its recitals and *travaux préparatoires*, is the sole source of the *sui generis* right in databases it is important that the European Court's views on the correct interpretation of the right are known so that all EEA national courts, in considering issues involving the *sui generis* right, should have a single and central source of guidance on the issues of interpretation raised by the Court of Appeal's referred questions.

### 6.11.1  The object of protection

Although article 7 of the Directive is headed 'Object of protection' the article does not expressly state what is to be protected. There are four possibilities:

(a) the database maker's investment in the obtaining, verification and/or presentation of the database's contents;

(b) the systematic or methodical way in which those contents have been arranged, and/or their individual accessibility;

(c) the whole or any substantial part of those contents; or

(d) any substantial information derived or derivable from consultation of or access to the database.

Article 7(1) provides:

Member States shall provide for a right for the maker of a database which shows that there has been qualitatively and/or quantitatively a substantial investment in either the obtaining, verification or presentation of the contents to prevent extraction and/or re-utilisation of the whole or of a substantial part, evaluated qualitatively and/or quantitatively, of the contents of the database.

The Court of Appeal has asked whether the expression 'substantial part of the contents of the database' in this context includes works, data or other materials derived from the database but which do not have the same systematic or methodical arrangement of, and individual accessibility to be found in, the database. The references to systematic or methodical arrangement and individual accessibility relate to the definition of a database in the Directive's article 1(2), which provides:

For the purposes of this Directive, 'database' shall mean a collection of independent works, data or other materials arranged in a systematic or methodical way and individually accessible by electronic or other means.

The Court of Appeal's questions thus appear to seek to establish whether what is to be protected under the *sui generis* right is limited to the qualities of arrangement and accessibility of the contents of a protected database, described by William Hill as its 'database-ness', or whether protection extends to works, data or other materials derived from the database. Recital 46 of the Directive states that the Directive should not give rise to the creation of a new right in the works, data or materials themselves. Since the terms 'data' and 'other materials' are broad, the Court of Appeal's question raises the possibility of protection extending to information derived from the database, including information relating to the dates of particular race meetings, courses, runners, jockeys, owners and other details.

Herein lies what may be the most important issue in the appeal: can the *sui generis* right, unlike copyright, protect information as such if the information has been extracted directly or indirectly from a protected database; and if it does so, can that protection continue, survive and follow the same information's being made available to the public in any manner, for example, through the racing press, into whoever's hands the information may come?

If the latter is the case, the *sui generis* right would appear to enable a database maker to invest in the obtaining, verification and/or presentation of collections of information and, having done so, to claim protection by the *sui generis* right not only of substantial parts of the resulting database but also of substantial information derived from consultation of that database. This could evolve into a method of obtaining control over substantial information by compiling it into a publicly available database.

### 6.11.2 Lawful-user rights and exceptions to the *sui generis* right

Article 8 of the Directive, which the Court of Appeal's reference does not quote, is headed 'Rights and obligations of lawful users', and article 9, also not referred to by the Court of Appeal, is headed 'Exceptions to the *sui generis* right'.

None of the article 9 exceptions applies to extraction for commercial purposes of the kind intended by William Hill, and the article 8 rights of lawful users, although extending to use for 'any purposes whatsoever', are limited to extracting and/or reutilizing insubstantial parts of a database's contents. The term 'lawful user' is not defined by the Directive, but the article 8 lawful-user right could not apply to William Hill's extraction and/or reutilization, on Laddie J's findings, since the extraction and/or reutilization by William Hill was not limited to insubstantial parts of the contents of the BHB database. Even if William Hill had been a lawful user using only insubstantial parts of the BHB database, William Hill would still have been restricted from performing acts which conflict with normal exploitation of the database or which unreasonably prejudice the legitimate interests of the maker (art 8(2)). These latter concepts are the subject of a question from the Court of Appeal, but in relation to article 7(5) (repeated and systematic extraction of insubstantial parts) and not in relation to article 8.

### 6.11.3 Competition-law issues

Article 13 of the Directive (which is quoted in the Court of Appeal's reference though not in a competition-law context) is headed 'Continued application of other provisions' and provides that the Directive shall be without prejudice to provisions concerning, amongst others, laws on restrictive practices and unfair competition. There is a possibility that, although BHB's *sui generis* right in its database may have been infringed by William Hill's activities to the extent that those activities are in relation to information which is in the public domain, attempts by BHB to enforce its rights in relation to that information may be trumped by European competition-law considerations, as was copyright in the *Magill* cases.[79] Early versions of the proposal for a database Directive included provisions for compulsory licensing of the *sui generis* right in those databases which were the sole source of the information they contain, but these provisions did not appear in the Database Directive as adopted.

In *Magill* compulsory licensing was required of copyright-protected material contained in broadcasting schedules developed by and in the control of broadcasters. In *BHB v William Hill* compulsory licensing is not a central issue. William Hill denies that the *sui generis* right extends to information extracted from a *sui generis* right-protected database after that information has been made generally available to the public, and on that view licensing, whether voluntary or compulsory, should not be necessary to authorize use of the information.

It may be that competition law either could prevent the *sui generis* right from applying to such information, or if the right applies could prevent it from being enforced. This is notwithstanding the narrow terms of article 8 of the Directive in relation to lawful-user rights in information made available to the public in any manner. Article 8(1) is expressed in terms of a restriction on the database maker's exercise of the *sui generis* right, and so as a limitation of it, rather than an express right for lawful users.

### 6.11.4 'Extraction' and 're-utilisation'

The Court of Appeal asks if these terms, as used in article 7, are limited to the extraction and/or reutilization of the contents of a database taken directly from that database, or whether they include the transfer to another medium and/or making available to the public of works, data or other materials derived indirectly from the database, without having direct access to it; and, in the case of reutilization, whether this is limited to the first making available to the public of the contents of that database.

These questions go back to the issues of protection of information where the information is not directly extracted from a protected database (see section 6.11.1 above).

---

[79] Case T-69/89 [1989] 4 CMLR 757 ECJ; ECJ 6 April 1995 Cases C-241/91P and C-242/91P.

### 6.11.5 'Substantial' and 'insubstantial'

The Court of Appeal asks a number of questions on these terms as used in article 7 in relation to parts of a database, including whether:

- 'substantial' means something more than insignificant; and
- 'insubstantial' means a part of a database which is not substantial.

William Hill has contended that the benefit it obtains from its use of information extracted is irrelevant as to whether or not that information is a substantial part of a protected database, and that whether a part of a database is a substantial part does not depend upon what the alleged infringer is doing with it. This is relevant to whether William Hill had extracted and/or reutilized any substantial part of the BHB database. Laddie J took the view that qualitative substantiality was to be measured by the importance of the parts taken: since accuracy and up-to-dateness were important to racegoers, and so to William Hill, then accuracy and up-to-dateness were to be taken into account in determining whether or not any parts of a database which were extracted and/or reutilized were substantial parts of that database.

If the information taken by William Hill were to be held insubstantial in these terms, William Hill might claim that they were lawful users, and so entitled to exercise the lawful-user right referred to in article 8 of the Directive (see section 6.11.2 above). If so, they would need to show that they were not performing acts which conflict with normal exploitation of the database or unreasonably prejudice the legitimate interests of the maker of the database. The Court of Appeal has referred the meaning of this latter expression to the Court of Justice, but in the context of article 7(5) and not of article 8. Article 7(5) provides:

The repeated and systematic extraction and/or re-utilisation of a substantial part of the contents of the database implying acts which conflict with a normal exploitation of that database or which unreasonably prejudice the legitimate interests of the maker of the database shall not be permitted.

### 6.11.6 Term of protection

Article 10(3) provides that:

Any substantial change, evaluated qualitatively or quantitatively, to the contents of a database, including any substantial change resulting from the accumulation of successive editions, deletions or alterations, which would result in the database being considered to be a substantial new investment, evaluated qualitatively or quantitatively, shall quality the database resulting from that investment for its own term of protection.

The Court of Appeal asks whether such a resulting database must be considered to be a new and separate database, including for the purposes of article 7(5). In such a case, William Hill has argued, repeated and systematic extraction and/or reutilization of insubstantial parts of the contents of a series of successive databases would not be an infringement in terms of article 7(5). In response to this argument, Laddie J had held that the BHB database was a single database in a state of constant evolution, rather than a succession of independent databases.

## 6.12 CONCLUSION

The appeal and the reference to the European Court in *British Horseracing Board v William Hill* centre on the object and extent of protection of the *sui generis* right, and in particular whether the right can extend to information derived directly or indirectly from a protected database. Copyright would be unlikely to protect the re-expression of such information: the position is less clear with the *sui generis* right which is intended to protect investment in the obtaining, verification and presentation of databases. If information which represents a qualitatively substantial product of that investment is not protected, is the right effective? If such information is protected, how long may that protection last? Does it attach to derived information? May it be followed into the hands of an innocent (in the sense of unknowing) reuser of the information? At what stage does the information enter the public domain so as to lose protection, and what effect will Community competition law have on the right?

There are other issues on substantiality, lawful-user rights and the concept of 'obtaining' the contents of databases, all of which need resolving.

Concerns have been expressed in the UK about the loss of the UK's copyright originality criterion of skill and labour, and the substitution of the higher standard of author's intellectual creation, thus potentially excluding computer-generated works of all kinds from copyright protection. This battle remains to be fought in relation to other forms of copyright-protected works, but appears to have been lost in relation to computer programs and in relation to databases within the Database Directive's definition of a database. The skill and labour criterion will, however, continue to apply for the time being to other literary works, including tables and compilations not falling within the Directive's definition of a database.

The Database Directive's transitional provisions for copyright and the *sui generis* right in databases have sweetened the pill:

(a) Databases which were in existence on 27 March 1996 can continue to be protected in the UK under UK copyright law during the residue of their respective terms, namely the author's life plus seventy years.

(b) If a post-1 January 1993 database fails to qualify for copyright protection for lack of human creativity it can still qualify for the *sui generis* database right protection if there has been sufficient investment by its maker in its obtaining, verification or presentation. The right of extraction under the *sui generis* database right is broad, and in some circumstances can amount to a right to control electronic searching of a database in much the same way as copyright controls transient copying, but subject to far-reaching lawful-user rights which are likely to be widely available.

(c) The ability to obtain successive fifteen-year terms of protection under the *sui generis* database right makes the disparity between the term of the author's life plus seventy years allowed for copyright and the fifteen-year term allowed for the *sui generis* database right less significant, leaving exposed only collections of static, non-copyright protected collections of materials which are incapable of being updated or re-presented.

(d) The definitions of extraction and reutilization for the *sui generis* right, combined with the traditional restricted acts for copyright, appear to give effective, though differently expressed, protection under each right against taking, adaptation, reformatting and other forms of reuse of databases by digital manipulation. This protection would seem to be available both for databases created by human authors and for databases which are computer-generated. These, in practice, may turn out to be the most important provisions of all.

There remain latent uncertainties in relation to competition between authors and makers having different rights in the same database. Who will take priority? Can each block the other's right to use or to license the database to third parties? What will be the effect on commissioned databases?

The Commission sees the Database Directive as a major plank in its platform of harmonized intellectual property rights for the Information Society in Europe. As digitization, the Internet, future information superhighways and the ability to store, forward, process and adapt large volumes of data emerge as commonplace realities, information is becoming a truly international commodity. Copyright is not intended to protect ideas or information as such, but control over processing of databases may provide a valuable form of secondary protection having that effect. The Court of Justice's responses to the Court of Appeal's questions should make clear the extent to which the *sui generis* right is intended directly or indirectly to protect information in databases.

A remaining concern is uncertainty about the future of the *sui generis* right internationally. Should the European Commission have opted for national treatment? Will reciprocity in practice be negotiable with non-Union countries? Would it have been better for Europe to have been generous, and to have made the *sui generis* right applicable to all databases within the European Union whether or not the rightholder is a Community national? The world seems to favour national treatment: a more generous approach by the European Union might have encouraged the development and use of non-European databases in the Union, to the general advantage of database rightholders, the public and the Union itself.

# 7

# PROTECTING CONFIDENTIAL INFORMATION

*Allison Coleman*

One of the main features of computers is their ability to store, manipulate and transmit data in ways that could not be achieved with manual records and storage systems. A result of this is to focus attention on data and on the information it contains and to follow this with questions about its position within the protective regime of the law. For example, to what extent is information treated as a commodity in its own right? How can or does the law control its use or abuse? The questions are legion and the answers varied.

This chapter focuses on the extent to which the law protects one special category of information which might be stored on a computer, namely confidential information. This category is traditionally given special treatment in law, but the advent of computing has aggravated the risks of its unauthorized use, disclosure or manipulation. The computer hacker is potentially a more intrusive animal than the burglar or more traditional spy.

Information processed by computers can be of many types; for example, it can be personal, business or governmental information, or perhaps a mixture of these. Similarly, information learned by computer operators and programmers can fall into any of these groups. Once information in any of those groupings is classified as confidential, certain general legal principles govern its use or disclosure by a confidant. This chapter sets out and explains these general principles, while acknowledging that there are sometimes special rules which apply to different types of confidential information. Because this chapter is aimed primarily at managers and computer scientists working in industry and their advisers, rather than at civil servants and governmental agencies, and because the confines of space make more extensive coverage impossible, where the rules diverge this chapter sets out the law relating to trade secrets rather than the rules which apply to the other categories of secrets.

In the world of high technology it is unduly insular to consider only English law, for computers and modern telecommunications links allow information to be moved around the world and across jurisdictional boundaries in but the blink of an eye. Lawyers and information managers therefore need to be familiar with themes and developments in other countries. While the basis of this chapter will be the law of England and Wales reference is also made to the laws of other countries, notably the United States and Canada, and also to proposals for law reform, for the law is never static and new concepts introduced into other legal systems often have an impact on our own.

It would also be remiss to look only at the civil action for breach of confidence. When a valuable asset such as commercial information is misappropriated, for example, by industrial espionage, the question arises as to whether a crime has been committed. The potential application of criminal law to is therefore also considered in this chapter (see section 7.4 below) and it will be seen that, perhaps surprisingly, the criminal law intervenes very little if purely information is 'stolen' or interfered with, as opposed to the tangible asset on which it is stored. This is an area which is ripe for reform, and in this context the proposals of the Law Commission for England and Wales to create a new offence of unauthorized use or disclosure of a trade secret are also considered (see section 7.4.3).

In other chapters it has sometimes been much easier to describe the law in its direct application to computers. For example, it is possible to analyse statutes and cases on copyright in computer programs. In the field of confidential information the law is generally old and computers are new, and there are relatively few reported English cases dealing specifically with computers and even fewer directly relevant statutes. Thus it is necessary to describe the law of confidence in other contexts and to apply it to computers by way of analogy. However there has been a steady trickle of cases in the United States in the last few years. Many of these apply comparable principles to those of English law and they also provide useful factual examples. They will therefore be cited at appropriate points.

## 7.1 THE CIVIL ACTION FOR BREACH OF CONFIDENCE

In English law three conditions must be satisfied before a civil action for breach of confidence can succeed:

(a) The information must be confidential.

(b) The information must have been disclosed in circumstances which give rise to an obligation of confidence.

(c) There must be an actual or anticipated unauthorized use or disclosure of the information.[1]

A fourth factor is sometimes added, namely that the claimant must suffer detriment. However it is uncertain whether this is an element of the action or whether it is something which the court takes into account when deciding the appropriate remedy. In any event its significance was reduced by Lord Keith in *Attorney-General v Guardian Newspapers Ltd (No 2)* who said:

> I would think it a sufficient detriment to the confider that the information given in confidence is to be disclosed to persons whom he would prefer not to know it, even though the disclosure would not be harmful to him in any positive way.[2]

Each of the three main elements of the action for breach of confidence will now be considered in turn.

### 7.1.1 What is confidential information?

Lord Greene MR in *Saltman Engineering v Campbell*[3] described confidential information as something which is not public property and public knowledge. This means that there is no need for absolute secrecy before information can qualify as confidential. Relative secrecy may suffice. Thus information may be confidential if it is inaccessible or if it is not readily available to the public. For example, programs developed to drive robots on a production line and known only to the employees of a particular firm may be confidential, as may be novel software methodologies[4] or even information which a journalist has gleaned by searching through old newspapers and publicly available documents such as birth certificates and wills. In the last example there is a new compilation of information or even a rediscovery of information which has ceased to be generally known. Either way, the law will protect the fruits of the journalist's labours until he chooses to put them into the public domain or until someone else does the same work and then puts the results of his own research into public circulation.

The extent of disclosure which will be needed before information comes into the public domain is a matter for determination by the court in the light of the facts of the case. However, once information is in the public domain it cannot be protected under confidentiality laws, as was decided in the UK *Spycatcher* case[5] and in the US case of *Public Systems Inc v Towry and Adams*[6] where the Alabama Supreme Court

---

[1] *Coco v AN Clark (Engineers) Ltd* [1969] RPC 41, per Megarry J.
[2] [1990] 1 AC 109, 256.                                         [3] (1948) 65 RPC 203.
[4] *Healthcare Affiliated Services Inc v Lippany* (1988) 701 F Supp 1142.
[5] See *Attorney-General v Guardian Newspapers Ltd (No 2)* [1990] 1 AC 109, but cf *Schering Chemicals v Falkman* [1982] QB 1.
[6] (1991) WL 184452.

ruled that a commercially available spreadsheet program using public data could not be protected under Alabama trade-secrecy laws.

The fact that relative secrecy is all that is needed before information can qualify as confidential contrasts with the requirement of absolute novelty in patent law where any prior publication, no matter how obscure, will destroy novelty and deny patentability.

The test of relative secrecy would seem to be an objective one, the matter being looked at by the court in the light of all the relevant circumstances. A different and more subjective test of confidentiality was suggested in *Thomas Marshall v Guinle*[7] by Sir Robert Megarry V-C, a judge whose decisions will feature prominently in this chapter. He said that there were four elements which might be of assistance in identifying confidential information in a trade or industrial setting:

(a)  The information must be information the release of which the owner believes would be injurious to him or of advantage to his rivals or others.

(b)  The owner must believe the information is confidential or secret, that is, not already in the public domain.

(c)  The owner's belief under the previous two heads must be reasonable.

(d)  The information must be judged in the light of the usage and practices of the particular industry concerned.

This test concentrates very heavily on the views of the 'owner' of the information. However, these views are objectively assessed under the third requirement that they must be reasonable, thus preventing overzealous protection of information which by objective standards is not the true subject matter of an action for breach of confidence.

### 7.1.2  Categories of confidential information

Any sort of information may be classified as confidential, but in practice confidential information tends to fall into three categories: personal information, governmental secrets and trade secrets. Whilst it is public policy to protect confidential information generally, each of these categories of information is also protected for special reasons which may not apply equally to the other classes. For example, the protection of personal information is closely tied up with the maintenance of privacy. Thus in *Argyll v Argyll*[8] the Duke of Argyll was not able to publish in a newspaper the secrets of his marriage to the Duchess of Argyll. It will be interesting to see how this area of the law is affected over the next few years by the Human Rights Act 1998. Traditionally the English courts have been very reluctant to develop a full-blown action for the protection of privacy, as witness *Kaye v Robertson* where Glidewell LJ said, 'It is well known that in English law there is no

---

[7]  [1979] Ch 227.        [8]  [1967] Ch 302.

right to privacy, and accordingly no right of action of a person's privacy'.[9] Now, however, with the enactment in the Human Rights Act of article 8 of the European Convention of Human Rights and the right to respect for private and family life, home and correspondence, one can expect the law on confidentiality and privacy to enmesh and interweave, as has already been seen in the area of data protection.[10]

One of the most fruitful sources for the development of the law covered in this chapter may be actions brought by celebrities to protect their commercial interests and merchandising activities, as in *Douglas v Hello!*[11] Here, the actors Catherine Zeta-Jones and Michael Douglas had given *OK!* magazine the exclusive right to publish photographs of their wedding. They took stringent precautions to prevent anyone else taking photos at the wedding, but nevertheless Mr Rupert Thorpe, son of the former politician Jeremy Thorpe, did so and sold the pictures to *Hello!* magazine, which published them before *OK!* had the opportunity to publish its 'official' photographs. As Pinto has pointed out,[12] *Douglas v Hello!* was in reality a commercial breach of confidence case and privacy was only used by the claimants to bolster their position.

The protection of governmental secrets gives rise to yet other issues of public policy, such as the preservation of national security, international diplomacy, politics and the reputations of governments and of public figures; plus questions of the freedom of the press to publish information in their own commercial interests and/or in the interest of free and informed debate. One issue which has been highlighted is the attitudes of different governments to freedom of information and the preservation of secrecy. This is appositely illustrated by the pursuit of Mr Peter Wright through the courts of the world by the representatives of the Thatcher Government in an attempt to prevent the publication of his book, *Spycatcher*.[13] This should be contrasted with the abandonment of a case by the Wilson Government after they lost at first instance in an action for breach of confidence against Richard Crossman for publishing Cabinet secrets.[14]

Trade secrets are valuable commercial assets and to a large extent they are protected for the same reasons as other intangible commercial assets such as patents and copyrights. These include rewarding innovation and effort, allowing recoupment of expenditure on research and development and curtailing unfair competition by limiting the opportunities for piracy. In the context of computing, trade secrets

---

[9] [1991] FSR 62, 66.

[10] See, further, Chapter 11 on data protection and Chapter 10 (section 10.4.1) on workers' privacy.

[11] [2003] WL 1822887.

[12] Timothy Pinto, 'The Influence of the European Convention on Human Rights on Intellectual Property Rights' [2002] EIPR 209, 214.

[13] See n 5 above. See also *Attorney-General v Blake* [2001] 1 AC 268 where the spy George Blake was held liable to account to the Crown for profits made on the sale of his autobiography, substantial parts of which were based on information acquired in the course of his duties and as a British intelligence officer, even though much of it was no longer confidential by the time of publication. The duty to account was based on a lifelong duty of confidentiality owed to the Crown by members of the Security Services.

[14] *Attorney-General v Jonathan Cape* [1976] QB 752.

may include the specifications for software or hardware, as well as more standard business information such as pricing policies, lists of customers and suppliers, the company's payroll, quotations and investments, any or all of which may be kept on an in-house computer or may be held on behalf of a client on the computer of a specialist bureau.

Because the protection of trade secrets will feature quite prominently in this chapter a definition should be attempted. It has proved notoriously difficult to define a trade secret, but one attempt at a non-exhaustive definition comes from a report of the Alberta Institute of Law Research and Reform and a Federal Provincial Working Party, as amended in a draft statute adopted by the Canadian Uniform Law Conference in 1988.[15] This definition has the advantage of reflecting case law in England and Wales, Canada and the United States of America, and thus can serve as an indicator of elements in all three jurisdictions. The draft statute states that:

(1) . . . trade secret, means information that

   (i)   is, or may be, used in a trade or business,

   (ii)  is not generally known in that trade or business,

   (iii) has economic value from not being generally known, and

   (iv) is the subject of efforts that are reasonable under the circumstances to prevent it from becoming generally known.

(2) For the purposes of the definition, trade secret 'information' includes information set out, contained or embodied in, but not limited to, a formula, pattern, plan, compilation, computer program, method, technique, process, product, device or mechanism.

The English Law Commission in a 1997 consultation paper on the misuse of trade secrets,[16] which considers whether there should an offence of misuse of a trade secret,[17] has suggested a somewhat looser definition of a trade secret. They think that the term should apply to information:

(a) which is not generally known;

(b) which derives its value from that fact; and

(c) as to which its 'owner' has indicated (expressly or impliedly) his or her wish to preserve its quality of secrecy.[18]

The Law Commission then sought views on:

(a) whether there should be an additional requirement that the information be used in a trade or business; and if so,

(b) the extent to which the definition should exclude professional secrets, and

(c) the extent to which the definition should extend to pure research.

---

[15] *Trade Secrets* (Report No 46, 1986). References in this chapter are to the version amended at the Canadian Uniform Law Conference in 1988. For the full text see Allison Coleman, *The Legal Protection of Trade Secrets* (ESC/Sweet & Maxwell, 1992), Appendix 2(a).

[16] Law Commission Consultation Paper No 150, *Legislating the Criminal Code: Misuse of Trade Secrets* (25 November 1997).

[17] See, further, section 7.4.3 below.

[18] Law Commission (n 16 above), para 1.29.

The view of the present author is that the definition should include the trade or business element of (a) above; that it should not necessarily exclude professional secrets; and that pure research should be protected, provided that it has actual or potential economic value. The Law Commission has promised a final report on the issue of regulating the misuse of trade secrets in 2003.

### 7.1.3 When will an obligation of confidence be imposed?

Generally, an obligation of confidence will be imposed whenever confidential information is disclosed for a limited purpose. The recipient of the information will then be under a duty to use the information for the limited purpose only, and if he discloses or uses the information for any other purpose he will be in breach of his obligation and is liable to be restrained by injunction or subject to other appropriate remedies. For example, in *Saltman Engineering v Campbell*[19] the claimants gave to the defendants confidential designs for tools which the defendants were to manufacture solely for the claimants. When the defendants manufactured the tools on their own account they were held to be in breach of an obligation of confidence. The court held that the designs had been handed over for a limited purpose only and the defendants were not entitled to use them or the information contained in them for any other purpose.

The same principles were applied in *Fraser v Thames Television*[20] where the claimants had disclosed in confidence to a television company an idea for their own show. When the defendants tried to use the idea for a series featuring other actresses without first obtaining the claimants' consent, they were held to be in breach of their obligation of confidence. A good example of the imposition of an obligation of confidence in the field of computers might be where a consultant programmer is engaged to develop programs which will be integrated with other programs devised in-house. Details of these programs will have to be disclosed to the consultant, but this disclosure would clearly be for the sole purpose of work for that organization and on the basis that he would not be free to use the information in work for other clients.

Problems can sometimes arise in determining the issue of to whom a duty of confidentiality is owed. In *Fraser v Evans*[21] the claimant, Fraser, wrote a report for the Greek Government. His contract stated that he was to keep confidential any information that he acquired while compiling the report, but the Greek Government did not enter into a reciprocal obligation to keep confidential information supplied by Fraser to them. After its delivery to the Greek Government Fraser's report was leaked by an unknown source to a newspaper, which proposed to publish an article about it. Fraser thought that the article might damage his reputation and he sought to restrain its publication on the ground of breach of confidence. The court held that, on the facts, no one owed a duty of confidentiality to Fraser despite his own categorization of the

---

[19] (1948) 65 RPC 203.      [20] [1984] QB 44.      [21] [1969] 1 QB 349.

information as being sensitive. Similarly, in the US case of *Bush v Goldman Sachs*[22] Bush had developed a computer model to restructure government bond debt through refunding. Bush was hired by one company to become part of its team tendering for the contract to reconstruct the bond debt of the city of Birmingham, Alabama. Bush's computer model was submitted to the city authorities as part of the tendering process. However, the contract was given to another company, Goldman Sachs. Goldman Sachs subsequently made use of Bush's model without his consent. However, an action for breach of confidence failed, first because Bush had failed to take positive steps to protect the confidentiality of the model, for example, by express notice of confidentiality in the tendering documentation; and secondly the court held that the city authorities, which had undoubtedly passed on the information to Goldman Sachs, owed no duty of confidentiality to Bush. Because they owed no duty to Bush they did not act in breach of duty in passing on the information to Goldman Sachs, which likewise could also not be held liable.

Precedent has not limited the range of circumstances in which an obligation of confidence can arise; it is a question of fact to be decided in each case, but there are guidelines. For example, in the commercial context a useful statement was made by Megarry J (as he then was) in *Coco v AN Clark (Engineers) Ltd*.[23] He said that where information of commercial or industrial value is given on a business-like basis or with a common object in mind such as a joint venture or the manufacture of articles by one party for another, the recipient is under a heavy burden if he seeks to refute the contention that he is bound by an obligation of confidence. Where confidential information falling into the other categories is disclosed this *dictum* is obviously not directly applicable, but use of the limited-purpose test described above should overcome any difficulties.

In *Coco v AN Clark (Engineers) Ltd* Megarry J gave another test for the circumstances giving rise to an obligation of confidence. He said that an obligation would lie when a reasonable man standing in the shoes of the recipient of the information would realize on reasonable grounds that the information was being given to him in confidence. It will be remembered that in *Thomas Marshall v Guinle*[24] Megarry V-C (as he later became) had defined information which could be classified as confidential. There he viewed the situation from the standpoint of the 'owner' of the information, but now when faced with the other side of the coin he said that the circumstances which give rise to an obligation were to be viewed from the position of the reasonable recipient. This shift in emphasis from the 'owner' to the recipient reflects the bilateral nature of the obligation of confidence and the mixed elements of subjectivity and objectivity in the various tests. These take into account not only the views of the parties to the action but also the public interest in the maintenance of confidentiality. In certain circumstances even if information has been classified as confidential an obligation of confidence will not arise if, for example, it would be against the public interest to keep the information confidential or if such a restriction

---

[22] (1989) 544 So 2d 873.     [23] [1969] RPC 41.     [24] [1979] Ch 227.

would prevent an ex-employee using the general knowledge and skill acquired in his former employment. The special position of employees will be considered in section 7.2.3.1 below, but the following section considers in greater detail the public interest which permits disclosure even of information which would otherwise be classified as being confidential.

### 7.1.4 The public interest in disclosure

The cases show that there is a clear public policy in favour of protecting confidential information. However, in certain circumstances that policy is overturned by one which holds that it is in the public interest that even confidential information should be disclosed, either to the public as a whole, for example, through the media, or to the appropriate authorities such as the police. For example, suppose a scientist has discovered a cure for AIDS or for cancer. Should he be allowed to lock it in his safe or store it on his computer with the intention of keeping it a secret for the rest of his life? If one of his employees proposes disclosing the secret in a medical journal, to a national newspaper or at a scientific conference, should the discoverer be able to restrain him from so doing by an action for breach of confidence? This section considers the factors which the court will take into account when assessing whether the disclosure is justified in the public interest, followed by an examinaton of the position of 'whistleblowing' employees and the protection given to them under the Public Interest Disclosure Act 1998 ('PIDA 1998') against victimization by their employers following a disclosure made in the public interest.

First, however, it is necessary to look at article 10 of the European Convention on Human Rights which contains the right to freedom of expression. This will play an increasing role in cases of breach of confidence, particularly in cases where press freedom is an issue. Article 10 provides:

1. Everyone has the right to freedom of expression. This right shall include freedom to hold opinions and to receive and impart information and ideas without frontiers . . .

2. The exercise of these freedoms, since it carries with it duties and responsibilities, may be subject to such formalities, conditions, restrictions or penalties as are prescribed by law and are necessary in a democratic society, for the protection of the rights of others[25] . . . for preventing the disclosure of information received in confidence . . .

However it should be noted that article 10 requires the courts to perform the same type of balancing exercise as in traditional cases of breach of confidence, and thus arguably the cases of the past can still be used as a guide to the practice of the future.

In cases of breach of confidence, the test for determining the public interest in disclosure has varied over the years. An early and much-quoted *dictum* comes from

---

[25] This includes their intellectual property rights ('IPRs'). See, further, article 1 of the First Protocol (the right to property). Whether confidential information can be classified as property is discussed in section 7.2 below.

the case of *Gartside v Outram* where Wood V-C said 'there is no confidence as to the disclosure of an iniquity'.[26] From this there arose what became known as the 'iniquity rule', which basically meant that a confidant was justified in breaching confidentiality and disclosing information in the public interest if it was related to some misconduct, and the closer this misconduct came to criminal or unlawful activity the better. But this is a rather narrow basis on which to permit disclosure and it may not, for example, permit the disclosure of the cure for cancer referred to in the previous example, for there the discoverer who wishes to keep the information out of the public domain is guilty of no criminal or unlawful conduct even though most would probably castigate his intentions as immoral.

Lord Denning led a movement away from the iniquity rule in *Initial Services v Putterill*,[27] *Fraser v Evans*[28] and *Schering Chemicals v Falkman*,[29] but there remained uncertainty as to the status of the old rule or the extent of any new rule until *Lion Laboratories v Evans*[30] where the Court of Appeal held that confidential information may be disclosed in circumstances where there was 'just cause or excuse', which is obviously a much broader notion than that of an iniquity.[31]

In *Lion Laboratories v Evans* the claimant company manufactured computerized electronic equipment known as the Lion Intoximeter which was used by the police to measure the level of alcohol in the breath of people suspected of drink-driving. Readings from the machine were used as a basis for prosecution. Confidential internal memoranda produced by the company indicated that readings from the machines were often inaccurate. Two of the claimants' employees gave copies of the memoranda to a national newspaper, the *Daily Express*, which at that time was conducting a campaign against the use of the Intoximeter by the police. The claimants sought an injunction to restrain publication of the information by the newspaper on the grounds of breach of confidence and breach of copyright. The actions failed as the Court of Appeal held that there was a public interest in the disclosure of the information, as it might lead to the reappraisal of a device which had the potential for causing wrongful conviction for a serious offence. They said that the defence of public interest was not limited to cases involving disclosure of an iniquity, iniquity being just one example of the public-interest exemption and not therefore an essential ingredient. The court based the defence on the wider ground of 'just cause or excuse' for disclosure, with the caution given by Lord Griffiths that the decision should not be treated as a 'mole's charter'. The court also made it clear that there was a difference between matters which, on the one hand, it was in the commercial interest of newspapers to publish and which might merely be of public interest to read and, on the other hand, matters which it was in the public interest to disclose. Only in the latter cases would the public interest permit disclosure of confidential information. Furthermore, the press might not always be the appropriate medium for a disclosure. In other cases it

---

[26] (1857) 26 LJ Ch 113, 114.          [27] [1968] 1 QB 396.          [28] [1969] 1 QB 349.

[29] [1982] QB 1.                                                       [30] [1985] QB 526.

[31] See also *W v Egdell* [1990] 1 All ER 835.

might be more appropriate to disclose the information to the police or other authorities. That was not, however, the case here where disclosure through the press would be allowed.

We do not know what happened to the employees in *Lion Laboratories*, but Yvonne Cripps has chronicled a number of cases where employees have lost their jobs as a result of similar disclosures and effectively have been prevented from working for anyone else ever again.[32] While equity may refuse an injunction to prevent the disclosure of information in the public interest, the common law has generally taken the approach that disclosure of confidential information is a breach of the implied duty of fidelity in the contract of employment, which may justify dismissal or other disciplinary action. The position of the employee has however recently been improved by the Public Interest Disclosure Act 1998 ('the PIDA 1998').

The PIDA 1998 amends the Employment Rights Act 1996. The 1998 Act protects a 'worker' from being victimized by the employer when the worker makes what the Act calls a 'protected disclosure'. A 'worker' is an individual who works under a contract of employment, or who contracts 'to perform personally services for another party to the contract whose status is not by virtue of the contract that of a client or customer of any business undertaking carried on by the individual'.[33] Self-employed computing consultants are therefore not covered by the Act, but they have no need of its protection, as they cannot of course be dismissed or otherwise victimized by an 'employer'. Programmers seconded from other firms are however covered, for the PIDA 1998[34] extends protection to, *inter alia*, agency and seconded employees; and also to many homeworkers and teleworkers, provided they do not ordinarily work outside Great Britain.[35]

A worker will be protected against victimization for disclosure if the worker makes (a) a qualifying disclosure (b) in certain prescribed circumstances. A 'qualifying disclosure' means any disclosure of information which, in the reasonable belief of the worker making the disclosure tends to show one or more of the following, which has occurred in the past, is occurring in the present, or is likely to occur in the future: a criminal offence; failure to comply with a legal obligation; a miscarriage of justice; danger to health and safety; environmental damage; or information showing concealment of any of these.[36] This is narrower than the 'just cause or excuse' test for public-interest disclosure set out in *Lion Laboratories* and reflects to a much greater extent the old and discredited 'iniquity' test. It is interesting that the legislature went for certainty of definition, rather than width of protection.

A qualifying disclosure made in appropriate circumstances to an appropriate

---

[32] Yvonne Cripps, *The Legal Implications of Disclosure in the Public Interest: An Analysis of Prohibitions and Protections with Particular Reference to Employers and Employees*, 2nd edn (Sweet & Maxwell, 1994), ch 1.

[33] Employment Rights Act 1996, s 230.

[34] PIDA 1998, s 1, inserting a new section 43K into the Employment Rights Act 1996.

[35] Employment Rights Act 1996, s 196(2), (3).

[36] PIDA 1998, s 1; Employment Rights Act 1996, s 43B.

person becomes a protected disclosure, entitling the worker to protection against victimization. The PIDA 1998 lists six cases where a disclosure by a worker is a protected disclosure. Basically, the Act encourages private or semi-private disclosures, either to the employer, or to the person committing the wrongful act, and many employers have produced Codes of Practice on Public Interest Disclosure which also specify other persons to whom disclosures may be made and the way the matter is to be handled. Only if it is of a more serious nature, or if the private or semi-private route has failed, may the employee be justified in disclosing to a wider audience, such as the press, but in this case close attention needs to be paid to the minutiae of the Act, for there are many pitfalls for the public-spirited, but poorly advised employee. Dismissal of an unprotected employee may not be unfair; and disciplinary action may not be in breach of contract. The PIDA 1998 therefore remedies many of the abuses highlighted by Cripps[37] and furthers the policy of permitting, and even encouraging, disclosure of otherwise confidential information in the public interest; but it is a cautious piece of legislation and it is to be hoped that the judiciary will not further restrict its ambit, for although they have defined public interest widely in the past, they have not also consistently championed the rights of the victimized employee.

## 7.2 JURISDICTION

There has been much debate as to the jurisdictional foundation of the action for breach of confidence, but quite remarkably the courts seem free to draw on most of the available jurisdictional bases of contract, equity, property and tort. In many instances the facts will lead quite naturally to the application of one of these bases, in others there may be several possibilities. This section outlines the various jurisdictional bases and indicates areas where they are most frequently employed in practice.

### 7.2.1 Express contractual obligations of confidence

Parties who are aware that information is confidential and that its unauthorized use or disclosure would be disadvantageous to them would be well advised to enter into express contracts of confidentiality with their confidants before making a disclosure. As well as setting out the terms on which the information is disclosed, the contract will also serve as a warning of both confidentiality and the serious intent of the discloser.

An express contract may be oral or in writing, although writing is clearly advantageous for evidential reasons. No particular form is necessary so long as the intent is clear, and it is common for the obligation of confidence to be set out in a letter or

---

[37] See n 32 above.

deed which, in practice, follows a fairly standard pattern. In return for the release of the information the confidant agrees to treat it as confidential and to use it only for the limited purpose intended. However, it is normal to qualify the agreement by providing that in three cases the obligation shall cease:

(a) If the information subsequently comes into the public domain other than by breach of confidence on the part of the confidant.

(b) If it was lawfully in the confidant's possession before the agreement.

(c) If it was acquired by him after the agreement from a third party who was not also bound by an obligation of confidence to the present discloser.

Confidentiality clauses are also commonly found in contracts dealing with an array of other matters such as contracts for the supply or maintenance of hardware or software, consultancy contracts, and agreements for the provision of data services.

It is not necessary to define in the contract all of the information which is to be regarded as being confidential, and indeed this will rarely be possible in practice. But if an injunction is sought to restrain breach of an obligation of confidence, it is important then to define carefully for the purpose of the proceedings information which is believed to be confidential and which it is alleged is, or is thought likely to be, improperly used or disclosed. For example, in *Amway Corporation Ltd v Eurway International Ltd*[38] the claimants alleged that all of the material in all of their sales promotion literature was confidential. The claim failed. The court held that the claimants had not disclosed the information to the defendants under an obligation of confidence, but even if they had, an injunction could not be granted to restrain use of such a generalized body of information or what the judge referred to as 'mere know-how'. The distinction between protectable confidential information and 'mere know-how' which cannot be protected is an important one, and is relied on heavily in employment cases (see section 7.2.3).

Another useful device for protecting confidential information is what can be described as a 'black box' contract. In *Paul (Printing Machinery) Ltd v Southern Instruments (Communications) Ltd*[39] the claimants supplied a telephone answering machine to one of the defendants under a contract for hire, which specified that the defendant was not to remove the machine from the address and position at which it was installed nor interfere in any way with the machine or with any of its electrical connections. In breach of this agreement one of the defendants allowed another defendant to remove it, take it apart and examine it. Damages would obviously not have been an appropriate remedy as the claimant clearly wanted to preserve the 'secrets in the box'. As a result the court granted an interlocutory injunction restraining the defendants from using or disclosing confidential information gleaned from the unlawful inspection.

This type of contract is obviously useful in the supply of computers or other tech-

[38] [1974] RPC 82. See also *FSS Travel and Leisure Systems Ltd v Johnson* [1999] FSR 505.
[39] [1964] RPC 118.

nologically advanced equipment where the secret parts can be shielded from view. In the absence of such agreement the law of confidence will not prevent the purchaser of equipment from reverse engineering a machine or disassembling a program.[40] Even copyright laws do not prevent a competitor from taking the ideas behind, for example, a computer program, copyright being aimed a protection of the form in which material is laid out rather than the ideas on which it is based.[41]

### 7.2.2 Implied contractual obligations

An obligation of confidence may also be implied into a contract. An implied term can provide the entire obligation of confidence or it may supplement an express term. An example of its supplementary role is *Thomas Marshall v Guinle*[42] where an employee was subject to an express clause prohibiting the disclosure of confidential information belonging to his employers. However, on the facts of the case the employee had been *using* the information for his own purposes and not *disclosing* it to others. The court held that the express term against disclosing confidential information could be supplemented by an implied term prohibiting its use.

Another case on the implied obligation of confidence, and one to which we shall return later, is *Schering Chemicals Ltd v Falkman*.[43] The facts were that the claimant was a drug company which manufactured a drug called Primodos. It had been suggested that the drug could have harmful effects on unborn children, and as a result the claimant suffered bad publicity. It engaged the first defendant to train its executives in television techniques and to put across effectively the claimant's point of view. The first defendant engaged the second defendant to help with the training courses. The claimants supplied a large amount of information on the drug to the first defendant and that in turn was passed on to the second defendant. It was acknowledged that the first defendant had received the information in confidence, but it was never established whether the second defendant gave an express undertaking of confidentiality.

Shortly after the training course, the second defendant proposed making a television programme about the drug for Thames Television. Much of the information which was to be included in the film had been supplied by the claimant for the training course but, importantly, most of it was already available from public sources. The claimant sought an injunction to restrain use of the information, arguing that it had been obtained in circumstances imposing an obligation of confidence and to use it in the film would amount to breach of confidence.

Lord Denning MR, who dissented, refused to imply an obligation of confidence on the ground that the information was publicly available. Shaw and Templeman LJJ disagreed. Shaw LJ said that the second defendant owed a fiduciary duty to the

---

[40]  See, eg, *Acuson Corp v Aloka Co Ltd*, 257 Cal Rptr 368, 209 Cal App 3d 1098, 209 Cal App 3d 425, 1989 Cal App Lexis 317, (1989) 2 The Software Law Bulletin 146.

[41]  See, further, Chapter 6.          [42]  [1979] Ch 227.          [43]  [1982] QB 1.

claimant and described his conduct as a 'flagrant breach of an elementary duty to honour confidences'. He said that the law did not grant 'a licence for the mercenary betrayal of business confidences'. As for the argument that the information was in the public domain and thus not confidential, he said this was 'at best cynical; some may regard it as specious'.[44]

Templeman LJ also held that the second defendant was under a duty of confidence, but instead of describing it as a fiduciary duty, he said, most importantly in the present context, that it was based on an implied promise. He said that the information had been given for one purpose only, and when the second defendant had agreed for reward to take part in the training course and had received the information from the claimant he came under a duty not to use that information, and in particular he impliedly promised not to use it for the very purpose which the claimant sought to avoid, namely bad publicity or publicity which it reasonably regarded as bad. Rather unusually, although the information was already in the public domain it remained confidential as between the parties to the action, and as the second defendant could not republish or recycle it without causing further harm, he would be in breach of his obligation of confidence if he used the information for another purpose. Furthermore, as Thames Television had acted with full knowledge of the facts, they could be in no better position than the second defendant, and they too would be restrained from using or disclosing the information.

### 7.2.3 The different obligations of confidence owed by employees and consultants

#### 7.2.3.1 *Employees*

Employees both generate and acquire confidential information in the course of a contract of employment. The general principle is that the employee holds the confidential information for the benefit of the employer.

Employment contracts do, however, present special problems, as here the contractual obligation of confidence is subject to the qualification that an employee is, after the termination of the contract of employment, free to use general knowledge and skill either for the employee's own benefit or for the benefit of others. As a result, the confidential character of information is probably more closely scrutinized in these cases than in almost any others. One of the most difficult questions in this area of the law is to determine the dividing line between confidential information and general knowledge and skill. For example, is the knowledge acquired by a computer-systems expert in the course of employment the employee's own to use as the employee pleases or is it an asset belonging to the employer? What is the position of firms of headhunters who seek to persuade highly skilled personnel to leave their present employment and to use their expertise for the benefit of others in return

---

[44] Ibid, 27, 28.

for greater reward? In today's competitive environment expertise is a valuable commodity, but to what extent is it really readily saleable?

An employee's obligation of confidence may be found in the express or in the implied terms of the contract of employment. This was illustrated earlier by the case of *Thomas Marshall v Guinle*[45] where it will be remembered that an express term prohibiting the disclosure of confidential information was supplemented by an implied term preventing the employee from using that information. In employment cases the implied obligation of confidence is part of the more general implied obligation of good faith and fidelity which every employee owes to the employer. This obligation exists during the term of the contract, but very importantly, it also continues after employment ceases. It is at its clearest and strongest during the subsistence of the contract, for here as Gurry argues[46] the employee's interest in enhancing his knowledge and skill 'interlocks' with the duty to develop and improve the employer's business. At this stage Gurry shows that the obligation of fidelity owed by an employee to an employer can be expressed in three propositions:

(a) An employee is bound not to disclose or use confidential information received in the course of employment for purposes which are against the interests of the employer.

(b) An employee must not compete with the employer or work for any of the employer's rivals.

(c) The employee is bound to disclose to the employer any valuable information which the employee receives in his capacity as an employee and which is unknown to his employer, and this will include any confidential information which would further the employer's trade.

The first two propositions are illustrated by *Hivac v Park Royal Scientific Instruments Ltd*[47] where five people who were employed by the claimants were working in their spare time for the claimants' rivals, the defendants. If this had continued they were almost certain to have disclosed to the defendants confidential information belonging to the claimants. As a result, the claimants succeeded in their action to restrain the defendants from continuing to employ the claimants' employees. Moonlighting is therefore discouraged.

After the contract of employment has been terminated the employee's implied duty of good faith and fidelity continues and he will still be required to keep confidential those secrets which he learnt during the former employment. However, at this stage the interest of the employee in using and developing general knowledge and skill usually diverges from the former employer's interest in the employer's own business. To return to the previous example, the computer-systems expert whose skills have been headhunted by a rival concern or who wishes to set up in business

---

[45] [1979] Ch 227.
[46] Francis Gurry, *Breach of Confidence* (Oxford University Press, 1984), p 179.
[47] [1946] Ch 169.

on his own account may not be prepared to make less than full use of all of the knowledge that he possesses, including knowledge of information classified by his former employer as being confidential, or indeed his new employment may be conditional on the full use of such knowledge. Here a number of policies conflict, namely the public policy in the maintenance of confidences as against policies favouring mobility of labour, the free flow of information and free competition. As a compromise, the first policy holds sway to the extent that a former employee is under a continuing obligation not to use or disclose confidential information belonging to the former employer, but the other policies ensure that he is free to use his general knowledge and skill.

There are a number of tests for determining the dividing line between confidential information and general knowledge and skill. In *Printers and Finishers v Holloway* Cross J said the question was whether the information could 'fairly be regarded as a separate part of the employee's stock of knowledge which a man of ordinary honesty and intelligence would recognise to be the property of his old employer, and not as his own to do as he likes with'.[48] More recently the Court of Appeal laid down guidelines in *Faccenda Chicken Ltd v Fowler*.[49] Neil LJ, giving the judgment of the court, said that in order to determine whether information could be classified as so confidential that an employee should not be allowed to use or disclose it for the benefit of a subsequent employer it was necessary to consider all the circumstances of the particular case, but the following were among those to which attention must be paid:

(a) *The nature of the employment.* Employment in a capacity where confidential information is habitually handled may impose a high obligation of confidentiality because the employee could be expected to realize its sensitive nature to a greater extent than if he were employed in a capacity where such material reached him only occasionally.

(b) *The nature of the information itself.* In order to be protected the information must be of a highly confidential nature; no other information could be protected even by a covenant in restraint of trade. The court said it would clearly be impossible to provide a list of matters which would be protectable as trade secrets. Secret processes of manufacture were obvious examples, but innumerable other pieces of information were capable of being trade secrets even though the secrecy of some information may only be short-lived. In addition, the fact that the circulation of certain information was restricted to a limited number of individuals may throw a light on the status of the information and its degree of confidentiality.

(c) *Whether the employer impressed upon the employee the confidentiality of the information.*

(d) *Whether the relevant information can be easily isolated from other information which the employee is free to use or disclose.* This factor should not be regarded as conclusive, as might have been suggested in earlier cases, but like the other

---

[48] [1964] 3 All ER 731, 735.      [49] [1987] Ch 117.

matters listed above it was one of the factors which the court should take into account.

The result of this test is that if information is not categorized as confidential under these criteria then it forms part of the employee's general knowledge and skill, and it may be easier to apply the factors listed in *Faccenda Chicken Ltd v Fowler* to employees in high-technology industries than it is to apply more general statements such as that in *Printers and Finishers v Holloway*. However, there are still many difficulties and each case must inevitably turn on its facts.

Neil LJ also made it clear that he was stating principles which would apply only when the ex-employee wanted to earn his living from use of the information in question. He left open the question of whether additional protection should be afforded if an ex-employee proposed not to use it in order to earn his living but merely to sell it to a third party. Such a distinction, if drawn, would be new to English law. It would also necessitate the development of a new set of principles of a complexity hitherto unforeseen. For example, what would be the position of a person who sold information in return for a consultancy for one day a week, or for one day a month, or for one day a year, or for just one day?

An alternative approach to reliance solely on an implied obligation to respect confidentiality, and hence a way around some of the difficulties described above, might be to use a contractual term to restrain the employee from working for competitors after he leaves his employment. However, the courts view such restrictions unfavourably and they will only be enforced if they are no wider than is reasonably necessary to protect the employer's interests in terms of the activities covered, the geographical area to which the restriction extends and the length of time it lasts.[50] For example, a hardware manufacturer whose business consisted solely of producing automated teller machines for use in the banking industry in the UK would be unable to restrict one of its programmers from working for any other hardware manufacturer in the world for ten years after leaving. It is important to note that if the restriction is too wide it is likely to be totally ineffective, thus allowing the employee to work for a direct competitor[51] and directing reliance back on the uncertain obligation of confidence. A better restriction would be against working on the production of automated teller machines and connected hardware for any business marketing its equipment in the UK. The length of time of the restriction should not last beyond the date when the employer's secret technology is likely to become obsolete.

The principles for interpretation of restrictive covenants were recently restated by the Court of Appeal in *FSS Travel and Leisure Systems Ltd v Johnson*.[52] Here, the defendant employee was a computer programmer who had worked on the claimant employer's computerized booking system, a system which had been devised especially for the travel industry. The system comprised 2,852 separate programs which

---

[50]  *Nordenfeldt v Maxim Nordenfeldt Gun Co* [1894] AC 535.
[51]  *Mason v Provident Clothing & Supply Co Ltd* [1913] AC 724.
[52]  [1999] FSR 505.

interacted with each other and were updated daily. The defendant had worked on 395 of them. It was a term of the defendant's contract of employment that for a period of one year after the termination of the contract, he would not work for any of the claimant's competitors. Mummery LJ, delivering the judgment of the Court of Appeal, said that the principles to be applied to cases such as the present one were to be found in three cases: *Littlewoods Organisation v Harris*;[53] *Office Angels Ltd v Rainer-Thomas*;[54] and *Lansing Linde Ltd v Kerr*.[55] They were as follows. The court will never uphold a covenant taken by an employer merely to protect himself from competition by a former employee. Instead there must be some subject matter which an employer could legitimately protect by a restrictive covenant. However, protection could be claimed for identifiable objective knowledge constituting trade secrets belonging to the employer, but which the employee has learned (or even created) during the course of employment. By way of contrast, and as described above in the context of the implied obligation of confidence, protection could not be legitimately claimed by way of a restrictive covenant for skill, experience, know-how and general knowledge acquired by an employee whilst working for the employer, even though that would better equip him to work for others in competition with the former employer. Once again, therefore, the critical question was whether the information the employer sought to protect came under the heading of trade secrets, or whether it was part of the employee's general knowledge and skill. Mummery LJ explained that in order to classify the information in question it was necessary to examine all of the evidence relating to: the nature of the employment; the character of the information; the restrictions imposed on its dissemination; the extent to which it was in the public domain; the damage likely to be caused by its use and disclosure to a competitor; and the extent to which the information in question is readily separable from the employee's general knowledge and skill. But crucially, it was also necessary to be very precise in pleadings and to provide solid evidence in proof of trade secrets, and this the claimant in this case had failed to do. It was notable that witnesses had described the skills the defendant possessed and emphasized what he could do, rather than what he knew; and from this the court concluded that FSS Travel and Leisure Systems were claiming to be entitled to control the exercise, after the termination of the contract of employment, of the skill, experience, know-how and general knowledge of their former employee. This, the court would not allow them to do, and the covenant was held to be invalid. Witnesses for the employer should therefore be schooled not to use the modern skills-based language, but to concentrate instead on hard fact.

Other ways in which an employee's competitive potential can be reduced and his ability to misappropriate trade secrets restricted is either to require a long period of notice to be given prior to termination of the contract, or to put the employee on 'garden leave'. 'Garden leave' entitles the employee to full pay and perks for a defined period (for example, twelve months) so long as he does not work for anyone

---

[53] [1977] 1 WLR 1472.   [54] [1991] IRLR 214.   [55] [1991] IRLR 80.

else. The employee may effectively be given a holiday. The enforceability of a garden-leave clause and its ability to protect confidential information was first tested in *Provident Financial Group plc v Hayward*.[56] At one time it was suggested that these clauses might be construed more flexibly than conventional restrictive covenants,[57] but more recently, in *William Hill v Tucker*,[58] Morritt LJ, giving the judgment of the Court of Appeal, said that they will be subject to similar controls to covenants in restraint of trade, for their effect is equally to keep an employee out of the labour market.

### 7.2.3.2 *Consultants*

An increasing number of people are now working in the computing industry as consultants, that is, as independent contractors rather than as employees. It is therefore necessary also to consider their position in relation to confidential information generated and acquired in the course of their work.

A well-drafted contract for services to be provided by a consultant should always deal with the ownership of IPRs generated in the course of the work and with the question of confidentiality. This is in the interests of both the consultant and the firm for which the work is to be done.

In the absence of express agreement it is necessary to fall back on ordinary principles of law. So far as confidential information is concerned this will be governed by implied contractual terms, as in the case of a contract of employment. A consultant should hold for the benefit of the firm for which he works all trade secrets generated or acquired in the course of the work and he should not use or disclose these trade secrets for any unauthorized purpose. Counterbalancing this is, however, the principle that a consultant, like an employee, is entitled to use for his own benefit and for the benefit of others his general knowledge and skill. Thus again we meet the thorny issue of what is a trade secret and what is general knowledge and skill. Where does the dividing line lie?

In the case of an employee, *Faccenda Chicken v Fowler*[59] laid down guidelines as to which information could be used for the benefit of the employee and others after termination of a contract of employment and which should be kept secret. However, there is nothing in *Faccenda Chicken* to indicate that those guidelines would apply equally to a consultant. If they do not apply, consultants are therefore in a different position to employees. Cases such as *Schering Chemicals v Falkman*,[60] discussed above, *Deta Nominees v Viscount Plastic Products*,[61] and *Surveys and Mining Ltd v Morrison*[62] have taken a rather hard line with consultants who have acquired confidential information whilst working for one client and then subsequently used that information for their own benefit or for the benefit of others. In

---

[56] [1989] 3 All ER 298.
[57] *Credit Suisse Asset Management Ltd v Armstrong* [1996] ICR 882, 892, CA, per Neill LJ.
[58] [1999] ICR 291.       [59] [1987] Ch 117.              [60] [1982] QB 1.
[61] [1979] VR 167.        [62] [1969] QdR 470.

each of these cases the courts have held that the consultant has acted in breach of an obligation of confidence.

If employees and consultants are treated differently several propositions follow. For example, while both consultants and employees can use their general knowledge and skill for the benefit of others, more information is likely to be held to be confidential and protectable in the case of consultants than in the case of employees. Viewing this from the point of view of a firm deciding to take on additional labour, it might be desirable therefore to take on independent contractors or consultants rather than to engage employees under short-term contracts.

### 7.2.4 The equitable obligation of confidence

There are many circumstances in which confidential information is disclosed and yet there cannot be said to be any contract between the discloser and confidant. This will normally be the case when personal confidences are exchanged between friends, and it will often be so when an inventor discusses an invention with potential financiers and business partners. In these circumstances any obligation of confidence will almost always be equitable. For example, in *Coco v AN Clark (Engineers) Ltd*[63] the claimant who had designed the 'Coco Moped' sought cooperation from the defendants in its development. The parties quarrelled before any agreement was reached, but features of the Coco Moped were later found in the defendant's mopeds. The court found that the information which the claimant gave to the defendants was not confidential but, had it been, Megarry J said that an equitable obligation would have been imposed if, applying the test which we met earlier, the circumstances were such that a reasonable man standing in the shoes of the recipient of the information would have realized on reasonable grounds that the information was being given to him in confidence.

Another example is *Seager v Copydex*[64] where the claimant, in the course of negotiations for marketing one type of carpet grip which he had invented, disclosed his design for a second grip and suggested the name 'Invisigrip'. This disclosure would seem to have been unsolicited. Negotiations foundered and the defendants decided to develop and market a carpet grip of their own. This they also called 'Invisgrip' and its design closely resembled the second grip described to them by the claimant. The claimant succeeded in an action for unauthorized use of confidential information. The court said that even if the plagiarism by the defendants was unconscious there were too many coincidences and too many similarities for the court to conclude that there had been anything other than a misuse of information given to the defendants by the claimant. Equitable principles were also applied recently by the Irish courts in *House of Spring Gardens v Point Blank Ltd*[65] where, because there were no Irish cases in point, the courts applied the doctrines of English law.[66]

---

[63] [1969] RPC 41.  [64] [1967] RPC 349.  [65] [1985] FSR 327.
[66] See, further, A Coleman, '*House of Spring Gardens v Point Blank*: "A Maze of Deception" ' [1988] EIPR 218.

### 7.2.4.1 *Unsolicited disclosures*

Cases on the equitable obligation of confidence highlight the problems which can arise from unsolicited disclosures. Some firms regularly receive ideas from outsiders about new products or improvements to their existing ranges, and while it is not proper that they should make free use of all confidences that come their way their subsequent activities should not, at the other extreme, always be inhibited by a prior unsolicited disclosure. Strong representations were made to the Law Commission on this point.[67] Evidence to the Commission showed that many firms adopted elaborate procedures in order to avoid an obligation of confidence. Some firms required the person submitting the information to sign a form recognizing that no obligation of confidence existed in relation to the information, the person submitting the information being limited to such rights (if any) which he may have to patent, copyright or design rights. Other firms were content to ensure that the person submitting unsolicited information appreciated that the recipient would remain free to exploit ideas involved if they had already been, or were in the future, independently discovered by the recipients or if they were in the public domain. In other words those firms who understood their legal position modified their relationship with the discloser of confidential information by express contract, whereas those who did not know the law often found themselves bound to respect confidentiality. To ameliorate the position of persons in the latter category the Law Commission recommended[68] that the law be changed, and that an obligation of confidence should come into existence only when the recipient of the information had given an express undertaking of confidence or where an undertaking could be inferred from the relationship between the parties or from the conduct of the recipient. However, this is arguably going too far and represents an unnecessary change. It is better to prefer confidentiality and to refute the obligation if necessary than to place barriers in the way of it arising in the first place.

### 7.2.5  Tortious obligations of confidence

So far tort has not featured very prominently in the cases on breach of confidence, but it assumes an important role in proposals for reform in three common-law jurisdictions, England and Wales, Canada and the United States.[69]

In each of these jurisdictions it has been suggested that henceforth, at least in certain areas, the action for breach of confidence should be based on tortious liability. In 1981 the English Law Commission recommended[70] that the present action for breach of confidence should be abolished and that it should be replaced by one new statutory tort of breach of confidence covering the unauthorized use or disclosure of

---

[67] Law Commission Report No 110, *Breach of Confidence* (Cmnd 8388) (HMSO, 1981), para 5.3.
[68] Ibid, para 6.14.
[69] See further Coleman (n 15 above), ch 2.
[70] Law Commission Report No 110 (n 67 above), para 6.2.

confidential information. In contrast to the reforms in the United States and Canada, the English Law Commission recommended that the new action should apply to all categories of confidential information. In the United States and Canada the various categories of information are now often treated separately. There, for example, the law of privacy has burgeoned in recent years, affecting the protection of personal confidences, and reform bodies now suggest that trade secrets should also be treated separately, recognizing the different interests involved and their greater affinity with the policies of intellectual property and unfair competition law than with the issues underlying, for example, privacy and governmental information. This section examines the reforms of trade-secrets law, following once again the theme of trade where the law diverges as between the different categories of confidential information.

In the United States and Canada an additional complication arises in that confidentiality is a matter for state or provincial law, unlike patents and copyrights, which are regulated federally. As a result, although there is a common core of principles underlying the action for breach of confidence laws do diverge across the country. There have been two main sets of proposals for uniform laws for the United States. The first came in the *Restatement of the Law of Torts* published in 1939. Like the later English Law Commission report this recommended that it should be a tort for a person to use or disclose a trade secret without privilege to do so. However, when the 1939 *Restatement* was updated the legal protection of trade secrets was omitted. The American Law Institute, which produces the *Restatements*, said that trade secrets had become a subject of such importance in its own right that it no longer belonged in that volume of the *Restatement* and that it should receive independent treatment in a separate Trade Practices *Restatement*, but regrettably this was never produced.

In a separate development, in 1979 the US National Conference of Commissioners on Uniform State Laws recommended the adoption of another set of uniform laws on trade secrets set out in a Uniform Trade Secrets Act, which could be enacted by individual state legislatures. This has now been adopted (sometimes with amendments) in at least thirty-five states.

The latest set of proposals for reform come from Canada in the Joint Report of the Alberta Institute of Law Research and Reform and a Federal Provincial Working Party (see section 7.1.2 above). The reforms suggested there reflect to a far greater extent the recent changes in US law than those recommended by the English Law Commission. This reflects a desire on the part of the Canadians to harmonize laws in North America, but it also means a break from Commonwealth jurisprudence which has traditionally been reflected in Canadian laws. At the date of writing no province of Canada has enacted the reform proposals, but the matter is by no means dead and changes are likely.

For present purposes one of the main differences between the various sets of proposals for law reform lies in the number of torts which each recommends. Both the *Restatement* and the English Law Commission recommend one; the Alberta Institute and the US Commissioners recommend two. Common to all was the

suggestion of a tort of unauthorized use or disclosure of a trade secret; but additionally the US Commissioners and the Alberta Institute recommend a second tort of
improper acquisition of a trade secret. This latter tort is very important as it charac-
terizes as a separate tort the act of industrial espionage. Under the *Restatement* and
the Law Commission proposals, improper acquisition *per se* is not a separate tort.
No liability attaches until information improperly acquired is used or disclosed,
although an injunction can of course be obtained to restrain anticipated use or disclosure. However, the improper acquisition of trade secrets is such an important issue
that it is considered in much greater detail below (see section 7.3) where both the
civil and the criminal aspects of the subject are considered. For the purposes of this
section, however, it can be concluded that although tort is not an important jurisdictional base for the action for breach of confidence at the moment it is likely to
become so in the future, and in some instances it may even supersede the contractual
and/or equitable obligations of the current law.

### 7.2.6 Confidential information as property

A fourth jurisdictional base for the action for breach of confidence is in property. So
far this has not featured prominently in English civil cases, although it has been used
quite often in US cases. However, there have been many attempts to classify confidential information as property for the purposes of the criminal law in order to found
charges of theft and other property-based offences (see section 7.4 below). In the
view of the present author, property in its traditional sense is not an ideal jurisdiction
for the action for breach of confidence. Contract, tort and equity are more appropriate in that they focus on entitlement rather than ownership and this more accurately
reflects rights over information than does property. However, here again, human-
rights legislation may well have a substantial impact on UK law. Article 1 of the
First Protocol to the European Convention on Human Rights provides that:

Every natural or legal person is entitled to the peaceful enjoyment of his possessions. No one
shall be deprived of his possessions except in the public interest and subject to the conditions
provided for by law and by the general principles of international law . . .

This section applies to patents,[71] and arguably to other statutory IPRs defined as
property rights such as copyright, designs, trade marks and applications for trade
marks, although whether these can strictly be categorized as 'possessions' is a matter
for debate. It could be argued by analogy that article 1 of the First Protocol could
also apply to know-how and to trade secrets which are frequently the subject of
licensing, and are bought and sold as commercial assets; but article 1 is much less
likely to apply to secret governmental information and certainly not to personal
information which may be classified as confidential.

---

[71] Application 12633/87 *Smith Kline and French Laboratories v Netherlands* 66 DR 70 (1990), E Com
HR, cited in Pinto (n 12 above), 212.

## 7.3  THE SPECIAL PROBLEM OF CONFIDENTIAL INFORMATION ACQUIRED BY IMPROPER MEANS

Before discussing the criminal law it is necessary to consider first one rather surprising gap in the protection of confidential information by the civil law. This occurs where confidential information is acquired by improper means by a person such as a spy or computer hacker who is under no pre-existing obligation of confidence. As we have seen, the emphasis of the English action is on breach of an obligation of confidence. In cases where there is an obligation to respect confidentiality there are few problems in founding liability providing all the other elements of the action are present. To use the familiar example, an employee or ex-employee who misappropriates his employer's confidential information in order to use it himself or to disclose to a trade rival, will be acting in breach of confidence and can be restrained by injunction or be subject to the other remedies of damages, an account, etc; and any third party who acquires information from the employee knowing that it has been disclosed in breach of an obligation will be similarly liable. Thus, the employee who gleans secrets from unauthorized use of a sector of his employer's computerized database can be made liable.

By way of contrast, where there is no obligation of confidence there can be no breach and no action. This causes problems, for example, where a spy gleans a secret from reading a confidential document, tapping a telephone or gaining unauthorized access to a computer network. The spy or hacker cannot, without a high degree of artificiality, be said to have voluntarily undertaken an obligation to respect the confidentiality of the information he has improperly acquired. Any obligation must be imposed involuntarily by the law, but here the law seems remarkably reluctant to intervene. A similar problem arises in the law of trusts. A trustee who misappropriates trust property acts in breach of a fiduciary obligation owed to a beneficiary under the trust. Breach of fiduciary duty allows the beneficiary to trace the property through other forms and into other hands. But if a thief who is not a trustee or other fiduciary misappropriates trust property, he breaks no fiduciary obligation and there is no right to trace in equity.

It is surprising that there have been few civil cases on the improper acquisition, use or disclosure of confidential information by persons who have no pre-existing obligation of confidence. After all, espionage is not particularly rare. For the lawyer looking for a precedent there are few guiding principles, only some broad-ranging statements, but these are not necessarily helpful even though they are often cited in this context. For example, in *Millar v Taylor* it was said that an injunction would be granted to prevent:

Surreptitious or treacherous publishing of what the owner never made public at all, nor consented to the publication of . . . Ideas are free. But while the author confines them to his study, they are like birds in a cage which none but he have a right to let fly.[72]

---

[72] (1769) 4 Burr 2303, 2378, 2379.

*Millar v Taylor* was, however, a case on the common-law right of property in the copyright in an unpublished work and although sometimes cited in the context of breach of confidence and information law it cannot be relied on as authority in this particular field. Another broad statement is to be found in *Ashburton v Pape* where Swinfen Eady LJ said:

The principle on which the Court of Chancery has acted for many years has been to restrain the publication of confidential information improperly or surreptitiously obtained or of information imparted in confidence which ought not to be divulged.[73]

Also, in *ITC Film Distributors v Video Exchange Ltd*[74] Walton J referred to a general rule that where A has improperly obtained possession of a document belonging to B the court will, at the suit of B, order A to return the document to B and deliver up any copies of it that A has made, and will restrain A from making use of such copies or the information contained in them. But again, although the *dicta* seems to be relevant both *Ashburton v Pape* and *ITC Film Distributors v Video Exchange Ltd* involved obtaining documents by a trick in order to use them in legal proceedings and arguably they are not directly applicable to the action for breach of confidence.

More recent cases have not clarified the position. In *Malone v Commissioner of Police of the Metropolis (No 2)*[75] the claimant's telephone was tapped by the Post Office at the request of the police. The claimant sought a declaration that he had a right of confidentiality in the information conveyed in the course of his telephone conversations and that recordings thereof were made in breach of confidence.

Sir Robert Megarry V-C, delivering the judgment of the court, drew a distinction between misuse of information: (a) by a person to whom the information was intended to be communicated (where presumably the obligation of confidence would be governed by contract or by the normal equitable principles described above); and (b) by someone to whom the claimant had no intention of communicating anything. It is of course into this latter category that the spy and the telephone tapper fall. However, Megarry V-C did not distinguish those who deliberately set out to acquire information and those who come across it accidentally, which is arguably very important in deciding whether to attach liability, and in the course of his judgment many of the examples given were of those who accidentally overhear and maybe these examples even unfairly trivialize the problem.

He said that a person who utters confidential information must accept the risk of any unknown hearing that is inherent in the circumstances of communication. Those who exchange confidences on a bus or a train run the risk of a nearby passenger with acute hearing or a more distant passenger who is adept at lip reading; those who speak over the garden wall run the risk of the unseen neighbour in a toolshed nearby; office cleaners who discuss secrets in the office when they think everyone else has gone home run the risk of speaking within earshot of an unseen member of staff who

[73] [1913] 2 Ch 469, 475.          [74] [1982] Ch 431.          [75] [1979] Ch 344.

is working late; those who give confidential information over an office intercommunication system run the risk of some third party being connected to the conversation.

His lordship then went on to say that he did not see why someone who has overheard some secret in such a way should be exposed to legal proceedings if he uses or divulges what he has heard. Furthermore, he said that no doubt an honourable man would give some warning when he realized that what he heard was not intended for his ears, but the court had to concern itself with the law and not with moral standards. Here he said he was dealing with only a moral precept and not with one that was legally enforceable.

Applying those general principles to telephone conversations, Megarry V-C argued that a speaker takes such risks of being overheard as are inherent in the system. By way of illustration he said that users of the telephone system knew that they might be overheard when using extension lines, private switchboards or as a result of 'crossed lines'. More modern examples not given by Megarry V-C would of course be misrouted e-mail or hacking. His lordship said that in recent years so much publicity had been given to the deliberate tapping of telephone lines 'that it is difficult to envisage telephone users who are genuinely unaware of this possibility'.[76] As a result he concluded that he did not see how it could be said that an obligation of confidence could be imposed on those who overhear a conversation 'whether by means of tapping or otherwise'. How, one might ask, would his lordship have viewed a case of computer hacking?

So far as tapping telephones was concerned, Megarry V-C expressly stated that he was only dealing with a case of authorized tapping by the police in connection with the detection of crime and his *dicta* on tapping must be limited accordingly,[77] but the judgment does remain disturbingly general on other methods of improper acquisition of confidential information and on the failure of the law to impose an obligation of confidence even where the improper acquisition is deliberate and for monetary gain.

In 1972, the report of an official inquiry into privacy chaired by Kenneth Younger ('the Younger Report')[78] concluded on the basis of the earlier cases that in English law it is highly uncertain whether a person who uses or discloses confidential information which he knows to have been improperly obtained can be made liable in an action for breach of confidence. They recommended that the law should be clarified and that an obligation of confidence should be imposed if the user or discloser of confidential information knew or ought to have known that it was obtained by illegal means. This was also the recommendation of the Law Commission in its preliminary Working Paper,[79] although there they referred to acquisition by unlawful means which they envisaged covering information obtained by means prohibited by the criminal law; taking without authority any object from which the information was

---

[76] Ibid.
[77] cf *Francome v Mirror Group Newspapers* [1984] 1 WLR 892.
[78] *Report of the Committee on Privacy* (Cmnd 5012) (HMSO, 1972).
[79] Working Paper No 58.

obtained; and possibly also information obtained by means of a trespass to land. The Law Commission changed their minds on this after consultation, and in their Final Report they said that improper acquisition should be only one of those circumstances which gave rise to an obligation of confidence and that obligation would be broken only by unauthorized use or disclosure.[80] They also defined 'improper means' much more narrowly than before. It is important to note in the present context that neither the Younger Committee nor the Law Commission in their Final Report suggested that the improper acquisition of confidential information in itself should be a tort, as is provided by the US Uniform Trade Secrets Act, recommended in Canada and discussed in section 7.2.5 above. It is recognized that in most circumstances it is the use or disclosure of the information which causes the greatest harm, and this may be the rationale of the conclusions of the Law Commission. However, in the view of the present author the earlier in the chain of activity the liability attaches the better. The Law Commission proposals have, of course, never been enacted and hence the problem in English law of trying to control the improper acquisition, use or disclosure of confidential information obtained in circumstances where there is no obligation of confidence remains.

One decision which could solve the dilemma, if it were followed here, is the Australian case of *Franklin v Giddins*.[81] The facts were that the defendant stole budwood cuttings from the claimant's genetically unique nectarine trees. An action was brought for the improper acquisition by the defendant of the confidential information embodied in the genetic coding in the wood. Dunn J in the Supreme Court of Queensland accepted that:

[t]he parent tree may be likened to a safe within which there are locked up a number of copies of a formula for making a nectarine tree with special characteristics . . . when a twig of budwood is taken from the tree it is as though a copy of the formula is taken out of the safe.[82]

Having thus classified it as a misappropriation of confidential information he went on to hold that the defendant had breached an obligation of confidence owed to the owner of the tree. He said, 'I find myself quite unable to accept that a thief who steals a trade secret, with the intention of using it in commercial competition with its owner, to the detriment of the latter, and so uses it, is less conscionable than a traitorous servant'.[83]

Thus unconscionability was brought into play to found an action, but this is no less vague a term than many others which have been used as bases of the action for breach of confidence in equity in other circumstances. As Professor Gareth Jones has argued,[84] equity should not be past the age of child-bearing, and the action for breach of confidence should be capable of extension to protect confidential informa-

---

[80] Law Commission Report No 110 (n 67 above), para 6.4 and Appendix A, cl 5.
[81] [1978] QdR 72. See also *Australian Broadcasting Corp v Lenah Game Meats Pty Ltd* (2001) 185 ALR 1; [2001] HCA 63, High Court of Australia.
[82] Ibid, 74.                                                                          [83] Ibid.
[84] (1970) 86 LQR 463, 482–3.

tion obtained by improper means regardless of whether there is a pre-existing rela-tionship of confidence.[85] This is particularly important now that information is assuming a greater role in technologically advanced communities. The defects of the present civil law leave a huge gap in the protection of confidential information in English law. The problem does not arise in the United States and would not arise in Canada if the reform proposals were enacted. It may be solved in the UK by the application of article 1 of the First Protocol to the European Convention on Human Rights and the right to property, discussed in section 7.2.6 above, but this depends on the classification of a trade secret as property and as a possession, a matter which, as we have seen, is highly controversial. In the next section we shall see that English criminal law also fails to punish the misappropriation of confidential information. There is an obvious need for reform.

## 7.4 THE CRIMINAL LAW

The analysis in this part of the chapter inevitably cuts across the divisions drawn in preceding sections, for information can be misappropriated not only by persons who have never been bound by an obligation of secrecy, such as by strangers engaged in industrial espionage, but also by those already under an obligation of confidence such as employees who disclose the trade secrets of their employers to trade rivals. In the latter situation, the prospect of making employees and ex-employees liable for misappropriating trade secrets highlights perhaps even more urgently than ever the need to distinguish carefully between an employee's general knowledge and skill, which he is of course entitled to use for the benefit of himself and others, and his employer's trade secrets which he cannot use or disclose, for in some legal systems the distinction could represent the line between criminal and legitimate activity.

Once again this account will concentrate mainly on the misappropriation of trade secrets. There are very different policy issues underlying the question of criminaliz-ing the acquisition of other categories of confidential information, and for reasons of space as well as emphasis no mention is made of the Official Secrets Act 1989 and the problems that it brings in its wake.

### 7.4.1 English law

In English law, if there is intentional interference with a tangible object, such as damage to or permanent deprivation of a computer disk or a piece of paper, or unau-thorized entry onto land with intent to do specified acts in relation to tangibles or

---

[85] A similar view was expressed, *obiter*, by Lord Goff (a co-author with Professor Jones of Goff and Jones, *The Law of Restitution*, 5th edn (Sweet & Maxwell, 1998)), in *Attorney-General v Guardian Newspapers Ltd (No 2)* [1988] 3 All ER 545, 658–9. And see also John Hull, *Commercial Secrecy: Law and Practice* (Sweet & Maxwell, 1998), pp 139–48.

people, then various criminal offences may be committed. But if only information is 'taken' or interfered with by reading, memorizing or photographing the tangible object on which the confidential information is stored, then no crime may be committed, unless it is a case of computer hacking, which is regulated by the Computer Misuse Act 1990.[86] As Sir Edward Boyle once remarked, 'It is not too much to say that we live in a country where . . . the theft of the board room table is punished far more severely than the theft of the board room secrets'.[87]

In English law, 'theft' of a trade secret is not a criminal offence. The main case is *Oxford v Moss*[88] where an undergraduate improperly obtained the proof of an examination paper before the examination was held. He read the paper and then returned it, retaining the information for his own use. He was charged with theft but was acquitted. Two reasons were given: first, for the purposes of the Theft Act 1968, information is not property, and only property can be stolen; and secondly, the university had not been permanently deprived of the tangible asset which had been taken, namely the piece of paper, and borrowing does not amount to theft. *Oxford v Moss* was followed in *R v Absolom*[89] where a geologist was acquitted of a charge of theft after he had obtained and tried to sell to a rival company details of Esso Petroleum's oil exploration off the Irish coast, information which was valued in evidence as worth between £50,000 and £100,000.

The emphasis in English law is clearly on the interference with a tangible asset, and because in neither *Oxford v Moss* nor *R v Absolom* was the owner of the information permanently deprived of such an asset there could be no successful prosecution for theft. However, even if a tangible asset such as a piece of paper or a computer disk is taken, the value of the tangible asset may in no way reflect the value of the information either in terms of damage to a business, if the secret is a trade secret, or of unwanted publicity if the information is of a personal nature; and if we look at the attitude of society towards crime, a charge of theft of a piece of paper worth a few pence is regarded as of far less importance than a charge of theft of information worth maybe thousands of pounds. Furthermore, when confidential information is misappropriated its owner loses the advantage of the exclusive right to control its use, yet this is not an asset protected by the English law of theft.

Other criminal charges may of course be relevant. For example, where confidential information is obtained by hacking this may amount to a criminal offence under section 1 of the Computer Misuse Act 1990. However, section 1 does not apply when data-storage media other than computers, such as filing cabinets, are accessed without authorization nor does it apply to access to programs or data which are, for example, on disks lying on a shelf in an office. The wrong to which section 1 is

---

[86] See, further, Chapter 8.
[87] The Rt Hon Sir Edward Boyle MP (later Lord Boyle) cited in Law Commission Consultation Paper No 150, *Legislating the Criminal Code: Misuse of Trade Secrets*, para 1.1.
[88] (1978) 68 Cr App R 183.
[89] *The Times*, 14 September 1983.

directed is a wrong against a particular computer, rather than being a wrong directed specifically and exclusively towards information as a commodity in its own right.[90]

### 7.4.2 Scottish law

A similar approach has been taken in Scotland. In *Grant v Procurator Fiscal*[91] the High Court of Justiciary said that there was no crime in Scots law of dishonest exploitation of the confidential information of another. Also, the court refused to exercise the inherent powers of the Scottish courts to create a new crime. In that case the defendant had made copies of computer printouts belonging to his employer and then offered to sell them to a rival concern. The printouts contained confidential information about the employer's customers. In the course of his judgment Lord Justice Clerk said that while the defendant may have breached an express or implied obligation of confidence owed to his employer under the civil law it would be quite another thing to categorize such behaviour as criminal. If it was to be criminalized it was a matter for Parliament and not for the courts.

### 7.4.3 Reforms

Until recently, there were few calls for the reform of English law. In 1972, the Younger Committee specifically rejected the suggestion that there should be a new offence of theft of information,[92] and when the Law Commission[93] were first asked to consider the law relating to breach of confidence their terms of reference limited them to the civil law alone. They made no recommendations for reform of the criminal law. By way of contrast the New Zealand Committee for Torts and General Law Reform said that the chief weakness of the New Zealand law relating to trade secrets was the lack of specialized criminal provisions. In the United States, many states have criminal statutes expressly protecting trade secrets;[94] and the Economic Espionage Act 1996 creates two federal offences of stealing trade secrets: one relating to the theft of trade secrets in general and the second aimed at economic espionage for the benefit of foreign governments. In Europe there are criminal offences in a number of Codes. For example article 17(1) of the German Act Against Unfair Competition (UWG) of 1909[95] states that an employee who wrongfully communicates an industrial or commercial secret is liable to be imprisoned for up to three years and to pay a fine. Similar provisions are to be found in article 418 of the

---

[90] If personal information is misappropriated the Data Protection Act 1998 may apply; see Chapter 11.
[91] [1988] RPC 41.
[92] Younger Report (n 78 above), p 149.
[93] Law Commission Report No 110 (n 67 above), para 4.10.
[94] eg, California, Colorado, Massachusetts, Minnesota, New York, Texas, Ohio and Pennsylvania. See Law Commission Consultation Paper (n 16 above), Appendix B, for an account of the criminal laws of France, Germany, Italy, Switzerland, Bulgaria, Poland, Romania, Scotland, Australia, Canada, USA and Korea.
[95] See Coleman (n 15 above), ch 7.

French Penal Code and article 162 of the Swiss Penal Code. In each of these Codes, communication of the secret to a foreigner increases the penalty. Interestingly, the civil laws of Japan dealing with the misappropriation of trade secrets have recently been reformed but there have been no changes to the criminal laws. Prosecutions have however been obtained under general criminal laws such as larceny and embezzlement.

The English Law Commission have recently studied the problem anew and in 1997 they produced a consultation paper on the misuse of trade secrets, as part of their ongoing review of English criminal law.[96] They provisionally concluded that trade secrets were valuable commercial assets which were inadequately protected by the civil law and that there was no distinction in principle between the harm caused by the misuse of a trade secret and the harm caused by theft. They proposed a new offence which would be committed by a person who used or disclosed a trade secret belonging to another without that other's consent, providing that the defendant knew that the information in question was a trade secret belonging to another, and was aware that the other did not consent to the use or disclosure in question. Importantly, in view of the difficult distinctions which have to be drawn, they proposed that the new offence should not extend to the use or disclosure of information which, under the law of confidence, constitutes an enhancement of an employee's (or independent contractor's) personal knowledge, skill or experience. This qualification is very welcome. Also, the new offence should not cover the use or disclosure of information acquired by independent development or solely by reverse engineering. Furthermore, innocent third parties should not be liable, and no offence should be committed where the disclosure was in the public interest, this term being widely drawn. The new offence proposed by the Law Commission concerns the use or disclosure of a trade secret. However, they invited views on whether the criminal law should also be extended to cover the acquisition of a trade secret and if so, how this should be done. The Law Commission's provisional recommendations are to be welcomed as reform is urgently needed. The Law Commission have promised a final report in 2003. Whether the political and economic climate has changed sufficiently to prompt the Government into action remains to be seen.

### 7.4.4 Canadian cases

Proposals to reform Canadian laws have similarly been slow to develop. There have been some interesting cases, but the proposals of the law-reform bodies for legislative change have sat on the shelf for some considerable time. This is surprising given the changes to US federal laws in the form of the Economic Espionage Act 1996. In the Canadian case of *R v Offley*[97] the Alberta Court of Appeal followed the English decision of *Oxford v Moss* and held that confidential information could not be stolen. Here, the defendant had been asked by the representative of a union to obtain the

---

[96] See n 16 above.          [97] (1986) 28 CCC (3d) 1.

details of the employees of an hotel. This information was contained in the employees' personal files and computer records held by the hotel company. They were regarded as being strictly confidential and were protected by the hotel's security arrangements. The defendant had contacted an employee of the hotel and asked him to copy the confidential information without removing or affecting the records themselves. The defendant was charged with three offences, namely counselling an employee of the hotel to commit fraud, theft and mischief to the private property of the hotel. The accused was acquitted on all three counts and the Crown appealed against the acquittals on the charges of counselling theft and counselling fraud. By a majority of two to one the Ontario Court of Appeal allowed the appeal and a conviction was entered for counselling theft.

Interestingly, the Ontario Court of Appeal in *R v Stewart*,[98] in contrast to the Alberta Court of Appeal in *Offley*, held that confidential information was property for the purposes of the offences of theft and fraud in Canadian criminal law. For example, Houlden JA said that while clearly not all information was property he could see no reason why confidential information that had been gathered through the expenditure of time, effort and money by a commercial enterprise for the purposes of its business should not be regarded as property and hence entitled to the protection of the criminal law. In *Offley* and *Stewart* we therefore have two contrasting decisions of two Courts of Appeal of Canadian provinces, the outstanding question being whether confidential information is property for the purposes of the criminal laws of Canada with its obvious implications also for the jurisdictional foundation of the civil obligation to respect confidentiality. The decision of the Supreme Court of Canada in *R v Stewart*[99] was therefore anxiously awaited.

On appeal, the Supreme Court of Canada rejected the notion that confidential information could be property. First, the Court said that although 'anything' (using that term in its technical sense in the Canadian Criminal Code) whether tangible or intangible could be the subject matter of a charge of theft, it must be of such a nature that it can be the subject of a proprietary right; and secondly, the property must be capable of being taken or converted in a manner that results in deprivation of the victim. Taking each of these elements in turn Lamer J, giving the judgment of the court, said that it had not been settled that property was the basis of the civil action for breach of confidence, but even if it had been it would not automatically follow that it would be so classified for the purposes of the criminal law. If it was property under the criminal law a large number of provisions of the Criminal Code would potentially apply to acts in relation to confidential information and a whole host of practical problems would ensue. He recognized that information of commercial value was in need of some protection under the criminal law, but this was a matter for Parliament and not for the courts. For policy reasons the court held that confidential information was not property for the purposes of the Canadian Criminal Code.

Secondly, the Supreme Court held that an intangible could not be 'taken' as such;

---

[98] (1983) 42 OR (2d) 225.       [99] (1988) 50 DLR (4th) 1.

nor could it be converted, as conversion required deprivation of its use and possession and if merely information was misappropriated (as opposed to the tangible on
which the information was stored) then the alleged owner was not deprived of the
information: henceforth, the information was merely shared. The only 'thing' that
the victim would be deprived of was the confidentiality of the information and in the
view of the court confidentiality could not be the subject of theft because it did not
fall within the meaning of 'anything' as previously defined. Confidentiality could
not be property, as it could not be owned only enjoyed. Furthermore, the court
rejected the argument of Cory JA in the Ontario Court of Appeal that there was a
right of property in confidential information which was the subject of copyright, as
were the employer's confidential lists in this case. Lamer J explained that copying a
list constitutes an infringement of copyright under the Copyright Act, but the rights
provided in that Act could never be taken or converted as required by the theft provisions as their owner would never suffer deprivation. Once again, there would only be
sharing and this was not enough.

The result of the Canadian Supreme Court decision in *Stewart* is that the question
of criminalizing the misappropriation of confidential information was referred back
to the Canadian legislature. Those countries which do not already criminalize this
type of conduct will inevitably have to consider doing so sooner or later, for with the
growth in the use of computers and the development of information as a commodity
in its own right the pressures will grow to afford information the same degree of
protection as other valuable assets. In Canada there is already a set of proposals for
legislative reform of this area of confidentiality. In 1986 the Alberta Institute of Law
Research and Reform and the Federal Provincial Working Party recommended not
only changes to the civil law but also the creation of new criminal offences relating to
the misappropriation of trade secrets. These new offences have the advantage of
being custom-built and hence avoid the difficulty of attempting to fit cases involving
intangible assets into an inappropriate conceptual framework which was developed to
accommodate tangibles. Thus, the report rejects the approach of the Ontario Court of
Appeal in *Stewart* and argues that property should not form the basis for liability.
These reforms are considered briefly in section 7.4.5 below as it remains possible that
they will be enacted in Canada, albeit with amendments, and they also form a good
starting point for reform in other common-law jurisdictions and a focus for debate.

### 7.4.5  Proposals for the reform of Canadian criminal law

First, it was decided that in order to achieve uniformity the same information should
be protected under both the civil and the criminal law (see section 7.1.2 above for the
text of the proposed definition of 'trade secret'). Secondly, it is recommended that
the new criminal offences should proscribe the non-consensual acquisition, use or
disclosure of a trade secret, that term being used in the sense both of what might
otherwise be called 'theft' of a secret and also of acts where the consent was fraudulently obtained, for example, where the victim was duped. Therefore, there are two

offences in the draft Bill covering the two aspects of non-consensual conduct, firstly a new section 301.3(1) of the Criminal Code would provide that:

Everyone who fraudulently and without colour of right acquires, discloses or uses the trade secret of another person, without the consent of that other person, with intent to deprive that other person (a) of control of the trade secret or (b) of an economic advantage associated with the trade secret is guilty of an indictable offence and is liable to imprisonment for ten years, or of an offence punishable on summary conviction.

Secondly a new draft section 338.1(1) would provide that:

Everyone who, by deceit, falsehood or other fraudulent means, whether or not it is a false pretence within the meaning of this Act, induces any person to disclose, or to permit another person to disclose or use, a trade secret, is guilty of an indictable offence and is liable to imprisonment for ten years, or of an offence punishable on summary conviction.

It was hoped by clearly defining the mental element which the accused must be shown to have that only the most reprehensible conduct would be caught by the new provisions. As an additional safeguard, it is provided that no one commits an offence under section 301.3 in respect of an acquisition, disclosure or use of a trade secret if:

(a) the trade secret was acquired by independent development or by reason only of reverse engineering; or

(b) the information was acquired in the course of that person's work, and the information is of such a nature that the acquisition amounts to no more than an enhancement of that person's personal knowledge, skill or expertise.

The proposed amendments to the Criminal Code contain two further offences aimed at, for example, the industrial spy who goes on what may be described as a 'shopping expedition' in order to acquire information, the precise character of which he does not know but which he thinks he may be able to sell or otherwise use. Subsequent reports suggest that these proposed offences are not popular among Canadian legislators and may be dropped from any draft Bills which come forward.

The Canadian proposals and the provisional conclusion of the Law Commission illustrate the moves in many countries to criminalize the misappropriation of trade secrets. Inevitably pressures from industry will mount to reform the law in this area, and the idea of adopting custom-built offences rather than extending existing property-based offences in order to found liability is a sound one. But there are strong reasons favouring the free flow of information and requiring the disclosure even of confidential information, and any shift in the balance needs to be carefully considered. Not least among the concerns are those affecting employees and the need to draw a very clear distinction between, on the one hand, the employer's trade secrets and, on the other hand, the employee's general knowledge and skill. Mobility of labour could be seriously damaged by overzealous prosecution of employees. This is particularly the case in high-technology areas such as computing, where skills and knowledge so frequently merge. We await with interest the final report of the Law Commission for England and Wales and the UK Government's response thereto.

# 8

# COMPUTER CRIME

*Ian Walden*

## 8.1  INTRODUCTION

The proliferation and integration of computers into every aspect of society has inevitably led to computer-related criminal activities. The computer may constitute the instrument of the crime, such as in murder and fraud; the object of the crime, such as the theft of processor chips; or the subject of the crime, such as hacking and distributing viruses. This chapter is concerned with how criminal law has adapted and been amended to address some of the issues raised by the involvement of computers in criminal activities.

The first part of the chapter considers some of the offences under English law that are relevant to crimes involving the use of computers. Such offences can generally be distinguished into three categories. The first category is traditional types of criminal offence that may be committed using computers as the instrument of the crime, referred to as computer-related crime, such as fraud. The second category concerns content-related crimes, primarily involving intellectual property and pornography. The third category is offences that have been established specifically to address activities that attack the integrity of computer and communications systems, such as distributing computer viruses. It is this final category that will be the primary focus of this chapter.

The second part of the chapter will examine issues relating to the prosecution of perpetrators of computer crime. To date, few cases have been brought before the courts, relative to the estimated incidence of such crime. Such paucity is generally seen as being due to a range of factors. First, there is a lack of reporting by victims, as commercial organizations avoid adverse publicity.[1] Second, a lack of experience among law-enforcement and prosecuting authorities.[2] Third, the transnational nature of computer crime and the associated jurisdictional problems contribute to the complexity of investigating and prosecuting offenders. Finally, computers, particularly when networked, create significant forensic challenges to law-enforcement agencies when obtaining evidence and subsequently presenting it before the courts.

## 8.2 COMPUTER-RELATED CRIMES

It is obvious that computers may play a part in the commission of nearly every form of criminal activity, from fraud to murder. This section will not review the broad range of English criminal law, but will focus on those areas of existing law which have given rise to particular problems where computers are involved, either because the legislation was drafted in an era before such technology was envisaged, or because statutory drafting has failed to be robust enough to address appropriately computer technology.

### 8.2.1 Fraud

The range of fraudulent activity is not substantially altered by the use of computers, although they may facilitate certain forms, such as securities fraud. Computers may be involved in any aspect of the fraudulent process, from altering information being input into a system or manipulating the operation of programs processing the information, to altering the output. Often, the computer is simply a modern tool by which the defendant's actions have been carried out.

In the majority of cases involving computer-related fraud, existing legislation has been an adequate instrument under which to prosecute. However, as with other areas of legislation, traditional statutory terminology can give rise to problems of application not anticipated before computers appeared. In certain jurisdictions, for example,

---

[1] See the US survey by CSI/FBI, which reported that only 32% of respondents who had suffered an intrusion had reported it to law-enforcement agencies (quoted in the National Criminal Intelligence Service report, *Project Trawler: Crime on the Information Highways* (1999), para 10, available at www.cyber-rights.org).

[2] See, generally, E Bell, 'The Prosecution of Computer Crime' (2002) 9(4) Journal of Financial Crime 308–25.

it is a requirement to show that a 'person has been deceived' for a fraud to be deemed to have occurred.[3]

Under English law, section 15 of the Theft Act 1968 states:

(1) A person who by any deception dishonestly obtains property belonging to another, with the intention of permanently depriving the other of it, . . .

(4) For purposes of this section 'deception' means any deception (whether deliberate or reckless) by words or conduct as to fact or as to law, including a deception as to the present intentions of the person using the deception or any other person.

Case law has further defined 'deception' to mean 'to induce a man to believe a thing which is false, and which the person practising the deceit knows or believes to be false'.[4] Where innocent persons have been involved at some moment in the fraud, such as the processing of computer output, there does not appear to be any problem with prosecuting under section 15.[5] However, where the process is completely automated, the courts have indicated that an offence may not be deemed to have taken place.[6] Where a machine has been deceived to obtain property, then the offence of theft is generally applicable. However, where a service is obtained from a machine, the absence of 'deception' is fatal to the founding of a criminal prosecution.[7] This problem has been reported in the Internet environment, where people have given false credit-card details during the online registration process for accessing services such as CompuServe.[8]

The Law Commission has examined this lacuna in English criminal law and has recommended that, rather than taking the approach of extending the concept of 'deception' to include machines,[9] a new offence related to theft should be established.[10] The Council of Europe Convention of Cybercrime has formulated an offence of fraud that avoids the concept of deception:

Each Party shall adopt such legislative and other measures as may be necessary to establish as criminal offences under its domestic law, when committed intentionally and without right, the causing of a loss of property to another by:

---

[3] eg, German Penal Code, s 263.

[4] *Re London and Globe Finance Corpn Ltd* [1903] 1 Ch 728, 732, per Buckley J.

[5] eg, *R v Thompson* [1984] 3 All ER 565.

[6] See *R v Clayman*, Times Law Reports, 1 July 1972. See also *R v Moritz*, 17–19 June 1981, Acton Crown Court (unreported), quoted in M Wasik, *Crime and the Computer* (Clarendon Press, 1991).

[7] See Theft Act 1978, s 1.

[8] Where the service is provided by a licensed telecommunication operator, an offence of fraudulent use of a telecommunication system would be applicable under the Telecommunications Act 1984, s 42.

[9] As adopted in the Value Added Tax Act 1994, s 72(6): '. . . making use of a document which is false in a material particular, with intent to deceive, includes a reference to furnishing, sending or otherwise making use of such a document, with intent to secure that a machine will respond to the document as if it were a true document.' See also the concept of 'induce' in the offence of forgery discussed at section 8.2.3 below.

[10] See Law Commission Consultation Paper No 155, *Legislating the Criminal Code: Fraud and Deception* (1999), paras 8.36–8.58.

a.  any input, alteration, deletion or suppression of computer data,

b.  any interference with the functioning of a computer system,

with fraudulent or dishonest intent of procuring, without right, an economic benefit for oneself or for another.[11]

The need to obtain property 'belonging to another' in the commission of a fraud also gave rise to a lacuna in English law in the House of Lords decision in *Preddy*.[12] The court acquitted the defendants of mortgage fraud on the basis that the process of altering the accounting data recorded in the accounts of the lending institution and the mortgagor, by the amount representing the loan, did not constitute the obtaining of property 'belonging to another'. Instead, the court characterized the process as one where property, as a chose in action, is extinguished in one place and a different chose in action is created in another place. This decision required the Government to push through emergency legislation creating a new offence of 'obtaining a money transfer by deception' to cover such activities.[13] However, *Preddy* illustrates the types of problem raised when trying to apply traditional criminal concepts to acts involving intangible information.

Theft will often be an alternative charge to that of fraud. However, as discussed in Chapter 7, English law does not view information *per se* to be 'property'. In *Oxford v Moss*[14] a student took a forthcoming examination paper from a lecturer's desk, photocopied it, and returned the original. The court held that the offence of theft had not been committed as the victim had not been permanently deprived of the asset, a copy had simply been taken. This issue has also been the subject of a Law Commission report, which has proposed the establishment of an offence of misusing a trade secret.[15]

### 8.2.2 Forgery

We use a broad range of documentation in our daily lives, from £20 notes to driving licences and insurance certificates. Creating forged versions of these documents is an obvious area of crime that has benefited from developments in computer technology. Most genuine documents are now created using computers, therefore computers provide the opportunity to amend them often in an undetectable manner. Current software-based products for digital manipulation provide a powerful tool for even the most amateur of forgers.[16]

---

[11]  European Treaty Series No 185, art 8. See, further, section 8.5.1 below.

[12]  [1996] 3 All ER 481.

[13]  Theft (Amendment) Act 1996. See also Law Commission Report No 243, *Offences of Dishonesty: Money Transfers* (1996).

[14]  (1979) 68 Cr App R 183.

[15]  Law Commission Consultation Paper No 150, *Legislating the Criminal Code: Misuse of Trade Secrets* (1997).

[16]  eg, Adobe's Photoshop 7.0.

Section 1 of the Forgery and Counterfeiting Act 1981 states:

A person is guilty of forgery if he makes a false instrument with the intention that he or another shall use it to induce somebody to accept it as genuine . . .

As relatively recent legislation, one could expect the Act to avoid the interpretative issues raised by the use of computer technology in respect of fraud, as discussed above. However, the leading English case concerning the use of computers to commit forgery, *R v Gold, Schifreen*,[17] illustrates the continuing problems faced by the legislative draftsman.

In *Gold*, the defendants gained unauthorized access to BT's Prestel service and discovered the password codes of various private e-mail accounts (including the Duke of Edinburgh's!). The defendants were prosecuted under the 1981 Act for creating a 'false instrument' by entering customer authorization codes to access the system. The Act defines an 'instrument' seemingly broadly to include 'any disc, tape, sound track or other device on or in which information is recorded or stored by mechanical, electronic or other means' (s 8(1)(d)). In addition, the meaning of 'induce' expressly avoids the need for a real person, as required in respect of 'deception': 'references to inducing somebody to accept a false instrument as genuine . . . include references to inducing a machine to respond . . .' (s 10(3)).

However, the House of Lords held that the electronic signals that comprised the identification codes, could not be considered tangible in the sense that a disk or tape were. It also held that the signals were present in the system for such a fleeting moment, that they could not be considered to have been 'recorded or stored':

The words 'recorded' and 'stored' are words in common use which should be given their ordinary and natural meaning. In my opinion both words . . . connote the preservation of the thing which is the subject matter of them for an appreciable time with the object of subsequent retrieval and recovery.[18]

In respect of the issue of whether somebody had been 'induced', the Court of Appeal in *Gold* had recognized that the prosecution's case could be rendered absurd because the machine being induced was also claimed to be the false instrument.[19]

It is also interesting to note that the Court of Appeal was highly critical of the application of the Act to such a set of circumstances:

The Procrustean attempt to force these facts into the language of an Act not designed to fit them produced difficulties for both judge and jury which we would not wish to see repeated.[20]

Such explicit recognition by the judiciary of the need to draft new legislation, rather than try to extend traditional terminology to fit computer technology, lent significant pressure to the calls for reform of the criminal law.

---

[17] [1988] 2 All ER 186.    [18] Ibid, 192C, per Lord Brandon.
[19] [1997] 3 WLR 803, 809G, per Lord Lane CJ. This question was not considered by the House of Lords.
[20] Ibid, 809H. Such sentiment was echoed by Lord Brandon in the House of Lords at [1988] 2 All ER 186, 192D.

## 8.3  CONTENT-RELATED OFFENCES

Computers and communication technologies are designed to process information. Such technologies have had a fundamental impact on national economies, particularly in the developed world, shifting them from a traditional industrial base towards an information base. Companies are increasingly valued not on their tangible assets, such as plant and materials, but their intangible assets, in the form of information. Such information is protected under a range of laws examined in this book, including copyright, database right, confidentiality and data-protection law. Some of these laws, such as copyright and data protection, have criminal sanctions as part of their enforcement regime.[21]

However, another form of information that has increased in economic value in our networked environment is pornography. The pornography industry has been estimated to contribute some $20 billion annually to the global economy.[22] The distribution of pornography using information systems, particularly the Internet, is one of the most prevalent forms of content-related computer crimes, as well as attracting a high public profile.

### 8.3.1  Pornography

In terms of a criminal activity, a distinction needs to be made between general pornographic imagery and specific sub-categories of pornographic material, such as child pornography, which has been the focus of law-enforcement activity and will be considered in this section.

As with computer-related offences such as fraud, English obscenity laws have sometimes struggled adequately to address computer-based activities and the unique features of computer-generated pornography. As a result, such laws have been subject to legislative amendment to close particular lacuna and to raise the level of penalties available. In 1994, for example, the Criminal Justice and Public Order Act, amended the Protection of Children Act 1978 and the Criminal Justice Act 1988 to extend offences in relation to the distribution and possession of indecent photographs of children to the concept of 'pseudo-photographs', created through the use of digital images (s 84).[23]

In addition, the courts have been required to consider to what extent the types of activities that occur across networks, such as the Internet, are adequately covered by existing legislation. In *R v Fellows and Arnold*[24] the court considered whether the legislation before the 1994 amendment had been made would enable computer data to be considered a 'copy of an indecent photograph' and whether making images

---

[21] See, further, Chapters 5 and 11 (sections 5.7.2 and 11.3.8 respectively).
[22] Quoted in 'Cashing in on Porn Boom', BBC News, 5 July 2001.
[23] See also the recommendations made by the Home Affairs Committee of the House of Commons, *Computer Pornography* (1st Report, Session 1993–4, HC No 126).
[24] [1997] 2 All ER 548.

available for downloading from a website constituted material being 'distributed or shown'. The court held that the statutory wording was drafted in sufficiently wide terms to encompass the use of computer technology.

In *Atkins and Goodland v Director of Public Prosecutions*[25] the court was required to consider a situation where the offending images upon which the prosecution was based were contained in the cache memory of the defendant's machine.[26] Such copies are generally created and stored automatically by the browser software, used to access the Internet, for reasons of efficiency. Expert evidence was submitted that most users of computers are unaware of the operation of the cache-memory feature.

Two issues for the court were whether the cache copies could be said to have been 'made' under section 1(1) of the Protection of Children Act 1978 or 'possessed' under section 160 of the Criminal Justice Act 1988. In a previous decision, *R v Bowden*, a court held that downloading and printing images from the Internet fell within the concept of 'making' since the term 'applies not only to original photographs but . . . also to negatives, copies of photographs and data stored on computer disc'.[27] However in *Atkins*, the prosecution could not prove that the defendant was aware of the cache copies and therefore liability for 'making' or 'possession' could only be found if section 1(1) or section 160, respectively, were construed as offences of strict liability rather than requiring knowledge. The court held that knowledge was required and therefore the appeal succeeded on this point. If the prosecution could have proved that the defendant was aware of the cache memory, perhaps by showing that the individual had altered the default settings for the caching function, then the conviction would likely have been upheld.

In a subsequent decision, *R v Westgarth Smith and Jayson*,[28] a similar argument to *Atkins* was advanced in respect of the receipt of an e-mail with an attachment containing a pornographic image. Here Smith's counsel argued that the 'making' involved in the receipt of an unsolicited e-mail was similar to that of the cache copy in *Atkins*. The court accepted this assertion in general terms, but held that this was not the situation before the court. In *Jayson*, the prosecution was able to prove that the defendant was aware of the caching function within his browser software. However, the court also held that the mere 'act of voluntarily downloading an indecent image from a web page on to a computer screen is an act of making',[29] whether or not there was an intention to store the images for subsequent retrieval. Such an approach should avoid future reliance on technical ignorance as a defence.

In addition to the obscenity laws, the act of sending such material across the public telephone network may also constitute an offence of improper use under section 43(1)(a) of the Telecommunications Act 1984.

---

[25] [2000] 2 All ER 425.
[26] Images were also found in a separate directory but charges relating to those saved images were dismissed for being brought out of time.
[27] [2000] 1 Cr App R 438, 444, per Otton LJ.          [28] [2002] EWCA Crim 683.
[29] Ibid, para 33, per Dyson LJ.

## 8.4  COMPUTER-INTEGRITY OFFENCES

When considering computer crime, most people think in terms of 'hacking' into systems and the distribution of 'viruses'. Such activities target the computers themselves, rather than use them as a tool to facilitate other crimes. With the spread of computerization and our consequential dependency, the adequacy of criminal law to deter such activities has had to be addressed by policy-makers and legislators. In most jurisdictions, the application of traditional criminal law is often uncertain or completely inappropriate. As such, *sui generis* legislation has been adopted to tackle the threat to the security of computer systems, their integrity, confidentiality and availability.

In the UK, the Computer Misuse Act 1990 became law on 29 August 1990. The direct origins of the Act are found in the Law Commission's report on computer misuse,[30] published in October 1989; additionally, the Scottish and English Law Commissions had published previous reports and working papers,[31] and a Private Member's Bill on the topic had been introduced during the previous parliamentary session.

In December 1989, Michael Colvin MP introduced a Private Member's Bill, with the tacit support of the Government, closely following the English Law Commission's recommendations. The primary motivation for Government support was possibly a belief that if the UK did not follow the example of many of its European partners, then the UK's position in the European information market could suffer. The fear is that if the UK does not have adequate legal protection for both systems and data, it will inhibit the growth of the domestic IT industry.

The 1990 Act introduced three new categories of offence: unauthorized access to computer material, unauthorized access with intent to commit a further offence and unauthorized modification.

### 8.4.1  Unauthorized access

The section 1 offence of unauthorized access is the basic 'hacking' or 'cracking' offence. Commission of the offence requires the *actus reus* of causing 'a computer to perform any function'. Some form of interaction with the computer is required, but actual access does not need to be achieved. This broad formulation means that simply turning on a computer could constitute the necessary act.[32]

The Act also does not define a 'computer', therefore potentially extending its scope to everyday domestic appliances and cars that incorporate computer technol-

---

[30] Law Commission Report No 186, *Computer Misuse* (Cm 819) (HMSO, 1989).

[31] Scottish Law Commission, *Report on Computer Crime* (Cm 174) (HMSO, 1987) and Law Commission Working Paper No 110 and Report No 186, *Computer Misuse* (Cm 819) (HMSO, 1988).

[32] Section 17(1) broadly defines 'function' to include alterations or erasure, copying or moving data, using it or producing output from the computer.

ogy.[33] The Law Commission found general support for the view that to attempt such a definition would be 'so complex, in an endeavour to be all-embracing, that they are likely to produce extensive argument'.[34] This position has also existed in other jurisdictions, such as France and Germany. One major exception to this approach has been the United States, where the Computer Fraud and Abuse Act contains the following definition:

an electronic, magnetic, optical, electrochemical, or other high speed data processing device performing logical, arithmetic, or storage functions, and includes any data storage facility or communications facility directly related to or operating in conjunction with such device.[35]

However, the UK's non-definitional approach may need to be reconsidered as a consequence of the Council of Europe Convention of Cybercrime,[36] which incorporates the following definition for a 'computer system':

any device or a group of inter-connected or related devices, one or more of which, pursuant to a program, performs automatic processing of data (art 1(a)).

The *mens rea* of the offence under section 1 comprises two elements. First, there must be 'intent to secure access to any program or data held in any computer'. Second, the person must know at the time that he commits the *actus reus* that the access he intends to secure is unauthorized. The intent does not have to be directed at any particular program, data or computer (s 1(2)).

The first prosecution under the new Act addressed the nature of the *actus reus* under section 1. In *R v Sean Cropp*[37] the defendant returned to the premises of his former employee to purchase certain equipment. At some point when the sales assistant was not looking, the defendant was alleged to have keyed in certain commands to the computerized till granting himself a substantial discount. During the trial, the judge accepted the submission of defence counsel that section 1(1)(a) required 'that a second computer must be involved'. He believed that if Parliament had intended the offence to extend to situations where unauthorized access took place on a single machine, then section 1(1)(a) would have been drafted as 'causing a computer to perform any function with intent to secure access to any program or data held in *that or any other computer*'.

Such an interpretation would have seriously limited the scope of the Act, especially since the majority of instances of hacking are those carried out within organizations.[38] The critical nature of this distinction led the Attorney-General to take the rarely invoked procedure of referring the decision to the Court of Appeal. The Court

---

[33] See J C Smith, *Smith & Hogan: Criminal Law*, 10th edn (Butterworths, 2002), p 727, where it is argued that a narrow view of what constitutes a computer should be adopted.
[34] Law Commission Report No 186 (n 30 above), para 3.39.
[35] 18 USC section 1030(e)(1). See also Singapore's Computer Misuse Act 1998, s 2(1).
[36] See, further, section 8.5.1 below.
[37] Snaresbrook Crown Court, 4 July 1991.
[38] See Audit Commission Report, *Ghost in the Machine: An Analysis of Fraud and Abuse* (1998) which found that nearly 25% of frauds were committed by staff in managerial positions.

of Appeal subsequently rejected the lower court's interpretation, stating that the 'plain and natural meaning is clear'.[39] It is interesting to note, however, that the Council of Europe Convention offence of 'illegal access' does permit Member States to limit the offence to 'exclude the situation where a person physically accesses a stand-alone computer without any use of another computer system'.[40]

The offence under section 1 is punishable on summary conviction by a fine of up to £2000 or six months in jail (s 1(3)).[41] A person can be found guilty of the basic section 1 offence where a jury could not find him guilty of an indictment under section 2 or section 3 (s 12). In addition, under section 44 of the Magistrates' Courts Act 1980, a person who 'aids, abets, counsels or procures the commission by another person of a summary offence shall be guilty of the like offence' which could be applicable, for example, against those who distribute passwords and other authorization codes via bulletin boards.

### 8.4.2  Intent to commit a further offence

The offence under section 2 involves the commission of a section 1 offence together with the intent to commit, or facilitate the commission, of a further offence. A relevant further offence is one for which the sentence is fixed by law, for example, life imprisonment for murder, or where imprisonment may be for a term of five years or more, for example, a computer fraud.[42] The access and the further offence do not have to be intended to be carried out at the same time (s 2(3)), and it also does not matter if the further offence was in fact impossible (s 2(4)). Upon conviction, a person could be sentenced to imprisonment for up to a five-year term (s 2(5)).

The following cases illustrate the range of situations that have arisen under the section 2 offence:

(a) In *R v Pearlstone*[43] an ex-employee used his former company's telephone account and another subscriber's account to defraud the computer-administered telephone system and place calls to the US.

(b) In *R v Borg*[44] an investment company analyst was accused of establishing dummy accounts within a 'live' fund-management system. The alleged 'further offence' was expected to be fraudulent transfers into the dummy accounts.

(c) In *R v Farquharson*[45] the defendant was prosecuted for obtaining mobile telephone numbers and codes necessary to produce cloned telephones. The computer

---

[39] *Attorney-General's Reference (No 1 of 1991)* [1992] 3 WLR 432, 437F.

[40] Explanatory Report to the Convention, para 50. (See, further, section 8.5.1 below.)

[41] A prosecution under section 1 is subject to certain time limits (s 11(2) and (3)) which were not complied with in *Morgans v DPP* [1999] 1 WLR 968, DC.

[42] ie, for a first offender aged 21 or over.

[43] April 1991, Bow Street Magistrates' Court, described in R Battcock, 'Prosecutions under the Computer Misuse Act 1990' (1996) 6 Computers and Law 22.

[44] March 1993; see Battcock (n 43 above).

[45] 9 December 1993, Croydon Magistrates' Court; see Battcock (n 43 above).

system containing this information was actually accessed by his co-defendant Ms Pearce, an employee of the mobile telephone company, who was charged with a section 1 offence. Farquharson was found to have committed the unauthorized access required for the section 2 offence even though he never touched the computer himself, but had simply asked Pearce to access the information.

Prosecutions under section 2 are likely to be relatively infrequent, since in many cases prosecutors will pursue a prosecution for the further offence rather than the unauthorized access, even though the individual may be initially charged with the section 2 offence. In addition, the perpetrator's act of unauthorized access may be sufficient to found a prosecution for an attempt to commit the further offence.[46]

### 8.4.3 Intent and authorization

In May 1993, the first classic 'hackers' were given six-month jail sentences for conspiracy to commit offences under sections 1 and 3 of the Computer Misuse Act 1990.[47] The defendants' activities were said to have caused damage, valued at £123,000, to computer systems ranging from those of the Polytechnic of Central London to NASA. In passing sentence the judge said:

There may be people out there who consider hacking to be harmless, but hacking is not harmless. Computers now form a central role in our lives, containing personal details ... It is essential that the integrity of those systems should be protected and hacking puts that integrity in jeopardy.

Such judicial sentiment is critical if the Act is to have a significant deterrent effect.

However, the jury acquitted one of the co-defendants in the same case, Bedworth, because defence counsel successfully argued that the necessary *mens rea* for a charge of conspiracy was absent because the defendant was an 'obsessive' hacker. This case was widely publicized and was seen by many as a potential 'hacker's charter'.[48] However, the decision seems to have arisen from a mistaken choice by the prosecuting authorities to pursue an action for conspiracy, rather than a charge under the Computer Misuse Act.

In addition to the *Bedworth* case, the issue of prosecution for the inchoate offences of incitement or conspiracy with others to commit an offence[49] arose in respect of the publication of *The Hacker's Handbook*, a popular guide to current developments in this area. Following the coming into force of the 1990 Act, the

---

[46] See Criminal Attempts Act 1981, s 1: 'If, with intent to commit an offence to which this section applies, a person does an act which is more than merely preparatory to the commission of the offence, he is guilty of attempting to commit the offence'. This provision was amended by the Computer Misuse Act 1990, s 7(3).

[47] *R v Strickland, R v Woods*, March 1993, Southwark Crown Court.

[48] See eg, 'Bedworth Case Puts Law on Trial', *Computing*, 25 March 1993, p 7.

[49] Criminal Law Act 1977, s 1.

publishers apparently decided to withdraw the book from circulation to avoid potential legal action.[50]

During the passage of the Computer Misuse Bill, an attempt was made to add a provision whereby hackers would be able to offer a defence if computer users had not implemented security measures.[51] A similar approach has been adopted in other jurisdictions, where the presence of security measures is a necessary element of the offence[52] and, indeed, the Convention on Cybercrime states that a party 'may require that the offence be committed by infringing security measures' (art 2). Whilst the amendment to the Bill was rejected, the issue of the existence of security measures does arise in the context of establishing whether access was 'unauthorised'. Under section 17(5) of the Act, access is considered to be 'unauthorised' if:

(a) he is not himself entitled to control access of the kind in question to the program or data; and

(b) he does not have consent to access by him of the kind in question to the program or data from any person who is so entitled

Where the accused is external to the victim's organization, showing knowledge of an absence of entitlement or consent is not generally an issue. However, where the accused is an employee of the organization, the burden is upon the prosecution to show that the accused knew that 'access of the kind in question' was unauthorized, rather than a misuse of express or implied rights of access, for example, an accounts clerk entering claims for false expenses. As noted by the Law Commission, 'An employee should only be guilty of an offence if his employer has clearly defined the limits of the employee's authority to access a program or data.'[53]

The interpretation of section 17(5) was first considered in detail in *DPP v Bignell*.[54] The case concerned two serving police officers who had accessed the Police National Computer ('PNC'), via an operator, for personal purposes. They were charged with offences under section 1 of the Computer Misuse Act 1990 and convicted in the Magistrates' Court. They successfully appealed to the Crown Court against their conviction, and this decision was the subject of a further appeal before the Divisional Court, which was dismissed.

The central issue addressed to the court was whether a person authorized to access a computer system for a particular purpose (for example, policing) can commit an offence under section 1 by using such authorized access for an unautho-

---

[50] See E Dumbill, 'Computer Misuse Act 1990: Recent Developments' (1992) 8(4) CL&P 107. See also *R v Maxwell-King*, Times Law Reports, 2 January 2001.

[51] See Standing Committee C, 14 March 1990. The following amendment was proposed by Harry Cohen MP: 'For the purposes of this section, it shall be a defence to prove that such care as in all the circumstances, was reasonably required to prevent the access or intended access in question was not taken.'

[52] eg Norwegian Penal Code, s 145, refers to persons 'breaking security measures to gain access to data/programs'.

[53] Law Commission Report No 186 (n 30 above), para 3.37.

[54] [1998] 1 Cr App R 1.

rized purpose (for example, personal). The Crown Court asserted that the Computer Misuse Act 1990 was primarily concerned 'to protect the integrity of computer systems rather than the integrity of the information stored on the computers . . .' and therefore such unauthorized usage was not caught by the Act. The Divisional Court upheld this view. First, Justice Astill stated that the phrase 'access of the kind in question' in section 17(5)(a) was referring to the types of access detailed in section 17(2): alteration, erasure, copying, moving, using and obtaining output. Second, the phrase 'control access' was referring to the authority granted to the police officers to access the PNC. He concluded that this did not create a lacuna in the law as the Data Protection Act 1984 contained appropriate offences in relation to the use of personal data for unauthorized purposes.[55]

This decision has attracted significant criticism and, as with *Sean Cropp*, was seen as significantly limiting the scope of the Act.[56] However, aspects of the decision were re-examined by the House of Lords in *R v Bow Street Magistrate and Allison (AP), ex p US Government*.[57] The case concerned an extradition request by the US Government of an individual accused of a fraud involving an employee of American Express who was able to use her access to the computer system to obtain personal identification numbers to encode forged credit cards. As in *Bignell*, defence counsel argued that an offence under section 1 had not been committed since the employee was authorized to access the relevant computer system. The House of Lords, whilst agreeing with the decision in *Bignell*, rejected the subsequent interpretation of section 17(5) made by Justice Astill.[58]

On the first issue, 'access of the kind in question', Lord Hobhouse stated that this phrase simply meant that the authority granted under section 17(5) may be limited to certain types of programs or data, and does not refer to the kinds of access detailed in section 17(2). Evidence showed that the employee at American Express accessed data in accounts for which she was not authorized, therefore the access she obtained was 'unauthorised access'. Second, 'control access' did not refer to the individual authorized to access the system, but the organizational authority granting authority to the individual. In the *Bignell* case, it was the Police Commissioner who exercised such control and, through employee manuals, specified that access was for police purposes only.

Whilst the decision in *Allison* clarifies the interpretation of 'control' under section 17(5), the court's acceptance of *Bignell* would seem to perpetuate the uncertain jurisprudence under the 1990 Act. First, Lord Hobhouse stresses the point that in *Bignell* 'the computer operator did not exceed his authority'[59] and therefore did not

---

[55] Data Protection Act 1984, s 5(6). See, generally, Chapter 11 on data protection.
[56] See, eg, D Bainbridge, 'Cannot Employees Also be Hackers?' (1997) 13(5) CLSR 352–4; and P Spink, 'Misuse of Police Computers' [1997] Juridical Review 219–31.
[57] [1999] 3 WLR 620.
[58] This interpretation had been followed by the Divisional Court from which the appeal had been made; see *R v Bow Street Magistrates' Court, ex p Allison* [1999] QB 847.
[59] [1999] 3 WLR 620, 627G.

commit an offence. This would seen irrelevant to the question of whether the Bignells were committing an offence under section 1, since the operator is simply an innocent agent.[60] Second, Lord Hobhouse recognizes that the concept of authorization needs to be refined, as 'authority to secure access of the kind in question', and the example given is where access 'to view data may not extend to authority to copy or alter that data'.[61] On this reasoning, it seems incongruous that the court should hold, by implication, that authority to view the data may not also be limited to particular circumstances. The Bignells knew that they were only authorized to access the PNC for policing purposes and knowingly misrepresented the purpose for their request.

### 8.4.4 Unauthorized modification

Obtaining access to a computer system clearly threatens the confidentiality of any information residing in it. However, the greater concern is often that such access enables a perpetrator to affect the integrity and availability of the information being processed by the system. The consequences of unauthorized modifications can range from mild inconvenience to life-threatening incidents, such as occurred in *R v Rymer* (1993) where a hospital nurse altered patient prescriptions.[62]

#### 8.4.4.1 *Criminal damage*

The offence of criminal damage may obviously be relevant in many situations where a computer is the subject of the crime. The value of a computer system normally resides in the information it contains, software and data, rather than the physical hardware.[63] However, as with the concept of theft, to what extent does the unauthorized deletion or modification of computer-based information constitute 'damage' to property, as required under section 1(1) of the Criminal Damage Act 1971?[64] The question was examined in *Cox v Riley*[65] where an employee deleted computer programs from a plastic circuit card that was required to operate a computerized saw. The court stated that the property (ie, the plastic circuit card) had been damaged by the erasure of the programs to the extent that the action impaired 'the value or usefulness' of the card and necessitated 'time and labour and money to be expended'[66] to make the card operable again.

This interpretation was upheld in *R v Whiteley* where the defendant was convicted of causing damage after gaining unauthorized access into the Joint Academic Network, used by UK universities, and deleting and amending substantial numbers

---

[60] See, eg, *R v Manley* (1844) 1 Cox 104.                     [61] [1999] 3 WLR 620, 626F–G.

[62] Battcock (n 43 above).

[63] Although the theft of computers for their processor chips has been significant during periods where market demand has exceeded supply.

[64] 'Property' under the 1971 Act means 'property of a tangible nature, whether real or personal' (s 10(1)).

[65] (1986) 83 Cr App R 54.                                        [66] Ibid, 58.

of files. It was argued, on his behalf, that the defendant's activities only affected the information contained on a computer disk, not the disk itself. However, the court stated:

What the Act [Criminal Damage Act 1971] requires to be proved is that tangible property has been damaged, not necessarily that the damage itself should be tangible.[67]

The alteration of the magnetic particles contained on a disk, whilst imperceptible, did impair the value and usefulness of the disk and therefore constituted damage. However, if the disk had been blank, any alteration would not necessarily be 'damage'.

Despite these successful prosecutions, the Law Commission considered that uncertainty continued to exist when prosecuting offences under the Criminal Damage Act 1971 which involved the misuse of computers and therefore proposed the creation of a new offence under the Computer Misuse Act 1990. One concern was the possibility of situations where it would be difficult to identify the tangible 'property' that had been damaged when altering data, for example, deleting information being sent across the public telephone network. A second major concern was that police and prosecuting authorities were experiencing practical difficulties 'explaining to judges, magistrates and juries how the facts fit in with the present law of criminal damage.'[68]

### 8.4.4.2  Computer Misuse Act 1990

The third substantive offence under the Computer Misuse Act 1990 is that of unauthorized modification of computer material. Section 3(1) provides that:

A person is guilty of an offence if—

(a) he does any act which causes an unauthorised modification of the contents of the computer; and
(b) at the time when he does the act he has the requisite intent and the requisite knowledge.

Conviction could result in imprisonment for up to a five-year term (s 3(7)). The offence was principally promoted by the spate of publicity and fear surrounding the use of computer viruses.

The concept of damage in the Criminal Damage Act 1971 is amended by section 3 to the extent that 'a modification of the contents of the computer' shall not be regarded as damage, and therefore an offence under the 1971 Act, if it does not impair the 'physical condition' of the computer (s 3(6)). In the case of removable data media, such as a computer disk or CD-ROM, deletion of data would only be an offence under section 3 if the storage medium were in the computer (s 17(6)). Once removed, any damage would be subject to the terms of the 1971 Act.

---

[67] (1991) 93 Cr App R 25, 28.
[68] Law Commission Report No 186 (n 30 above), para 2.31.

The 'unauthorised modification' offence creates a substantial discrepancy with the situation prior to the 1990 Act, since conviction under the Criminal Damage Act could be punishable by imprisonment for up to ten years (s 4). In addition, liability for criminal damage could arise through the defendant 'being reckless as to whether any such property would be destroyed' (s 1(1)), without the requirement for the prosecution to show intent. Such reckless damage is often a feature of 'hacking' cases, where a hacker inadvertently deletes or alters files and data during the course of his activities, causing the victim substantial loss.[69] The restricted scope of the offence under section 3 significantly limits the penalties that such consequences can attract. However, the Law Commission considered that the section 3 offence should be limited to those engaged in intentional acts of sabotage and noted that those causing inadvertent damage would already be guilty of the offence under section 1, which should be a sufficient deterrent.

As with the offence under section 1, the offence of unauthorized modification comprises three elements: 'unauthorised modification' of contents, 'requisite intent' and 'requisite knowledge'.

The first element can obviously be further broken down into 'unauthorised' and 'modification'. Whether an act is unauthorized or not is clearly a potentially difficult issue where the person carrying out the act is part of the organization against whom the offence is being committed and has certain 'authorisation' to use the computer system in question.[70] The 'requisite knowledge' element, defined at section 3(4) as knowledge that any modification he intends to cause is unauthorized, also relates to the question of authorization. The interpretation provisions in the Act in section 17 provide guidance as to the nature of authorization required under section 3:

(8) Such a modification is unauthorised if—

    (a) the person whose act causes it is not himself entitled to determine whether the modification should be made; and

    (b) he does not have consent to the modification from any person who is so entitled.

The nature of any 'modification' may be permanent or temporary (s 3(5)) and is further elaborated at section 17(7):

(7) A modification of the contents of any computer takes place if, by the operation of any function of the computer concerned or any other computer—

    (a) any program or data held in the computer concerned is altered or erased; or

    (b) any program or data is added to its contents;

and any act which contributes towards causing such a modification shall be regarded as causing it.

Section 3(2) elaborates the meaning of 'requisite intent':

(2) For the purposes of subsection (1)(b) above the requisite intent is an intent to cause a modification of the contents of any computer and by so doing—

---

[69]  Law Commission Report No 186 (n 30 above), para 3.62.
[70]  See the discussion of 'authorisation' at section 8.4.3 above.

(a)  to impair the operation of any computer;
(b)  to prevent or hinder access to any program or data held in any computer; or
(c)  to impair the operation of any such program or the reliability of any such data.

As with the offence under section 1, the intent need not be directed at any particular program, data or computer (s 3(3)).

Section 3(2) suggests the requirement for a dual intention, that of causing a modification and that of causing an impairment. This was illustrated in the *Sean Cropp* case. In the Crown Court, the judge had agreed with defence counsel's argument that the defendant's actions more appropriately fell under the offence of unauthorized modification rather than that of unauthorized access. However, in the Court of Appeal, Lord Taylor put forward the opinion that the only form of modification that could be applicable to the defendant's actions was with respect to the impairment of the reliability of the data, and went on to note:

That would involve giving the word 'reliability' the meaning of achieving the result in the printout which was intended by the owner of the computer. It may not necessarily impair the reliability of data in a computer that you feed in something which will produce a result more favourable to a customer than the store holder intended.[71]

This statement clearly recognizes the requirement for dual intention and also seems to support the Law Commission's stance that 'the offence should not punish unauthorised modifications which improve, or are neutral in their effect'.[72]

However, the meaning of the term 'reliability' has subsequently been revisited in *Yarimaka v Governor of HM Prison Brixton; Zezev v Government of the United States of America*.[73] The case concerned the hacking into the systems of the financial information company Bloomberg, and the subsequent attempt to blackmail its founder Michael Bloomberg. In the course of extradition proceedings, defence counsel for Zezev challenged the validity of the section 3 charge. It was submitted that the purpose of section 3 was confined to acts which 'damage the computer so that it does not record the information which is fed into it'.[74] In this case, the defendant fed false information into the system concerning the source of certain information and as such he did not alter or erase the data, the apparent mischief against which the section was directed. A clear similarity could be drawn between this situation and the position in *Sean Cropp*. In the former, false information was also input into the computer to benefit the perpetrator, and yet Lord Taylor was of the opinion that this does not 'necessarily impair the reliability of the data in a computer'. In *Yarimaka*, Lord Woolf did not feel inclined to make a distinction between an intention to modify and an intention to impair, stating '[i]f a computer is caused to record information which shows that it came from one person, when it in fact came from someone else, that manifestly affects its reliability'.[75] Such an approach, whilst chiming

---

[71]  *Attorney-General's Reference (No 1 of 1991)* [1992] 3 WLR 432, 438A.
[72]  Law Commission Report No 186 (n 30 above), para 3.72.
[73]  [2002] EWHC 589 (Admin).        [74]  Ibid, para 14.        [75]  Ibid, para 18.

with common sense, would seem to generate uncertainty regarding the scope of the section 3 offence.

The first major prosecution brought under section 3 was *R v Goulden*.[76] In this case, Goulden installed a security package on an Apple workstation for a printing company, Ampersand. The package included a facility to prevent access without use of a password. Goulden made use of this facility as part of his claim for fees totalling £2,275. Due to the computerized nature of their printing operations, Ampersand were unable to function for a period of a few days. They claimed £36,000 lost business as a result of Goulden's actions, including £1,000 for a specialist to override the access protection. The court imposed a two-year conditional discharge on Goulden and a £1,650 fine. (The judge also commented that Goulden's actions were 'at the lowest end of seriousness'!)

In *R v Whitaker*[77] the courts were required to consider the extent to which the unauthorized modification offence could be applied against an owner of intellectual property. The case concerned a software developer and his client, and arose when the developer initiated a logic bomb designed to prevent use of the software following a dispute over payment. The defendant programmer argued that since under the contract he had retained all intellectual property rights in the software (with title transferring upon payment), he had the requisite right to modify the software. The court held that, despite the existence of copyright in the software, the nature of the development contract constituted a limitation on the exercise of the developer's rights. The court did recognize, however, that such an action would have been permitted if it had been explicitly provided for in the contract, ie, the licensee was made aware of the consequences of a failure to pay. He was therefore found guilty of an offence under section 3. This was an important decision, since the software industry is increasingly resorting to such techniques as a means of ensuring payment for their services.

The first prosecution of a virus writer, one of the original targets of section 3, was of Christopher Pile, also known as 'the Black Baron', in 1995.[78] An interesting feature of the case was that Pile was found guilty of the offence even though he had no knowledge of which computers were affected by his viruses (for example, 'Pathogen') and had not targeted any specific computer.

One issue that has arisen concerning the offence of unauthorized modification is its applicability to the carrying out of so-called 'denial of service' attacks launched against commercial websites, such as eBay and Amazon. Such attacks are designed to disrupt the operation of the site by deliberately flooding the host server with multiple requests for information.[79] There has been concern that the existing offence

---

. [76] *The Times*, 10 June 1992.

[77] 1993, Scunthorpe Magistrates' Court; see Battcock (n 43 above).

[78] Plymouth Crown Court, 1995; see Battcock (n 43 above).

[79] Such actions should be contrasted with the sending of multiple requests for supposedly legitimate purposes, eg, a competitor checking current prices. See, eg, *eBay v Bidders Edge* (2000) 100 F Supp 2d 1058 (ND Cal) where eBay successfully obtained an injunction on the basis of a claim for trespass to chattels.

would not necessarily cover such activities, since the submission of requests is not in itself an unauthorized activity. As a consequence, a Private Member's Bill was introduced into Parliament in May 2002, which would specifically address such activities under a new offence.[80] However, the Bill is unlikely to be adopted.

### 8.4.4.3  Civil remedies
In Singapore, the Computer Misuse Act 1993, based on the UK Act, expressly grants a court the power to make an order against a person convicted of an offence to pay compensation to any party that has suffered damage from the offending activity.[81] Similarly, in the US, section 1030(g) of the Computer Fraud and Abuse Act provides that 'any person who suffers damage or loss . . . may maintain a civil action . . . to obtain compensatory damage and injunctive relief or other equitable relief'. In the UK, no such provisions are contained in the Computer Misuse Act, although the courts have the power within their general jurisdiction to make compensation orders.[82]

### 8.4.4.4  Terrorism
As noted in the Introduction (section 8.1 above), concern about societal dependence on computer and communication technologies has been one of the drivers behind new legislative initiatives in the area. Clearly one aspect of such concerns relates to terrorism and the possibility that computer-based attacks may be launched against a nation's critical infrastructure, such as the systems operating power stations and air-traffic control systems. As a consequence, recent legislation has redefined the concept of what constitutes a terrorist act to include actions 'designed seriously to interfere with or seriously disrupt an electronic system'.[83] In addition, a recent EU draft Decision on computer crime has proposed that causing 'substantial damage to part of the critical infrastructure of the Member State' should be considered an aggravating circumstance giving rise to greater penalties.[84] Member States are left to designate what constitutes 'critical infrastructure'.

In the comparatively short time since coming into force, the Computer Misuse Act 1990 has been successfully applied against the range of offences for which it was envisaged. However, concerns continue to exist over the attitude of the judiciary towards convicting and sentencing for such offences. In terms of increasing the effectiveness of the Act, further successful prosecutions will give organizations the confidence to make use of the Act to deter such activities and pursue perpetrators.

---

[80]  Computer Misuse (Amendment) Bill [HL], introduced by the Earl of Northesk, 1 May 2002.
[81]  Computer Misuse Act 1993 (amended in 1996 and 1998), s 13.
[82]  Powers of Criminal Courts (Sentencing) Act 2000, s 130.
[83]  Terrorism Act 2000, s 1(2)(e).
[84]  See section 8.5.2 below.

## 8.5  INTERNATIONAL HARMONIZATION

Computer crime has an obvious international dimension and governments have recognized the need to ensure that legal protection is harmonized among nations. Attempts have been made within various international organizations and fora, such as the G8 Member States,[85] to achieve a harmonized approach to legislating against computer crime and thereby try to prevent the appearance of 'computer crime havens'. The first major attempt was under the auspices of the Organisation for Economic Co-operation and Development. It published a report in 1986, which listed five categories of offence that it believed should constitute a common approach to computer crime.[86] However, the most significant institution in the field has been the Council of Europe, although the European Union has also recently become active.

### 8.5.1  Council of Europe

In 1985, a select committee of experts, the European Committee on Crime Problems, was established under the auspices of the Council of Europe to consider the legal issues raised by computer crime. The final report was published in September 1989.[87] As part of the Committee's work, it produced guidelines for national legislatures on a 'Minimum List of Offences Necessary for a Uniform Criminal Policy'.[88] These eight offences were seen by all Member States to be the critical areas of computer misuse that required provisions in criminal law. In addition, the report put forward an 'optional list' of four offences that failed to achieve consensus among Members, but was thought to be worthy of consideration.[89] The report was published with a Council of Ministers' Recommendation urging governments to take account of the report when reviewing and initiating legislation in this field.[90]

Following the Recommendation, the Council of Europe shifted its attention to the issue of prosecution of computer crime and the particular problems faced by law-enforcement agencies. In 1995, for example, it adopted a Recommendation address-

---

[85]  eg, G8 Recommendation on Transnational Crime. The Recommendation was endorsed at the G8 Justice and Interior Minister's Meeting in Canada, 13–14 May 2002 (www.g8j-i.ca). See, in particular, Part IV, Section D, 'Hi-Tech and Computer-Related Crimes'.

[86]  *Computer-Related Criminality: Analysis of Legal Policy in the OECD Area* (report DSTI-ICCP 84.22 of 18 April 1986).

[87]  *Computer-Related Crime* (report by the European Committee on Crime Problems, Strasbourg, 1990).

[88]  The list of offences: computer fraud; computer forgery; damage to computer data or computer programmes; computer sabotage; unauthorized etc access; unauthorized interception; unauthorized reproduction of a computer program; unauthorized reproduction of a topography.

[89]  ie, alteration of computer data or computer programs; computer espionage; unauthorized use of a computer and unauthorized use of a protected computer program.

[90]  Recommendation No R(89) 9, 13 September 1999.

ing issues of search and seizure, the admissibility of evidence and international mutual assistance.[91]

Despite these various initiatives, Council of Europe Recommendations are not binding legal instruments on Member States and inevitably, therefore, such harmonizing measures have had limited effect. However, the growth of the Internet as a transnational environment for the commission of crime has refocused the attention of policy-makers on the need for harmonized criminal laws in the area. As a consequence, in April 1997, the Council of Europe embarked on the adoption of a Convention in the area, which Member States would have an obligation to implement.

In November 2001, the Council of Ministers adopted the Convention on Cybercrime, which was opened for signature in Budapest on 23 November 2001, and has since been signed by thirty of the forty-four members of the Council of Europe.[92] However, of particular significance to the status of the Convention, four non-members were involved in the drafting process, the United States, Japan, South Africa and Canada, and became signatories. The Convention also contains a mechanism whereby other non-members can sign and ratify the Convention. Once five states have ratified the Convention, through implementation into national law, it shall enter into force (art 36(3)).[93]

The Convention addresses issues of substantive and procedural criminal law, which Member States are obliged to take measures to implement in national law, as well as issues of international cooperation.

In terms of offences, section 1 distinguishes three categories of offence:

(a) 'Offences against the confidentiality, integrity and availability of computer data and systems': illegal access, illegal interception, data interference, systems interference and misuse of devices (arts 2–6).[94]

(b) 'Computer-related offences': forgery and fraud (arts 7–8).

(c) 'Content-related offences': child pornography and infringements of copyright and related rights (arts 9–10).

Relevant aspects of these provisions have been examined in other sections of this chapter. In addition, the Convention addresses related liability issues in relation to attempts and aiding or abetting (art 11) and corporate liability (art 12).

Section 2 of the Convention addresses procedural provisions that Member States are obliged to implement in national law. These include measures to enable the

---

[91] Recommendation No R(95) 13 'concerning problems of procedural law connected with information technology'.
[92] European Treaty Series No 185 and Explanatory Report (available at www.coe.int). Number of signatories as at 16 September 2002.
[93] Three of the ratifications have to be Council of Europe Members. As at 16 September 2002, only one ratification, by Albania, had been made.
[94] Devices, including passwords, being produced or used with the intent to commit one of the offences within the category.

'expedited preservation of stored computer data' (art 16); 'expedited preservation and partial disclosure of traffic data' (art 17);[95] the production and search and seizure of computer data (arts 18–19); the 'real-time collection of traffic data' (art 20); and the interception of content data (art 21). Section 3 addresses the issue of jurisdiction (art 22).[96]

In terms of international cooperation, the Convention addresses issues of extradition (art 24), mutual legal assistance between national law-enforcement agencies (arts 25–34) and the establishment of a permanently operational network of points of contact to support such assistance (art 35).

The comprehensive nature of the Convention, as well as the geographical spread of its signatories, means it is likely to remain one of the most significant international legal instruments in the field of computer crime for the foreseeable future.

### 8.5.2 European Union

Many aspects of criminal law have historically been outside the competence of the European Union. However, under Title VI of the Treaty on European Union issues of 'police and judicial co-operation in criminal matters' have now been brought within the EU's sphere of activities. At a special meeting of the European Council in October 1999, Member State governments agreed that efforts should be made to reach common positions with respect to definitions of criminal offences and appropriate sanctions for particular areas of crime, including computer crime.[97] Subsequently, the Commission adopted a Communication on computer crime that included proposals for legislative measures in the area;[98] as well as a Communication on 'Network and Information Security'.[99]

In April 2002, the Commission published a proposal for a Council Framework Decision on 'attacks against information systems'.[100] As with the Convention on Cybercrime, the proposal addresses issues of both substantive and procedural law, although its focus is on the former.

In terms of substantive offences, the proposal is only concerned with activities aimed against the integrity of systems, not with content-related or computer-related crimes. It proposes offences of illegal access and illegal interference. In respect of illegal access, the proposal mandates the optional position taken under the

---

[95] ' "Traffic data" means any computer data relating to a communication by means of a computer system, generated by a computer system that formed a part in the chain of communication, indicating the communication's origin, destination, route, time, date, size, duration, or type of underlying service' (art 1(d)). See, further, section 8.7.1 below.

[96] See section 8.6 below.

[97] Press Release C/99/0002, Presidency conclusions, Tampere European Council 'on the creation of an area of freedom, security and justice in the European Union', 15–16 October 1999.

[98] Communication from the European Commission to the Council and the European Parliament, 'Creating a Safer Information Society by Improving the Security of Information Infrastructures and Combating Computer-related Crime' COM (2000) 890 final, section 7.1.

[99] COM (2001) 298 final, 6 June 2001.

[100] COM (2002) 173 final, 19 April 2002.

Convention that for the offence to be committed either the 'information system' is subject to 'specific protection measures' or there is intent to cause damage or obtain an economic benefit (art 3).

While the Convention states in general terms that sanctions for the commission of an offence should be 'effective, proportionate and dissuasive' (art 13), the draft Decision goes further and mandates a term of imprisonment of at least a year in 'serious cases', ie those involving damage or economic benefit (art 6). This minimum term would meet the threshold required in extradition proceedings.[101] Where aggravating circumstances exist, the draft proposes the minimum term of imprisonment should be raised to four years. Aggravating circumstances include where the activity is carried out within the framework of a criminal organization; where substantial economic loss or physical harm or damage to critical infrastructure is caused, or substantial proceeds result (art 7(1)).

Concerning procedural issues, the draft Decision simply requires Member States to establish permanently operational points of contact (art 12). However, EU Member States have addressed issues of mutual legal assistance in a separate Convention, which includes issues such as the interception of communications.[102]

Whilst the draft Decision is intended to be consistent with the Convention on Cybercrime, the nature of the European Union permits of more comprehensive harmonization between Member States than that achievable within the Council of Europe.

## 8.6  JURISDICTIONAL ISSUES

Computer crime often has an extraterritorial aspect to it that can give rise to complex jurisdictional issues involving people and the commission of acts in many different countries. Such issues are either addressed explicitly in the governing legislation, or are left to general principles of international criminal law.

In terms of legislation, for computer-integrity offences, the Computer Misuse Act 1990 asserts jurisdiction through the concept of a 'significant link' being present in the domestic jurisdiction, that is, the UK. An offence will have been committed if the accused, the accessed computer or the unauthorized modification is in the domestic jurisdiction.[103] Where computer-related offences have been committed, such as fraud or forgery, Part I of the Criminal Justice Act 1993 provides for jurisdiction on the basis of a 'relevant event' occurring in England and Wales (s 2(3)). A 'relevant event' means 'any act or omission or other event (including any result of one or more acts or omissions) proof of which is required for conviction of the

---

[101] See, further, section 8.6 below.

[102] Convention of 29 May 2000 on Mutual Assistance in Criminal Matters between the Member States of the European Union, OJ C197/1, 12 July 2000.

[103] Computer Misuse Act 1990, ss 4 and 5. Sections 6 and 7 of the 1990 Act address the territorial scope for the inchoate offences, ie, conspiracy, attempt or incitement.

offence' (s 2(1)).[104] In cases of child pornography, the Sexual Offenders Act 1997 bestows domestic jurisdiction if the act is also an offence in the jurisdiction where the act has been committed and the defendant is a British citizen (s 7).[105]

Both the Convention on Cybercrime and the EU draft Decision address the question of establishing jurisdiction. Article 22 of the Convention states that jurisdiction should exist when committed:

a. in its territory; or
b. on board a ship flying the flag of that Party; or
c. on board an aircraft registered under the laws of that Party; or
d. by one of its nationals, if the offence is punishable under criminal law where it was committed or if the offence is committed outside the territorial jurisdiction of any State.

The fourth scenario, based on the nationality of the offender, is generally referred to as the 'active personality' principle, and is often applicable in civil-law jurisdictions.[106] The draft Decision also adopts the territorial and 'active personality principle', as well as situations where the beneficiary of the offence is a legal person with its head office in the Member State (art 11). The draft Decision also qualifies the concept of territoriality in similar fashion to the Computer Misuse Act 1990, requiring the presence of either the offender or the information system.

The Citibank fraud in the early 1990s is illustrative of some of the issues that can arise when prosecuting transnational criminal activities. In 1994 Citibank suffered a significant breach of security in its cash-management system, resulting in funds being transferred from customer accounts into the accounts of the perpetrator and his accomplices.[107] The eventual sum involved was $12 million, although the vast majority, $11.6 million, was transferred subsequent to the discovery of the breach as part of the efforts to locate the perpetrators. After significant international cooperation between law-enforcement agencies, an individual was identified. Vladimir Levin was arrested in the UK and, after appeals, was subsequently extradited to the United States.[108]

In an action for extradition the applicant is required to show that the actions of the accused constitute a criminal offence exceeding a minimum level of seriousness in both jurisdictions, that is the country from which the accused is to be extradited and the country to which the extradition will be made; sometimes referred to as the 'double criminality' principle. Under the Extradition Act 1989, the offence must be punishable by a minimum of twelve months' imprisonment in both states

---

[104] These provisions came into force on 1 June 1999.

[105] See also the Sexual Offence (Conspiracy and Incitement) Act 1996, where citizenship is irrelevant.

[106] Explanatory Report (n 40 above), para 236. See, generally, I Bantekas, S Nash and M Mackarel, *International Criminal Law* (Cavendish Publishing, 2001).

[107] The system, called the 'Financial Institutions Citibank Cash Manager' ('FICCM'), provided large institutional customers with dial-in access from any geographic location to the online service, based on a system in Parsipenny, New Jersey. Once accessed, customers could carry out a range of financial transactions, including the execution of credit transfers between accounts.

[108] *R v Governor of Brixton Prison and Another, ex p Levin* [1996] 4 All ER 350.

(s 2).[109] Both the Convention and draft Decision provides that Member States should establish jurisdiction over offenders that they refuse to extradite.[110]

In *Ex p Levin* the defendant was accused of committing wire and bank fraud in the United States. No direct equivalent exists in English law, and therefore Levin was charged with sixty-six related offences, including unauthorized access and unauthorized modification under the Computer Misuse Act. However, as discussed previously in this chapter, even where similar offences exist, a particular computer-related activity may not be deemed to fall within the terminology of existing criminal law. Levin's counsel argued, for example, that one of the offences cited by the extradition applicant, under the Forgery and Counterfeiting Act 1981, had not been committed, based on an earlier decision by the English courts in *Gold*.[111]

A second jurisdictional issue in *Levin* revolved around the question of *where* the offences were held to have taken place. Counsel for the defendant claimed that the criminal act occurred in St Petersburg at the moment when Levin pressed particular keys on the keyboard instigating fraudulent Citibank transfers, and therefore Russian law applied. Counsel for the extradition applicant claimed that the place where the changes to the data occurred, the Citibank computer in Parsipenny in the United States, constituted the place where the offence took place. The judge decided in favour of the applicant on the basis that the real-time nature of the communication link between Levin and the Citibank computer meant that Levin's keystrokes were actually occurring on the Citibank computer.[112] Such an approach would suggest that a message-based system of communication, such as e-mail, operating on a 'store-and-forward' basis, might produce a different result if an interval in the course of committing the act could be shown to exist. In *Governor of Pentonville Prison, ex p Osman*,[113] for example, the court held that the sending of a telex constituted the act of appropriation and, therefore, the place from where the telex was sent was where the offence was committed. The nature of computer and communications technologies may therefore create legal uncertainty about where an act occurs, which is likely to be a common ground for challenge by defendants.

## 8.7 FORENSIC ISSUES

The investigation of computer crimes and the gathering of appropriate evidence for a criminal prosecution can be an extremely difficult and complex issue, due primarily

---

[109] See also the Computer Misuse Act 1990, s 8(1) and *R v Bow Street Magistrates' Court, ex p Allison* [1999] QB 847, where the court held that the Computer Misuse Act 1990, ss 2 and 3, were extradition crimes (confirmed by the House of Lords at [1999] 3 WLR 620, 625G). On 14 November 2002 the Government introduced an Extradition Bill into Parliament that will likely replace parts of the 1989 Act.

[110] Convention (n 102 above), art 22(3) and Decision (n 100 above), at 11(4).

[111] See section 8.2.2 above. See also *R v Governor of Brixton Prison and Another, ex p Levin* [1996] 4 All ER 350, 360E–361E.

[112] Ibid, 363A.                                      [113] [1989] 3 All ER 701.

to the intangible and often transient nature of data, especially in a networked environment. The technology renders the process of investigation and recording of evidence extremely vulnerable to defence claims of errors, technical malfunction, prejudicial interference or fabrication. Such claims may lead to a ruling from the court against the admissibility of such evidence.[114] A lack of adequate training of law-enforcement officers will often exasperate these difficulties.

In terms of obtaining evidence, relevant data may be resident on the computer system of the victim, the suspect and/or some third party, such as a communication service provider. Alternatively, evidence may be obtained in the process of its transmission between computer systems. Specific procedural rules address access to both sources of evidence.

### 8.7.1 Search and Seizure

Data stored on the computer system of the suspect is generally obtained through the execution of a court order for search and seizure.[115] A search-and-seizure warrant can give rise to problems where the relevant material is held on a computer system being used at the time of the search, since any attempt to seize the material for further examination may result in either the loss or alteration of the evidence.[116] The volume of material potentially contained on the hard disk of a computer subject to a warrant can raise issues as to the scope of the warrant. In *R v Chesterfield Justices and Others, ex p Bramley*[117] the potential vulnerability of the police was exposed when the court held that the Police and Criminal Evidence Act 1984 did not contain a defence to an action for trespass to goods in respect of items subject to legal privilege being seized during the execution of a search warrant. Subsequently, in *H v Commissioners of Inland Revenue*,[118] it has been held that *Bramley* only extends to situations involving legally privileged material, not any situation where irrelevant material is seized in the course of taking a computer as evidence.[119]

To remedy the potential liability established by *Bramley*, the Government added provisions to the Criminal Justice and Police Act 2001. The Act grants law-enforcement agencies the right to remove material, including material potentially outside the scope of a warrant, where it is 'not reasonably practicable' to separate it (s 50(1)(c)). An exhaustive list of relevant factors is provided for determining whether it is 'reasonably practicable', including 'the apparatus or equipment that it would be

---

[114] Police and Criminal Evidence Act, s 78.

[115] eg under the Computer Misuse Act, s 14, or the Police and Criminal Evidence Act 1984, ss 8, 19–20.

[116] See, generally, the *Good Practice Guide for Computer Based Evidence* published by the Association of Chief Police Officers. See also US Department of Justice Report, *Searching and Seizing Computers and Obtaining Electronic Evidence in Criminal Investigations* (July 2002) available at www.usdoj.gov/criminal/cybercrime.

[117] [2000] 2 WLR 409, DC.

[118] [2002] EWHC 2164 (Admin).

[119] Although the officer should then make a copy of the hard disk, eg, through imaging, and then return the original (per Burnton J, ibid, para 40).

necessary or appropriate to use for the carrying out of the determination or separation' (s 50(3)(d)), which would presumably encompass the various software tools used in computer forensics. The Act details a number of safeguards for the handling of such data that are designed to protect the defendant's rights under the European Convention on Human Rights.[120]

Another aspect of the use of search warrants in a networked environment concerns the geographical scope of such warrants. Under the Police and Criminal Evidence Act 1984, a constable may require 'any information which is contained in a computer and is accessible from the premises to be produced in a form in which it can be taken away . . .' (s 19(4)).[121] This provision would seem to enable law-enforcement officers to obtain information held on remote systems, since the reference to 'a computer' would seem to extend to a remote computer that can be accessed via another computer on the premises. Such a position has also been adopted in the Convention on Cybercrime, which states that the right to search and access should extend to any other computer system on its territory which 'is lawfully accessible from or available to the initial system' (art 19(2)).

However, where the remote computer is based in another jurisdiction, important issues of sovereignty and territoriality arise. In *United States v Gorshkov*,[122] for example, the FBI accessed computers in Russia, using surreptitiously obtained passwords, to download data.[123] In transborder circumstances, article 32 of the Convention on Cybercrime provides that authorization of the state in which the data resides is not required in order to:

a.  access publicly available (open source) stored computer data, regardless of where the data is located geographically; or

b.  access or receive, through a computer system in its territory, stored computer data located in another Party, if the Party obtains the lawful and voluntary consent of the person who has the lawful authority to disclose the data to the Party through that computer system.

The former would presumably be applicable where information was contained on a public website. The latter would extend, for example, to a person's e-mail stored in another country by the service provider. These two situations were the only examples upon which all parties to the Convention could agree, but does not preclude other situations being authorized under national law.[124]

In the early 1990s, certain UK-based electronic bulletin boards, containing illegal material such as virus code, began placing messages at the point of access to the site stating that 'law-enforcement officials are not permitted to enter the system'. Such a

---

[120]  See, further, D C Ormerod [2000] Crim LR 388, where he suggests off-site sifting be carried out by an independently appointed legal adviser.

[121]  See also section 20, which extends this provision to powers of seizure conferred under other enactments.

[122]  (2001) WL 1024026 (WDWash).

[123]  The court held the Fourth Amendment was not applicable to such actions and even if it was, the action was reasonable in the circumstances.

[124]  See Explanatory Report (n 40 above), paras 293–4.

warning was considered to be an effective technique in restricting the police from monitoring the use made of such bulletin boards.[125] As a consequence, in 1994 the Computer Misuse Act was amended to prevent law-enforcement agencies committing a section 1 offence of unauthorized access:

nothing designed to indicate a withholding of consent to access to any program or data from persons as enforcement officers shall have effect to make access unauthorised for the purposes of the said section 1(1).

In this section 'enforcement officer' means a constable or other person charged with the duty of investigating offences; and withholding consent from a person 'as' an enforcement officer of any description includes the operation, by the person entitled to control access, or rules whereby enforcement officers of that description are, as such, disqualified from membership of a class or persons who are authorised to have access.[126]

The scope of this exception should perhaps have been more narrowly drafted so as not to legitimize the use of 'hacking' and related techniques by law-enforcement agencies to circumvent data security measures utilized on remote systems. Such proactive techniques by investigators, as well as the deliberate alteration or modification of information held on a remote system, should perhaps be subject to specific procedural controls, akin to interception regimes.

Even when data has been lawfully obtained, a further problem that investigators increasingly face is that seized data may be protected by some form of security measure, such as a password or encryption, which renders it inaccessible or unintelligible. In the US, for example, when the notorious hacker Kevin Mitnick was finally arrested, many of the files found on his computers were encrypted and investigators were unable to access them.[127]

Obtaining access to protected data has been addressed by a combination of approaches in the UK. First, under the Regulation of Investigatory Powers Act 2000, a notice may be served on a person requiring that they disclose the information in an 'intelligible form' (s 49). Prior to this provision, the law only required that information be provided in a 'visible and legible form'.[128] Second, where necessary and proportionate, a person may be required by notice to disclose the 'key'[129] that would enable the investigators to render the information intelligible themselves (s 51). Failure to comply with either such notice is an offence (s 53). Third, under a separate but related initiative, the Government has established a National Technical Assistance Centre, which is designed to provide the necessary technical expertise to law-enforcement agencies to try and access protected data without the involvement of the person at all.

---

[125] See Home Affairs Committee Report No 126, *Computer Pornography*, p xii, paras 31–2 (HMSO, February 1994).
[126] Criminal Justice and Public Order Act 1994, s 162, amending the Computer Misuse Act 1990, s 10.
[127] See, generally, www.freekevin.com.           [128] Police and Criminal Evidence Act 1984, s 19.
[129] ' "[K]ey", in relation to any electronic data, means any key, code, password, algorithm or other data the use of which (with or without other keys)—(a) allows access to the electronic data, or (b) facilitates the putting of the data into an intelligible form' (s 56(1)).

The most common third-party source of evidence is communication service providers, such as an Internet Service Provider. Data stored on the systems of a communications service provider is currently accessed either under the Data Protection Act 1998, which provides a voluntary mechanism to enable the disclosure of stored personal data without the third party incurring liability,[130] or the Police and Criminal Evidence Act 1984.[131] However, the Regulation of Investigatory Powers Act 2000 ('RIPA 2000') contains new powers that, when implemented, will establish a new regime to enable law-enforcement agencies to require the disclosure of 'communications data' from communication service providers. 'Communications data' includes 'traffic data' (s 21(6)),[132] such as a telephone numbers, data concerning usage of the service and any other data held on the person by the service provider (s 21(4)).

### 8.7.2 Interception

As well as stored data, evidence may be obtained during its transmission between computers across communication networks. Such evidence may comprise the content of a communication, such as a list of passwords, or the attributes of a communication session, such as the duration of a call or the location of the caller.

Interception of the content of a communication is governed in the UK under RIPA 2000. The Act makes it an offence to intercept a communication being transmitted over a public telecommunications system without a warrant issued by the Secretary of State; or over a private telecommunication system without the consent of the system controller (s 1). An interception is lawful, however, where both the sender and recipient have consented to the interception (s 3(1)); or it is carried out by a communications service provider 'for purposes connected with the provision or operation of that service or with the enforcement . . . of any enactment relating to the use of . . . telecommunications services' (s 3(3)). This latter provision renders lawful an interception carried out by a telecommunications operator to prevent fraudulent use of a telecommunication service or its improper use, under the Telecommunications Act 1984 (ss 42, 43).[133]

The RIPA 2000 regime is not primarily designed to tackle the activities of those intercepting communications in the furtherance of their criminal activities; rather its purpose is to control the interception practices of law-enforcement agents and the use of intercepted material as evidence. The European Court of Human Rights has

---

[130] Section 29(3).

[131] Section 9 concerning access to 'special procedure material'. See *NTL Group Ltd v Ipswich Crown Court* [2002] EWHC 1585 (Admin).

[132] This definition attempts to draw a clear distinction between the content of communication and its attributes. See, further, the European Commission-funded report, *Study on Legal Issues Relevant to Combating Criminal Activities Perpetrated Through Electronic Communications* (2000), section 5 (available at europa.eu.int/ISPO/eif/InternetPoliciesSite/Crime/Study2000/Report.html).

[133] See *Morgans v DPP* (n 41 above).

twice found UK law to be in breach of the Convention in respect of protecting the right of privacy of those who have been subject to interception.[134]

An interception warrant should only be issued by the Secretary of State on the grounds of national security, 'serious crime'[135] or the 'economic well-being of the United Kingdom' (s 5); and must identity a particular subject or a set of premises (s 8(1)). A procedure for scrutiny exists through the office of the Interception Commissioner, and a right of appeal to an Interception Tribunal.

One unique feature of the UK interception regime is that it does not generally permit information obtained through an interception to be adduced as evidence in legal proceedings (s 17).[136] Such evidence is for the purpose of an investigation, not for any subsequent prosecution. The reasoning behind such a provision is to protect from disclosure information about the investigative activities of law-enforcement agencies. Such activities would enter the public domain if intercept evidence was used in court and became subject to challenge by a defendant's counsel. Conversely, interception evidence is not inadmissible where a service provider under the Telecommunications Act 1984 carries out the interception,[137] or if the evidence comes from an interception carried out in another country,[138] since neither would reveal anything about the activities of UK law enforcement.

The interception rules would not cover the practice of 'electronic eavesdropping', where emissions from computer VDU screens are surreptitiously received and reconstituted for viewing on external equipment,[139] since they are not in the course of transmission to a recipient. However, 'electronic eavesdropping' would probably constitute a form of 'surveillance', which is governed under a separate Part of RIPA 2000.[140] By contrast, the Convention on Cybercrime states that interception shall include 'electromagnetic emissions from a computer system' (art 3).

As discussed in the previous section, access to communications data held by a communications service provider is to be governed by a new regime to be established under RIPA 2000. However, such communications data will only be available to be accessed by investigators if the service provider has retained such information. Generally, such data is retained for relatively short periods of time, due both to the

---

[134] ie *Malone v United Kingdom* [1984] 7 EHRR 14 and *Halford v United Kingdom* [1997] IRLR 471. See, further, Chapter 12.

[135] ie '(a) . . . an offence for which a person who has attained the age of twenty-one and has no previous convictions could reasonably be expected to be sentenced to imprisonment for a term of three years or more; (b) that the conduct involves the use of violence, results in substantial financial gain or is conduct by a large number of persons in pursuit of a common purpose.' (s 81(3)).

[136] However, it may be retained for certain 'authorised purposes' (s 15(4)), eg, if 'it is necessary to ensure that a person conducting a criminal prosecution has the information he needs to determine what is required of him by his duty to secure the fairness of the prosecution', and may be subsequently disclosed to the prosecutor or trial judge (s 18(7)).

[137] eg *Morgans v DPP* (n 41 above).

[138] See *R v P and Others* [2001] 2 All ER 58.

[139] See, generally, O Lewis, 'Information Security and Electronic Eavesdropping: A Perspective' (1991) 7(4) CLSR 165–8.

[140] Part II, 'Surveillance and Covert Human Intelligence Sources'.

cost to the provider as well as compliance with data-protection rules.[141] With heightened concerns about the threat of terrorism, the issue of the potential unavailability of evidence has led to calls for obligatory data retention to be imposed on communication service providers.[142] As a consequence of the events of 11 September 2001, provisions were incorporated in Part 11 of the Anti-terrorism, Crime and Security Act 2001 establishing a regime for a voluntary code of practice on retention to be agreed between the Secretary of State and communication service providers, with the alternative possibility of mandatory directions being imposed. However, such a scheme has yet to be adopted, amid concerns that the provisions would breach European data-protection and human-rights laws.[143]

### 8.7.3 Mutual Legal Assistance

The investigation and prosecution of cross-border computer crimes will usually require mutual assistance between national law-enforcement agencies and prosecuting authorities. In *Levin*, for example, assistance was required not only from the St Petersburg police, but also the local telephone company. Obtaining such assistance in a timely and efficient manner will often be critical to the success of an investigation involving computers. Historically, however, procedures for mutual legal assistance have been notoriously slow and bureaucratic. Such procedures are currently governed by the Criminal Justice (International Co-operation) Act 1990 which provides for the provision of evidence and extends the powers of search and seizure to materials relevant to an overseas investigation or proceedings.[144]

As discussed in section 8.5 above, many of the international harmonization initiatives have been designed to address the procedural issues related to the investigation of a crime, as much as the substantive offences themselves. Through initiatives such as the establishment of national points of contact available twenty-four hours a day, seven days a week, it is intended to ensure that investigations can be carried out in a manner reflecting the nature of the technology involved.

Prosecutors will often be challenged to prove the reliability of the computer-derived evidence presented. Auditable procedures may need to be adhered to, usually supported by independent expert witnesses, to show that the computer systems generating any evidence, either under the direct control of the investigators (for example, a seized hard disk) or remotely accessed (for example, a website), were operating properly; that a link can be made between the evidence and the

---

[141]  See, further, Chapter 11 (section 11.3.9).

[142]  See, eg, the NCIS document, 'Looking to the Future, Clarity on Communications Data Retention Law: Submission to the Home Office for Legislation on Data Retention' (21 August 2000). The document was leaked to the *Observer* and is available at www.fipr.org.

[143]  See the evidence submitted by the Home Office to the All-Party Parliamentary Internet Group inquiry on data retention at www.apig.org.uk.

[144]  On 19 November 2002, the Government introduced the Crime (International Co-operation) Bill into Parliament, which will amend and repeal aspects of the 1990 Act.

accused,[145] and how the evidence was collected and maintained by the investigators until trial.[146]

## 8.8 CRIMINAL EVIDENCE

While the previous section examined the gathering of evidence, the logical next step concerns its use in the prosecution of the perpetrator of the crime. It is beyond the scope of this chapter to discuss English evidential rules in criminal proceedings, such as the distinction between real and hearsay evidence.[147] However, particular issues arise in respect of the use of computer-derived evidence that are pertinent to our discussion of computer-based crime.

Until recently, English law had special rules governing the admissibility of computer records in criminal proceedings. These rules presented an increasing obstacle to the prosecution of computer-based crime and led to their eventual repeal. However, while the challenge of admissibility has broadly disappeared, many of the issues raised in relation to the admissibility requirement continue to be relevant in respect of questions concerning the probative value of computer-derived evidence.

Under the Police and Criminal Evidence Act 1984, all computer evidence had to comply with section 69:

(1) In any proceedings, a statement in a document produced by a computer shall not be admissible as evidence of any fact stated therein unless it is shown—

(a) that there are no reasonable grounds for believing that the statement is inaccurate because of improper use of the computer;

(b) that at all material times the computer was operating properly, or if not, that any respect in which it was not operating properly or was out of operation was not such as to affect the production of the document or the accuracy of its contents;

To satisfy a court that the conditions under section 69(1) had been met, it was necessary to obtain either a signed statement or oral testimony from a person who occupies 'a responsible position' in relation to the operation of the computer system.[148]

The broad nature of the language used in section 69(1) presented obvious opportunities for a party to challenge computer-derived evidence. The conditions were therefore the subject of significant consideration by the courts.

In a networked environment, one issue that arose is the extent to which section

---

[145] eg, *R v Woollhead*, *The Herald*, 9 March 1995, quoted in Spink (n 56 above).

[146] See P Sommer, 'Evidence from Cyberspace: Downloads, Logs and Captures' (2002) 8(2) Computer and Telecommunications Law Review 33–42.

[147] See *R v Wood* (1983) 76 Cr App R 23 which held that when computers are operating in a mechanistic way, as automatic recording systems or simply as calculating tools, the evidence is real, not hearsay. See, generally, *Cross and Tapper on Evidence*, 9th edn (Butterworths, 1999).

[148] Police and Criminal Evidence Act 1984, Sch 3, Pt II, paras 8 and 9. See *R v Shephard* [1993] 1 All ER 225.

69(1) was to be complied with in respect of each and every machine involved in the processing of the evidential information. In *R v Cochrane*[149] the court upheld an appeal concerning a prosecution for theft of monies from a building society's cash machines because the Crown were unable to adduce evidence about the operation of the company's mainframe computer as well as the cash machine itself. However, identifying all the relevant computers could be problematic in an open networked environment such as the Internet. In *R v Waddon*[150] the court held that the computers involved in the transmission of an image across the Internet were not involved in its 'production' when printed from the investigator's computer and therefore did not require certification under section 69. Network-derived evidence does however raise the possibility of challenge both in respect of the provenance of any data and the nature of any intermediate processing that may have occurred.

In *Ex p Levin*, defence counsel challenged certain evidence presented by Citibank on the grounds that since the accused had improperly used the computer, the requirements of section 69(1)(a) could not be satisfied. The court rejected this argument noting that 'unauthorised use of the computer is not of itself a ground for believing that the statements recorded by it were inaccurate'.[151] Clearly, where more extensive and/or unintended modifications were involved, the value of such computer-derived evidence could be open to challenge on such grounds.

Section 69(1)(b) also required that a computer must have been 'operating properly' at the 'material time'. In *Connolly v Lancashire County Council*[152] audit records were submitted with respect to the correct operation of a computerized weighing bridge. However, the records related to an examination of the weighbridge system carried out nearly three months prior to the date of the alleged offence. The records were not accepted by the courts as evidence that the system was operating properly at the 'material time'. A party may therefore need to be able to show that any system from which evidence is derived was functioning appropriately at the time the evidence was generated, for example, through audit records.

A final aspect that has been addressed by the courts is the admissibility of computer-derived evidence where a part of the computer is found to be malfunctioning. In *DPP v McKeown and Jones*[153] an Intoximeter used to analyse the amount of alcohol in a person's breath was found to have an inaccurate clock. In the Divisional Court, the defendants successfully argued that the clock's inaccuracy rendered the statement detailing the level of alcohol present in the defendant inadmissible on the grounds that section 69(1)(b) could not be complied with. This was subsequently overturned in the House of Lords, with Lord Hoffmann stating:

A malfunction is relevant if it affects the way in which the computer processes, stores or retrieves the information used to generate the statement tendered in evidence. Other malfunctions do not matter.[154]

---

[149] [1993] Crim LR 48.                                        [150] [2000] All ER (D) 502.
[151] [1996] 4 All ER 350, 359C. It is interesting to note that the judge refers to the recording of statements, whereas section 69(1) is only concerned with the production of statements.
[152] [1994] RTR 79.                    [153] [1997] 1 WLR 295.                    [154] Ibid, 302.

Despite the generally favourable attitude of the courts to the admission of computer-derived evidence, considerable disquiet had been voiced against the section 69 conditions. In response, the Law Commission proposed reform of the rules to reintroduce the pre-1984 maxim *omnia praesumuntur rite esse acta*, a common-law presumption that things have been done properly.[155] The presumption effectively shifts the burden of proof with respect to the reliability of computer evidence from the party submitting the evidence to the party against whom the evidence is being adduced; therefore considerably reducing the likelihood of a challenge being raised. A similar reform was adopted with respect to the admissibility of computer evidence in civil proceedings by the Civil Evidence Act 1995, repealing the special provisions for computer evidence under section 5 of the Civil Evidence Act 1968. The repeal of section 69 came into force in April 2000.[156]

## 8.9 CONCLUSION

Public perception of computer crime contrasts sharply with reality. The news and entertainment media have promoted the image of the 'hacker' as an almost Robin Hood-like figure attacking the computers of big-brother organizations. The reality of computer crime is that such activities encompass a broad range of perpetrators: the traditional criminal fraternity, exploiting the power of a new tool; disgruntled employees utilizing their inside knowledge; the curious and thrill-seekers treating the medium as a challenge; and those engaged in industrial espionage and information warfare.

Nation states have generally needed to react to the phenomena of computer crime by updating their criminal law, whether through amendments to existing statutes or the adoption of *sui generis* offences. However, prosecutors, the judiciary and juries continue to struggle to comprehend the nature of computer-related crime and computer-derived evidence. Over recent years, policy-makers have shifted their focus from the need for appropriate offences to the needs of law-enforcement agencies in a networked environment.

From a commercial perspective, legislation addressing computer misuse is a final resort to which companies are generally reluctant to turn. The impact that such a prosecution may have on a company can be substantial, often affecting the systems upon which the company is reliant, consuming considerable management time and effort, and generating adverse publicity.

Perpetrators of computer crime usually exploit weaknesses in the systems either being used or attacked. Inadequate security procedures, physical, organizational and logical, continue to be a central feature in the vast majority of examples of computer

---

[155] See Law Commission Consultation Paper No 138, *Evidence in Criminal Proceedings: Hearsay and Related Topics* (HMSO, 1995) and Law Com No 245 (HMSO, 1997), Part XIII and recommendation 50.
[156] Youth Justice and Criminal Evidence Act 1999, s 60.

crime. The growth of the Internet, with the prospect of 'always-on' connectivity for large segments of population, presents very significant new and enhanced security threats to individuals, and society as a whole, as well as challenges to law-enforcement agencies.

# 9

# E-COMMERCE

*Chris Reed and Gavin Sutter*

## 9.1 INTRODUCTION: WHAT IS E-COMMERCE?

The term 'e-commerce' (or 'electronic commerce') has become commonly associated with the Internet, but it would be a mistake to assume that it is a new phenomenon. Prior to the development and widespread commercial use of the Internet, other technologies based on private or closed electronic networks were already in use to provide electronic communications between commercial entities which in turn were used to enter into binding agreements or contracts.

Electronic Data Interchange ('EDI'), a system of electronic communications between commercial parties where the communications take place over a closed system and are governed by a set of previously agreed contracts, was perhaps the most commonly used technology. Other communications systems existed and continue to exist within certain defined industries, and these too constitute a form of e-commerce. Quite aside from these closed networks, new techniques and protocols are being developed that allow users to create virtual private networks ('VPN's) across the Internet; these too can and almost certainly will be used in a manner similar to those of closed networks.

The Internet, by contrast, is an open network which permits communication between parties without the need for both to subscribe to the same closed network. Due to its widespread use and purportedly well-educated and affluent user group, it is an attractive medium for both business-to-business and business-to-consumer commerce. Quite aside from the possibility of using it to make contracts, the wide reach of the Internet presents an attractive medium through which commercial entities can advertise and market their wares.

Given the increasing use of electronic networks by commercial entities, all of which have differing aims and uses, what aspects of this use amount to e-commerce? What does the term mean?

Though the question is easy to ask it is very hard to answer, or at least to answer in a definite manner. This is not due to any difficulty in understanding what is meant by the question. Rather it is due to the difficulty of categorizing the subject matter into discrete topic areas.

Electronic network activity is very simple to define in a generic sense. It can be summarized as activities carried out across some form of electronic network, such as the Internet or the closed networks used for EDI, whatever those activities may be. E-commerce presents much more of a problem[1] as its definition depends on the differing views taken as to what is and what is not commerce or commercial activity. Taken at its most generic sense e-commerce could be said to comprise commercial transactions, whether between private individuals or commercial entities, which take place in or over electronic networks. The matters dealt with in the transactions could be intangibles, such as data or information products,[2] or tangible goods such as books and T-shirts. The only important factor is that some or all of the various communications which make up these transactions take place over an electronic medium. The communications could involve any part of the commercial process, from the initial marketing to the placing of orders and even through to the background transaction processing.[3] Whether these communications take place via EDI, or across other forms of electronic network such as the Internet or indeed a combination of these systems, is irrelevant. All that matters is that the commercial transactions utilize some form of electronic communication.

---

[1] See the discussion in *Defying Definition* (US Department of Commerce) (www.technology.gov/digeconomy/6.htm).

[2] Data products are often combinations of both the tangible and the intangible, for instance a CD-ROM which contains a database.

[3] *Sacher Report* (OECD, 1997), p 20, gives a generic yet comprehensive definition which forms a good starting point from which to proceed: 'Definitions of electronic commerce vary considerably, but generally, electronic commerce refers to all forms of commercial transactions involving organizations and individuals that are based upon the processing and transmission of digitized data, including text, sound, and visual images. It also refers to the effects that the electronic exchange of commercial information may have on the institutions and processes that support and govern commercial activities. These include organizational management, commercial negotiations and contracts, legal and regulatory frameworks, financial settlement arrangements, and taxation among many others.'

## 9.2 E-COMMERCE: GENERAL ISSUES

### 9.2.1 Contract formation

The question of contract formation across electronic networks is problematic to say the least. This is due not only to the interjurisdictional issues that arise as a natural result of the borderless nature of the networks, but also to the issues that arise when considering the terms of any contract that might be formed. Such issues arise because of the need to consider any overriding legislation which may affect the freedom to contract in the jurisdiction in which the contract was formed or under the law chosen in the contract.

The ease and flexibility of communicating across electronic networks allows users to enter into agreements with each other with little if any difficulty. The issue is therefore not whether the users can enter into agreements. The issue that must be addressed is whether these agreements can constitute contracts.[4] Though it is valid to ask what *law* applies to contracts formed across electronic networks, which courts have *jurisdiction* and what *terms* apply, these are not the most important issues. The fundamental question, and one which is rarely asked, is *whether or not* a contract was actually formed. This naturally leads to the questions of *where* that contract was formed and *when*.[5] Until these questions are answered it makes no sense even to attempt to ask what laws or jurisdictions apply. If contracts were not formed then any discussion on which laws apply is completely irrelevant. This is an obvious point, perhaps, but one which is often overlooked.

The basic principles of contract law are very well understood and can be applied readily to most traditional contracting scenarios to give answers to these questions. Unfortunately, applying these principles to e-commerce across electronic networks often poses more questions than answers because the application of standard contractual principles to electronic transactions can either provide unwelcome results, or in the worst case a series of mutually contradictory results.

One of the main requirements of contract law, at least from a commercial point of view, is that it should provide for some degree of certainty as to the relationship and obligations that lie between the contracting parties. The degree of certainty may not, and indeed need not, be absolute. What is required is sufficient certainty so that the risks and obligations are ascertainable and thus the parties can engage in a risk/benefit analysis and decide whether or not to proceed with their agreements.

In any contract the parties need to be able to determine several factors, whether these are implicit or explicit. These are rules of contract formation, choice of law,

---

[4] Agreements that are legally enforceable in a court of law as opposed to simply having moral force.

[5] It is of no use whatsoever to suggest that somewhere in the soup of electronic communications that make up a series of messages a contract was formed but it is not known exactly where or when; just that a contract was somehow formed. In order for a contract to exist the exact instant when it came into existence must be identifiable, and not merely be a vague and nebulous occurrence. It must be a definite and identifiable event.

choice of jurisdiction, terms and conditions, enforceability of the agreement, the identities of the contracting parties, whether the contract can bind third parties, and, perhaps most important of all, whether or not a contract has actually been formed.

Not all electronic transactions or communications result in the formation of a contract. Although a number of attempts have been made to classify electronic messages according to the different legal problems raised,[6] for our purposes it is sufficient to note three broad categories, set out below.

### 9.2.1.1 *The transmission of mere information*

Generally, the sender does not intend a message of this type to have legal consequences. Examples might range from the trivial ('Our Chairman will arrive on the 1520 flight') to the vital ('Maximum safe operating pressure: 130 p.s.i.').

The only legal problem arising from this type of message is the potential liability where the sender owes a duty to the recipient to take care to ensure that the information is correct, and as a result of his carelessness the recipient suffers loss.[7]

### 9.2.1.2 *The transmission of unilateral notices*

This type of communication will be intended to have a legal effect and will in most cases be made in performing an existing contract. Typical examples of this category might be invoices, which are often a prerequisite for payment, or a notice under a charterparty that a ship is ready to load, thus fixing the laytime and demurrage periods.

The sort of legal questions that this type of communication will raise are threefold:

(a) Is it effective as a notice? This will often depend on whether the notice is required to be in writing, or if a signature is needed.

(b) When (and possibly where) does it take effect, ie, is the sending or receipt the legally significant point?

(c) If its sending or contents are disputed, can these facts be proved?

One important unilateral notice is the Customs declaration. The penalties for false or non-declaration are severe, so the legal effect of such a notice is easily apparent. The required form and contents of Customs declarations are set out in national legislation, which will thus answer the question of whether it is possible to replace the paper documents with an electronic transmission. Over recent years many jurisdictions have introduced systems for electronic customs declarations which are designed to produce the necessary evidence and authentication for these documents.[8]

---

[6] eg, R Goode and E Bergsten identify five types of communication: (a) communications having no legal significance; (b) communications having legal significance; (c) communications operative to transfer ownership, control or contract rights; (d) communications required by law; and (e) communications requiring legal authority or licence. ('Legal Questions and Problems to be Overcome', in H Thomsen and B Wheble, *Trading with EDI: The Legal Issues* (IBC, 1989), pp 131–3.)

[7] *Hedley Byrne v Heller & Partners* [1963] 2 All ER 575.

[8] eg, the UK HM Customs & Excise CHIEF system at www.hmce.gov.uk/business/importing/chief/about.htm.

### 9.2.1.3  *Contract-formation messages*[9]

Where, for example, goods are ordered using an electronic message, the intended result will be the formation of a contract. In most cases such messages are part of a series including negotiation, ordering and acceptance. This type of communication raises the largest number of legal questions, in particular:

(a) Can this particular type of contract be formed using electronic messages? There may be requirements such as writing or signature, depending on the national legislation. For example, in the UK a contract of marine insurance must be embodied in a marine insurance policy signed by the insurer,[10] and in the United States a contract for the sale of goods for a price of $500 or more must be evidenced in writing and signed by the party against whom it is to be enforced.[11]

(b) When, and more important, where, was the agreement made? This may decide which national law is to apply to the contract or which court has jurisdiction, if there is no effective choice-of-law or forum clause.

(c) If the terms of the contract are later disputed, will it be possible to prove what was agreed?

Unless particular formalities such as writing are specifically required (see section 9.2.2.1 below), the general rule of English law and of most other jurisdictions is that a contract is formed when the parties reach an agreement on its terms, and this can be done orally, as our everyday experience in shops demonstrates. There is thus no theoretical objection to using electronic messages for this purpose. In English law, the process of formation is analysed into two stages: the offer, when one party sets out the terms on which he is prepared to contract, either in one document or by express or implied reference to a preceding course of negotiations; and the acceptance, when the other party agrees to these terms without attempting to amend them in any way. If both parties satisfactorily perform their side of the bargain there is no need to involve the law. However, there are three types of dispute which might arise, and which can be resolved by examining the formation process:

(a) One party believes a contract to have been concluded, but the other disputes it.

(b) Both agree that a contract has been formed, but disagree as to its terms.

(c) The parties disagree as to when and where the contract was formed.

In order to understand how English law will deal with these disputes, a number of basic principles of contract law must be borne in mind:

---

[9] See also A D Murray, 'Entering into Contracts Electronically: The Real WWW', in L Edwards and C Waelde (eds), *Law and the Internet: A Framework for Electronic Commerce*, 2nd edn (Hart Publishing, 2000).

[10] Marine Insurance Act 1906, ss 22–4.

[11] Uniform Commercial Code, s 201(1).

(a) Unless otherwise stated, an offer remains open for a reasonable time or until it is accepted or rejected by the other party.

(b) An offer may be withdrawn (unless there has been some payment to keep it open, ie, an option) at any time before it is accepted, but this withdrawal is only effective when it reaches the other party.[12]

(c) A counter offer, ie, the suggestion of different terms, brings the original offer to an end, and no contract is formed until the new offer is accepted.[13] If the parties engage in a so-called 'battle of the forms' where each purports to contract on its own terms, the set of terms that applies will be those contained in the last offer made before acceptance.[14]

(d) The contract is formed when, and where, acceptance takes place.

In applying these principles to electronic communications, it must also be noted that whilst offers and withdrawals of offers must actually be communicated to the other party[15] the rules governing acceptances are quite different. Where acceptance is made by some instantaneous means such as face-to-face communication or telephone, it too must actually reach the offeror. It has been held that telex communications are instantaneous, and thus contracts made by telex are made where the telex is received.[16] This rule is certain to apply to electronic communications where there is a direct link between the parties. The contract-formation law of other jurisdictions will differ in detail. All these issues are normally addressed in national laws, and most jurisdictions adopt roughly similar principles.

The position may, however, be different if the network across which the transmission is made stores the acceptance message for an appreciable period before it is delivered to the offeror. As common-law lawyers learn at an early stage, if an acceptance is made in written form the 'postal rule' applies. This provides that the acceptance takes place when the letter is posted, whether or not it ever arrives.[17] Might the postal rule apply to such an electronic message of acceptance?

There are two justifications suggested for the postal rule. The first is that it is an *ad hoc* method for solving what would otherwise be a more difficult question (for instance, if the rule were that the letter had to be received, would it be relevant that it arrived but was never read, or not read before withdrawal of the offer?). Even if this justification is the correct one, the dictum of Lord Brandon in *Brinkibon Ltd v Stahag Stahl und Stahlwarenhandelgesellschaft mbH* suggests that the postal rule might apply to electronic acceptances:

The cases on acceptance by letter and telegram constitute an exception to the general principle of the law of contract [on grounds of expediency] . . . That reason of commercial expediency

---

[12] *Byrne v Van Tienhoven* (1880) 5 CPD 344.

[13] *Hyde v Wrench* (1840) 3 Beav 334.

[14] *Butler Machine Tool Co v Ex-Cell-O Corporation* [1979] 1 WLR 401.

[15] *Byrne v Van Tienhoven* (1880) 5 CPD 344.

[16] *Entores Ltd v Miles Far East Corporation* [1955] 2 QB 327.

[17] *Adams v Lindsell* (1818) 1 B & Ald 681; *Household Fire Insurance v Grant* (1879) 4 Ex D 216.

applies to cases where there is bound to be a substantial interval between the time when the acceptance is sent and the time when it is received. In such cases the exception to the general rule is more convenient, and makes on the whole for greater fairness, than the rule itself would do.[18]

The second justification is that the offeror has impliedly agreed that the accepting party may entrust the transmission of his acceptance to an independent third party, the postal authorities, and that therefore the offeree has done all that the offeror requires for acceptance when he posts his letter. This too would suggest that acceptance takes place when the message is received by the system provider's computer. The clearest analogy to using a store-and-forward messaging system is with acceptance by telegram; it is necessary for the message actually to be communicated to the telegram service, normally by telephone (an instantaneous method of communication), but once it has been received by the service acceptance is complete.[19]

The postal rule is not unique to Anglo-American law; for example, in Spain the postal rule applies to acceptances in commercial transactions,[20] though in non-commercial transactions an acceptance is not effective until it is received.[21] Other jurisdictions apply the requirement of receipt to all types of contract.[22]

Where the postal rule applies, the author's opinion is that the time of acceptance is the time the electronic message was received by the network, and the place of acceptance will therefore be that node of the network which received the message. In most cases this is likely to be in the same jurisdiction as the acceptor, but not inevitably—it is easy to conceive of a Scottish company accepting an offer from a US company using a closed electronic-messaging system such as an EDI system, or indeed a private network based on an open electronic network such as the Internet,[23] where the message of acceptance is sent to a computer in England. The contract would be formed in England, and subject to agreement to the contrary might therefore be subject to English law, at least in respect of its formation. Fortunately, the English courts have accepted that it is permissible for the parties to stipulate what acts will constitute acceptance,[24] which suggests that it would be beneficial for e-commerce contracts to provide exactly when a message will be taken to have effect and which law is to govern the performance of the contract. Where the electronic transaction is subject to a different law, it will be necessary to assess whether, under that law, it is possible for the parties to agree what steps will lead to the formation of a valid contract and include an appropriate term to that effect in their contract. With

---

[18] [1982] 1 All ER 293, 300.
[19] *Re London & Northern Bank* [1900] 1 Ch 200.
[20] Spanish Commercial Code, art 54.
[21] Spanish Civil Code, art 1262(2).
[22] See, eg, Swiss Code of Obligations, art 35; Italian Civil Code, art 1335. The Italian Code adopts a further refinement, that it is sufficient for the acceptance to reach the offeror's premises provided he is then likely to receive it.
[23] eg, VPNs that operate across the Internet.
[24] *Holwell Securities Ltd v Hughes* [1974] 1 WLR 155.

regard to the EDI community there appears to be general agreement that an EDI message should not have operative effect until it is received.[25]

Within Europe, many of these uncertainties should be reduced as Directive 2000/31/EC on certain legal aspects of information society services, in particular electronic commerce, in the Internal Market ('the E-Commerce Directive') is implemented in national law.[26] Article 9(1) provides:

> Member States shall ensure that their legal system allows contracts to be concluded by electronic means. Member States shall in particular ensure that the legal requirements applicable to the contractual process neither create obstacles for the use of' electronic contracts nor result in such contracts being deprived of legal effectiveness and validity on account of their having been made by electronic means.

The Directive does not attempt to define the formation process, but article 10(1) requires the supplier to explain to the customer the steps which will give rise to a contract and make its terms available, while article 11(1) requires orders to be acknowledged and provides that both these communications are only effective when received.

### 9.2.2 Formalities in the Underlying Transaction

It has already been pointed out (see section 9.2.1.3 above) that certain types of contract require particular formalities to be observed if they are to be enforceable. The most common of these are that the contract must be made or evidenced in writing or in a document, and that it must be signed.

#### 9.2.2.1 Writing, documents and signatures

*General problems.* Unless there is legislation which specifically provides to the contrary,[27] 'writing' under English law requires the communication to be in some visible form.[28] However, if all that is required is a 'document'[29] then, unless this is also defined in the legislation or case law governing the transaction to require visible form, there seems no reason why it might not be produced electronically.[30] The laws of most other countries also require certain types of transaction to be made in writing and signed. This is often limited to sales of real property, but in Greece, for example, a wider range of commercial transactions require written and signed documents. France has a particular problem in that transactions carried out by persons other than

---

[25] UNCID Rules, art 7(a) (see further section 9.3.4 below).

[26] See, eg, UK Electronic Commerce (EC Directive) Regulations 2002, SI 2002/2013.

[27] eg, the Unidroit Convention on International Factoring 1988, art 1(4)(b), defines notice in writing to include 'any other telecommunication capable of being reproduced in tangible form'.

[28] Interpretation Act 1978, Sch 1.

[29] In civil proceedings this is defined as 'anything in which information of any description is recorded' (Civil Evidence Act 1995, s 13).

[30] See Goode and Bergsten (n 6 above), pp 136–8.

traders need written proof if their value exceeds 5,000 francs.[31] This presents a problem for the retail use of electronic messaging, but can also affect commercial use because professionals such as architects are not classified as traders.

In an attempt to deal with problems of formalities, it is worth including a provision , at least in B2B contracts which provides:

(a) That all communications between the parties are deemed to be in writing.

(b) That use of the prescribed authentication procedures is deemed to be the signature of the appropriate party.

Whether the first provision is legally effective must be open to doubt as most national laws are adamant that 'writing' demands visible marks on a physical carrier and it might therefore seem to be equivalent to providing that 'for the purposes of this contract, night shall be deemed to be day'. However, in the common-law jurisdictions at least, a provision of this type may raise an estoppel between the parties to the Interchange Agreement, and thus prevent either of them from denying the validity of an electronic transaction on the ground that the law requires the transaction to have been made in writing. This would be the case even though both parties know that under their law the electronic messages do *not* amount to writing.[32] It should be noted, though, that:

(a) The estoppel will not bind a third party, who will be able to plead the lack of writing as a defence and, as a corollary, will not be able to found his own action on the estoppel.

(b) The estoppel will not be effective if the result would be to declare valid a transaction which is in fact void according to the law for lack of formalities.[33] This will not be so, however, if the requirement for writing is imposed by the law solely to protect the parties to the transaction, as opposed to the public interest.[34]

By contrast, the second provision stands a good chance of being effective if national law does not specifically demand that signatures be in manuscript form. For example, because English law permits signatures to be typewritten or made via a stamp,[35] there seems no reason to insist on a handwritten signature. Attention should instead be focused on the purpose of the signature; to authenticate the message as originating

---

[31]  French Civil Code, art 1341.

[32]  'The full facts may be known to both parties; but if, even knowing those facts to the full, they are clearly enough shown to have assumed a different state of facts *as between themselves* for the purposes of a particular transaction, then their assumption will be treated, as between them, as true, in proceedings arising out of the transaction. The claim of the party raising the estoppel is, not that he believed the assumed version of the facts was true, but that he believed (and agreed) that it should be *treated as true*'; see G Spencer-Bower and A K Turner, *The Law Relating to Estoppel by Representation*, 3rd edn (Butterworths, 1977), p 160, citing *Newis v General Accident Fire & Life Assurance Corporation* (1910) 11 CLR 620, 636, per Isaacs J (High Court of Australia).

[33]  See, eg, *Swallow & Pearson v Middlesex County Council* [1953] 1 All ER 580.

[34]  Spencer, Bower and Turner (n 32 above), pp 142–4.

[35]  See, eg, *Chapman v Smethurst* [1909] 1 KB 927.

from the purported sender. If this is a correct statement of the function of a signature under English law[36] cryptography (see section 9.2.2.2 above) offers the possibility of producing digital signatures that are more difficult to forge than handwriting.[37]

*Digital signatures.*   The issue of authentication, and consequently the use of digital signatures, is vital for two reasons. Parties who wish to engage in e-commerce and enter into an electronic contract will not usually have any means of verifying the other's identity. Quite aside from the issue of establishing the validity of each other's purported identity to their mutual satisfaction the parties must have some way of authenticating or signing contracts in an electronic form as evidence of intent if nothing else. These two requirements are separate and need to be treated as such.

Parties can agree between themselves whether or not they will accept a data string[38] as evidence of intent. In effect they can themselves agree on the validity of an electronic signature between themselves. However their agreement will not bind a third party unless that third party agrees to be so bound.

Though the parties might agree between themselves to accept a digital signature, the signature itself may not necessarily prove to be acceptable before a court. The uncertainty on this point has so far proved to be a major stumbling block to the widespread use of digital signatures. In order to be effective parties must be able to sign documents electronically or digitally and to enforce these signatures before a court of law. The digital or electronic signatures must be as acceptable as hard copy signatures and accorded the same rights before a court of law.

In order to determine whether digital signatures may be used the situation regarding hard-copy signatures must be examined to determine whether it is possible to use digital versions. Unfortunately the situation regarding hard-copy signatures is not particularly clear. Though it is possible to define what a signature is in civil jurisdictions, common-law jurisdictions cannot do so. Instead they look more to the function of the signature for a particular class of document.[39]

Specifically the signatures must have validity before a court of law. As with ensuring the sufficiency of electronic data or electronic messages for contract formation, this is an area which the parties cannot deal with between themselves. Regulatory intervention is the most effective way of ensuring that the electronic form of a signature is held to be legally valid and so treated as a hard-copy equivalent.

---

[36] See *Goodman v J Eban Ltd* [1954] 1 QB 550; *London County Council v Vitamins, Ltd*; *London County Council v Agricultural Food Products Ltd* [1955] 2 QB 218; *Ringham v Hackett and Walmsley* (1980) 10 Legal Decisions Affecting Bankers 206; *Bartletts de Reya (A Firm) v Byrne, The Times*, 14 January 1983.

[37] Digital signatures are mathematical functions of the digital form of a message. In order to act effectively as a signature they must be producible only by the sender. In theory, all digital signatures are capable of forgery—what gives them their effectiveness is that it is computationally infeasible to do so.

[38] In other words a digital or electronic signature.

[39] A signature is only recognized as such if it fulfils the functions of a signature that are required by that document.

The starting point for most laws about electronic signature is article 7(1) of the UNCITRAL Model Law on Electronic Commerce 1996, which provides:

Where the law requires a signature of a person, that requirement is met in relation to a data message if:

(a) a method is used to identify that person and to indicate that person's approval of the information contained in the data message; and

(b) that method is as reliable as was appropriate for the purpose for which the data message was generated or communicated, in the light of all the circumstances, including any relevant agreement.

This text does not mandate any particular technological signature method. However, the current trend in laws and legislative proposals is to link the question of signature validity with certification of identity, and to introduce licensing schemes for certification authorities. This enables national law to recognize as valid ID certificates issued by a foreign certification authority by approving the relevant licensing scheme.

Over the next few years a global system of digital-signature law will largely have been put in place. Already there is legislation in Europe,[40] Singapore[41] and the US,[42] to name but a few of the jurisdictions which have introduced legislation. The general shape of the global digital-signature regime is already becoming clear:

(a) An important element is the establishment of a digital-signature infrastructure, in which bodies known as certification authorities take evidence of a person's identity (for example, by requiring production of a passport or identity card), and then issue an electronic ID certificate which links that person to his digital signature key. In many instances voluntary licensing schemes are introduced, and a digital signature which refers to an ID certificate issued by a licensed certification authority may be given greater legal weight.[43]

(b) The second part of the regime is the introduction of laws which define as valid[44]

---

[40] EU Directive 1999/93/EC on a Community framework for electronic signatures, OJ L13 p 12, 19 January 2000.

[41] Electronic Transactions Act 1998.

[42] See the Electronic Signatures in Global and National Commerce Act 2000, 15 USC 7001 (usually known as the E-Sign Act).

[43] See EU Directive 1999/93/EC on a Community framework for electronic signatures, OJ L13 p 12, 19 January 2000, arts 2 and 5.

[44] Note that the UK's Electronic Communications Act 2000 does not follow this trend. Although it is likely to result in a voluntary licensing scheme for certification authorities (see www.cst.gov.uk/cii/datasecurity/electronicsignatures/tscheme.shtml for details of the scheme project), it does not specifically validate resulting digital signatures. Instead, section 7(1) provides only that such a signature shall be 'be admissible in evidence in relation to any question as to the authenticity of the communication or data or as to the integrity of the communication or data'. This approach in practice produces the result that an electronic signature is legally equivalent to a handwritten signature because under English law a handwritten signature is merely an evidential method of authenticating a document; see C Reed, *Digital Information Law: Electronic Documents and Requirements of Form* (CCLS, 1996), ch. 5. However, the UK solution will be less satisfactory to digital signature users than that adopted in article 5(1) of Directive

any digital signature which is supported by an ID certificate issued by a qualifying certification authority. These laws may be technology-neutral, in the sense that they do not prescribe a particular technical standard which must be adopted but merely describe the requirements which a certificate and its issuing certification authority must meet. Some laws, however, mandate the use of particular technical standards.[45]

### 9.2.2.2 Record-keeping requirements

A user is likely to see little benefit from adopting e-commerce if the record-keeping requirements of its national law or the law of its trading partner force him to use paper documents in order to comply with the law. As a general rule, record-keeping laws are mandatory, and if they prohibit electronic record keeping there is little that can be done. However, if e-commerce is possible under a country's record-keeping laws, then in respect of EDI the Interchange Agreement should set out what records each party is to keep, and the information that each is to supply to the other, so as to enable both parties to keep their records in accordance with the law.

The accounting laws of Europe fall broadly into two types: those which permit, or at least do not prohibit, the keeping of accounts in electronic form; and those which require accounts to be maintained on paper. This split is, interestingly, largely geographical. The northern states tend to fall into the first category, while the southern states (with the exception of Spain) fall into the second.

Thus Denmark has accounting laws which specifically facilitate computerized record keeping, requiring only that the annual accounts should be in hard copy form,[46] and Ireland[47] and the UK[48] specifically permit computerized accounting. Belgium still retains some hard-copy requirements, but the trend is clearly towards permitting the use of electronic documents. This is not universal in the Northern European countries, however, as in some cases there is still a legacy of accounting or tax laws which require the production or receipt of paper (see below).

In the southern states, accounting laws generally require the books of account to be maintained on paper. France, stretching from the North Sea to the Mediterranean, is a hybrid case. Electronic accounts have been permitted since 1983,[49] but in the end need to be printed out to comply with the law. In Italy accounting records can probably be kept electronically, though this is an interpretation of the law which has

---

1999/93/EC, which in addition to making them admissible as evidence provides that certain types of certified signature shall 'satisfy the legal requirements of a signature in relation to data in electronic form in the same manner as a handwritten signature satisfies those requirements in relation to paper-based data'.

[45] eg, Utah Digital Signature Rules (r 154-10 of the Utah Commerce, Corporations and Commercial Code), r 301(4)(a); German Digital Signature Act (Signaturgesetz), s 14(4), German Digital Signature Ordinance (Signaturverordnung, made under the Digital Signature Act 1997, s 19, in force 1 November 1997), s 16(6).

[46] Danish Book-Keeping Act 1986 and Instruction No 598 of 1990.

[47] Irish Companies (Amendment) Act 1977, s 4.

[48] UK Companies Act 1985, s 723(1).

[49] French Decree of 29 November 1983, art 2(2).

not been tested in the courts, but it is clear that the information in those records will still need to be printed out in order to produce the compulsory hard-copy books.[50]

Greece was until recently the most extreme case, with very complicated and formal accounting requirements. Accounting software was subject to stringent regulation and software suppliers could be fined if they fail to comply with the law.[51] Computerization of accounting in Greece was at that time merely an automated method of producing the compulsory hard-copy books.

Most of the countries which permit accounts to be kept electronically do so without restriction, other than that the accounts must satisfy the company's auditors. However, German law contains stringent requirements to ensure that the accounting software prevents subsequent alteration, and in Belgium formal accounts must be kept in hard-copy form, though working accounts can be electronic.[52] Belgian law therefore contains special provisions which allow credit institutions to keep bank-account records, records of insurance policies, etc, in electronic form and prove them by producing copies.

The laws of some European states, however, have not been amended to permit modern forms of bookkeeping. The need to maintain printed books of account was restated in Italy in a Supreme Court decision,[53] and in Portugal a number of categories of obligatory accounts must be kept on paper.[54] Some categories of books must be sealed and authenticated by a government official before they can be used in the courts or government offices so as to comply with the Portuguese Stamp Tax Act.[55] However, the Portuguese Government appears to be attempting to interpret existing laws to permit electronic record keeping, although the compulsory categories of paper records still remain on the statute book. Even in Austria, which does not formally require accounting records to be kept in any particular form, the tax authorities can require printouts at any time and the annual accounts must be signed,[56] which implies a manuscript signature on paper and therefore hard-copy accounts. Article 11 of the Austrian VAT Act also requires invoices to be 'documents', which demands that they be in hard-copy format. However, the Ministry of Finance has ameliorated the harshness of this rule by permitting regular EDI users to produce summary invoices as hard copy for VAT purposes. The same will probably hold true for e-commerce providers in general.

UK legislation contains extensive requirements for writing and signatures,[57] though in general these apply to communications with governmental and administrative bodies rather than commercial communications. Section 8 of the Electronic Communications Act 2000 confers on ministers the power to repeal many of these provisions, and proposals for what should be repealed are now starting to appear. By summer 2003, nearly 20 Statutory Instruments had been passed reforming the law in

[50] Italian Civil Code, arts 2214 et seq.
[51] Greek Code of Fiscal Elements, arts 22–5.
[52] Belgian Act of 17 July 1975.
[53] Cass 16 November 1991 (Italy).
[54] Portuguese Commercial Law Act 1988, art 25.
[55] Portuguese Stamp Tax Act, arts 130, 195 and 196.
[56] Austrian Commercial Code, art 194.
[57] See, generally, Reed (n 44 above).

areas such as taxation,[58] intellectual property law,[59] and social security.[60] Completion of this process is likely to take several more years because each SI makes detailed changes to one or more pieces of legislation, rather than attempting global reform of the area.

### 9.2.3 Compliance with national laws

In theory there is no limit on the circumstances in which a jurisdiction might claim to apply its laws to the e-commerce activities of a supplier from a different jurisdiction, although practical enforcement of those laws against a foreign enterprise may be difficulty or impossible. However, governments usually attempt to limit the extraterritorial effect of their laws through the principle of comity, which requires that a state should not claim to apply its legislation to persons within another state unless it is reasonable to do so. The standard approach to maintaining comity is to apply a state's laws only to *activities* undertaken within the state, but determining the location where e-commerce activities take place is extremely difficult. Traditional tests for localization of commercial activities look for particular trigger events, the most common of which include:

(a) the place of delivery of products sold;
(b) the place where services were performed;
(c) the place where a purchaser took steps towards concluding a contract; and
(d) whether the supplier 'targeted' the jurisdiction in question.

All of these are largely metaphysical concepts where products and services are supplied online, or where products are advertised and contracts concluded via a website.

Increasingly, there is a recognition that attempts to localize e-commerce activities are inappropriate, and that some alternative basis for maintaining comity must be found. The most promising alternative seems to be that of accepting 'country of origin' regulation, coupled with an appropriate degree of harmonization or convergence of national laws.

The most striking example of country-of-origin regulation is found in articles 3 and 4 of Directive 2000/31/EC on electronic commerce, which provide:

Article 3

1. Each Member State shall ensure that the Information Society services provided by a service provider established on its territory comply with the national provisions applicable in the Member State in question which fall within the coordinated field.

---

[58] See eg Income and Corporation Taxes (Electronic Communications) Regulations 2003, SI 2003/282.
[59] See eg Patents Act 1977 (Electronic Communications) Order 2003, SI 2003/512.
[60] See eg Social Security (Electronic Communications) (Child Benefit) Order 2002.

2. Member States may not, for reasons falling within the coordinated field, restrict the freedom to provide Information Society services from another Member State . . .

Article 4

1. Member States shall ensure that the taking up and pursuit of the activity of an Information Society service provider may not be made subject to prior authorisation or any other requirement having equivalent effect . . .

A number of exceptions to this principle are set out in the Annex to the Directive, but its general effect can be expressed quite simply. An e-commerce business in one Member State is free to do business with residents of every other Member State provided that it complies with its own national laws, even if its activities would contravene the laws of the purchaser's Member State. Thus, for example, a UK e-commerce business cannot be subject to action for breach of Germany's Act Against Unfair Competition simply on the ground that its website is visible to German customers and it does business with German consumers.

This adoption of the country-of-origin principle is only possible because of the large degree of harmonization which has already taken place in fields such as consumer protection, and because the Directive's other provisions on commercial communications (articles 6 and 7) and the provision of information about the business (article 5) introduce common controls on the potentially controversial aspects of these activities. How far the principle will be adopted on a global scale depends very much on the degree to which the economic pressures exerted by e-commerce result in convergence of these aspects of the laws of other jurisdictions.

## 9.3 BUSINESS-TO-BUSINESS E-COMMERCE

Business-to-business e-commerce has, until recently, been undertaken solely via proprietary networks, and is usually referred to as Electronic Data Interchange ('EDI'). Open networks, and in particular the Internet, are increasingly becoming the communications medium of choice for business, and the term EDI is likely to fall gradually into disuse. This has not yet occurred, however, and so in this section the term EDI is used for convenience of expression.[61]

EDI is, at the simplest level, nothing more than a technology for exchanging information. One computer is linked to another and a stream of data is sent across the link. At this level, the only distinction from, say, a fax message is that the recipient can easily edit his copy.

Where EDI becomes interesting, both commercially and legally, is if the messages are structured in such a way that they can be processed automatically.[62]

---

[61] The replacement term has been settled upon as 'B2B [business-to-business] e-commerce'. Its equivalent for consumer transactions is 'B2C'.

[62] This is somewhat different to networking methods, such as the Internet where a large proportion of messages are meant to be processed by the human mind. However, the technologies exist that can easily

The most common use of such messages is to carry out trade, particularly international trade, and it is in this sense that the term EDI is most commonly used. This also gives rise to the alternative term 'paperless trading', which is particularly common in the United States.[63]

Structured EDI messages offer their users two potential benefits, benefits which can be of immense commercial value, for example:

(a) The abolition (or near abolition) of the physical, paper documents which previously effected the transaction. Estimates of the costs involved in producing and processing this paper range as high as 10 per cent of the value of the goods.

(b) The complete automation of the ordering/delivery/payment cycle.

### 9.3.1 Replacing paper

To take an example, suppose a motor manufacturer has a need to purchase parts from a supplier. In a paper-based system a human being examines the stock inventory, decides which parts are needed, and informs the purchasing department. The purchasing department issues an order to the supplier. Payment may need to be effected through a documentary credit, necessitating further communications between the manufacturer, one or more banks, and the supplier. Once the supplier has the parts ready to ship he must engage a carrier, thus generating further documentation which must be processed by all the parties involved in the transaction.

The EDI ideal is quite different. Here the manufacturer's stock-control system automatically generates the order when stocks of any part are low. The order is sent without any human intervention to the supplier's computer, which accepts the order and commences manufacture. The payment mechanism is set up in a similar way, again with little or no human intervention, as is the contract of carriage. To perform the contract the only physical movement is that of the goods from the supplier's premises to those of the manufacturer. All the messages which would have been placed on paper and circulated along the chain of banks to the manufacturer are replaced by structured EDI messages which are processed automatically, the relevant portions being copied to accounting and other computer systems.

This technology exists and is in use, though not in quite such a perfect form as the example above. The benefits it brings are increasing the pressure for its adoption, as large customers force their suppliers to adopt EDI. The time saved in the ordering process makes 'just in time' ordering possible, cutting stocks held to the bare minimum. It also offers the flexibility of production seen in the Japanese motor industry where a production line can be switched from one model to another in a very short

---

be put into use to allow messages to be structured in such a way that they too can be processed automatically. Not only is this increasingly being used by interactive sites on the Internet but it is possible to create a virtual private network across the Internet that behaves in a manner similar to EDI.

[63] See, eg, B Wright, *The Law of Electronic Commerce* (Little, Brown & Co, 1991).

space of time. The manpower savings are also potentially large, as EDI prevents the redundant manual processing of information in stock control, purchasing and accounts departments.

To achieve this aim, the legal relationships set up by lawyers must make it possible to carry out the transaction without needing to generate any paper. Whether this is possible or not will depend very much on the legal barriers which are posed by the national laws involved, and whether those barriers can be surmounted by provisions in the Interchange Agreement (see section 9.3.4 below). If the provisions of national laws make it necessary to document discrete parts of the transaction on paper or, worst of all, require duplication of, for example, invoices by generating them as both EDI messages and hard copy, the client will need to be advised so that he can decide whether the use of EDI for that transaction is appropriate.

### 9.3.2 EDI and networks

Whilst it is possible to set up dedicated EDI links with each of one's trading partners, this rarely makes sense in practice. The volume of communications is likely to be too small to be economical. For this reason most EDI users communicate via a Value Added Network Service ('VAN'), although as mentioned above the Internet is increasingly favoured as a communications technology. Most of the issues discussed in this section do not apply to Internet communications because there is no identifiable network provider who can be made responsible for elements of the communications process.

In the VAN model the user's computer system generates the messages to the network, rather than directly to the intended recipient. The network's computer systems ensure, using the address information which is part of the message structure,[64] that the message is delivered to the addressee's computer. The delivery may be near-instantaneous or may take several hours, depending on the number of time zones which separate the parties and the level of service contracted for. In most cases there will be an element of 'store and forward' which, as we have seen, raises potential problems when forming contracts using EDI.

Additionally, the VAN may not be the only network involved, as the technology exists for a sender using one VAN to communicate with an addressee using another via a 'gateway' between the two VANs. The address segment of the message contains the information required to route the message to the gateway, and thence to the addressee across his own VAN. Linking VANs in this way raises interesting liability questions, as the nature of the legal relationship between the sender and the addressee's VAN is unclear.

---

[64] See I Walden (ed), *EDI and the Law* (Blenheim OnLine, 1989), Appendix E, for examples of message structures.

### 9.3.3 Network agreements

The legal issues raised by EDI[65] fall into two basic categories; those that arise between the user and the network provider(s) and those that arise between users themselves. The relationship between a user and the VAN to which he connects is primarily contractual. Sa'id Mosteshar identifies four main responsibilities of the network provider:

(a)  Conveyance of the message in the correct format and protocol.
(b)  Safeguarding against corruption of the message.
(c)  Securing that the message is conveyed to the recipient.
(d)  Preserving the confidentiality and security of the message.[66]

The method by which these responsibilities are to be carried out will largely be covered by the 'User Handbook', the technical manual for connecting to the VAN. It is most likely that the contract between user and network provider will contain an obligation that the user's communications with other users of the network should comply with the technical and operational requirements of the User Handbook, but even if this is not expressly stated it is likely that the users will be contractually bound to each other under the principle in *Clarke v Dunraven*.[67] The effect of the agreement will be to create a contract between each user and all the other users, either because entering into the agreement amounts to a standing offer to future users to be bound which is accepted by joining the system, or perhaps more logically, by impliedly giving the system provider authority to contract as agent on behalf of the user.

The contract may also make express provision for the level and quality of service to be provided, though in most cases VAN operators will seek to exclude much, if not all, of their liability for breach of these obligations.[68] These exclusions will be subject to the Unfair Contract Terms Act 1977 ('UCTA 1977'), and may also be limited in scope by the terms of the network operator's telecommunications licence.

The VAN operator's contractual liability to the user will primarily be based on section 13 of the Supply of Goods and Services Act 1982 ('SGSA 1982') which will imply into the contract an obligation to take reasonable care in supplying the service contracted for. This obligation may be breached in a number of ways:

---

[65] These problems have been examined on an international scale in TEDIS (Trade Electronic Data Interchange Systems), discussed further at section 9.3.4 below; see *The Legal Position of the Member States with respect to Electronic Data Interchange* (EC Commission, 1991) and subsequent publications under the project.

[66] S Mosteshar, 'Liability Issues of EDI', in Walden (n 64 above), p 50.

[67] [1897] AC 59.

[68] One of the few exceptions to this practice is SWIFT (the Society for Worldwide Interbank Financial Telecommunications). SWIFT is a closed network for electronic funds transfer, used only by the banks which own it or organizations sponsored by a member. SWIFT limits its liability to 3,000 million Belgian francs per loss or series of losses caused by SWIFT's negligence, error or omission; see S Petre, 'Network Providers' (1990) 7 CL&P 8, note 18.

(a) if the system goes down;

(b) if a message is not transmitted;

(c) if it is sent to the wrong person;

(d) if it is intercepted or copied by an unauthorized person; or

(e) if it is garbled in transmission.

In each case, however, the system provider will only be liable for breach of the implied term if the problem was caused by a lack of care. Such negligence might take one of two forms: a failure to be sufficiently careful in selecting the hardware and software which comprises the system, or a failure to take sufficient care in operating the system. Provided the hardware and software are from reputable sources, then unless the system provider is also the designer of the hardware or software a defect in either will not normally render him in breach.

Although there is no doubt that this term will be implied into the contract between the system provider and each user, it is less clear that the users are providing services to each other. It is probable that their contractual liability to other users, in the absence of a formal interchange agreement, is limited to observing the terms of their agreement with the VAN operator.

### 9.3.4 Interchange agreements

The purpose of an interchange agreement is to set out the terms on which the communicating parties agree to undertake EDI.[69] It is important to make a distinction between the interchange agreement, which deals only with the details of the communication process, and the underlying commercial transaction such as a sale of goods, which is entered into and performed using that communication process. Although in the United States it is not uncommon for both to be dealt with in the same agreement, this practice arose from the way EDI has developed there, through large customers forcing their suppliers to trade with them via EDI. In Europe the practice has been rather different. Industry groupings such as ODETTE[70] or CIDX[71] have developed protocols for EDI, and this has focused attention on the communications aspect of EDI rather than the underlying transaction. This separation makes theoretical and practical sense, as EDI can be used for many different types of underlying transactions without changing the agreement on interchange.

As the purpose of the interchange agreement is to bind the parties to a particular, structured form of communication, there are a number of issues which it must address. Because different industry sectors will inevitably have different specific

---

[69] The interchange and user agreements inherent in EDI set this system apart from the general use of the Internet where agreements to cover the use and provision of networking services cover only the access from the user to the provider's network and usually warrant nothing further. With EDI the provider can guarantee a level of service and messaging reliability. Without the use of VPN technologies, ISPs can only warrant the performance of their own systems and not those of other ISPs.

[70] The motor industry—www.odette.org.

[71] The chemicals industry—www.cidx.org.

requirements, no universal standard is achievable. However, a number of organizations have produced model interchange agreements which provide a useful starting point for negotiations, and on an international level the International Chamber of Commerce has produced the Uniform Rules of Conduct for Interchange of Trade Data by Teletransmission ('the UNCID Rules'). Within the EC, DG XIII initiated the TEDIS[72] project which examined the technical and legal issues involved in EDI. As part of its work, TEDIS produced a model interchange agreement whose suggested provisions reflect best practice among the EDI community.[73]

A detailed examination of interchange agreements is beyond the scope of this chapter[74] but the main areas which such an agreement should cover are:

(a) A requirement to adhere to the technical procedures of the chosen communication link. This is normally done by reference to the VAN User Handbook. Where the Internet is used, these matters will need to be dealt with in detail in the Interchange Agreement rather than being left to a third-party document.

(b) Agreement on a particular protocol for the message format, for example, an EDIFACT message.

(c) Agreement on acknowledgements of messages and any confirmations of their content that are required.

(d) Agreement on which of the parties takes responsibility for the completeness and accuracy of the communication. As we have already seen, it is likely that the parties will wish the received version of a message to be operative, rather than that transmitted. For this reason it will be important that the technical safeguards listed in (a) to (c) above are incorporated to ensure that transmission takes place and that errors are immediately detected. Whilst message corruption is almost certain not to produce an apparently sensible message with an entirely different meaning, it is quite conceivable, for example, that a '£' symbol could be replaced by a '$' symbol, or that an entire block of text could be lost. As, in general, it is the received version which is operative, the onus to ensure correct transmission must be on the sender.

(e) Agreement on security and confidentiality.

(f) Agreement on data logs and the storage of messages.

(g) Agreement on which country's law is to apply to the communications process.

---

[72] Council Decision 87/499/EEC of 5 October 1987 introducing a communications network Community programme on trade electronic data interchange systems ('TEDIS'), OJ L285/35, 8 October 1987.

[73] Recommendation 94/820/EC of 19 October 1994 relating to the legal aspects of electronic data interchange, OJ L338, 1994.

[74] For more detail, see Walden (n 64 above), chs 5, 6.

## 9.4 BUSINESS-TO-CONSUMER E-COMMERCE

Commercial e-commerce, where both parties to any contract are businesses, is the easiest situation to deal with as the parties can in general agree to what they wish with few constraints. In general where two or more commercial entities enter into agreements at arm's length then they can usually agree to whatever terms they so wish. The position can differ considerably with other types of contract, notably where one of the parties acts as a consumer.

Consumer-protection legislation, such as that commonly found within EU Member States,[75] often imposes limits on the terms and conditions that may be excluded or varied and these cannot be overridden by agreement. Any terms which attempt to avoid the legislative provisions are automatically void. The position is somewhat different within the United States where it is possible, in some circumstances, to contract out of the provisions provided certain formalities are met.

In its early versions the Distance Selling Directive[76] presented several problems for businesses that wished to sell goods or supply services to consumers, the problems principally being in the requirement to provide prior information about the contract to the consumer in written form. This would automatically negate some of the benefits of contracting over the Internet, namely the elimination or reduction of large amounts of paperwork. This has now changed to a requirement to provide the required information in any way appropriate to the means of communication,[77] a vast improvement on the previous versions. The Directive also gives consumers the right, in certain circumstances, to withdraw from the contract within seven days from the date of performance of the contract[78] and requires that consumers receive written confirmation[79] of the information previously supplied prior to the contract[80] itself.

---

[75] See the Council Directive 93/13/EEC of 5 April 1993 on unfair terms in consumer contracts, OJ L95, 21 April 1993. This is implemented within the UK by the Unfair Terms in Consumer Contracts Regulations 1994, SI 1994/3159.

[76] Directive 97/7/EC of the European Parliament and of the Council of 20 May 1997 on the protection of consumers in respect of distance contracts.

[77] Article 4(2).

[78] Article 6(1). The date from which the seven-day period runs depends on whether the contract is for the sale of goods or the supply of services.

[79] Article 5(1).

[80] Articles 5 and 6 still pose problems for some Internet contracts. Where the contract is clearly for the sale of goods then no real issues arise as the information required by article 5 can be supplied on delivery of the goods themselves under article 6(1). Where the contract is clearly for the supply of services then again no issues arise. Indeed article 5(2) removes the requirement for written confirmation where the 'service is to be performed through the use of a means of distant communication'. However, the situation is not so clear-cut when it comes to supplying information, computer code or software over the Internet. The Directive does not explicitly define these as either services or goods, though it does make mention of what could be regarded as shrink-wrapped software, that is software packages bought off the shelf or by mail order or whatever, in article 6(3). The issue here is that there is some confusion as to the status of computer code or software. Software or computer code which is stored and supplied on a physical medium such as a tape or disk would most probably be treated as a good, in the same way as a music tape,

In order to determine whether or not overriding terms and conditions apply the law and jurisdiction of the contract must be established, as the rules of that jurisdiction will determine the question. This holds even if the parties have attempted to predetermine the jurisdiction and governing law. Such an agreement can only be valid if the choice is not void within the applicable law of the contract itself.[81] In reality, however, this will rarely pose a problem as in general the law of a contract for a consumer transaction will be held to be that of the consumer.[82]

Consumer regulation is an all-pervasive topic which has several aims. Contrary to many views, commercial concerns often welcome some degree of consumer protection. Not only does it give consumers the confidence to interact and enter into commercial transactions with the commercial entities, but it also informs the commercial entities of what they can do and how they can act.

One view of the regulatory framework for consumer protection is that its purpose is to provide some redress in the balance of bargaining power between the consumer and a commercial entity. The idea is simply that the consumer should not be over-reached by the commercial entity[83] and to this end commercial entities are often prevented from excluding certain rights and warranties that are granted to the consumer. Another object is to provide a competitive regulatory framework within which the consumers and commercial entities are free to interact as they wish. So long as neither breaches the framework, the parties will have freedom to operate within that framework to contract for that which each party wants.

The framework can also be viewed as a form of protection for commercial entities. By operating within the consumer-protection framework, the liabilities of the commercial entities for faults or flaws in their services or goods may be capped or controlled.

The general perception of e-commerce among consumers is that it poses a greater degree of risk than other more standard forms of commerce. Measures for consumer protection could help to allay these fears and encourage the take up of e-commerce. This would bring benefits to all actors in the activity, to the economic development of the jurisdiction, to the economic activity of the commercial entities, and to a greater degree of freedom of choice for the consumer.

---

record or CD is treated as a good. The value is in the intangible information contained in the medium and not the medium itself. However, the confusion arises when looking at information, computer code or software that is supplied electronically over the Internet as a stream of bits. If this is held as a good, then article 5(1) might present a problem, as the benefits sought by transacting over the Internet, of paperless transactions, is reduced. If this is held as a service then article 5(1) may not apply through article 5(2). Some EC competition-law cases seem to point to the electronic supply of computer code or software as being a supply of a service, as does EU VAT law, but the courts have yet to decide the matter.

[81] As an example in the UK, see UCTA 1977, s 27(2).

[82] For instance, see the Rome Convention on the Law Applicable to Contractual Obligations, codified in OJ C27, 26 January 1998 p 34, art 5.

[83] The Unfair Terms in Consumer Contracts Regulations 1994, SI 1994/3159, go further than UCTA 1977 in that it applies to any contractual term in a consumer contract rather than simply to exclusion clauses. Regulation 3 ('Terms to which these Regulations apply') makes this quite clear.

Consumer protection need not be seen as a burden. Indeed in some jurisdictions where consumer protection is quite weak commercial entities have taken it upon themselves to offer consumers extra rights or warranties over those of competitors. The effect has been to establish a quality or superior feel to the product or service. The service becomes regarded as superior and so attracts more customers. A similar result could easily occur in e-commerce.[84]

Paradoxically, e-commerce will most likely be an area where under-regulation could have as detrimental an effect as over-regulation for a jurisdiction. If a jurisdiction were to provide no consumer protection, or a degree of consumer protection which was perceived as being inadequate, then consumers and users might not wish to enter into transactions with commercial entities situated in that jurisdiction. Commercial entities would then be faced with three possibilities. They could remain in the jurisdiction and lobby for greater consumer protection; they could themselves offer a degree of consumer protection as a selling point to attract consumers; or they could move to a jurisdiction which offered a greater degree of consumer protection. Due to the current perception of consumers that e-commerce bears a greater degree of risk than other forms of commerce, commercial entities would most probably move to a jurisdiction with stronger consumer protection simply in order to allay those fears. The option of simply offering a degree of protection would not be realistically available, as this would only be enforceable by contract if at all.

Similar issues would face commercial entities which faced overbearing regulations for consumer protection. Should the regulations prove to be too burdensome the commercial entity can easily move to another jurisdiction to conduct trade.

## 9.5 REGULATORY ISSUES

### 9.5.1 Payment

All the major banks now offer electronic banking products to their corporate customers, which allow accounts to be manipulated from a PC at the customer's premises. These permit payments to be made through:

(a) BACS, which operates a three-day clearing cycle;

(b) CHAPS, for same day inter-UK payment; and

(c) SWIFT for same-day (or near same-day, depending on time differences) payment internationally.

These products can be used for making payments arising out of electronic transactions, but a number of points need to be noted:

---

[84] This might occur through self-regulatory schemes which audit the e-commerce website and operations for consumer-protection compliance. An early example was the UK *Which?* Webtrader certification scheme, now closed—see www.which.net/webtrader/index.html.

(a) It was initially difficult to link an electronic networking system, such as EDI or an Internet-based system, with the electronic banking product, the banks generally insisted in their terms and conditions that the electronic banking service could only be accessed using the software provided by the bank. The reasons for this were:

(i)   to preserve the integrity of the banks' own systems, using the inbuilt security features of the software; and

(ii)  to ensure that the bank did not make payments following unauthorized instructions apparently emanating from a customer for which it would be liable to the customer—again, this is linked to the security and authentication features of the software.

In recent years, however, software which enables these linkages has become available. It is essential that the account and software licence terms are coordinated so that the allocation of risk between business, bank, and software provider is clear and explicit.

(b) Electronic payments are normally irrevocable. So far as traditional payment methods such as cheques are concerned, it is clear that the bank makes payment as its customer's agent, and therefore its authority as agent to pay can be withdrawn at any time until the payment is made.[85] However, certain types of paper payment, in particular the use of cheques with a cheque card, are not capable of countermand by the customer. The reason for this is the agreement by the customer, as part of the terms and conditions for the issue of the card, that he will not countermand cheques which are guaranteed with that card. There is some doubt whether this stipulation does in fact prevent countermand of the cheque, but whether it does or not the effect so far as the customer is concerned is the same.[86] It is therefore clear that if the bank includes in its contract with the customer an obligation not to countermand electronic payments, that obligation will be in practice effective to prevent the customer stopping payment. Such an obligation is likely to be found in the terms and conditions of all electronic banking products. Even if there is no express agreement that the payment may not be countermanded, the customer would have to give actual notice to the bank that it is to stop payment,[87] before the payment is made and almost certainly at a reasonable time before payment so as to give the bank the opportunity

---

[85] Bills of Exchange Act 1882, s 75, codifying the pre-existing common law; see, eg, *Williams v Everett* (1811) 14 East 582; *Warlow v Harrison* (1859) 1 E&E 309.

[86] If the customer is not able to countermand the cheque, the cheque will be paid and the bank will be entitled to debit his account. If he is entitled to countermand the cheque, he will be in breach of his contract with the bank and thus liable to pay damages. As the bank, by issuing the card to the customer, makes a unilateral contract with payees who accept the cheque card as guarantee (*Carlill v Carbolic Smoke Ball Co* [1893] 1 QB 256), it will be contractually obliged to pay those people. The loss it suffers by reason of the customer's breach of the obligation not to countermand is therefore the amount it is forced to pay out, ie, the value of the cheque.

[87] *Curtice v London City and Midland Bank Ltd* [1908] 1 KB 293.

to process the countermand.[88] It seems clear from the leading cases on revocation of payments[89] that payment cannot be countermanded once the banks become irrevocably committed to each other to process the transfer through the clearing system. The time at which this occurs will depend very much on the method of payment selected by the customer. As a general rule, both CHAPS and SWIFT messages are irrevocable once confirmed by the recipient, but BACS messages may be revoked until part way through the second day of the clearing cycle.

(c) The effect of an electronic payment in discharging the underlying debt may be rather different from its paper analogy. For example, although the receipt of a cheque by the creditor is a conditional discharge of the debt, the mere issue of a payment instruction by the payer does not as a general rule discharge the obligation. The essence of payment is that the funds should be available to the recipient for his unfettered use. If for some reason of national law or banking practice the money is not available to the creditor,[90] the fact that it has been transferred to his bank will not amount to payment, and thus not discharge the debt.[91]

Whether any particular form of payment is conditional or unconditional depends on the terms of the contract under which payment is due, and in general will need to be inferred from the surrounding circumstances. In *Re Charge Card Services Ltd*[92] Charge Card Services operated a credit-card scheme, 'Fuel Card', for the purchase of petrol and other motor supplies from garages. On the company's liquidation the question arose as to whether the use of the card discharged the user's liability to pay the garage, so that the garages were left to prove in the liquidation, or whether it was conditional payment so that on the liquidation of the company the condition was not fulfilled and the garages' rights to payment from the users revived. The court held that because the card was generally used to pay for small purchases where the supplier and customer were not known to each other, and there was no obligation on the customer to supply his address, the intention of the contract between garage and card user was that use of the card would amount to complete payment:

[T]he supplier and customer have for their mutual convenience each previously arranged to open an account with the same company, and agree that any account between themselves may, if the customer wishes, be settled by crediting the supplier's and debiting the customer's account with that company . . . [T]he customer must be discharged, at the latest, when the supplier's account with the company is credited, not when the supplier is paid.[93]

[88] G A Penn, A M Shea and A Arora, *Banking Law* (Sweet & Maxwell, 1987), vol I, para 6.26.

[89] See *Momm v Barclays Bank International Ltd* [1976] 3 All ER 588; *Delbrueck and Co v Manufacturers Hanover Trust Co* (1979) 609 F 2d 1047.

[90] See, eg, *The Chikuma* [1981] 1 All ER 652 where, through the peculiar provisions of Italian law, money transferred to the recipient's account was only available to him in the first instance on payment of interest to the bank. The court held that this did not amount to payment of the obligation.

[91] See R Goode, *Payment Obligations in Commercial and Financial Transactions* (Sweet & Maxwell and Centre for Commercial Law Studies, 1983), pp 11–19.

[92] [1986] 3 All ER 289.

[93] Ibid, 304, per Millett J.

The question which therefore needs to be answered, which can only be done by interpretation of the agreement between creditor and debtor for electronic payment, is whether the creditor has agreed to accept some third party's contractual obligation as satisfaction of the debt, or whether the agreement requires the funds actually to become available to the creditor. This point can be important because the effect of an electronic payment message sent from one bank to another is that:

(i)   the message does not normally transfer any funds as between the banks *per se*;

(ii)  instead, the message gives rise to a contractual obligation on the sending bank to clear that payment through the central bank (for example, the Bank of England) at some later time (the close of business for CHAPS transfer, the close of the clearing cycle for BACS transfers).

If the proper interpretation of the agreement between creditor and debtor is that creditor has agreed that receipt of a payment message by his bank amounts to payment, he has effectively agreed to the substitution of the sending bank's obligation for that of the debtor, so that the debt is discharged.

This can be important in a transaction where late payment gives rise to legal rights, such as the right to bring a charterparty to an end, as payment would have been made perhaps some days before the funds actually became available to the creditor. This occurred in *Mardorf Peach & Co Ltd v Attica Sea Carriers Corporation of Liberia*[94] where the Court of Appeal held that payment was complete when the debtor's bank's payment order (which the arbitrator found to be equivalent to payment in cash) was received by the creditor's bank. Here, the obligation to pay was expressed to be by payment into the payee's account. The case illustrates that the agreement between debtor and creditor as to the mode of payment is definitive; if the payee agrees that payment to his agent (ie, his bank) will suffice, payment will be complete when the agent receives the funds.

(d) Current systems for the electronic transfer of funds have no method of ensuring that payment is made only against the security of documents of title. Electronic payments are simply internal accounting exercises on the computers involved, and until dematerialized bills of lading and other documents of title are devised, no electronic equivalent of the letter of credit is possible.[95]

Business customers will be able to use the electronic banking products discussed above to make payment for electronic transactions, but it is still not common for consumer customers to manage their bank accounts in this way. An e-commerce supplier which wishes to receive electronic payment from its consumer customers will therefore need to use some third-party service, such as a credit-card provider. It is clearly possible to accept credit-card payments using any electronic networking service, or even using the Internet, as all that is required is for the

---

[94] [1976] 2 All ER 249, 255.     [95] See Reed (n 44 above), ch 8.

purchaser to transmit his card number and expiry date. This is already common practice when purchasing by telephone. However, because electronic messages are transmitted by copying them to all the computers in the chain of transmission, electronic credit-card payments present major security risks to the card holder. Visa and Mastercard have for some time been working on systems which are intended to reduce these risks. As an alternative, payment in digital cash[96] was much heralded during the late 1990s as the way forward in providing an effective way of receiving payment from consumers. As of 2003, however, digital cash appears largely to have failed to gain acceptance by consumers, and many of the most high-profile projects have entered receivership. At the time of writing, consumer e-commerce payments are still predominantly made using traditional credit and debit cards.

### 9.5.2 Advertising and promotion

Advertising regulations present a great problem to entities involved in offering commercial services across the Internet or some other public electronic network. The issue does not really occur with EDI as the purpose of EDI is to transport and process electronic messages according to a predetermined agreement and for a predetermined process. By contrast, the Internet is simply a vast communications medium that is available to the public. EDI tends to be private to a small and defined user group and EDI messages are not made available to the public.

Almost every jurisdiction has advertising regulations of some form which aim to control not only the content of the material that is published in the form of an advertisement, but also the subject matter that may be advertised. These controls can vary, from requiring the material to be presented in the national language through to requiring certain information to be presented in a certain form. The penalty for breaching the controls can vary from a civil offence to a serious crime. Except where these controls originate from an international forum, they invariably apply only to the relevant jurisdiction.

By placing a webpage containing an advertisement on the Internet a commercial entity is effectively advertising across the globe. As such it will almost certainly be in breach of an advertising regulation in a jurisdiction somewhere on the planet irrespective of whether or not it complies with the regulations of the jurisdiction within which the advertisement was placed on the Internet. As a consequence it may well be held to be in breach of various advertising regulations in differing jurisdictions simply because users in that jurisdiction may access the page. Two particular areas of advertising will cause regulators a great deal of concern.

---

[96] See C Reed and L Davies, *Digital Cash: The Legal Implications* (Centre for Commercial Law Studies, 1995), published under the Information Technology Law Unit's Internet Law Research Project; L Edgar, 'Electronic Payment Systems', section 7.1, in J Hornle and I Walden (eds), *Ecommerce Law and Practice in Europe* (Woodhead, 2000).

### 9.5.2.1 *Financial advertising*

Regulations which purport to control financial advertising can be very stringent,[97] and incorrect information published in an advertisement will result in a breach of them. One of the major attractions of the Internet is the ease with which users can offer financial services to other users wherever they are located. Most users can pay for these services by using credit cards, bank transfers and the like, without having any real regard to their actual physical location.[98] Though this availability is obviously a great leap in terms of competition within the markets for financial services, regulators of financial services may have great cause for concern. Regulations to control financial advertising are not designed to keep the advertising of such services to a minimum so much as to protect investors from fraud and malpractice and to prevent them from being mislead or exposed to undue risk without their knowledge.

Some investors are highly informed about financial markets and are quite able to make decisions for themselves regarding the risks and pitfalls of investment opportunities, and consequently need little regulatory protection. Most investors, however, are not that sophisticated. One of the problems of financial advertising on the Internet is that in general it does not target specific investors but rather is open to all who access it. It targets all potential investors. Regulators will thus have a wholly valid interest in attempting to regulate financial advertising to ensure that the unsophisticated investor is protected or at least warned of the dangers inherent in unknown or poorly understood financial products and services.

Within the UK the Financial Services Authority takes the pragmatic and realistic view that the Internet is simply a means of communication. Consequently this has the immediate effect of bringing within its remit any activity controlled by the Financial Services and Markets Act 2000 which is carried out over the Internet. Indeed the Authority holds that the provisions of the Act apply equally to the Internet as they do to other forms of communication.[99] In the main this causes few problems and could be seen as an enlightened position although it partly comes about by accident due to the wide drafting adopted within certain definitions of the Act itself. The result is that the financial regulations, and in particular the securities laws and regulations, automatically apply to the Internet.

Were this to be the only issue arising from the view expressed by the Financial Services Authority, this would be all that there is to analyse the regime within the UK aside from a description of that regime itself. Fortunately, or unfortunately as the case may be, the use of the Internet in the area of financial services, and securities in

---

[97] See the Financial Services and Markets Act 2000, ss 19 and 21.

[98] The limitations are not so much to do with the physical location of the users as to do with the ease with which the users can pay for the services. Providing that they can make payment in the required form or currency, users may effectively purchase products from wherever they choose. Whether or not they will incur tax or other liabilities is besides the point.

[99] See 'Carrying on Investment Business over the Internet' and 'Treatment of Material on Overseas Internet World Wide Web Sites Accessible in the UK but not Intended for Investors in the UK', Guidance 2/98, both available from www.fsa.gov.uk.

particular, raises issues which pose difficult problems for the Financial Services Authority.

The Financial Services and Markets Act 2000, which replaced the Financial Services Act 1986, was drafted partly with the Internet in mind, however, the Internet itself is not explicitly regulated within the new Act. Instead the aim was to draft the Act in such a manner that its provisions remained as far as possible technologically neutral in order to 'future proof' them against new technical developments, both in terms of services and the underlying technologies irrespective of how these services are offered. It is in providing for this flexibility that the specific nature of the Internet was taken into account when the Act was drafted.

The Act itself aims to build upon and extend the regime that currently exists under the Financial Services Act 1986. This regime covers most, if not all, of the activities concerning securities over the Internet through the accident of wide drafting rather than by design. One consequence of this is the wide jurisdiction which exists under the present regime and which proves somewhat problematical.

### 9.5.2.2 *Medical advertising*

As with other forms of commercial activity, so too for pharmaceutical and biotechnology companies, the Internet presents an attractive medium to attempt to circumvent the standard restrictions that currently exist within different jurisdictions and advertise directly to the consumer.[100] The rules differ quite widely between jurisdictions as different regulators take differing views on what should and should not be allowed. Some regulators simply monitor and police the statements and claims made concerning authorized medical products and treatments, whilst others strictly prevent any publication or dissemination of information to consumers about such products in all but the most limited cases.

Within the UK the restrictions and controls on advertising medicines are particularly stringent.[101] Quite aside from the general controls placed on advertising medicines to the medical profession,[102] specific advertising to the general public is strictly controlled or, more usually, absolutely prohibited.[103] The regulations are

---

[100] A recent attempt was made by a Canadian biotechnology company to use the services of a United States agency to spam ('to spam' is to send unsolicited commercial e-mail or unsolicited news data) thousands of users on the Internet using user lists obtained from ISPs. They attempted to do this using a mail server in the UK. The posting of the messages within the UK fell foul of the Medicines Act 1968.

[101] Medicines Act 1968, s 92.

[102] Ibid, s 95, grants Ministers the appropriate powers to introduce regulations to prohibit the advertising of medicines. It is a criminal offence to breach the regulations promulgated under this section.

[103] See the Medicines (Advertising of Medicinal Products) Regulations 1975, SI 1975/298; the Medicines (Advertising of Medicinal Products) (No 2) Regulations 1975, SI 1975/1326, as amended by the Medicines (Contact Lens Fluids and Other Substances) (Advertising and Miscellaneous Amendments) Regulations 1979, SI 1979/1760; the Medicines (Labelling and Advertising to the Public) Regulations 1978, SI 1978/41, as amended by the Medicines (Advertising) Regulations 1994, SI 1994/1932; and the Medicines for Human Use (Marketing Authorisations etc) Regulations 1994, SI 1994/3144. Aside from controlling the wording and descriptions which can be applied to various medicines the regulations also strictly prohibit certain medicines from being marketed or advertised to the general public.

designed to prevent consumers from coming in to contact with information about which they would not be able or have the knowledge to make an informed judgment. Medical professionals, on the other hand, are specifically trained and have the requisite knowledge to be able to make informed opinions about medical products and treatments. Thus the regulations are designed to restrict most of the advertising to the professional journals that are aimed at these professionals as they are best placed to make the required decisions on the merits of the products or services.

Where direct advertising to consumers is allowed, the regulations control the type of information that is allowed and the way in which the information itself may be displayed. By setting out these stringent requirements consumers are protected from being unduly swayed towards or against a medical treatment or product without seeking medical advice, an action which could have a serious and detrimental effect on their health and well-being.

Quite aside from controlling the type of information which is published to consumers, the regulators also have the valid wish to limit access to medical treatments and products in their jurisdictions to those which have been tested and approved by them. In some circumstances this may be to control the costs to a public health scheme of providing those treatments. In the majority of cases, however, any restriction has to do with valid concerns over the suitability and safety of the treatment in question. Making information about medical treatments available across the Internet, and in some cases making the treatments themselves available, would circumvent these controls which are put in place for the reasons of public safety.

## 9.6 INTERNET INTERMEDIARIES: LIABILITY IN THE INFORMATION MARKETPLACE

As discussed above, Internet-based e-commerce creates new opportunities not only for the advertising and sale of physical goods, but also for the sale of information itself. Often in an Internet transaction a third party—an Internet Service Provider ('ISP')—will be involved in some respect. ISPs are by far the most high-profile Internet intermediaries, a state of affairs which may be put down to the fact that without their services the average individual, and many small to medium-sized enterprises, would be unlikely to be able to participate in e-commerce. The involvement of ISPs in Internet transactions inevitably raises questions of potential liability. This section considers a range of these issues, most particularly the issue which has caused most debate at the time of writing: liability in respect of dealing with content provided by third parties.

### 9.6.1 What is an ISP?

When one examines the issue of the legal liabilities of ISPs, one has first to determine what is currently understood by the term 'ISP'. Initially, the answer to this question would seem quite straightforward, but if one engages in just a little research, almost immediately any answer begins to take on more complex dimensions. For example, the *Webopedia*[104] provides the following definition of an ISP:

. . . a company that provides access to the Internet. For a monthly fee, the service provider gives you a software package, username, password and access phone number. Equipped with a modem, you can then log on to the Internet and browse the World Wide Web and USENET, and send and receive e-mail.

In addition to serving individuals, ISPs also serve large companies, providing a direct connection from the company's networks to the Internet. ISPs themselves are connected to one another through Network Access Points ('NAPs').[105]

On its face this would seem like a reasonably adequate definition of an ISP, one that many Internet users might once have recognized as fitting perfectly the company that provided them with access to the Internet. However, beyond the 'provides access to the Internet' of the opening sentence, today this definition appears both simplistic and inaccurate, for as the Internet hardware and software technologies have developed and become more sophisticated, so too have the standard business models of the companies that provide access to it. Now, therefore, the answer to the ISP question posed above has become a much more complex one than that which might have been given five years ago.

Contemporary ISPs may supply solely Internet access,[106] such companies being referred to as access-only ISPs, interactive computer service providers ('ICSPs'),[107] or enhanced service providers ('ESPs').[108] However, increasingly they may provide a bundle of communications services including telecommunications[109] and television.[110] They may provide access via traditional telecommunications systems requiring an analogue dial-up modem, via traditional telecommunications systems using ADSL (Asymmetric Digital Subscriber Line)[111] modems or ISDN (Integrated Services Digital Network) Terminal Adaptors[112] to

---

[104] Online dictionary and search engine at www.pcwebopedia.com/.

[105] See www.pcwebopedia.com/TERM/I/ISP.html.

[106] eg, Freeserve (www.freeserve.net) and AOL (www.aol.com).

[107] US Telecommunications Act 1996, 47 USC, s 223(e)(6).

[108] K Werbach, 'Digital Tornado: The Internet and Telecommunications Policy', March 1997, FCC OPP Working Paper No 29, pp 32–3.

[109] eg, British Telecom (www.bt net) and AT&T (www.att.net).

[110] eg, COGECO (www.cgocable.net) and Cox Communications (www. cox.com).

[111] 'Asymmetric Digital Subscriber Lines (ADSL) are used to deliver high-rate digital data over existing ordinary phone-lines. A new modulation technology called Discrete Multitone (DMT) allows the transmission of high speed data. ADSL facilitates the simultaneous use of normal telephone services, ISDN, and high speed data transmission, eg, video'; K Kimmo Saarela, 'ADSL', www.cs.tut.fi/tlt/stuff/ads1/pt-adsl.html at www.cs.tut.fi/tlt/stuff/adsl/node5.html.

[112] 'ISDN allows multiple digital channels to be operated simultaneously through the same regular phone wiring used for analog lines. The change comes about when the telephone company's switches can support digital connections. Therefore, the same physical wiring can be used, but a digital signal, instead of an analog signal, is transmitted across the line. This scheme permits a much higher data transfer rate than analog lines'; see R Becker, 'ISDN Tutorial', at www.ralphb.net/ISDN/index.html at www.ralphb.net/ISDN/advs.html.

provide high-speed service,[113] through a broadband cable network requiring a cable modem,[114] or through a combination of dial-up and satellite service.[115] They may provide just a connection to the Internet,[116] or they may provide other services through 'portal sites' via the World Wide Web ('WWW'),[117] where the actual services are usually supplied by third parties.[118] Technical innovations are appearing apace, and developments such as Hotline[119] mean that even the 'standard' software set ups provided by ISPs, usually based around a web browser, may be far from a permanent fixture.

### 9.6.2 ISPs and civil liability

In their most basic form, ISPs are the 'glue' that binds the Internet together, via their supply of TCP/IP packet-switching services, which allow third parties to communicate data packets across the 'network of networks'. To facilitate such information transactions, ISPs will provide services to one or more of the parties, including fundamental communications services such as access and information storage. ISPs, and indeed other Internet intermediaries, may also provide additional services to facilitate transactions between end-users, such as the provision of search facilities and indexes. Where these basic or additional services are found to be defective, liability will normally be based on the established legal principles of contract and tort, although it may not be immediately apparent how best to apply existing principles to forms of service previously unconsidered by legislators and the courts. Indeed, in the case of certain types of enhanced service, such as those involving provision of software, the courts may struggle to determine whether the service provided is in fact legally to be considered a 'service'.[120]

A more problematic issue is raised by the role of ISPs and other intermediaries in relaying information through their systems. Determining their liability for loss of the information stored in relayed packets is one matter, determining liability for the nature of the information content of those packets, where that content has been determined by a third party, is quite another. ISPs and other intermediaries usually operate using software which processes information automatically. As such, they are

---

[113] eg, Bell Sympatico High Speed Edition (hse.sympatico.ca/en/fs–main.htm), British Telecom Home Highway (www.homehighway.bt.com).

[114] eg, the iHome network and its franchises (www.home.com), Cable London (www.cable london.co.uk/residential/internet/index.html) and Cable Internet (www.cableinet.net).

[115] eg, DirecPC (www.direcpc.com).

[116] eg, West Dorset Internet (www.wdi.co.uk), CIX Ltd (www1.cix.co.uk).

[117] Portal sites offer pre-selected, ready-made links throughout the Internet, essentially making the information source transparent to the user. Such portals are content aggregators. They add value to that content by organizing it within a unified framework.

[118] eg, AOL's CompuServe (www.compuserve.com/gateway/default.asp), Demon Internet Ltd (www.demon.net).

[119] See Hotline Communications Ltd (www.BigRedH.com/index2.html).

[120] Consider the difficulties faced by the court in *St Albans City and District Council v International Computers Ltd* [1996] 4 All ER 481. See, further, Chapter 1 (section 1.2.1.14).

usually transferring the information without obtaining, or seeking to obtain, knowledge of either its content, or the nature of the transaction of which it is a part. This lack of knowledge, however, does not necessarily render them immune to legal action where the third-party information content infringes another third party's rights, for there are often good reasons for aggrieved claimants to pursue the intermediary rather than the other third party:

(a) Information intermediaries are often seen as potentially more lucrative targets for litigation than the originators of the offending information content. This perception may be based on the unofficial first rule of litigation, 'never sue poor people', or, in the case of large intermediaries, because the claimants suspect that it will be cheaper for the intermediary to pay them to drop the case than to fight it.

(b) The question of jurisdiction may play a role, for example, if the originator of the offending information is in a foreign jurisdiction while the intermediary is in the claimant's home jurisdiction, or if the intermediary is in a jurisdiction that has a reputation for favourable outcomes in cases similar to that brought by the claimant.[121]

(c) The outcome the claimant desires may be more effectively obtained by action against the intermediary. For example, where the desired outcome is the prevention of further access to the offending information, taking action against one originator may have minimal effect, whereas action against the intermediary may result in complete or partial blocking of all potential originators.[122] Action against an intermediary may also be part of a wider strategy by a claimant to 'chill' the willingness of other intermediaries to carry the same information.[123]

Any intermediary who provides Internet transaction services is faced with the risk that his actions or inaction may result in the failure of the transaction. In such circumstances, it may be that he will be forced to compensate one or other of the parties to that transaction for any resulting losses. For ISPs that risk is two-fold: first, there may simply be a communications failure which prevents the transaction from ever taking place. This may be considered a failure of 'basic service provision'. For a compensation claim in respect of such a failure to succeed, it will need to identify a

---

[121] Consider, eg, the well-publicized possibility of jurisdiction or forum shopping in libel cases; see F Auburn, 'Usenet News And The Law' [1995] 1 Web JCLI at webjcli.ncl.ac.uk/articles1/auburn1.html.

[122] This was the aim of the Bavarian *Land* government when it took action against CompuServe officials in 1995 in an attempt to stop CompuServe providing access from within Germany to neo-Nazi newsgroups (mainly in the United States). This achieved some limited measure of success, as CompuServe was initially forced to suspend worldwide access to those newsgroups. See U Sieber, 'Criminal Liability for the Transfer of Data in International Networks: New Challenges for the Internet (Part I)' (1997) 13 CLSR 151. However, given the distributed nature of the Internet, the wide array of intermediary options for accessing information on it, and the perception of many governments that allowing such cases to be brought might damage Internet growth, such apparent victories are all too likely to be transitory, as indeed was the victory here. (See 'CompuServe Ex-Official's Porn-Case Conviction Reversed', Associated Press, 17 November 1999.)

[123] See *Religious Technology Center v Netcom* (1995) 33 IPR 132.

duty on the part of the intermediary to ensure that such failures could not occur. In the absence of specific legislative provision imposing such liability on Internet intermediaries, such a duty could only arise in contract or in tort. While many types of intermediary may operate in the absence of any contractual agreement between them and communicating parties,[124] commercial ISPs are highly likely to have express terms delineating the extent of their liability. Where such terms attempt to limit an ISP's liability, this is likely to be to the bare minimum that the company's lawyers think will pass muster before the courts. Where either express terms relating to liability are included or they are ruled void, contract law in most jurisdictions will imply a term that the ISP must take *reasonable* care in the provision of services to its user.[125] The mere fact of a failure alone will not generally be enough for an action to lie against an ISP unless a competent ISP could reasonably have been expected not to fail.

Secondly, there may be a failure of some additional service. As the Internet industry has grown and developed, increasingly ISPs, in a bid to gain a competitive edge, have offered additional services beyond mere service provision. Such enhanced services are sometimes available to all comers via the World Wide Web, but can be restricted to the ISPs clients.[126] They may include the provision of:

(a) Customized software for accessing Internet services, including parental controls, dedicated chat rooms, roaming capabilities, and instant messaging.

(b) Space on the ISP's servers for client web pages, and data storage.

(c) Information services such as news, weather, and financial data.

Generally these enhanced services will be governed by express contract terms, normally incorporated into a 'click-wrap licence' which appears prior to the downloading of software or with each new session using a specific service. In the absence of express terms, the situation becomes more complex. Where the ISP is providing a non-contractual service, or the service is being delivered by other Internet intermediaries who have no express contract with an end user, there are only limited circumstances in which a contractual duty might be owed. In some cases the courts may be

---

[124] Not all parties offering ISP services will necessarily have a clear contractual arrangement covering communications sent by their end users. For example, a university offering such services to staff and students may well not have a contract for service between university and network users. Notably, however, many university regulations and guidelines now contain statements such as 'Whilst every reasonable endeavour is made to ensure that the computing systems are available as scheduled and function correctly, no liability whatsoever can be accepted by Academic Services computing for any loss or delay as a result of any system malfunction, howsoever caused.'

[125] eg, SGSA 1982, s 13. Some ISPs explicitly spell this out, eg, BT's Internet's 'Terms & Conditions' (guest.btinternet.com/html/termsconditions.html) provides: '11.3 In performing any obligation under this Contract, our duty is only to exercise the reasonable care and skill of a competent Internet service provider.'

[126] AOL, for example, offers a range of pricing packages for its services. A client can purchase: '(a) Four pricing variants on basic access to AOL's services, plus Internet access. (b) Additional premium services, on top of one of the four basic variants. (c) Access to AOL's services and premium services, via another ISP. A range of informational services are also available for free from AOL's webpage, to anyone with Internet access.'

prepared to imply a contract between the intermediary and the end-user. This is rare, but not unknown, at least in the common-law jurisdictions, even where the parties have had no previous dealings.[127] Much would turn on the closeness of the relationship between the intermediary and end user.

For example, where the intermediary was an Internet host supplying the ISP with transmission facilities, and his sole connection with an end-user of the ISP was the reception of information packets for onward transmission, it seems unlikely that a court would be prepared to imply a contract between him and that end-user in the event of a loss of information. That would involve the implication of contracts between every Internet host and all users whose packets arrive at their servers. Taken to its logical conclusion, this would potentially produce millions of individual contracts, none of whose terms could easily be identified as they would all need to be implied by the courts.

Additionally, in jurisdictions where the applicable law recognizes the concept of enforceable contractual obligations for the benefit of a third party, this might create a contractual duty owed by a host to the customers of those ISPs with which it has an express interconnection agreement (for example, if it provides the ISP with a connection to the Internet on a chargeable basis).[128] However, even if such a contractual duty were found to exist, again it would be at most a duty to take reasonable care in the forwarding of packets. Proof of breach would always be extremely difficult.

If bringing a successful case against an Internet host intermediary would be difficult in contract, it would be even less likely in tort, due to the extreme difficulty of demonstrating that the intermediary owed the user a tortious duty of care. This is because losses resulting from an information transaction are highly likely to be pure financial losses, and many jurisdictions will not impose a duty of care to avoid pure financial losses unless there is some clear pre-existing non-contractual relationship between the parties. The fact that the Internet operates using a packet-switching protocol (TCP/IP), allowing individual information packets from the same communications to be routed via a multiplicity of different routes and hosts to ensure the best chance of delivery, means that a user cannot predict with any certainty which intermediaries will be involved in the transaction, other than his ISP and that of the party with whom he is communicating, and as such there can be no duty of care to him on the part of the other hosts involved. Even if the failure or malfunction of Internet communication at issue were to have the capacity to cause physical injury or property damage, it would not be foreseeable that a failure on their part might cause such loss. This is because the intermediaries involved in transporting the communication would have no knowledge of the nature of the transaction, as it would appear

---

[127] In the UK, see *Clarke v Dunraven* [1897] AC 59 (a yacht owner's act of entering for a sailing race created an implied contract between himself and all the other entrants in which they agreed to abide by the rules of the race).

[128] For the UK, see now the Contracts (Rights of Third Parties) Act 1999, discussed in Chapter 3 (section 3.3.3).

as just a set of not necessarily related packets to them. Foreseeability of this kind is normally a prerequisite for a duty to arise. Even if, by some means it could be proven that a particular intermediary did owe a duty to one or other of the communicating parties, the fault-tolerant nature of the Internet would tend to militate against any breach of that duty causing loss. In the common-law jurisdictions at least, this will mean that there is likely to be an insufficient causal link between the breach and the loss, with damages unrecoverable as being too remote.

In addition to potential liability arising from the provision of its service, an ISP may owe other legal obligations, not least in the area of consumer protection. Another obligation that has received much media and industry attention in recent years, not least because of its importance to the development of e-commerce, is that of informational privacy. This may be granted by law, as in the case of the EU Data Protection Directive and attendant national legislation,[129] or may be incorporated or implied into the contract between ISP and user.[130] Chapter 11 explores in depth the implications of this Directive in the context of information technology and the Internet.

### 9.6.3 ISP liability for third-party-provided content

The range of laws that impose civil, or in some cases criminal, liability in respect of information content is extremely wide. However, in most jurisdictions, a common feature of such laws is that mere intermediaries will not be held liable for their contravention in the same way as an individual who originates the information, or who instigates its transmission or copying. In many circumstances, as with the concept of 'common carrier' status commonly applied to telecommunications companies in the United States, if the intermediary simply provides a regular service for information transport, without discriminating as between types of users, or exercising any control over the content of information, he is likely to be granted a degree of immunity from information-content laws. In contrast, newspaper publishers who exercise editorial functions, in deciding both who and what will and will not be published, expose themselves to the full gamut of information-content legislation, from the obvious aspects such as copyright, obscenity and indecency, and defamation through to the intricacies of advertising and securities laws, and obscurities such as the law relating to blasphemy.

The difficulty with Internet intermediaries and ISPs is that the nature of the forms of communication that they provide often go well beyond the simple carriage of information commonly found with basic telecommunication services, without necessarily remotely approaching the degree of carrier involvement to be found in

---

[129] Directive 95/46/EC on the protection of individuals with regard to the processing of personal data and on the free movement of such data, OJ 1995 L281/31 (www2.echo.lu/legal/en/dataprot/directiv/directiv.html). See, further, Chapter 11.

[130] See, eg, Sprint Canada's terms and conditions at www.sprint.ca/general/terms.php3 and www.sprint.ca/general/privacy.php3.

the communications process in the print and broadcast media. This has led to a certain degree of international judicial and legislative uncertainty as to the precise standard to which ISPs and other Internet intermediaries should be held with regard to responsibility for the content of their services. Although, as will be seen, this uncertainty initially led to cases where ISPs were effectively held to broadcast and print-media standards of liability for content, the international trend is moving towards a much more limited standard. The main reason for this shift in attitude has been increasing legislative action relating to the Internet on the part of many national governments, which have been concerned to ensure that the application of existing national laws to Internet intermediaries will not unnecessarily impede the growth of e-commerce.

In general terms, an intermediary's liability for the information content of communications or resources which have originated from a third party will be derived from one or more of three types of activity: copying, possession or transmission. In the case of copyright infringement, carrying out any of the three actions without the permission of the copyright owner will potentially be an infringing act. In the case of obscenity or indecency laws the act of copying may not give rise to liability, but possession and transmission may. In terms of defamation law, making copies of or possessing potentially defamatory content is unlikely to raise liability issues, but the act of transmission probably will.

### 9.6.3.1 *Copyright*

A very basic formulation of the way that the copyright laws of most nations relate to electronic communications is that 'there will be a copyright infringement when an individual copies a work held in electronic format without the authority of the copyright holder'.[131] The key problem with this formulation, as far as ISPs and intermediaries are concerned, is that both the TCP/IP protocol underlying the Internet, and the technologies which overlay it, rely extensively, if not entirely, on the ability to make copies of information. Thus ISPs and intermediaries can only operate by copying information. If the intermediary is merely part of the communications chain, it copies received packets into memory (and probably onto disk) and then sends fresh copies to the next host in the chain. If it is hosting a resource, it initially makes a copy of that resource onto its disks, and then makes further copies when the resource is requested by a user. If those copies are of a work protected by copyright, the intermediary, by making copies not specifically authorized by the rightsholder, is technically infringing that copyright.

It was argued that such transient or evanescent copies, in RAM, because of their

---

[131] Berne Convention, art 9(1): 'Authors of literary and artistic works . . . shall have the exclusive right of authorising reproduction of these works, in any manner or form'; UK Copyright, Designs and Patents Act 1988 ('CDPA 1988'), s 16(1): 'The owner of the copyright in a work has . . . the exclusive right . . . (a) to copy the work . . .'; 17 USC, s 106: '. . . the owner of copyright under this title has the exclusive rights . . . (1) to reproduce the copyrighted work . . .'.

lack of permanence, could not be said to breach copyright.[132] In fact, many copyright laws can be, and have been, interpreted such that even supposedly evanescent copies in computer memory can be deemed to be sufficient copying for a finding of infringement.[133] Of course, in the course of their daily operations, many ISPs and Internet intermediaries will make not just evanescent copies in RAM, but will make further copies on a range of storage media, for example, hard disks when caching a resource, or DAT tapes when making back-up copies of a resource. The first US court to consider the matter, in *Playboy Enterprises v Frena*,[134] held that a bulletin-board operator who encouraged users to use the board to upload and download images in which *Playboy*-owned copyright, had infringed *Playboy*'s copyright by the direct copying the system undertook when storing and transmitting images. The problem with this particular interpretation of what precisely is taking place when information is being uploaded or downloaded from Internet hosts is that although, as a matter of technical fact, the host is copying or reproducing the work, via its software, the commands that are being sent to that software instructing it to make the copies are in fact given by a third party. In other words, a third party is operating the host's computer system remotely. Thus, when instructions to make an infringing copy of information are sent to an Internet host by a third party, the owner of the host will very likely have neither knowledge of the infringement relating to that information, nor any intent to infringe that information.[135]

This lack of knowledge, or lack of intent, was often emphasized by the ISPs in the early case law. However, they were soon to discover that it did not necessarily mean that they would escape liability for the infringement. The judiciaries in the UK and the United States, for example, have long tended towards a position that lack of intention to infringe is not a defence in copyright actions. In some of the ISP cases, it appears that that rigid position may have shifted slightly, with the courts recognizing that there might be a minimal mental element in copyright infringement, ie, an inten-

---

[132] The argument was especially pertinent in relation to US law where 17 USC s 101 states: ' "Copies" are material objects . . . in which a work is fixed by any method . . . and from which the work can be perceived, reproduced, or otherwise communicated, either directly or with the aid of a machine or device' and 'A work is "fixed" in a tangible medium of expression when its embodiment . . . is sufficiently permanent or stable to permit it to be perceived, reproduced, or otherwise communicated for a period of more than transitory duration'.

[133] *MAI Systems Corp v Peak Computer Inc* (1993) 991 F 2d 511 (9th Cir), cert dismissed (1994) 114 S Ct 671. (Copyrighted software program at issue was 'fixed' in RAM because the computer user was able to view a representation of the program's information, including the system error log, after loading the program into the computer's RAM); *Triad Systems Corp v Southeastern Express Co* (1994) 31 USPQ 2d 1239 (NDC); *Advanced Systems of Michigan Inc v MAI Systems Corporation* (1994) 845 F Supp 356, 363 (ED Va). See A Morrison, 'Hijack on the Road to Xanadu: The Infringement of Copyright in HTML Documents via Networked Computers and the Legitimacy of Browsing Hypermedia Documents' (1999) 1 Journal of Information, Law and Technology (JILT) (www.law.warwick.ac.uk/jilt/99-1/morrison.html).

[134] (1993) 839 F Supp 1552 (MD Fla). Also www.Loundy.com/CASES/Playboy–v–Frena.html.

[135] See *Marobie-FL Inc d/b/a Galactic Software v National Association of Fire Equipment Distributors and Northwest Nexus Inc* (1997) 983 F Supp 1167 (ND Ill) (defendant not guilty of direct infringement because it did not initiate the copying of claimants work, its systems were merely used to create a copy by a third party). Also at www.Loundy.com/CASES/Marobie–v–NAFED.html.

tion to make a copy. This position was exemplified by the case of *Religious Technology Center v Netcom On-Line Communications Services Inc.*[136] Here, an infringement action was brought by representatives of the Church of Scientology against Netcom, an ISP, which hosted a newsgroup, alt.religion.scientology, to which a customer had posted verbatim extracts of material in which the Church of Scientology claimed copyright. The judge expressly rejected the allegation that the ISP had infringed directly and refused to follow *Playboy Enterprises v Frena*, on the ground that Netcom could only be guilty of direct infringement if it had caused the infringing copies to be made:

the mere fact that Netcom's system incidentally makes temporary copies of plaintiff's [claimant's] works does not mean Netcom has caused the copying.[137]

In *Playboy Enterprises, Inc v Webbworld*[138] however, the judge noted the principle raised in the *Netcom* case that an ISP or Internet intermediary might not have any control over the information to which it gave access, but concluded that:

Even the absence of the ability to exercise such control, however, is no defense to liability. If a business cannot be operated within the bounds of the Copyright Act, then perhaps the question of its legitimate existence needs to be addressed.[139]

Whilst this might perhaps be true of the website that the defendants in *Webbworld* ran, as it provided access by subscription to images obtained from adult newsgroups, which are notorious for egregious copyright infringements,[140] it was a harsh approach in relation to the average ISP's potential liability for breach of copyright. However, even if the trend in US cases[141] tended to suggest that ISPs, and other Internet intermediaries, such as Bulletin Board Service ('BBS') operators, should escape direct liability, it was clear that they might still be held to be contributory or vicarious infringers where they are vicariously liable for the users' acts or have authorized or contributed to the copying.[142]

---

[136] (1995) 907 F Supp 1361 (ND Cal). Also at www.Loundy.com/CASES/RTC–v–Netcom.html.

[137] Ibid, 1368. See, further, on contributory infringement, E A Burcher and A M Hughes's casenote, '*Religious Tech Ctr v Netcom On-Line Communications, Inc.* Internet Service Providers: The Knowledge Standard for Contributory Copyright Infringement and The Fair Use Defense' (1997) 3 Rich J L Tech 5 (www.richmond.edu/jolt/v3il/burhugh.html).

[138] (1997) 968 F Supp 1171 (ND Tex). Also at www.loundy.com/CASES/PEI–v–Webbworld.html.

[139] Ibid, 9.

[140] See also *Playboy Enterprises, Inc v Russ Hardenburgh, et al* (1997) 982 F Supp 503 (ND Ohio) (a bulletin-board service operator was held liable for infringement of the copyright in *Playboy*'s images, on the basis of his executive position, and his authority to control the bulletin board's content—there was no evidence that he personally approved the uploading of the images. He was also liable for contributory infringement as he had at least constructive knowledge that infringing activity was likely to be occurring on the bulletin board).

[141] The trend in other jurisdictions is more difficult to ascertain, either because there have been no cases decided, or because the cases that have been decided carry uncertain precedental value. See H Paynter, and R Foreman, 'Liability of Internet Service Providers for Copyright Infringement' (1998) 21(2) University of NSW Law Journal (www.austlii.edu.au/au/other/unswlj/thematic/1998/vol21no2/paynter.html).

[142] See *Sega Enterprises Ltd v Sabella* (1996) WL 780560 (ND Cal); *Sega Enterprises Ltd v MAPHIA*

Vicarious liability is predicated upon a pre-existing relationship between the defendant and the direct infringer, and not on the defendant's involvement in the infringing activity—the link essentially being that the defendant potentially benefits from the infringer's activities:[143]

If someone has the 'right and ability' to supervise the infringing action of another, and that right and ability 'coalesce with an obvious and direct financial interest in the exploitation of copyrighted materials—even in the absence of actual knowledge' that the infringement is taking place—the 'supervisor' may be held vicariously liable for the infringement. Vicarious liability is based on a connection to the direct infringer (not necessarily to the infringing activity).[144]

Yet in the case of ISPs, it is unlikely that a court will find sufficient relationship between a user and a transmission host to ground such liability.[145] Equally, even though a defendant may appear to authorize infringement by providing the necessary facilities for copying knowing that some users of that service will use it to make infringing copies,[146] this will probably not be sufficient to persuade a court that authorization is intended, in circumstances where the equipment might also be used for non-infringing purposes and where the provider cannot control the use made by the copier.[147]

The US doctrine of contributory infringement is based on 'the basic common law

---

(1996) 948 F Supp 923 (ND Cal) (BBS operators knew their boards were being used to copy Sega's games and actively participated in that use by soliciting users to upload games and selling copiers to assist in the making of copies). See also *Marobie-FL Inc d/b/a Galactic Software v National Association of Fire Equipment Distributors and Northwest Nexus Inc* (1997) 983 F Supp 1167 (ND Ill) (defendant not vicariously liable for copyright infringement unless it has the right and ability to supervise the infringing activity and also has a direct financial interest in such activities). See, further, K Tickle, 'The Vicarious Liability of Electronic Bulletin Board Operators for the Copyright Infringement Occurring on Their Bulletin Boards' (1995) 80 Iowa Law Review 391.

[143] The most common example would be that of employer and employee, but any relationship in which the defendant expects to benefit from the infringer's acts might give rise to vicarious liability, thus, for example, vicarious liability could arise from an independent contract or via a licence, eg, *PRS v Bradford Corporation* [1917–1923] Mac CC 309; *Australasian PRA v Miles* [1962] NSWR 405 (liability of an organizer of an entertainment for infringement of performance rights by musicians); *Shapiro, Bernstein & Co v HL Green Co* (1963) 316 F 2d 304, 307 (2d Cir) (a company leasing floor space to a record department was liable for the record department's sales of 'bootleg' records despite the absence of actual knowledge of the infringement, because of the company's beneficial relationship to the sales). See also the 'dance hall cases', *Dreamland Ball Room, Inc v Shapiro, Bernstein & Co* (1929) 36 F 2d 354 (7th Cir); *Famous Music Corp v Bay State Harness Horse Racing & Breeding Ass'n, Inc* (1977) 554 F 2d 1213 (1st Cir); *KECA Music, Inc v Dingus McGee's Co* (1977) 432 F Supp 72 (WD Mo).

[144] Information Infrastructure Task Force Working Group on Intellectual Property Rights (Chair: Bruce A. Lehman), *Intellectual Property and the National Information Infrastructure: The Report of the Working Group on Intellectual Property Rights* (1995) (available at www.uspto.gov/web/offices/com/doc/ipnii).

[145] *Cubby Inc v CompuServe Inc* (1991) 776 F Supp 135 (SDNY).

[146] *Moorhouse v University of NSW* [1976] RPC 157.

[147] *CBS Songs UK Ltd v Amstrad* [1988] RPC 567; *Sony Corp of America v Universal Studios, Inc* (1984) 464 US 417. See, however, the contrary argument voiced in F Macmillan et al, 'Copyright Liability of Communications Carriers' (1997) 3 Journal of Information, Law and Technology (JILT) (elj.warwick.ac.uk/jilt/commsreg/97–3macm).

doctrine that one who knowingly participates or furthers a tortious act is jointly and severally liable with the prime tortfeasor . . .'[148] and thus the defendant must (a) have knowledge of the infringement, and (b) have induced, caused or materially contributed to the third party's infringing conduct.[149] This was a key point raised by the court in the *Netcom* case. Here it was held that if Netcom had knowledge that infringing material was passing through its servers and failed to take action to prevent the dissemination of that material, it might be liable as a contributory infringer. The deciding factor would be the host's actual knowledge of the infringement:

[If the host] cannot reasonably verify a claim of infringement, either because of a possible fair use defense, the lack of copyright notices on the copies, or the copyright holder's failure to provide the necessary documentation to show that there is a likely infringement, the operator's lack of knowledge will be found reasonable and there will be no liability for contributory infringement for allowing the continued distribution of the works on its system.[150]

The uncertain state of affairs that was developing out of the case law in the United States led ISPs to hope that the Working Group on Intellectual Property Rights, set up in 1994 as part of the US Department of Commerce's Information Infrastructure Task Force, would support their assertion that online service providers should not be held liable for copyright infringement, since they had no way of policing what was transmitted on their networks. The ISPs argued that:

(a) The volume of material on any ISP's system was too great to monitor or screen.

(b) Even if an ISP was willing and able to monitor the material on its system, it would not be able reliably to identify infringing material.

(c) Failure to shield ISPs would impair communication and availability of information.

(d) Exposure to liability for infringement would drive ISPs out of business, causing the Internet to fail.

(e) The law should impose liability only on those ISPs who assumed responsibility for the online activities of their subscribers.

However, when that Working Group reported in 1995,[151] the ISPs were dismayed to discover that the concerns of a more powerful lobby group, that of the copyright

---

[148] *Screen Gems-Columbia Music, Inc v Mark Pi Records Inc* 256 F Supp 399 (SDNY, 1966), cited in K A Walton, 'Is a Website like a Flea Market Stall? How *Fonovisa v Cherry Auction* Increases the Risk of Third-Party Copyright Infringement Liability for Online Service Providers' (1997) 19 Hastings Comm Ent LJ 921, 926.

[149] *Gershwin Publishing Corp v Columbia Artists Management, Inc* (1971) 443 F 2d 1159, 1162 (2d Cir); *Sega Enterprises Inc v MAPHIA* (1994) 857 F Supp 679 (ND Cal).

[150] *Religious Technology Center v Netcom On-Line Communications Services Inc* (1995) 907 F Supp 1361, 1374 (ND Cal). For a detailed analysis of the potential liability of intermediaries as contributory infringers, see Burcher and Hughes (n 137 above).

[151] Information Infrastructure Task Force (n 144 above).

owners, had won the day. The Working Group decided that it would be undesirable to reduce the copyright liability of ISPs as this might prematurely halt the development of marketplace tools that could be used to lessen their risk of liability and the risk to copyright owners, although they suggested that circumstances under which service providers should have reduced liability might be identified in the future.

The Working Group noted that:

(a) Millions of files travel through a network in a given day, but believed that other industries were faced with similar situations and coped without reduced liability.[152]

(b) Online service providers could take appropriate action when notified of the existence of infringing material on their systems and therefore limit their liability for damages to those for innocent infringement.

(c) Online service providers were in the best position to know the identity and activities of their subscribers and to stop unlawful activities.

(d) Other businesses with similar risk factors had been able to take appropriate precautions to minimize their risk of liability through indemnification agreements and insurance.

In the event, the legislative response to the recommendations of the Working Group on Intellectual Property Rights, and their proposed amendments to the Copyright Act was muted,[153] not least because of the protests that some of the other proposed measures provoked.[154] It was not until the passage of the Digital Millennium Copyright Act of 1998 (see below), that the issue of ISP liability for copying was addressed by the US legislature to the satisfaction of US ISPs.

Under UK law, the fact that an ISP is in possession of infringing copies made by a third party may, in some circumstances, lead to liability for infringement of the copyright owner's rights. This liability is known as secondary infringement, and stems from section 23 of the CDPA 1988. This states that there will be an infringement where the possession is in the course of a business; and the defendant knows or has reason to believe that the material held is an infringing copy. Most ISPs clearly operate on a commercial basis, and will thus fall within the definition of a business under the first leg of the test.[155] However, the question of possession remains uncertain. If an ISP is merely routing information packets constituting infringing material,

---

[152] eg, the position of photo-processing laboratories.

[153] Although the National Information Infrastructure Copyright Protection Act of 1995 was considered by the both the Senate and House of Representatives in the 104th Congress, it was not passed by either House and was not reintroduced in the 105th Congress. For criticism of the Act, see, W M Melone, 'Contributory Liability for Access Providers: Solving the Conundrum Digitalization Has Placed on Copyright Laws' (1997) 49(2) Federal Communications Law Journal (www.law. indiana.edu/fclj/pubs/v49/no2/melone.html).

[154] For a brief overview of other criticisms, see P Samuelson, 'The Copyright Grab', *Wired* 4.01, January 1996.

[155] CDPA 1988, s 178.

it is unclear whether the transient possession will suffice for liability under section 23, or whether more long-term possession is necessary. Certainly, even if possession could be proven, it would be extremely difficult for the rightsholder to prove that an ISP had specific knowledge about the copyright status of individual packets. An ISP's liability arising from possession is therefore likely to be limited by practical constraints to circumstances where it hosts resources, such as webpages and Usenet postings, or where it provides caching services.

The question of knowledge is less certain. Copyright infringement has long been endemic on the Internet,[156] either because users are unaware of the restrictions imposed by copyright, or because they are aware of the limited likelihood of their being held to account for infringement. As a result, almost every ISP, and especially those which host third-party websites, carry Usenet newsgroups, and cache resources will inevitably have a certain number of infringing copies on its servers. Yet the fact that there is a high likelihood of infringing copies, does not mean that an ISP can be automatically held to have sufficient knowledge of any particular infringement to give rise to liability under section 23. The cases under the legislation prior to the CDPA 1988[157] give strong support to the theory that actual knowledge of the infringement in question is required,[158] and that a general constructive knowledge that some copies may be infringing will not be sufficient.[159]

This can make determining the liability of an ISP, in circumstances where the rightsholder claims that the ISP was given notice of infringing material, difficult to determine. If the notice identifies specific infringing material, such as a .jpg or .gif picture file on a webpage, or a computer program on a 'warez' FTP site, the matter is easy to resolve, as the ISP can either delete or block access to the resource, reducing the likelihood of the rightsholder bringing legal action. If the ISP were to refuse to delete or block access to the resource the rightsholder would have no difficulty proving continued possession with actual knowledge. However, this circumstance is probably the exception rather than the rule, as with many infringements the rightsholder may only be able to determine that the infringing material is being distributed via a particular newsgroup or third-party website, and its notice can only indicate that if an ISP carries that newsgroup or caches resources requested from the website, it will come into possession of infringing copies.[160] In those circumstances, it would seem that the UK courts would be unwilling to accept that a notice couched in such general terms would be sufficient to fix a person with knowledge such that any

---

[156] Indeed, on the more exotic Usenet hierarchies, such as alt.binaries.pictures.erotica.* and alt.binaries.warez.* the scale of infringement is such that over 90% of postings are likely to involve infringing material.

[157] Copyright Act 1956, s 5 (infringement by importation, sale etc of copies known to be infringing).

[158] *Hoover plc v George Hulme Ltd* [1982] FSR 565.

[159] *Columbia Picture Industries v Robinson* [1987] Ch 38.

[160] For an example of an even vaguer notice, consider the form letter sent by Lucasfilm to hundreds of ISPs regarding infringing materials from the film *Star Wars: Episode I: The Phantom Menace*, discussed in D Goodin, '*Star Wars* Rekindles Net Debate', *CNETNews.com*, 2 May 1999, news.cnet.com/news/0-1005-200-341957.html.

infringing copies which appeared on their systems would be capable of leading to liability.[161]

The issue of liability for further transmission of infringing materials has in the past been equally fraught. An ISP may undertake two forms of transmission which have copyright implications. These are forwarding packets received from another host; and transmitting a copy of a resource hosted by the intermediary, following a user request. This transmission involves copying of the material, and thus can be considered as a potential infringement. However, the copies made are evanescent, with the ISP's copy normally being deleted once the material has been sent. While in some jurisdictions such copying has resulted in an infringement,[162] other jurisdictions have explicitly stated that no such infringement takes place.[163] This situation is further complicated by the fact that national laws have often granted an exclusive right of distribution as part of the copyright 'bundle of rights', making it at least arguable that the transmission of infringing packets of information might breach this exclusive right. In practice, this was often not the case as the relevant statutory provisions, drafted in a pre-Internet era, were not couched in suitable terminology. This has been remedied within the European Union by the Copyright in the Information Society Directive[164] This Directive provides a range of exclusive rights to copyright holders in respect of the use of their material online. These include the 'reproduction right',[165] the 'right of communication to the public',[166] and the 'distribution right'.[167] Such exclusive rights could well place ISPs in a difficult position. Furthering a general trend towards limiting liability for ISPs, however, that same Directive also provides a range of exceptions and limitations, including:

Temporary acts of reproduction . . . which are transient or incidental, which are an integral and essential part of a technological process whose sole purpose is to enable . . . a transmission in a network between third parties by an intermediary . . . shall be exempted from the reproduction right . . .[168]

The general provisions limiting the liability of intermediaries in respect of transmission, caching and hosting of content provided by third parties found in the E-commerce Directive (and the UK implementing legislation) will also apply equally to infringing copies as to other unlawful material. These provisions are discussed in

---

[161] *Hoover plc v George Hulme Ltd* [1982] FSR 565 (under the Copyright Act 1956).

[162] See, eg, UK Copyright, Designs and Patents Act 1988, s 17(6).

[163] *Religious Technology Center v Netcom On-Line Communications Services Inc* (1995) 907 F Supp 1361, 1368 (ND Cal)

[164] 2001/29/EC.

[165] '. . . the exclusive right to authorise or prohibit direct or indirect, temporary or permanent reproduction by any means and in any form, in whole or in part . . .' (art 2).

[166] '. . . the exclusive right to authorise or prohibit any communication to the public of their works in such a way that members of the public may access them from a place and at a time individually chosen by them . . .' (art 3).

[167] '. . . the exclusive right to authorise or prohibit any form of distribution to the public by sale or otherwise . . .' (art 4).

[168] Article 5.

detail below (see section 9.6.3.2). The USA has enacted very similar provisions with respect to copyright only;[169] the US approach to civil liability in respect of other types of third-party provided content is, as we shall see, very different.

### 9.6.3.2 *Defamation*

The primary difficulty with establishing an ISP's liability for defamation is that national defamation laws differ so widely. It is possible to state with some certainty that in most, if not all, jurisdictions, the fundamental basis of defamation liability is the publication of untrue information, that liability will be based on the extent of the damage to the reputation of the person referred to in that information, and that a person's reputation cannot be damaged unless the information is disseminated to people other than the author. Once one ventures beyond these basic principles, national defamation laws rapidly diverge. English law[170] imposes liability regardless of whether the publisher of a statement knew or ought to have known it was defamatory[171] whereas under Finnish law a distinction is made between intentional and negligent defamation.[172] Unlike English law, Scots law[173] provides that the defamatory statement need only be communicated to the pursuer for an action to lie and justify an award of at least nominal damages.[174] Under US law a statement referring to a public figure will only be defamatory if malice can be proved on the part of the maker of the statement.[175] These national differences make it difficult for an Internet publisher to assess in advance whether material is likely to give rise to liability.

Because of these disparate divergences, the differing provisions of national law will not be considered in detail here, and the discussion below will start from the assumption that an ISP has transmitted a defamatory statement, either from a website which it hosts or caches, or as one of the hosts in the transmission chain from the offending website. The potential risk to ISPs of transmitting defamatory information is high, because of the way in which the Internet works and, more importantly, because of the ways in which users communicate using the Internet technologies.[176] The important question is whether that risk of (usually inadvertent) transmission translates into liability on the part of the ISP in addition to the original author of the statement.

In the traditional media, publishing is seen as requiring positive input on the part of the publisher (such as arranging for the printing of a work, sending out copies, selling copies, etc). This positive input approach meshes with the approach of those

---

[169] See the US Digital Millennium Copyright Act, s 512.
[170] See, further, D Price, *Defamation: Law, Procedure and Practice* (Sweet & Maxwell, 1997).
[171] *Hulton & Co v Jones* [1910] AC 20.
[172] Finnish Penal Code, ch 27, ss 1–8.
[173] See, further, K Norrie, *Defamation and Related Actions in Scots Law* (Butterworths, 1995).
[174] *Mackay v McCankie* (1883) 10 R 537.
[175] *New York Times Co v Sullivan* (1964) 376 US 254.
[176] See L Edwards, 'Defamation and the Internet', in L Edwards and C Waelde (eds), *Law and the Internet: Regulating Cyberspace* (Hart Publishing, 1997), pp 184–8.

legal authorities that define publication as the communication of the statement to at least one person other than the claimant.[177] However, as we have noted in relation to copyright (see section 9.6.3.1), many Internet-based transactions are neither initiated nor controlled by the ISP, as the commands that are being sent to the ISP's hardware and software instructing it to make the copies are in fact given by a third party. This has provided the courts with two potential perspectives as to the process that is occurring, either:

(a) the user is controlling the software running on the ISP's system, and is thus responsible for the transmission; or

(b) the transmission is undertaken by software which is in the possession of and under the overall control of the ISP, making it responsible for the transmission.

The latter perspective was adopted by the UK courts in *Godfrey v Demon Internet Ltd*.[178] Here the defendant ISP was sued for a defamatory statement carried in a newsgroup hosted on its server. Demon argued that it was not a publisher, as it merely provided the infrastructure necessary for the newsgroup posters to exchange views. The court, in rejecting this line of defence, held that because Demon had chosen to receive and store the newsgroup, and had the power to delete messages from it, it was at common-law a publisher, subject to any specific defences under the Defamation Act 1996 (discussed below).

While Demon's defence with regard to newsgroups failed, where ISPs do not store defamatory material in readily ascertainable forms like newsgroups or webpages, or simply transmit the material, it is not really accurate to say that they 'publish' it in the sense that we would understand it in the physical world. The term 'publication' in national libel laws, however, is sometimes used in a more technical legal sense to include the role of those persons who play an important role in the dissemination of the statement. In general, this broader interpretation means that, in addition to the author of the statement, publishers and editors are nearly always liable, and in some jurisdictions some degree of liability may also be imposed on distributors, such as printers, booksellers, libraries and newsagents.

Assessing the liability of ISPs with regard to the transmission of defamatory material thus involves an examination of the functions, or business practices, that the ISPs themselves have adopted, as this will often influence the application of the law by the courts. There are essentially three levels of activity that can be separated out:[179] the ISP as 'information carrier; (2) the ISP as 'information distributor'; and (3) the ISP as 'information controller'.

---

[177] 28 *Halsbury's Laws of England*, 4th edn, 'Libel and Slander', para 60.

[178] *The Times*, 20 April 1999.

[179] See also Edwards (n 176 above), p 192, and C Waelde, L Edwards, 'Defamation and the Internet: A Case Study of Anomalies and Difficulties in the Information Age' (1996) 10(2) International Review of Law Computers and Technology 263.

(1) *The ISP as 'information carrier'*. Here the ISP merely moves information from one place to another, without examining its contents. Most jurisdictions recognize that certain types of organization have such a limited role in the dissemination of statements that they should be granted immunity from defamation claims. Classic examples of such organizations are postal services and telecommunications organizations. Article 12 of the European E-commerce Directive provides that where an ISP is a 'mere conduit', a 'pass-through provider' which merely passes on information provided by a third party or provides access to a communications network, it will not be liable in respect of the content of the transmission.[180]

The E-commerce Directive also addresses the subject of caching in a similar manner. Cached information is that which is:

the subject of automatic, intermediate and temporary storage where that storage is for the sole purpose of making more efficient onward transmission of the information to other recipients of the service upon their request . . .[181]

Cached information usually takes the form of a temporary copy of a recently visited website, stored locally to facilitate more rapid access by the user. The Directive provides a similar immunity in relation to liability for such content on the part of intermediaries. The immunity here, however, is qualified insofar as ISPs are obliged, on receipt of 'actual knowledge' of the fact that information has been removed at the original source, or access to it there disabled, or that such removal has been ordered by a court, to ensure that it is also deleted or disabled on their servers.

(2) *The ISP as 'information distributor'*. Here the ISP's main function is the transportation of information, but the law presumes the ISP to have had the opportunity of examining the content of that information. The actual operational difference between an 'information distributor' ISP and an 'information carrier' ISP may be negligible. Thus the difference in their liability is based entirely on a legal presumption. Where a jurisdiction adopts an 'information distributor' model of defamation liability, the ISP will usually have a legal obligation to meet certain additional conditions in order to avoid liability. Simply taking no steps to monitor or control the content of the information it conveys to users will leave it exposed to liability. Following the passage of the Defamation Act 1996, UK defamation law is a clear example of the information distributor model. Here ISPs will generally not be considered to be publishers,[182] but will not escape liability unless they are able to demonstrate that they did not know and had no reason to believe the statement was defamatory,[183] and that they took 'reasonable care in relation to its publication'.[184] Article 14 of the E-commerce Directive (and the associated UK

---

[180] See also the UK Electronic Commerce (EC Directive) Regulations 2002, SI 2002/2013, reg 17.
[181] Article 13; see also the UK Electronic Commerce (EC Directive) Regulations 2002, SI 2002/2013, reg 18.
[182] Defamation Act 1996, s 1(3).     [183] Ibid, s 1(1)(b).     [184] Ibid, s 1(1)(c).

implementing legislation[185]) applies this standard of liability to a wide range of content, including defamation.[186]

(3) *The ISP as 'information controller'.*   Where an ISP makes a concerted effort to examine the information content it transmits, and to take action to prevent transmission if the content is unlawful, it will be liable if that 'editorial' function fails to stop the transmission of a defamatory statement.[187] This would certainly be the position under UK law,[188] and most likely under the laws of many other countries.

The liability of ISPs in the first and third categories is fairly clear. However, difficulties can arise when a jurisdiction's laws blur the line between the second and third categories. The Defamation Act 1996 provides a salutary example of this. ISPs are obliged to take some minimum steps to monitor information content to obtain liability protection under section 1(1), and once they are apprised of defamatory content on their servers they must take all reasonable steps to remove or deny access to it.[189] Yet, if UK ISPs begin monitoring in any depth, they open themselves to the contrary risk that they fall outside section 1(3), and will thus treated as publishers.[190]

With the passage of the Electronic Commerce (EC Directive) Regulations,[191] another potential difficulty for ISPs has been at least partially addressed. The concept of 'actual notice' is a key part of the immunities provided by the Directive in relation to caching and hosting unlawful content, including defamatory material. However, the Directive does not give any guidance as to what might constitute actual notice, something which was the subject of much criticism by the Internet industry during the UK Government's consultation prior to the introduction of the Regulations. Regulation 22 does provide the UK with some indication as to the scope of such notice by setting out a non-exhaustive list of factors which a court will consider in determining whether actual notice has been issued to the service provider. These include whether the service provider has received a notice through any means of contact that the service provider has made available in compliance with regulation 6(1)(c). Regulation 6(1) requires the service provider to make certain information available to the user 'in a form . . . which is easily, directly and perma-

---

[185]  See the UK Electronic Commerce (EC Directive) Regulations 2002, SI 2002/2013, reg 19.

[186]  The Directive articles on intermediary liability apply to all forms of civil liability, including copyright, while the UK Regulations take this a step further and apply to all forms of content generally, including criminal liability.

[187]  *Stratton Oakmont, Inc v Prodigy Services Co* (1995) 23 Media Law Rep (BNA) 1794, 5 CCH Computer Cases 47,291 (NY Sup Ct) (defendant bulletin board claimed in its advertising that it offered a family service, and that all its discussion groups were moderated. When the moderation process had failed, because Prodigy held itself out as exercising editorial control, the court held that it was liable for a statement defaming the claimant). D P Miranda, 'Defamation in Cyberspace: *Stratton Oakmont, Inc v Prodigy Services Co*' (1996) 5 Alb LJ Sci & Tech 229.

[188]  Defamation Act 1996, s 1(2): ' "editor" means a person having editorial or equivalent responsibility for the content of the statement or the decision to publish it'.

[189]  *Godfrey v Demon Internet Ltd, The Times,* 20 April 1999; see also the UK Electronic Commerce (EC Directive) Regulations 2002, SI 2002/2013, reg 19.

[190]  See, further, Edwards (n 176 above), p 194.                                   [191]  SI 2002/2013.

nently accessible'. Regulation 6(1)(c) refers to contact details of the service provider, including e-mail addresses, which permit rapid and direct communication. This requirement can be easily fulfilled by placing an obvious link on an institution's homepage which points to e-mail, telephone and other contact details. A dedicated e-mail address for dealing with complaints may be helpful, provided that it is checked at least daily for incoming mail. Other factors which a court should consider under regulation 22 are:

> (b) the extent to which any notice includes—
>> (i) the full name and address of the sender of the notice;
>> (ii) details of the location of the information in question; and
>> (iii) details of the unlawful nature of the activity or information in question.

This at least provides some guidance as to what constitutes 'actual notice', although the Internet industry remains unhappy in large part that the guidance remains insufficiently certain, prior to case law arising on this point. The lack of clarification as to what is sufficient to satisfy the requirement to 'act expeditiously to remove or to disable access to the information' in question is another source of complaint regarding lack of clarity. For example, if a complaint arises over a weekend and is dealt with promptly on the first working day thereafter (say the complaint is e-mailed on Saturday morning, and dealt with when the ISP's legal office reopens on Monday morning), is that expeditious enough? Or must it be within twenty-four hours? Or the same day? These matters remain to be clarified by the courts.

The USA has dealt with ISP liability for defamation (as well as other types of content) in a markedly different manner. Outside of the provisions in relation to copyright (see section 9.6.3.1), there exists a very wide immunity for ISPs. This lies in what remains of the Communications Decency Act 1996. Section 230 of the Act provides:

> No provider or user of an interactive computer service shall be treated as the publisher or speaker of any information provided by another information content provider.

> [It is the policy of] the US to preserve the vibrant and competitive free market that presently exists for the internet and other interactive computer services, *unfettered by federal or state regulation* . . . Congress made a policy choice . . . not to deter harmful online speech through the separate route of imposing tort liability on companies that serve as intermediaries for other parties' potentially injurious messages . . . the specter of tort liability in an area of such prolific speech would have an obvious chilling effect. Congress . . . chose to immunize service providers to avoid any restrictive effect.

This provision was originally to be found in the context of others designed to create new offences in relation to online pornography, in particular its availability to minors, and was intended to encourage ISPs to act as 'good Samaritans' by monitoring and removing 'indecent' content from their servers. In a landmark ruling by the US Supreme Court,[192] the other sections of this Act were found unconstitutional and

---

[192] *Reno v ACLU* (1997) US Supreme Court No 96-511; see supct.law.cornell.edu/supct/html/96-511.ZS.html.

were struck out. The full extent of the immunity in section 230, which remains in force, was illustrated in the case of *Zeran v America Online*,[193] where the ISP was held not liable for defamatory postings which it hosted, despite having received actual notification and failing to act to remove them.[194]

### 9.6.4 ISPs and criminal liability

#### 9.6.4.1 *Obscenity/Indecency*

If one were to take media reports about Internet information content at face value, one might be justified in believing that the primary activity on the Internet is the provision, distribution, and downloading of obscene and indecent materials, notably pictorial pornography.[195] Whilst it is certainly possible to locate such material with relative ease,[196] media statements as to its prevalence usually considerably overstate its role and status on the Internet. Despite this exaggeration, the result of the extensive coverage that the topic has received has placed the question of ISP liability for its possession and transmission firmly on the political agenda. There are, however, a number of difficult issues to address when considering the issue of liability. To begin with, there is no international understanding or definition of the type of material that would be considered 'obscene', 'indecent', or even 'pornographic'.

In the US, 'obscenity' is limited to sexual material, and requires the material to appeal to the prurient interest, as defined by reference to the standards of the local community, and to depict sexual conduct defined by the applicable state law.[197] This classification is not based on the potential effects of the material, but on whether it contravenes locally determined standards of acceptable sexual depiction. This leads to the somewhat unfortunate result that material which is unobjectionable in one US state may be viewed as obscene in another, with potentially deleterious effects for the publishers. In the traditional media, publishers can largely avoid falling foul of locally determined standards, by adjusting their distribution networks accordingly.

---

[193] (1997) 129 F 3d 327 (4th Cir).

[194] *Zeran* has been followed in *Blumenthal v Drudge* (1998) 992 F Supp 44, 51–2 (despite AOL's editorial control over a gossip columnist, the ISP was not liable for defamatory content as 'Congress has made a different policy choice by providing immunity, even where the interactive service provider has an active, even aggressive role in making available content prepared by others . . .') and *Ben Ezra, Wenstein & Co v America Online* (DNM 1999) (AOL to face no legal liability in respect of erroneous stock values of plaintiff corporation: '*Zeran* plainly immunizes computer service providers like AOL from liability for information that originates with third parties').

[195] And not just the media; see M Rimm, 'Marketing Pornography on the Information Superhighway' (1995) 83 Georgetown Law Journal 1849–1934 (archived at TRFN.pgh.pa.us/guest/mrstudy.html). This study caused immense controversy when first published, making the cover of *Time* magazine and being widely quoted during the passage of the ill-fated US Communications Decency Act. However, it was rapidly exposed as, at best, methodologically flawed. See, further, www2000.ogsm.vanderbilt. edu/cyberporn.debate.html.

[196] Yahoo, the popular search engine, contains a number of index pages to such material. See, eg,www.yahoo.com/Business-and-Economy/Companies/Sex/Directories/.

[197] See *Miller v California* (1973) 413 US 15.

For an ISP, this approach may simply be untenable, as those using or accessing a potentially objectionable Internet service might be based anywhere in the US.[198]

In the UK, by contrast, the term is not limited to sexual material, but applies to any material whose:

effect . . . is, if taken as a whole, such as to tend to deprave and corrupt persons who are likely . . . to read, see or hear the matter contained or embodied in it.[199]

Thus, while the depiction of sexual acts in pictorial or textual form is the most obvious form of potentially obscene material, UK case law demonstrates that action can also be taken against pamphlets and books about the use of drugs,[200] and material showing scenes of violence.[201]

Equally, the question of the standard that one might use to establish whether material is, or is not, pornographic is a highly contentious one and one that over the years has created some unusual alliances.[202] An example of the type of definition that may be used is 'offensive, degrading, and threatening material of an explicitly sexual or violent nature'. However, it is clear from the debates and the case law over the years that one person's 'offensive, degrading, and threatening material' may well be another's great work of literature,[203] great work of art,[204] protected social, political, or sexual statement, or holiday snaps.[205]

Where child pornography is concerned, while most jurisdictions are united in their prohibition of it, their national standards tend to be equally divergent. The rationales often provided for prohibiting such pornography include: that children

---

[198] This problem is clearly demonstrated by the case of *United States v Thomas* (1996) 74 F 3d 701 (6th Cir), cert denied, 117 S Ct 74, where a BBS operator was extradited from California to Tennessee to face criminal charges. It was stated in argument that the material, which was stored on a computer in California, was not obscene by Californian community standards, but the court determined that the appropriate standards by which to test for obscenity were the standards of Tennessee, the place in which the material was received and viewed.

[199] Obscene Publications Act 1959, s 1(1).

[200] *John Calder (Publications) Ltd v Powell* [1965] 1 All ER 159 (book concerning the life of a drug addict in New York held to be obscene); *R v Skirving and Another* [1985] 2 All ER 705 (book concerned with the use and abuse of cocaine and which contained detailed explanations, instructions and recipes for obtaining the maximum effect from ingesting the drug held to be obscene).

[201] *DPP v A & BC Chewing Gum Ltd* [1967] 2 All ER 504 (depiction of violent activity on chewing-gum cards held liable to tend to deprave or corrupt children, and thus to be obscene).

[202] eg, on this issue, but one would suspect few others, US feminist writers Catherine McKinnon, author of *Only Words* (Harvard University Press, 1994), and Andrea Dworkin, author of *Pornography: Men Possessing Women* (The Women's Press, 1981), agree with US Christian fundamentalist groups that certain materials are pornographic, though for very different reasons.

[203] eg, *Lady Chatterley's Lover* (*R v Penguin Books* [1961] Crim LR 176); *Last Exit to Brooklyn* (*R v Calder & Boyars Ltd* [1969] 1 QB 151).

[204] In June 1998, British police seized a book, *Mapplethorpe*, from the library at the University of Central England. It contained photographs of homosexual activity and bondage scenes taken by the internationally renowned photographer and artist Robert Mapplethorpe. Despite the fact that the book was widely acknowledged as serious artistic work, the police told the University that its contents might contravene the Obscene Publications Act 1959. In the event, no charges were brought.

[205] There have been a number of reports of film processors reporting to the police pictures of nude children taken by family members on holiday. These reports are however difficult to substantiate.

may be harmed in the making of the materials; that the materials may be used to persuade children that sexual activity with adults is acceptable; and that the material may encourage paedophiles to act out their fantasies. Thus, while, broadly speaking, depictions of minors engaged in sexual conduct will usually be held to be unlawful *per se*, regardless of local community standards, or the likelihood that the depictions might deprave and corrupt, there are significant differences between national rules.[206] Hence, depictions of adults who appear to be minors, and computer-manipulated depictions based on non-obscene images of minors and adults may be prohibited in some jurisdictions,[207] in others the actual participation of a minor may be required.[208] Equally, in some jurisdictions,[209] only pictorial child pornography is covered, whilst in others written child pornography is also illegal.[210] There is also no international agreement on the age of sexual consent. In the UK a minor for these purposes is a person under sixteen years of age, but in Tennessee[211] and Canada,[212] the relevant age is set at eighteen years.

This plethora of laws and approaches to obscene and indecent material can place ISPs and Intenet intermediaries in a difficult position with regard to its possession and transmission, particularly where those ISPs have an international presence, such as AOL and CompuServe. They may find themselves being held liable in one jurisdiction in which they operate, for activities that are perfectly legal in their other jurisdictions of operation.

*Possession by an ISP.*    In principle, in most jurisdictions, mere possession of an obscene article will not constitute an offence. That having been said, some jurisdictions, such as the UK, do make a distinction between child pornography and other

---

[206] In Canada, the situation has been complicated by the case of *R v Sharpe* where the British Columbia Court of Appeals upheld a lower-court ruling that the Canadian federal child pornography law, as currently drafted, breached constitutional rights that guarantee freedom of expression and the protection of privacy. It said the law was also flawed because it had the potential to penalize people for possessing and creating material that may merely be the products of the imagination and not intended for distribution. The court stated that 'Making it an offence to possess expressive material, when that material may have been created without abusing children and may never be published, distributed or sold, constitutes an extreme invasion of the values of liberty, autonomy and privacy protected by the rights and freedoms enshrined in the Charter'; *R v Sharpe* (BCCA 1999 416), judgment of 30 June 1999, para 171. See, further, Anon, 'Kiddie-Porn Law Headed to Top Court: BC Appeal Judges Decide 2-1 in Favour of Man Found with Child Pornography', *The Globe and Mail*, 1 July 1999, and www.courts. gov.bc.ca/jdb-txt/ca/99/04/c99-0416.html.

[207] Adults depicted as minors: 18 USC, s 2256(B) (US); computer-manipulated depictions: Protection of Children Act 1978 and the Criminal Justice Act 1988, s 160, both as amended by the Criminal Justice and Public Order Act 1994, ss 84 and 86 (UK); 18 USC, s 2256(C) (US). The constitutionality of the Child Pornography Protection Act 1996's prohibition on possession of child pornography was recently upheld by the United States First Circuit Court of Appeals in *US v Hilton* (1999) 167 F 3d 61.

[208] See *R v Sharpe* (n 206 above).

[209] eg, the UK.

[210] eg, New Zealand where child pornography is addressed in the Films, Videos and Publications Classification Act 1993, No 94-SNZ 1993. Publication is defined in this respect to include written materials.

[211] Tennessee Code, s 39-17-901(8).

[212] Section 163.1(1)(a) of the Canadian Criminal Code, RSC 1985, c C-46.

obscene or indecent material, with the possession of the child pornography constituting an offence in and of itself.[213] Where mere possession is not criminalized, prosecutors must usually show that some further element of intent is involved, this usually being an intent to distribute or exhibit the article. Sometimes that intent alone is sufficient to ground a criminal action,[214] whereas in some jurisdictions a more specific intent, that of distribution for gain must be proven.[215] Where child pornography is at issue, possession with intent to distribute is normally regarded as a more serious offence than mere possession.[216]

In circumstances where the basis of liability is possession, ISPs will only run the risk of liability for third-party content if they host or cache the offending material on their servers. In this situation, the act of possession will be committed in the jurisdiction where the server is physically located. It is possible that there may be a further risk involved where the ISP controls a server from a different jurisdiction, if the determination as to the jurisdiction in which the material is held is made by reference to the place of control, rather than the physical location of the data. As yet, however this type of issue does not appear to have arisen in any legal proceedings.

If an ISP is found to be in possession of obscene or indecent material, a prosecutor may also then additionally have to prove that the ISP knew that the file held on its server was unlawful.[217] Proving this with regard to an ISP's hosted and cached resources might very well prove difficult as it would, in most circumstances, almost certainly be uneconomic for an ISP to check all its files for obscene content. Under the UK Obscene Publications Act 1964 it is a defence for the accused to show that he has not examined the article and thus has no reasonable grounds for suspicion that his possession of it amounted to an offence. Whether this suggests that UK ISPs should simply abdicate any responsibility for checking of content is a moot point, for a criminal court might take the view that a deliberate policy of not undertaking any scrutiny of content negated the defence of lack of reasonable grounds for suspicion. The question of ISP liability in respect of criminal liability for third-party provided content has been clarified to a fair degree by the provisions of the Electronic Commerce (EC Directive) Regulations in relation to caching and hosting.[218] While the Directive to which they give force deals only with civil liability,[219] the UK Regulations also apply the same qualified immunities to criminal liability.

An alternative approach, and one seemingly favoured by UK ISPs, has been a

---

[213] See the UK Criminal Justice Act 1988, s 160, as amended by Criminal Justice and Public Order Act 1994, s 84(4) to cover 'pseudo photographs'. See also the California Penal Code, s 311.11(a).

[214] See, eg, California Penal Code, s 311.2(a); under, s 311.2(b) possession with intent to distribute for gain, where the subject is a minor, is a more serious offence.

[215] See, eg, the UK Obscene Publications Act 1964, s 1(2).

[216] See the California Penal Code, s 311.1(a) (possession with intent to distribute), s 311.2(b) (intent to distribute for commercial consideration).

[217] See, eg, the California Penal Code, s 311.11(a).

[218] See, further, section 9.6.3.2 above and the Electronic Commerce (EC Directive) Regulations 2002, SI 2002/2013, regs 18, 19.

[219] Criminal-law matters are beyond the remit of the European Parliament.

combination of hotlines for individuals to report illegal materials, and other self-regulatory mechanisms such as Codes of Conduct for their clients, with coordination through a UK self-regulatory body for ISPs, the Internet Watch Foundation.[220] Whilst this approach almost certainly cannot totally prevent the storage and transmission of illegal material via an ISP's servers, it would appear to have reduced the amount of such material on UK ISPs to a level with which the authorities and law-enforcement agencies are willing to live, whilst not imposing too rigorous an economic burden on the ISPs themselves.

Where intent to distribute is required for liability, the issue of whether an ISP, whose primary role is the transmission of data packets, has the requisite intention by virtue of possessing a copy of the file arises. This issue was handled in UK law by amendments to section 1(2) of the Obscene Publications Act 1964.[221] However, because the offence under section 1(2) is only committed if the intention is to distribute for gain, a website host will only be criminally liable under this section if it has paid subscribers, and possibly only if access to the offending website requires a separate subscription.

*Transmission by an ISP.*    It is clear that the primary purpose of most obscenity laws is to prevent the distribution of pornographic material, presumably on the ground that if individuals are prevented from distributing it, at least some of the motivation for producing it in the first place will be lost. As such, the laws clearly target distributors over possessors. This is where the aims of the legislators and courts clash most obviously with the role of ISPs, as the primary purpose of ISPs is the paid transmission of information. From the ISPs' point of view, and depending upon their particular business model, the more people sending and receiving information, or the more information that is sent, the better, regardless of the content of that information. Legal measures that slow the flow of information dissuade people from using the medium, or impose higher costs on the service, are all undesirable. From the point of view of lawmakers, for national content laws to have any meaning, they must be applied to all media, or the distributors of undesirable content will simply shift their focus to the weakly regulated medium. The difficulty lies in determining what constitutes reasonable regulation within a new medium, and in ensuring that the financial burden of any regulation does not destroy the growth of that medium.[222]

Three different approaches to that dilemma can be ascertained from existing laws. The first approach criminalizes the knowing distribution of obscene material.[223] This approach allows ISPs to plead ignorance of the content of the material that they host

---

[220] See www.iwf.org.uk, especially www.iwf.org.uk/stats/stats.html.

[221] See the Criminal Justice and Public Order Act 1994, s 168 and Sch 9, para 3.

[222] For an interesting, if unconventional, assessment of this balance see P Johnson, 'Pornography Drives Technology: Why Not to Censor the Internet' (1996) 49(1) Federal Communications Law Journal, www.law.indiana.edu/fclji/pubs/v49/no1/johnson.html.

[223] See, eg, the Tennessee Code, s 39-17-902(a): 'It is unlawful to knowingly . . . prepare for distribution, publish, print, exhibit, distribute, or offer to distribute, or to possess with intent to distribute or to exhibit or offer to distribute any obscene matter . . .'

or retransmit, providing that they do not monitor the contents of their servers. Problems may arise, however, if the relevant law defines knowledge to include constructive knowledge.[224] Hosting Usenet newsgroups such as those in the alt.binaries.pictures.erotica.* hierarchy, or alt.sex.bestiality, or webpages with names such as *.supersex.com/cumming.html and *.gang-bang.com/hardcoreXXX/Ebony would suggest, fairly strongly, constructive knowledge.

The second approach criminalizes distribution of obscene material for gain, subject to a defence of lack of knowledge or reasonable suspicion of contents.[225] This would potentially catch ISPs who carried the Usenet newsgroups and websites listed above, but would seem to permit ISPs not to have to filter all the files on, and transmissions to and from, their systems.

The third approach criminalizes knowing distribution of obscene material, but provides a specific exemption from liability for intermediaries who merely provide access to other servers without participating actively in the production or distribution of the material.[226]

This model is gradually becoming more prevalent, a recent example being the German Federal Law to Regulate the Conditions for Information and Communications Services 1997 ('the Multimedia Law'). Under article 5(3) of the Multimedia Law, ISPs are provided with a blanket immunity from liability except insofar as they are aware that certain material is unlawful and fail to comply with a legal duty to block access to it.[227] Intermediaries who host material, however, are liable under article 5(2) for unlawful content if (a) they know that the content is unlawful, and (b) it is technically possible for the intermediary to block access and it is reasonable to expect such blocking to be effected.[228] Liability for material distributed from the intermediary's own servers, for example, from a hosted website, remains based on knowledge of the intermediary. The effect of this approach is to provide criminal sanctions against an intermediary who knowingly hosts or caches obscene material, but removes the danger of liability from those intermediaries who merely act as transmitters of third-party originated packets, whatever the intermediary's state of knowledge. This degree of immunity, however, may be predicated on a

---

[224] See the Tennessee Code, s 39-17-901(1): 'Actual or constructive knowledge: a person is deemed to have constructive knowledge of the contents of material who has knowledge of facts which would put a reasonable and prudent person on notice as to the suspect nature of the material.'

[225] See, eg, the UK Obscene Publications Act 1959, s 2(1).

[226] See, eg, the California Penal Code, s 312.6(a): 'It does not constitute a violation of this chapter for a person or entity solely to provide access or connection to or from a facility, system, or network over which that person or entity has no control, including related capabilities that are incidental to providing access or connection. This subdivision does not apply to an individual or entity that is owned or controlled by, or a conspirator with, an entity actively involved in the creation, editing, or knowing distribution of communications that violate this chapter.'

[227] German Multimedia Law 1997, art 5(4): 'any duties to block the use of illegal content according to the general laws remain unaffected, insofar as the service provider gains knowledge of such content . . .'

[228] See F W Bulst, 'Hear No Evil, See No Evil, Answer for No Evil: Internet Service Providers and Intellectual Property: The New German Teleservices Act' [1997] European Intellectual Property Law Review 32.

fairly simple ISP business model, where the ISP simply provides Internet access. Providing more sophisticated services may still leave an ISP or Intenet intermediary open to more stringent rules.[229]

Some jurisdictions impose criminal liability for the transmission of obscene, indecent or other unlawful material through their national telecommunications laws. Since Internet communications are often carried across telecommunications networks, these laws will also potentially be applicable. Examples of such laws are 18 USC, section 1465[230] and section 43 of the UK Telecommunications Act 1994.[231] Such offences are usually only committed by the sender of the material, which suggests that an ISP, which merely transmits packets originating outside its systems, cannot be liable.[232] Matters become less certain when the ISP hosts a website—it may be perceived that the ISP does send the material, in that its software responds to requests for the obscene resource by transmitting it to the requesting user,[233] although it would seem more logical to decide that the true sender is in fact the controller of the resource.

### 9.6.4.2 *Publication restrictions*

Another area concerning information content where the potential criminal liability of ISPs remains uncertain, due largely to a lack of decided case law, is that of criminal contempt of court.[234] Criminal contempts essentially fall into five categories:

---

[229] This appears to be the situation in France, where the French Telecommunications Law of July 1996 provides those supplying basic ISP services with a limited immunity for content liability. In the situation where an intermediary hosts webpages for third parties, an increasingly common option for ISPs, a court ruled in 1998 that in providing file storage and transfer facilities at the disposal of the public the intermediary was no longer a mere access provider, and became responsible for the content of its site even in the absence of knowledge: Tribunal de grande instance de Paris, référé, 9 juin 1998 et Cour d'appel de Paris, 14éme Chambre, section A, 10 février 1999, *Affaire Estelle Hallyday c Altern* (France) (www.legalis.net/legalnet/judiciaire/decisions/ca–100299.htm).

[230] Offence of using a means of interstate commerce for the purpose of transporting obscene material.

[231] Offence of using a public telecommunications system to send grossly offensive, threatening or obscene material. See T Gibbons, 'Computer Generated Pornography' [1995] 9 International Yearbook of Law Computers and Technology 83.

[232] This supposition is supported by the UK Electronic Commerce (EC Directive) Regulations 2002, SI 2002/2013, reg 17, which provides an immunity for intermediaries acting as a 'mere conduit', transmitting content provided by a third party from one place to another at the request of the third party and without exercising any form of control over the material or selection of its recipient.

[233] This may be the correct interpretation of the UK Indecent Displays (Control) Act 1981, s 1(1), which creates an offence of publicly displaying indecent matter in public or in a manner which permits it to be visible from any public place (s 1(2)). Although section 1(3) exempts places which exclude those under 18 and make a charge for admission, this does not apply to the section 1(1) offence. It has been suggested that this might impose liability for websites, on the grounds that they can be accessed from terminals in public places; see G Smith (ed), *Internet Law and Regulation*, 2nd edn (FT Law & Tax, 1997), p 260.

[234] In England and Wales, a distinction is drawn between 'civil' and 'criminal' contempts. In broad terms, civil contempt relates to circumstances where parties breach an order of court made in civil proceedings, for example, injunctions or undertakings, and as such are not relevant here. Criminal contempt, in contrast, is aimed at various types of conduct that might interfere with the administration of justice, and is designed to have both a punitive and deterrent effect. See G Smith (ed), *Internet Law and Regulation* (FT Law & Tax, 1996) and A Charlesworth, 'Criminal Liability', in C Armstrong (ed), *Electronic Law and the Information Society* (Library Association, 1999), pp 120–49.

(a) The publication of materials prejudicial to a fair criminal trial.

(b) The publication of materials prejudicial to fair civil proceedings.

(c) The publication of materials interfering with the course of justice as a continuing process.

(d) Contempt in the face of the court.

(e) Acts which interfere with the course of justice.

Whilst the law of contempt of court has been largely developed by the judiciary through the common law, it has been modified to some extent by the Contempt of Court Act 1981.[235] This makes it an offence of strict liability to publish a publication which 'includes any speech, writing, broadcast, cable programme or other communication in whatever form, which is addressed to the public at large, or any section of the public'[236] where such a publication 'creates a substantial risk that the course of justice in the proceedings in question will be seriously impeded or prejudiced'.[237]

The fact that it is an offence of strict liability means that an offence occurs even where the person making the publication did not intend to interfere with the course of justice. The broad definition of 'publication' would cover USENET messages, e-mail messages sent to mailing lists and webpages. The publication of material relating to a case will only be an offence where it occurs when the case is still *sub judice*. The statutory 'strict liability' rule is only applied during the period that the case is 'active' and the definition of 'active' is laid down in the Act. However, in circumstances where an individual knows, or has good reason to believe, that proceedings are imminent, and publishes material which is likely or calculated to impede or prejudice the course of justice before the point laid down in the Act as the time when the case is 'active', may still constitute a common-law contempt.

Defences to the 'strict liability' offence are:

(a) A person will not be guilty of contempt of court under the strict-liability rule as the publisher of any matter to which that rule applies if at the time of publication (having taken all reasonable care) he does not know and has no reason to suspect that the relevant proceedings are active.[238]

(b) A person will not be guilty of contempt of court under the strict-liability rule as the distributor of a publication containing any such matter if at the time of publication (having taken all reasonable care) he does not know that it contains such matter and has no reason to suspect that it is likely to do so.[239]

(c) A person is not guilty of contempt of court under the strict-liability rule in respect of a fair and accurate report of legal proceedings held in public, published contemporaneously and in good faith.[240]

---

[235] However the 1981 Act does not codify or replace entirely the common law. It does, however, apply to Scotland (s 15).

[236] Contempt of Court Act 1981, s 2(1).

[237] Ibid, s 2(2).

[238] Ibid, s 3(1).

[239] Ibid, s 3(2).

[240] Ibid, s 4(1).

The enforcement of the law of contempt has been rendered more difficult in modern times, by the ability of individuals to publish material, in both traditional[241] and digital media, in countries outside the court's jurisdiction. The Internet has in many ways exacerbated this situation. A prime example of this concerns the 1993 murder trials in Ontario, Canada, of Karla Homolka and Paul Bernado. During the trial of Karla Homolka for the murders of two teenaged girls, Kristen French and Leslie Muhaffy, the court ordered a publication ban on reports of the trial in Ontario, in order to ensure a fair trial for Homolka's husband Paul Bernado (aka Paul Teale), also charged with the murders.[242] Despite the ban, however, information was widely available due to coverage by US newspapers, cable and TV stations, and at least one website based at a US university.[243] A Usenet newsgroup set up to disseminate and discuss information about the trial, alt.fan.karla-homolka, was censored by many Canadian universities, which were concerned about their liability to contempt proceedings.[244]

Whilst denying access to webpages is more difficult than cutting off newsgroups, it has been suggested with regard to the Internet that where the court cannot bring contempt proceedings against the original publisher, it may seek to do so against the ISP that distributed the material within the court's jurisdiction. Of course, in addition to the defence to distribution of a contempt discussed above, the defences to liability set out in the E-commerce Regulations will also be potentially available to an ISP.[245]

## 9.7 E-COMMERCE AND THE JURISDICTION QUESTION

A general rule of contract formation is that parties are free to contract as they wish, including the freedom to agree the laws and the jurisdiction[246] which they wish to govern the contract. They do this not only to ensure that they will know the laws which govern the contract but also that they know the rules and procedure of the courts which may have to determine any dispute that arises as a consequence of the

---

[241] Consider, for instance, the *Spycatcher* saga, where the book in question was freely available outside the UK, but could not be published or excerpted in the UK. The judicial ban was imposed by preliminary injunction to ensure that the main trial, where the UK Government sought to prevent publication of the allegations made in the book, was not rendered meaningless by prior publication in the UK. It is likely that a similar UK publication ban today would be rendered ineffective by Web publication within hours. See, eg, the events surrounding the case *Nottinghamshire County Council v Gwatkin*, 3 June 1997, Ch D (unreported), and *Cyber-Rights & Cyber-Liberties (UK) Newsletter* Issue Number 2, June 1997 at www.leeds.ac.uk/law/pgs/yaman/newslet2.htm.

[242] See Action No 125/93, *R v Bernardo* [1993] OJ No 2047 at www2.magmacom.com/djakob/censor/mediaban.txt. Also C Walker, 'Cybercontempt: Fair Trials and the Internet' (1997–8) 3 Oxford Yearbook of Media and Entertainment Law 1.

[243] Information from www.cs.indiana.edu/canada/karla.html.

[244] Information from www.cs.indiana.edu/canada/BannedInCanada.txt.

[245] See Regulations 17–19.

[246] These are two separate issues. Parties can choose a jurisdiction without choosing a law or choose a law without choosing a jurisdiction, but this is rare and can be dangerous.

contract. However, the fact that the parties can choose the law or jurisdiction does not necessarily mean that the choice is valid or enforceable[247] and this is why the actual location of the contract formation has such an important bearing on this matter. The contractual terms which purport to define the law and jurisdiction must be valid and the question of validity is determined by the laws of the jurisdiction in which the contract is formed regardless of any term within the contract itself. This point is often forgotten but it is vital. Every jurisdiction has rules which govern the freedom of parties to choose the law or jurisdiction[248] of a contract and it is these rules which will determine whether or not the terms or choices themselves are valid.[249]

The borderless nature of the Internet gives rise to legal issues for commercial transactions which occur over, or in some way involve use of the Internet. If a transaction takes place between computers or parties in different jurisdictions then the question arises as to which laws govern the transaction. This is compounded by the problem that the involvement of different jurisdictions is not immediately apparent. Another question which must be asked is: where was the contract formed, or even was a contract formed at all? And the question which must always be asked is: does the jurisdiction in which any agreement was entered into recognize that agreement as a legally valid contract?

Attempts have been made to deal with the question of choice of law and jurisdiction in electronic contracts. Some of the more interesting are the attempts made in the draft revision of the Uniform Commercial Code. Articles 2, 2A and 2B contain several interesting elements. Of particular interest is the inclusion of provisions to deal with the default choice of law and jurisdiction[250] of any contracts entered into

---

[247] Unfair Terms in Consumer Contracts Regulations 1994, SI 1994/3159, reg 3(7) states that: 'These Regulations shall apply notwithstanding any contract term which applies or purports to apply the law of a non-Member State, if the contract has a close connection with the territory of the Member States.'

[248] The Brussels Regulation (Council Regulation (EC) No 44/2001 of 22 December 2000 on jurisdiction and the recognition and enforcement of judgments in civil and comercial matters, OJ L12/1, 16 January 2001) applies to Member States of the European Union and governs the choice of jurisdiction for civil and commercial matters within the European Union. The basic rule in Art 2(1) is that a defendant may always be sued in the courts of the country where he is domiciled, which for a company is the country of incorporation. Additional jurisdictions are also available, depending on the nature of the claim. For example, in matters relating to contracts the defendant may also be sued in the jurisdiction in which the contract is to be performed.

An additional point which is relevant to e-commerce is the special rule for consumer contracts in Art 15(1)(c) which allows the consumer to sue in his home courts if the business 'directed' its activities there. The meaning of this provision is disputed, ranging from an assertion that a website which is accessible in a jurisdiction is by definition directing its activities there, to the other extreme that a business which does not intend to sell in a particular country is not directing its activities there even if it does in fact sell to customers in that country. This uncertainty will ultimately need to be resolved by either amending legislation or a judgment of the European Court of Justice.

[249] The choice may be valid but the term in which that choice is made may itself be invalid. In this case the whole term falls apart and the choice disappears into the great courtroom in the sky. Equally the term may be valid but the choice of law invalid. The term survives but is completely ineffective.

[250] Section 2B–108: '(a) A choice-of-law term in an agreement is enforceable. (b) If an agreement does not have a choice-of-law term, the following rules apply: (1) In an access contract or a contract providing

which come under the code. Though the provisions are interesting they would appear to be unworkable in most jurisdictions outside of the United States and its commonwealth and in any case the draft revision will only bind states and territories that enact the provisions. The call by the United States for the international adoption of the UNCITRAL Model Law would help in enabling the common provisions to be satisfied and so be applicable in many more jurisdictions. The Model Law, however, does not go so far as to attempt to solve the jurisdictional questions. Indeed the Model Law would be an incorrect forum to do so as it is simply concerned with the mechanisms of contract formation. It should not deal with jurisdictional issues in a prescriptive manner as these are issues which are within the sole competence of individual states to adjudicate according to their own rules on the conflicts of laws.

Jurisdiction will be a central issue in many cases on intermediary liability. Differing cultural values and norms inevitably give rise to differing legal standards of content regulation, a fact which often raises problems for those who distribute material online. During 2000, Internet giant Yahoo was sued in the French courts in respect of Nazi memorabilia and neo-Nazi materials being sold via its auction site. The site was based in the US but, as is the nature of the Internet, available worldwide, including in France, where it is illegal to offer such items for sale. The French courts ordered Yahoo to block the availability of pages offering such items from view by French-based Internet users.[251] A Californian court later granted an injunction to Yahoo to the effect that the French judgment would not be enforced within the USA.[252] As it turned out, in the end Yahoo decided to ban the sale of Nazi-related material altogether from sale on its auction sites, but this did not prevent Timothy Koogle, former chairman and chief executive of Yahoo US, from being arrested in France and facing charges of justifying war crimes before a criminal court in Paris.[253] This case indicates the difficulties which can arise where differing

for delivery of a copy by electronic communication, the contract is governed by the law of the jurisdiction in which the licensor is located when the contract becomes enforceable between the parties. (2) A consumer contract not governed by subsection (b)(1) which requires delivery of a copy on a physical medium to the consumer is governed as to the contractual rights and obligations of the parties by the law of the jurisdiction in which the copy is located when the licensee receives possession of the copy or, in the event of nondelivery, the jurisdiction in which the receipt was to have occurred. (3) In all other cases, the contract is governed by the law of the State with the most significant relationship to the contract. (c) If the jurisdiction whose law applies as determined under subsection (b) is outside the United States, subsection (b) applies only if the laws of that jurisdiction provide substantially similar protections and rights to the party not located in that jurisdiction as are provided under this article. Otherwise, the rights and duties of the parties are governed by the law of the jurisdiction in the United States which has the most significant relationship to the transaction. (d) A party is located at its place of business if it has one place of business, at its chief executive office if it has more than one place of business, or at its place of incorporation or primary registration if it does not have a physical place of business. Otherwise, a party is located at its primary residence.'

[251] *LICRA v Yahoo* (Tribunal de Grande Instance de Paris, 22 May 2000). For an unofficial English translation, see www.juriscom.net/txt/jurisfr/cti/yauctions20000522.htm

[252] *Yahoo v LICRA* (US District Court for the Northern District of California, San Jose Division Case no C-00-21275 JF, Judgment filed 7 November 2001). Available online at www.eff.org/Net_culture/Global_village/LICRA_v_Yahoo/20011107_us_distct_decision.pdf.

[253] *Le Monde*, 8 January 2003. The criminal court later dismissed all charges, finding that Yahoo had never tried to 'justify war crimes [or] crimes against humanity'. See www.cdt.org/jurisdiction.

national content regulations compete to regulate online content which is available internationally.

For defamation, the question of where publication takes place is key to determining the appropriate jurisdiction in which an action should be brought. As regards libel actions in the traditional print media, the UK courts appear to take the line that publication will be deemed to have occurred in every jurisdiction in which the publisher ought to have foreseen it would be made available. This excludes copies brought privately into jurisdictions where it was not otherwise foreseeable that the publication would be made available.[254] This makes sense from both a practical point of view, in that a print-media publisher will be aware of both the distribution chain for his product, and the number of physical copies made, and from a pragmatic legal point of view, in that the potential damage done to an individual's reputation by the odd personal copy that is transported into jurisdictions not served by the publisher, will necessarily be limited. With publications made via the Internet, however, the situation becomes more complex. The place at which an online publication is made may be either:

(a) The place at which the material is uploaded to the ISP's servers. In this case, a single jurisdiction would be regarded as the place of publication; or

(b) The place at which it is downloaded and read, which could potentially be anywhere in the world.

In *Shevill and Others v Presse-Alliance SA*[255] the European Court of Justice held that where the Brussels Convention 1988 applies,[256] a defamation action may be brought both where the publication occurred and where the claimant suffered damage to his reputation. The latter place is most likely to be interpreted as where the defamatory statement was read, ie, the location of the viewer. On that basis, ISPs (and authors) will inevitably be exposed to liability in every country of the world, although *Shevill* suggests that a court may only award compensation for the damage to the claimants reputation in its jurisdiction, and not damages for all losses worldwide. In the case of Internet defamation, that will probably be sufficient to make it worthwhile for intermediaries to be sued in a 'claimant-friendly' jurisdiction. Indeed, in *Shevill* the Advocate-General of the European Court of Justice expressed exactly this point, saying:

. . . the English courts could even find themselves in danger, by reason of their 'generosity' towards victims of defamation, of becoming the natural choice of forum in such matters.[257]

---

[254] *Shevill and Others v Presse-Alliance SA* [1992] 1 All ER 409, CA, [1995] 2 WLR 499, ECJ.
[255] [1995] 2 WLR 499.
[256] Where the Brussels Convention does not apply, the English courts have the power to stay proceedings on the ground that there is insufficient connection with the jurisdiction, eg, if the publication in England is small in comparison to worldwide publication; *Berezovsky v Forbes Inc, The Times*, 19 January 1998.
[257] Opinion of Advocate-General Leger, para 56.

More recently, the Australian High Court has held the place of publication to be the point of downloading. In *Dow Jones & Co Inc v Joeseph Gutnick*[258] the court considered that the focus of defamation is upon the damage which it causes to reputation. A defamation can only cause such harm when 'comprehended by the reader, the listener or the observer', thus publication of a defamation is a bilateral process which can only be complete once the publisher has made the article in question available *and* it is available for perusal by a third party. Internet material is not available to the reader in a comprehensible form until it has been downloaded onto the computer of an individual who has acquired it from the server using an Internet browser. The place where the information is downloaded is the place where damage to reputation may be done, therefore, the court held, that will, as a rule, be the place where the tort of defamation is committed.

## 9.8  CONCLUSION

The Internet as we know it, basically the World Wide Web, is now just about a decade old. In that time, it has moved from a leftfield information resource to a broadly commercial advertising medium and forum across which the undertaking of actual commercial transactions has become routine. Much progress in relation to legal regulation of this sector has been made during the last several years, although this is still a developing area of law. The importance of properly drafted contracts remains paramount; there is still a key role for the commercial lawyer to play.

While the position of the commercial service providers with respect to legal liability is becoming clarified, there remain many unanswered questions and grey areas requiring interpretation by the courts. As new technological advances, such as the advent of third-generation mobile phones with streaming video and wireless Internet-access capabilities, bring about increasing convergence between different sectors, commercial considerations will encourage ISPs to continue to add more enhanced services to their standard packages, potentially opening up new areas of liability in the process. The shape of the law regulating e-commerce to come is far from set in stone.

[258] [2002] HCA 56.

# 10

# EMPLOYMENT RIGHTS IN AN INFORMATION SOCIETY

*John Angel*

## 10.1 INTRODUCTION

Employment lawyers are used to considering employment rights largely in the context of unfair dismissal, redundancy, discrimination and trade-union laws. This chapter will show that the new Information Society demands an extension of the fields of law traditionally viewed as employment law in the light of radical techno-logical developments in our society.

What do we mean by an Information Society? Firstly, it is one where an increasing proportion of society's wealth is made up of 'information' rather than tangible goods. Secondly, it is one which enables much of traditional work, commerce and leisure to be undertaken anywhere and at any time at a person's choice. This wireless, global connectivity is made possible largely through digital technology which converts information, including sound, images, and even smells, as well as text, into similar formats for transporting anywhere at incredible speeds through broadband telecommunications systems. It is no less than an 'Information Revolution', on a par with the Industrial Revolution of the nineteenth century. Already today, a person can take his multimedia computer and mobile phone to most places in the world and communicate by voice or visually, without the need to plug into anything. Bearing in mind our employment laws were largely developed on the basis of the Industrial Revolution there is need for a reappraisal and this chapter sets out to examine two main areas. First, if the wealth of organizations is now largely based on information rather than tangible assets then the rules relating to 'ownership' need to be re-examined to see what rights apply as between employer and worker. Secondly, the increasing trend to more flexible approaches to work facilitated by new technology will be examined in the context of laws facilitating this development. This requires an understanding of new fields of law arising from the radical changes happening in our society.

## 10.2  CONTRACT OF EMPLOYMENT

Before considering this new analysis, there needs to be a brief review of the basis of any employment relationship, namely the contract of employment. Such contracts comprise both express and implied terms. With the advent of the Information Society described in section 10.1 above, the only constant is continuing change brought about by new technology and the need to be flexible to stay competitive. Most employment contracts today have express flexibility and mobility clauses to facilitate this constant need for change. Even where they are absent, the courts are predisposed towards flexibility where the purpose is the efficient running of the enterprise.

In *Cresswell v Board of Inland Revenue*[1] a group of tax officers brought an action against the Inland Revenue for refusing to pay them unless they worked a new computerized system for administering PAYE. The court found that the employer had not broken the contract since there was an implied contractual duty on the part of the employees 'to adapt themselves to new methods and techniques'[2] of working. The employer had in turn an obligation to train the employee, if the change required it.

The *Cresswell* case related to doing the same job but using a computer. Where the job definition is required to change substantially, then unless there is an express flexibility clause covering the change, employers cannot insist on a unilateral variation of the contract. However, the dismissal of an employee who refuses to accept such a change would not necessarily be unfair. Where the old job, in effect, disappears because the requirement to do the job has ceased or diminished, this may be a redundancy situation, and provided the dismissal is carried out in a way which is procedurally fair, then an employer can dismiss without breaching the law.[3] Even if there is not a redundancy situation, insisting on changes to the job might still be fair where there is a business need for reorganization.[4]

---

[1] [1984] IRLR 190.                                      [2] Ibid, 199.
[3] Employment Rights Act 1996, s 98(1), (3); and see *Polkey v AE Dayton Services Ltd* [1987] IRLR 503, HL.                              [4] Employment Rights Act 1996, s 98(4).

Increasingly in this information age, workers are not employees, but independent contractors. In order to maintain flexibility and keep costs down, many enterprises use contractors for specialist requirements as and when needed, and only retain a 'core' workforce. How is the status of a worker determined? Historically, the test to determine whether a contract was one of employment or for services was whether or not the employer controlled or had the right to control the job that the employee did and the way it was done. The 'control' test became outdated with a more skilled workforce and the concept of empowerment, and the courts then considered the extent to which workers were an 'integral part of the business' as opposed to being merely an accessory to it. More recently, the courts have moved to a multiple-factor test, one which retains the test of control, but combines it with a test of mutual obligation. So, factors like whether or not there is an entrepreneurial element in the relationship,[5] the degree of control, the risk of loss and chance of profit, the provision of equipment, methods of tax and National Insurance payment, and the intentions of the parties,[6] are matters which will be taken into account.

The implementation of the European Working Time Directive[7] by the Working Time Regulations 1998,[8] which gives entitlements to 'workers', together with DTI guidelines,[9] helps further define who are the genuinely self-employed.[10] Someone who is pursuing a business activity on his own account is such a person and factors to be taken into account to determine this include:

- whether he is paid on the basis of an invoice or similar demand for payment rather than receiving wages;
- how he is taxed;
- whether he can decide not to accept work;
- whether he is free to do the same type of work for more than one enterprise;
- whether he provides his own tools and equipment;
- whether he has his own helpers;
- what degree of financial risk he takes;
- what degree of responsibility for investment and management he has; and
- whether and how far he has an opportunity of profiting from sound management in the performance of their task.

Difficulties often arise where employment agencies are involved and individuals hire themselves out through their own limited companies. In addition to applying the

---

[5] *Market Investigations Ltd v Minister of Social Security* [1968] 3 All ER 732; *Nethermere (St Neots) Ltd v Taverna and Gardiner* [1984] IRLR 240, CA.

[6] *O'Kelly v Trusthouse Forte plc* [1983] IRLR 369, CA.

[7] Directive 93/104/EC of 23 November 1993 concerning certain aspects of the organization of working time, OJ L307, 13 December 1993.

[8] SI 1998/1833.

[9] *A Guide to the Working Time Regulations* (DTI, September 1998) (URN 98/894).

[10] In *Byrne Brother (Formwork) Ltd v Baird and Others* [2002] IRLR 96 the fact that a contract provided that in certain circumstances services could be provided by someone other than the contractor himself did not prevent the worker being subject to the Regulations.

above tests the courts will first seek to ascertain whether there was a contract of any kind between the individual and the company for whom the work is performed.[11] Mutuality of obligation and control are the irreducible minimum legal requirements for the existence of such a contract of employment.[12]

The fact that employment status is relevant as to whether workers are eligible for statutory employment rights and that the various rights often treat this question in different and inconsistent ways has resulted in the UK Government issuing a consultation document in relation to the subject.[13]

As will be appreciated from the following discussion, employment status is a key factor in an Information Society.

## 10.3 INTELLECTUAL PROPERTY RIGHTS AND EMPLOYEES

### 10.3.1 Copyright

The fundamental property laws of an Information Society are those which relate to intellectual property, and the most important intellectual property right ('IPR') is copyright (see Chapter 5). One of the big issues with all proprietary rights relates to their ownership. The general rule under sections 9 and 11(1) of the Copyright, Designs and Patents Act 1988 ('CDPA 1988') is that information (which may be literary, dramatic, musical or artistic) which amounts to an original work, such as a book, marketing brochure, CD or a legal opinion, will first be owned by the person who creates it. The legal standard in the UK for establishing 'copyright' is low and does not involve any element of creativity, only that the work has not been copied. All such works are made by people, except computer-generated works. Where these people are employees who make the works during the course of their employment, the employer is the owner of copyright in the work.[14]

Two issues arise here. First, with the increasing use of contractors, who owns the copyright? This is particularly relevant where a work is created by a number of people, some of whom are employees and some contractors. For example, in *John Richardson Computers Ltd v Flanders*[15] there was a dispute over the copying of a computer program and the plaintiff first had to establish that he owned the copyright in the program. This was quite difficult because the program was developed over a period of time by different people, some employees, some contractors (of whom some were ex-employees), and generally the software company had not entered into express assignments of IPRs. The court found that the plaintiff had an equitable

---

[11]  See *Hewlett Packard Ltd v O'Murphy* [2002] IRLR 4.
[12]  See *Montgomery v Johnson Underwood Ltd* [2001] IRLR 269.
[13]  'Discussion Document on Employment Status in Relation to Statutory Employment Rights' (DTI, July 2002) (URN 02/1058) available at www.dti.gov.uk/er/individual/statusdiscuss.pdf.
[14]  CDPA 1988, s 11(2).
[15]  [1993] FSR 497.

interest in nearly all parts of the program not developed by employees, and that the contractors held their rights in trust for the company. However, there is no guarantee of such a finding which depends on the facts of each case. The increasing use of contractors in all parts of business makes it much more difficult to protect company property, and could give rights to some workers which previously were taken for granted as being 'owned by the employer'.

If the employer wishes, he may allow the employee to be the first owner of the copyright under the CDPA 1988.[16] In these times of scarce expert high-tech resources, some employees will be in strong negotiating positions and may insist on owning their own works.

The second issue relates to whether or not the work is undertaken 'in the course of employment'. In these days of homeworking, possibly using one's own computer, it will not be so obvious whether the work has been undertaken by an employee in the course of employment. The position may be apparent from the job description. However, the trend towards more general descriptions with increased flexibility and mobility, could make this more uncertain. A basic test is whether the skill, effort and judgment expended by the employee in creating the work are part of the employee's normal duties (express or implied) or within any special duties assigned to him by the employer. If the answer is 'no', then the employee will be the first owner of the work, even if he has used his employer's equipment or received help from the employer. In *Stephenson Jordan & Harrison Ltd v MacDonald*[17] an employed accountant gave some lectures which he later incorporated into a book. It was held that, even though his employer had provided secretarial help, the copyright in the lectures belonged to the accountant because he was employed as an accountant to advise clients and not to deliver public lectures. However, part of the book was based on a report that the accountant had written for a client of his employer, and it was held that the copyright in this part belonged to the employer. So employers need to draft job descriptions carefully and keep them up to date. Also, where there is any doubt as to first ownership, agreement should be reached before the employee starts the work.

Today many works are created by computers. Where the computer assists a person in making the work, the rules on ownership are the same as for any other work. Where the computer generates the work without human intervention, the author is 'the person by whom the arrangements necessary for the creation of the work are undertaken'.[18] If such an author is an employee, then the employer-ownership rule applies.

In an Information Society much of our knowledge and information is obtained from published databases such as law reports and journals. The articles or cases in such databases are usually owned by their authors, where copyright also usually resides, unless they are employees. However, the compilation (ie, the arrangement

---

[16] CDPA 1988, s 11(2).          [17] [1951] 69 RPC 10; [1952] RPC 10.          [18] CDPA 1988, s 9(3).

and selection) of such material may also give rise to copyright.[19] In some EU countries, the intellectual effort involved in compiling a database is regarded as too low for the work to attract copyright. As a result of the inconsistent approach in Member States and the recognition of the need to protect the investment of makers of databases, which can so easily be copied in this technological age and which are regarded as economically and socially beneficial to the EU, a Directive to protect makers has been adopted.[20] Under article 3(4), a database created by employees in the execution of their duties following instructions given by employers will entitle the employer to exercise all economic rights in the database, unless otherwise provided by contract. The Directive has now been implemented in the UK by the Copyright and Rights in Databases Regulations 1997.[21] Databases that do not qualify for copyright might qualify for the new *sui generis* or database right under these Regulations. Again there is the usual provision that a database made by an employee in the course of his employment will (in the absence of any agreement to the contrary) automatically be the property of the employer.

One final and rather different point on copyright relates to the use of works rather than their creation. Under the CDPA 1988, organizations which in the course of business possess copyright materials without a licence may be guilty of a criminal offence.[22] This is a considerable problem with computer software, which can so easily be copied if not properly controlled. Most organizations go in fear of committing such an offence, particularly as employees often install software on their workstations and it is common practice to copy software from someone else's PC. Where an employer knows such activity is going on and copyright is being infringed, then not only the company but also the directors and officers of the company will be committing an offence. Today, software audits are a regular feature of asset-management systems designed to reduce this risk.

### 10.3.2 Moral rights

The Berne Convention incorporated a new set of IPRs based on continental systems known as 'moral rights',[23] and these were introduced into English law by the CDPA 1988. They provide authors with two rights: to be identified as the author of a copyright work (right of paternity),[24] and to object to any derogatory treatment of the work (right of integrity).[25] However, there are a number of exceptions which include employees who produce works in the course of their employment. Employees have no right of paternity nor of integrity in relation to such works unless the

---

[19] CDPA 1988, s 3(1)(a).
[20] Directive 96/9/EC on the legal protection of databases, OJ L77, 27 March 1996. See, further, Chapter 6.
[21] SI 1997/3032.                                                        [22] CDPA 1988, s 107(1).
[23] Article 6 *bis* of the Paris text of the Berne Convention for the Protection of Literary and Artistic Works, 24 July 1971.
[24] CDPA, s 77.                                                          [25] Ibid, s 80.

author/employee had at some time been identified with the works; and even here the extent of the right is simply to insist that there is a clear and reasonably prominent indication that the work has been subjected to treatment to which the author has not consented.[26] Other exceptions relate even to contractors, like reporting current events,[27] publications in newspapers, magazines or similar periodicals[28] and computer programs, including computer-generated works.[29]

Moral rights generally operate to allow a person to be identified with his own work or to object to interference with the work. There is also a right against false attribution which involves the converse situation.[30] This right is not affected by employment status, although it is unlikely to apply to employees if their names are not associated with copyright works in the first place, because they have no moral rights.

It is questionable whether a signatory to the Convention can exclude moral rights for employees, as there is no such right under article 6 *bis*, and it would be interesting to see the result of a challenge before the European Court of Human Rights. Some EU countries do not exclude moral rights for employees, so those employers with European workforces may find that different rules apply.

### 10.3.3 Patents

Copyright is not the only IPR subject to 'the employer ownership' rule. Employees' inventions will belong to their employers, even where they are made outside normal duties, where the task is specifically assigned to the employee and an invention might reasonably be expected to result from carrying out those duties.[31] Also, an invention made in the course of the employee's duties which, at the time of making the invention, was such that the employee had a special obligation to further the interests of the employer's undertaking, will belong to the employer.[32] The rule will not apply where the invention is made outside the employee's normal duties and where he has not been assigned any relevant specific duties; for example, a salesperson inventing a new product.[33]

What is less well known is that an employee who has made an invention can claim compensation from the owning employer where a patent has been granted in certain circumstances. These are where the patent is of 'outstanding benefit' to the employer, having regard, *inter alia*, to the size and nature of the employer's undertaking, and if it would be just for the employee to be awarded compensation of an amount representing a 'fair share' of the benefit derived or expected to be derived by

[26] Ibid, ss 79(3) and 82.    [27] Ibid, ss 79(5) and 81(3).
[28] Ibid, ss 79(6) and 81(4).    [29] Ibid, ss 79(2) and 81(2).
[30] Ibid, s 84.    [31] Patents Act 1977, s 39(1)(a).
[32] Ibid, s 39(1)(b).
[33] eg, *Harris' Patent* [1985] RPC 19, *Reiss Engineering Co Ltd v Harris* [1985] IRLR 232 where the inventor of a valve made while he was working out his redundancy notice, was the manager of the valve department.

the employer from exploiting the patent itself or by assigning it.[34] A claim for compensation can be made under the Patent Rules.[35] Cases normally go before the Comptroller of Patents who determines the amount of compensation according to the provisions set out in the Patents Act.[36] These provisions also apply where the invention initially belonged to the employee and he has subsequently assigned it to the employer or granted an exclusive licence to him.

Employees rarely seem to use this right. This is surprising considering the number of registered patents and applications for patents made each year, and the fact that some patents can make enormous sums for their owners, for example, in the pharmaceutical industry. No doubt, one of the difficulties is that inventions are not made single-handedly, and there may be problems deciding who should receive compensation and how it should be shared between employees in, say, a research and development team. Also, it is difficult for employees to determine whether the patent is of outstanding value as all the evidence tends to be held by the employer. Patent attorneys or agents are careful to find out whether employees could have a claim at the time of preparing the application and will try to ensure that employees are 'compensated' at this stage before any outstanding value can be established. Any payments made would be taken into account by the Comptroller, and morally and ethically employees tend to consider that they have received recompense and do not take matters further. Not surprisingly, there have been few cases and of the reported decisions the author is not aware of a single employee who has succeeded.[37] Common reasons given for failure include the fact that, where an employer is very large, it is difficult to show outstanding benefit, as even relatively large revenues attributed to the patent will still be very small compared to annual turnover.

One way of avoiding the compensation provisions is for the employer not to apply for a patent and to rely on the law of confidence. Furthermore, a contracting-out clause in relation to inventions owned by the employee or the compensation provisions, will be unenforceable against an employee,[38] unless a trade union, of which the employee is a member, negotiates a payment for compensation for inventions in a collective agreement.[39]

### 10.3.4 Design rights[40]

Both registered (aesthetic appeal) and unregistered design (utilitarian, including semi-conductor chips) rights are subject to the employer-ownership rule.[41] This

---

[34] Patents Act 1977, ss 40 and 41.          [35] SI 1990/2384, r 59 using Patents Form 2/77.
[36] Patents Act 1977, s 41(4).
[37] Examples include *Memco-Med Ltd's Patent* [1992] RPC 403, *GEC Avionics Ltd's Patent* [1992] RPC 107 and *British Steel plc's Patent* [1992] RPC 117.
[38] Patents Act 1977, s 42.          [39] Ibid, s 40(3).
[40] Article 1(b) of Directive 98/71/EC of 13 October 1998 on the legal protection of designs, OJ L289, excludes computer programs from the definition of 'product' and the scope of the Directive.
[41] Registered Designs Act 1949, s 2(1B), as amended by CDPA 1988, and CDPA 1988, s 215(3), as amended by the Design Right (Semiconductor Topographies) Regulations 1989, SI 1989/1100.

goes even further with unregistered designs where the commissioner is the first owner.[42]

### 10.3.5 Confidential information

So far we have examined the old rules, which employment lawyers will be familiar with even if they are not referred to regularly. They will become increasingly important as information plays a more important role in wealth creation. However, there is a newer analysis being prompted by the advent of the Information Society.

The starting point is in the law of confidence. This subject has already been covered in Chapter 7 but will be further analysed and extended here in a way which is particularly relevant to employment rights in an Information Society.

Employees both generate and acquire confidential information in the course of employment. The concern here is with confidential information associated with industrial and commercial activity, often known as 'trade secrets'. The general principle is that the employee holds the confidential information for the benefit of his employer. However, relying on this principle in employment relationships presents special problems as the contractual obligation of confidence (whether express or implied under the duty of good faith) is subject to the qualification that an employee is, after the termination of his employment, free to use his 'knowledge and skill' either for his own benefit or for the benefit of others. This remains true even though during his employment such information which is learned must be treated as confidential. Some trade secrets, however, are so confidential or can be described as so entitled to protection that a continuing duty of confidence applies even beyond the termination of employment. This classification was considered by the court in *Faccenda Chicken Ltd v Fowler*.[43]

The problem is distinguishing between trade secrets and knowledge and skills that employees can take with them. In *Fowler* the Court of Appeal laid down guidelines as to how to determine whether information could be classified as confidential. The court said attention should be paid to

(1) the nature of the information itself, for example, a secret process or confidential customer list;

(2) the nature of the employment, for example, there will be a higher obligation on a more senior employee or one who habitually handles sensitive data;

(3) whether the employer made it known to the employee that the information was of a confidential nature, for example, by marking it confidential; and

(4) whether the information can be easily isolated from other information the employee is free to use.

The problem with this approach to classification is that it provides little guidance as

---

[42] CDPA 1988, s 215(2).     [43] [1985] 1 All ER 724.

to what precisely distinguishes a trade secret from information in the second category (skill and competence), although it does show that such information will be given less protection. In *Lansing Linde Ltd v Kerr*[44] the court spoke in terms of information that would be liable to cause real harm if it was disclosed to a competitor, provided it was used in a trade or business and the owner had either limited the dissemination of the information or at least not encouraged or permitted widespread publication. The court stressed the need to take account of the changing nature of the business and the need to take account of 'the wider context of highly confidential information of a non-technical or non-scientific nature'.[45]

The computer industry has provided some examples of cases which provide some further clarification of this difficult issue. In the South African case *Northern Office Microcomputers v Rosenstein*[46] the Supreme Court recognized the difficulty in deciding where to draw the dividing line. The court considered that computer programs, which were not commonplace, should be eligible for protection as trade secrets. However, the protection given by the law of trade secrets in the context of ex-employees should be of a limited nature only, and should not extend beyond the employer's 'lead-time', the time to develop the program. In other words, the advantage the employer has in getting his product to market first should be protected and nothing more. The court went on to find that, in many cases, the employer's trade secrets were no more than the result of the application by an employee of his own skill and judgment, but if the employee was engaged specifically to produce that information then it could still amount to a trade secret. But, if the material was commonplace, there would be nothing to stop the ex-employee deriving the same or similar material again as long as he did not simply copy his employer's material. The employee would not have to 'wipe the slate of his mind clean' on the termination of his employment.

In *Ibcos Computers v Poole*[47] the court observed that source code of a computer program is normally kept confidential by software houses and that customers do not themselves usually get the code and that it was confidential.

These cases also involved questions of copyright infringement and substantial copying of computer programs which were worked on by an ex-employer. In the *Flanders* case[48] it was accepted that the employee/programmer had a deep knowledge of the plaintiff's program, and that while he could not carry in his memory substantial parts of the source code, he would have remembered all the main routines. Despite this finding it was held that there was no substantial copying. Breach of confidence was not pleaded. If it had been, the plaintiff might have succeeded in confidence where he did not in copyright law.

More recently in *FSS Travel & Leisure Systems Ltd v Johnson*[49] an employer in the business of designing and marketing software for the travel industry attempted to constrain a computer programmer from joining a competitor. The Court of Appeal

---

[44] [1991] 1 All ER 418.       [45] Ibid.            [46] [1982] FSR 129.
[47] [1994] FSR 275.            [48] [1993] FSR 497.  [49] [1998] IRLR 382.

dealt with the question of whether an employer has trade secrets which are legitimately protectable by the imposition of a restrictive covenant against an employee.
The court had to decide whether there are trade secrets which can fairly be regarded
as the employer's property, as distinct from the skill, experience, know-how and
general knowledge which can fairly be regarded as the property of the employee to
use without restraint for his own benefit or in the service of a competitor. The court
found that the distinction necessitates examination of all the evidence relating to the
nature of the employment, the character of the information, the restrictions imposed
on its dissemination, the extent of use and disclosure in competition to the employer.
In each case it is a question of examining closely the detailed evidence relating to the
employer's claim for secrecy and deciding, as a matter of fact, on which side of the
boundary line it falls. It is not sufficient for the employer to assert a claim that it is
entitled to an accumulated mass of knowledge which in the relevant business the use
and dissemination of which is likely to harm the employer.

In *PMS International plc & McKenhnie plc v Whitehouse & Willenhall
Automation Ltd*[50] drawings, quotations, price costings and business strategies were
considered to rank as trade secrets. In *Faccenda Chicken v Fowler* more mundane
information such as sales information, convenient routes to customers, and customer
orders was found not to be of a confidential nature, relying on the implied duty of
fidelity instead.

However, there must be a fine line between such information and trade secrets.
An express provision in a contract of employment, or a clear indication that the
employer regards such information as confidential, may tip the balance and provide
an additional cause of action in cases involving the copying of computer programs,
which often involve ex-employees.

Another weakness of confidentiality is its difficulty in enforcement, whether or
not there is an express provision in the contract, particularly in post-termination situations. As a result there is an increasing trend towards introducing non-competition
or restraint-of-trade clauses in contracts of employment for employees at all levels,
which can be easier to enforce provided they are reasonable.[51]

The new employer can also be liable for the ex-employee's misuse of confidential
information. This was the position in *Ibcos*, where Barclays Mercantile Highland
Finance was aware that Mr Poole had taken the source code. Where such a breach is
discovered, the new employer would be advised to disregard the code developed in
breach. It may require re-engineering the program through a clean-room approach as
was done by the employer in the US case *Computer Associates v Altai*.[52] This only
left the copyright claim which is much more difficult to prove, particularly for non-
literal copying.

What is the position of consultants? A well-drafted contract for services should
always deal with ownership of IPRs generated in the course of the consultant's

[50] [1992] FSR 489.
[51] Except in the circumstances found in *Rock Refrigeration Ltd v Jones*, *The Times*, 17 October 1996.
[52] (1992) 23 USPQ 2nd 1241 (2nd Cir).

work, as will be appreciated from the discussion so far. Also, it should deal with the question of confidentiality. In the absence of express agreement it is necessary to fall back on ordinary principles of law. So far as confidential information is concerned this will be governed by implied contractual terms, as in the case of a contract of employment. A consultant should hold for the benefit of the company for which he works, all trade secrets generated or acquired in the course of the work, and he should not use or disclose these trade secrets for any unauthorized purpose. Counterbalancing this is the principle that a consultant, like an employee, is entitled to use for his own benefit and for the benefit of others his general knowledge and skill. So again there is the thorny issue of what is a trade secret and what is general knowledge and skill. Where does the dividing line lie? Cases like *Schering Chemicals Ltd v Falkman Ltd*[53] would suggest that a rather harder line is taken by courts with consultants who have acquired confidential information in the course of work undertaken for others. In *Schering Chemicals* consultants were used to undertake damage-limitation sales training for the defendant in relation to a drug which had been withdrawn from the market. Their contract included a confidentiality clause. They in turn contracted out some of the training to the defendant, who also accepted the information was confidential. The defendant used the confidential information to make a film for TV. The defendant was held to be in breach of an obligation of confidence to the plaintiff with whom he had no direct contract, even though the disclosures in the film were found to be in the public interest, but only where the information was not from public sources. Could this make it even more attractive for firms to use contractors?

The point should be made that the obligation of confidence arising from a contract of employment is not all one way. In many cases, the employer will owe a duty of confidence to his employee. An employer will hold information concerning an employee such as performance rating, salary and career details. This information should not be divulged to others without the employee's permission, except where disclosure is permitted by express provision (for example, attachment of earnings), or implied (for example, salaries paid by a bureau). The protection given by data-protection laws will be discussed later in this chapter (see section 10.4.1) and in Chapter 11.

The obligation of confidence here could be considered as an extension of the duty of mutual respect and trust between employees and employers. There are few cases on this aspect of the employer's duty. In *Dalgleish v Lothian and Borders Police Board*[54] a local authority sought information on the names and addresses of persons employed by another public-sector body, for the purposes of ensuring payment of taxes. A Scottish court granted an interdict (injunction) restraining the disclosure of the information on two alternative grounds. First, that the contract of employment did not authorize such disclosures and secondly, under the general principles of confidentiality irrespective of contract.

---

[53] [1982] QB 1.          [54] [1991] IRLR 422, CS.

Another illustration could be where employers operate suggestion schemes. An employee could be said to have waived his rights, if any, in the information he has disclosed under such a scheme if his employer uses the information. However, if the employer does not use the information it seems that a duty of confidence could arise. In *Prout v British Gas plc*[55] an employee submitted an idea for a new design of a bracket for warning lamps placed around excavations. The bracket was supposed to be vandal-proof. Mr Prout was given an award by British Gas under a suggestion scheme, but later the company said it had no interest and agreed to allow Mr Prout to apply for a patent on his own behalf. In spite of this, later British Gas decided to use the suggestion. On the issue of confidence it was held that there was a contractual or equitable duty of confidence imposed on the employer. Although this duty would normally end once the idea was used in public for the first time without objection from the employee, a fresh duty could arise if the employee gave notice to apply for a patent and would continue until the filing date of the application. In this particular case it was held that the employer was in breach of confidence by making use of the invention.

This case has interesting implications for employers who do not use 'ideas' coming from their employees. There is no copyright protection in ideas, only in original works. So the rule that the employer owns IPRs does not apply. If we assume employees are under a duty of good faith to disclose ideas which could be beneficial to the employer's business, then where the employer does not use or rejects the idea, is the employee free to use or exploit it? In an information age this is a serious issue. The answer may depend on whether the idea itself is confidential information, which is the only IPR (other than perhaps patents) which can protect, in effect, ideas.

The duty of confidence has already proved to be an important right in the Information Society. Like other common-law rights it has demonstrated adaptability in the face of new technology. However, it is not reliable enough as once confidential information is in the public domain, the protection is lost, which is clearly an even bigger issue in these days of the Internet.


## 10.4 NEW EMPLOYMENT ISSUES IN THE INFORMATION AGE

Having considered whether workers have any rights in relation to the information assets of their employers we now move to the second part of our examination. Technology has facilitated new employment developments and created some new employment challenges. This section examines some of these in order to illustrate how new laws are becoming part of the employment-law arena and how traditional employment concepts must adapt to Information Society developments in the employment field. The particular areas which will be considered are: workers' privacy, teleworking, computer misuse at work, knowledge management and outsourcing.

[55] [1992] FSR 478.

## 10.4.1 Workers' privacy

Many activities performed routinely in the employment context entail the processing of the personal data of workers, which will sometimes include very sensitive information. This processing will almost certainly fall within the scope of the EU Directive on the protection of individuals with regard to the processing of personal data and on the free movement of such data (Directive 95/46/EC) ('the Data Protection Directive') and has been the subject of an Article 29 Working Party Opinion.[56] The Opinion considers that the monitoring of a worker's e-mail or Internet access by the employer falls within the Directive's scope as does the processing of sound and image data in the employment context and video surveillance of workers. Employers still keep manual records and if these form part of a 'personal data filing system' they will also fall within the Directive's scope.

It follows that the processing of workers' personal data are subject to the fundamental principles concerning data protection described in Chapter 11.

The Data Protection Directive provides consent as one of the means for legitimizing the processing of personal data. The problem in the employment context is whether workers or prospective workers can give the 'freely, specific and informed' consent necessary under the provisions of the Directive bearing in mind the real nature of the employment relationship where the worker is subordinate and dependent. For example, a worker or prospective worker is often in the position where it is not possible to refuse, withdraw or modify consent due to the employer's position of power and the worker's fear of loss of promotion prospects or job offer. Given the imbalance in power in the employment relationship it has been argued that consent alone is not an adequate safeguard, particularly in relation to the processing of sensitive data.

This issue has been the subject of a Commission Communication[57] and two stages of consultation[58] which have also identified particular issues for medical data, drug and genetic testing and monitoring and surveillance. It raises the question as to whether the Data Protection Directive adequately addresses the protection of workers' personal data. For example, testing of workers for drug and substance abuse is increasingly prevalent in some Member States whose laws tend to allow testing of a worker or prospective worker to ensure that he is fit to work. However what about rules as to the further processing of such data, or what happens if a worker refuses to undergo tests, and what are the consequences if he gives inaccurate or incomplete answers on questions related to the matter?

In the UK the Information Commissioner has recognized the issue by producing an Employment Practices Data Protection Code ('EPDP Code') under powers

---

[56] Opinion 8/2001 on the processing of personal data in the employment context adopted on 13 September 2001.

[57] Protection of workers' personal data, published on 31 July 2001.

[58] Second stage issued on 31 October 2002. For the complete text of the consultation decision, see europa.eu.int/comm/employment_social/news/2002/oct/data_prot_en.html.

granted by the Data Protection Act 1998 ('DPA 1998').[59] It covers recruitment and selection, employment records, monitoring at work and medical testing[60] and provides guidance in the context of the Data Protection Principles. Monitoring at work proved one of the most controversial sections of the Code during the consultation process and as it is linked with the interception of communications it is dealt with later in this chapter (see section 10.4.1) and Chapter 8 (see section 8.5).

There are other privacy laws which affect workers which are referred to in Chapter 11. In particular it is worth noting that location data is becoming widely used by employers in particular to monitor the whereabouts of their employees at any given time. The data may be obtained from a number of sources such as the vehicle the worker is driving or the equipment the worker is using, for example a GSM mobile phone. Article 9 of the Directive concerning the processing of personal data and the protection of privacy in the electronic communications sector (Directive 02/58/EC) ('the Privacy and Electronic Communications Directive') now covers such data, making it necessary to process with consent or where the data are made anonymous. Clearly the problem concerning the imbalance of power identified above still arises despite this new provision.

### 10.4.1.1 *Relationship of workers' privacy to human rights*
The application of human rights to workers' personal data was established by the European Court of Human Rights in the case *Niemitz v Germany*:

Respect for private life must also comprise to a certain degree the right to establish and develop relationships with other human beings. There appears, furthermore, to be no reason of principle why this understanding of the notion of private life should be taken to exclude activities of a professional or business nature since it is, after all, in the course of their working lives that the majority of people have a significant, if not the greatest, opportunity of developing relationships with the outside world. This view is supported by the fact that, as was rightly pointed out by the Commission, it is not always possible to distinguish clearly which of an individual's activities form part of his professional or business life and which do not.[61]

This adds another dimension to privacy at work and whereas before the coming into force of the Human Rights Act 1998 the Convention's rights could only be vindicated at European level[62] now in the UK, for example, the rights are exercisable before the national courts under the 1998 Act.

### 10.4.1.2 *Relationship of workers' privacy to employment law*
There is a clear connection between data protection and employment law. There are

---

[59] Under section 51(3) the Commissioner has power if he considers it appropriate to introduce codes of practice as to good practice after full consultation. Under section 51(9) 'good practice' is defined as 'such practice . . . as appears . . . desirable having regards to the interests of data subjects and others, and includes (but is not limited to) compliance with' the DPA 1998. Under section 51(5) the code may describe the 'class of persons to whom it is to relate'.

[60] For medical testing, still to be introduced at the time of writing.

[61] 23 November 1992, Series A No 251/B, para 29.

[61] See, eg, *Halford v United Kingdom* [1997] IRLR 471.

criteria for making data processing legitimate under article 7 of the Data Protection Directive. For example, the criteria which requires that processing is necessary for the performance of a contract to which the data subject is party. Employment relationships are based on a contract of employment between the employer and worker. To meet its obligations under the contract to, for example, pay the worker, the employer must process some personal data often through a processor or payroll bureau.

Another criteria is where processing is necessary for compliance with a legal obligation. Employment law may impose legal obligations on the employer, which necessarily require the processing of personal data. The employer may be under a legal obligation to make certain disclosures of personal data, for example, to tax authorities, discrimination regulators or to process data in connection with social security payments.

The UK Information Commissioner's EPDP Code is extremely comprehensive and detailed and covers areas of personnel practice outside the strict remit of data protection. In effect it is a code of good industrial or information practice in the workplace which has been arrived at after years of consultation with trade unions, employers' representative bodies and others. In the UK employment tribunals are required to apply tests to determine whether an employee's rights have been infringed. For example, in a case concerning unfair dismissal the tribunal has to determine whether the dismissal was fair or unfair, 'having regard to the reason shown by the employer'. Its decision must depend on 'whether in the circumstances (including the size and administrative resources of their undertaking) the employer acted reasonably or unreasonably in treating their reason as a sufficient reason for dismissing the employee'.[63] The provision adds that the question must be determined in accordance with equity and the substantial merits of the case. In applying the test employment tribunals are viewed as 'industrial or information juries' applying accepted standards of business which apply at the relevant time and place. In order to help in their determinations they will seek guidance from ACAS codes of practice as to these standards as well as previous cases. These codes are limited to certain activities like dismissal. In contrast the Information Commissioner's employment code's coverage is much greater and may well be used by tribunals in the future to help to determine cases.

### 10.4.1.3 *Relationship of workers' privacy to confidentiality*

*Data Protection Registrar v PLP Motors Ltd*[64] illustrates the overlap between data protection and confidentiality in the employment context. The defendant recruited an employee from one of his competitors. Shortly after joining the company, the employee passed on names and addresses of his former employer's customers to the defendant's marketing department. This information was used in a direct marketing

---

[63] Employment Rights Act 1996, s 98(1) and (4).
[64] Decision given on 24 April 1995 (unreported).

campaign, and the Data Protection Registrar (now the Information Commissioner) received a complaint from a recipient of the mailshot. The Registrar brought proceedings against the defendant under the Data Protection Act 1984 for obtaining the information unlawfully. The company was found to have secrets. Whereas claims for breach of confidence are difficult to prove and are potentially expensive, a criminal prosecution under the Data Protection Act at someone else's expense, and which may be quicker, is an attractive alternative.

### 10.4.1.4 *Monitoring and surveillance of workers*

The Data Protection Working Party in its Opinion 8/2001 stated 'there should no longer be any doubt that data protection requirements apply to the monitoring and surveillance of workers whether in terms of email use, internet access, video cameras or location data'. More recently the Data Protection Working Party has produced a working document on the surveillance and monitoring of electronic communications in the workplace.[65]

These reports conclude that the fundamental data-protection principles apply to this activity. Any monitoring, especially if it is conducted on the basis of article 7(f) of the Data Protection Directive, must also satisfy article 6 and be a proportionate response by an employer to the risks it faces, taking into account the legitimate privacy rights and other interests of workers. Any personal data held or used in the course of monitoring must be adequate, relevant and not excessive for the purpose for which monitoring is justified. Therefore any monitoring should be carried out in the least intrusive way. It must be targeted on the area of risk, taking into account the rules about data protection and, where applicable, the principle of the secrecy of correspondence.[66] Also monitoring, including surveillance by camera, must comply with the transparency requirements of article 10. So workers must be informed of the existence of the surveillance, the purposes for which personal data are to be processed and other information necessary to guarantee fair processing.

These principles are reflected in the 'Monitoring at work' section of the UK Employment Practices Data Protection Code. However in the UK the position is complicated by the Regulation of Investigatory Powers Act 2000, discussed in Chapter 8 (see section 8.7.2) which prohibits the interception of communications unless undertaken lawfully. In the employment context, the Lawful Business Practice Regulations[67] specify the circumstances in which interception can take place lawfully and this is reflected in the Code.

This part of the Code is concerned primarily with activities which involve 'watching over' workers, often but not necessarily by automated means. So it addresses: watching workers by means of CCTV cameras, for example, to ensure

---

[65] Adopted on 29 May 2002 (5401/01/EN/Final WP 55).

[66] See also articles 7 and 8 of the EU Charter of Fundamental Rights, signed and proclaimed in Nice on 7 December 2000.

[67] The Telecommunications (Lawful Business Practice) (Interception of Communications) Regulations 2000, SI 2000/2699.

that health and safety rules are being complied with; randomly opening an individual worker's e-mails, for example, looking for evidence of harassment of other workers; using automated checking software to collect information about workers, for example, to find out whether particular workers are sending or receiving inappropriate emails; and examining logs of websites visited to check, for example, that individual workers are not downloading pornography.

### 10.4.2 Teleworking

Teleworking is well suited to an Information Society and there is already evidence of its increasing importance in the EU[68] and to the UK economy.[69] On 16 July 2002 the European-level Social Partners signed a Framework Agreement on teleworking.[70] In the 'General Considerations' part of the Agreement, the social partners see

telework both as a way for companies and public service organisations to modernise work organisation, and as a way for workers to reconcile work and social life and giving them greater autonomy in the accomplishment of their tasks. If Europe wants to make the most out of the information society, it must encourage this new form of work organization in such a way, that flexibility and security go together and the quality of jobs is enhanced, and that the chances of disabled people[71] on the labour market is increased.

The voluntary agreement aims at establishing a general framework at the European level to be implemented by the members of the signatory parties in accordance with national procedures and practices specific to management and labour. The agreement provides a definition and scope of telework as 'a form of organising and/or performing work, using IT, in the context of an employment contract/relationship, where work, which could also be performed at the employer's premises, is carried out away from those premises on a regular basis'. A teleworker is any person carrying out telework whether an employee or other worker.

In a recent study[72] three main types of teleworker were identified:

(1) the home-based teleworker who spends most or all of his working time at home;

(2) the mobile worker, ie someone who works at multiple locations, who travels extensively, but has an office base at home; and

(3) the occasional teleworker who works at the office most of the time but occasionally works from home.

---

[68] See the *Benchmark Report following up the 'Strategies for Jobs in the Information Society'* (European Commission, 7 February 2001) (SEC (2001) 222).

[69] See the Labour Force Survey, Spring 2001.

[70] Social Partners Framework Agreement on Teleworking (July 2002, No 038) implemented through the voluntary route foreseen in article 139 of the EU Treaty.

[71] See Directive 2000/78/EC establishing a general framework for equal treatment in employment and occupation. The EU has developed a Disability Strategy in its Communication 'Equality of Opportunities for People with Disabilities: A New Community Disability Strategy 1996' endorsed in a resolution of the Council of Ministers in December 1996.

[72] 'Teleworking' (IDS Study 729, May 2002).

From a legal perspective the framework agreement recognizes employment areas which need additional consideration.

### 10.4.2.1 *Contractual negotiations*

Telework is voluntary for the worker and the employer concerned. Teleworking may be required as part of a worker's initial job description or it may be engaged in as a voluntary arrangement subsequently. In both cases, the employer provides the teleworker with relevant written information in accordance with the Directive on an employer's obligation to inform employees of the conditions applicable to the contract or employment relationship (Directive 91/533/EEC), including information on applicable collective agreements, description of the work to be performed, etc. The details of telework normally requires additional written information on matters such as the department of the undertaking to which the teleworker is attached, details of his immediate superior or other persons to whom he can address questions of a professional or personal nature, reporting arrangements, etc.

If telework is not part of the initial job description, and the employer makes an offer of telework, the worker may accept or refuse this offer. If a worker expresses the wish to opt for telework, the employer may accept or refuse this request. This passage to telework only modifies the way in which work is performed and should not affect the teleworker's employment status. A worker's refusal to opt for telework should not be a reason in its own right for terminating the employment relationship or changing the terms and conditions of employment of that worker. If telework is not part of the initial job description, the decision to pass to telework may be reversible by individual and/or collective agreement. The reversibility could imply returning to work at the employer's premises at the worker's or at the employer's request. The details of this reversibility could be established by individual and/or collective agreement.

In relation to other employment conditions, teleworkers should benefit from the same rights, guaranteed by applicable legislation and collective agreements, as comparable workers at the employer's premises. However, in order to take into account the particular requirements of telework, specific complementary collective and/or individual agreements may be necessary.

### 10.4.2.2 *Data protection and privacy*

The employer would be responsible for taking the appropriate measures, notably with regard to software, to ensure the protection of data used and processed by the teleworker for business purposes. The employer may need to inform the teleworker of all relevant legislation and company rules concerning data protection. It is the teleworker's responsibility to comply with these rules.

The employer would need to respect the privacy of the teleworker. For example, if any kind of monitoring system is put in place, it needs to be proportionate to the objective etc (see, further, section 10.4.1 above).

### 10.4.2.3 *Equipment and software*

As a general rule, the employer is responsible for providing, installing and maintaining the equipment necessary for regular telework unless the teleworker uses his own equipment. If telework is performed on a regular basis, the employer would usually compensate or cover the costs directly caused by the work, in particular costs relating to providing communications with the employer, customers and others. The employer would usually provide the teleworker with appropriate technical support, and cover by insurance, loss or damage to the equipment and data used by the teleworker. The teleworker would be expected to take good care of the equipment provided to him and would not be expected to collect or distribute illegal material via the Internet.[73] The Directive on the minimum safety and health requirements for work with display screen equipment (Directive 90/270/EEC) would need to be complied with.

The employer as a licensee of IPRs, will usually have the right to allow their teleworker to use software as part of a site or other licence on or off the employer's premises and on a teleworker's own computer. Company confidential information will also be held on such equipment by employees. The termination of the employment relationship will give rise to a number of issues, from protecting the company's property to ensuring that there are no breaches of licence agreements. These issues will usually be covered by the contract of employment and personnel procedures on termination, including obtaining undertakings from employees to the effect that there are no breaches. Software and digital information are always difficult to check, particularly as even deleted files can be recovered. However, it is important to be able to demonstrate that action has been taken so that licences are not breached, and such assurances are often obtained in termination agreements, which may also include the right to enter the teleworker's premises to make any appropriate seizures.

### 10.4.2.4 *Health and safety*

The employer is responsible for the protection of the occupational health and safety of the teleworker in accordance with the Directive on the introduction of measures to encourage improvements in the safety and health of workers at work (Directive 89/391/EEC) and relevant daughter Directives, national legislation and collective agreements.[74] This would involve the employer informing the teleworker of the company's policy on occupational health and safety, in particular requirements on visual display units. The teleworker would be required to apply these safety policies correctly. In order to verify that the applicable provisions concerning health and safety are correctly applied, the employer, workers' representatives and/or relevant authorities would need access to the teleworkplace, within the limits of national legislation and collective agreements. If the teleworker is working at home, such

---

[73] See further Chapter 8.

[74] For the UK, see Health and Safety (Display Screen Equipment) Regulations 1992, SI 1992/2792; Electricity at Work Regulations 1989, SI 1989/635.

access would need to be subject to prior notification and his agreement. The teleworker is entitled to request inspection visits.

### 10.4.2.5 *Organization of work*
Within the framework of applicable legislation, collective agreements and company rules, the teleworker will, in effect, manage the organization of his working time. The workload and performance standards of the teleworker should be equivalent to those of comparable workers at the employers' premises. The employer would need to ensure that measures are taken preventing the teleworker from being isolated from the rest of the working community in the company, such as giving him the opportunity to meet with colleagues on a regular basis and to have access to company information.

### 10.4.2.6 *Training*
Policies will need to be established giving teleworkers access to training and opportunities for career development comparable with other workers at the employer's premises and subject to similar appraisal policies as these other workers. Teleworkers will require appropriate training to use the technical equipment at their disposal and in the environment of telework. The teleworker's manager and other work colleagues may also need training for this form of work and its management.

### 10.4.2.7 *Trade-union and collective-rights issues*
Teleworkers have the same collective rights as workers at the employer's premises so they will need to be able to communicate with workers representatives, stand for election to bodies representing workers, etc. Teleworkers are included in calculations for determining thresholds for bodies with worker representation in accordance with European and national law, collective agreements or practices. The establishment to which the teleworker will be attached for the purpose of exercising his collective rights needs to be specified if not already clear. Worker representatives should be informed and consulted on the introduction of telework in accordance with European and national legislation, collective agreements and practices.

### 10.4.2.8 *Working Time Regulations 1998*
The Working Time Regulations 1998[75] will have some impact on the flexibility of teleworking, although they do not seem to apply to the self-employed and many other categories of workers. If opt-out agreements are used they will only be effective if up-to-date records are maintained, which will increase the need to computerize record keeping, particularly for those who work remotely.

---

[75] SI 1998/1833.

## 10.4.3 Computer misuse at work

In the Information Society workers tend to use computers as essential 'tools of the trade'. These tools potentially give workers access to the trade secrets of the organizations they work for and the possibility of disrupting operations on a scale never achievable before. Therefore new ways of protecting organizations are necessary.

As will be appreciated from the cases quoted in Chapter 8 many computer crimes are committed by employees, ex-employees or their accomplices, usually where the employee has or did have some level of authorization to access his employer's computer system. Whether an offence under the Computer Misuse Act 1990 or other crime is committed will often depend on how an employer has set the boundaries of authorization so it is clear what is the level of permitted access. This may be found in the contract of employment or staff handbook with prior warnings as to the consequences of breach, but in practice the boundaries are often not clear and this can lead to difficulty in obtaining convictions.

Whether or not a criminal offence is committed unauthorized access to the firm's computers, or to parts of the system to which the employee is not entitled to access, is likely to be a breach of an employer's disciplinary rules and an act of gross misconduct providing the employer with a potentially fair reason to dismiss.

In *Denco Ltd v Joinson* an employee who had limited access to the firm's computer discovered another employee's password which gave greater access. Late one night, while legitimately using the computer for his own work, he used the password and tried (unsuccessfully) to gain access to certain financially important information. He had worked for the company for twenty-one years and was dismissed for gross misconduct. The EAT found that

. . . in the modern industrial world if an employee deliberately used an authorised password in order to enter or attempt to enter a computer known to contain information to which he is not entitled, then that of itself is gross misconduct which prima facie will attract summary dismissal, although there may be some exceptional circumstances in which such a response might be held unreasonable. Basically this is a question of 'absolutes' and can be compared with dishonesty. However, because of the importance of preserving integrity of the computer with its information it is important that management should make it abundantly clear to its workforce that interfering with it will carry severe penalties.[76]

## 10.4.4 Building a knowledge culture

As the scope and scale of knowledge-intensive business expands rapidly there is a need to develop new strategies for managing knowledge. Most of these strategies today are based on finding technology vehicles for processing the knowledge. However this is only part of the solution. Knowledge relates to the experience of employees in formal education and continuing personal development (codified

---

[76] [1991] IRLR 63 (EAT).

knowledge), the cumulative experience of working with clients/customers (tacit knowledge) and explicit knowledge of the job.

It is increasingly becoming clear that the design by an employer of a strategy and policies for its human resources is essential to support and complement the technical processes.[77] In the recruitment process candidate profiles may need to identify individuals who are team players prepared to share their experiences. Training and development programmes may need to reinforce the importance of sharing knowledge. Appraisal schemes may need to set targets for capturing knowledge. Reward schemes may need to recognize the time spent on contributing to knowledge management.

These developments can result in tension between achieving results in the 'normal' job and time spent on knowledge management. For example, lawyers will be under pressure to use their time on fee-earning work and knowledge capture will rarely have the same priority. Because organizations realize that their competitive future may depend on sharing knowledge, provision may be necessary in the contract of employment to achieve the objective by obliging managers and employees to undertake this vital part of the job.

Once an employee shares his knowledge and uses the knowledge of others through a system of knowledge management, does this have any implications for the 'experience and skills' that an employee can use once he leaves the employment of that organization? This is a new dimension to the discussion as to what is confidential information examined earlier in this chapter (see section 10.3.5). We will need to wait and see how the courts deal with this new development.

### 10.4.5 Technology outsourcing

Chapter 2 deals with the outsourcing of information systems and discusses one of the major components of an outsourcing deal, namely the transfer of employees. Outsourcing is a new business development and is particularly important in the IT field. When the Acquired Rights Directive[78] was first considered by the European Commission outsourcing, as we know it today, was hardly recognized as a new business practice. The implementation of the Directive in the UK through the Transfer of Undertakings (Protection of Employment) Regulations 1981[79] ('TUPE 1981') was similarly introduced without any real appreciation of the developments described in Chapter 2. In fact early editions of this book did not cover outsourcing as such. Therefore the significance of outsourcing as a major area of employment practice is also a recent development.

---

[77] See Laurie Hunter, Phil Beaumont and Matthew Lee, 'Knowledge Management in Scottish Law Firms' (2002) 12(2) Human Resource Management Journal.

[78] Directive 77/187/EEC on the approximation of the laws of the Member States relating to the safeguarding of employees' rights in the event of transfers of undertakings, businesses or parts of businesses.

[79] SI 1981/1794.

Directive 98/50/EC amended the 1977 Acquired Rights Directive to cope with the development of outsourcing. UK courts have been able to interpret TUPE 1981 in a way which has recognized some of these developments. This is easier in a common-law system but more difficult in civil-law systems, hence the need for an EU approach to reform. Therefore it is perhaps not surprising that the UK Government is still pondering how to reform TUPE 1981 in light of the 1998 Directive, despite the consultation process having been completed some time ago, as it may not be so pressing as for other jurisdictions.[80]

In an Information Society organizations are finding it expedient to outsource many of their peripheral business functions. This development is resulting in the transfer of millions of workers between organizations. TUPE 1981 enables many of these workers to retain their employment rights despite the transfers.

## 10.5 CONCLUSION

Employment rights in an Information Society are no longer restricted to traditional industrial concepts around termination of employment, discrimination, collective rights, etc. Information technology is changing the workplace and is a significant part of wealth creation in its own right. Therefore it is necessary to reappraise existing property and employment rights in this changing environment. Also new laws dealing with the impact of these changes on society, which are in themselves providing new employment rights, need to be recognized as part of the plethora of laws affecting working relationships. Of particular note is the fact that many of the new employment rights are not restricted to 'employees' but encompass all workers which follows the trend in employment to more flexible contracting arrangements.

---

[80] See *Transfer of Undertakings (Protection of Employment) Regulations 1981: Government Proposals for Reform* (DTI, September 2001) (URN 0111158).

# 11

# DATA PROTECTION

*Ian Walden*

Throughout this chapter the reader will be introduced to the key elements which go towards an understanding of data-protection law. The first two sections will consider the nature of the subject itself, primarily from a European perspective, as well as reviewing the international instruments which address data-protection issues. The final substantive section will focus on UK law, specifically the Data Protection Act 1998.

## 11.1  SUBJECT MATTER

Data-protection law as a distinct legislative field is predominantly a European phenomenon. Currently such laws exist in some twenty-five European countries,[1] and of these, a number have already revised or amended their original legislation, sometimes more than once. Outside Europe other industrialized nations, such as Australia, Japan and Canada, have adopted data-protection laws, but they are in the minority of trading nations and their laws tend to be less all-embracing than the European approach.

---

[1] Austria, Belgium, Czech and Slovak Republics, Denmark, Finland, France, Germany, Greece, Guernsey, Hungary, Iceland, Ireland, Isle of Man, Italy, Jersey, Luxembourg, The Netherlands, Norway, Poland, Portugal, Spain, Sweden, Switzerland and the UK.

One of the most straightforward definitions of data protection is given in the UK Government's explanatory report, appended to the draft of the Council of Europe Convention on Data Protection:

> ... the legal protection of individuals with regard to automatic processing of personal information relating to them.[2]

An alternative definition of data-protection legislation has been proposed by the Office of the Information Commissioner. The Deputy Commissioner has defined data protection as 'fairness legislation', not requiring a balance between data users and data subjects, but simply being fair to an individual.[3]

However, an expanded definition of data protection has been put forward by some less-developed countries. It has been suggested that data protection is a legal regime that should also be applied to information pertaining to states. Resolutions at Latin American and African conferences have proposed that 'information and knowledge affecting national sovereignty, security, economic well being and socio-cultural interests should be brought within the ambit of data protection'.[4]

Indeed, until the recent European Union Directive, the UK Government's definition would not have been sufficient to cover the variations of data-protection legislation within Europe, or between industrialized nations. Some countries, such as Denmark, Austria and Italy extend the protection afforded under data-protection laws to legal persons, such as companies and trade unions, as well as individuals. In other countries, including France and the Netherlands, data-protection laws have always applied to manual records, as well as computer data. While in non-European countries, such as Australia and Japan, data-protection laws were limited to public-sector data-processing activities, not the private sector.[5]

Within Europe, the 1981 Council of Europe Convention on data protection has been the foundation upon which national legislation and the 1995 EU Directive has been constructed.[6] Two distinct motives underpinned the 1981 Convention: the threat to individual privacy posed by computerization; and the desire to maintain a free flow of information between trading nations. The Convention therefore attempts to reconcile the article 8 right of privacy under the European Convention on Human Rights with the principle of the free flow of information, viewed as an element of the right to freedom of expression under article 10 of that Convention.[7]

Indeed, in the course of the Parliamentary debates on the UK Data Protection Act

---

[2] Convention for the Protection of Individuals with regard to Automatic Processing of Personal Data, Strasbourg, 28 January 1981 (European Treaty Series No 108) (Cmnd 8341) (HMSO, 1981), Explanatory Report, p 5.

[3] CBI Conference, London, 4 March 1988.

[4] Intergovernmental Bureau for Informatics, TDF 270, p 55.

[5] In 2000, the Australian federal Privacy Act was amended to extend its provisions to most of the private sector.

[6] See, further, section 11.2.1 below.

[7] See Council of Europe Recommendation No R(91)10, 'Communication to third parties of personal data held by public bodies', Explanatory Memorandum, para 10.

1984, the Under-Secretary of State at the Home Office, clearly put forward these two objectives:

[T]he Bill is drafted to fulfil two purposes. The first is to protect private individuals from the threat of the use of erroneous information about them—or indeed, the misuse of correct information about them—held on computers. The second is to provide that protection in a form that will enable us to satisfy the Council of Europe Convention on Data Processing so as to enable our own data processing industry to participate freely in the European market.[8]

### 11.1.1 Data protection and privacy

Since the Warren and Brandeis formulation of privacy as the 'right to be let alone',[9] considerable effort has been devoted to establishing an exhaustive definition of the constituent components of a right to privacy.[10] Article 12 of the United Nations Universal Declaration of Human Rights states that every individual has a right to privacy, yet fails to define the term. However, what does seem to be agreed upon in the literature is the extent to which the meaning of 'privacy' is dependent on a nation's culture.

The classic contrast to the British attitude to privacy is Sweden. Sweden has had 'freedom of information' legislation since 1776, and a social-security system based on the existence of a mandatory, unique personal identifier for each citizen, something which would not seem acceptable in this country at the present time.[11]

However, is there a significant difference between the principles upon which data-protection legislation is based and those that lie behind a 'right to privacy'?

Data protection and privacy are clearly substantially overlapping concepts, although certain distinctions have been drawn. In the 1978 Lindop Report on data protection, for example, the following distinction was made:

a data protection law should be different from that of a law on privacy: rather than establishing rights, it should provide a framework for finding a balance between the interests of the individual, the data user and the community at large.[12]

Such a balancing act can be recognized in the two motives that underpin the Council of Europe Convention. The report also gave the example of the use of inaccurate or incomplete information when making decisions. While within the proper scope of data protection, in terms of good information practices, such issues do not necessarily raise privacy issues.[13]

---

[8] 443 Parl Deb, HL (5th ser) 509 (1983) (statement of Lord Eton).
[9] See S D Warren and L D Brandeis, 'The Right to Privacy' (1890) IV(5) Harvard Law Review 193–220.
[10] See, eg, A Westin, *Privacy and Freedom* (Bodley Head, 1975) and R Wacks, *Personal Information: Privacy and the Law* (Clarendon Press, 1993).
[11] However, see the current debate generated by the Home Office consultation paper on 'entitlement cards'.
[12] *Report of the Committee on Data Protection* (Chairman: Sir Norman Lindop) (Cmnd 7341) (1978), p xix. (See, further, section 11.3.1 below.)          [13] Ibid, para 2.03.

As well as certain substantive distinctions between data-protection and privacy laws, a procedural distinction can also be seen, particularly within Europe. An assertion of privacy, as a right, is generally made by an individual before a court, which is required to exercise its discretion often through a process of balancing conflicting rights and taking into consideration principles such as proportionality. By contrast, data-protection laws, whilst granting individuals specific rights, are generally enforced through the intervention of a regulatory authority, with a supervisory remit over the actions of those that process personal data. This has led, arguably, to the profile of concerns of the authority, whether as an individual or as a collective body, becoming a surrogate for the interests of individuals.

Despite differences between the concepts, data-protection jurisprudence has inevitably extended to wider questions regarding an individual's 'right to privacy'. In Germany, for example, a Constitutional Court decision declared unconstitutional an act that had authorized the Government to undertake a comprehensive population census. The court declared that each data subject has a right to 'determine in general the release and use of his or her personal data'; therefore establishing a constitutional right of individual 'informational self-determination'.[14] The decision led to a fundamental revision of the German Data Protection Act. It has also been noted that some judicial opinion within the European Commission of Human Rights has begun to use the Council of Europe Convention on data protection to enliven and strengthen article 8 of the Human Rights Convention.[15]

In the UK, prior to 1998, any concept of a right of privacy resided primarily within the equitable action for breach of confidence, however inadequately, rather than the statutory framework established under the Data Protection Act 1984.[16] However, two legal developments in the UK have driven data protection and privacy ever closer together. First, the European Directive, upon which the Data Protection Act 1998 was based, expressly recognizes its origins in the right of privacy as expressed in article 8 of the European Convention for the Protection of Human Rights and Fundamental Freedoms.[17] Second, the Convention itself was incorporated into UK law by the Human Rights Act 1998, which imposed an obligation upon the courts, as public authorities, not 'to act in a way which is incompatible with a Convention right' (s 6(1)). As a consequence, the UK courts have increasingly been called upon to interpret questions of data protection and confidentiality law in privacy-related terms.[18]

---

[14] Judgment of December 15, 1983, Bundesverfassungsgericht [BVerfG], 65 Entscheidungen des Bundesverfassungsgericht [BVerfGE] 1, at p 43.

[15] P Hustinx, 'The Role of the Council of Europe', paper delivered at Privacy, Laws and Business Conference on Data Protection in Ireland, The Netherlands and Switzerland (19 October 1988) in the possession of the author.

[16] See *Kaye v Robertson* [1991] FSR 62.

[17] See Directive 95/46/EC, recital 10 and art 1.

[18] See *Douglas v Hello! Ltd* [2001] QB 967.

## 11.1.2  Data protection and freedom of information

One area of law that has developed an intricate relationship with data protection and privacy laws is that concerning freedom of information or access to official information. The potential conflict between these areas of law is obvious: data protection and privacy laws are primarily concerned with restricting the disclosure of information, while laws concerning freedom of information are designed to facilitate access to information. Generally, privacy is one of a number of recognized exemptions under regimes for freedom of information.[19]

Historically, data protection and freedom of information have been subject to distinct legal regimes. The primary exception to this has been Canada, where a number of provinces within the Federation have enacted statutes that embrace both freedom of information and data protection.[20] However, as has been noted, there are potential disadvantages of addressing these areas separately:

. . . the coexistence of access to official information legislation and data protection legislation may come into conflict especially where they are administered separately by different organs and under different criteria.[21]

Recognizing the synergies between laws concerning data protection and freedom of information, when the UK Government put forward the draft legislation which eventually became the Freedom of Information Act 2000, is was decided to place the regulatory functions created under the Act with the existing Office of the Data Protection Commissioner in a new entity known as the Office of the Information Commissioner (s 18).[22] In addition, specific exemptions from the right of access were granted for 'personal information' under the new regime for freedom of information (s 40).

Although the Freedom of Information Act does not enter fully into force until 2005 (s 87(3)), we can expect the integrated regulator to treat these overlapping though distinct areas of law with a common approach.

## 11.2  INTERNATIONAL ACTIVITY

The nature of the global economy inevitably means that large amounts of personal data cross national borders every day, either over communication networks, such as the Internet, or through the manual transfer of media, such as hard disks in notebook computers and personal digital assistants. Such transfers will predominantly occur in

---

[19]  eg, in the United States, 5 USC, s 552(b)(6), (7).

[20]  eg, Quebec (1982), Ontario (1988), Saskatchewan (1991), British Columbia (1992) and Alberta (1994).

[21]  Council of Europe Assembly Recommendation 1037 (1986) on data protection and freedom of information, para 10.

[22]  See, further, section 11.3.4 below.

the absence of any form of effective control or supervision by any regulatory authority. However, such transfers could obviously pose a threat to individual privacy, not least because national data-protection laws may be circumvented by transferring data to so-called 'data havens' that lack such protections.

In order to discourage organizations from avoiding data-protection controls and to guarantee a free flow of information, inter-governmental organizations, including the Council of Europe, the OECD, the United Nations and the European Union, have been active in attempting to achieve harmonization for data-protection legislation.

### 11.2.1 The Council of Europe

The Council of Europe has been the major international force in the field of data protection since the 1981 Convention for the Protection of Individuals with regard to Automatic Processing of Personal Data.[23] Of the forty-four members of the Council of Europe, some thirty-three have signed the Convention, and have therefore accepted an obligation to incorporate certain data-protection principles into national law. The Convention came into force on 1 October 1985 when five countries (Sweden, Norway, France, the Federal Republic of Germany and Spain) had ratified it.

The Council of Europe has been involved in the field since 1968, when the Parliamentary Assembly passed Recommendation 509 (68), asking the Council of Ministers to look at the Human Rights Convention to see if domestic laws gave adequate protection for personal privacy in the light of modern scientific and technical developments. The Council of Ministers asked the Committee of Experts on Human Rights to study the issue, and they reported that insufficient protection existed.

A specialist Committee of Experts on the Protection of Privacy was subsequently asked to draft appropriate resolutions for the Committee of Ministers to adopt. Resolution 22 (1973) covered the 'ground rules' for data protection in the private sector while Resolution 29 (1974) focused on the public sector. In 1976, a new Committee of Experts on Data Protection was established. Its primary task was to prepare a Convention on the protection of privacy in relation to data processing abroad and transfrontier data processing. The text of this Convention was finalized in April 1980, and opened for signature on 28 January 1981.

The Convention is based around a number of basic principles of data protection, upon which each country is expected to draft appropriate legislation. Such legislative provision will provide for a minimum degree of harmonization between signatories, and should therefore prevent restrictions on transborder data flows for reasons of 'privacy' protection.

Since 1981, the Committee of Experts on Data Protection has been primarily involved in the drafting of sectoral rules on data protection. These form part of an

---

[23] See n 2 above.

ongoing series of recommendations issued by the Committee of Ministers designed to supplement the provisions of the Convention.[24] In addition, the Convention was amended in 1999, to enable the European Communities to accede;[25] while an additional protocol was adopted in 2001 'on Supervisory Authorities and Transborder Data Flows'.[26]

The major weakness of the Convention is its lack of enforceability against countries that fail to uphold the basic principles. No enforcement machinery was created under the Convention, and therefore any disputes have to be resolved at the diplomatic level. However, to date, no such disputes have been reported.

### 11.2.2 OECD

The OECD (the Organisation for Economic Co-operation and Development) was established in 1961, and currently comprises thirty of the leading industrial nations. The nature of the organization has meant that interest in data protection has centred primarily on the promotion of trade and economic advancement of member states, rather than 'privacy' concerns *per se*.

In 1963, a Computer Utilization Group was set up by the Third Ministerial Meeting and aspects of the Group's work concerned with privacy went to a subgroup, the Data Bank Panel. This body issued a set of principles in 1977. In the same year, the Working Party on Information Computers and Communications Policy ('ICCP'), was created out of the Computer Utilization and Scientific and Technical policy groups. Within this body, the Data Bank Panel became the 'Group of Government Experts on Transborder Data Barriers and the Protection of Privacy' with a remit 'to develop guidelines on basic rules governing the transborder flow and the protection of personal data and privacy, in order to facilitate the harmonisation of national legislation'.

The OECD Guidelines were drafted by 1979, adopted in September 1980, and endorsed by the UK Government in 1981.[27]

The Guidelines are based, as with Council of Europe Convention, upon eight, self-explanatory, principles of good data-protection practice. The Guidelines are simply a recommendation to countries to adopt good data-protection practices in order to prevent unnecessary restrictions on transborder data flows; they have no formal authority. However, some companies and trade associations, particularly in the United States and Canada, have publicly adhered to the Guidelines.

---

[24] Some 12 Recommendations have been published, including the use of personal data in 'automated medical data banks' (R(81) 1); 'scientific research and statistics' (R(83) 10); 'employment records' (R(89) 2) and 'payment' (R(90) 19); 'the communication to third parties of personal data held by public bodies' (R(91) 10); 'telecommunication services' (R(95) 4) and 'protection of privacy on the Internet' (R(99) 5).

[25] See, further, section 11.2.4 below.

[26] European Treaty Series No 181, opened for signature on 8 November 2001.

[27] OECD, 'Guidelines on the Protection of Privacy and Transborder Flows of Personal Data' (OECD, 1980).

### 11.2.3 United Nations

While its historic Universal Declaration of Human Rights of 1948 was the first international instrument to recognize a right to privacy, the United Nations only comparatively recently focused on the human-rights aspects of the use of computer technology. In 1989, the General Assembly adopted a set of draft 'Guidelines for the regulation of computerized personal data files'.[28] These draft guidelines were subsequently referred to the Commission on Human Rights' Special Rapporteur, Mr Louis Joinet, for redrafting based on the comments and suggestions received from member governments and other interested international organizations. A revised version of the Guidelines was presented and adopted in 1990.[29]

The Guidelines are divided into two sections. The first section covers 'Principles concerning the minimum guarantees that should be provided in national legislations'. These 'principles' echo those put forward by both the Council of Europe Convention and the OECD Guidelines, except for three additional terms:

(a) Principle of non-discrimination: sensitive data, such as racial or ethnic origin, should not be compiled at all;

(b) Power to make exceptions: justified only for reasons of national security, public order, public health or morality; and

(c) Supervision and sanctions: the data-protection authority 'shall offer guarantees of impartiality, independence *vis-à-vis* persons or agencies responsible for processing . . . and technical competence'.

The second section considers the 'Application of the guidelines to personal data files kept by governmental international organisations'. This requires that international organizations designate a particular supervisory authority to oversee their compliance. In addition, it includes a 'humanitarian clause', which states that:

a derogation from these principles may be specifically provided for when the purpose of the file is the protection of human rights and fundamental freedoms of the individual concerned or humanitarian assistance

Such a clause is intended to cover organizations such as Amnesty International, who hold large amounts of personal data, but would be wary of sending information out to a data subject on the basis of an access request made while the person was still imprisoned.

---

[28] Resolution 44/132, on 15 December, 1989.
[29] Adopted by the Commission on Human Rights, Resolution 1990/42 (6 March 1990); subsequently by the UN Economic and Social Council, Resolution 1990/38, 14th Plenary Session (25 May 1990), and finally by the UN General Assembly, Resolution 45/95, 68th Plenary Session (14 December 1990).

## 11.2.4 European Union

Despite an interest and involvement in data protection and privacy issues for nearly two decades, from both the European Parliament and the Commission, the emergence of a binding legal instrument in the area only occurred in 1990.

The European Parliament's involvement in data-protection issues has primarily been through its Legal Affairs Committee, though the issue has been subject to parliamentary questions and debates over previous years. In 1976, the European Parliament adopted a resolution calling for a Directive to ensure that 'Community citizens enjoy maximum protection against abuses or failures of data processing' as well as 'to avoid the development of conflicting legislation'.[30]

In 1977 the Legal Affairs Committee established the Sub-Committee on Data Processing and the Rights of the Individual. The Sub-Committee, produced the 'Bayerl Report' in May 1979.[31] The resultant debate in the European Parliament led to recommendations being made to the Commission and the Council of Ministers concerning the principles that should form the basis of the Community's attitude to data protection.[32] These recommendations called on the European Commission to draft a Directive to complement a common communications system; to harmonize the data-protection laws and to secure the privacy of information on individuals in computer files.

In July 1981, the European Commission recommended that all Members sign the Council of Europe Convention and seek to ratify it by the end of 1982.[33]

A second parliamentary report, the Sieglerschidt Report, was published in 1982.[34] The report noted 'that data transmission in general should be placed on a legal footing and not be determined merely by technical reasons'.[35] It recommended the establishment of a 'European Zone', of members in the EEC and Council of Europe, within which authorization prior to the export of data would not be needed. It also indicated that initiatives, such as a Directive, were still necessary. Following the report, a resolution was adopted by the European Parliament, on 9 March 1982, calling for a Directive if the Convention proved inadequate.[36]

In July 1990, the European Commission finally published a proposal for a Directive on data protection.[37] It was published as part of a package of proposals:

---

[30] Resolution on the protection of the rights of individuals in connection with data processing, OJ C100, 3 May 1976, p 27.

[31] Named after the rapporteur. *Report on the Protection of the Individual in the Face of the Technical Developments in Data Processing* (1979–80 Eur Parl Doc (No 100) 13) (1979)).

[32] OJ C140, 5 June 1979, p 34.

[33] Commission Recommendation 81/679/EEC of 29 July 1981 relating to the Council of Europe Convention for the protection of individuals with regard to automatic processing of personal data, OJ L246/31, 29 August 1979.

[34] *Second Report on the Protection of the Rights of the Individual in the Face of Technical Developments in Data Processing* (EP Doc 1-548/81, 12 October 1981).

[35] Ibid, p 7.

[36] OJ C87/39, 5 April 1982.

[37] OJ C277, 5 November 1990.

(a) A recommendation that the European Community adheres to the Council of Europe Convention on data protection.[38]

(b) A declaration applying data-protection principles to Community institutions.[39] This was subsequently embodied within article 286 of the European Community Treaty and a supervisory authority, the European Data Protection Supervisor, was subsequently established.[40]

(c) A draft Directive addressing data-protection issues in the telecommunications sector.[41]

(d) A draft Council decision to adopt a two-year plan in the area of security for information systems.[42]

After considerable controversy and political debate at all stages of the legislative process, the general framework Directive on data protection was finally adopted by the European Parliament and Council on 24 October 1995.[43] Member States had to implement the Directive by 24 October 1998, although only five managed to adopt legislation by that date.[44] The provisions of the Directive are considered below (see section 11.3) in the context of the UK's implementing statute, the Data Protection Act 1998.

The primary justification for Commission action was as part of the Single Market programme, under article 95 (formerly article 100a) of the European Community Treaty. In 1990, only eight of the (then) twelve Member States had passed data-protection legislation. Even between these eight considerable divergence existed in terms of the scope of protection; the nature of the obligations imposed on data users and restrictions on the use and export of data. Such differences were seen as a potential obstacle to the development of an integrated European Information Market. The Commission also expressed its desire to protect the rights of individual data subjects, 'and in particular their right to privacy' (art 1(1)). The Directive is therefore limited to the protection of natural persons, rather than legal persons.[45]

---

[38] In 1996, however, the European Court of Justice held that that the Community can not adhere to the European Convention on Human Rights: Opinion No 2/94 [1996] 2 CMLR 265. The Convention has subsequently been amended to enable adherence: 'Amendments to the Convention for the protection of individuals with regard to automatic processing of personal data (ETS No 108) allowing the European Communities to accede', adopted by the Committee of Ministers, in Strasbourg, on 15 June 1999.

[39] Commission Declaration on the application to the institutions and other bodies of the European Communities of the principles contained in the Council Directive concerning the protection of individuals in relation to the processing of personal data (COM (90) 314 final), OJ C277/74, 5 November 1990.

[40] See Regulation No 45/2001 of the European Parliament and of the Council of 18 December 2000 on the protection of individuals with regard to the processing of personal data by the Community institutions and bodies and on the free movement of such data, OJ L8/1, 12 January 2001.

[41] See section 11.3.9 below.

[42] Adopted as Council Decision 92/242/EEC of 31 March 1992, in the field of information security, OJ L123, 8 May 1992.

[43] Directive 95/46/EC on the protection of individuals with regard to the processing of personal data and on the free movement of such data, OJ L281/31, 23 November 1995 ('the Data Protection Directive).

[44] ie, Greece, Italy, Portugal, Sweden and the UK, although the UK Act had not entered into force.

[45] However, see, further, section 11.3.9 below.

## 11.2.5 Transborder data flows

Despite the international initiatives outlined above, many important trading nations still lack comprehensive data-protection laws, extending in particular to private-sector use of personal data, such as the USA and Japan. Where countries do not have legislation or, indeed, where the level of protection is of a different nature (for example, extending only to public-sector data), an issue arises as to whether transfers of personal data should be permitted to jurisdictions that do not have 'equivalent' or 'adequate' protection.[46]

Where a recipient country does not have substantive data-protection legislation, could an individual's rights be ensured through other means? If a functional approach were adopted, a transfer could take place to countries without specific legislation where it can be shown that other forms of protection exist in the recipient country, such as constitutional or sectoral legal provisions and/or that the real risk to personal data is low, due to one or a combination of alternative forms of control, such as industry self-regulatory codes of practice, data security measures or contractual protection.

Since the Council of Europe Convention, particular interest has been shown in the use of contractual terms between the sender and recipient of personal data as a mechanism for achieving 'equivalent' protection. In 1992, the Council of Europe's Committee of Experts on data protection published a set of model contractual provisions which were designed to replicate, as far as possible, the principles of the Convention on data protection in a set of enforceable contractual provisions.[47] The clauses are primarily intended for situations where a contracting party, in a jurisdiction bound by the Council of Europe Convention, wishes to export personal data to a party based in a jurisdiction that has not legislated for data protection. Subsequently, other organizations have issued similar model terms, designed specifically to achieve 'adequate' protection.[48]

However, the role of contracts in protecting the transborder flows of personal data has been extended significantly under the Data Protection Directive. The Directive states that safeguards enabling a data controller to derogate from the requirement for 'adequate' protection 'may in particular result from appropriate contractual clauses' (art 26(2)). In addition, the Commission had the right to decide that certain terms offered sufficient protection (art 26(4)); and subsequently the Commission has adopted two decisions concerning such model contractual clauses.[49]

---

[46] The Convention uses the term 'equivalent' (art 12(3)(a)) while the Directive uses the term 'adequate' (art 25(1)).

[47] Council of Europe, 'Model Contract to ensure equivalent data protection in the context of transborder data flows' (T-PD (92) 7), October 1992.

[48] eg, International Chamber of Commerce, Model clauses for use in contracts involving transborder data flows (1999) (see www.icc.org).

[49] Commission Decision 2001/497/EC on standard contractual clauses for the transfer of personal data to third countries, under Directive 95/46/EC, OJ L181/19, 4 July 2001, and Commission Decision 2002/16/EC to processors established in third countries, OJ L6/52, 10 January 2002.

The major issue when looking to rely on contractual safeguards is whether such provisions can be sufficiently enforceable by, or on behalf of, the data subject whom they are intended to protect. The data user exporting the data is unlikely to suffer damage from any breach of such contractual terms, and therefore has little incentive to either police the agreement or sue for any breach. In addition, until recently, the primary obstacle under English law to a third party, such as a data subject, acting against the importing data user has been the privity of contract rule, whereby only the parties to a contract can enforce its obligations.[50]

The use of contractual terms to achieve harmonized protection for personal data between jurisdictions is a solution being strongly promoted by industry. Companies perceive contractual terms as a practical means of extending data-protection rights and obligations to jurisdictions where the adoption of comprehensive data-protection laws appears unlikely. The widespread adoption of such terms will, however, depend on the attitude of the appropriate national data-protection authorities.[51]

## 11.3  THE UK DATA PROTECTION ACT 1998

### 11.3.1  A history of legislative activity

In 1961, Lord Mancroft introduced a Right of Privacy Bill, which can be seen to mark the beginning of a twenty-three-year history that finally led to the successful passage of the Data Protection Act 1984. This first Private Member's Bill was followed by four others until the Government finally decided to establish a formal committee of inquiry into the area.

In May 1970, a Committee on Privacy was appointed under the chairmanship of Kenneth Younger. The Committee's purview was limited to the private sector, despite the Committee's request that it be extended to encompass the public sector as well. The final report ('the Younger Report') was completed and presented to Parliament in July 1972.[52]

During its establishment, the Committee set up a special Working Party on Computers. The Working Party concluded that:

Put quite simply, the computer problem as it affects privacy in Great Britain is one of apprehensions and fears and not so far one of facts and figures (para 580).

Indeed, their report went on to note that the most credible anxieties were those held about computers in the *public* sector, an area outside the Committee's scope. The Committee noted that areas of concern were with universities, bank records and

---

[50]  The Contracts (Rights of Third Parties) Act 1999 has removed this obstacle.

[51]  See *Transfers of Personal Data to Third Countries: Applying Articles 25 and 26 of the EU Data Protection Directive* (24 July 1998), a report adopted by the Working Party comprising the EU Member State data-protection authorities, established under article 29 of the Data Protection Directive. And see, generally, europa.eu.int/comm/dg15/en/media/dataprot/adopted.htm.

[52]  *Report of the Committee on Privacy* (HMSO, 1972) (Cmnd 5012).

credit agencies. The Committee recommended that an independent body ('Standing Commission') composed of computer experts and lay persons should be established to monitor growth in the processing of personal information by computer, as well as the use of new technologies and practices.

In response to the Younger Report, the Government promised a White Paper. However, it was three years before the White Paper, *Computers and Privacy*[53] was presented to Parliament in December 1975. In it, the Government accepted the need for legislation to protect computer-based information. Despite the concerns expressed in the Younger Report with regard to manual records, the Government felt that computers posed a special threat to individual privacy:

6. The speed of computers, their capacity to store, combine, retrieve and transfer data, their flexibility, and the low unit cost of the work which they can do have the following practical implications for privacy:

(1) they facilitate the maintenance of extensive record systems and the retention of data on those systems;

(2) they can make data easily and quickly accessible from many distant points;

(3) they make it possible for data to be transferred quickly from one information system to another;

(4) they make it possible for data to be combined in ways which might not otherwise be practicable;

(5) because the data are stored, processed and often transmitted in a form which is not directly intelligible, few people may know what is in the records, or what is happening to them.

The Government also issued a second White Paper, *Computers: Safeguards for Privacy*,[54] which agreed with the comments made by the Younger Report with regard to the concerns generated by public-sector information.

Rather than establish a standing commission to monitor the use of personal data, the White Paper proposed legislation to cover both public- and private-sector information systems. The creation of a Data Protection Authority was also proposed, to supervise the legislation and ensure that appropriate safeguards for individual privacy were implemented. In order to provide a detailed structure for the proposed data-protection authority, the Government established a Data Protection Committee, under the chairmanship of Sir Norman Lindop, which reported in 1978.[55]

The Lindop Report proposed that a number of data-protection principles should form the core of the legislation, with a Data Protection Authority being responsible for ensuring compliance with those principles. In particular, the Authority would be required to draft codes of practice for various sectors, based on consultations with interested parties and associations, which would then become law, as statutory instruments. Failure to comply with a code would lead to criminal sanctions. Overall, the Lindop Report was concerned to produce a flexible solution which

---

[53] Cmnd 6353.     [54] Cmnd 6354.     [55] See section 11.1.1 above.

would not act so as to hold back the growing use of computers within both the public and private sector.

After the fall of the Labour Government in 1979, legislation on data protection was further delayed. Finally, in 1982, the Government issued the White Paper, *Data Protection: The Government's Proposals For Legislation.*[56] The approach put forward in the White Paper was much less thorough than that proposed in the Lindop Report. The idea of a data-protection authority was replaced by an individual Registrar of Data Protection. The White Paper also rejected the idea of statutory codes of practice. Although they saw the value of such codes, the Government felt that the length of time necessary to create an adequate range of statutory codes of practice would be unacceptable.

The Data Protection Act of 1984 received the Royal Assent on 12 July 1984. The provisions of the Act were phased in over a three-year period, with the Act becoming fully operational on 11 November 1987.

With the adoption of the Data Protection Directive, the Government had an obligation to transpose it into national law by 24 October 1998. The Government chose to enact new primary legislation and repeal the 1984 Act, rather than amend the 1984 Act through secondary legislation. The Data Protection Act 1998 received Royal Assent on 16 July 1998. While it repealed the 1984 Act, transitional provisions effectively meant that processing carried out prior to 24 October 1998 continued to be subject to the 1984-style regime until October 2001. The 1998 Act did not enter into force until 1 March 2000, when the necessary ministerial orders under the Act had been drafted.[57]

The following sections primarily consider the provisions of the 1998 Act, although reference will also be made to the 1984 Act, since much of the case law under the previous regime continues to be applicable when considering the implications of such legislation.

### 11.3.2  Terms

The 1998 Act is concerned with personal data. 'Personal data' consists of data that relates to a 'living individual' who can be identified from that data, or from that and other data or information in, or likely to come into, the possession of the data user. 'Data' includes information processed by computers, contained in 'relevant filing systems' and 'accessible records'.

In contrast to the 1984 Act, the term 'relevant filing system' extends the scope of the legislation to manual records as well as computer records. To constitute a 'relevant filing system' the set of information must be 'structured, either by reference to individuals or by reference to criteria relating to individuals, in such a way that specific information relating to a particular individual is readily available' (s 1).

---

[56] Cmnd 8539.

[57] For all the relevant primary and secondary legislation, see S Chalton, S Gaskill, H Grant and J Walden (eds), *Encyclopedia of Data Protection* (Sweet & Maxwell) (looseleaf service).

The term 'accessible records' has been incorporated in order that the UK Government can comply with the European Court of Human Right's decision in *Gaskin v United Kingdom*.[58] In this case, the Court held that certain records relate to 'private and family life' in such a way that the issue of access falls within the ambit of article 8 of the European Convention on Human Rights. The Government has defined the types of records which it believes fall within the scope of the *Gaskin* decision, including health and educational records (s 68 and Sch 12).

The Freedom of Information Act 2000 has subsequently amended the definition of 'data' by adding another category of the term: information recorded by a 'public authority', which does not fall within any of the other categories, ie, unstructured manual records.[59] Access by data subjects to such 'unstructured personal data', under section 7, is qualified by the need for the request to contain a description of the data being sought, and where the estimated cost of compliance exceeds an amount prescribed by the Secretary of State the data need not be supplied.[60] Such records are also exempt from many of the Data Protection Act's provisions,[61] including six of the eight data-protection principles.

Under the 1984 Act, the 'processing' of personal data is limited to processing 'by reference to the data subject'.[62] Such a limitation is not present in the 1998 Act's definition of processing which follows the all-encompassing definition in the Data Protection Directive:

any operation or set of operations which is performed upon personal data, whether or not by automatic means, such as collection, recording, organisation, storage, adaptation or alteration, retrieval, consultation, use, disclosure by transmission, dissemination or otherwise making available, alignment or combination, blocking, erasure or destruction (art 2(b)).

The 1998 Act is primarily concerned with three categories of persons:

(a) 'Data subjects': the individual which is the subject of the personal data.

(b) 'Data controllers': a person who, whether alone, jointly or in common with others, 'determines the purposes for which and the manner in which' the data are processed.[63]

(c) 'Data processor': a third party who simply processes personal data on behalf of a data controller without controlling the contents or use of the data.

---

[58] (1990) 12 EHRR 36.

[59] Freedom of Information Act 2000, s 68.

[60] Ibid, s 69(2), inserting a new section 9A into the Data Protection Act 1998.

[61] Ibid, s 70, inserting a new section 33A into the Data Protection Act 1998.

[62] See *Equifax Europe Limited v The Data Protection Registrar* (1991) (case DA/90 25/49/7) where the Data Protection Tribunal held that the phrase 'processing by reference to data subject' meant that 'the object of the exercise is to learn something about individuals'.

[63] In *Data Protection Registrar v Francis Joseph Griffin, The Times*, 5 March 1993, QBD, the court held that limitations imposed on an individual's use of personal data for his own purposes, either contractual or professional, does not necessarily prevent him from being a separate registrable 'data user' under the 1984 Act.

Under the regime established by the Data Protection Directive, a key concept is that of 'data subject's consent'. If the data controller obtains consent then he is broadly free to process the personal data. The Directive defines 'data subject's consent' as being freely given, specific and informed. It supplements this in the substantive provisions when referring to consent as being 'unambiguously' given (arts 7(1) and 26(1)(a)). Such terminology would seem to provide little opportunity for a data controller to rely on the implied consent of the data subject, on the basis, for example, that a data subject has not ticked an 'opt-out' box on an application form. Significantly, however, the 1998 Act does not include any definition of 'consent'. In justification of this position, the Government has stated:

> The Government are content for the issue of whether consent has been validly given to be determined by the courts in the normal way . . . It is better for the courts to decide according to ordinary principles of law than for the Act to contain specific consent provisions.[64]

However, this absence may provide data controllers with greater flexibility with respect to claiming the consent of the data subject through implication, although the courts would have to consider the terminology used in the Directive when interpreting the application of the Act.

Provisions concerning so-called 'sensitive data' were contained in the 1984 Act, but were never brought into operation by the Secretary of State.[65] Under the new Act, section 2 defines eight categories of 'sensitive personal data', including: data concerning a person's racial or ethnic origin; their political and religious beliefs; trade-union membership; physical and mental health; and criminal convictions. The processing of sensitive data is subject to additional controls.[66]

### 11.3.3 Data-protection principles

The Data Protection Act 1984 was built around certain data-protection principles, an approach that the EU Directive and the 1998 Act reiterate. These principles are intended to be good practices that data controllers should comply with in order to protect the data they hold, reflecting both their interests and those of their data subjects. These principles are fundamental to an understanding of the basis of data-protection law in Europe. The 1998 Act contains a limited redraft and renumbering of the 1984 principles, and data controllers have a duty to comply with the principles, except where an exemption exists (s 4(4)).

The first principle requires fair and lawful processing, with the additional requirement that one of the conditions in Schedule 2 (and Schedule 3 where sensitive data is processed) is present. These conditions primarily relate to the issue of lawful

---

[64] Comments made by Mr Hoon (Parliamentary Secretary, Lord Chancellor's Department), 12th sitting of Standing Committee D, 4 June 1998 (morning).

[65] 1984 Act, s 2(3).

[66] See Schedule 3 and the Data Protection (Processing of Sensitive Personal Data) Order 2000, SI 2000/417.

processing. Schedules 2 and 3 therefore substantially extend the concept of 'lawful' processing under the 1984 Act (see, further, section 11.3.8 below).

The basic position under Schedules 2 and 3 is that, except where the data controller has the consent of the data subject, the processing of personal data must be 'necessary' for one of the specified purposes, such as 'the performance of contract to which the data subject is a party'. The burden will be upon the data controller to show evidence of such necessity.

Under the Data Protection Directive, a data controller is required to provide certain information to the data subject, either when the data are collected from the data subject (art 10), or where the data were not obtained from the data subject (art 11). These provisions have been incorporated into the Act within the concept of 'fair' processing, as part of the interpretation provisions. As with 'lawful' processing, this constitutes a significant extension to the interpretation of 'fairness' under the 1984 Act.

In *Innovation (Mail Order) Limited v Data Protection Registrar*[67] the Data Protection Tribunal stated that 'fair obtaining' means that at the time that information is collected, the data user needs to inform the data subject of certain matters that will enable the individual to decide whether to provide the information or not. In particular, this includes information about the intended uses for the data, unless such use could be considered obvious.

Whilst the Directive refers only to the data controller providing such information to the data subject 'except where he already has it', the Act also enables the data controller to comply with the obligation by making the information 'readily available' to the data subject. The manner in which this phrase is interpreted may have important implications for a controller in terms of the procedural mechanisms it establishes, such as the use of Intranet-based techniques to disseminate information to employees.

Where the data controller has not obtained the data from the data subject himself, the controller is exempt from the requirement to provide information where it would involve either 'disproportionate effort', or the recording or disclosure is required under a non-contractual legal obligation.[68]

Under the second principle, data controllers must obtain data only for specified and lawful purposes, and must not carry out any further processing which is incompatible with those purposes. For example, a contravention of this principle would be for an organization to notify the holding of personal data for purposes of personnel management, and use it additionally for marketing purposes.

The third principle requires a data controller to hold only personal data that is 'adequate, relevant and not excessive in relation to that purpose or those purposes'.

The fourth principle requires that all personal data 'shall be accurate and, where

---

[67] 29 September 1993 (case DA/92 31/49/1).

[68] See the Data Protection (Conditions under Paragraph 3 of Part II of Schedule 1) Order 2000, SI 2000/185.

necessary, kept up to date'. If, for example, an organization purports to keep a list of undischarged bankrupts, but makes no effort to seek information on persons discharging themselves from bankruptcy, it will be contravening this principle.

The fifth principle states that personal data 'shall not be kept for longer than is necessary for that purpose or those purposes'. This principle implies that data should be destroyed or rendered anonymous when the specified purpose(s) for which they were collected has been achieved.

The sixth principle requires processing to be carried out in accordance with the rights of data subjects under the Act (see, further, section 11.3.6 below).

The seventh principle addresses issues of data security, requiring data controllers to take 'appropriate technical and organisational measures' against unauthorized or unlawful processing, and accidental loss, destruction or damage to the data. Regard must be had to the state of technological development and the cost of implementing such measures. Data controllers should also take measures to ensure that employees are reliable and, if using a data processor, written contractual obligations must be provided to ensure that the processor complies with the seventh principle and does not process the data except on the instructions of the data controller (Sch 1, Pt II, paras 11–12).

The obligation upon data controllers not to transfer personal data to countries which do not have an 'adequate' level of protection, as required by article 25 of the Directive, is implemented in the Act through a new eighth principle:

Personal data shall not be transferred to a country or territory outside the European Economic Area unless that country or territory ensures an adequate level of protection for the rights and freedoms of data subjects in relation to the processing of personal data.

The principle is accompanied by an interpretation section (Sch 1, Pt II, paras 13–15) and by Schedule 4, which details situations where the principle is not applicable.

Data controllers will also be required to notify the Commissioner of those countries outside the EEA to which they transfer, or intend to transfer, personal data. This will enable him to take proactive steps against transfers to countries perceived as providing inadequate protection. The eighth principle will require an assessment of 'adequacy' on a country-by-country basis.

In procedural terms, where a data controller intends to transfer personal data, the first issue that will need to be addressed is whether the transfer falls within one of the criteria specified in Schedule 4. If it does, then the eighth principle would not be applicable.

Schedule 4 substantially echoes the derogations provided for under article 26(1) of the Directive, ie, either where the data subject has given consent, or where the transfer is necessary for a particular reason (for example, to perform a contract with the data subject). Article 26(2) provides an additional circumstance arising where a Member State, through the offices of the Information Commissioner, authorizes 'a transfer or a set of transfers of personal data to a third country which does not ensure an adequate level of protection'. Such authorizations will only arise where the data controller 'adduces adequate safeguards'. The initiative is clearly upon the individual data controller to seek such authorization before making a transfer.

Under the Act, article 26(2) of the Directive has been implemented through two distinct procedural situations:

(a)  the transfer 'is made on terms of a kind approved by the Commissioner'; or
(b)  the transfer 'has been authorised by the Commissioner'.

The former is addressed to the possibility that the Commissioner could approve the use of certain contractual terms, which would then be considered suitable to cover a 'set of transfers' carried out by the data controller over a period of time (see, further, section 13.2.5 below). The latter procedure seems to presume some form of case-by-case prior authorization process.

The Commissioner is required to notify the European Commission and the other Member States of all approvals and authorizations granted. Objections may be lodged against such decisions and the European Commission, through its Committee procedure (under article 31(2)), may make a determination prohibiting such an authorization. Therefore, any approval or authorization a data controller obtains from the Commissioner must be viewed as qualified, subject to this consultation process. The Commissioner is also obliged to notify data controllers of any Community finding in respect of non-EEA countries that are considered either to have 'adequate' protection or not (s 51(6)). To date, findings of adequacy have been made for three countries: Hungary, Switzerland and Canada, as well as for US-based organizations who have signed-up to the 'Safe Harbor' Agreement.[69]

Where a transfer *does* fall within the scope of Principle 8, then a data controller will need to assess whether the 'country or territory' to which the transfer is to be made ensures an adequate level of protection. The interpretation provision, Part II of Schedule 1, provides a non-exclusive list of criteria relevant to the making of such an assessment, echoing the terminology of article 25(2). Of particular interest is paragraph 13(g), which states:

any relevant codes of conduct or other rules which are enforceable in that country or territory (whether generally or by arrangement in particular cases)

This is phrased in broad enough terms to include contractual mechanisms, as rules may be 'enforceable' through contractual agreement. Such an interpretation suggests there-fore that contractual mechanisms will be a factor in cases where the eighth principle is applicable, as well as those where it does not apply because a derogation is sought. The procedural advantage of complying with the eighth principle is the avoidance of the need for the Information Commissioner to notify the European Commission and the other Member States.[70]

---

[69] Commission Decision 2000/250/EC of 26 July 2000 pursuant to Directive 95/46/EC of the European Parliament and of the Council on the adequacy of the protection provided by the Safe Harbor privacy principles and related frequently asked questions issued by the US Department of Commerce, OJ L215/7, 25 August 2000.

[70] See, generally, 'Guidance Note: The Eighth Data Protection Principle and Transborder Data Flows' (Office of the Information Commissioner, July 1999), available at www.dataprotection.gov.uk.

## 11.3.4 The Information Commissioner

The 1998 Act renamed the supervisory authority 'the Data Protection Commissioner', which has subsequently been renamed 'the Information Commissioner'.[71] The Commissioner has a number of duties and enforcement powers under the Act. Under the 1984 Act, the Data Protection Registrar had a duty to promote observance of the data-protection principles. This has been significantly broadened to a general duty to promote 'good practice', defined as:

'good practice' means such practice in the processing of personal data as appears to the Commissioner to be desirable having regard to the interests of data subjects and others, and includes (but is not limited to) compliance with the requirements of this Act' (s 51(9))

One mechanism for such promotion is the development of codes of practice. Under the 1998 Act, the Commissioner can draft such codes rather than merely encourage trade associations to do so (s 51(3)(b)). The first code proposed by the Commissioner is in the area of employer/employee relations. This is likely to be an important implementation tool for the Commissioner and will result in a proliferation of the number of codes.[72] Under the proposed orders, compliance with a code of practice is likely to confer a number of procedural benefits. The Commissioner has the power to carry out 'good practice'-based assessments, with the consent of the data controller (s 51(7)).

The Commissioner has the power to pursue administrative remedies, in the form of notices issued against data controllers, and/or criminal remedies for the commission of offences under the Act (see section 11.3.8 below). In terms of investigating compliance with the Act, the Commissioner can issue an 'information notice' against a data controller requiring the provision of specific information (s 43). Where necessary, the Commissioner can apply to a court for a warrant to access, search and seize material held by an individual or organization (Sch 9). While the Commissioner can instigate a prosecution for an offence under the Act, he can not commence civil proceedings against a data controller where a data subject's statutory rights have been breached.

The Act also provides the Commissioner with the ability to serve an 'enforcement notice' against a data controller that has failed to observe any of the data-protection principles (s 40). The notice specifies the nature of the breach that has occurred and outlines the measures that will need to be taken in order to correct the breach. If the data controller fails to comply with the notice, then an offence is committed (s 47).

Any person who is, or believes himself to be, directly affect by any processing of personal data may require the Commissioner to carry out an 'assessment' of whether

---

[71] See section 11.1.3 above. The first Registrar was Eric Howe. He was replaced by Elizabeth France in August 1994. A new Information Commissioner, Richard Thomas, was appointed from 2 December 2002.

[72] There are currently some 30 codes of practice. See the *Encyclopedia of Data Protection* (n 57 above).

the Act is being complied with (s 42). If provided with sufficient information to identify the relevant processing, the Commissioner has a duty to make such an assessment.

Under the 1984 Act, a Data Protection Tribunal was established to hear appeals by data controllers against any notice issued against them by the Registrar. Data subjects had no such right of appeal. This position is broadly maintained under the 1998 Act, although data subjects will now have the right to appeal to the, now renamed, Information Tribunal where they are 'directly affected' by the issuance of a certificate exempting data from the Act's provisions for reasons of national security (s 28(4)–(5)).[73]

### 11.3.5 Data controller notification

Under the 1984 Act, the Registrar was required to establish a public register of all data users and computer bureaux. The principal functions of the register were to identify systems and facilitate supervision and compliance with standards (as well as generating income!) The Office of the Data Protection Registrar initially estimated the number of registrations to be around 300,000; however, just over half that number were received. Much criticism was levelled at the registration process from both data users and subjects.

Under the 1998 Act, data controllers are required to continue to notify the Information Commissioner in a similar fashion to the previous registration system, although, as noted by the Home Office, 'notification will be an element of the main regime rather than triggering application of that regime'.[74] The Act prohibits processing without notification (s 17), except for:

(a) manual data processed as part of a 'relevant filing system' or an 'accessible record';

(b) where the Secretary of State has, in 'notification regulations', exempted categories of processing from the notification obligation as 'unlikely to prejudice' data subject rights and freedoms;[75] or

(c) the processing is for the *sole* purpose of maintaining a public register.

Such notification shall include 'the registrable particulars' (for example, name, address and description of purposes for which the data are being processed (s 16(1))) and 'a general description of measures to be taken for the purpose of complying with the seventh data protection principle'. Controllers also have a duty to notify the Commissioner of any changes relating to such matters. The Commissioner shall

---

[73] See *Norman Baker MP v Secretary of State for the Home Department* (2001) UKHRR 1275 where a certificate was overturned by the Information Tribunal.

[74] See the Home Office's *Consultation Paper on Notification Regulations* (August 1998), para 8.

[75] See the Data Protection (Notification and Notification Fees) Regulations 2000, SI 2000/188, reg 3 and Sch, paras 2–5 ('Notification Regulations').

maintain a register of notifications which shall be made available to the public for inspection,[76] although this only includes the 'registrable particulars', not the information relating to data-security measures (s 19(2)). Considerable controversy has surrounded the need to supply a description of security measures. Data controllers are obviously concerned to limit the amount of information disclosed; whilst the Commissioner needs to obtain sufficient detail to make the process meaningful.

Processing may be classified as 'assessable processing', under the terms of an Order yet to be issued by the Secretary of State, where such processing will be likely either to cause 'significant damage or distress to data subjects', or to 'prejudice the rights and freedoms of data subjects' (s 22). The Government has indicated that it is considering whether such controls may be necessary for processing involving data matching, genetic data and private investigation activities. Processing such data will require the data controller to notify the Commissioner, as with any other form of data, but then delay commencement for a period of twenty-eight days, which can be extended for a further fourteen days by the Commissioner. Whilst unable to prohibit such processing, the Commissioner will be able to issue an enforcement notice where the processing is considered to be non-compliant with the Act.

One innovation under the Data Protection Directive, imported from German data-protection law,[77] is the possibility that a controller may be exempted from the notification obligation through the appointment of a 'personal data protection official' to act as an internal supervisory authority. However, the Government found little private-sector enthusiasm for the idea and, therefore, the Act simply grants the Secretary of State the power to issue an Order at some point in the future.[78]

Exemption from notification does not take the relevant processing outside the terms of the Act, since data controllers will still be required to comply with the data-protection principles. In addition, even where a data controller is exempt from notification, for example, by processing only manual data (s 17(2)) or under the Notification Regulations, the data controller may be required to provide details of its 'registrable particulars' to any person who submits a request in writing (s 24(1)). Such information is to be provided free of charge, within twenty-one days. The potential burden involved in meeting this obligation may convince many data controllers to notify voluntarily their details to the Commissioner (s 18).[79]

### 11.3.6 Data subjects' rights

The 1998 Act extends and amends existing rights given to data subjects and provides data subjects with additional rights, in line with the Data Protection Directive.

---

[76] See www.dataprotection.gov.uk.

[77] Gesetz zur Fortentwicklung der Datenverarbeitung und des Datenschutzes (Bundesgesetzblatt 1990 I, p 2954), s 28.

[78] Government White Paper, *Data Protection: The Government's Proposals* (Cm 3725) (July 1997), para 5.11.

[79] Ibid, para 5.10.

### 11.3.6.1 *Subject access*

A data subject is entitled to be informed by any data controller whether processing of his personal data is being carried out and to be given copies, 'in an intelligible form', of any such data (s 7). However, the requirement to provide information to the data subject is significantly enhanced over that required under the 1984 Act regime. Under the 1998 Act, the following information must be supplied:

(a)  the personal data being processed;

(b)  the purpose(s) for which data are being processed;

(c)  the recipients or classes of recipients to whom data may be disclosed; and, where relevant,

(d)  the logic involved in any automated decision taking.

In the event that the data subject then requests a copy of such information, the data controller must also provide the data subject with 'any information available to the data controller as to the source of those data' (s 7(1)(c)(ii)).

Such information adds significantly to the value of the access right. Under the 1984 Act, such contextual information was only indirectly and imperfectly made available to the data subject through the data user's registration entry. The onus was placed on the data subject to figure out the likely source of their personal data, how it is used and to whom it may be disclosed. The 1998 Act's provisions require the direct provision of specific information on a per request basis. This will require significant additional processing overhead for data controllers responding to subject access requests.

The information must be supplied in 'permanent form' unless this is either impossible or would involve a disproportionate effort, or the data subject agrees otherwise (s 8(2)). Any terms that are not intelligible without an explanation must be accompanied with an appropriate explanatory note. The only amendments that may be made to the information held by the data controller once an access request has been received and before it is supplied are: those that would have occurred in the normal course of events (s 8(6)); those required to respect third-party personal data (see below) or information subject to an exemption from access (see section 11.3.7 below).

A data controller is not required to supply such information unless he has received a request in writing and any prescribed fee (s 7(2)). The Act provides the Secretary of State with the ability to prescribe different levels of fees, which have been laid down in the Data Protection (Subject Access) (Fees and Miscellaneous Provisions) Regulations 2000:[80]

(a)  The general maximum fee is £10;

(b)  For requests concerning an individual's financial standing from a credit-reference agency the fee is £2;

---

[80]  Act, s 7(11) and SI 2000/191.

(c) For requests in respect of educational records, a sliding scale is detailed in the Schedule, with a maximum of £50;[81] and

(d) For health records the maximum fee is £50, although no fee may be charged in certain circumstances.[82]

As well as submitting a request in writing and paying any required fee, the data subject can be required to provide any information the data controller may 'reasonably require' in order to satisfy himself of the identity of the requesting party (s 7(3)). Such an authentication process is clearly required in order to prevent unauthorized disclosures; however, it could be abused in order to frustrate access requests.

In addition, information must be provided that indicates the location of the information (s 7(3)). So, for example, a requesting data subject would be expected to notify the data controller of his relationship to the data controller, for example, as a customer or ex-employee. Such information could also extend to an indication of methods of communication used in any interaction with the data controller, such as e-mail.[83]

The data controller has an obligation to provide the requested information within a prescribed period (s 7(8)). The standard period is forty days, although different periods are prescribed for requests from credit-reference agencies (ie, seven working days) and educational records (ie, fifteen school days).[84]

Concerns about the operation of the subject access provisions, particularly the exemptions from subject access, have been raised in a consultation paper recently published by the Lord Chancellor's Department, the Government department responsible for data-protection policy.[85] The process is designed to uncover whether 'any "running" adjustments are needed to take account of legal and technological changes' (para 5).

### 11.3.6.2 *Third-party personal data*

The subject access provisions also address the issue of the provision of requested information that includes personal data relating to another individual. Coverage of the issue is in considerably greater detail than under the 1984 Act, possibly reflecting the problems experienced by data controllers in the past.

In determining whether 'information relating to another individual who can be identified from that information' will be disclosed through the subject access

---

[81] See Commissioner's compliance advice on 'Subject Access: Education Records in England' (November 2001).

[82] Under the initial regulations, the £50 maximum applied only to requests made before 24 October 2001 (reg 6(1)(c)). However, transitional provision was subsequently deleted, leaving £50 as the maximum permitted fee; see the Data Protection (Subject Access) (Fees and Miscellaneous Provisions) (Amendment) Regulations 2002, SI 2002/3223. See also the Commissioner's compliance advice on 'Subject Access and Health Records' (version 2.1) (13 November 2001).

[83] See the Commissioner's compliance advice on 'Subject Access and Emails' (version 1) (14 June 2000).

[84] SI 2000/191, paras 4(1)(b) and 5(4) respectively.

[85] *Data Protection Act 1998: Subject Access* (October 2002).

request, the data controller must take into account 'any other information which, in the reasonable belief of the data controller, is likely to be in, or come into, the possession of the data subject making the request' (s 8(7)). This is likely to prove difficult for data controllers to apply, and it may require them to demand further information from the data subject prior to responding to their access request. A data controller is obliged to provide such information to the data subject as he can without 'disclosing the identity of the individual concerned'.

The 1984 Act only permitted disclosure of third-party identifying information where the data user was 'satisfied that the other individual has consented'. This is extended under the 1998 Act to include situations where 'it is reasonable in all the circumstances to comply with the request without the consent of the other individual'. The Act elaborates a non-exhaustive list of factors that may be relevant to such a determination, such as any duty of confidentiality owed to the other individual (s 7(6)). A data controller will need to establish appropriate internal procedures to handle subject access requests for information which contain data on third parties, in order to evidence the appropriateness of any decision to disclose or withhold data.

### 11.3.6.3 *Right to prevent and restrict processing*

One common misperception about the data-protection regime is that it grants a data subject a general right to prevent a data controller from processing his personal data. Neither the 1984 nor the 1998 Acts grant such a broad right. Under the Data Protection Act 1998, provided that a data controller legitimately processes the data in compliance with the data-protection principles, particularly the first principle concerning fair and lawful processing, a data subject can only prevent the processing of his personal data in two specific circumstances: where the processing is likely to cause damage or distress and where the purpose of the processing is for direct marketing.

Under article 14(a) of the Directive, a data subject has the right to object to the processing of his data 'on compelling legitimate grounds' and, if the complaint is 'justified', the data controller is obliged to stop such processing. The Act has specified the scope of such legitimate grounds as causing, or likely to cause: (a) 'substantial damage or substantial distress to him [the data subject] or to another' and where (b) such damage is 'unwarranted' (s 10(1)). Where such circumstances arise, the data subject may give notice to the data controller in writing and, in the event of dispute, apply for a court order requiring the data controller to stop such processing (s 10(4)).

Article 14(b) of the Directive grants data subjects a specific right to object to processing for the purpose of direct marketing, 'or to be informed before personal data are disclosed for the first time to third parties or used on their behalf for the purposes of direct marketing'. The Act clearly implements the first part of this provision, by granting the data subject a right to require the data controller to cease processing for the purposes of direct marketing (s 11(1)). However, the further element (in quotations) is not present in the Act, which would appear to be a significant limitation of the rights being granted to the data subject.

Data subjects have a new right in respect of automated decision taking, such as credit-reference scoring and the use of psychometric testing for screening applicants (s 12). The Act gives data subjects an entitlement to notify a data controller not to take decisions which 'significantly affect' the data subject and are based 'solely' on automated processing. In the absence of notification, a data controller must proactively notify the individual, 'as soon as reasonably practicable', where such a decision *was* taken and give them the opportunity to require the data controller to 'reconsider the decision or to take a new decision otherwise than on that basis'. However, this right of notification does not apply where the Secretary of State has exempted particular circumstances, or the following conditions are met:

(a) the decision is an aspect of entering into, or performing, a contract with the data subject (s 12(6)(a)); or

(b) the automated decision-making is required under an enactment (s 12(6)(b)); and

(c) the decision grants the request of the data subject (s 12(7)(a)); or

(d) steps have been taken to protect the data subject's interests, for example, there is a procedure for appeal (s 12(7)(b)).

The operation of these provisions seem unnecessarily complex, and will create compliance uncertainties and procedural overheads for data controllers whilst offering minimal effective protection for data subjects.

### 11.3.6.4 *Compensation*

The 1998 Act extends the grounds upon which a data subject may recover compensation. Under the 1984 Act, compensation could only be awarded by a court in situations of inaccuracy, loss, destruction or unauthorized disclosure or access.[86] The 1998 Act substantially broadens this right to '*any* contravention by a data controller of *any* of the requirements of this Act' (s 13). Compensation can extend to any 'distress' suffered by the individual, although only as a supplement to damage. Compensation may be for distress alone only where the contravention relates to processing for the 'special purposes' (see, further, section 11.3.7 below).

The Information Commissioner has noted that the concept of 'damage' includes 'financial loss or physical injury'.[87] The courts were obliged to consider the scope of the compensation provisions in *Campbell v Mirror Group Newspapers Limited*[88] where a concurrent claim for damages arose under section 13 of the Data Protection Act 1998 and for breach of confidence. The court noted that the concept of 'damage' under section 13 'means special or financial damages in contra-distinction to distress in the shape of injury to feelings'.[89] The court in *Campbell* also found that the plaintiff had suffered both primary and aggravated damage, ie 'increased distress and injury',

---

[86] 1984 Act, ss 22–3. See, further, *Lord Ashcroft v Attorney-General and Department for International Development* [2002] EWHC 1122.

[87] See Commissioner's publication, *Data Protection Act 1998: Legal Guidance*, section 4.5.

[88] [2002] HRLR 28.                                          [89] Ibid, para 123.

suffered as a result of the defendant's conduct subsequent to the breach giving rise to the action, although the level of award was minimal.[90]

It has been suggested that this provision may not comply with the Data Protection Directive because the concept of 'damage', under article 23(1), has been interpreted too narrowly. The European Commission's Article 29 Working Party on data protection has stated:

> It should be borne in mind that 'damage' in the sense of the data protection directive includes not only physical damage and financial loss, but also any psychological or moral harm caused (know as 'distress' under UK and US law).[91]

Whether the Government's interpretation is non-compliant, or whether such issues of relief are beyond the competence of EU law, may have to be resolved before the European Court of Justice. It should also be noted that a data subject may have a right to bring the Government before a national court for a failure to protect an individual's rights under the Data Protection Directive, and this could rise to a compensatory award.[92]

Where the data controller is a 'public authority', a concurrent claim could be brought before the UK courts under the Human Rights Act 1998. Section 6(1) of the Human Rights Act states that it is 'unlawful for a public authority to act in a way that is incompatible with a Convention right'. In *R (Robertson) v Wakefield Metropolitan District Council*,[93] for example, the authority was found to be acting in breach of the Data Protection Directive and the 1998 Act, as well as an individual's right to respect for private life under article 8(1) of the Convention, by selling the electoral register without permitting an individual right to object. Section 8 of the Human Rights Act 1998 provides that a court may grant 'such relief or remedy, or make such order, within its powers as it considers just and appropriate', including an award of damages.[94] A court could therefore make an award of damages that reflects non-pecuniary injury such as distress, without making an award in respect of pecuniary damage. Indeed, such a situation arose in the *Gaskin* case, where the European Court of Human Rights awarded £5,000 as compensation for non-pecuniary injury in respect of emotional distress and anxiety, even though the claim for pecuniary damage was rejected.[95] Therefore, the remedy available under the Human Rights Act, whilst co-existing with the remedy provided for under section 13 of the Data Protection Act 1998, is considerably wider.[96]

---

[90]  This was subsequently overturned on appeal at [2002] EWCA Civ 1373.

[91]  Working Document, 'Judging Industry Self-Regulation: When Does it Make a Meaningful Contribution to the Level of Data Protection in a Third Country?', adopted by the Working Party on 14 January 1998.

[92]  eg, *Francovich and Others v Italy* [1991] ECR 1-5357. See also *Wakefield* (n 93 below), para 19.

[93]  [2002] 2 WLR 889.

[94]  Subject to a general limitation that the principles applied by the European Court of Human Rights must be taken into account (s 8(4)). In *R (Robertson) v First Secretary of State*, *The Times* 11 August 2003, the Court held that regulations permitting the sale of electoral registers to credit reference agencies struck an appropriate balance between human rights and the public interest.

[95]  (1990) 12 EHRR 36, paras 57–8.

[96]  The issue was recognized by the court in *Wakefield* (n 93 above), para 44, as raising 'some difficult questions', but was left for further submissions, the outcome of which is unreported.

### 11.3.6.5 *Rectification, erasure, destruction and blocking*

The 1984 Act gave data subjects the right to apply to the courts for an order requiring a data controller to rectify or erase inaccurate data. The 1998 Act extends this to rectification, erasure, destruction and blocking of incomplete and inaccurate data (s 14).

The Directive also requires that data subjects be given the right to 'obtain from' data controllers notification to third parties, to whom data have been disclosed, of any rectification erasure and blocking, unless this is impossible or involves a 'disproportionate effort' (art 12(c)). However, the Act has qualified this provision. Imposition upon a data controller of an obligation to notify third parties lies within either the discretion of the court, or an enforcement notice issued by the Commissioner, but not with the data subject. This would seem to be potentially non-compliant with the Directive.

### 11.3.6.6 *Enforced subject access*

An important new protection for data subjects, not present in the Directive, is the issue of enforced subject access. This is the practice whereby potential employees ask individuals to supply them with a copy of their criminal record, obtained through the exercise of the individual's subject access right to the Police National Computer. The Commissioner has indicated disapproval of such practices, but was unable to prevent them under the 1984 Act.[97] The Government's White Paper announced its intention to prohibit such practices and the Act creates an offence where the requirement relates to criminal records, prison records and DSS records (s 56). Where 'health records' are concerned any contractual term requiring the provision of such information is rendered void (s 57). The offence contains the following features:

(a) the data subject has to have been required to provide the information, rather than such information being requested;

(b) it applies in only certain types of situations: employment, placing of contracts and the provision of goods, facilities or services to the public;

(c) defences exist where the requirement was authorized by law, or was in the public interest.[98]

However, the offence does not come into force until sections 112, 113 and 115 of the Police Act 1997 are all brought into force.[99] These provisions provide for the establishment of a criminal records agency to issue 'criminal record certificates'. These certificates will provide an alternative mechanism to obtain data about criminal

---

[97] See DPR Guidance Note 21, 'The use of the subject access provisions of the Data Protection Act to check the criminal records of applicants for jobs or licences', GN21-JB-3/89; see also the Tenth Report of the Data Protection Registrar (June 1994), Appendix 2.

[98] The public-interest defence does not include the prevention or detection of crime, due to the Police Act 1997 (1998 Act, s 56(4)).

[99] The Police Act 1997 (Commencement No 9) Order 2002, SI 2002/413, brought into force sections 113 and 115 on 1 March 2002. Although section 112 was not included in this Commencement Order it was brought into force in Scotland on 31 July 2002 (see SI 2002/124).

convictions and, therefore, the practice of enforced subject access is allowed to continue until the new system has been established.

### 11.3.7 Exemptions

Three broad categories of exemption are provided for in the Act:

(a) General exemptions from the majority of the Act's provisions, for example, the processing of personal data for reasons of national security (s 28).

(b) Exemptions from the 'subject information provisions' under section 7 and the information obligations under the first data protection principle, for example, for the prevention and detection of crime (s 29).[100]

(c) Exemptions from the 'non-disclosure provisions', for example, data made public under enactment (s 34) or required by law or in connection with legal proceedings (s 35).[101]

This section reviews some of the key areas where exemptions are applicable.

#### 11.3.7.1 'Special purposes'

One of the most significant exemptions relates to personal data processed for the 'special purposes', defined under section 3 of the 1998 Act as the purposes of journalism, artistic purposes and literary purposes. This exemption arises from article 9 of the Data Protection Directive, which stresses the need to balance the right of privacy against the need to protect freedom of expression.[102] However, it also reflects wider Government policy, which places a high priority upon the protection of freedom of expression and a clear intention not to allow data-protection laws to prejudice such freedom. This exemption is also affected by the Human Rights Act 1998 and article 10 of the European Convention on Human Rights.

Data processed for a 'special purpose' will be exempt from compliance with certain of the Act's requirements, including the data-protection principles, the subject access right, and the right of rectification, blocking, erasure and destruction. However, these exemptions will only operate where all of the following conditions apply:

- the processing is *only* for one or more of the 'special purposes';
- the processing is 'with a view to publication';
- the data controller 'reasonably believes' that publication is in the public interest 'having regard in particular to the special importance of freedom of expression';[103] and

---

[100] See also the Data Protection (Miscellaneous Subject Access Exemptions) Order 2000, SI 2000/419.
[101] See, further, *Totalise plc v Motley Fool Ltd & Interactive Investor* [2002] 1 WLR 1233.
[102] See also Recommendation 1/97, 'Data Protection Law and the Media', of the Article 29 Working Party (n 51 above).
[103] An assessment of whether such a belief was reasonable will take into account any relevant, or desig-

- the data controller 'reasonably believes' that compliance with the exempted provisions would be incompatible with the 'special purposes' (s 32(1)).

The scope of this provision was extensively examined in *Campbell v Mirror Group Newspapers Ltd.* At first instance, the judge held that the phrase 'with a view to publication' limited the scope of the exemption to journalistic activities prior to publication, preventing the use of 'gagging injunctions' and related actions, but did not provide protection against a breach of the Act once publication had occurred.[104] On appeal, the court rejected this interpretation on the basis that 'giving the provisions of the sub-sections [(1) to (3)] their natural meaning and the only meaning that makes sense of them, they apply both before and after publication'.[105]

Where a data subject commences civil proceedings against a data controller, the controller can raise a defence based on this exemption. In such an event, the court would be obliged to stay the proceedings pending a determination by the Commissioner whether the processing is only for the special purposes or with a view to publication (s 32(5)). The Information Commissioner has strongly criticized the complexity of the mechanism by which this exemption will operate, since it shifts the burden of proof between the various parties and could provide the data controller with a legitimate mechanism to delay proceedings for an unnecessary period of time.

### 11.3.7.2 *Research*
Research data may be exempt from the subject access provisions. The research exemption includes data held for 'statistical and historical purposes'. As with the 'special purpose' exemption, certain conditions must exist:

(a) the data are not to be processed 'to support measures or decisions with respect to particular individuals';

(b) 'substantial' damage or distress must not be, or be likely to be, caused (collectively referred to as the 'relevant conditions'); and

(c) the research results 'are not made available in a form which identifies data subjects'.

### 11.3.7.3 *Domestic purposes*
Under the Directive, the processing of data for purely domestic purposes is considered outside the scope of its application. The Act provides that data controllers processing personal data 'only for the purposes of that individual's personal, family or household affairs (including recreational purposes)' are exempt from the data-protection principles, the rights of data subjects (Pt II) or the notification obligations (Pt III). However, they may be subject to an 'information notice' or 'special information notice' issued by the Commissioner.

---

nated, code of practice (s 32(3)), eg, the Press Complaints Commission Code of Practice; see Data Protection (Designated Codes of Practice) (No 2) Order 2000, SI 2000/1864.

[104] [2002] HRLR 28, para 95, per Morland J.                    [105] Ibid, para 121, per Lord Phillips.

While such an exemption makes sense from an enforcement perspective, it may also raise difficult issues in respect of drawing a clear line between regulated and non-regulated personal data. In an Internet environment, for example, a person may post photographs of his family members or a list of his local five-a-side football team on his website. At what point does a personal activity enter the public sphere?

### 11.3.7.4 *Commercial purposes*

For private-sector data controllers, there are some important exemptions designed to reflect the needs of commerce:

(a) 'confidential references' given or to be given for the purposes of either (i) the education, training or employment, or prospective education, training or employment of the data subject; (ii) the appointment or prospective employment of the data subject to an office; or (iii) the provision or prospective provision of a service by the data subject;[106]

(b) processing for the 'purposes of management forecasting or management planning';

(c) processing relating to the provision of a 'corporate finance service', or

(d) processing 'of records of the intentions of the data controller in relation to any negotiations with the data subject' (Sch 7).

Management forecasting and planning is not defined, which leaves data controllers with a potentially broad, although uncertain, scope to withhold information. However, under both the management and negotiation exemptions, the data controller will need to show that providing subject access 'would be likely to prejudice' the activities in question.

## 11.3.8 Enforcement

The Data Protection Act 1998 creates or gives rise to the possibility of criminal prosecution under six different categories of offence:

(a) Processing without notification (s 21(1));

(b) Notification information must be accurate (s 21(2));

(c) Failure to comply with a notice (s 47);

(d) Unlawful obtaining or procurement of data (s 55);

(e) Requiring the provision of certain records (s 56); and

(f) Obstructing or failing to assist a person in the execution of a warrant (Sch 9, para 12).

---

[106] The recipient of the reference would be subject to section 7(4), regarding 'information relating to another individual', eg, references given in confidence could not be disclosed.

These offences can be further divided into offences of strict or absolute liability; and those that require the data user to have acted 'knowingly or recklessly'.[107]

As well as a data controller being prosecuted for an offence, a 'director, manager, secretary or similar officer' can also be found personally liable, where the offence was committed with 'the consent or connivance of or to be attributable to any neglect on the part' of any such individual (s 61).

Under the 1984 Act, the vast majority of prosecutions were brought against data controllers who had failed to register or to renew their registration. However, in 1996, in *R v Brown*[108] the House of Lords was required to give an important judgment on the interpretation of the word 'use' in section 5(2)(b) of the Act:

A person in respect of whom such an entry is contained in the register shall not . . . (b) hold any such data, or use any such data held by him, for any purpose other than the purpose described in the entry.

The case involved a police officer who was also associated with a debt-collection agency. It was alleged that, on two occasions, he obtained information from the Police National Computer about the ownership of certain cars relating to two debtors being pursued by the agency. On the first occasion, the car was owned by a company, and therefore no personal data was retrieved. In the second, no evidence was shown that he had made subsequent use of the information retrieved. He was charged on two counts, one of improper use and attempted improper use in contravention of section 5(2)(b) of the 1984 Act. At his first trial he was found guilty, and he appealed to the Court of Appeal. They upheld his appeal and the case then came before the House of Lords.

The central issue before the Lords was whether the retrieval of personal data onto a screen constituted 'use' under the Act. The Lords decided, by a three-to-two majority, that the natural and ordinary meaning of the word 'use' should be adopted. 'Use' was therefore seen to require some element of subsequent use, which could not be shown to have taken place in this case. Lord Griffiths, dissenting, argued that a broad construction should be taken otherwise the purpose of the Act would not be achieved: to protect an individual's right to privacy.[109] The decision was seen as a serious limitation in the protection afforded by the 1984 Act. However, under the 1998 Act, the activity carried out by Brown would be the offence of unlawful obtaining (s 55).

Under the 1984 Act, data users took a number of appeals against 'enforcement notices' to the Data Protection Tribunal. The most interesting decisions were concerned with the credit-reference and utility industries, and continue to be applicable precedents under the 1998 Act.

---

[107] See, further, *Data Protection Registrar v Amnesty International (British Section), The Times*, 23 November 1994 and *Information Commissioner v Islington London Borough Council* [2002] EWHC 1036 (Admin).
[108] [1996] 1 All ER 545.
[109] Ibid, 554G–J.

The former Registrar was in a long-running dispute with the four UK credit-reference agencies concerning the definition of what information it is 'fair' for the agencies to consider when assessing a person's eligibility for credit. In particular, the Registrar was concerned with the use of information relating to past residents of a person's accommodation. In *CCN Systems Ltd v Data Protection Registrar*[110] the Registrar had issued an enforcement notice to the appellants, requiring them to cease to provide information relating to applicants for credit that was based purely on their address. The practice of CCN and other credit-reference agencies was to provide not only details of the applicant's credit record, but also details of others (whether they bore the same name or not) who formerly or subsequently resided at the applicant's current or previous address. CCN appealed against this notice on the ground that the processing they undertook was not unfair.

The case was concerned primarily with the issue of what is 'fair processing'. The question was whether the processing undertaken by the appellants extracted data which were *relevant* to the decision whether to grant credit. CCN argued that such data were relevant to the credit decision because, on the statistical evidence present, adverse information against third parties at the same address increased the likelihood *in the aggregate* that applicants in that category would default on the loan. On the other hand, the Registrar argued that the proper test was whether the information was relevant *to the particular applicant*, and it was clear that for any individual case such third-party information did not generally increase the risk of default. In coming to its judgment on this point, the Tribunal held:

In our view, in deciding whether the processing . . . is fair *we must give first and paramount consideration to the interests of the applicant for credit—the 'data subject'* in the Act's terms. We are not ignoring the consequences for the credit industry of a finding of unfairness, and we sympathise with their problems, but we believe that they will accept that they must carry on their activities in accordance with the principles laid down in the Act of Parliament [emphasis added].

The Tribunal therefore held that CCN's processing was unfair in this respect, and disallowed the appeal on that point. It was particularly influenced by the fact that in some cases the inquirer never saw the raw data, and thus had no opportunity to make a separate assessment of their relevance, because CCN offered a number of credit-scoring systems which gave the inquirer only a credit score, based in part on this third-party information.

However, the Tribunal did hold that the enforcement notice had been too wide, as certain types of third-party information would be relevant and thus fairly extracted if there was a clear connection with the applicant for credit. The enforcement notice was therefore amended so as to permit the extraction of certain types of third-party information, such as individuals who share the same surname.

---

[110] 25 February 1991 (case DA/90 25/499).

The most important principle to be extracted from this judgment is that 'fairness' must always be assessed in relation to the data subject. The mere fact that such processing is to the advantage of the data user is not a relevant consideration.

Enforcement notices have also been issued against companies in the gas and electricity industries. In the *British Gas* case,[111] the Registrar took action against the gas supplier over the use of its customer data for marketing purposes. The Data Protection Tribunal was required to consider whether such processing was both unlawful and unfair, in breach of the first principle.

On the issue of lawfulness, the Registrar had previously stated that processing requires that 'a data user must comply with all relevant rules of law, whether derived from statute or common law'.[112] The Tribunal was therefore asked to consider whether such processing could be considered unlawful by virtue of either (a) a statutory limitation on the use of the data rendering the processing *ultra vires*; (b) breach of an implied contractual provision; or (c) breach of an equitable obligation of confidence between British Gas and its customers. The Tribunal held that none of these obligations were present and, therefore, the processing was not unlawful.

On the issue of fair processing, two key issues arose. First, with respect to whether customers had been appropriately informed that their data would be used for marketing purposes. The Tribunal held that it was not unfair to process customer data for marketing gas and gas-related products, including electricity, since it may be considered 'reasonably obvious' to customers that their personal data may be used in that way. However, disclosure of such data to third parties for marketing purposes would not be fair. Second, British Gas provided customers with the opportunity to 'opt-out' of having their data used for marketing purposes through the use of a separate form sent with customers' bills. On this issue the Tribunal held that it would be unfair for British Gas to imply consent from a customer's failure to return this opt-out form, since customers would have positively to send the form back to British Gas even though they may pay their bill through another mechanism (for example, their bank) which does not require communication with British Gas. As subsequently stated by the Registrar:

The fact that the data subject must 'signify' their agreement means that there must be some active communication between the parties. Data controllers cannot infer consent from non-response to a communication, for example from a customer's failure to return or respond to a leaflet.[113]

Although the concepts of fair and lawful processing are significantly more specific under the 1998 Act, the issues raised by these Tribunal decisions continue to be relevant and applicable.

---

[111] *British Gas Trading Limited v The Data Protection Registrar* (24 March 1998). See also *Midlands Electricity plc v The Data Protection Registrar* (7 May 1999). See, further, www.dataprotection.gov.uk or the *Encyclopedia of Data Protection* (n 57 above).

[112] See DPR Guideline 4, 'The Data Protection Principles' (Third Series, November 1994), para 1.18.

[113] Data Protection Registrar, *An Introduction to the Data Protection Act 1998* (October 1998), ch 3, section 1.6.

### 11.3.9 Telecommunications and data protection

As noted in section 11.2.4 above, when the European Commission published its first proposal for a Directive in the field of data protection in 1990, it also published a proposal for a sectoral Directive addressing the use of personal data within the telecommunications sector. The Commission was of the opinion that the general Data Protection Directive would not be sufficient to address concerns about the use of personal data made within particular areas. It was envisaged, therefore, that the general Directive would be supplemented by a series of sectoral Directives, similar to that proposed for the telecommunications sector. Such proposals have not been forthcoming. However, the proposal for the telecommunications sector was eventually adopted, as Directive 97/66/EC,[114] although this measure is in the process of being replaced by a new measure, Directive 02/58/EC, which was recently adopted and which Member States were obliged to transpose into national law by 31 October 2002.[115]

Directive 97/66/EC was implemented in the UK by the Telecommunications (Data Protection and Privacy) Regulations 1999.[116] It contains provisions supplementing the general Directive, imposing additional obligations upon data controllers in the telecommunications sector to those already contained within the general Directive. It is beyond the scope of this chapter to detail all the provisions of the existing legislation and the new Directive, however the key themes are outlined below.

Though sectoral in nature, the scope of Directives 97/66/EC and 02/58/EC is broad, addressing four distinct privacy relationships within a communications environment, between:

(a) the service provider and his customer or 'subscriber';
(b) a subscriber and the actual user of a service;
(c) users; and
(d) a user and the state.

First, the use of communication services generates significant amounts of personal data about the attributes of a communication session (for example, the number of the person called, time of call and duration), as well as the content of the communication itself, which could be of significant value to the service provider. Under Directive 97/66/EC, a service provider is restricted in its ability to process such communication attributes (referred to as 'traffic' and 'billing data') to a much greater degree than that provided for under the general obligation to process data fairly and lawfully

---

[114] Directive 97/66/EC of the European Parliament and of the Council concerning the processing of personal data and the protection of privacy in the telecommunications sector, OJ L24/1, 30 January 1998.
[115] Directive 02/58/EC of the European Parliament and of the Council concerning the processing of personal data and the protection of privacy in the electronic communications sector, OJ L201/37, 31 July 2002.
[116] SI 1999/2093.

(see section 11.3.4 above). In addition, the definition of a 'subscriber' extends protection to legal persons (for example, a corporation) as well as individuals (art 2(a)).

'Traffic data' must be erased or rendered anonymous upon termination of the call. 'Billing data'[117] may only be retained until 'the end of the period during which the bill may lawfully be challenged or payment may be pursued', and can only be processed for limited purposes, for example, fraud detection (art 6). Under the new Directive 02/58/EC, these restrictions have been slightly loosened, to enable continued processing for the provision of so-called 'value added services'.[118]

One form of communications attribute addressed in detail in the new Directive is the processing of 'location data', ie, data which identifies the geographical location of a user. With the growth of mobile telephony, concerns have been raised about the potential abuse of location data to infringe privacy. Processing restrictions are therefore imposed on service providers, including the obligation to provide users with the ability to block the disclosure of such data (art 9).

The second privacy relationship is that between the 'subscriber' and 'users' of the service. Clearly a user of a telephone may have legitimate reasons why he may not wish data relating to its use to be disclosed to the subscriber, such as a child calling a counselling helpline. The Directives require that Member States ensure that users have alternative means for making calls and paying for such calls, which would include, for example, certain numbers not appearing on itemized bills.

A third category of privacy relationship is that between users of a communications service, ie, the called and the calling party. Modern digital telephony enables data to be displayed to the recipient of a call concerning the number from which the call was made: generally referred to as 'caller line identification' ('CLI'). However, a calling party may have a legitimate reason to want to prevent the disclosure of such information. As a consequence, the Directives require that users be given, 'via a simple means, free of charge', the ability to prevent the display of such CLI data.[119] Conversely, the privacy rights of the called party must also be maintained and therefore the called party must have the ability: (a) to reject calls which fail to display the calling party's CLI; and (b) prevent disclosure of the CLI data related to the equipment they are using for receipt of the call.

Another aspect of the privacy relationship between users that has become of increasing concern among the general public over recent years is that of unsolicited contact. Forms of unsolicited contact, including 'cold calling', faxing and e-mails (generally referred to as 'spam') are primarily used as a direct-marketing technique. As such, the problem has been addressed in a number of consumer-protection

---

[117] Defined in the Annex.

[118] Value added service 'means any service which requires the processing of traffic data or location data other than traffic data beyond what is necessary for the transmission of a communication or the billing thereof' (art 2(g)).

[119] In the UK, this can generally be achieved through inputting certain numbers into the handset.

measures at an EU level, as well as Directives 97/66/EC and 02/58/EC.[120] The Directives restrict the use of such unsolicited communication techniques without the prior consent of the subscriber.

The final privacy relationship addressed in the Directives is that between the state and users. This relates to issues of the confidentiality of communications, ie the content, and restricts any form of interception. Member States may provide for lawful interception by the state where necessary to protect national security, the prevention and detection of crime and related circumstances;[121] as well as by data controllers in the course of a 'lawful business practice'.[122]

One major criticism of Directive 97/66/EC was the uncertain application of its provisions to modern communication technologies such as e-mail. The terminology used in certain of the provisions has given rise to legal uncertainty. For example, use of the term 'call' in relation to unsolicited contact was viewed as not extending to e-mail-based communication by the Department of Trade and Industry in its consultation document on the implementing regulations; while the Commissioner issued guidance stating that in her view e-mail was included.[123] Recognizing such uncertainty, as well as the pace of development in the telecommunications market, in July 2000, as part of a broader reform of the regulatory framework for the telecommunications sector, the European Commission issued a revised Directive, Directive 02/58/EC, which was formally adopted in July 2002.

## 11.4 CONCLUSION

Data-protection law became a high-profile political issue during the late 1970s and early 1980s as European countries began to adopt legislation and companies voiced fears that the spread of such laws would act as an obstacle to the international flow of data, even as a deterrent to the adoption of computer systems altogether. Reality, particularly in the age of the Internet, would suggest that such fears were unfounded. However, the adoption and implementation of the Data Protection Directive has given new life to the debate. A full-scale trade row nearly arose between the EU and the United States over the extent to which US companies could avoid potential restrictions on international data flows by agreeing to abide by a set of self-regulatory principles.

When the first national data-protection law was passed in Sweden in 1973, the major privacy fears were generated through the use of large mainframe computers. Currently developments such as the Internet, CCTV and the use of genetic data are

---

[120] See Directive 1997/7/EC on the protection of consumers in respect of distance contracts, OJ L144/19, 4 June 1997, art 9; and Directive 2000/31/EC on certain legal aspects of information society services, in particular electronic commerce, in the Internal Market, OJ L178/1, 17 July 2000, art 7.

[121] See, further, Chapter 8 (section 8.7.2).

[122] See, further, Chapter 10 (section 10.4).

[123] 'Telecoms Guidance: Legal Advice', para 1.7.

some of the current areas of concern. Such rapid technological change renders data-protection laws vulnerable to an accusation of obsolescence. However, the promotion of general principles of good information practice, together with an independent supervisory regime, should enable the law to maintain sufficient flexibility to achieve an appropriate balance between the need to protect the rights of individuals to control how data about them is used and the needs of an increasingly networked economy.

# 12

# EC COMPETITION LAW AND THE NEW ECONOMY OF INFORMATION TECHNOLOGY

*Steve Anderman*

## 12.1 INTRODUCTION

The contribution to innovation by new developments in information technology ('IT') has been huge, helping to improve living standards and competitiveness within the European Union. It therefore calls for an antitrust policy and regulation which takes pains not unduly to inhibit the innovative process.[1] At the same time, the commercial exploitation of innovative IT can on occasion take anticompetitive forms creating a conflict with competition policy which is charged with preserving effective competition on 'markets'.[2] How have the EU competition authorities resolved this conflict?

---

[1] See, eg, C Veljanowski, 'EC Antitrust in the New Economy: Is the European Commission's View of the Network Economy Right?' [2001] ECLR 115.

[2] See, eg, M Monti, 'Competition and Information Technologies', speech to Barriers to Cyberspace, Kangaroo Group, Brussels, 18 September 2000.

Economists have repeatedly pointed out that industries in the new economy have different characteristics from those in the old.[3] First, products competing in the new economy are often confronted by increasing returns to scale rather than the diminishing returns of traditional markets.[4] The costs of the first prototype copy of a product are extremely high while the marginal cost of each subsequent copy is minuscule by comparison.[5] It has been estimated for example that '[t]he first disk of Windows to go out the door cost Microsoft $50 million; the second and subsequent disks cost $3.'[6] Secondly, products in the new economy, such as IT software, are often heavily protected by intellectual property rights ('IPRs') and tend to produce strong market leaders often achieving the position of industrial standards.[7] This would normally argue for careful monitoring by the competition authorities.[8]

However, economists have further argued that the process of competition in markets in the new economy is different in kind to that in the old; it takes the form of competition *for* the market rather than the traditional form of competition *in* the market.[9] Competition in high-technology markets consists of a rivalry between products designed to replace one another rather than remain in competition in the same market. As Schumpeter described it, this form of competition is 'dynamic competition' which involves a process of 'creative destruction' which strikes 'not at the margins of the profits of existing firms but their foundations and their very lives'.[10] In the IT field there is undoubtedly evidence of succeeding generations of products achieving the status of industrial standards only to disappear and be replaced by competitors: Wang and dedicated word processors gave way to Wordstar and PCs. Wordstar in turn was ousted by DOS/Word Perfect which in turn was displaced by Windows and Word. Visicalc gave way to Lotus 1-2-3 which in turn was displaced by MS Excel, etc.

It has been further argued by economists that markets subject to this new and radically different type of competition should be treated differently by the competition authorities. The case has been made that, although monopolies or market dominance may be inevitable in such markets, such concentrations of market power are *inherently* 'fragile'[11] in the face of the new type of competition. Indeed, some econ-

---

[3] See, eg, D Evans and R Schmalensee, 'Some Economic Aspects of Antitrust Analysis in Dynamically Competitive Industries' at www.nber.org/books/innovation2/evans 5-1-01.pdf.

[4] Brian Arthur, 'Increasing Returns and the New World of Business', in Dale Neef (ed), *The Knowledge Economy* (Butterworth-Heinemann, 1997), p 75.

[5] See eg C Shapiro and H Varian, *Information Rules: A Strategic Guide to the Network Economy* (Harvard Business School Press, 1999), p 20.

[6] Arthur (n 4 above), p 75.

[7] C Ahlborn, D Evans and A Padrilla, 'Competition Policy in the New Economy: Is European Competition Law up to the Challenge?' [2001] ECLR 156.

[8] See, eg, Steve Anderman, *EC Competition Law and Intellectual Property Rights: The Regulation of Innovation* (Oxford University Press, 2000).

[9] R Schmalensee, 'Antitrust Issues in Schumpeterian Industries' (2000) 90 Am Econ Rev (Papers and Proceedings) 192, 193.

[10] J A Schumpeter, *Capitalism, Socialism and Democracy* (HarperCollins, 1984), p 82.

[11] See Schmalensee (n 9 above), p 193.

omists have even argued that the pace of innovation is so fierce that it contains a strong element of *self-correction* making such markets workably competitive even where markets shares are high, as they invariably tend to be, and where barriers to entry are strong in part because of the use of IPRs protection.[12] The theory is that the market power of the dominant 'product system' will always be offset and disciplined by entrants seeking to displace it.

From the European perspective, much of the argument that the inherent fragility of market leadership in the new economy does away with the need for regulation of markets by the competition authorities has not been viewed as credible in view of the evidence. The Commission's view is that even if creative destruction may take place eventually, there are periods where 'fragile' market power sustains itself for years, as in the case of Microsoft and Intel, etc. Even during their 'temporary' periods of extensive market power, therefore, the conduct of these undertakings needs to be regulated using the usual measures of competition policy.[13]

Moreover, even if market dominance may ultimately be at risk owing to the process of competition for markets, the presence of 'network effects' and 'network externalities' in the sale of complementary products in systems in new-economy industries represents a new type of competition concern. An important characteristic of new-economy industries is that they are based on 'systems' of complementary products rather than single products and the marketing of these complementary products can produce both direct 'network effects' and indirect 'network effects' or 'network externalities'. Direct 'network effects' are simply the effects of the purchase of one component of a system upon other components of the system. The more buyers of a product, the more advantageous the product is to the consumer. A good example of this is the fax machine or the text-messaging facility on mobile telephones. The more users of the product there are, the more attractive it will be to all users, new and existing.[14] This is the phenomenon of positive direct 'network effects'.

The indirect 'network effects' or 'network externalities' are the less obvious feature. 'Network externalities' are a process by which some innovative products experience a lift off in their rivalry with other products as an increase in their customer base interacts with their cluster of 'complementary' products in a mutually reinforcing way. Either the increase in customer base triggers an increase in applications of the product or an increase in applications triggers an increase in customer base but the effect of the initial catalyst is to set in motion a mutually reinforcing cycle. For example, take the case of Microsoft's Windows and its application products. It certain cases, an increase in demand for Windows applications can trigger off an increase in demand for Windows as an operating system ('OS'): the more applications available on

---

[12] See, eg, D Teece and M Coleman, 'The Meaning of Monopoly: Antitrust Analysis in High Technology Industries' [1998] Antitrust Bull 801.

[13] See, eg, Monti (n 2 above).

[14] M Katz and C Shapiro, 'Technology Adoption in the Presence of Network Externalities' (1986) 94 Journal of Political Economy 822.

Windows, the more Windows sells, the more Windows sells, the more the makers of applications make applications for Windows. This mutually reinforcing process has been described as a 'positive feedback loop'. In the Microsoft case, a US District Court found that the network effects of applications compatible with Windows on PC users created an 'applications barrier to entry' to other PC operating systems.[15]

In certain cases, this mutually reinforcing process can gather momentum or 'snowball' to the point where the product and its applications, ie, the product system, eventually 'tips' a market and becomes the market standard.[16] In the event competing products or systems can end up being either ejected from the market or reduced to low market shares irrespective of their technical superiority.[17]

There is an obvious difference in the rivalries between systems of products which are 'closed' and those which are 'open' or interoperable. The Betamax/VHS rivalry offers a good example of competition between 'closed systems' of products, ie, products which are not interoperable with products of another system.[18] In that rivalry Betamax was completely ejected from the consumer market. Another example of a rivalry between closed systems is that between Sony Play Station, Microsoft X Box and Nintendo.

In the computer software field, apart from Apple Macintosh, most creators of major IT products in systems have chosen for commercial reasons to opt for 'open' systems, ie, systems with component products which are interoperable with the products of other systems. This is pre-eminently true of the ISPs on the Internet. Nevertheless, even open systems can produce 'tipping' effects. In such cases, the market can 'tip' and a market standard can develop without the losers being completely ejected from the market but instead driven down to extremely low market shares. In the recent US Microsoft case, for example, the Federal District Court, which tried the case, accepted that the market share of the Windows operating system was 94 per cent of all Intel chip PCs worldwide. Word had about 94 per cent of the word-processing market and Microsoft's Internet Explorer had captured more than 84 per cent of the market for web browsers.

Consequently, in the new economy of IT markets, as in the old economy, competition policy will continue to apply using all of the traditional measures of EC competition law but requiring adaptation to the characteristics of the new economy.

In the first place, once a market has 'tipped', article 82 of the Treaty applies. This article regulates the conduct of firms which have already achieved a position of

---

[15] *United States v Microsoft* (1996) 84 F Supp 2d 9, 20 (DDC)

[16] See, eg, B Arthur, 'Competing Technologies, Increasing Returns, and Lock in by Historical Events' (1989) 99 Econ Jnl 116.

[17] See, eg, Arthur (n 16 above). See also R Peritz, 'Towards a Dynamic Antitrust Analysis' (paper given at the American Antitrust Institute Annual Conference, 1 July 2002, Washington, DC). This conclusion has been disputed. See, eg, S Liebowitz and S Margolis, 'Are Network Externalities a New Source of Market Failure?' (1995) 17 Research in Law and Economics 1. However, it has also been acknowledged as a theoretical possibility. See, eg, J Church and N Gandall, 'Complementary Network Externalities and Technology Adoption' (1993) 11 Intl Jnl Indus Org 239.

[18] See, eg, Arthur (n 16 above).

market dominance to ensure that they are not abusing the rules of fair competition during their period of 'temporary' market power. Achieving dominance is not unlawful itself but once a firm achieves dominance in a market, it has a 'special responsibility' not to act abusively towards its competitors as well as customers. Article 82, the counterpart of section 2 of the Sherman Act, prohibits a range of abuses of dominant market positions such as tie-ins, predatory and discriminatory pricing, refusals to supply and license. In an exceptional case, the European Commission has the power to order a compulsory licence of a database or the provision of copyright-protected information. This legislation is enforced by the Directorate General Competition ('DG Comp') of the European Commission.

Secondly, since network effects have a potential to snowball and eventually tip a market in favour of one contender, sometimes irrespective of technical superiority, the Merger Task Force of DG Comp has decided to give weight to the need to protect markets in the 'pre-tipping' stage from two anticompetitive threats when assessing pre-notified mergers. First, where a merger between two competitors will result in too few firms being left in the post-merger product market, the merger will be denied to prevent anticompetitive collusion. Secondly, where a merger between non-competitors in different markets is found to be a 'strategic alliance', ie, an alliance which is designed to create an advantage by capturing portals to related product markets, the merger could be denied. On the other hand, where mergers between non-competitors offer increased efficiencies of scale and scope or consist of sharing the risks and costs of research and development mergers will often be allowed. These latter motives for mergers are viewed as pro-competitive by the Task Force.

Finally, article 81, the counterpart to section 1 of the Sherman Act, regulates agreements between firms that have the object or effect of preventing, restricting or distorting competition. In relation to IT, the most relevant fields of application of article 81 are vertical joint ventures, research-and-development joint ventures, exclusive distribution agreements for hardware and software products and technology transfers through licensing agreements as well as multiparty agreements involving cross-licensing. Article 81 is also enforced by DG Comp.

## 12.2 ARTICLE 82 AND IT

Article 82 of the Treaty prohibits any abuse by one or more undertakings of a dominant position within the Common Market or in a substantial part of it. The examples of abuse given in article 82 include unfair pricing, discriminatory pricing and tie-ins. However, article 82 also extends to such abuses as exclusive dealing, predatory pricing, refusals to supply and license. The application of article 82 to regulate innovation and even IT protected by IPRs appear to be authorized by article 82(b) which declares it to be an abuse by dominant firms to limit 'production, markets or technical development to the prejudice of consumers'.

Once a market has 'tipped' and a firm has achieved market dominance by establishing what is effectively a market standard, the competition concern under article 82 is that the firm may unfairly use its dominant power in a market to deny competitors access to markets. This can include conduct designed unfairly to exclude existing competitors in the market in which a firm is already dominant. It can also include activities designed to leverage its dominance improperly in a dependent downstream market, or 'aftermarket', by precluding access to competitors.[19] A special concern of article 82, in the field of IT in which a market has 'tipped', is with the question of preserving interoperability for downstream competitors facing firms with dominant positions in the form of industrial standards in upstream markets.

### 12.2.1  The relevant market, dominance and IPRs

Under article 82 DG Comp begins its assessment of dominance by measuring it on a particular market, the 'relevant market'. A relevant market is defined by choosing a product and determining whether other products are substitutable or interchangeable with that product and therefore fall within that market. If the initial product chosen for this investigation is a single product, say a banana[20] or a rubber tyre[21] or vitamin A[22] then the Commission applies a test of substitutability including the familiar SSNIP test[23] as a method of determining whether other products are in the same market.

If, however, as in the IT field, a product is a complex product, or a commercially designed 'system' consisting of component parts, there is an initial issue of discretion in determining the relevant product with which to begin the process of defining a market. Is the starting point for investigation, ie, the 'relevant product', to be the 'system' as a whole, or will each component be taken as a relevant product with which to start the investigation of the relevant market? In the case of Microsoft, was its web browser 'integrated' with its Windows desktop platform or were they to be treated as separate products? In the Microsoft cases, both the US District Court and the European Commission found that there were three types of markets: the market for Intel chip PCs; the market for operating systems for PCs such as Windows; and individual markets for different applications ('APIs') such as web browsers, servers and multi-utility media players.

---

[19]  In either case, a dominant firm, whether the dominance is reinforced by an IPR or not, may compete on the merits even if such a marketing strategy results in increased levels of dominance in both markets. This would certainly be true if the dominant firm wins custom by low but non-predatory prices reflecting efficiencies. See, eg, *AKZO v Commission* [1991] ECR I-3359.

[20]  *United Brands v Commission* [1978] ECR 207.

[21]  *Michelin v Commission* [1983] ECR 3461.

[22]  *Hoffman La Roche v Commission* [1978] ECR 1137.

[23]  This test assumes hypothetically a small but significant but non-transitory increase in price, say 5% or more, in a particular product and then looks at the response (elasticity) of demand for alleged substitute products. If the demand for another product is assessed as likely to rise proportionately in response to the price increase for the first product, then both are viewed as being in the same market.

To the extent that DG Comp opts to start its market definition with components as separate products rather than systems of products, it defines markets narrowly and that naturally makes it easier to find dominance. The Commission's practice of defining markets narrowly is not directed solely at IT giants. It is part of a wider tendency to regulate essential infrastructures which create dependency relationships or 'lock-ins' in 'after-markets', such as maintenance markets, spare-parts markets, consumable markets and application markets. The Commission's actions, as openly argued by the Commission in the *Magill*[24] case, however, are in part prompted by a desire to use article 82 to supervise effective competition in markets in the new economy of IT and telecommunications. In its definition of markets, the Commission has increasingly acknowledged the existence of 'technology markets' and the possibility that IPRs such as patents or copyright can confer dominance or reinforce market standards in such markets.[25]

### 12.2.2 Dominance, industrial standards and *de facto* monopoly

Once systems of products are defined as consisting of separate products in separate markets, it is easier to find that one product is dominant in a particular market. The narrow market definition can result in high market shares. And the Commission's assessment of 'dominance' starts with an estimation of the market share of the product in its market. The concept of dominance is not the same as a complete monopoly. A firm can be dominant with a market share as low as 50 per cent and in very unusual cases as low as 40 per cent. However, in extreme cases, dominance can take the form of a *de facto* monopoly in which there are no actual competitors in the market or very large market shares. In such cases, the European Court of Justice has held that very large market shares can be 'save in exceptional circumstances, evidence of a dominant position'.[26]

Once the Commission obtains a market-share assessment, it then looks to see whether there are any 'plus factors' reinforcing the market power of the firm with a high market share. One important 'plus factor' consists of a market where the market shares of all or most of the actual competitors are low. Normally, only sizeable competitors, or those backed by resources from say a multinational of which they are a subsidiary, constitute real competition in the market. Other 'plus factors' are the 'barriers to entry' for potential competitors, ie, possible new entrants to the market. One such barrier can be IPR protection reinforcing exclusive use of the product by the incumbent firm. Another major barrier to entry can be extensive financial resources of an incumbent firm since this would deter entrants. A third can be the extent of its vertical integration. In the new economy, network effects analysis has drawn attention to a further barrier to entry, one created by other products in the

---

[24] [1991] ECR II-485.
[25] See, eg, *IBM Undertaking* [1984] 3 CMLR 147; *Digital/Olivetti* 1994 OJ L294 10; *Shell/Montedison*, 8 June 1994.
[26] See *Hilti v Commission* [1994] ECR I-667, para 91.

system. In the Microsoft case in the USA, for example, the high market share of Microsoft's Windows OS in the Intel chip PC market was reinforced by an 'applications barrier to entry' caused by the fact that so many applications worked with Windows.[27]

In the new economy, a key issue is to determine when a high market share coincides with a *de facto* monopoly which is also an 'essential facility', that is a product which is an indispensable infrastructure for or input into another product, whether good or service, produced by competitors.[28] To be an 'essential facility' the product must be irreplaceable, ie, there are no alternatives to it and the owner of the second product cannot realistically create one himself. Normally, 'essential facilities' are tangible products such as ports, tunnels, etc. In the IT field they can be informational products such as software.

In the IT field, the position of IPR-protected market leadership and market standards lends itself to a diagnosis of 'super dominance' or 'essential facility'. The *IBM* case in 1984[29] established the principle that where a firm is dominant to the point where its product is an industrial standard, it has obligations to supply code information to allow interoperability to competing firms in secondary markets. IBM was the owner of the Systems 370 mainframe CPU system and its main memory, as well as the producer of applications or peripheral software for its systems. The Commission proceeded under the theory that IBM's Systems 370 mainframe product not only made it dominant in its market but in fact amounted to an essential facility for the 'peripherals' market of applications interoperable with such mainframes.

This diagnosis could also be seen in the *Microsoft* case in the US in 1994[30] and again in 1999.[31] The latter *Microsoft* case in the USA involved, *inter alia*, the market for web browsers. The *Microsoft* case in Europe focused on the server and multimedia utility player markets. In both cases, there were three separate markets. The hardware market, ie, the market for Intel chip PCs, the PC operating system market, ie, the market in which the Windows platform dominated and the separate market for each of the relevant applications: web browsers; servers and multimedia utility players. As a result of its finding three separate markets, the Commission proceeded under the theory that Microsoft enjoyed a practically undisputed market dominance in the market for Intel chip PC operating systems, which is the equivalent of an 'essential facility'.[32]

---

[27]  *United States v Microsoft* (1999) 253 F 3d 34 (DC Cir).

[28]  See, eg, *B&I Line v Sealink Harbour* [1992] 5 CMLR 255.

[29]  *IBM* [1984] OJ L118/24; [1984] 2 CMLR 342.

[30]  *Microsoft* IP (94) 643; [1994] 5 CMLR 143.

[31]  See n 27 above.

[32]  IP/01/1232. Note that the 'essential facilities' doctrine in the USA is narrower in scope than that in the EU. See J Venit and J Kallaugher, 'Essential Facilities: A Comparative Approach' [1994] Fordham Corp Law Inst 315.

### 12.2.3 Article 82 and the concept of abuse

The narrow definition of 'markets' under article 82 has also influenced the approach taken to abuse and this has been particularly true in the case of the exercise of IPR-protected products in the IT field because of the desire to preserve interoperability. At the core of the Commission's approach is the definition of restrictions on innovation as an abuse. Article 82(b) prohibits conduct by a dominant undertaking which limits 'production, markets, or technical developments to the prejudice of consumers'.

The mere possession of a dominant position is not viewed as abusive under EU law. What is abusive is the use of that market power unjustifiably to deny access to markets to competitors. The dominant firm has a special responsibility not to prevent or erode the already weak levels of competition on markets by conduct which is not competition on the merits ('using normal trading methods').[33]

Over the years the European Court of Justice has made it clear that this reasoning applies not only to markets in which a firm is dominant, 'primary markets', but also to 'secondary markets'. For example, it has found it to be abusive conduct for a firm to acquire control over potentially competing innovative technology by another firm[34] because this would preclude its access to the market. The Court has also accepted that abusive conduct can consist of conduct by dominant firms in secondary markets, or 'aftermarkets', particularly those which are dependent on the product in the primary market. In such cases, the firm which is dominant in the primary market is prohibited from acting to 'leverage' its power in the primary market to exclude existing competitors in the secondary market and to deny access to new entrants in those markets.[35] The main abuses under article 82 relevant to the IT field are those which are designed to prevent downstream innovation: refusals to supply or license software or to provide information allowing full interoperability to competitors in secondary markets; discriminatory licensing; and 'tie-ins' or 'bundling' of products.

#### 12.2.3.1 *Refusals to license or provide code information allowing interoperability*
In 1984 the *IBM* case indicated that the Commission was prepared to act on the assumption in the field of IT that a firm, whose IT product was an industrial standard, and who refused to supply code information to allow full interoperability to competing firms in secondary markets, could be acting abusively under article 82(b). IBM as the owner of the Systems 370 mainframe CPU system and its main memory as well as the producer of applications or peripheral software for its systems was charged with abusive conduct in withholding or delaying comparable information

---

[33] See *Michelin v Commission* [1983] ECR 3461, 3511; see too *Hoffman La Roche v Commission* [1979] ECR 461, 541.
[34] See *Tetra Pak v Commission* [1990] ECR II-309.
[35] See *ICI and Commercial Solvents v Commission* [1974] ECR 223; see too *Tetra Pak International v Commission* [1994] ECR II-0755.

about interfaces to other creators of software usable with Systems 370 mainframes and related IBM products and thereby creating an artificial advantage for itself in those secondary markets. The Commission dropped its charges under article 82 in return for a five-year undertaking from IBM whereby IBM agreed to supply full interface information to competitors at the time its own divisions received it.[36]

The law applied by the Commission to the *IBM* case derived from the earlier case of *Commercial Solvents*.[37] In that case Commercial Solvents, a multinational, used its monopoly over the production of a chemical raw material to refuse supply to an existing manufacturer in the secondary market of chemical products made from the raw material. The European Court of Justice found that such an act was abusive under article 82(b) because Commercial Solvents was using its dominance in the primary market to eliminate all competition in the secondary market by refusing to supply an existing customer where it had the capacity to continue to supply that competitor as well as its own subsidiary which was entering the secondary market.

What was noteworthy about the IBM undertaking in the mid-1980s was that it applied the obligation of interoperability more widely than *Commercial Solvents*. It applied it to all competitors, existing and new entrants. The Commission gave little weight to the right of IBM as the inventor of the mainframe system to prevent competing manufacturers of peripheral applications for the IBM system from enjoying the position of 'free riders' who had not contributed to the costs of researching and developing the system. It gave priority to interoperability over reward-incentives to innovation, seeking only to ensure that IBM as the owner of the essential infrastructure received a fair and reasonable return for any licences.

A decade later, Microsoft was charged with unlawfully 'leveraging' its monopoly market power against competitors[38] both in the USA and in Europe. The charge in 1994 against Microsoft was that it used its dominance to raise barriers to entry and foreclose innovation to competitors in the primary market of PC operating systems. The tactic it used was to charge the original equipment makers ('OEMs') a royalty for the Microsoft Windows and MS-DOS for each PC sold (a 'per processor license') even when the OEMs did not load the Microsoft software. The practice did not preclude OEMs from pre-installing other operating systems, as for example an exclusive contract might have done. However, it meant that if an OEM did install a competing operating system, the cost would be higher since consumers would have to pay for two operating systems even though only one was to be used. This anti-innovative practice raised concerns under US antitrust law as well as EU competition law. After negotiations between Microsoft, the US Department of Justice and the European Commission, a settlement was reached whereby Microsoft undertook *inter alia* to end its 'per processor' licensing practices for its current versions of Windows and MS-DOS and use only 'per copy' licences.

---

[36]   *IBM* [1984] OJ L118/24; [1984] 2 CMLR 342.
[37]   [1974] ECR 223.
[38]   *Microsoft* IP (94) 643; [1994] 5 CMLR 143.

More recently, the US Department of Justice and eighteen states brought a case against Microsoft[39] under the Sherman Act for using almost identical tactics for its Windows operating system and web browser product, Internet Explorer, against Sun Microsystem's Netscape Navigator. In this case, Microsoft used its market power in the Windows OS market to limit access to Netscape Navigator in the market for web browsers by *inter alia* using per processor licences.

Finally, Microsoft has also been investigated again in Europe in 2000 and 2001[40] when Sun Microsystems, one of Microsoft's most important competitors in the work group server market, complained to the Commission alleging that Microsoft was providing inadequate information about interface codes for Sun to equip its servers and its multimedia utility to interoperate smoothly with Microsoft's Windows platform. After an investigation, the Commission issued a Statement of Objections alleging that Microsoft was abusing its dominant position in the Windows OS market by refusing to supply the technical information necessary to achieve interoperability with its software to Sun servers, etc, and thereby limiting competition in the work group server OS market and the multimedia utility market to the prejudice of consumers.[41]

### 12.2.3.2 *The IPR complication*

What framework does EC competition law use to strike a balance between the entitlement of IP rightholders to exercise their exclusive rights over IP-protected innovative products and its attempts to ensure that effective competition and innovation is maintained on markets? In principle, in the IT sector these two fields of law are often thought to be reconcilable because each in its own way contributes to consumer welfare and innovation.[42] However, in the case law of the European Court of Justice, the Court of First Instance and in the decisions of the European Commission, it appears that at points of conflict the logic of the reward/incentive function of IPRs tends on occasion to be subordinated to the logic of preserving effective competition on 'markets'.

Where IPRs coincide with an essential infrastructure or input, it has been accepted by the European Court of Justice that the normal exercise of IPRs is not an abuse; there must be 'exceptional circumstances'. The judicial concept of 'exceptional circumstances' has led to a clear tendency to differentiate the concept of abuse in relation to IPRs depending on whether the market was a 'primary' one in which the IPR holder is dominant or a 'secondary' one in which the dominant firm has undue influence because of the 'essential facility' nature of its dominance in the

---

[39] *United States v Microsoft* 253 F 3rd 34 (DC Cir) cert denied 122 S Ct 350 (2001).

[40] IP/01/1232. This statement also alleged that Microsoft may have acted illegally by incorporating its new multimedia utility, Media Player, into its Windows PC operating system.

[41] A further Statement of Objections was issued by the Commission on 30 August 2001 which merged with the earlier procedure. A 'Statement of Objections', in the Commission's own words, is a formal step in European antitrust procedure and does not prejudge the final outcome. A final decision is awaited from the Commission.

[42] See, eg, *Atari Games Corp v Nintendo of America, Inc* 897 F 2d 1572, 1576 (Fed Cir 1990).

primary market. In the primary market, the IPR will normally give its holder a right of exclusive use to make or sell the product.[43] In the secondary market, however, the IPR holder may be required to supply or even license its protected product under certain conditions.

The landmark case for information products was '*Magill*' or *RTE, BBC and ITV v Commission*.[44] Magill was a compiler of a comprehensive weekly television guide combining the contents of the three individual weekly television guides sold separately by the respective television companies. After losing an action for copyright infringement at the national level, Magill successfully made a complaint to the Commission on the grounds that the refusal of the television companies to license the programme listings was abusive conduct under article 82 and won an order for a compulsory licence of the listings material from the television companies to produce the guide. The case, a *cause célèbre*, went to the Court of First Instance which affirmed the Commission's order. On further appeal to the European Court of Justice, the television companies were supported in their arguments by the IPO representing software makers internationally. The appeal resulted in a lengthy opinion by the Advocate-General recommending reversal. The European Court of Justice however decided that the order for a compulsory licence should stand. The Court held that copyright itself did not justify a refusal to license in the 'exceptional circumstances' where there was consumer demand for the new product, where the television companies had a *de facto* monopoly over the listings by virtue of their scheduling of television programmes, where a licence of the listings was an indispensable input for the comprehensive television guide and where they were not themselves supplying the product to consumers. The Court went on to say that an owner of a *de facto* monopoly over a product such as television listings for which there were no substitutes and which was indispensable to the provision of another product in a secondary market could not use its monopoly in one market to eliminate competition in the second market reserving that second market for itself.

After *Magill*, the 'exceptional circumstances' in which an IPR holder could commit an abuse under article 82 seemed initially as if it might extend to at least two different types of cases. First, an IP rightholder, who enjoyed a *de facto* monopoly of an indispensable input, and who used its IP-protected product to block innovation by unjustifiably refusing to supply or license a competitor seeking to introduce *a new product* on a secondary market could be acting abusively. This would apply even where the owner of the IP-protected product had no previous dealing with the new entrant because it would have the effect of foreclosing access to a secondary market of that new product.

Secondly, where a dominant firm with an IPR-protected *de facto* monopoly in the form of an indispensable input refuses to supply or license a competitor in a second dependent market *with whom it had been dealing* with a view to reserving that

---

[43] See, eg, *Volvo UK Ltd v Veng AB* [1988] ECR 6211.
[44] [1995] ECR I-743.

secondary market for itself, that might constitute an abuse even in the absence of a new product by the third party. This conclusion derived from earlier cases such as *Commercial Solvents* which involved a cutting off of supplies and/or licences to existing customers, but its inclusion in *Magill* made it possible to regard it as extending to a refusal to supply to or possibly even license a new customer or competitor. There was some language in the case suggesting that both these conditions were cumulative and not separate[45] but it was not entirely clear whether this was because of the facts or was the view of the Court about the minimum requirements of the test of exceptional circumstances more generally.

The *Magill* case itself offered little guidance to the question of what defence the IP rightholder could put forward to this abuse. In its treatment of the issue of 'justification' for the refusal to license, the European Court of Justice, in *Magill*, made clear that the mere ownership of an IPR would not as such justify a refusal to license in 'exceptional circumstances'. It also indicated that the mere fact that the owner had never dealt with the competitor before was not such a justification. However, it offered no guidance about the positive grounds for justification for a refusal to supply or license which has the effect of blocking a downstream market. It only made clear that the right to exclusive use as a reward to invention did not apply automatically in the second market as it did in the first.

The obvious contenders for justification under the reasoning of other article 82 cases were where the firm seeking compulsory access was a credit risk, where there were objective grounds to worry about quality control and where there were health-and-safety risks, all sound commercial objections which would need to be proved to be well founded[46] in the sense that the grounds were established as factual and that the resort to refusal was proportionate to the threat.[47]

In the subsequent case law, the European Court of Justice and the Court of First Instance made it a point to reiterate that a refusal to license by a dominant firm would only be abusive in the strict conditions of the 'exceptional circumstances' test as articulated in *Magill*. Thus, in *Oscar Bronner GMbH & Co KG v Mediaprint*[48] the European Court of Justice reiterated the importance of a proper test of dominance, stressing the need for it accurately to reflect 'essential facilities' criteria.[49]

---

[45]  Ibid, para 57: 'In the light of all those circumstances the Court of First Instance did not err in law in holding that the appellant's conduct was an abuse of a dominant position'.

[46]  See, eg, *Tetrapak Int'l SA v Commission* [1996] ECR I-5951, para 37.

[47]  See, eg, *Sega and Nintendo* (EC Commission, 1997).

[48]  [1998] ECR I-7791.

[49]  The European Court of Justice held that where a newspaper proprietor asked for access to another proprietor's home-delivery service, a finding of abusive refusal of access using *Magill* as a precedent for the limits to the exercise of any property right, including an IPR, could not be made unless: (i) the refusal of the service in the home-delivery market would be likely to eliminate all competition in that market on the part of the person requesting the service; (ii) there was no objective justification for the refusal; and (iii) the service in itself was indispensable to carrying on that person's business, inasmuch as there was no actual or potential substitute in existence for the home-delivery scheme. The lack of substitutes had to be strictly proved and the test of indispensability was not be confused with mere economic non-viability owing to the small size of the competitor (paras 41 and 45).

In *IMS Health Inc v Commission*[50] the issue was raised whether the 'new product' condition was essential to a finding of exceptional circumstances in which a compulsory licence could be obtained. In *IMS* the Commission ordered a compulsory licence of information contained in a database, consisting of an '1860 brick structure' which provided a format for storing regularly updated information about the sales of pharmaceutical products in Germany region by region. The beneficiaries of the compulsory licences were firms started *inter alia* by former senior management to market regional sales data services based on the brick-structure database. The Commission distinguished between the brick-structure database, which it found to be protected by copyright, and the related market of regional sales data services. It then found that the IMS 1860 brick structure was an essential facility because it had become a market standard demanded by customers including the wholesalers as well as the pharmaceutical companies and that it was not economical for competitors in the second market of selling regional sales data services to reproduce it. It found that the refusal to license was abusive because once the tests of essential facility and two markets were met, it was not necessary that the competitors in the second market were offering a product which was new in relation to the product offered by IMS. IMS appealed to the Court of First Instance which stayed the order of compulsory license pending the result of the appeal because there was a serious doubt that the decision would be upheld, in part because the Commission had proceeded on the supposition that the new product requirement was not an indispensable condition of the test of exceptional circumstances.

The *IMS* case could eventually decide that in the case of new entrants to a secondary market, to qualify for a compulsory licence of an IPR-protected product, the competitor in the downstream market must provide a new product innovation and not merely replicate the IPR holder's own product in that secondary market. This interpretation would certainly be consistent with the actual facts of *Magill* and would seem at first sight to offer an intriguing reconciliation between competition law and IPRs based on their mutual interest in innovation by stressing that 'exceptional circumstances' include only cases of new products or 'follow up' innovation and not 'me too' competition.

However, this decision would not exhaust the possibilities of 'exceptional circumstances' under which article 82 will apply to the exercise of IPRs where they shore up 'essential facilities'. Article 82 will also apply to cases of predatory conduct by a dominant firm, such as that alleged in the *Microsoft* case, when it uses its dominance to disrupt its supply of information or its exclusive copyright to refuse to license to an existing contractor/competitor in the secondary market with the purpose of foreclosing that market. This would be particularly true where that existing competitor is an innovating competitor, such as Netscape Navigator in the browser market or the Sun Microsystems server in the server market. In such a case, in fact it would be the dominant firm which would be the one with the 'me too' prod-

---

[50] Case T-184/01 (10 August 2001).

uct and would be entering the market by anticompetitive means, 'leveraging' its dominance, rather than by using the methods associated with 'competition based on the merits'. If the dominant firm chose to compete legitimately using the methods of 'competition on the merits' it would continue to 'supply', ie, license or inform its existing customers (now competitors) in the downstream market as well as to introduce its own product on the market. As long as it has the capacity to supply, and enjoys an essential facility, it has a special responsibility under article 82 to do this. When the European Court of Justice stated in *Magill*, 'it can be an abuse for a dominant undertaking with a de facto monopoly to reserve for itself a secondary market by excluding all competition on that market by denying access to the basic information which was indispensable to the publication of the guide',[51] it could not have intended to restrict this *principle* solely to competitors with *new* products in the secondary market. For that would rule out a case, such as the above, where a dominant firm refuses to license a firm with which it has been dealing essentially as a pretext for anticompetitive conduct.[52]

In other words, the test of 'exceptional circumstances' must continue to include refusals to supply or license *existing* downstream operators with predatory intent, as was the case with *Commercial Solvents*, and subsequent decisions by the European Court of Justice.[53] What remains to be established in the IT field is whether under article 82(b) a dominant firm with an IP-protected product is entitled to refuse to license *new* downstream competitors who are merely replicating the product already offered by the incumbent essential-facility holder in the downstream market or has a wider obligation under EC competition law of not impeding interoperability. What is clear is that article 82 will apply the rules of compulsory access to cases like that of *Microsoft* where an essential-facility holder refuses to supply either a licence or full interface code information to existing competitors with whom it has had previous dealings.

### 12.2.4 Refusals to supply interface information and the Computer Software Directive

The interoperability imperative in the IT field has been taken into a further dimension by the Computer Software Directive.[54] It seems to suggest that there may in principle be a distinction to draw between the scope of copyright protection between the source codes of software and the object codes of software. Under article 6(1), software users are entitled to reproduce and translate a software program even without the rightholder's authorization when such acts are 'indispensable to obtain the information necessary to write and produce a new program which will be interoperable with

---

[51] N 44 above, para 56.

[52] cf *Antitrust Guidelines to Intellectual Property Licensing* (US Department of Justice Antitrust Division/Federal Trade Commission, 6 April 1995), s 3.1, n 14.

[53] See, eg, *Centre Belge d'Etudes de Marche (CBEM) v Telemarketing* [1985] ECR 3261. See too *Otter Tail Power Co v United States* 410 F 2d 1081 (7th Cir 1983).

[54] Directive 91/250/EEC on the legal protection of computer programs, OJ L122, 17 May 1991.

the protected program but will be independent of it'. This provision permits unauthorized 'decompilation' of a program for the limited purpose of creating a new program, ie, one which when completed would not infringe the rights of the owner of the original program. It is true that under article 6(1)(a) it requires that the decompilation must be performed by a 'licensee or by another person having the right to use a copy of the program'. Moreover, it offers some protection to the rightholder by requiring the decompiler under article 6(2)(c) to obtain authorization from the rightholder when the interface codes are to be used 'for the development, production or marketing of a computer program substantially similar in its expression . . .'.

Nevertheless, it is noteworthy that the decompilation right applies independently of a finding of dominance. A software developer may be able to treat an existing software product for certain purposes almost as if it was an essential facility even though it is not irreplaceable and indispensable This legislation operates essentially in the domain of copyright law rather than competition law. Where, however, patent protection is applied to software programs, article 6 will apply. It is only where dominance is established that article 82 will apply concurrently to the parties.

### 12.2.5 Refusals to license or supply interface information and the Database Directive

The Community's Database Directive[55] has introduced a *sui generis* form of copyright protection for the content of databases which has been more explicitly reconciled with competition law's concerns with interoperability. Article 13 makes it clear that the provisions of the Directive are subject to the 'laws on restrictive practices and unfair competition'.

Recital 43 explains it as follows:

in the interest of competition between suppliers of information products and services, protection by the sui generis right must not be afforded in such a way as to facilitate abuses of a dominant position, in particular as regards the creation and distribution of new products and services which have an intellectual, documentary, technical, economic or commercial added value; whereas therefore the provisions of this Directive are without prejudice to the application of Community or national competition rules.

In contrast with the Computer Software Directive, therefore, in the case of a copyright-protected database, a finding of dominance or even 'super dominance' would appear to be a prerequisite for an order of interoperability.

### 12.2.6 Refusals to license or supply interface information as discrimination under article 82(c)

Under article 82(c) it can be an abuse to apply dissimilar conditions to equivalent

---

[55] Directive 96/9/EC on the legal protection of databases, OJ L77, 27 March 1996.

transactions with other trading parties, without justification,[56] thereby placing them at a competitive disadvantage. Under article 82(c) a failure to provide access comparable to that provided by the dominant firm to its own subsidiary or to other customers can be abusive conduct. For example in the *IBM* case in 1984 the Commission found that by delaying disclosure of interface information on new IBM products while taking orders for them, IBM had created an artificial advantage for itself and denied its competitors an opportunity to adapt their products to the new IBM mainframe computers. The Commission accepted IBM's undertakings particularly in relation to interface information.[57] *IBM* was a settlement, not a Commission decision. Nevertheless it seemed to reach that settlement based on a theory that there was a duty on IBM, as a dominant firm with the equivalent of an essential facility, to enable producers of compatible products to continue to compete with IBM in secondary markets. Moreover, IBM was charged with discriminating between different users of IBM software and refusing to supply certain software-installation services to non-IBM central processor units.

The facts alleged in the *Microsoft* case in Europe also raised an issue whether Microsoft's refusal to license its software to Sun to allow interoperability with Sun's Solaris OS while at the same time giving such licences to Sun's more Microsoft-friendly rivals such as Compaq and SGI, both hardware and (UNIX) software vendors, was abusive discriminatory behaviour under article 82(c).[58] Similarly, Microsoft allegedly withheld information from Sun which would have enabled its server using Sun Solaris OS to interoperate with Microsoft Windows 2000. This conduct allegedly discriminated in favour of Microsoft's own server and OS. Microsoft's refusal to license Sun and provide information to allow full interoperability between the Sun server and Windows 2000 could, if proved, also be abusive conduct under article 82(c) because it distinguishes between Sun and other server makers.[59]

### 12.2.7 Tie-ins

Under article 82(d) it can be an abuse for a dominant firm to insist upon the purchase of one product as a condition of purchasing another, ie, to bundle two separate products together. Under article 82, tie-ins are viewed as abusive because they exclude competitors as well as limit the freedom of choice of consumers.

---

[56] Simply to discriminate between a subsidiary and rivals with the aim of preventing competition from rivals is not a valid justification under article 82(c). See, eg, *British Midland v Aer Lingus* [1993] 4 CMLR 596.

[57] *IBM* [1984] OJ L118/24; [1984] 2 CMLR 342.          [58] IP/00/906.

[59] Under 82(c), a lower level of dominance than *de facto* monopoly might be enough to find abusive certain forms of discrimination by dominant IP rightholders in downstream markets in favour of the the dominant firm's own product in the downstream market. In that case, if the downstream operator has been dependent upon the dominant firm in the sense of being locked in and faced with heavy switching costs to change, it might be found to be abusive to discriminate by a firm with lower levels of dominance than market standard or tipped dominance in the primary market. Cf *United Brands v Commission* [1978] ECR 207.

In the European Commissioner's settlement with IBM in 1984, article 82(d) was used as part of the regulatory framework which resulted in IBM agreeing to discontinue its practice of 'bundling' the main memory function with the sale of its System 370 CPUs by including the price of its main memory function in the price of its CPU and refusing to sell them separately. In the *Microsoft* settlement of 1999, Microsoft was accused of bundling its sales of Windows systems with its web browser product in a similar way. PC makers given a licence for Windows were charged for the Internet Explorer web browser whether or not they wanted to have it. This would not prevent users adding the Netscape Navigator facility but then they would nevertheless have to pay for the Microsoft web browser as part of their purchase of the pre-installed Windows system.

Whether the two products are illegally 'bundled' or legally integrated is an important issue. In the *Microsoft* case in the US the 1994 consent decree provided an exception for integrated products. In the *Microsoft* case in 2001, Microsoft was accused of unlawfully tying by 'commingling' the code for its Windows operating system and its Internet Explorer browser which made them impossible for users to separate and to be sold separately. The DC Circuit Court of Appeals required three findings to conclude that there was unlawful tying conduct. First, Microsoft had to have significant market power in its OS market. Secondly, Windows and Internet Explorer had to be 'separate products'. Third, the commercial effects of the tie had to be 'not insubstantial'. However, the Court also held that in approaching the issue of tying in computer software bundles the courts should apply a 'rule of reason', ie, a balancing of pro-competitive and anticompetitive effects rather than a *per se* rule once the requirements were met, thus singling out the IT sector for especially lenient treatment and widening the scope of intellectual-property protection within it.[60]

Under article 82(d), the Commission has much greater discretion to decide when a commercially integrated system can be unbundled into separate components and separate products. An insistence by a dominant firm owning a key component of the system can be viewed as illegally bundling or tying-in other products of the same system.[61] In the most recent Microsoft case in Europe, the Commission alleged that Microsoft unlawfully tied sales of its Windows OS to its Media Player. Media players are software which allows users to access audio and video files without excessive download times. Media Player could not be uninstalled by OEMs and was effectively 'tied' to the sales of the Windows OS. Microsoft was charged by the Commission with the abuse of illegally tying the two products together reducing the freedom of choice of PC manufacturers and consumers and preventing free competition on the market on the basis of quality and price.[62]

---

[60] See H Hovencamp, 'IP Ties and Microsoft's Rule of Reason' [2002] Antitrust Bulletin 369.
[61] See, eg, *Hilti v Commission* [1994] ECR I-667.
[62] IP/01/1232.

## 12.2.8 The concept of remedies and ensuring interoperability

Once the Commission finds that there has been an infringement of article 82 it has the power to levy a fine of up to 10 per cent of the worldwide turnover of the undertaking committing the abuse as well as to require that undertaking to bring that infringement to an end.[63] In *Magill* the remedy chosen by the Commission was a compulsory licence on terms which were 'reasonable and non-discriminatory'. It chose this remedy only because an order to supply the information in the listings would not have allowed their use and therefore would not have ended the infringement. The only way the Commission could be sure that Magill could publish the new product in the secondary market and that the parties would end the infringement was to require a licence to publish along with the supply of the listings.

In the IT field the attitude to remedies has been more strongly influenced by the imperative of interoperability. In the *IBM* settlement in 1984, the Commission insisted on undertakings by IBM to provide full interface information to all applications makers comparable to that provided to its own subsidiary operating in a downstream market. The purpose of that settlement was to ensure that the dominant firm, particularly where it operated in a downstream market, adhered to the principle of fair and non-discriminatory treatment of competitors in that market. In the later *Microsoft* cases the issues of shaping a competition law remedy to ensure interoperability became more controversial.

In the *Microsoft* case in the USA after the District Court judge's remedy of compulsory division of Microsoft into two companies was overturned by the Circuit Court, the Department of Justice, together with half of the litigating states, negotiated a consent decree with Microsoft which stipulated that Microsoft had to cease a number of monopolistic practices. The decree also placed three positive obligations upon Microsoft to assist dependent competitors to achieve full interoperability with Microsoft products. First, Microsoft was required to supply ISVs, Internet Access Providers and OEMs, among others, with the Application Protocol Interfaces ('APIs') and related documentation used by Microsoft middleware to interoperate with a Windows OS product in a timely manner. Secondly, there was an obligation to license to third parties, on reasonable and non-discriminatory terms, any communications protocol implemented in a Windows OS product when it is installed on a client computer and used to interoperate 'natively', ie, without the installation of additional software code, with a MS OS product. Finally, Microsoft agreed to give a compulsory licence to ISVs, etc, of any IPRs owned or licensable by Microsoft that was required to exercise any of the options or alternatives expressly provided to them under the final judgment on reasonable and non-discriminatory terms.[64]

The difficulty was that these obligations were subject to a wide proviso on security to the effect that Microsoft would not be required to disclose or license to third

---

[63] Council Regulation No 17, art 3.
[64] See Second Revised Final Proposal of 6 November 2001, III.D–F.

parties portions of APIs documentation or layers of communications protocols *inter alia* 'if their disclosure would compromise the security of a particular installation'.[65]

The nine dissenting states who continued to litigate after the Department of Justice consent decree with Microsoft concluded that the settlement did not provide an adequate remedy. It did little more than prohibit past misdeeds and did nothing to prevent Microsoft from future anticompetitive conduct adjusted to new technological and marketplace developments. They were also concerned with the wide security proviso. They therefore proposed mandatory timely disclosure by Microsoft of interoperability interfaces to ISVs, IAPs, OEMs, etc in 'whatever media Microsoft customarily disseminates such information to its own personnel' for the purpose of allowing non-Microsoft software and applications to interoperate with Microsoft Platform software as well as disclosure of all APIs etc 'necessary for interoperability'. They were concerned to provide compulsory disclosure with fewer provisos related to security which could be used to avoid disclosure. They suggested the appointment of a Special Master as part of the enforcement mechanism to deal swiftly with disputes over the disclosure obligation.[66] Finally, they included express prohibitions on actions by Microsoft which it knows, or reasonably should know, will directly or indirectly interfere with or degrade the performance or compatibility of any non-Microsoft middleware when interoperating with Microsoft platform software other than for good cause.[67]

The dissenting states were of the view that this latter remedial model was more likely to secure effective compliance. The European Commission is likely to aim for a remedy taking a similar form to that proposed by the dissenting states rather than the looser remedy provided in the Department of Justice settlement. At all events, what is clear is that in the IT field there is a propensity to provide a remedy to ensure that the owners of essential infrastructure or industrial standard software do not curb interoperability with related products by competitors without justification.

This use of competition policy does have the effect of overriding property rights but it does so based on the public interest that competitive markets will create a better balance between 'second generation' innovation and IPR-protected 'first generation' innovation. It puts in place severe limits to the use of such a remedy but retains it as a last resort in extreme cases of imbalance between the two types of innovation should all else fail.

## 12.3 MERGER POLICY AND INNOVATIVE MARKETS IN THE PRE-TIPPING STAGE

As long as an individual firm achieves market leadership under its own steam by

---

[65] Ibid, III.J.
[66] See Plaintiff Litigating States' First Amended Proposed Remedy, 4 March 2002, sections 2–4.
[67] Ibid, section 5.

producing an innovative product by its own research and development and combining this product with other self-generated complementary products, EC competition law will not interfere with the process of establishing market dominance even through it is achieved by a combination of system effects and negative externalities. The theory is that achieving dominance by internal growth, ie, a process of investment in research and development and individual innovation, is lawful partly because the exploitation of IP protection can be viewed as a form of competition on the merits and partly because the acquisition of dominance by efficient performance is lawful. Consequently, before the point of dominance, and before the market 'tips', competition law will not interfere with any *single firm's* efforts to compete by individual performance with rival systems. It may also allow *collaboration* in various forms, for example, acquisitions and joint ventures, or acquisitions of minority shareholdings where they are designed to promote the technological development of the parties.

The main concern of competition policy in product markets in the 'pre-tipping' stage is with the attempts of firms to achieve dominance by collaboration with other firms in such forms when they are designed primarily to enhance 'network externalities' and thereby enhance their prospects of 'tipping' the relevant market.

EC competition policy recognizes that there is a need for many, if not most, high-technology firms to collaborate in the form of joint ventures, outright mergers or partial acquisitions simply to share high research-and-development investment costs, high production costs and high economic risks in order to bring a new product to the market. In fact, collaboration for purely financial motives is generally regarded as 'pro-competitive', in the sense that it enables new products to be introduced that would otherwise not be developed and marketed. Hence, EC competition law provides a Block Exemption Regulation for research-and-development joint ventures, subject to market-share limits, which now allows the joint venture to continue through to the marketing phase. It is also beginning to look more positively at forms of cooperation such as patent pools where they are genuinely pro-competitive and are not disguised cartels or efforts to foreclose markets.

Where, however, an alliance is formed either as a merger or a joint venture primarily as an attempt to achieve market dominance and strategic network effects, the EC competition authorities are more likely to intervene using either the Merger Control Regulation or article 81 of the Treaty. Both competition measures are based on a market analysis and are used to ensure that collaboration between firms does not create a product market which effectively forecloses competition by rivals, as well as to ensure they do not improperly influence the autonomous process whereby markets are 'tipped' into adoption of market standards.

### 12.3.1 Merger policy and new-economy markets

In the new economy, as in the old, the Merger Control Task Force of the European Commission applies a dominance-based test to its appraisal of mergers. If a newly merged entity with a European Community dimension would: (1) be dominant in a market which is at least a substantial part of the Common Market; and (2) that dominance will prevent effective competition in that market, the merger will be found to be 'incompatible' with the Common Market and will either be disapproved or the parties will be asked to divest operations or be subject to 'behavioural restrictions' or commitments as the price of approval. In such situations IPRs get caught in the crossfire and licensing discretion can be curbed.

The presence of a dominance test requires that the Commission must first define the relevant market in which the merger will compete. It then also requires an assessment of the market power or degree of dominance of the newly merged entity in that market. The test is comparable to that under article 82 with one important difference. The Commission assesses these issues prospectively in the context of mergers but on the basis of past conduct in the case of article 82.

In the new economy, as in the old, the Merger Task Force also continues to prevent competing firms merging 'horizontally' into concentrations of economic power in a particular product market. A good example of this policy is offered by the Commission's rejection of the WorldCom/MCI merger because the merger would have had the effect of reducing the number of 'backbone' ISPs in the hierarchy of ISPs on the Internet in a situation in which there were only four ISPs.

The 'backbone' ISPs consist of the private companies who stepped into the breach to provide the links connecting the different networks that constituted the Internet once the National Science Foundation withdrew in the mid-1990s as the financier of the Internet's 'backbone'. Their reciprocal arrangements gave them the capacity to 'provide connectivity anywhere on the Internet solely through their own peering arrangements with other networks'[68] without having to pay for a 'transit service' from any provider. These backbone companies also offered access services to paying subscribers creating a hierarchy consisting of a small group of backbone ISPs which peered or interconnected on a traffic-exchange basis with other backbone ISPs and a second tier of ISPs which paid access charges to the 'top level' ISPs.

The Commission defined the geographic market for the Internet as worldwide but the relevant product market was the market for the provision of 'top level' or 'universal' connectivity, ie, the 'backbone' or peering ISPs. The Commission further found that the product market was highly concentrated with a big four consisting of WorldCom, MCI, Sprint and GTE/BBN[69] and that WorldCom together with MCI would control more than 50 per cent of that market. It found that the merger if not altered would lead to a dominant position in the market for top level or universal connectivity[70] but accepted that if MCI divested itself of its Internet-related activities, in particular its Internet backbone operations, the merger could go ahead because the number of backbone ISPs would remain at four. It made plain its concerns that the merged entity if not altered 'would control market entry by denial

---

[68]  See WorldCom/MCI 99/287/EC Commission Decision of 8 July 1998, point 23.
[69]  Ibid, point 102.                                    [70]  Ibid, point 135.

of new peering requests, foreclosure or the threat of foreclosure of peering agreements and/or their replacement with paid interconnection.'[71]

When MCI WorldCom tried a year later to merge with Sprint, the Commission prohibited the merger because it found after an extensive investigation that 'the merger would, through the combination of the merging parties' extensive networks and large customer base, have led to the creation of such a powerful force that both competitors and customers would have been dependent upon the new company to obtain universal Internet connectivity.[72] The parties argued that defining the peering ISPs as a separate market was inappropriate because it did not take full account of the structure of the Internet and the ability to gain universal connectivity through the 'transit' or paid-for carriage. The Commission, however, did not accept that paid for and free carriage on the Internet were substitutes concluding that the quality of the paid-for service would be significantly inferior as data had to pass through more hoops.

WorldCom and Sprint also argued that there were no barriers to building backbone ISP capacity. The Commission could not accept this vision of unlimited potential competition. Instead, they indicated their traditional competition concern with the potential foreclosure effects of the high concentration as well as the new-economy concern with network externalities causing a snowballing effect enhancing MCI/WorldCom/Sprint's dominance. This as Veljanovski has pointed out[73] was reinforced by the success of MCI/WorldCom in winning its customers back from Cable & Wireless to whom MCI's backbone operation was divested in response to the Commission's condition.

Although the Commission encountered major new methodological issues in defining the relevant product market and in calculating the market shares of the top-level ISPs, it was guided by traditional considerations of the competition risks associated with high horizontal concentration both in defining the acceptable structural remedies in the first merger and prohibiting the second merger altogether. Yet, as pointed out by Ungerer,[74] the Merger Task Force was also aware of the risks of a 'snowball effect' in this sector of the Internet economy '. . . in that MCI WorldCom would be better placed than any of its competitors to capture future growth through new customers, because of its attractions for any new customer of direct connection with the largest network, and the relative unattractiveness of competitor offerings owing to the threat of disconnection or degradation of peering which MCI WorldCom's competitors must constantly live under'.[75]

Along with pursuing this traditional remit of 'horizontal' merger policy, the Merger Task Force now has become active in preventing the possibility of strategic

---

[71]  Ibid, point 119.

[72]  IP/00/668, 28 June 2000 (see www.europe.eu.int).

[73]  See C Veljanovski, 'EC's Vodafone Decision Signals Policy Departure' (2000) Global Competition Review, June/July, pp 19–21.

[74]  H Ungerer, 'Access Issues under EU Regulation and Antitrust Law: The Case of Telecommunications and Internet Law' (Research Paper, WCFIA Fellows Program 1999/2000, Harvard University), p 40.

[75]  WorldCom/MCI 99/287/EC Commission Decision of 8 July 1998, point 86.

network effects being achieved by 'vertical' integration in innovation markets. In dealing with mergers particularly in the media and telecoms sector, the Commission has evolved a strategy of avoiding firms gaining 'gatekeeper' status through mergers. A paradigm example is offered by the attempt by Microsoft to acquire a substantially increased minority share in the cable company Telewest from 9.3 per cent to above 15 per cent. Microsoft had already acquired full ownership of another cable company, Liberty Media. The Commission regarded Microsoft's interest in Telewest as part of a strategic plan to acquire minority stakes in cable companies in many countries either by itself or through its strategic alliance with AT&T for the purpose of influencing the decisions of the cable companies to adopt Microsoft's software package for television set-top boxes for cable television. Microsoft's software MSTV package was interoperable with its Windows platform and the wider adoption of the MSTV software package by cable companies would have encouraged even more application software writers to write for the Windows platform.

Since Microsoft's history indicated that it often hindered interoperability with other systems providers, the Commission was concerned about the network externalities that might arise from the Microsoft strategy. The Commission took the view that Microsoft's new substantial minority shareholding, if allowed, would be used to influence Telewest to adopt Microsoft's MSTV software in Telewest's next generation of television set-top boxes for cable television. This, the Commission concluded, created the risk that MSTV software could dominate the market for next-generation television set-top boxes for cable TV and foreclose competition.

This case offered an example of the Commission being prepared to use merger policy to preclude strategic alliances attempting to gain control of portals or other 'gateways'. Merger policy always attempts to anticipate the consequences of mergers whether in new or old product markets and in Microsoft/Telewest 'the potential role of network effects raised a . . . plausible threat of "tipping" the market for set-top box software packages towards monopolization.'[76] Microsoft reacted to the Commission's intention to stop the acquisition by abandoning its original plan but retaining a lower stake in Telewest, below the 15 per cent level, thus taking the transaction outside the jurisdiction of the Merger Control Regulation.

Similarly, in the vertical merger between AOL and Time Warner, the Commission was prepared to give its approval to the merger only after AOL offered to dispose of its joint-venture links with the German media company Bertelsmann. Part of the problem was that Time Warner had been planning to merge its music recording and publishing activities with EMI before the AOL/Time Warner merger. EMI, Time Warner and Bertelsmann together had about 50 per cent of the music publishing rights and the Commission took the view that there was a risk that AOL would have been placed in a position of gatekeeper in the emerging Internet market for delivering music online.

---

[76] B Bishop and C Caffera, 'Merger Control in "New Markets" ' (2001) 22(1) European Competition Law Review 32.

Only after the abandonment of the EMI/Time Warner merger, and on the condition that Time Warner severed its links with Bertelsmann, would the Commission allow the AOL/Time Warner merger to proceed.

The gatekeeper-control policy was also evident in the conditions the Commission placed on the acquisition of the Canadian firm Seagram by the French telecoms and media company Vivendi.[77] Since Vivendi had Canal+ as a subsidiary, the merger would have given Canal+ preferential or, possibly exclusive, rights to the Universal film rights owned by Seagram, which would have strengthened Canal+'s dominant position in the pay-TV market in a number of countries. The Commission required the newly merged firm, as conditions of the merger, to limit the first window rights of Canal+ to a fixed proportion of Universal film productions and to divest its stake in British pay-TV company BskyB. The Commission's idea was to place BskyB (and Fox Studios) in a position to compete with Canal+ (and Universal) rather than to coordinate with them.

Even where the Commission accepts that early leadership is not likely to be durable, it continues to seek assurances of access to third parties in cases where the new entity shows a potential to be a 'gatekeeper'. For example, in the recent merger of Vodafone/Mannesmann which created the first advanced pan-European mobile service, the Commission acknowledged that the newly merged firm would have a short-lived period of leadership owing to competition from third-generation mobile technology. Nevertheless the Commission insisted upon the divestiture of Orange by Mannesmann as well as detailed conditions to facilitate access to competitors, for a limited period of three years, as the price of approving the merger. The divestiture initially could be viewed in the tradition of avoiding merger-created dominance in a particular market. Thus if the issue were viewed solely from the perspective of national markets for mobile telephony services, the divestiture of Orange had the effect of precluding high-market shares in second-generation mobile services in Belgium and the UK.

Yet the Commission's analysis of the relevant market and dominance was not traditional. The Commission found that the relevant product market was a 'seamless pan European mobile telecommunications service' even though this service was not yet in operation.[78] The Commission also found that Vodafone/Mannesmann would have a dominant position in this prospective market. It would bring together ten networks in fifteen countries in the EU even after the divestiture of Orange. Other mobile networks would have difficulty in replicating Vodafone's geographical coverage or 'footprint'.[79] It was unimpressed with the argument that the relevant product markets were separate national markets. The Commission was adamant that it would not allow a merger to place the new entity in a position to dominate an industry in which hitherto national mobile telephony networks had roaming agreements on a

---

[77] See, eg, *Canal+ and Bertelsmann* OJ C168 (1995) (Commission).
[78] See Veljanovski (n 73 above), p 19.
[79] Ibid.

non-exclusive basis and therefore customers had a choice of networks in each country. Its assessment was that the merger threatened the openness of international roaming services.

The Commission therefore required Vodafone/Mannesmann to take on obligations to keep separate accounts, to design systems to facilitate interconnection including rules preventing unfair pricing to new users and to accept arbitration of interconnection disputes as the price of a green light from the Commission. The Commission accepted that the mobile telephony sector was dynamic and therefore limited the access undertakings to the three-year period. Indeed within months Orange/France Telecom produced a rival system. The case nevertheless offered a dramatic example of the willingness of the Commission to use an analysis of post-merger actions to anticipate the tipping effects of strategic alliances.

## 12.4 ARTICLE 81 AND AGREEMENTS BETWEEN FIRMS IN NEW-ECONOMY MARKETS

### 12.4.1 Article 81 generally

Article 81(1) of the Treaty prohibits agreements, decisions of trade associations or concerted practices that prevent, restrict or distort competition. If an agreement or joint venture can be shown to be non-restrictive or non-distortive of competition, it will be cleared by the Commission and regarded as legally valid. Most joint ventures are caught by article 81(1) and require exemption under article 81(3) from the Commission in order to be free of the risk of non-enforceability under article 81(2) and to provide sufficient reassurance to parties to commit funds to the venture.

Article 81(3) formally recognizes the pro-competitive value of innovative agreements by stipulating that to obtain exemption, an agreement must contribute 'to improving production and distribution of goods and promoting technical progress'. Article 81 however also requires two other conditions to be met. First, the agreement must not contain restrictions on competition which are not 'indispensable to the attainment' of the above objective. Secondly, the agreement must not afford the parties to it 'the possibility of eliminating competition in respect of a substantial part of the products in question'. Under article 81, therefore, the Commission has the task of balancing the innovative benefits of an agreement with its risks of denial of access to a particular market to entrants and existing competitors. In the field of research-and-development agreements, technology agreements and exclusive agreements to distribute computer hardware and software products,[80] article 81 regulates principally through the device of Block Exemption Regulations.

---

[80] Agreements for the exclusive distribution of IT hardware and software are regulated by article 81 under a Block Exemption Regulation for Vertical Agreements (1999/C 270/07) and a set of Guidelines on Vertical Restraints issued by the European Commission (1999/C 270/12). Detailed discussion of these provisions are beyond the scope of this chapter.

The main tests under article 81 used by the Commission in processing joint ventures which do not fall under any of the Block Exemption Regulations are three in number. First, will there be any loss of actual or potential competition between the parents themselves or between the parents and the joint venture? Does the joint venture aim to produce an entirely new product or does it aim to produce a product which overlaps with the commercial activities of the parties to the joint venture? In other words, is there a real need for cooperation to get the venture off the ground? Secondly, are there any 'spill over' effects that might lessen competition in other markets owing to the actual and potential competition between the parents of the joint venture? Thirdly, does the joint venture foreclose any third parties from entry to the market?

### 12.4.2 Joint-venture policy in the B2B sector

A new focus of the monitoring of joint ventures under article 81 as well as under the Merger Control Regulation has occurred in the case of vertical joint ventures in Internet-related markets. One such development has been the Commission's concern with B2B information exchanges. B2B marketplaces have become quite common and are viewed as generally pro-competitive activities because they help to reduce search and information costs, improve inventory management and increase the possibility of lower prices for the ultimate consumer. Yet they can have negative effects on competition, particularly when the information sharing leads to the exchange of market-sensitive information on prices and quantities, because this can lead to the coordination of pricing activity, the archetypal cartel practice. It can also lead to restrictions on competition *vis-à-vis* their competitors.

The B2B sector offers an excellent field in which to observe how the Commission has applied the rules of article 81 to the new economy.[81] The first Commission case, *Myaircraft.com*[82] was brought under the Merger Regulation but because it was a joint venture it was assessed under article 81. The case, which concerned a joint venture between Honeywell and UTC to supply aerospace parts and services to aircraft manufacturers, primarily raised the important issue of how the market for a particular B2B service was to be assessed in relation to its functionally equivalent 'bricks-and-mortar service'. Are these different modes of distribution to be defined as separate markets or co-existing and competing services in the same market? In *Myaircraft.com* the Commission decided that the relevant market was aerospace parts and services and that e-commerce was only 'one segment among the many modalities by which companies transact business' in the same market.[83] As we shall see, that is not inevitably the case in B2B operations. Much will depend on the commercial facts of the service and the market.

---

[81] See the discussion by E Vollebregt, 'E-Hubs: Syndication and Competition Concerns' [2000] ECLR 437.

[82] M.1969 UTC/Honeywell/12/Myaircraft.com.

[83] Ibid, paras 11–13.

The Commission went on to find that the restrictions on competition contained in the joint venture were 'indispensable' and therefore pro-competitive 'ancillary restraints' in the meaning of article 81(3). The joint venture required both the parents, Honeywell and UTC: (1) not to use the services of any competitor of Myaircraft.com for the purchase and sale of aftermarket parts and the performance of aftermarket services; (2) not to make any consulting resources available to competing aerospace B2B platforms; (3) not to promote any competitor of the joint venture; and (4) not to acquire an equity interest in any competitor after reducing their shareholding in Myaircraft.com. All were accepted as legitimate ancillary restraints by the Commission.

Another early candidate for scrutiny in the B2B sector was the joint venture, *Covisint*,[84] created by the major motor manufacturers including Ford, Daimler Chrysler, General Motors, Renault and Nissan, later joined by PSA Peugeot Citroen. Covisint, in the Commission's words, is 'an electronic marketplace intended to provide the automotive industry with procurement, collaborative product development and supply chain management tools'. By using IT and the Internet, it can reduce costs and improve efficiency in the supply chain. The car makers intending to make use of Covisint account for about 61 per cent of worldwide car production

There were three main features of the Covisint joint venture that convinced the Commission to conclude that it did 'not currently restrict competition within the meaning of article 81(1) and to send the parties a comfort letter to that effect'.[85] The first was that it was an exchange managed by purchasers rather than sellers and could therefore be distinguished from other B2B exchanges such as Supply On which are set up by the sellers of components. The second was that there were sufficient firewalls and security rules to prevent the communication and exchange of confidential information. The third was that Covisint was 'open to all firms on a non-discriminatory basis', was 'based on open standards' and allowed 'both shareholders and other users to participate in other B2B exchanges'.[86]

A similar concern to ensure openness in e-commerce agreements under article 81 can be seen in the *Identrus* case decided by the Commission in late 2001.[87] This case concerned an agreement between a number of European and non-European banks creating a global network for the authentication of electronic signatures and other aspects of e-commerce transactions. The Commission examined the agreement and 'cleared' it of any appreciable restriction of competition under article 81 because it entailed no foreclosure risks since other competing systems provided competitive checks and participants in Indentrus were free to join such systems.[88]

---

[84] Case COMP/38.064 (OJ C49, 15 February 2001); press release IP/01/1155, 31 July 2001.

[85] See *XXXIst Report on Competition Policy* (European Commission DG Competition, 2001), pp 42–3.

[86] Ibid, p 43.

[87] Case COMP/37.462 (OJ L249, 19 September 2001).

[88] *XXXIst Report* (n 85 above), p 35.

Another group of vertical joint ventures in Internet-related markets were three cases concerning T-Online. T-Online, Deutsche Telecom's Internet subsidiary, is the leading ISP in Germany with 52 per cent of the market followed by AOL with 20 per cent and Freenet, Tiscali and Arcor with about 10 per cent each. T-Online also operates the country's most visited Internet portal by a wide margin.

T-Online initially created a joint venture with the two largest tour operators in Germany, TUI Group and C&N Touristic (now renamed Thomas Cook).[89] T-Online was to hold 51 per cent of the shares with the two tour operators dividing the remaining shares equally.

TUI and C&N are vertically integrated tour operators acting in several EU countries. They provide tour operating and travel agency services, hotels, cruises and other services. They are number one and two in most of the relevant travel markets with only one major competitor, REWE, holding a similar market share.

T-Online Travel, the joint venture, was to operate an online travel agency linked to T-Online's Internet portal, t-online.de. It was intended to offer a range of travel services including package holidays, last-minute holidays, flights and hotel accommodation. These services were to be supplied by TUI and C&N as well as other operators in response to online bookings by consumers.

The first competition issue was what was the relevant market? Was it only online travel agencies or all travel agencies? The Commission's initial market investigation suggested that there were two different markets. First, with Internet penetration expected to rise significantly from 29 per cent in early 2001, it was also expected that a significant share of package tours would be sold online. Secondly, there were significant differences in the characteristics of the two types of travel service. Traditional agencies offered individual advice on complex travel products, for example, flight, hotel and car rentals, and availability checks, comparisons and price checks were done by staff in the agencies. They also had access to the Computer Reservation System ('CRS') with its powerful booking engine. Online travel sites were available twenty-four hours, seven days a week but offered less functionality than the CRS; they tended to cater for relatively standardized travel products such as last-minute holidays or flight/hotel packages to short-haul destinations.

Thirdly, there were major differences in cost structures. Online travel agencies require significant sunk costs initially for advertising and technology, but their variable costs were smaller allowing them to pass on significantly lower prices to consumers than the traditional agencies.

The other Internet-related market product markets affected by the joint venture were the ISP market and Internet portal market. Here too there were issues of whether the ISP and Internet portal markets were separate, vertically integrated markets or not, but the Commission appeared to view them in these terms.

The net result of this analysis was that the joint venture raised concerns that competing online travel agencies would be foreclosed from the access enjoyed by

<hr />

[89] Case COMP/M.2149 (2001).

the two leading package holiday brands within the joint venture; they would be given preferential treatment in respect of promotions, price reductions, capacity during peak periods of demand, supporting pictures and logos, etc. T-Online, using its strong position in the ISP/portal market, would have carried out a commercial strategy of using T-Online Travel as a preferred, if not exclusive, distribution channel for the two tour operators.

The Commission refused to accept behavioural remedies from the parties to the joint venture and referred it to the Phase II proceedings. In response the parties restructured the joint venture to take it outside the jurisdiction of the Merger Control Regulation. Under the new agreement, T-Online was given sole control with the two tour operators' shares reduced to less than 12.5 per cent each

The new agreements were then investigated by the Commission under article 81.[90] This investigation confirmed that online travel agency services were a separate market from traditional travel agencies. It also confirmed that there was a distinction between portal markets and ISP markets. The portal market was viewed as an advertising market whilst the ISP market was a relationship market covering the commercial relationship between the ISP and the subscribers/Internet users.

The Commission found that there were no appreciable restrictions on competition on the online travel agency services market caused by the agreement. The German portal market had a range of competitors to T-Online as a portal provider. The tour operators could advertise on their own websites as well as third-party portals and/or online travel agents and therefore there was no exclusivity contrary to article 81. Moreover, there was no exclusivity of access offered via T-Online Travel in favour of T-Online ISP subscribers.[91]

### 12.4.3 Research-and-development joint ventures within the Block Exemption

Research-and-development agreements which extend beyond pure research and development to commercialization and marketing can be exempted under the new Research and Development Block Exemption Regulation[92] subject to certain conditions. The first is that the parties' share must be below 25 per cent of the relevant market since with a market share above 25 per cent the Commission considers that the risk of foreclosure could result in restraints on innovation and coordination between firms for anticompetitive purposes. Hence, above a market share of 25 per cent, the parties must seek individual exemption. Secondly, the research-and-development agreements must not contain certain hardcore restrictions. There must be no limits to the capacity of each party to carry out independent research and development. There can be no 'no-challenge clause' in an agreement. There can be no limit on the right of each party to license to third parties. In these and other respects, EC

---

[90] Case COMP/C-2/38.161 (2001).

[91] The third Internet joint venture involving T-Online was its joint venture with Bild.de, the online edition of Germany's largest tabloid newspaper (Case B6-144/01 Bild.de/T-Online).

[92] 2659/2000.

competition law acts as a heavy regulator of research-and-development agreements, possibly discouraging investment in such joint ventures which might have been encouraged by a more user-friendly legal framework.

### 12.4.4 Technology transfers and the Block Exemption

The current framework for IPR licensing is provided by the Technology Transfer Block Exemption Regulation.[93] Unlike the more flexible requirements of the Antitrust Guidelines for the Licensing of Intellectual Property in the USA, the Technology Transfer Regulation operates on the principle that to qualify for exemption and legal enforceability under article 81, the agreement must fit squarely within the rules of the Regulation. If a licensing agreement does not fit within the Regulation, the parties are left only with the alternative to petition the Commission for individual exemption, an often long and laborious process.

The Regulation limits its exemption only to patent licences or know-how licences or mixed patent/know-how licences. It allows other IPRs as part of the licensing package only under conditions that require that these other IPRs are essentially there to contribute to the objects of the other main forms of licensing. The Regulation also distinguishes between territorial and non-territorial restraints. It treats territorial restraints quite strictly creating *per se* violations in the form of blacklisted contractual provisions where contractual exclusivity for licensees prevents licensed goods, once placed on the market, from circulating freely from country to country within the Common Market. It also regulates improvement clauses and non-compete clauses strictly to ensure even-handed treatment for licensee and licensor.

The current Regulation thus adds to a picture of close regulation of intellectual property by EC competition law. Unless, the clauses in IPR licensing agreements conform strictly to the detailed requirements of the individual articles in the Regulation, either the agreement as a whole or the individual clause will be void and unenforceable. The Regulation is due for revision in 2003 and is expected to become more flexible and user-friendly in relation to licensing in many respects, but competition policy will remain in place as a regulator of technology transfer licensing agreements.

### 12.4.5 Patent pools and other forms of multiparty cooperation between competitors

Patent pools and other forms of multiparty licensing agreements such as standards-setting institutes are viewed as potential competition concerns by the Commission because of their capacity for preventing entry to markets and artificially raising prices above competitive levels. Both patent pools and cross-licensing agreements in respect of know-how are excluded from the Technology Transfer Block Exemption

---

[93]  240/96.

(art 5). Moreover, such schemes have been refused exemption where the Commission finds that they may have anticompetitive effects.[94] On the other hand, where such agreements can contribute to production, technical or economic progress, multiparty forms of collaboration involving cross-licensing can be exempted or found not to be a concern of the competition authorities and receive a 'comfort letter'.[95] Similarly, the coordination of standard setting by the European Telecommunications Standards Institute's IPR policy has been approved after its compulsory cross-licensing policy was challenged and closely examined.[96] The Commission's *Guidelines on Horizontal Agreements* set out the principles that apply to reconcile standard-setting agreements with the concern of article 81 that such agreements shall not limit innovation.[97]


## 12.5  CONCLUSION

The competition policies of the Commission under articles 81 and 82 as well as under the Merger Control Regulation continue to regulate the conduct of firms in the new economy as in the old. This occurs because in the new economy, the commercial strategy of firms gets caught in the crossfire of the measures used by competition policy to maintain competitive markets.

Thus, as we have seen, where agreements are made between firms, either in the form of joint ventures or acquisitions, the Commission seems to be alert to stop alliances which are designed to achieve strategic control over 'gateways' to related markets which could place parties in a position to foreclose competition in those markets. Both merger policy and joint-venture policy officials are on the lookout to ensure open access and interoperability in high-technology markets using measures which include demanding imaginative forms of undertakings by the parties before approving even vertical collaborations or mergers between firms. This may at times place the Commission in the position of appearing more like a regulator than a competition authority but it is a measure of the need for competition policy to maintain access to markets even where they are 'innovative'.

There is a noticeable measure of overlap between article 82 and mergers policy in regulating markets in the new economy, particularly the common view of dominance taken by the authorities enforcing both aspects of competition policy. We have seen how the enforcement of article 82 operates retrospectively by regulating the conduct of firms which have already achieved monopoly market power in a market in the sense that they are a market standard and that the market has already tipped in their favour. Merger policy in the EU is based on a prospective test of

---

[94] See, eg, *Video Cassette Recorders Agreements* [1978] 2 CMLR 160; *IGR Stereo Television* (Commission's *XIth Report on Competition Policy* (1984), para 94).
[95] See, eg, MPEG-2 OJ [1998] C229/6 (technology to improve video-signal quality).
[96] OJ [1994] C76/5; [1995] 5 CMLR 352.
[97] OJ 2001 C3/2.

*dominance* which has a serious prospect of significantly impeding competition on a market. It has been used to inhibit vertical acquisitions of complementary products and processes on secondary markets which can lead to foreclosure of markets by the tipping process as well as the more traditional acquisitions of competing technologies on primary markets. As with the article 82-type of regulation, the existence of IPRs is regarded as incidental to the market power of the entity being formed. If the actual market power of a firm in one market is reinforced by an IPR, it will be treated as if its intangible property rights are no different than its tangible property rights. The negative effect of this type of curb on innovation or the incentives to innovation is thought to be counterbalanced by the maintenance of access to markets by competitors. At this point in its development, the EC competition authorities have not succumbed to the arguments for 'creative destruction' and fragile monopolies as a basis for the relaxation of competition concerns about foreclosure of markets.

In the course of this relationship, EC competition law has evolved into a role as residual protector of the function of *diffusion* of IPRs in the economy. As is well known, IPRs have their own internal checks and balances between the protection of exclusive rights and diffusion for 'follow up' innovation taking the form, for example, of publishing the patent claim during the protected period and limiting the protected period of exclusive use to twenty years and rights of fair use of copyright-protected matter. Along with this internal balance within IPR legislation, competition law has been thrust into the role of an external protector of the diffusion element of innovation because of its own logic of preserving competitors in secondary markets dependent on essential facilities by compulsory supply or licence remedies, ensuring that the scope of IPR protection in licensing and research-and-development agreements is not too restrictive of competition by parties to such agreements and by controlling mergers both horizontal and vertical which would lead to foreclosure of competition in high-technology markets. The methods used by EC competition law can be attacked on the grounds that their choice of markets is sometimes arbitrary, their findings of dominance is sometimes suspect and their definitions of abuse ignores the full entitlement of IPR holders to obtain what the market will bear. The riposte of competition authorities is that while there may be some arbitrariness in their definition of markets, the arguments for looser definitions would run the risk of allowing private concentrations of power too free a rein to extinguish competition to the prejudice of consumers as well as competitors. This controversy is likely to run and run and in the case of competition law it will ultimately be the judges in the Community courts who will decide how the balance is struck.

# Index